Microsoft®
Management
Console
Design and Development Kit

PUBLISHED BY
Microsoft Press
A Division of Microsoft Corporation
One Microsoft Way
Redmond, Washington 98052-6399

Library of Congress Cataloging-in-Publication Data pending.

Printed and bound in the United States of America.

1 2 3 4 5 6 7 8 9   WCWC   5 4 3 2 1 0

Distributed in Canada by Penguin Books Canada Limited.

A CIP catalogue record for this book is available from the British Library.

Microsoft Press books are available through booksellers and distributors worldwide. For further information about international editions, contact your local Microsoft Corporation office or contact Microsoft Press International directly at fax (425) 936-7329. Visit our Web site at mspress.microsoft.com.

Acquisitions Editor: Eric Stroo
Project Editors: John Pierce and Denise Bankaitis

In loving memory of

Abigail Miller Busche

September 5, 1974 ~ January 31, 2000

Contributing Writers
Robert Corrington, Shawna Davis, Wendy Davis, Rob Frankland, Lauren Gallagher,
Kevin Hintergardt, Derek Jacoby, Radha Kotamarti, Tom Martino, Tony Romano, Peter Shier

Technical Editors
Mary Browning, Annette B. Hall, Julie Lang, Erin Rodabough, Margery Spears

Technical Consultants
Glen Anderson, Eugene Baucom, Gloria Boyer, Kris Durgin, Paul Elrif, Anandha Ganesan, Gary Geiger, Winn Gilmore, Daphne
Guericke, Vivek Jhaveri, Kirk Lang, Michael Maston, Mike Miller, Jon Newman, Bruce Prang, Gautam Reddy, Jeff Robison,
Robert Rodrigues, Autumn Sheppard, Tammy Snow,
Carla Sornson, Rick Swaney, Stephen Todd, Tim Toyoshima, Brett Zalkan

Production
Mark Anable, Sean Hyde, Gary Kraut, Kali Kucera, Jessica Vu

Graphic Designers
Dan Ballard, Corrina Barber, Abigail Busche, David Hose,
Kelly King, Susan Roth, Gavin Schmitz, Kristie Smith, Carol Whittlesey

Print Production Specialist
Kathleen Liekhus

Indexers
Lee Ross, Tony Ross

User Education Group Manager
Stefan Sierakowski

User Education Manager
Alan Boner

User Education Lead
Erika Somm

Contents

Part 3   Snap-in Help

Part 4 Building Snap-ins with C++

Part 5   Building Snap-ins with Visual Basic

Foreword

The rapid acceptance of Microsoft Windows NT as an enterprise-caliber server product has brought an enormous number of tools, technologies, and solutions to the platform. Windows NT is being deployed in more and more mission-critical environments every day. Manageability is key to the success of these installations. It is with this fact in mind that Microsoft Management Console (MMC) was envisioned and developed. As the environment becomes more sophisticated, it has become essential that we provide a single entry point for managing the Windows platform. Before MMC, administrators were faced with a wide array of nonintegrated and dissimilar tools that they had to learn and configure in order to manage their environments. With the MMC console, we have provided a one-stop-shopping approach which brings together platform tools as well as tools provided by management vendors across the industry. If you or your company is developing solutions for managing Windows NT, then this is the book for you. Building and deploying MMC snap-ins will allow your products to integrate with other Microsoft management tools in this common shell. This integration and consistency will reduce the learning curve for you and for your customers as they deploy management solutions on the platform.

Manageability is more than just tools, so it is important to understand the overall architecture for manageability on the Windows platform. The more you understand the platform and leverage built-in technologies, the quicker you will be able to deliver solutions that integrate well with built-in services. MMC provides the visual tools for administrators, but there are many other key technologies that are important for delivering manageable Windows solutions. These include Windows Management Instrumentation (WMI) and the Active Directory. The Active Directory is used for locating resources across the enterprise; WMI is used for managing these resources.

The Active Directory can best be thought of as the "Yellow Pages" for the enterprise. Released with Windows 2000, it is a valuable technology for locating users and other management resources (printers, machines, services, and so on). When you need to locate resources in the environment, the Active Directory is the place to go. Over time, more and more components will be locatable through the directory, which will increase the level of manageability and consistency across enterprise components and services.

WMI provides the instrumentation layer for the platform, plus a broad suite of management infrastructure which includes a rich eventing architecture and scripting support for instrumented components. WMI is a valuable resource for accessing and managing resources across the platform. Over time, Microsoft will continue to enhance support for WMI-enabled components. As you begin to design and architect management solutions for Windows, the best path is to follow the three-tier architecture with MMC as the client user interface (UI) tier, WMI interfaces as the middle tier, and the managed component on the server tier. This will allow you to deliver solutions that provide UI as well as being scriptable (using WMI). Providing easy-to-use UI is important, but providing the ability to script these solutions is just as important. The WMI interfaces you develop will also provide access to your components by industry-wide management products.

Microsoft will continue to improve and integrate MMC, WMI, and the Active Directory, so your efforts here will be leveraged moving forward. Thanks and welcome to Windows!

Casey Kiernan
Director–Distributed Management
Microsoft Corporation

Preface

Welcome to the *Microsoft Management Console Design and Development Kit*. This book provides an introduction to Microsoft Management Console (MMC) and information about how to create and distribute snap-ins.

A Short History of MMC

Here is a short history of MMC in the words of its creator, Tony Romano:

> Microsoft Management Console (MMC) is a relatively simple environment for server administration that indicates nothing of the complex path by which it came into existence.

> In June 1996, Mike Miller and I finished working on the Windows NT 4.0 Network Control Panel (NCP) and I was moving on to my next project. I was to design and implement the routing administration for the Routing and Remote Access Service (RRAS). As usual I had a plethora of requirements from our Program Manager (PM), with some being quite unique. The original design was to add property pages to the NCP if the computer had RRAS installed so that RRAS would be administered in the same fashion as the network configuration.

> One of the requirements the PM listed was to give outside developers the ability to add their own property sheets for custom routing protocols that extend RRAS's capabilities. This sounded fairly straightforward. But, with time and many discussions, the number of items that needed to get extended went far beyond what we could do in NCP. It was now around October, and we decided that we needed to take a new direction.

> I thought that using a user interface based on Windows Explorer with an extension model was the way to go. After further thought, I realized that many administration tools could also use this model, including the NCP that we had just created. Developers are forever needing Windows service or event log information in whatever new tool they're developing, but there was no integrated way to reuse these other components.

I worked with Wayne Scott, another developer, to get a prototype done. It was very simple, but it gave us a visual way to convey the idea. The prototype was completed and I demonstrated it to the RRAS team. After the demonstration, Thomas Payne, my manager at the time, asked me to talk to another PM, Dan Plastina. He stated that Dan was working on some new Windows NT ideas that were very similar and we should hook up. And...

Well, I never did get to do the RRAS admin, because now I was on a new mission with a team of people creating Windows NT's next generation of administration. MMC was created so administration tools can coexist with each other, giving users and developers a consistent visual and programmatic interface. In addition, we built in the ability for one snap-in to extend another snap-in independent of each other. This is valuable for people who need to extend a snap-in that has already shipped.

This book provides the resources you need to plan, design, implement, and deploy management tools through MMC snap-ins. The professionals who are affected by MMC include people in diverse roles such as user interface and usability designer, system administrator, system architect, and administration tool developer.

The book covers the user interface guidelines, MMC Software Development Kit (SDK), C++ and Visual Basic samples, and the Snap-in Designer for Visual Basic. The recent addition of Visual Basic support now completes the goal of making the widest range of developers able to create snap-ins.

Who Should Read This Book

MMC was created to provide an easy and consistent way to administer computer and network systems. Although MMC has no management capabilities on its own, the snap-ins you create to use with it can do virtually any computer or network management task. These snap-ins are the central subject of this book.

Whether you are developing a snap-in for internal use or for commercial distribution, you must make many decisions along the way. This book will aid you in making informed decisions regardless of whether you are a snap-in planner, a designer, or a software developer who is tasked with actually coding the snap-in.

How This Book Is Organized

This book contains a huge amount of information, some of which is specific to particular audiences. Although the book can be read from cover-to-cover, many readers will be interested primarily in certain parts. To help you identify which parts of the book may be of interest to you, the following sections provide an overview of each part.

Part 1: Planning Guide

The first two chapters in this part provide a foundation for all the other material in this book, and therefore are essential reading for everyone. They include an introduction to the MMC user interface (UI) and the snap-in development process.

The next three chapters provide an overview of a snap-in's UI from a programmer's viewpoint, tips on testing snap-ins, and a brief synopsis of how to distribute snap-ins to end users.

Part 2: Design Guidelines

Chapters 6 through 14 explain how to design the UI elements for snap-ins. Note that the MMC UI is based on the Windows UI, but is unique in some ways. For instance, the namespace and taskpad user interface elements are unique to MMC and are discussed in detail. MMC-specific requirements are provided for UI elements, such as property sheets, that are used throughout Windows applications. Each chapter ends with a list of guidelines for creating the graphical user interface element under discussion.

Part 3: Snap-in Help

This section provides step-by-step guidance for creating online Help for your snap-in.

Part 4: Building Snap-ins with C++

Developers can create snap-ins using the MMC COM SDK and any programming language that supports function calls, although the most commonly used language is C++. Note that the MMC COM SDK is part of the MMC SDK (which is part of the Microsoft Platform SDK available at http://msdn.microsoft.com/library).

These chapters provide a programmer's guide for MMC snap-ins that are based on the Component Object Model (COM). Snap-ins have been written in many languages that support COM, such as C++, Visual Basic, Java, and Delphi. Microsoft provides samples and support only for C++. The MMC COM SDK makes use of the Microsoft-supported C++ development environment to provide access to the COM interfaces.

Several sample snap-ins built using the MMC COM SDK are discussed. The code for these samples is on the companion CD-ROM.

The companion CD-ROM contains the C++ MMC development environment and COM SDK, which are part of the MMC SDK. Note that the reference portion of the MMC COM SDK documentation is only available in electronic format on the CD-ROM. The programmer's guide is available both in the book and in electronic format on the CD-ROM.

Part 5: Building Snap-ins with Visual Basic

Developers can also create snap-ins using the Snap-in Designer for Visual Basic, which provides all the functionality of the MMC COM SDK. Although you can access the COM interfaces directly with Visual Basic, the snap-in designer offers much easier access to these interfaces. The Snap-in Designer for Visual Basic is an ActiveX designer. An ActiveX designer is an in-process ActiveX object that extends the functionality of the Visual Basic integrated development environment (IDE). As with all ActiveX designers, the Snap-in Designer for Visual Basic consists of a design-time component and a run-time DLL. See Chapter 32, especially the "What is an ActiveX Designer?" section, for more information on ActiveX designers.

These chapters provide a programmer's guide and reference for the MMC interfaces that are specific to Visual Basic. Included is a discussion of several sample snap-ins built with the Snap-in Designer for Visual Basic. The code for these samples is on the companion CD-ROM.

This part includes an overview of the Visual Basic Object Model, which appears in its entirety on the companion CD-ROM. The Snap-in Designer for Visual Basic documentation in this book also appears in electronic format on the CD-ROM.

The companion CD-ROM contains the Snap-in Designer for Visual Basic product, which is part of the Platform SDK. The Snap-in Designer for Visual Basic can only be used in conjunction with Microsoft Visual Basic version 6.0 or later.

How to Use This Book

The way you use this book depends to a great degree on the part you play in the development of a snap-in.

If you are involved in the planning of a snap-in you should read Chapters 1 through 6. Chapter 6 presents planning steps as well as an overview of the MMC namespace and its elements.

If you are involved in both the planning and the design of a snap-in you should read Chapters 1 through 15 (Parts 1 through 3).

For technical information about developing a snap-in using C++, use the printed information in Part 4 (which is duplicated in electronic format) and use the information on the CD-ROM for SDK reference material and sample code.

For technical information about developing a snap-in using Visual Basic, use the printed information in Part 5 (which is duplicated in electronic format) and use the information on the CD-ROM for sample code and the complete Visual Basic Object Model.

Using the Companion CD-ROM

The CD-ROM included with this book contains the following:

Microsoft Accessibility SDK
This SDK contains all the tools referenced in Chapter 14, "Accessibility and Localization," to test your snap-in for usability by people with disabilities. Click **Accessibility** on the CD-ROM's splash screen to install the SDK on your computer.

This book in online format
The complete book, both text and graphics, in online format. This allows full-text search of the contents. Click **Book Online** to open the folder.

This book in ASCII text format
A set of text files containing Chapters 1 through 15 of the book. This ASCII text version of these chapters is provided for use with systems designed to make the text accessible to users with visual disabilities. Click **Book Contents (Text)** to open the folder.

Icons
A set of icons for use in your snap-ins. Click **Icons** to open the folder.

Internet Explorer 5.01
This is required to run MMC 1.2. It also contains the reader for the online version of the book. Click **Internet Explorer 5.01** to install it on your computer.

Microsoft Management Console version 1.2
Click **Microsoft Management Console** to install it on your computer.

Microsoft Platform SDK
This is a special build of the Microsoft Platform SDK that installs the samples, documentation, and build environment for MMC and WMI. It includes all the C++ and Visual Basic samples that appear in the book. Click **Platform SDK** to install it on your computer.

System Requirements

To use the tools and run the samples on the companion CD-ROM, you will need the following:

To run MMC 1.2

- Microsoft Internet Explorer version 5.01 or later

To build the C++ sample snap-ins

- Microsoft Windows 2000, Windows NT 4.0, or Windows 98 operating system
- Microsoft Visual C++ version 6.0, or properly installed C++ compiler, linker, and resource compiler that are compatible with Microsoft Visual C++ 6.0
- Microsoft Platform SDK, Windows 2000 RC1 or later version
- Microsoft Management Console version 1.1 or later

To build the MMC Snap-in Designer for Visual Basic sample snap-ins

- Microsoft Windows 2000, Windows NT 4.0 with Service Pack 3 or later, or Windows 95/98 operating system
- Microsoft Visual Basic version 6.0
- MMC Snap-in Designer for Visual Basic
- Microsoft Management Console version 1.1 or later

Sample Code

Pieces of sample source code are included in the MMC COM SDK and the Snap-in Designer for Visual Basic portions of the book to illustrate how to implement various elements of a snap-in. The sample code appears in a special monospace font as shown here:

```
HRESULT CComponent::CreatePropertyPages(
            /* [in] */ LPPROPERTYSHEETCALLBACK lpProvider,
            /* [in] */ LONG_PTR handle,
            /* [in] */ LPDATAOBJECT lpIDataObject)
{
    CDelegationBase *base = GetOurDataObject(lpIDataObject)-
        >GetBaseNodeObject();

    return base->CreatePropertyPages(lpProvider, handle);
}
```

The companion CD-ROM contains the complete code for the sample snap-ins presented in the book.

Other Resources

This book covers the entire snap-in development process from planning to software development. The resources listed here are divided into those that are available as traditional books and those that are available electronically, and cover design, development, and usability.

Books

Design

Cooper, Alan. *About Face: The Essentials of Interface Design.* Foster City, CA: IDG Books Worldwide, Inc., 1995.

Cooper, Alan. *The Inmates Are Running the Asylum: Why High-Tech Products Drive Us Crazy and How to Restore the Sanity.* Indianapolis, IN: Sams, 1999.

Fernandes, Tony. *Global Interface Design: A Guide to Designing International User Interfaces.* Boston, MA: AP Professional, 1995.

Mandel, Theo. *The Elements of User Interface Design.* New York: Wiley, 1997.

Microsoft Corporation. *Microsoft Windows User Experience: Official Guidelines for User Interface Developers and Designers*. Redmond, WA: Microsoft Press, 1999.

Microsoft Corporation. *The Windows Interface Guidelines for Software Design*. Redmond, WA: Microsoft Press, 1995.

Mullet, Kevin, and Darrell Sano. *Designing Visual Interfaces: Communication Oriented Techniques*. Englewood Cliffs, NJ: SunSoft Press, 1995.

Rogerson, Dale. *Inside COM*. Redmond, WA: Microsoft Press, 1997.

Shneiderman, B. *Designing the User Interface: Strategies for Effective Human-Computer Interaction*. Reading, MA: Addison-Wesley, 1987.

Zetie, Carl. *Practical User Interface Design: Making GUIs Work*. London; New York: McGraw Hill Book Company, 1995.

Development

Chappell, David. *Understanding ActiveX and OLE*. Redmond, WA: Microsoft Press, 1996.

Grimes, Richard, and Alex Stockton. *Beginning ATL COM Programming*. Chicago, IL: Wrox Press, 1998.

McKay, Everett N. *Developing User Interfaces for Microsoft Windows*. Redmond WA: Microsoft Press, 1999.

Usability

Beyer, H. and K. Holtzblatt. *Contextual Design: Defining Customer-Centered Systems*. San Francisco, CA: Morgan Kaufmann, 1998.

Nielsen, J. *Usability Engineering*. Boston, MA: Academic Press, 1993.

Rubin, J. *Handbook of Usability Testing: How to Plan, Design, and Conduct Effective Tests*. New York: Wiley, 1994.

Wixon, D and J. Ramey. *Field Methods Casebook for Software Design*. New York: Wiley Computer Pub., 1996.

Electronic Resources

MMC

Microsoft Management Console home page. Available
http://www.microsoft.com/management/mmc.

MMC public newsgroup. Available "microsoft.public.management.mmc."

Windows NTServer Management Services page. Available
http://www.microsoft.com/ntserver/management/.

Design

ACM SIGCHI: Special Interest Group on Human-Computer Interaction.
Available http://www.acm.org/sigchi/.

MSDN Online: User Experience and Interface Design Resources. Available
http://msdn.microsoft.com/ui/default.asp.

Yahoo Human-Computer Interaction index. Available
http://dir.yahoo.com/Science/Computer_Science/Human_Computer_Interaction_
HCI_/.

Yahoo User Interface index. Available
http://dir.yahoo.com/Science/Computer_Science/User_Interface/.

Development

Microsoft Developer Network (MSDN) home page. Available
http://msdn.microsoft.com.

Usability

Microsoft Corporation: Usability Research site. Available
http://www.microsoft.com/usability/.

MSDN Online Web Workshop: Improving Web Site Usability and Appeal.
Available
http://msdn.microsoft.com/workshop/management/planning/improvingsiteusa.asp.

"Usable Web: 741 links about Web usability." Available
http://www.usableweb.com.

P A R T   1

Planning Guide

Everyone should read the first two chapters of this section. They lay the foundation for the material in the other parts of the book. Chapters 3 through 5 provide a high-level overview of a snap-in's user interface (UI), and offer sound advice to prospective snap-in developers on testing snap-ins and distributing snap-ins to customers. While these three chapters cover essential material for developers, they can be skipped by others more eager to begin the "Design Guidelines" section of the book.

While most of the material in Chapters 3 through 5 is equally applicable to developers using C++ and those using Visual Basic, special attention is called to topics that the two development environments handle differently. This is particularly true of Chapter 5, which deals with deploying snap-ins.

The electronic version of the MMC SDK is provided on the companion CD-ROM. The SDK also contains this Planning Guide section. As a result, some of the language and terminology in this section is similar to that found in the SDK portions of this book (Parts 4 and 5).

C H A P T E R   1

Introducing MMC

This chapter introduces Microsoft Management Console (MMC) and includes a brief background of its development. It concludes with an overview of the graphical user interface elements used in MMC.

Administration Solutions

Administration of a single computer or a network of computers has evolved in many directions over the past few years. In the not-too-distant past, an administrator of single computers only needed to be concerned with a few relatively simple tasks such as checking the integrity of a hard disk or ensuring modem connectivity. For networked systems, the most common task for administrators was ensuring access to shared files and other network resources such as printers.

Today both stand-alone and networked system administration have become increasingly complex. Stand-alone systems typically have access to the Internet, a host of new peripherals (video cameras, removable storage drives, DVDs, and so on), and multiple software applications that require at least intermittent attention. Networked systems can provide services locally as well as globally by using the Internet. Although these systems have many of the same administration issues as stand-alone systems, they additionally must deal with a host of new ones related to server and network administration.

Underlying this plethora of new technology are multiple administration programs, each with its own unique user interface. It is not always easy to find the administration program required for a particular application or peripheral. In addition, administration program user interfaces are not customizable to fit the knowledge and skill level of the administrator, adding to the training and supervisory loads of experienced administrators. All of these issues contribute to a long learning curve for new system administrators and a high frustration level for current system administrators.

A typical server administrator uses a wide range of applications to keep a server running smoothly. These applications control such things as databases, printers, networks, Internet connectivity, telephones, computer hardware, automated software installations, and user accounts. Each application has a different user interface. It can be difficult to find the application needed to do the task at hand. For instance, an application appearing on the **Start** menu can easily be buried under a menu item not usually associated with the task at hand.

In summary, computer system and network administrators face these problems:

- Administration tools can be hard to find.
- Each administration tool has its own unique user interface.
- In general, tools cannot be customized to the knowledge or skill level of the intended user.

Planning Guide

A Computer Administration Solution

Microsoft has long recognized the increasing complexity and difficulty of computer administration. MMC is a significant part of the solution to these problems. Microsoft first shipped MMC version 1.0 with the Microsoft Windows NT 4.0 Option Pack for Windows NT Server. MMC 1.1 shipped in Microsoft SQL Server 7.0 and Microsoft Systems Management Server 2.0. MMC 1.2 is bundled with Windows 2000 and runs on all 32-bit and 64-bit Windows operating systems.

The goal of MMC is to minimize the cost of administering Windows-based computers, and to provide a simple, consistent, and integrated user interface and administration model. One of the strengths of MMC is its ability to support task delegation scenarios. Usability research and customer surveys suggest that there are several distinct types of administration, and that many problems need to be handed off from one administrator to another as the problem is resolved. In the following descriptions, note that one person might perform any or all of these roles, particularly in a small organization employing only a few administrators.

First-tier administrator
Provides help desk support and performs day-to-day administrative tasks such as creating users, restarting workstations (but not servers), and working with end users.

Second-tier administrator
Uses monitoring and troubleshooting tools on a daily basis. Administrators working at this level are often considered to be the experts in solving server problems and usually have in-depth knowledge of an organization's network and server applications. Unusual or complex problems are escalated to this level from the first tier.

Third-tier administrator
Evaluates and rolls out new server applications, designs and defines new operational and support procedures, and develops administration tools as necessary. Critical or cross-application problems may be escalated to this level from the first- or second-tier administrators.

Although system administration is not always so clearly categorized within an organization, there is usually a hierarchy of administrative tasks that are assigned according to the skill and experience level of the administrator.

How MMC Manages Administration Problems

You can use Microsoft Management Console (MMC) to create, save, and open administrative tools (called MMC *consoles*) that manage the hardware, software, and network components of your Windows system.

MMC does not perform administrative functions, but hosts tools that do. The primary type of tool you can add to a console is called a snap-in. Other items that you can add include ActiveX controls, links to Web pages, folders, taskpad views, and tasks.

It provides a multiple-document interface (MDI) in which each window is a *view*. Each view can contain one or more administrative components that supply the management behavior. Each administrative component is a *snap-in*.

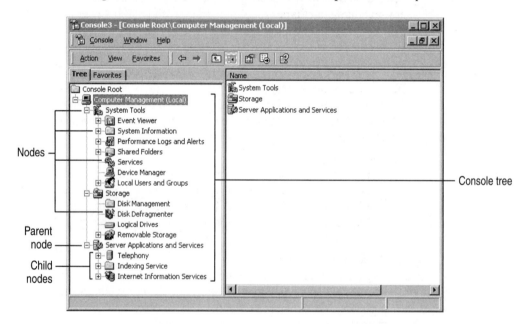

Figure 1.1   MMC console

Figure 1.1 shows an MMC console that contains a tree structure in the left pane. Each branch of the tree is a *node*. The *console tree* contains a hierarchy of nodes. Each node is the *parent* of any nodes that lie one level below it in the tree hierarchy. The nodes below a parent node are *child* nodes.

By using snap-ins in MMC consoles, administrators no longer need to hunt for administration tools and the tools can have a common user interface. The guidelines provided in this book are critical for the creation of snap-ins with a common user interface. This lessens the administrator's learning and training curve.

Snap-ins

An MMC console has no native system or network management functionality, but rather provides a common user interface for whatever management functionality it is populated with in the form of snap-ins.

A snap-in is a Component Object Model (COM) in-process server dynamic-link library (DLL). This COM interface is situated between MMC and the snap-in. MMC does not care how the snap-in communicates with the managed service. Snap-ins can communicate with the managed service through any data protocol that the managed service supports. MMC has no knowledge of the mechanism used for this communication. Both Microsoft developers and independent software vendors (ISVs) can create snap-ins.

There are two types of snap-ins:

Stand-alone
> A stand-alone snap-in, when loaded in a console, can perform its designated management task as the only snap-in loaded in the console.

Extension
> An extension snap-in adds functionality to a stand-alone snap-in. Extension snap-ins can add their own nodes as children of the stand-alone snap-in's node. They can also add context menu items, toolbar buttons, property pages, and taskpad tasks to the stand-alone snap-in's node. Depending on the item being extended, an extension snap-in can further be classified as any combination of the following:

- Namespace extension
- Context menu extension
- Toolbar extension
- Menu button extension
- Property page extension
- Taskpad extension

It is possible for a snap-in to operate as a stand-alone snap-in and also to extend the functionality of another snap-in as an extension snap-in. Snap-ins that take this double role are *dual-mode* snap-ins. For example, the Event Viewer snap-in reads the event logs of computers. If the Computer Management snap-in's computer object exists in the console, the Event Viewer snap-in automatically extends each instance of the computer object and provides appropriate event logs. When the Event Viewer snap-in is used as a stand-alone snap-in, an administrator must manually provide a computer name when the snap-in is opened, and the snap-in simply provides the event logs of this one computer.

MMC Console Creation

MMC has two modes, *author mode* and *user mode*. Author mode permits full control of the MMC environment, including the ability to add or remove snap-ins, create taskpad views, and change many options through the **Customize View** and **Options** dialog boxes. User mode offers three alternative access models that progressively restrict the user's ability to alter the console's contents and appearance.

A system administrator can create a tool that consists of a console with one or more snap-ins and save it (as an .msc file) for future use or for sharing with other administrators. This tool might be used to delegate tasks to others in the organization, to improve workflow, or to coordinate completion of tasks. Separate tools might be created to handle daily, weekly, and monthly administrative tasks. These scenarios illustrate that all the elements necessary to complete a task are together in one easy-to-find place.

MMC User Interface Elements

This section presents a brief description of the major MMC graphical user interface (GUI) elements. More details appear in subsequent chapters of this book.

MMC-Specific GUI Elements

Two GUI elements are unique to the MMC console—the namespace and the taskpad. The *namespace* provides the context for all MMC activity. A *taskpad* is a graphical way of presenting actions that can be performed on a selected item in the scope pane.

Namespaces

Below the standard toolbars in the MMC console are two panes as shown in
Figure 1.2. The pane on the left contains the console tree and the pane on the right
contains details about the selected node in the console tree. Together, these panes
form the *namespace*.

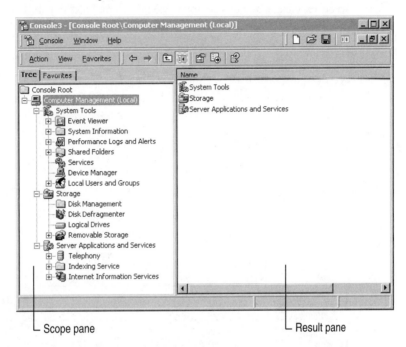

Figure 1.2   MMC console namespace

In this book, the left pane is called the *scope pane* and the right pane is called the
result pane to be consistent with the programming documentation.

Note MMC Help refers to these two panes as the console tree and the details
pane, respectively. These are the end-user terms for the panes.

The console tree in the scope pane contains the snap-ins that make up the
management tool. For the currently selected node in the console tree, the result
pane contains the child nodes, information about the node, or a user interface to
perform a task on the node.

For more information about the MMC namespace, see Chapter 6, "Namespaces,"
and Chapter 16, "MMC COM Programmer's Guide Overview."

Taskpads

Because of the object-oriented nature of the console tree, users tend to search for the object they want to manage rather than for a particular task to accomplish. New users may find it easier to follow a task-based approach. At other times, you may want to combine pieces from several different snap-ins to accomplish a task. In either case, you can create an MMC taskpad to fill your need.

Figure 1.3   MMC taskpad example

Figure 1.3 shows the System Log console taskpad. Note that if you create multiple taskpads for a single node, each taskpad has its own tab at the bottom of the result pane, as shown.

For more information about MMC taskpads, see Chapter 11, "Console Customization and Taskpads"; Chapter 20, "Using Different Result Pane View Types"; and Chapter 34, "Developing Snap-ins."

Common GUI Elements

Because MMC is a standard Windows application, MMC and its snap-ins follow Windows GUI standards whenever they apply. The elements covered in this section are found in many Windows applications.

Menus

A snap-in's menus follow the standard Windows conventions, as specified in the *Microsoft Windows User Experience* book. A snap-in creates the right-click context menu for an item, and then MMC builds the corresponding console **Action** menu for that item. The context menu must include the **View** menu as a cascading menu item as shown in Figure 1.4.

Figure 1.4   Event Viewer context menu and Action menu

Note that the only difference in these menus is the inclusion of the **View** cascading menu on the context menu. If the node is selected, the context menu and the **Action** menu are identical (except, of course, for the **View** menu).

For more information about snap-in and MMC console menus, see Chapter 7, "Menus"; Chapter 21, "Working with Context Menus"; and Chapter 34, "Developing Snap-ins."

Toolbars

The MMC console contains two standard Windows toolbar frames, the *console* toolbar frame and the *snap-in* toolbar frame, as shown in Figure 1.5.

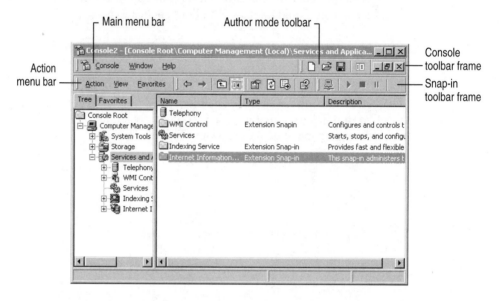

Figure 1.5   MMC console and snap-in toolbars

Although you cannot make changes to the main menu or the author mode toolbar in the console toolbar frame, you can add drop-down menus and command buttons to the snap-in **Action** menu bar and snap-in toolbars in the toolbar frame. For each node, you can create one or more sets of command buttons (toolbars).

For more information about MMC toolbars, see Chapter 8, "Toolbars"; Chapter 22, "Working with Toolbars and Menu Buttons"; and Chapter 34, "Developing Snap-ins."

Wizards

In an MMC snap-in, use wizards to automate complicated tasks or to provide a helping hand for novice users. You can display a wizard at any time, for instance, when you add a snap-in to a console, or in response to a menu or toolbar command. Figure 1.6 shows the first page of the New Scope Wizard from the Windows 2000 DHCP snap-in.

Figure 1.6   First page of the New Scope Wizard

For more information about MMC wizards, see Chapter 12, "Wizards"; Chapter 23, "Adding Property Pages and Wizard Pages"; and Chapter 34, "Developing Snap-ins."

Property Sheets

In an MMC console, a property sheet is often used to set or view properties of a node, as shown in Figure 1.7. Note that a property sheet always includes the **OK**, **Cancel**, and **Apply** buttons by default.

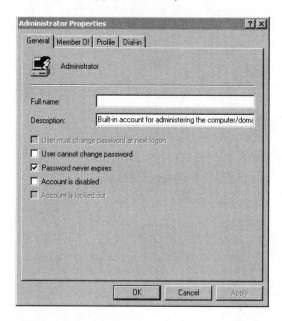

Figure 1.7   Services snap-in property sheet

For more information about snap-in property sheets and property pages, see Chapter 10, "Property Sheets"; Chapter 23, "Adding Property Pages and Wizard Pages"; and Chapter 34, "Developing Snap-ins."

Dialog Boxes

Use a dialog box to obtain the user input needed to complete a task. Figure 1.8 shows a dialog box from the Windows 2000 Active Directory Users and Computers snap-in.

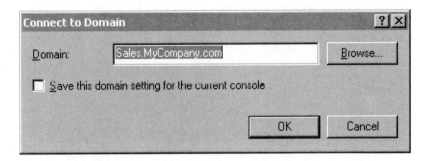

Figure 1.8   Dialog box from Active Directory Users and Computers snap-in

For more information about snap-in dialog boxes, see Chapter 13, "Dialog Boxes and Message Boxes."

C H A P T E R   2

Creating Snap-ins

To create a Microsoft Management Console (MMC) snap-in, a developer must write code and save the file as a dynamic-link library (DLL) using the tools and techniques spelled out in the MMC Software Development Kit (SDK).

Before any coding can begin, a certain amount of planning is required. (For more information, see Chapter 6, "Namespaces" and Appendix A, "Snap-in Design Planning.") Much of this planning centers on design issues.

The Role of Design in Snap-in Development

Design is an ambiguous term. Ask five different people what the role of design is, and more than likely you will get five different answers. For snap-in development, design is a process that involves several different people addressing different aspects of a problem to achieve common goals. Whether you are creating a snap-in for the first time or revising an existing snap-in, these goals of product development are well-recognized. A product should be:

- Useful: needed and used.
- Usable: easy to learn and use.
- Desirable: wanted by its intended audience.
- Feasible: possible to build economically and on time.

It is difficult to completely meet these goals, but in the process of working toward them, you acquire information that improves the quality of your finished product. For instance, before you can determine if your product meets the needs of users, you need to determine who the potential users are and the needs they have. The research you pursue in determining who the users are can also help define an intuitive approach to the task your snap-in performs. When you ask the users what they need and develop the product with that in mind, you have realistically defined the market for your product.

The design guidelines presented in Part 2 of this book complement those detailed in *Microsoft Windows User Experience*. Use these two books for guidance in creating graphical user interface (GUI) elements for your snap-in. Note that if you discover differences in their recommendations, for snap-in design, you should follow the guidelines set forth in this book.

As you work toward these design goals, you should constantly test the product with real users to assess your progress. Design becomes an iterative process and forms a contract between end users and developers that results in an easy-to-use, robust product. This holds true whether you are developing an MMC tool for your staff of five or a console file that will be commercially distributed and potentially have thousands of users.

Consoles and Snap-ins

Remember that MMC by itself provides no management functionality. It acts as a host to snap-ins that provide the functionality for management tasks. This section provides some basic information about MMC and snap-ins so that you can decide whether your functionality belongs in MMC, in Control Panel, or as a stand-alone application.

Console Files

Developers and end users can save an MMC multiple-document interface (MDI) window—a console populated with one or more snap-ins—as a file with an .msc extension. Anyone in author mode can create such a console file and tailor its look and feel for those that use the tool. You can save the file with any combination of the following settings:

- **Add/Remove Snap-ins** is disabled.
- MMC console controls are not displayed.
- Console tree and scope pane are hidden.
- A taskpad is the only visible interface.

This ability to build custom tools (saved console files) enables administrators to provide tools that are appropriate to users' skill levels and to control the ways in which users can gain access to and manipulate data. For example, you might create a console file populated with tools to perform specific first-tier administrative tasks. For more information about saved console files, see Chapter 5, "Deploying Snap-ins," and Chapter 29, "Distributing Your Snap-in."

Snap-ins

Without a snap-in loaded, an MMC console has no management functionality. The snap-in provides the interface to the management task and the access to programs and data required to perform the task.

A snap-in is implemented as a Component Object Model (COM) in-process server. The compiled code is linked to create a DLL. MMC interacts with snap-ins using several MMC-defined programming interfaces. The MMC interfaces allow snap-ins to share a common hosting environment (consoles) and provide cross-application integration.

Using the WMI and Active Directory Technologies

Snap-ins can communicate with the managed objects using whatever interface those objects support (DCOM, RPC, LDAP, and so on), but you should use Windows Management Instrumentation (WMI) and Active Directory directory service wherever possible. These interfaces encourage uniform access, including scripting, for the underlying functionality provided by the snap-in.

One outcome of their use is to keep the data management application programming interfaces (APIs) separate from the user interface layer (snap-ins). A snap-in should simply function as a way to invoke management services that are defined by an API.

Planning Guide

A snap-in can use two complementary technologies (WMI and Active Directory) to interact with other applications, services, hardware, data, and devices. Figure 2.1 illustrates the use of these technologies with MMC to access a variety of objects. Note that one snap-in uses Active Directory to locate all the SQL servers available and select two to perform a service. The snap-in then uses WMI to actually interact with the servers to perform the task.

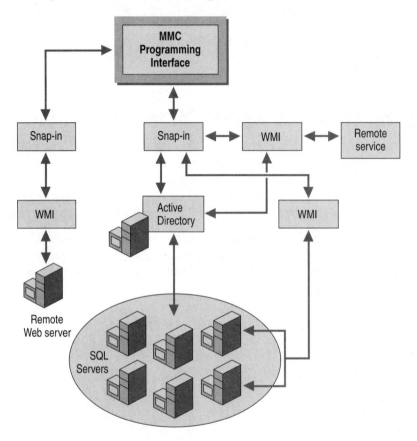

Figure 2.1   MMC, Active Directory, and WMI

Windows Management Instrumentation

WMI is Microsoft's implementation of the Web-Based Enterprise Management (WBEM) standard.

WBEM is an industry initiative, overseen by the Distributed Management Task Force (DMTF), to develop a standardized, nonproprietary means for accessing and sharing management information in an enterprise network. It is intended to alleviate the problems usually associated with collecting management and diagnostic data that can include different types of hardware, protocols, operating systems, and distributed applications.

In the context of MMC and snap-ins, WMI offers a simple interface to management data that includes:

- A rich and consistent model of the Windows operating system's behavior, configuration, and status.
- A COM API that supplies a single point of access to all management information.
- Interoperability with other Windows 2000 management services.
- A flexible architecture that enables vendors to extend the information model to cover new devices, applications, and services.
- A rich query language that enables SQL-based queries of the information model.
- A scriptable API that allows seamless local and remote system administration.

As Figure 2.1 suggests, snap-in developers can use WMI as the interface to local and remote managed objects. The underlying WBEM technology ensures access to virtually all objects in an enterprise network.

For more information about WMI, visit the MSDN Online Downloads Web site at:
http://msdn.microsoft.com/developer/sdk/wmisdk/default.asp.

Active Directory

Active Directory Service Interfaces (ADSI) is the primary API for Active Directory directory services. Active Directory provides the following:

Location transparency
> Finding information about a user, group, networked service, or resource, without knowing addressing information.

Information on people and services
> Storing user, group, organization, or service information in a structured hierarchical tree.

Rich query
> Locating objects of interest by querying for properties of the objects.

High availability
> Locating a replica of the directory at a location that is the most efficient for a read/write operation.

Snap-in developers can use ADSI to gain access to objects stored in the directory as COM objects. Active Directory adds a powerful component to distributed application management by providing a way to transparently access objects on the enterprise network.

For more information about Active Directory, visit the Microsoft Windows 2000 Web site at
http://www.microsoft.com/windows2000/

WMI and Active Directory Interoperability

These two technologies, WMI and Active Directory, can act in concert to make a snap-in developer's work much easier. Both offer a data store, a query engine, and an index engine. However, the uses for the data stores and engines are very different.

Active Directory provides a replicated, highly available store, optimized for fast access to largely static information. It holds the information necessary to locate users, systems, and devices in the enterprise, along with meta-information about the network and environment that is not available elsewhere.

WMI provides access to detailed system and device information for managed objects in the enterprise. It supports both static and dynamic properties, methods, and events for its managed objects.

Snap-ins can use Active Directory to locate objects in the enterprise and WMI to gather information from those objects, making enterprise management more centralized and accessible, and therefore easier.

When to Use Snap-ins

You can create snap-ins, utility programs, and wizards with similar functionality, but snap-ins are intended for administrative tasks. To help you decide if a task is appropriate for a snap-in, here are some guidelines:

Create a snap-in when the task:

- Requires privileged access.
- Is administrative in nature.
- Involves configuration of a service.
- Extends another snap-in.

Create a program for Control Panel when the task:

- Is end-user oriented rather than administrative.
- Does not need to be automated.
- Requires high, centralized visibility.
- Does not rely on another Windows user interface.

In some cases, you can create a wizard that a user can gain access to by using a snap-in. For example, create a wizard if a task:

- Is focused and involves several steps.
- Is performed with moderate frequency.
- Has high visibility.
- Can be accomplished with a simple nonbranching set of steps.

Snap-in Development Tools

You can create snap-ins in any development environment that supports producing COM components. Some of the most common development environments are Microsoft Visual C++ 5.0 and 6.0, and Microsoft Visual Basic 6.0. Each development tool has slightly different requirements, as follows:

Visual C++ 5.0
Current Microsoft Platform SDK; MMC SDK (included on the companion CD-ROM); must use LINK.exe

Visual C++ 6.0
Current Platform SDK; MMC SDK

Visual Basic 6.0
MMC Snap-in Designer for Visual Basic (included on the companion CD-ROM)

For up-to-the-minute updates on development requirements, visit the Microsoft Management Console Web site at:
http://www.microsoft.com/management/mmc/

The MMC COM Programmer's Guide (for C++ programmers) and the MMC Snap-in Designer for Visual Basic (for Visual Basic programmers) form Part 4 and Part 5, respectively, of this book. A brief overview of each is included here.

MMC COM Programmer's Guide

The MMC COM Programmer's Guide is part of the MMC SDK. Because a snap-in is a COM in-process server DLL, you should be familiar with creating COM DLLs before starting work with the SDK.

In addition, the reference portion of the MMC SDK documentation covers approximately 30 COM interfaces that you need to become acquainted with, although you may need only a few for your snap-in. You need to know what each interface does so that you can choose the ones you need. Snap-ins implement some of these interfaces and expose them to MMC. MMC implements the remaining interfaces and exposes them to snap-ins to use.

For more information, see Part 4 later in this book and the MMC COM SDK on the companion CD-ROM.

MMC Snap-in Designer for Visual Basic

The MMC Snap-in Designer for Visual Basic is an ActiveX designer that enables you to write a snap-in using Visual Basic without having to use the complex code required for developing a snap-in using C++. When you install the snap-in designer, it creates a new project type called "Snap-in" in Visual Basic 6.0 (the only version that supports the designer).

The development process is very similar to the one used to create applications with typical Visual Basic forms. Although much of the complex code required for C++ snap-ins has been simplified, you lose none of the snap-in functionality.

For more information, see Part 5 later in this book and the Visual Basic Object Model on the companion CD-ROM.

Designing Exchange

Each of Chapters 6 through 13 of this book presents a different snap-in GUI element. Each element's use is explained and guidelines are presented for how that element should be implemented for snap-ins.

In Chapter 6, a process for designing a snap-in (or any other software product) is introduced. The process is detailed in Appendix A, "Snap-in Design Planning." Each step of that process further defines the final product.

Because the process is iterative, some design chapters conclude with a section called "Designing Exchange." In most cases, this section briefly recounts some of the experiences of the Microsoft Exchange group in developing that particular GUI element for an Exchange snap-in. The purpose of these sections is to illuminate some of the real-world tradeoffs that are constantly made in the design process. The hope is that reading about the Exchange team's experiences will give you, the snap-in developer, extra insight that will be reflected in the quality of snap-ins in the marketplace.

C H A P T E R   3

Analyzing the Snap-in User Interface

In Chapter 1, the graphical user interface (GUI) elements of an MMC snap-in were introduced. These elements are displayed to an end user differently than to the developer. While the design guidelines presented in Part 2 of this book help you create a seamless end-user environment, it might be helpful to understand some of the details of MMC snap-in development.

The type of detailed information that you need for designing a user interface (UI) depends on the snap-in development environment you choose; however, there are many basic GUI concepts that apply regardless of the development environment. This chapter explores these concepts by studying the following GUI elements:

- Scope panes
- Result panes
- Context menus
- Toolbars and menus
- Property sheets
- Wizards
- Taskpads

Scope Panes

As described in Chapter 1, the console tree is composed of nodes that represent containers and objects and is understood from a programming point of view to be made up of nodes. The top-level node of every stand-alone snap-in is a *static node,* which is maintained by MMC. When opening a saved console, MMC displays the title and icon of the node even if the snap-in itself has not been loaded.

The static node is a parent node. The nodes below it are *child* nodes. These child nodes can be placed in the tree either by the stand-alone snap-in or by a namespace extension. These nodes are dynamic because MMC does not know about them until they are added. They are generally added only when their parent node is double-clicked or expanded.

Because of the dynamic nature of child nodes, adding a childless node to the console causes the extension snap-in to notify MMC that a plus sign should not be displayed in the tree. If an extension snap-in later inserts a child into that node, then MMC changes the tree automatically to display the plus sign.

Result Panes

When a user clicks a node in the scope pane, MMC allows the snap-in that added the node to display a view in the result pane for that node. The snap-in that added the node is the *primary snap-in.* Note that the concept of a primary snap-in is different than that of a stand-alone snap-in. Every stand-alone snap-in is also the primary snap-in for at least one node, but a namespace extension snap-in is the primary snap-in for the nodes that it has added. Any node in the scope pane can display several different result pane views:

- **Standard result list view**

  The default result pane view type is a standard result list view (or simply *list view*). A list view displays a collection of items, each consisting of an icon and a label, and provides several ways to display and arrange the items. Unlike the scope pane, in which a snap-in adds items only once, the primary snap-in is expected to insert its result list items each time the scope node is clicked. This allows the result items to be considerably more dynamic than the scope items. For instance, if a scope node is selected in more than one multiple-document interface (MDI) window, the result list need not necessarily be the same.

  A special type of standard list is a *virtual list.* In a virtual list, the snap-in provides only as many items as are currently shown. When the user scrolls up or down, the snap-in is asked for additional items. This type of list is particularly well suited for large numbers of result items. Note that only the primary snap-in can add list items; extension snap-ins cannot add list items.

- **Taskpad view**

  A taskpad is a simplified GUI presentation of actions that can be performed within a snap-in. Taskpads are used for such tasks as starting wizards, opening property pages, performing menu commands, running command lines, and opening Web pages.

  For more information about Taskpads, see "Taskpads" later in this chapter.

- **Custom OCX view**

  A snap-in can start an OCX control in the result pane of an MMC console.

- **Custom Web page**

  The result pane of an MMC console can host HTML pages that are located either locally in MMC, or on an external Web server.

Wherever possible, you should design a snap-in to use a standard result list view rather than a custom OCX view or a Web page. Taskpads can be used to supplement a standard result list view. If the standard list simply does not provide enough user interface flexibility, then you should use an OCX or an HTML page. For more information, see the guidelines in Parts 4 and 5 of this book).

Context Menus

When the user right-clicks either a scope node or a list view item in the result pane, MMC displays a context menu. MMC builds the context menu by first adding its own menu items, then allowing the primary snap-in to add its own menu items, and finally by allowing any extension snap-ins to add their menu items. When the user clicks a context menu item, MMC forwards the user's action to the primary snap-in.

When the user right-clicks a scope node, MMC first allows the primary snap-in to add its items. The primary snap-in can add menu items and submenus to the top of the context menu as well as to the **All Tasks**, **New**, and **View** submenus. MMC then allows each extension snap-in to add its items to the **All Tasks** and **New** submenus only. Extension snap-ins cannot add menu items to the top of the context menu or to the **View** submenu. Next, MMC displays the context menu and forwards the user's selection to the primary snap-in.

Instead of adding common MMC menu commands to the context menu directly, the primary snap-in can enable certain *standard verbs*. MMC standard verbs include, for example, delete, copy, and paste. Using standard verbs properly is important. Since MMC controls the placement, text, and toolbars for these commands, consistency from snap-in to snap-in is ensured.

Planning Guide

Action and View Menus

The **Action** and **View** menus in the snap-in toolbar frame display the same
context menu items that appear in the item's right-click context menu. The snap-
in cannot discern between a user gaining access to these items through the **Action**
and **View** menus and a user gaining access through the context menu.

The **Action** and **View** menus behave differently, however, depending on whether
the nodes are accessed through the console tree or through the **Favorites** menu.
When a node is clicked in the **Favorites** menu, the ordinary context menu items
and the **Action** menu pertain to the **Favorites** node, not to the console tree node
from which the **Favorites** node was selected. Consequently, you cannot access the
context menu for the node through **Favorites**.

Toolbars and Menus

When the user clicks a node, the primary snap-in adds its menu items to the
context menu and its snap-in toolbar to the snap-in toolbar frame. Next, extension
snap-ins do the same. When the user clicks a menu item, MMC forwards the
user's selection to the primary snap-in. As in the context menus, the primary snap-
in can add MMC standard verbs so that MMC automatically creates toolbar
buttons for those items.

Property Sheets

When a user right-clicks a scope node or a result pane item and then clicks
Properties, MMC allows the primary snap-in to add property pages to it. MMC
then gives any extension snap-ins the same opportunity. If any snap-ins add
property pages, MMC displays a property sheet with each property page as a tab
on the property sheet. Any user action made on a particular property page is
forwarded to the snap-in that added that page.

A stand-alone snap-in can also display a property page independent of the **Properties** command. In this case, the snap-in that requests the property sheet must explicitly tell MMC to allow extension snap-ins to add their own property pages.

There are several options regarding how to implement snap-in Help on property sheets. For more information, see Chapter 15, "Creating Online Help."

Wizards

Any stand-alone or extension snap-in can display a wizard in response to a user action. Generally, wizards are invoked from a context menu command or by a toolbar button. When the user clicks a scope node or a result pane item and then performs an action that invokes a wizard, MMC allows the primary snap-in to add wizard pages to the wizard. Any user action entered in a particular wizard page is forwarded to the snap-in.

Note that in contrast to property sheets, MMC does not permit extension snap-ins to add their own pages to a wizard that is displayed by another snap-in.

Taskpads

There are two types of taskpads: *snap-in taskpads* and *console taskpads*. Snap-in taskpads were introduced in MMC 1.1 and have been largely replaced by console taskpads in MMC 1.2. Console taskpads offer many advantages: ease of creation, performance, display consistency, and ability of the user to customize the taskpad. In MMC 1.2, there is little reason for choosing snap-in taskpads over console taskpads.

Planning Guide

Snap-in Taskpad

A snap-in taskpad is implemented as a view on the selected scope node, and that view is represented as an HTML page in the result pane. The taskpad HTML page lists actions that can be performed on the selected node. Each action is represented as a task consisting of an image, a label, a description, and a mechanism for commanding the snap-in to perform the associated action.

There are three types of snap-in taskpads:

- **Standard**

  MMC provides a default taskpad that displays the taskpad title and tasks.

- **Standard list view**

  MMC provides a standard list view taskpad (*listpad*) that displays the taskpad title, a list control that displays items that can be selected, and tasks that can perform actions on the selected items.

- **Custom**

  Your snap-in can provide its own HTML page that displays tasks to perform as well as other elements.

If a particular node has a taskpad view, it is the responsibility of the primary snap-in to provide the user with a mechanism for gaining access to the taskpad. One solution is to add a menu item to the node's **View** context submenu. Note also that you can set a snap-in's default properties to display a taskpad automatically when a node is clicked.

When a taskpad view for a selected node is displayed in the result pane, MMC allows the primary snap-in to set up and add tasks to the taskpad. MMC then allows any extension snap-ins to add their own tasks to the taskpad. Note that for listpads, only the primary snap-in is permitted to insert items into its listpad's list view.

When the user clicks one of the tasks on the taskpad, MMC forwards the user's selection to the snap-in that added the task.

Console Taskpad

Console taskpads are introduced in MMC 1.2. The user can use a console taskpad to run tasks such as starting wizards, opening property pages, performing menu commands, running command lines, and opening Web pages.

Console taskpads are implemented by MMC. That is, MMC takes care of setting up a console taskpad for a particular node.

To create a console taskpad, the user right-clicks a scope node and then, on the shortcut menu, clicks **New Taskpad View**. The user, through the New Taskpad View Wizard and the New Task Wizard, then enters the requested information that MMC needs to create the console taskpad. By using the New Task Wizard, the user can choose as tasks either menu commands, shell commands, or navigation shortcuts.

The menu commands that the user can choose from are the *same* context menu items that are present in the context menu of the selected scope node. MMC receives these menu commands from snap-ins in exactly the same way that it receives context menu items. That is, there is a one-to-one relationship between a menu command and a context menu item.

When the user chooses a menu command as a task and later clicks that task in the console taskpad, MMC forwards the user's action to the snap-in that added the menu item (menu command) associated with the selected task.

For more information about console taskpads and their use, see Chapter 11, "Console Customization and Taskpads." Snap-in taskpads are discussed in the SDK section of this book, but since they are effectively replaced by console taskpads, snap-in taskpads are not recommended in the design guidelines.

Planning Guide

C H A P T E R   4

Testing Snap-ins

There are many good books available on how to effectively test software to ensure a quality product. This chapter does not attempt to duplicate the contents of such books. Rather, it calls on the experience of snap-in testers to identify areas that deserve special attention when testing snap-ins. For information for developers about identifying the areas in snap-in code that should be checked at code review, see "Testing Program Code" later in this chapter.

Note The content of this chapter is primarily intended for snap-in developers and testers. If your interest is primarily snap-in design, you may want to skip ahead to Part 2, "Design Guidelines."

Testing the User Interface

Most of the items in this section relate to navigation within the namespace; a few are more general in nature.

Testing tasks that should be performed on the user interface for a snap-in are:

- Check for duplication of keyboard shortcuts.
- Double-click each node in the scope pane and each result item and ensure that an appropriate default verb is applied.
- With **Console Root** selected, right-click each node in the scope pane and select each of the node's context menu items to test the navigation.
- Click the **Back** and **Forward** buttons to navigate between nodes that display different view types such as list view, OCX, and taskpad. The most important task is the navigation between different view types on a single node in the scope pane. Be sure that such navigation does not cause problems.
- Add items from each node of the scope pane and from each view of each node to the **Favorites** list. Add these items as navigation tasks to a console taskpad. This tests both the functionality of the **Favorites** list and the use of taskpads for navigation.

- Expand your entire tree without selecting any nodes. Click **Console Root** and press the asterisk (*) key.

- Run your snap-in with the desktop set to different color depths. Ensure that all of the toolbar buttons, console tree icons, result item large icons, and result item small icons appear correctly.

- Ensure that the appropriate toolbar buttons are enabled when selecting nodes in the scope pane, result items, and multiple items. If a toolbar is never appropriate for a selection, it should be hidden. If a toolbar button is not appropriate for the current state of the selection, it should appear dimmed.

- If your snap-in supports multiselection, select several result items and verify that the proper context menu appears for each item. Repeat this procedure for scope items in the result pane and for a mixture of scope and result items in the result pane.

- Verify that the text in the status bar and description bar is correct while selecting different nodes in the scope pane, result items, and context menu items.

- If your snap-in is MMC 1.1-compatible, run tests with both Internet Explorer 4.0 and Internet Explorer 5. Pay particular attention to property pages, wizards, snap-in Help, and taskpads.

- When dragging a node, ensure that the "prohibited" icon is correctly displayed for invalid drop targets.

- If your snap-in uses the same OCX control for multiple nodes in the scope pane, ensure that the OCX control's state is correct when navigating between the different nodes and when the OCX control is displayed in multiple views.

Result Pane

The following tests involve interaction with the result pane in a snap-in:

- Set a multicolumn list view in the result pane to **Details** and sort the list by clicking different column headers.

- Change a result item in one view and confirm that the change is applied to the same result item in all views. Try several different items and use these actions: rename, delete, cut/copy/paste, menu commands provided by the snap-in, apply changes from a property page, and add new items.

- Insert all columns for the result pane, including the columns that need to be hidden initially (these can be inserted as hidden columns). This makes it possible for the user to configure all inserted columns from the **Columns** dialog box and to choose which ones to display.

- Check that appropriate toolbar buttons are enabled when the result pane background is selected.

- Check that appropriate verbs are enabled in the **Action** menu when the result pane background is selected.

- Check that appropriate verbs are enabled in the **Action** menu when an OCX control is selected in the result pane and when a taskpad is selected in the result pane.

- Check that appropriate toolbar buttons are enabled when an OCX control is selected in the result pane and when a taskpad is selected in the result pane.

Taskpads

These are the minimal test suggestions for console taskpads, which are new to MMC 1.2:

- Create console taskpads to check that they work optimally. You may need to make node type or clipboard format changes to optimize performance.

Property Pages

MMC property pages differ in some ways from standard Windows property pages. For more information about MMC property page user interface guidelines, see Chapter 10, "Property Sheets." Perform the following tests on your snap-in property pages:

- Display pages using both small and large fonts in both low and high resolutions.

- Display a page for a list item, click a different node in the scope pane, and then click **Apply** on the property sheet.

- Display a page for a list item, click a different node in the scope pane, return to the original node, and then display properties for the same list item again. MMC should simply set the focus to the existing sheet. Click **Apply** on the property sheet.

- If your snap-in supports multiselection property pages, then perform the preceding tests using a multiple selection.

- If your snap-in supports multiselection property pages, then display a property sheet for a large number of selected items.

- For a node in the scope pane, open a property page for its result items in different views. Ensure that the same property page is opened in each view.

- Open the property pages for several different nodes. Ensure that the property page is the correct one for each node and that no two nodes share the same property sheet.

- Delete an item that has a property page open, and then apply changes from that property page. Ensure this situation is handled gracefully.

- Ensure that changes to the properties of an item are correctly updated in all views.

- Check that extension snap-in property pages are the same size as their parent's property pages.

Console Files

Because anyone can save a console file in author mode, the following tests should be performed by a wide range of administrators, developers, and testers:

- Save a console file with each of the snap-in nodes selected and ensure that the node is still selected when the console file is reopened.

- Save a console file with each of the snap-in nodes at the root of a view.

- Add multiple instances of your snap-in to the same console file and ensure all functionality remains intact.

- Save a console file containing your snap-in for each of the MMC user modes. Ensure that no major functionality of your snap-in is blocked when the user cannot gain access to toolbars or the scope pane.

- Ensure that the icon for a saved console file is not the default MMC icon.

- Close a view after opening a property page, and then apply changes. Then, open the view to see if the changes were applied.

- Perform drag-and-drop operations between different instances of your snap-in within the same console file to ensure that no problems occur.

- Shut down console windows with your snap-in selected in the following ways: each node in the scope pane selected, result pane background selected, any OCX control your snap-in uses selected, and with multiple result items selected. Be especially careful of nodes that display toolbars or menu buttons. Ensure that no problems occur.

- Ensure that your saved console file title agrees with the name in the **Start** menu.

- If your snap-in implements asynchronous insertion into the namespace, try saving a console file with a scope item at the bottom of the expanded tree selected.

- If your snap-in modifies the display name of its static node, ensure that this text is does not change when the snap-in is saved into a console file.

Planning Guide

Extension Snap-ins

These tests help ensure that your extension snap-in works with its parent snap-in. Note that these tests do not apply to stand-alone snap-ins.

- Ensure that the user interface of the extension snap-in follows the user interface of the parent snap-in.
- Ensure that the extension snap-in does not duplicate the functionality of the parent snap-in.
- Ensure that the extension snap-in does not duplicate menu item names or property page names for any parent snap-ins it extends.

Help Issues

Perform these tests to ensure that Help is available for your end users:

- Call the MMC **IDisplayHelp** interface to properly display context-sensitive Help in the merged MMC HTML Help collections file.
- Start Help to ensure that either **ISnapInHelp** or **ISnapInHelp2** is implemented to give MMC the name of your Help file.
- For Microsoft Visual Basic developers, test Help by pressing F1 on a scope item and on a list item. If you are using merged Help, ensure that your **SnapIn.DisplayHelpTopic** calls display the correct topics.
- Turn on the "autosync" option in Help. (This option is automatically set on Windows 2000 servers, but is not set on clients.)
- Ensure that an extension snap-in provides its own Help file and exposes all fields of the About information.
- In **About Help**, ensure that all the fields are exposed and that their text is not longer than the allotted space (that is, ensure that the text is not truncated).
- Test F1 Help on each of your scope pane nodes, result nodes, result pane background, OCX views, multiselected result items, and property pages to ensure that all of these items have context-sensitive Help implemented.
- If context-sensitive Help does not work, ensure that the HTML Help file table of contents is a binary file. Snap-in context-sensitive Help does not work without a binary table of contents.

Testing Snap-ins to a Console File

The following tests are recommended to ensure that your snap-in can be added to a console properly:

- Ensure that a snap-in is not registered with a full path name, because if the user renames the folder that contains the snap-in, the user must use Regsvr32 again to register the snap-in.

- Be sure to run tests both after adding your snap-in using the **Add/Remove Snap-in** dialog box and after adding it by using the console file.

- If your snap-in is a primary snap-in, try running it with different extensions enabled and disabled.

Testing Program Code

This section does not present specific tests. Rather, it points out areas of code that you should test to ensure that your code properly executes the scenario described in each bulleted item.

C++ Code Only

The following considerations apply only to C/C++ developers:

- Namespace extensions have a special responsibility. Only a single instance of a namespace extension is created for a single instance of the snap-in that it is extending, regardless of the number of nodes that it extends. Thus, a namespace extension needs to maintain several "trees" of nodes, one per node being extended. Ensure that this logic is coded into the snap-in from the start.

- Check data objects and cookies using the macros **IS_SPECIAL_DATAOBJECT** and **IS_SPECIAL_COOKIE** to ensure that the special data objects and special cookies are handled appropriately. Every snap-in should handle a NULL cookie because MMC uses this value to refer to the static node belonging to a stand-alone snap-in. Every snap-in should handle a NULL data object because some notifications such as MMCN_DESELECT_ALL and MMCN_PROPERTY_CHANGE send a NULL data object by default.

- For history and view persistence to work well, ensure the snap-in handles MMCN_RESTORE_VIEW appropriately.

- Check that **IComponentData::Notify**, **IComponent::Notify**, and **IExtendControlbar::ControlBarNotify** return S_FALSE to notifications they do not handle.

- For data objects, support the new CCF_NODEID2 clipboard format, not the old CCF_NODEID format.

- If you use Wizard97 wizards, ensure that you implement **IExtendPropertySheet2::GetWatermarks** and that it returns S_OK.

- If you are using Microsoft Foundation Classes (MFC), you should call **AFX_MANAGE_STATE**. If you don't make this call, the module and thread state will be wrong and it is very difficult to debug the problem.

- Snap-ins can return S_OK from **IComponent::CompareObjects** only if the two objects exposing an **IDataObjects** interface for comparison refer to the same object.

- The notification handler for a snap-in should return S_FALSE by default. The S_FALSE value triggers the default operation for the notification. Failure to follow this strategy could limit future functionality.

C++ and Visual Basic Code

The following considerations apply to both C++ and Visual Basic developers:

- Publish your clipboard formats and node types to allow extensions to be written to your snap-in. For more information about gaining free exposure for your snap-in on the Microsoft Web site, send e-mail to: **snapreq@microsoft.com**

- Do not change the node selected in the scope pane when your snap-in receives a selection or expand notification.

- *For Visual Basic developers*: If you add a childless node, ensure that **HasChildren** is set to **False** so that the plus sign (+) is hidden in the console tree.

  For C++ developers: If you add a childless scope pane node, ensure that the **SCOPEDATAITEM.cChildren** member is set to 0 so that the plus sign is hidden in the console tree.

C H A P T E R   5

Deploying Snap-ins

After you have coded and tested your snap-in, you are ready to deliver it to your end users. This means that you need to:

1. Gather the files needed for your snap-in (create a package).

2. Save the files to some medium for distribution (deploy the snap-in).

3. Provide some way for end users to install the snap-in on their local systems.

Note This chapter is primarily intended for snap-in developers. If you are not a developer, you may want to skip ahead to Part 2, "Design Guidelines."

There are three primary setup technologies you can use to distribute your snap-ins to end users:

1. Microsoft Windows Installer
   Prepares and deploys packages for computers running Windows 95 or later and Windows NT 4.0 or later. It includes the ability to create installer-based setups on any 32-bit Windows operating system.

2. Microsoft Visual Basic Package and Deployment Wizard
   Prepares packages and deploys packages for application programs using the Visual Basic programming system. It includes the creation of installer programs to copy application programs including the Visual Basic programming system—in this case snap-ins—onto the users' computers.

3. Proprietary or third-party installation package
   You may choose to use a third-party installation program or write your own scripts to package, deploy, and install snap-ins.

The following sections provide details about using these methods with snap-ins as well as special concerns about distributing saved console files.

Using Windows Installer

Microsoft Windows Installer is a setup technology used in a number of Microsoft applications, including Microsoft Office 2000. The Microsoft Windows 2000 directory services provide the ability to store a snap-in installation in the directory and to download it automatically when the user tries to open a console file that references that snap-in. This is the preferred methodology for distributing snap-ins. Windows Installer exists on all 32-bit Windows operating systems and can be used for your setup even if you do not intend to use the directory for distribution.

In Windows 2000, group policies enable administrators to grant access to tools and functionality on a group basis, for either computers or users. The Microsoft Windows 2000 directory services use these group policies to control access to application installations. You must provide a policy file (*.adm) that sets the appropriate permissions for each snap-in to be distributed.

Snap-in users can distribute a saved console file to recipients who may not have installed all the snap-ins referenced in the console file. When a user performs an action that requires a snap-in that is not locally installed, MMC's integration with Windows Installer makes it possible for the snap-in to be downloaded automatically and installed on the user's local computer.

For more information about using Windows Installer for snap-in and saved console file installation, see Chapter 29, "Distributing Your Snap-in," and the Microsoft Platform Software Development Kit (SDK).

The following section provides an overview of how to use Windows Installer to distribute saved console files.

Distributing Saved Console Files

If you are running only on Windows 2000 operating systems with an Active Directory directory service enabled, the Windows Installer information in the previous section allows you to distribute only the saved console files that you are interested in. The snap-ins referenced in those saved console files are downloaded automatically. This also allows you to wrap your saved console files in a Windows Installer package and assign them to users. Alternatively, you can leave your saved console files on a shared network drive and have all users gain access to them from there; this might make updates to the saved console files easier.

If you must support a mixed environment where Windows 2000 application deployment is not available, then you should include the saved console files in the Windows Installer package that includes your snap-ins. In this case, ensure that all snap-ins referenced in the saved console file are locally installed before the user opens the file.

Using the Package and Deployment Wizard

Use the Visual Basic Package and Deployment Wizard to create a package and setup program for a snap-in created in Visual Basic. Note that the following files are needed for a Visual Basic snap-in installation:

- Snap-in dynamic-link library (DLL) created by Visual Basic
- Snap-in designer runtime (mssnapr.dll)
- Visual Basic 6.0 runtime (msvbvm60.dll)

You can also use the Package and Deployment Wizard to create a package for a saved console file. Before you start, place the console file (.msc) in a directory that contains a snap-in project, and then use the following procedure:

▼ **To create a package for a saved console file**

1. On the Visual Basic **Tools** menu, click **Package and Deployment Wizard**.
2. In the **Select Project** drop-down list box, click the snap-in project you want to use. Or, click the **Browse** button to locate the snap-in project.
3. Click **Next** to continue to the page entitled "Package and Deployment Wizard–Included Files," and then click **Add**.
4. In the **Files of type** drop-down list box, click **All Files**.
5. Select the saved console file (.msc), and then click **Open**.
6. Proceed to the Start Menu Items page, and then click **New Item**.
7. In the **Target** drop-down list box, click the .msc file you want to use.
8. In the **Name** text box, type the name you want for your icon, and then click **OK**.
9. Click **Finish** to close the Package and Deployment Wizard.

Using a Proprietary or Third-Party Installation Package

If you do not want to use Microsoft Windows Installer or the Package and Deployment Wizard, you can use any third-party installation program or your own scripts to create the package and install the snap-in. The process for Visual Basic snap-ins is slightly different from that for snap-ins developed using COM interfaces (coded with C++).

COM Snap-ins

▼ **To deploy a snap-in developed with C++**

1. Copy your snap-in's DLL to your target directory.

2. Use Regsvr32.exe.
   On computers running Windows 95 or later, Regsvr32 is located in the System folder. On computers running Windows NT 4.0 or later, Regsvr32 is located in the System32 folder.

Registering your snap-in's DLLs adds all the necessary entries to the registry. For more information, see Chapter 17, "Building the Basic Snap-in Framework."

Visual Basic Snap-ins

▼ **To deploy a snap-in developed using Visual Basic**

1. Copy your snap-in's DLL to your target directory.

2. If the Visual Basic runtime (msvbvm60.dll) is not installed on the computer, install it in the system folder.

3. Copy mssnapr.dll to:
   \Program Files\Common Files\Microsoft Shared\SnapInDesigner.

4. To register both DLLs, double-click Regsvr32.
   On computers running Windows 95 or later, Regsvr32 is located in the System folder. On computers running Windows NT 4.0 or later, Regsvr32 is located in the System32 folder.

Important The designer runtime (mssnapr.dll) must be registered *before* your snap-in's DLL. If it is not registered first, registration of your snap-in's DLL will fail.

Registering your snap-in's DLLs adds all the necessary entries to the MMC registry keys under:
HKEY_LOCAL_MACHINE\SOFTWARE\Microsoft\MMC
For more information, see Chapter 32, "Snap-in Designer for Visual Basic."

P A R T   2

Design Guidelines

No matter what role you play in the development of snap-ins in your organization—manager, computer administrator, designer, developer, or tester—the material in these chapters can be helpful to you. It offers precise guidelines for creating snap-in user interfaces as well as a complete discussion of namespace creation. The user interface style guidelines stated here are the same as those in *Microsoft Windows User Experience* except in cases where MMC has unique requirements.

New to MMC 1.2 are console taskpads that can be created by anyone who uses MMC. These new taskpads enable you to tailor snap-ins to your audience or to a variety of audiences. Chapter 11 provides the details.

Many chapters contain very detailed size and spacing specifications for snap-in user interface features. These specifications are provided in both dialog units (dlus) for C++ developers and twips for Visual Basic developers.

CHAPTER 6

Namespaces

A namespace contains objects and containers organized in a hierarchy. Users can browse through a namespace, create new objects, edit the properties of existing objects, and move objects from one container to another. In MMC, objects and containers can be used to represent applications, services, server groups, users, security groups, devices, and other things that an administrator might want to configure or monitor.

A well-organized namespace helps users locate and perform their tasks quickly and easily. When designing a namespace, consider the following:

- Which similar or related objects could be grouped together?

- Does the user need to be able to reorganize or rename containers in the namespace?

- How could the namespace be broken up into smaller units that could be delegated for administration?

- Where and how would other snap-ins want to extend the functionality of your snap-in's namespace?

By designing your administration tools as collections of small, dual-mode snap-ins, you give your users the flexibility to create custom consoles that expose only the functionality necessary for them to carry out their tasks. For example, a junior administrator that manages and monitors a group of file servers doesn't need all of the functionality of the Computer Management snap-in and its extensions. A senior administrator could create a custom console that includes the Computer Management snap-in along with the Shared Folders and Event Viewer extension snap-ins, but exclude all of the other extension snap-ins. Thus the junior administrator is given access to the tools and functionality needed for his specific role, but no more. For more information about customized console files, see Chapter 11, "Console Customization and Taskpads."

Your snap-in's namespace and functionality can be extended in a variety of ways. The Event Viewer snap-in in Windows 2000 was designed with extensibility in mind. You can easily include it in your snap-in's namespace. Your snap-in can control several aspects of the Event Viewer snap-in. It can refocus the Event Viewer to the logs on another computer and specify the filter criteria.

This chapter describes techniques for designing the namespace for a new snap-in and for extending the namespaces of existing snap-ins.

Namespace Elements

This section describes in detail the various elements of the namespace, such as objects and containers, and how they are organized.

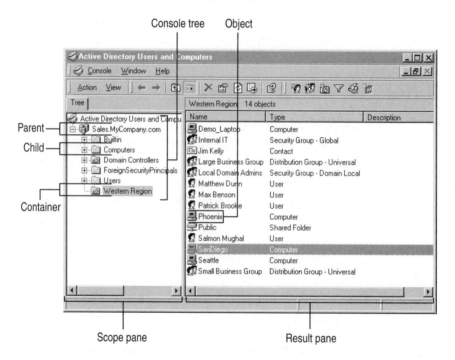

Figure 6.1   Active Directory Users and Computers snap-in

As discussed in Chapter 1, with the exception of the *console root* node, the MMC namespace is created entirely by snap-ins. Every stand-alone snap-in and many extension snap-ins add objects and containers to the namespace. The namespace in a particular console file is the result of one or more snap-ins. MMC displays the namespace in the scope pane and result pane. As shown in Figure 6.1, the scope pane contains the console tree.

Users navigate the console tree in the same way they navigate Windows Explorer. Clicking the plus sign (+) to the left of a node opens (expands) the next level of the console tree. Double-clicking a container node in the scope or result pane has the same effect. Clicking the minus sign (–) closes (collapses) the previously open level.

Adding Snap-ins to a Console

When you start MMC, the console tree displays a single node, the console root. Its icon is an open folder, as shown in Figure 6.2.

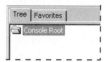

Figure 6.2   Console root

When a console is in author mode, stand-alone snap-ins can be added to or removed from the console. Every stand-alone snap-in has a top-level node, sometimes referred to as the *static node*. When a stand-alone snap-in is added to the console, the snap-in's top-level node is displayed under the console root. Figure 6.3 shows several stand-alone snap-ins added to the console.

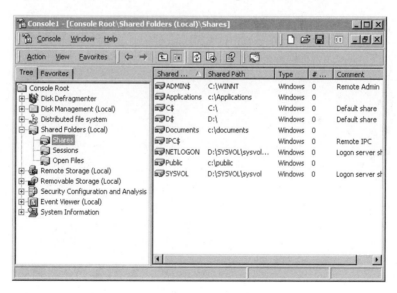

Figure 6.3   Console with multiple stand-alone snap-ins

Although extension snap-ins do not have static nodes, they can extend the namespace of another snap-in by adding additional nodes to the console tree. Extension snap-ins can also add commands to menus, buttons to toolbars, and property pages to another snap-in's property sheet. MMC does not support adding additional pages to another snap-in's wizard. When a stand-alone snap-in is added, all of its currently registered extension snap-ins are included by default.

Stand-alone snap-ins and extension snap-ins often use the Windows clipboard to pass data back and forth between them. For example, when a user retargets the Computer Management snap-in to another computer, the Computer Management snap-in passes the name of the target computer to all of its extension snap-ins. Each of the extension snap-ins retargets itself to the specified computer.

Many snap-ins append the name of the computer they are currently focused on to the name of the snap-in's top-level node. For example, when the Computer Management snap-in is targeted at a computer named WEB01, the top-level node is named Computer Management (WEB01).

For more information about adding stand-alone snap-ins to a console, see Chapter 11, "Console Customization and Taskpads."

Containers

As described earlier, a namespace consists of objects and containers. Containers can have subcontainers and objects. Containers are used to logically organize similar or related objects and are often represented by a folder icon. For example, in the Microsoft SQL Server snap-in shown in Figure 6.4, the Databases container holds all the SQL databases. Any object in the tree can become a container if an extension snap-in adds tree items beneath it.

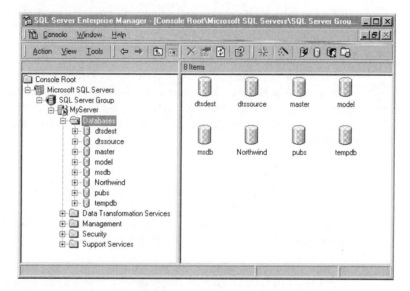

Figure 6.4   Microsoft SQL Server Enterprise Manager console tree

Naming Objects and Containers

Container names and object names should be nouns. Because containers typically hold multiple instances of a single object type, containers are often named by using the plural of the object type. For example, a Service object might reside in a Services container. Neither container names nor object names should be verbs or sentence fragments. Creating a namespace containing nodes with names such as Start Service, Create Scope, or Add User is highly discouraged. Verbs and sentence fragments should be reserved for commands on the **Action** or **View** menus. Delete, Send Request, and Clear Logs are good names for menu commands.

User-Customizable Namespaces

In many cases, container hierarchy is predefined and fixed by the snap-in developer. Users cannot create their own containers, rename existing containers, or move objects from one container to another. It is nearly impossible to design a single namespace that is ideal for every type of customer; especially if the namespace is large and complicated like the ones found in the Internet Information Services (IIS), SQL Server, and Microsoft Exchange Server snap-ins.

Some snap-ins enable users to create their own containers. This extra flexibility gives administrators the freedom to easily create deep or shallow namespaces and to rename and move things around; it also aids considerably in creating customized console files for delegation. For example, a senior administrator can create a new container in the Active Directory Users and Computers snap-in (these containers are called *organizational units*), place several users, security groups, printers, and computers in that organizational unit, and then create a custom console for the junior administrator who is responsible for managing those resources.

Functional Containers

Containers can be more than just organizational buckets. In some snap-ins, properties or commands are available on containers. When the top-level node of the Event Viewer snap-in is selected, the **Connect to another computer** and **Open Log file** commands are added to the **Action** menu.

Some containers, such as the organizational units found in the Active Directory Users and Computers snap-in, have security permissions associated with them. Like the permissions on files and folders, permissions can be used on a container to restrict access to the subcontainers and objects within it.

A Tools Container

Microsoft Systems Management Server 2.0 (SMS) includes a snap-in and a number of additional utility programs. The SMS team wanted to enable administrators to access these programs from within the SMS snap-in, and also to provide a place in the namespace for third-party companies to add their own tools. As shown in Figure 6.5, the SMS team added a Tools container to the snap-in's namespace. When a user double-clicks the Network Monitor node, the Network Monitor program is started.

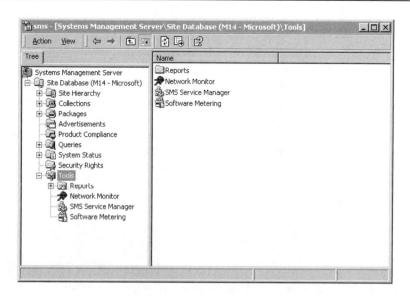

Figure 6.5   Microsoft Systems Management Server's Tools container

Adding a Tools container is preferable to adding a **Tools** menu button. A Tools container can be extended by other snap-ins. A taskpad can be added to the Tools container. The programs listed under the Tools node can be added to a taskpad as a task. For a complete list of the limitations of menu buttons, see Chapter 7, "Menus."

Inheriting Settings from a Parent Container

The top-level node of the Internet Information Services (IIS) snap-in supports master properties that act as default values for all new and existing Web or FTP sites. In this case, the subcontainers are inheriting settings from their parent container. Moving a Web site container up a level would break the inheritance model. However, the snap-in could optionally support a level of grouping under the IIS node. This would give an administrator the flexibility of grouping related Web sites together.

Using Favorites

Users and snap-in developers can use MMC Favorites to provide shortcuts to important or frequently visited nodes buried in a deep namespace. For more information, see Chapter 11, "Console Customization and Taskpads."

Result Pane

When a node in the console tree on the left is selected, additional information is often displayed in the result pane on the right. The snap-in has the option of displaying the information as a standard list view or as a custom view.

Standard List Views

List view is the simplest and most often-used view in the result pane. A list view can show objects or subcontainers. MMC supports the Windows common list view options **Large Icons**, **Small Icons**, **List**, and **Details**. **Details** is the recommended default view. Figure 6.6 shows the **Details** view for the Computer Management snap-in.

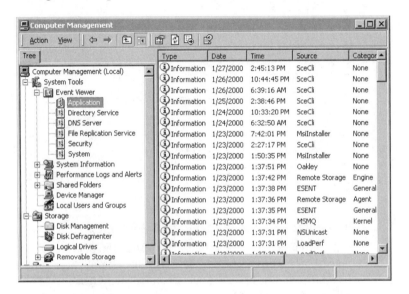

Figure 6.6   Details list view for Computer Management

MMC 1.2 enables users to select and order the columns they want to display in the standard **Details** view. Figure 6.7 shows the dialog box that appears when a user clicks **Choose Columns** on the **View** menu.

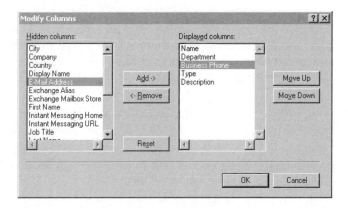

Figure 6.7   Modify Columns dialog box

Column selection is not available in MMC 1.1 snap-ins. MMC 1.2 provides column selection without any additional programming by the snap-in. For more information, see "Using List Views" in Chapter 20.

There is no limit to the number of columns a snap-in can offer the user. By default, display the most commonly used columns and hide the remaining columns. Note that users cannot hide or reorder the first column.

Icons are used in the first column to indicate object type and sometimes status. Icons by themselves are rarely sufficient to communicate their meaning. Too many different icons can make it difficult for a user to learn and remember all of them. Cultural differences can also make it difficult to understand the meaning of an icon.

Adding an additional column with a text description of the icon is a simple yet effective way to eliminate these problems. Consider offering the following columns by default:

- **Type**–Some objects share the same icon. Providing the user with a **Type** column helps the user determine the exact object type. The Active Directory Users and Computers snap-in uses the same icon for multiple types of security groups and distribution lists because they are closely related. Proving a **Type** column makes it easy for the user to distinguish between them and also makes it easy for a user to sort the result pane by type.

- **Status**–Most snap-ins need to indicate the current state of an object (for example: offline, disabled, and so on). Adding a **Status** column and communicating the state of an object through words makes it easier for a user to identify and understand the object's state. For more information about icons to indicate status, see Chapter 9, "Icons."

Taskpads

MMC 1.2 introduced console taskpads. You use taskpads to provide alternative navigation and task discovery. They can also be used to launch executable files, run scripts, and access Web pages. You create console taskpads using the New Taskpad View Wizard in MMC author mode. For more information about taskpads, see Chapter 11, "Console Customization and Taskpads."

Custom Views

The standard list view is not always the best way to present information about the selected node in the console tree. Sometimes you may want to present the results in a more graphical way, such as a network topology map. Sometimes you may want to show an error message because your snap-in can't show the results due to an error. For these reasons and more, MMC gives your snap-in the ability to create custom views in the result pane. Snap-ins have the option of displaying an HTML page or an OCX control in the result pane.

When designing a custom view, keep in mind that you are responsible for ensuring that your snap-in behaves in a usable and consistent manner. If your snap-in provides a custom view, it will be in complete control of the result pane, but less able to seamlessly integrate with MMC enhancements or other snap-ins. If only a custom view is offered for a specific node, other snap-ins are unable to extend that node and taskpads won't be able to take advantage of functionality offered in the result pane.

If you choose to create a custom view, consider offering a standard list view as well, and add an entry on the **View** menu so that users can toggle between the standard list view and your custom view.

When designing your custom view, avoid including controls that look like the standard list view. Also, do not permit direct editing of properties in the result pane. Properties in custom views should be edited on property pages implemented using the MMC property page interfaces; the property pages can then be extended by other snap-ins.

Figure 6.8 shows the Indexing Service hosting a simple HTML page in the result pane. This HTML page enables users to perform test queries against a catalog.

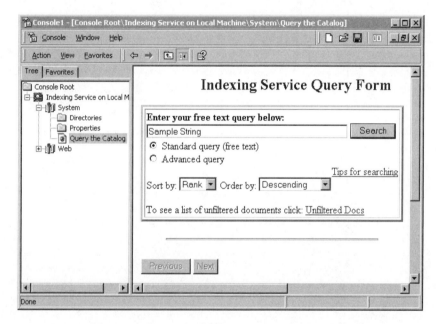

Figure 6.8   Indexing Service snap-in showing custom HTML view in result pane

When presenting a custom view, especially when using HTML pages, ensure that the navigation model always provides a way to return to the initial page without pressing the MMC **Back** button.

Message Pages

MMC 1.2 introduced an OCX control that gives your snap-in the ability to display simple messages in the result pane. As shown in Figure 6.9, message pages can be used to display error messages or provide information about what to do next. For more information about snap-in message pages see Chapter 13, "Dialog Boxes and Message Boxes."

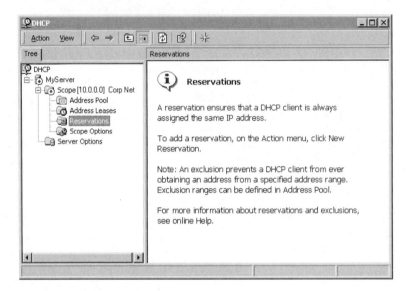

Figure 6.9   Message page in the result pane

Windows on the Namespace

MMC is a multiple-document interface (MDI) application. Each new window is essentially a view onto the same underlying namespace. Any given window can contain the entire namespace or only a portion of it. More than one window can show the same portion of the namespace, but this will result in multiple copies of an object being displayed rather than multiple objects. For instance, if two windows display the same object, and you request a property sheet on the object from one window, and then request a property sheet on the same object from the second window, only a single property sheet is displayed.

Filtering the Namespace

If a namespace is very large or if you want to hide advanced or less frequently used nodes in the namespace, consider adding filtering capabilities to your snap-in. You could provide filtering at the top-level node that is then applied to all of the nodes below it. On the other hand, you could offer filtering on each container. No matter which method you choose, be sure to implement and document the method for extension snap-ins so that they can participate in or drive the filtering process. If your snap-in has advanced or less frequently used nodes in the namespace, you may want to consider supporting filtering and having the filter enabled by default.

If your snap-in supports some type of filtering, be sure it adheres to the following guidelines:

- Add a **Filter Records** command to MMC's **View** menu. Also, add an **All Records** command to the **View** menu as a convenience for the user. This enables the user to quickly toggle back and forth between the filtered and unfiltered views (see Figure 6.10).

Figure 6.10   View menu with filtering options added

- Add a **Filter** button to the toolbar. Doing so will make it easier for a user to discover this capability.

- Ensure that the user always knows the current state of the filter. Consider adding text to the MMC description bar as shown in Figure 6.11. By default the description bar is hidden. To show the description bar, click **Customize** on the **View** menu and select the check box labeled **Description bar**.

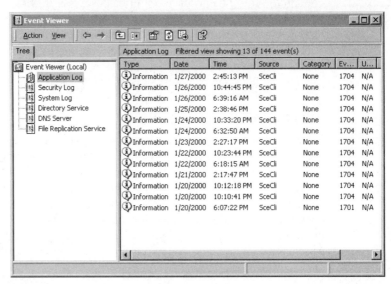

Figure 6.11   Event Viewer, Filtered View reported in description bar

- When a filter is applied, the scope and result panes are typically refreshed. Whenever possible, store the user's currently selected node just prior to the refresh. If that node is hidden because of the filter, put the focus on the next likely candidate, such as the next closest peer node or the parent node.

It is important that namespace filtering be limited to the namespace and not carry over into other elements of the snap-in. In other words, do not use the methods described above to hide advanced or less frequently used property or wizard pages.

Additional Guidelines

The following additional guidelines apply to namespaces and result pane views:

Use menus and toolbars to open secondary windows

Selecting a command from a menu, pressing a toolbar button, or double-clicking a node in the result pane are the only approved methods for launching a secondary window. Do not launch secondary windows when a user simply selects (single-clicks) a node in the console tree or in the result pane. If populating the result pane takes several moments, use the MMC status bar to indicate progress. Never display a modal progress dialog box.

Represent an item only once in the console tree.

Multiple instances of the same object can lead to user confusion about its purpose and use. If your design produces multiple object instances, try changing the design to eliminate the problem.

Try to limit the number of levels in the namespace to six or fewer.

After six levels it is harder to navigate and can result in users getting lost in the namespace. Note that in Figure 6.12, the Off-line Media node is at the fifth level.

Figure 6.12   Namespace levels

Extending Snap-ins

The majority of the administration tools in Microsoft Windows 2000 are MMC snap-ins. You can leverage their functionality by taking advantage of MMC's extension model. You can extend another snap-in, such as Computer Management, or you can have one of the Windows 2000 snap-ins, such as Event Viewer, extend your snap-in.

Both Computer Management and Event Viewer use the Windows clipboard to pass configuration data back and forth. For example, you can retarget the Event Viewer to another computer by passing it a new computer name via the Windows clipboard. For developer information about extending snap-ins, see "Registering and Unregistering a Snap-in" in Chapter 17 or visit MSDN Online at http://msdn.microsoft.com/.

The remainder of this section describes at a high level how to extend the Computer Management and Active Directory snap-ins and how to add the Event Viewer to your snap-in's namespace.

Extending Computer Management

The Computer Management snap-in is the administrator's primary configuration tool. It is designed to target a single computer. With a very small amount of development effort, you can extend this snap-in and ensure that all administrators will be able to get the functionality they need to manage your service or application.

Computer Management has three nodes that you can extend: System Tools, Storage, and Services and Applications. In Figure 6.13, the Windows 2000 Disk Defragmenter, developed by Executive Software International, extends the Computer Management Storage node.

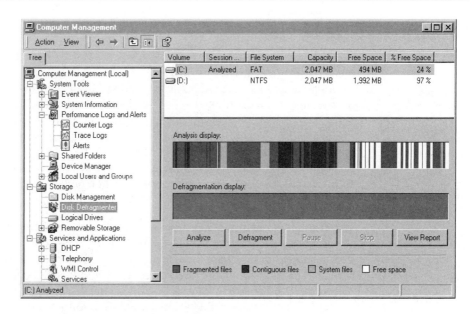

Figure 6.13   Computer Management snap-in

You cannot extend the static node of this snap-in with a namespace extension. You can, however, extend the static node with a context menu extension or add property pages to its property sheet.

System Tools and Storage

The System Tools node contains the tools that exist on computers running Windows 2000. These tools include the Event Viewer, Device Manager, and Local Users and Groups extension snap-ins. The Storage node contains all of the extension snap-ins related to disks; for example, Disk Management and Removable Storage.

To extend the System Tools and Storage nodes, register your snap-in under the appropriate node type. Next, design your snap-in so that it accepts configuration data from the Computer Management snap-in via the Windows clipboard.

Services and Applications

This node is used by snap-ins that optionally install on the system or are only installed on computers running Windows 2000 Server. Traditional end users would not interact with these snap-ins in everyday system use. This node is dynamically populated, depending on which computer the snap-in is focused on. For example, if the computer is a Domain Name System (DNS) server, a node will automatically appear for DNS management.

Extending Active Directory

In most cases you use *display specifiers* to extend the Active Directory service. Display specifiers are objects that hold Active Directory user interface information and provide a flexible mechanism to meet the needs of the various user groups in the distributed network. The advantage of using display specifiers is that your extension snap-in will appear both in MMC and in the shell. The disadvantage of using display specifiers is that your extension snap-in will always appear on the property page or context menu of the item you are extending. You do not have a choice at run time to decide what will appear. Display specifiers are fully explained in the "Active Directory" section under "Networking and Directory Services" in the Microsoft Platform SDK.

If you choose to extend the Active Directory Users and Computers snap-in using the MMC extension mechanisms, there are some areas to which you need to give special attention. Be aware that the node types of the nodes in Active Directory are the class globally unique identifiers (GUIDs) for each node's object in the directory. (See "Snap-in Namespace" in Chapter 16 for more information on GUIDs.) You are responsible for making the appropriate registrations for that node type. You should also pay particular attention to the **DSOBJECTNAMES** structure described in the "Active Directory" section of the Microsoft Platform SDK. This structure is given to you as a clipboard format and enables you to identify the directory object that a node in the MMC namespace represents.

Using Event Viewer as an Extension

To add the Event Viewer to your snap-in's namespace, register it as a namespace extension to the node type that you want to extend. Use a clipboard format to tell the Event Viewer what node name to use and what filter conditions to set.

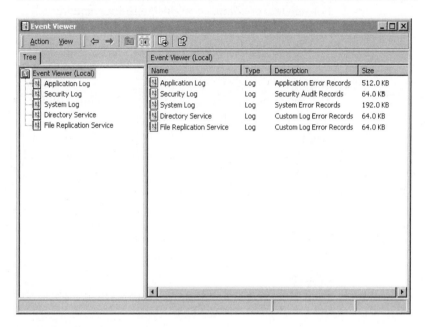

Figure 6.14   Event Viewer snap-in

Namespace Coding References

If you are creating a snap-in using C++, see Chapter 19, "Working with the Scope Pane," and Chapter 20, "Using Different Result Pane View Types," for additional information about namespaces.

If you are creating a snap-in using Visual Basic, see "Nodes," "Result Views," and "List Views" in Chapter 34, "Developing Snap-ins," for additional information about namespaces.

Namespace Design Process

Designing a namespace is an iterative process that involves the following steps:

Planning
Formulate a preliminary product definition and identify the audience.

Research
Make contact with potential users in order to help focus the design of the namespace to meet their needs.

Definition
Determine the user roles the snap-in will support and create some scenarios that simulate how the snap-in will be used.

Concept
Test prototype namespace designs with users and use the feedback to refine the prototypes.

Detail
By the time the process has reached the detail phase, elements of the user interface (UI) such as toolbars, property sheets, and wizards should be well-defined. Testing at this point can take several iterations to ensure that the namespace meets the design goals.

Finalization
Minor UI changes sometimes take place in order to make the product ready for delivery to customers.

At each stage of the process, test and refine your ideas. This process is covered in greater detail in Appendix A, "Snap-in Design Planning." The "Designing Exchange" section that follows takes you through this process by following the evolution of the Microsoft Exchange 2000 Server namespace design.

Designing Exchange

As this book was being written, Microsoft Exchange 2000 Server was under development. The Exchange namespace design followed the steps outlined in "Namespace Design Process."

Planning Phase

In the planning phase the Exchange team evaluated what was and what was not working in the current product, Microsoft Exchange Server version 5.5 and its namespace (shown in Figure 6.15). The team looked at past usability tests and conducted new tests with current users.

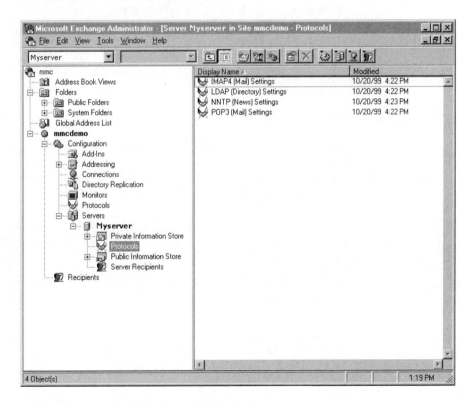

Figure 6.15   Original Exchange 5.5 namespace

Research Phase

During the research phase, the team conducted a series of site visits to help identify roles and tasks for the administrators who would use the namespace. From the research they identified these roles:

Account manager—First-tier administrator
Adds, deletes, and modifies user data; performs some message tracking and monitoring.

Day-to-day operator—Second-tier administrator
Performs message tracking, monitoring, and some user-management tasks; handles daily backups.

Exchange engineer—Third-tier administrator
Handles configuration, deployment, and troubleshooting.

Network manager—Fourth-tier administrator
Handles architecture, infrastructure planning, and evaluation of software and hardware needs.

Definition Phase

The Exchange team used this time to create scenarios that helped them further define how users would interact with and navigate the namespace. Using the roles and tasks discovered in the research phase, they created realistic scenarios that included diagrams of the relationships in the scenarios.

Concept Phase

In this phase, the Exchange team created both paper and electronic prototypes of possible namespaces and tested them with users. Three such prototypes are described in this section. The namespace shown in Figure 6.16 was organized around tasks rather than objects. The team was trying new ideas to see how usable they were.

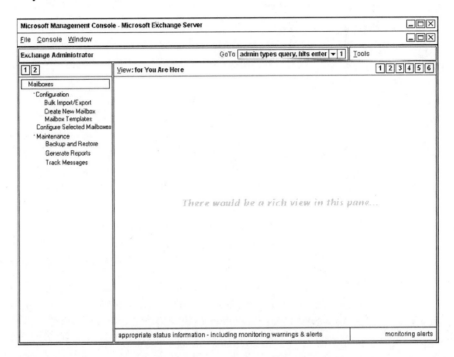

Figure 6.16   Early task-based Exchange namespace

Problems with this design centered on the cost of implementation and on the fact that the design did not have a good extensibility or scalability model. A few months later, the Exchange team began testing a new namespace, shown in Figure 6.17, that more closely conformed to MMC guidelines. In a series of four or more tests, users were able to find the objects that they needed to complete given tasks.

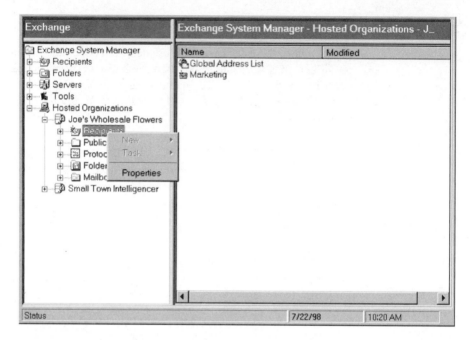

Figure 6.17   First object-based Exchange namespace

Some months later, a new Visual Basic prototype namespace (shown in Figure 6.18) was tested with users at several Exchange conferences. This new namespace moved the individual queue nodes beneath the Protocols node. It proved to be very difficult for users to find the individual queues because they were several levels deeper than they had previously been.

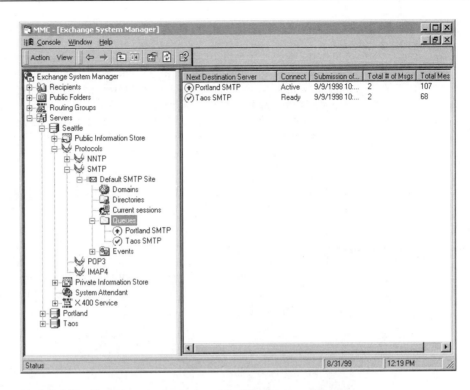

Figure 6.18   Exchange namespace used at Exchange conferences

This series of tests resulted in changes to the namespace, but did not resolve several issues. For example, there was no clear-cut resolution of the depth at which individual queues would reside. The tests did, however, move subsequent prototypes toward more realistic user-influenced designs. There was no attempt to fully flesh out the user interface, but rather an emphasis on making sure that the structure of the namespace met the needs of the users through repeated testing of alternatives.

Detail Phase

The detail phase, in which user interface elements were developed, led to the introduction of too many new features. This sometimes occurs when new product features are being added too quickly and threaten to make the user interface too complex to be usable. The addition of new features in this case meant the addition of new nodes, which forced objects that had been two levels deep to become six or seven levels deep. User testing and some common sense led to namespace revisions that brought these nodes up several levels.

In this stage, you should test the scenarios to make sure that the UI elements needed to accomplish the tasks within the scenario are present and operate appropriately.

Finalization Phase

In the finalization phase, the design is stable and only minor cosmetic and UI changes should take place. Figure 6.19 shows the state of the namespace as Exchange neared this phase.

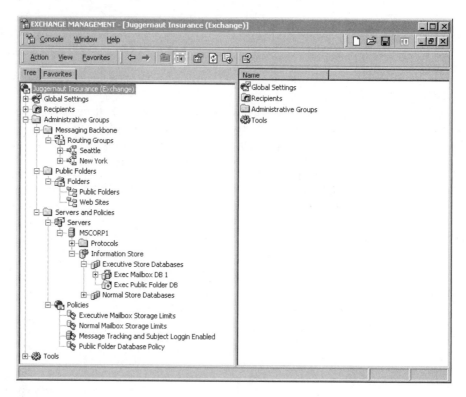

Figure 6.19   Nearly final Exchange namespace

Namespace Design Review

This section offers a capsule review of the information in this chapter.

- Design your administration tools as a collection of small, dual-mode snap-ins.

- Name containers and objects using nouns, never verbs or sentence fragments.

- Enable users to create their own containers to improve customization and aid delegation.

- Add a Tools container instead of a **Tools** menu button.

- Limit the number of levels in the namespace to six or fewer.

- Use Favorites to provide shortcuts to important or frequently visited nodes buried in a deep namespace.

- Offer columns for the most important or interesting properties.

- Offer **Type** and **Status** columns when appropriate.

- Do not place a property sheet in the result pane.

- If your snap-in offers a custom view, be sure to provide a standard list view as well.

- Instead of using a dialog box, consider using a message page to display simple messages in the result pane.

- If your namespace is large and complicated, or if you want to hide advanced or less frequently used nodes in the namespace, consider adding filtering capabilities to your snap-in.

- Add namespace-filtering commands to the **View** menu. Do not use the **View** menu to hide property pages or wizard pages.

- Ensure that the user is always aware of the current state of the filter by writing it to the description bar.

- Represent an item only once in the console tree.

- Use menus and toolbars to open secondary windows. Do not launch secondary windows when a user simply selects (single-clicks) a node in the console tree or in the result pane.

- When appropriate, extend Computer Management and include Event Viewer in your namespace.

- Do not put an OCX control that looks like a list view in the result pane.

Design Guidelines

CHAPTER 7

Menus

Chapter 6, "Namespaces," discussed the organization and arrangement of objects that make up the namespace and the snap-in. Menus provide the interface for the operations or commands applied to the objects in the namespace.

The primary means of interacting with Microsoft Management Console (MMC) menus is through right-clicking objects in the namespace to display the context menu commands associated with them and by using the **View** menu to change the view of the objects.

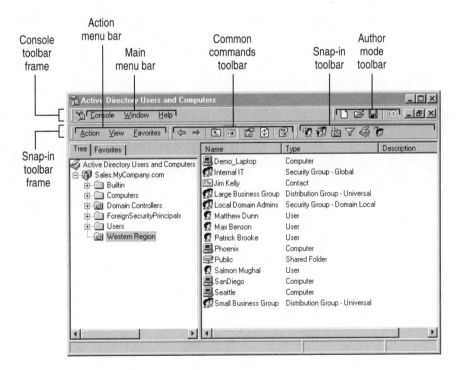

Figure 7.1   MMC menu bars

MMC organizes all toolbars and menu bars into two places, the console toolbar frame and the snap-in toolbar frame shown in Figure 7.1. For more information about console and snap-in toolbars, see Chapter 8, "Toolbars."

The menus and the toolbar in the console toolbar frame are used to customize the entire console. Individual snap-ins cannot extend any of these menus or toolbars. The main menu bar contains the **Console**, **Window**, and **Help** menu buttons.

The snap-in toolbar frame contains the menus and toolbars that apply to the snap-ins. The Action menu bar contains the **Action**, **View**, and **Favorites** menus. The **Action** and **View** menus are customized by individual snap-ins. The **Favorites** menu lists shortcuts to nodes in the console tree. For more information about the **Favorites** menu, see Chapter 11, "Console Customization and Taskpads."

The difference between the two toolbar frames is readily apparent when the child console window is minimized, as shown in Figure 7.2. The console toolbar frame is attached to the parent window, whereas the snap-in toolbar frame is attached to the child console window.

For each node, you can also provide a context menu that is tailored to your snap-in, as shown in Figure 7.2. The rest of this chapter offers guidelines for the structure and content of context menus, the **View** menu, and the **Action** menu.

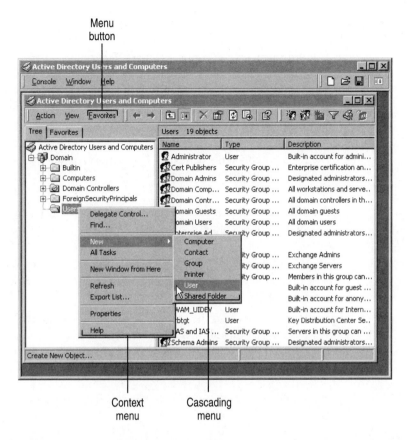

Figure 7.2   MMC nonmaximized child window with context menu displayed

Action Menu

The **Action** menu offers commands that affect objects in the namespace. Examples of these commands might be **New Printer, Reconcile Database,** and **Properties**. MMC provides the **Action** menu primarily for those users who are unfamiliar with context menus or who prefer drop-down menus.

Commands on the **Action** menu are organized into four areas:

- The top of the menu is dedicated to the most frequently used commands provided by the primary snap-in. Extension snap-ins cannot add commands here.

- The **New** cascading menu contains less frequently used commands that create new objects or containers. Extension snap-ins can add menu items to this menu.

- The **All Tasks** cascading menu contains less frequently used commands that perform actions other than creating new objects or containers. Extension snap-ins can add menu items to this menu.

- The bottom portion of the menu is dedicated to common commands provided by MMC as instructed by the snap-in. These include commands such as **Refresh** and **Properties**. For more information about these commands, see "Standard Verbs" later in this chapter.

For more information about the contents and form of an **Action** menu, see "Context Menu" later in this chapter.

View Menu

The **View** menu contains commands that change the way the namespace is displayed in the control tree and in the result pane. For example, if your snap-in supports filtering or custom views of the result pane, you would put these commands on the **View** menu. Figure 7.3 shows a typical **View** menu.

Figure 7.3   Default View menu

MMC supports the four standard Windows list view options (**Large Icons**, **Small Icons**, **List**, and **Detail**). You should use the **Detail** view as the default view for standard list views. If the other three views are not useful, you have the option of hiding them. For more information, see Chapter 20, "Using Different Result Pane View Types."

The **View** menu is also used to toggle between standard and custom views. For example, if a snap-in provides a custom view that can show the network topology map, the **View** menu could look like the one shown in Figure 7.4.

Figure 7.4   View menu supporting custom Network Map view

Providing **View** menu items to enable and disable filtering offers an easy way to customize the console tree and the result pane. For example, if your snap-in supports filtering, you could add a **Filter** command to the **View** menu (see Figure 7.5). The **Filter** command could display a secondary window that enables the user to enter filter criteria. Your snap-in could also offer an **All Records** command that shows all of the records without eliminating the filter criteria. This method enables the user to quickly toggle back and forth between the filtered and unfiltered views.

Figure 7.5   View menu with Filter command

View menu items should not be used for restricting access to property pages or for hiding items on context menus.

Since the primary snap-in owns and controls the contents of the result pane, the primary snap-in is the only one that can add or remove items from the **View** menu. Extension snap-ins cannot add or remove items from the **View** menu.

Context Menu

A *context menu* (also known as a *shortcut menu*) is the menu a user sees upon right-clicking a container or an object. The context menu displays only the commands that are specific to the currently selected item. For example, right-clicking a database object in the namespace causes commands such as **Purge** and **Backup** to appear on the context menu, whereas right-clicking a job object causes context menu commands such as **Start** or **End** to appear.

On a selected object, the **Action** menu and the context menu are identical with one exception: the **View** cascading menu does not appear on the **Action** menu because it is also exposed on the top **View** menu.

Figure 7.6 illustrates the structure of a context menu and shows where snap-ins and extension snap-ins can add commands.

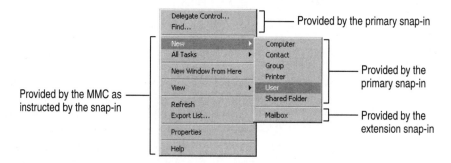

Figure 7.6   Context menu overview

The primary snap-in should list its most frequently used commands at the top of the context menu. Less frequently used commands should be listed on the **New** or **All Tasks** cascading menus. In addition, extension snap-ins can add commands to the **New** or **All Tasks** cascading menus.

Standard Verbs

MMC provides eight standard verbs (cut, copy, paste, delete, properties, refresh, print, and rename) that can be included on the **Action** and context menus. When a snap-in enables a standard verb, the corresponding context menu item and toolbar button are added. For more information about standard verbs, see Chapter 21, "Working with Context Menus," and Chapter 30, "MMC COM Reference."

Table 7.1 lists each of the standard verbs available to the context menu, the corresponding toolbar button, and a brief description of the function it performs.

Table 7.1   Standard Verbs

Command	Button	Function
Cut		Sends a cut command to the snap-in.
Copy		Sends a copy command to the snap-in.
Paste		Sends a paste command to the snap-in.
Delete		Sends a delete command to the snap-in.
Properties		Sends a command to the snap-in to display the object's property sheet.
Refresh		Sends a refresh command to the snap-in to update the current display.
Print		Sends a command to the snap-in to print the contents of the result pane for the current object.
Rename	none	Makes the name of the current object in the console tree available for editing.

Help is always available on the context menus. If desired, a snap-in designer can also provide context-sensitive Help. If a snap-in does not provide a custom handler, the default MMC Help topic is displayed. The **Help** menu displayed on the context menu is equivalent to the user pressing the F1 button on the keyboard. The context-sensitive Help and the F1 button provide the user with the same help based on the selected object or container in the namespace.

If your snap-in offers a command that has the same or similar functionality as a standard verb, use the standard verb. Do not create duplicate or similar commands. For example, delete is a standard verb provided by MMC. To provide a consistent Windows user experience, you should always use the delete standard verb instead of using similar words such as remove, eliminate, abolish, or destroy.

Design Guidelines

Frequently Used Commands

The primary snap-in should list its most frequently used commands at the top of the context menu. Limit the number of commands at the top of the context menu to 10. Listing more than 10 commands may cause the menus to scroll or wrap when viewed on a 640x480-resolution display. Place the frequently used commands at the top of the context menu grouped together by category or command similarity. Extension snap-ins cannot add commands here.

If you have more than 10 commands, list the less frequently used commands on the **New** and **All Tasks** cascading menus. Less frequently used commands that create new objects or containers should be listed on the **New** cascading menu. Extension snap-ins can add menu items to this menu. Less frequently used commands that perform actions other than creating new objects or containers should be put on the **All Tasks** cascading menu. Extension snap-ins can also add additional commands to this menu. Both the **New** and **All Tasks** cascading menus are hidden when they contain zero menu items. A command should be displayed only once on the context menu. Do not put a command at the top of the context menu and then again on the **New** or **All Tasks** cascading menus.

Note In MMC 1.1, the items above the first separator line are duplicated in the **All Tasks** menu. Usability tests show that this confuses users and as a result, it is not recommended.

Standardizing Menu Commands

Use the following tips to help standardize your context menus:

Provide description text for all context menus for MMC to show in the status bar.
MMC will display the menu description in the status bar. Provide the text for the menu and the text for the description. Use this text to clarify any confusing commands.

For a selection of multiple objects, enable only those commands that apply to all the objects.
If multiple objects are selected, enable only the commands that perform an action appropriate for all the selected objects.

There is a difference between adding an object and creating an object.
Snap-in designers must always be careful to apply the correct terms to menus and buttons. The proper terminology helps the user to easily locate and execute the needed commands. For example, to add objects that already exist, use **Add** plus the object reference. To create an object that previously did not exist, use **New** before the object reference. Do not use the command **Create**.

If the top menu commands require additional grouping, add separators.

Some commands may require additional separation. Keep the number of additional separators to a minimum.

Hide menu items; do not disable them.

If a command is unavailable or inappropriate for the currently selected node in the namespace, the command should be hidden. Do not display disabled commands on a context menu. This guideline is different for toolbar button commands. For guidelines on disabling toolbar buttons, see Chapter 8, "Toolbars."

Include a confirmation dialog box for destructive operations.

Provide a confirmation dialog box with **Yes**, **No**, and **Cancel** buttons for destructive menu commands such as "Delete host" or "Purge data."

Follow the *Microsoft Windows User Experience* book for guidelines on the use of ellipses.

Use ellipses for starting wizards. The book does not discuss wizards, but does cover other ellipses guidelines at length.

Menu Buttons

MMC provides three menu buttons (also known as *menu titles*): **Action**, **View**, and **Favorites**. Snap-ins can add their own menu buttons to the Action menu bar. For instance, some snap-in developers add a **Tools** menu button.

Although a snap-in can add a menu button, the use of menu buttons is discouraged for the following reasons:

- A menu button is specific to a particular snap-in and cannot be extended by another snap-in.

- There are accessibility issues with menu buttons. Menu buttons allow the snap-in to draw the entire menu and are exposed as command buttons. When the command button is pressed, MMC hands the coordinates onscreen to the snap-in and it draws the menu. This does not properly expose the control as a menu and screen readers tend not to read the snap-in-added menu.

- If you create and save a console file and hide the standard menus (Action menu bar), the added menu button will not be hidden.

- Button menus cannot appear on console taskpads.

- When a user has multiple snap-ins loaded into a console at the same time, moving between snap-ins causes a jumping effect within the snap-in toolbar frame.

As mentioned in Chapter 6, "Namespaces," if you feel that your snap-in requires a place to store context-independent tools, add a System Tools node at or near the root of the namespace.

Design Guidelines

Menu Coding References

For more information about creating snap-in menus using C++, see Chapter 21, "Working with Context Menus."

For more information about creating snap-in menus using Microsoft Visual Basic, see "Menus" and "Menu Buttons" in Chapter 34, "Developing Snap-ins."

Menu Design Review

This section offers a review of the information in this chapter.

- Use standard verbs where possible. Do not use similar or duplicate commands.
- Use only one level of cascading menus.
- Hide menu items, rather than disable them.
- Place the most frequently used commands at the top of the context menu list. Limit the number of menu items to 10. Place additional or less frequently used command menu items on the **New** or **All Tasks** cascading menus.
- A command should appear only once on the context menu. Do not place a command at the top of the context menu and then again on the **New** or **All Tasks** cascading menus.
- Do not use **View** menu items for restricting access to property pages or for hiding items on the context menus.

C H A P T E R   8

Toolbars

Toolbars, like menus, provide an interface for the operations or commands applied to objects in the namespace. Since the toolbar buttons are located on the top of the console, they provide the most discoverable way of advertising the commands to the user.

A toolbar is contained in a *toolbar frame*, which can contain multiple toolbars and menu bars.

MMC has two toolbar frames, as shown in Figure 8.1, the console toolbar frame and the snap-in toolbar frame.

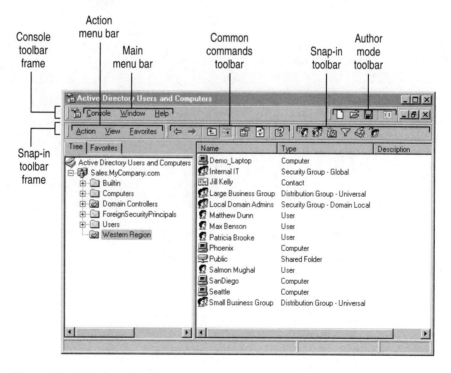

Figure 8.1   MMC toolbar frames

Console toolbar frame

The console toolbar frame contains the main menu bar and the author mode toolbar. A snap-in cannot alter the contents of the console toolbar frame.

Snap-in toolbar frame

The snap-in toolbar frame contains the Action menu bar, the common commands toolbar, and one or more snap-in toolbars. A snap-in can alter the contents of the common commands toolbar and display one or more snap-in toolbars. It can also add a menu button to the Action menu bar, but this practice is discouraged because the button cannot be extended by another snap-in, causing accessibility problems. For more information, see "Common Commands Toolbar" later in this chapter. For more information about menu buttons, see Chapter 7, "Menus."

If the snap-in toolbar frame is too small after a window is resized, MMC automatically adds an additional row to the frame.

The contents of the toolbar frames can change depending on the mode of the console and the settings in the **Customize View** dialog box. When creating a custom console, you can choose to hide the Action menu bar, the common commands toolbar, and snap-in toolbars. For more information, see Chapter 11, "Console Customization and Taskpads."

Figure 8.2 shows a simplified console file saved in user mode with the main menu and author mode toolbars hidden.

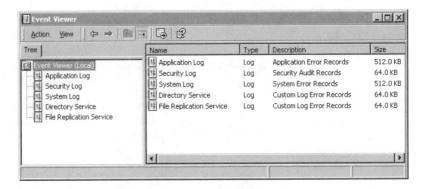

Figure 8.2   Console file with menus and toolbars hidden

Common Commands Toolbar

The common commands toolbar provides toolbar buttons for enabling the MMC standard verbs (cut, copy, paste, delete, properties, refresh, print, and rename). When a snap-in enables a standard verb, the corresponding context menu item and toolbar button are added. Neither stand-alone nor extension snap-ins can add new toolbar buttons to the common commands toolbar. For more information about standard verbs, see Chapter 7, "Menus."

As shown in Table 8.1, MMC also displays several additional toolbar buttons on the common commands toolbar. These toolbar buttons are always visible. Snap-ins cannot enable, disable, or remove any of these buttons.

MMC disables and enables the **Back, Forward**, and **Up one level** commands based on the context.

Table 8.1   Additional Common Commands Toolbar Buttons

Command	Icon	Function
Back	⇦	Retraces the selection of previously selected objects up the console tree.
Forward	⇨	After moving back, retraces the selection of previously selected objects down the console tree.
Up one level	🔼	Moves one level up the console tree.
Show/Hide Console tree/Favorites		Toggles visibility of the console tree and **Favorites** folder; default position is pressed in (set), which displays the console tree.
Export list		Copies the contents of the result pane for exporting to a text file.
Help		Commands HTML Help to search for and display a Help topic about the selected object.

Design Guidelines

Snap-in Toolbars

Snap-in toolbars are created by the snap-in to provide a convenient space to place its most frequently used commands.

✓ The commands offered by a snap-in in the snap-in toolbar should be the same as the commands that appear at the top of the context menu. Like the context menus, these commands should be grouped logically on the toolbar. Use separators if necessary to emphasize groupings. Although a snap-in can offer multiple snap-in tools, you should limit yourself to just one. For an extension snap-in to display a toolbar button, it must create its own toolbar to host the button. Extension snap-ins cannot add or remove toolbar buttons from another snap-in's toolbar.

Minimizing Toolbar Jumping

A snap-in can display many different types of objects in the result pane, such as users, computers, or printers. It is likely that different commands are available for each of the different object types. For example, the **Reset Password** command is available on the user object, while **Reset Account** is available on the computer object.

As the user selects objects of different types in the result pane, different commands and their associated toolbar buttons can be hidden and shown. Hiding and showing toolbar buttons might cause them to *jump*, or change position, from left to right and back again. This behavior is distracting and can cause the user to mistakenly select an incorrect button. For example, suppose that two objects display the same set of three toolbar buttons, and one of the objects adds a fourth button to the left of the original three. As a user changes selection between the two objects, the set of three buttons will appear to jump right and left as the fourth button is displayed and hidden.

To eliminate this behavior, simply enable and disable the toolbar buttons as the user selects different objects in the result pane.

As the user selects nodes of different types in the console tree, the same jumping behavior can occur in the snap-in toolbar buttons. To minimize this jumping effect, if 50 percent or more of the nodes in the namespace use the same toolbar buttons, the snap-in should simply enable and disable those buttons rather than hide and show them. Note, however, that the associated context menu items should be hidden, but never disabled. For more information about context menus, see Chapter 7, "Menus."

Note that the preceding guidelines apply only to small, heterogeneous namespaces. The more dissimilar the object types and commands, the less appropriate these guidelines are. Active Directory directory service, for example, could contain hundreds of different object types in the namespace. If all of the possible commands were represented in the snap-in toolbar frame, it would quickly become overloaded with dozens of buttons. For large and complicated namespaces with lots of different object types, the toolbar buttons should follow the same guidelines as the context menu items. Show and hide toolbar buttons as appropriate; do not enable and disable them.

Snap-in Toolbar Guidelines

The following guidelines apply to snap-in toolbars and the snap-in toolbar frame:

✓ **Place the most frequently used commands on a snap-in toolbar.**
Place the items that are at the top of a snap-in's context menu on a toolbar.

Use ToolTips to display the names of toolbar buttons.
Any control that does not display a text label should be identified through its ToolTip; they are especially useful for toolbar buttons.

For a selection of multiple objects, enable only those commands that apply to all of the objects.
If multiple objects are selected, enable only the commands that perform an action appropriate for all of the selected objects.

Add separators within a toolbar to group related commands.
Group commands logically on the toolbar, as they are grouped on the context menu. Add separators if necessary to emphasize groupings.

Include a confirmation dialog box for destructive operations.
Because the incorrect toolbar button can be selected inadvertently, provide a confirmation dialog box with **Yes**, **No**, and **Cancel** buttons for destructive commands such as **Delete host** or **Purge data** on a toolbar.

For more information about icons in snap-in toolbars, see Chapter 9, "Icons."

Toolbar Coding References

For more information about creating snap-in toolbars using C++, see Chapter 22, "Working with Toolbars and Menu Buttons."

For more information about creating snap-in toolbars using Microsoft Visual Basic, see Chapter 34, "Developing Snap-ins."

Toolbar Design Review

This section offers a review of the information in this chapter. The design features denoted with a check mark in this list and in the chapter text are likely to become logo requirements.

✓ ▪ Place the most frequently used context-sensitive commands on a toolbar. These commands should be the same ones that appear at the top of the associated context menu.

▪ On a snap-in toolbar, when multiple objects are selected, enable only those commands that can perform an action on all selected objects.

▪ Use ToolTips to display the names of toolbar buttons.

▪ Limit to 10 the number of buttons added by a single snap-in.

▪ As the user selects different object types, disable buttons rather than hide them.

▪ Provide a confirmation dialog box for destructive commands on a toolbar.

▪ Add separators within a toolbar to group similar or related commands.

C H A P T E R   9

Icons

For snap-in development, there are three icon types to consider: snap-in icons, namespace icons, and toolbar icons. The snap-in or product icon appears in a number of places and anchors your snap-in to the namespace. The namespace icons facilitate navigation by providing logical icons that differentiate containers and objects. Toolbar button icons make the most important commands visible by pictorially representing the operation. You can use existing icons or create new icons that are appropriate to the objects that the snap-in manages.

The information in this chapter is tailored to icons used in MMC. For more general information about creating Windows icons, see *Microsoft Windows User Experience*, especially Chapter 14, "Visual Design."

General MMC Icon Guidelines

Icons are most often used in creating the namespace. For common containers such as folders and common objects such as computers, use the established Windows icons included on the CD-ROM that accompanies this book.

When you create an icon, adhere to the following visual guidelines:

- Create 16x16-pixel and 32x32-pixel icons. Follow the Windows interface guidelines for "Icon Design" in Chapter 14 of *Microsoft Windows User Experience* when creating these icons. Note that the MMC guidelines differ from the *Microsoft Windows User Experience* guidelines in a few areas.

- MMC does not require 48x48-pixel icons. Your snap-in or product icon should be 48x48 if it appears outside of MMC. (If you have created one with your icon set, you do not have to remove it.)

- MMC does not require 256-color versions of your icons. Use the colors from the Windows 16-color system palette. MMC icons appear in 16x16-pixel size the majority of the time and the benefits of the 256-color icon size are diminished at that size. If you already have a 256-color icon, MMC displays it in 16- and 24-bit display modes.

- Design icons one pixel smaller than the pixel grid in either width or height. This allows space for the possibility of adding status, graphic overlay, the shortcut icon, or secondary icons, and allows users with visual impairments to identify the shape of a secondary element more clearly. The extra pixel of space also allows better spacing of icons in the namespace.

- Create each icon, 16x16 and 32x32, individually to avoid distortions that can occur when resizing an icon.

- Make sure the icons are clearly distinguishable in color and monochrome monitor settings, as well as in high-contrast display schemes. For more information on accessibility issues, see Chapter 14, "Accessibility and Localization."

- Center the icon in the 16x16-pixel or 32x32-pixel space.

- If you use an overlay graphic to denote status, do not change the size or position of the underlying graphic. The overlay is always placed in the lower-right corner. Maintaining a consistent location aids users in recognizing important status information.

When you create an icon, adhere to the following conceptual guidelines:

- Keep the icon simple by using only one or two objects to communicate its concept.

- Use real-world objects to represent abstract ideas so that the user can draw from previous learning and experience.

- Make sure the graphic you use is not culturally biased. A graphic can have different meanings in different cultures or might have no meaning at all.

- Avoid incorporating letters or words in the graphic because they might not easily translate across languages.

- Avoid incorporating a mouse pointer in the graphic because it might confuse users about the location of their own mouse pointer.

- If you are creating a set, or *family*, of icons, make the style and meaning consistent. You can do this by repeating their common graphic elements and avoiding using unrelated elements.

- Test the ability of users to recognize the icon as the object it represents.

Note that you can get the best possible results by employing a graphic designer who has experience in icon design.

Namespace Icons

MMC namespaces contain *objects* and *containers*. They are organized and presented in a hierarchical form similar to the way Microsoft Windows Explorer displays files and folders.

A well-organized namespace makes it easy for users to find what they are looking for and to perform their tasks. A great deal of care and thought needs to go into the creation of the namespace icons. The tree should consist of unique icons to represent objects, and folder icons for containers. If the object icons are simple and distinct, they can more readily be located by a user browsing a console tree with many hierarchical levels and large numbers of objects. Using folder icons to denote container nodes also assists the user in navigating the tree.

Following these guidelines when choosing whether to use folders or unique icons to represent nodes in the namespace helps you to create an easy-to-navigate namespace:

Use unique icons to represent objects in the namespace.
Selective use of unique icons makes them more effective. A unique icon then takes on a special meaning that the user associates with that icon. Servers and databases use unique icons that represent physical objects.

Use a unique icon to represent the top-level node, also known as the snap-in or product node.
In Figure 9.1, the Active Directory directory services icon is used for the top-level node. This usage automatically places the icon on the console title bar and in the **Start** menu when you save the console file. Using a unique icon for the top-level node makes your snap-in easy to find in the **Start** menu.

Use folder icons to represent containers in the namespace.

The namespace shown in Figure 9.1 illustrates the recommended method for using folders as containers.

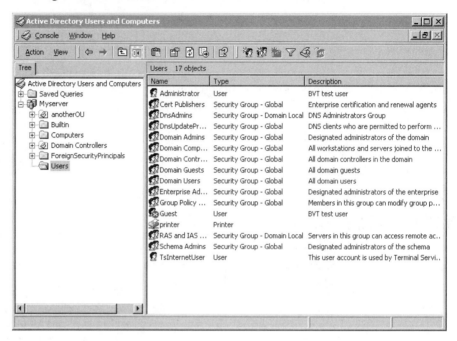

Figure 9.1   Folders used in namespace

The folder for Domain Controllers contains an extra graphic element, which seems to violate the icon guidelines. In this case, it illustrates the one exception to adding an overlay on a folder. Active Directory has two types of containers (folders). The first is a standard container and the other (the folder with the graphic overlay) contains objects (called *organizational units*) to which you can apply policies. So, if you have a technical reason for differentiating your folders, you can use a graphic overlay like the one shown in Figure 9.1. Because the effectiveness of an icon is significantly reduced at the small size contained within the frame of the folder, we recommend that you overlay a slightly larger icon on the bottom right of the folder as shown in Figure 9.2. You should use this type of overlay with as few folders as possible and keep your objects distinct from folders. Note that we do not recommend using status overlays in conjunction with folders containing a special overlay icon.

Figure 9.2   Larger icon overlay for folders in namespace

Use standard icons for existing objects and for new objects that are similar to an existing object.

Standard icons such as servers are established images that are easily recognized and associated with their object. Creating a new icon by using, for example, a server icon with a meaningful overlay helps the user quickly understand the intended function of the object and provides a familiar context for the user to learn the new icon. For more information, see the list of standard icons in Appendix B and on the companion CD-ROM.

Figure 9.1 shows the Users node with multiple object types displayed in the result pane. The Active Directory snap-in uses three main Group object types: Domain Local, Global, and Universal. Each of these groups can also be set to a secure enabled or secure disabled state. Instead of trying to design six different icons to communicate six different types and states, directory services simplified the user experience by using one visual concept for Group and relied on the type column in the result pane to differentiate between Group types and states.

Figure 9.3 shows the open Event Viewer folder with each event log represented by the same unique icon. Note that even though the logs contain different information, the designers chose to use the same unique icon for each log, rather than create a different icon for each log file.

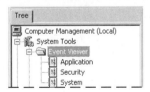

Figure 9.3   Event Viewer log icons

Do not the use same unique icon for a container and one of its children.

The obvious exception is the folder icon. However, by carefully planning your console tree, you can avoid using a unique icon for both a container and its children. If avoiding such usage is difficult you might consider redesigning the namespace to avoid the problem.

Use status overlays on unique icons to indicate state.

In the namespace, show the status of an object by overlaying a graphic on the object's icon. This *graphic overlay* (also called an *annotation*) should be placed in the lower-right corner of the icon. Figure 9.4 shows a server icon with a warning status overlay and Figure 9.5 shows the same icon with a critical status overlay.

Figure 9.4   Warning server status graphic overlay

Figure 9.5   Critical server status graphic overlay

These status overlays must be small, but meaningful. They are generally 11x11 pixels for 16x16-pixel icons and 15x15 pixels for 32x32-pixel icons. For icons that display status indicators, make sure the icon is recognizable even if the lower-right corner is covered. The main icon should remain in the same position in the 16x16- or 32x32-pixel grid as it did without a status indicator.

The status text indicated by the status graphic must appear in the **Status** column of the result pane **Detail** view. This enables visually impaired users to gain access to this information. For more information, see Chapter 14, "Accessibility and Localization."

Table 9.1 shows each status icon as it appears alone and as an overlay, with the overlay placement and name of the icon.

Table 9.1   Status Icons

Icon	Overlay	Placement	Name
N/A	N/A	▤	Normal
⊗	⊗	▣	Critical/Error
⚠	⚠	▤	Warning
ⓘ	ⓘ	▤	Information
✔	✔	▤	Completed/ Finished
⌛	⌛	▤	Busy

There is no overlay for the Normal icon because it would call special attention to the object, which is not necessary when the state is unchanged or normal. The Completed/Finished icon is best suited for indicating that a process, job, or task has completed or finished and the object is changing from a busy state to a finished state. This icon should appear for short time periods, and then the object icon should change to a Normal icon. Use the Busy icon when an object is waiting for the status to change, such as when a snap-in is connecting to a service on a remote computer. If this state change occurs very quickly, you can use the icon either alone or as an overlay. If the state change takes a longer period of time, consider using the Busy icon by itself, replacing the object icon until the state returns to normal. The larger icon better notifies the user of the state change.

These icons can appear by themselves, as they do in the Event Viewer (see Figure 9.6) to quickly and clearly communicate the type of event.

Figure 9.6   Status icons in Event Viewer

Do not create open and closed states for most icons.
There are only a few images, such as those of a folder or book, for which the open and closed states can be successfully depicted visually. For this reason, it is best not to create open and closed icons for most objects.

Extension snap-in icons should stay in the same style as the primary snap-in icons.
Try to maintain the icon family visual style used by the primary snap-in.

Other Names for Status Icons

When communicating information about the state of an object, the icon by itself does not sufficiently communicate all of the information. Add a **Status** column to the **Details** view to describe the current state in words. Doing so will help reinforce the meaning of the status icon.

In practical use, these icons can be used for a wide variety of related states. Table 9.2 lists standard status icons with their standard names in bold and the related states that they can represent. Using these icons for their related states reduces the number of icons you have to create and also promotes the use of these icons as standards.

Table 9.2   Standard Status Icons: Related States

Icon	Related States		
⊗	**Error**	Frozen	Unreachable
	Critical	Requires attention	No contact
	Offline	No data	Bad
	Failed	Data loss	Not present
	Inactive	Corrupt	Not loaded
	Not authenticated	Broken	Unavailable
	Connection lost	Revoked	Refuse
	Disabled	Stopped	Unauthorized
	Down		
⚠	**Warning**	Yield	Conflict
	Pause	Danger	Confusion
	Unknown	May need attention	
✔	**Completed**	Finished	
⧗	**Busy**	Pausing	Waiting
	Starting	Progressing	Busy
	Stopping	In process	Resuming

Snap-in Icons

Snap-in or product icons appear at the top of their tree hierarchy and provide an opportunity for product branding inside MMC. In a namespace that has multiple snap-ins, the snap-in icon helps users locate your snap-in. Snap-in icons also appear in the following places:

- **Start** menu
- Taskbar
- Desktop
- Title bars of windows

Create snap-in icons as 16x16-, 32x32-, and 48x48-pixel icons in 16 colors. Figure 9.7 shows the Active Directory Users and Computers icon used in the **Start** menu, in the taskbar, on the desktop as a shortcut, and in the title bar of the MMC window.

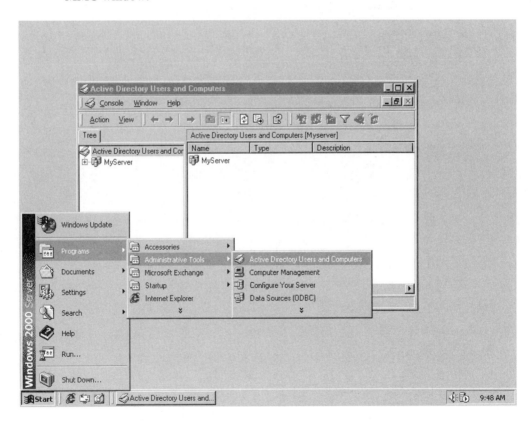

Figure 9.7   Snap-in icons

Design Guidelines

Use an icon that best represents the functionality of the snap-in. If possible, incorporate a standard icon into the snap-in icon. Keep in mind when designing the icon that status overlays and the shortcut icon can be added. To ensure that any secondary elements in an icon are not concealed by status overlays or shortcut icons, place secondary elements in the upper-right or upper-left corner. The following figures show correct placement of icons as well as an example of a problem caused by not following this strategy.

Figure 9.8 shows the Active Directory Sites and Services snap-in icon in both 32x32 and 16x16 pixels, with the shortcut icon and a status icon added correctly.

Figure 9.8   Example of correctly placed secondary elements in 16x16-pixel and 32x32-pixel icons

Figure 9.9 shows an example of how placing a secondary element in the lower-right corner instead of an upper corner can cause problems. In this case, the status icon covers the secondary element.

Figure 9.9   Example of incorrectly placed secondary element

Toolbar Icons

Snap-in toolbars provide the space for the snap-in to place its most frequently used commands. A well-crafted toolbar icon effectively visually communicates the purpose of the command. Design the icons for a toolbar as a set and consider how they will work together to make commands discoverable. Toolbar icons only need to be provided in 16x16-pixel size and are only displayed in 16-color mode.

In addition to using the guidelines provided for general icons, follow these guidelines for toolbar icons:

- Create the icon with two states, enabled and disabled.

Figure 9.10   Examples of toolbar icons rendered in the correct flat style.

- Create a black border around the entire image of the icon as shown in Figure 9.10. This flattens out an icon by eliminating the highlight and shadow. There are exceptions, such as the delete icon "X" which is rendered in a flat style but has no border and uses the red color to add meaning to the icon.
- Create the icon in a two-dimensional flat style.
- Test the icon for visibility on a light-gray background.
- Note that the MMC toolbar icons differ from the *Microsoft Windows User Experience* guidelines in a few areas:
  - MMC does not require 256-color versions of your toolbar icons. Use the colors from the Windows 16-color system palette. Do not include the 256-color icons, because they look very different next to the 16-color icons.
  - MMC does not require the larger 20x20-pixel icon size.
  - MMC does not require grayscale versions of the icons. All icons are to be rendered using the 16-color palette. MMC does not show color change when the pointer moves over the toolbar buttons.

For more information about toolbar buttons, see Chapter 7, "Menus." For a full list of toolbar icons, see the companion CD-ROM.

Icon Design Review

This section offers a review of the information in this chapter.

- Design the entire set of icons for a product to look like a family of icons.

- Use the same icon to represent similar containers and objects.

- Design icons with status overlays and the shortcut icon in mind. Make sure the secondary elements are still visible even if an overlay icon is added. Reserve the lower-right corner for status overlays and the lower-left corner for the shortcut icon.

- Design icons one pixel smaller than the pixel grid in either width or height.

- Create both 16x16- and 32x32-pixel icons as originals. Do not try to size a 16x16-pixel icon to make a 32x32-pixel icon or vice versa because that causes blurring.

- Make sure the icons are clearly visible in color and monochrome monitor settings, as well as in high-contrast display schemes.

- Use real-world objects to represent abstract ideas so that users can draw from previous learning and experience.

- When designing 16-color toolbar images:

  - Use the Windows 16-color palette.

  - Place a black border around the graphic, except for icons like delete that do not require a border.

  - Make images flat in appearance, with little dimension or shading.

- Reuse the same icon for similar containers and objects.

- Do not use the same icon for a parent and any of its children.

- Use unique icons consistently.

- Do not represent *every* item in the console tree with the folder icon.

- Avoid creating too many icons.

- Use a folder for containers.

C H A P T E R   1 0

Property Sheets

Users can view or change an object's attributes or settings by using the object's property sheet. MMC property sheets are both *modeless*, enabling the user to gain access to other windows while the property sheet is open, and *extensible*. Although snap-ins can display some properties in the result pane, property sheets enable users to see and change all the properties of a given object in a single location.

This chapter provides an overview of and guidelines for the creation of MMC property sheets. For more information about creating Windows property sheets, see *Microsoft Windows User Experience*.

Property Sheet Elements

A typical property sheet contains a title bar, one or more tabbed property pages, and command buttons. Figure 10.1 shows a typical property sheet.

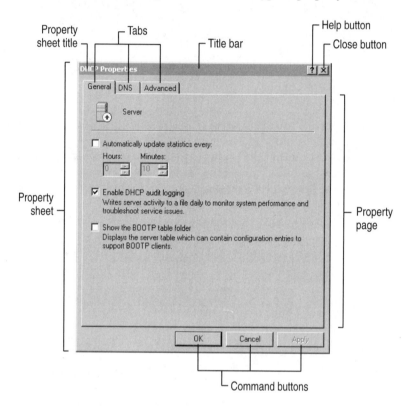

Figure 10.1   Typical property sheet

Property Sheet Title Bar

The title bar text of the property sheet identifies the object. An object's property sheet title bar contains the title bar text, a **Help** button to open context-sensitive Help (if used), and a **Close** button as shown in Figure 10.1. By default, MMC generates the title bar text by using the name of the currently selected object followed by the word *Properties*. For example, if the object name is Customer Database, MMC automatically sets the title to Customer Database Properties.

If an object has no name, create the title bar text by using the object's type name followed by the word *Properties*. If the property sheet applies to several objects of the same type, use the objects' type name. When the type name cannot be applied—for example, when the selection includes different types of objects—substitute the word *Selection* for the type name.

If the title bar text is too long to fit in the title bar, the title is truncated and an ellipsis is appended to the end. The full title then is displayed in a ToolTip when the pointer moves over the title bar. Try to keep the name short to avoid truncation.

The title bar should not include the path of the object. The user can display the path by holding down the CTRL+ALT keys while moving the pointer over the property sheet title bar.

Design Guidelines

Property Sheet Command Buttons

Most property sheets enable the user to make changes on one or more property pages, and then apply the changes to the object. To provide for this in a snap-in developed using Microsoft Visual Basic, add the **OK, Cancel, Apply,** and **Help** command buttons to the lower-right corner of the property sheet, right-aligned with the right edge, in the order presented in the following table.

Command	Action
OK	Applies all pending changes and closes the property sheet window.
Cancel	Discards any pending changes and closes the property sheet window. Does not cancel or undo any changes that have already been applied using the **Apply** button.
Apply	Applies all pending changes and leaves the property sheet window open. Enable this button when a user makes a change to a property.
Help	Displays conceptual or procedural Help for the property sheet in a pop-up window. Note that Help is not provided for individual property pages. This button is optional.

The **OK**, **Cancel**, and **Apply** buttons are automatically displayed on the property sheet for snap-ins developed using Microsoft Visual C++. If you decide to use Help on a property page, you can add a **Help** button that follows the **Apply** button. If the primary snap-in doesn't offer property sheet-level Help, but an extension snap-in has requested Help, a **Help** button is displayed for the property sheet. This button is disabled until the property page that requested Help is selected. For more information about using Help on property pages, see Chapter 15, "Creating Online Help."

If you create a secondary window from a property page, make sure changes are not automatically applied when the user closes the secondary window. Apply changes only when the user clicks the **OK** or **Apply** buttons on the property sheet.

Note A **Close** button on a property sheet title bar is not the same as a **Cancel** button. If the user clicks **Close** before clicking **Apply**, display a message prompting the user to apply or discard the changes. Include a **Cancel** button on the message box that enables the user to cancel the closing of the property sheet.

Property Pages

A property page can contain both editable and static properties, such as the Event Viewer snap-in shown in Figure 10.2.

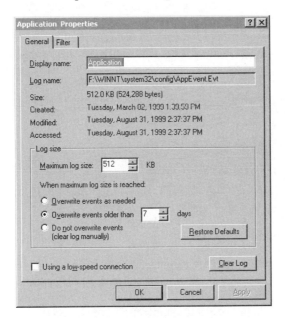

Figure 10.2   Static and editable properties

Use property pages to categorize and group properties. Each property page has a title that is displayed on the tab. Users click the tabs to switch from one page to the other. Try to keep property page tab labels to one or two words. If it is necessary to abbreviate the name on a tab, spell out the name on the top of the property page.

Arrange the properties and property pages from the most frequently used to the least frequently used. If properties are targeted for use by advanced users, place these properties on a property page titled **Advanced** or place them in a secondary dialog box that is displayed by clicking a button labeled **Advanced**. If you have properties that are rarely changed by the user, you can place them in a secondary dialog box as well.

Icons

The first page of a property sheet is usually the page dealing with nonspecific properties and is labeled **General**. Regardless of the tab name, for every first property page on a property sheet, include the icon that represents the node to which the properties belong. The icon should be presented in 32x32-pixel and 16-color format, and should appear as shown in Figure 10.3. You can include a read-only edit control with the borders turned off that repeats the name of the node to the right of the icon. A user's changes to the name of the container or object should also be reflected here. For more information about the specific placement of these elements on the page, see "Property Page Layout" later in this chapter.

Figure 10.3   General page icon

Avoid using icons on property pages other than the first page, except when you need to notify the user of potential side effects of a change. For instance, you can provide an alert icon and explanatory text to warn the user of changes that are either irreversible or not readily apparent. In these cases, place a standard alert icon (warning or critical) to the left of the text.

When the user clicks **Change Mode** as shown in Figure 10.4, a warning confirmation dialog box appears. Because confirmation dialog boxes are typically ignored, and because it is critical to capture the user's attention and ensure that the user understands the implications of clicking **Change Mode**, an alert icon and text are added.

For more information about alert icons, their meanings, and their appropriate uses, see Chapter 13, "Dialog Boxes and Message Boxes."

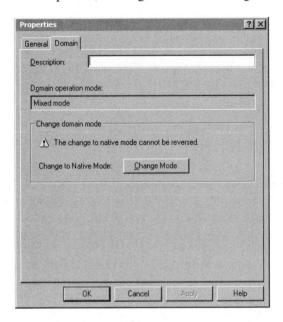

Figure 10.4   Warning icon placement in property sheet

Properties and Extension Snap-ins

An extension snap-in can add a property page to another snap-in's property sheet. This page is placed after the last page currently on the sheet. To identify which snap-in provided a given property page, press CTRL+ALT while moving the pointer over the tab of the property page.

If a node of your snap-in has no properties, but you believe an extension snap-in might need to add property pages to that node, you should create a property sheet without any property pages. This is so that the **Properties** command appears on the context menu. If none of the extension snap-ins provides any property pages, MMC displays a default page stating that there are no properties for the selected node. If any of the extension snap-ins provide property pages, the default page is hidden and only the extension property pages are displayed. For more information about how to implement this mechanism, see the MMC SDK.

Property Page Interactions

If a user attempts to reopen a property sheet that he or she already has open on the desktop, the snap-in brings the open sheet to the front. In some cases, the snap-in might not be able to tell if another copy of the property sheet for the same object is open. Such a situation might occur if, for example, the user is running separate MMC instances or multiple snap-ins in the same MMC instance. In such cases, the snap-in opens another instance of the property sheet.

Because an object's state can change at any time, you should check the current state of the selected object before displaying a property sheet. Provide appropriate actions based upon the object's state when displaying its property sheet.

For example, if a user tries to apply property changes to an object whose state has changed since the user opened the property sheet, you can, of course, save the changes. However, it may be preferable to detect the difference and notify the user that the object's state has changed. The message should direct the user to open a new instance of the property sheet (reflecting the object's current state), and then copy and paste the changes to the new instance. When the user dismisses this message, the snap-in should leave the original property sheet open with only the **Cancel** button active.

Property Page Layout

For most of the elements discussed in previous chapters, layout is applied automatically by MMC. However, MMC does not automatically arrange controls on individual property pages. Measurements for arranging controls are presented in this chapter. These measurements also apply to the design of dialog boxes. For more information, see Chapter 13, "Dialog Boxes and Message Boxes," and *Microsoft Windows User Experience*.

Provide enough space in your design so that when the property pages are localized, they continue to look as you intended. For more information, see *Microsoft Windows User Experience*.

Measurements in this section are expressed in dialog units (dlus), which are used by C/C++ programmers. Several tables for converting the measurements from dlus to twips are provided for Visual Basic programmers. For more information about twips, see Chapter 35, "Programming Techniques." For more information about dlus, see *Microsoft Windows User Experience*.

Property Page Size

When developing Windows applications, you usually have a choice of three standard sizes for a property page. However, in MMC, the recommended size of a property page is 252 dlus wide and 218 dlus high, as shown in Figure 10.5.

Just before a property sheet is displayed, all of the property pages are collected from the primary snap-in and its extension snap-ins. If one or more of these property pages is larger than the recommended size, each of the pages is resized to match the size of the largest property page by adding vertical and/or horizontal space to the smaller pages.

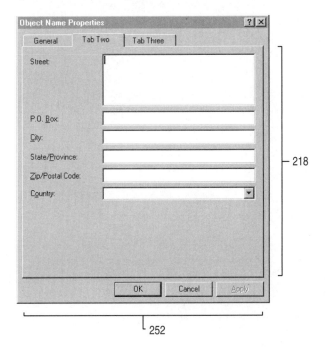

Figure 10.5   Recommended height and width of an MMC property page

Table 10.1   Visual Basic Dimensions for Property Page Height and Width

dlus	Small font twips	Large font twips
218	5300	5220
252	5660	6040

Design Guidelines

Placement of Controls, Text, and Graphics

The next three sections describe the specifications for spacing controls on property pages. The sample resource file from which Figures 10.6 through 10.11 are derived is provided on the companion CD-ROM.

General Property Page

Figure 10.6 illustrates the placement of controls, text, and an icon on a **General** property page.

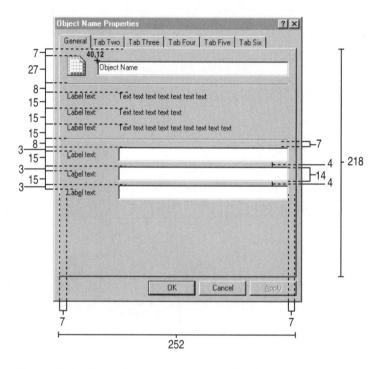

Figure 10.6   General property page specifications

Table 10.2   Visual Basic Dimensions for the General Property Page

dlus	Small font twips	Large font twips
3	60	60
4	80	80
7	160	160
8	180	180
12	280	280
15	360	360
27	640	640
40	960	960
218	5300	5220
252	5660	6040

Figure 10.6 illustrates the following minimal standards for placing controls and text on a **General** property page. Note that the borders of a control (text box, button, and so on) are included in the measurement of control height.

- Place the top-left corner of the icon (in 32x32-pixel, 16-color format) that represents the object at the (7, 7) coordinates.

- Place an edit control that displays the node name at the (40, 12) coordinates. If the currently selected node cannot be renamed, set the edit control to read-only.

- Place a separator line (1x238 dlus) at 27 dlus from the top of the icon.

- Place the top of the first control or text following the separator line at 8 dlus below the line.

Secondary Property Page

Figures 10.7 through 10.11 illustrate various examples of the placement of controls and text at the top of a secondary property page and in the body of all property pages.

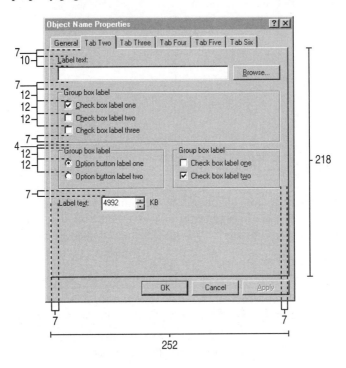

Figure 10.7   Secondary property page specifications

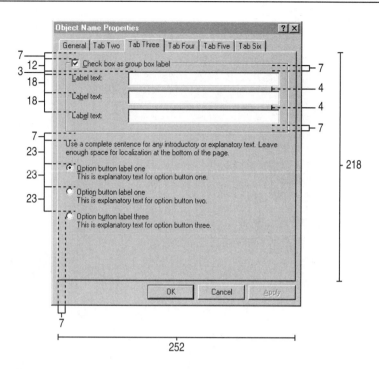

Figure 10.8   Secondary property page specifications

Design Guidelines

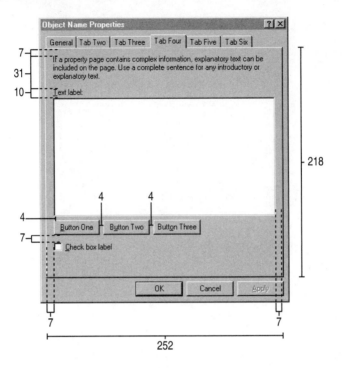

Figure 10.9   Secondary property page specifications

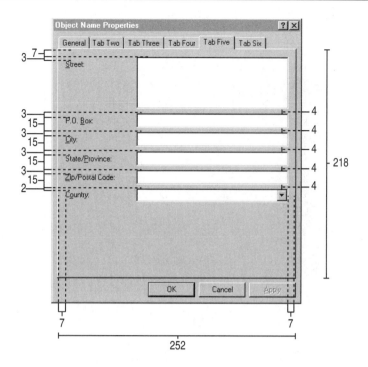

Figure 10.10   Secondary property page specifications

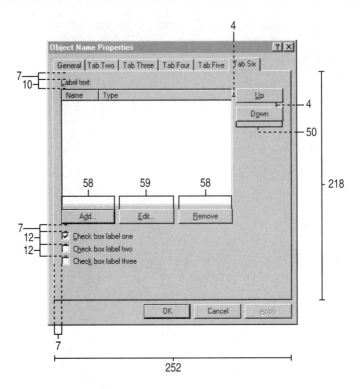

Figure 10.11   Secondary property page specifications

Table 10.3   Visual Basic Dimensions for Secondary Property Pages

dlus	Small font twips	Large font twips
2	40	40
3	60	60
4	80	80
7	160	160
10	240	240
14	320	320
15	360	360
218	5300	5220
252	5660	6040

Figures 10.7 through 10.11 illustrate the following minimal standard for placing controls and text at the top of a secondary property page. Note that the borders of a control (text box, button, and so on) are included in the measurement of control height.

- Place the initial control or text on the page at 7 dlus below the top line of the page (excluding the tabs).

All Property Pages

Figures 10.6 through 10.11 illustrate the following minimal standards for placing controls and text on any property page. Note that the borders of a control (text box, button, and so on) are included in the measurement of control height.

- Use the system font for all text.
- Indent all content 7 dlus from all borders of the page.
- Leave 7 dlus of space between paragraphs of text.
- Leave 4 dlus of space between text boxes, drop-down list boxes, and other controls when the controls are related.
- Leave at least 7 dlus of space between text boxes, drop-down list boxes, and other controls that are not related.
- The standard height of an edit control is 14 dlus.
- The standard size of a button is 50x14 dlus, although you can alter the length as shown in Figure 10.11.
- If a change to be made by a user is either irreversible or not readily apparent, add text explaining the nature of the change and place an alert icon before the text as shown in Figure 10.4.
- If a property sheet contains complex pages, include some explanatory text on each page.

Design Guidelines

Property Sheet Coding References

For more information about creating snap-in property sheets using C++, see Chapter 23, "Adding Property Pages and Wizard Pages."

For more information about creating snap-in property sheets using Visual Basic, see Chapter 34, "Developing Snap-ins."

Designing Exchange

The administration tools for Microsoft Exchange Server 5.5 are not based on MMC guidelines. The Microsoft Exchange 2000 Server administration tools are MMC-based. This section shows how administration tools can be built using MMC and redesigned to follow the MMC 1.2 user interface guidelines.

Exchange Server 5.5 IMAP4 Property Pages

Figures 10.12 and 10.13 show some of the property pages for the Internet Message Access Protocol 4 (IMAP4) for Exchange Server 5.5.

Figure 10.12   Example of incorrect type and icon sizes in an Exchange Server 5.5 IMAP4 General property page

The icon and the typeface in the property page in Figure 10.12 are not the correct size and there is no separator line.

Figure 10.13   Example of incorrect type and icon sizes in an Exchange Server 5.5 IMAP4 secondary property page

The secondary property page is shown in Figure 10.13. It should not have an icon, and the spacing between graphical user interface elements is different from the guidelines described earlier in this chapter. In particular, the property page size is much larger than the recommended size for MMC.

Exchange 2000 IMAP4 Property Pages

Figures 10.14 and 10.15 show the Exchange 2000 Server property pages for IMAP4. These property pages are based on MMC and follow MMC user interface guidelines. Compared to the early versions of the property pages, the information in the newer versions is presented on fewer tabs and is easier for users to use.

Figure 10.14   Exchange 2000 IMAP4 General property page

The icon and separator are in the correct location, the typeface is correct, and there is sufficient space for localization.

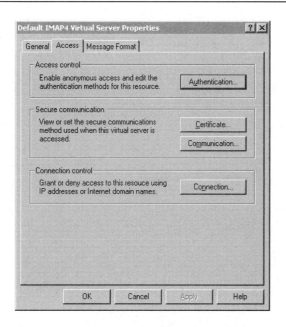

Figure 10.15   Exchange 2000 IMAP4 Access property page

The **Access** property page, shown in Figure 10.15, takes the place of four property pages (**Authentication**, **Diagnostics Logging**, **Idle Time-out**, and **Anonymous**) in the original property sheet.

Property Sheet Design Review

This section offers a review of the information in this chapter.

- Use the MMC property sheet provider to create snap-in property sheets.
- Use the system font for all text.
- Avoid large blocks of text on a property page.
- Group similar properties on the same property page.
- Make sure that the property sheet can be started from the context menu and from the properties toolbar button.
- If it is necessary to abbreviate the name on a tab, spell out the name on the top of the property page.

CHAPTER 11

Console Customization and Taskpads

Much of this book focuses on creating snap-ins. However, snap-ins must be added to an MMC console file (.msc file) before they can be used. While snap-ins are the primary type of tool you can add to a console, you can also add ActiveX controls, links to Web pages, taskpads, and folders for organizing the namespace.

This chapter focuses on how to customize snap-ins to address the needs of different users and contexts. Since you can customize the view and contents of console files, while planning a snap-in you should consider who will be using the snap-in and the roles of these users within an organization. For instance, you might customize a console to simplify the view for a novice user, restrict a junior-level administrator to certain snap-ins or functionality, create shortcuts to frequently used nodes, or add additional instructions to help a user complete a task.

After you create, customize, and save a console, you can use it on your local computer, send it to other users through e-mail, post it on your network, or publish it in the directory service or on the World Wide Web. For more information about deploying console files, see Chapter 5, "Deploying Snap-ins."

Customizing the Console

The primary elements used to customize MMC consoles are the **Add/Remove Snap-in** dialog box, **Customize View** dialog box, **Options** dialog box, **Modify Columns** dialog box, **New Window From Here** command, **Favorites,** New Taskpad View Wizard, and New Task Wizard. The wizards used to create taskpads and tasks are discussed later in this chapter.

My Custom Console

This section guides you through the creation of a custom console using some of the basic MMC customization options. Figure 11.1 shows the console before customization, and Figure 11.3 shows the same console after completing the steps described below. The resulting console, shown in Figure 11.3, is too stripped-down to be useful; it is provided for demonstration purposes only.

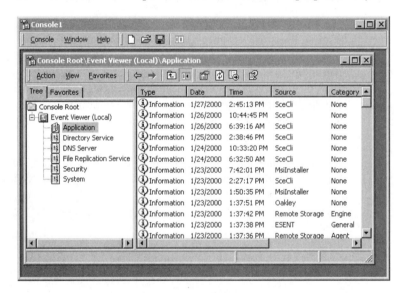

Figure 11.1   Event Viewer snap-in before customization

The overly simplified console shown in Figure 11.3 hides the common commands toolbar, Action menu bar, main menu bar, author mode toolbar, scope pane, and some unnecessary columns in the result pane. The title of the console is renamed from **Console1** to **My Custom Console** and a new icon is specified.

To try this yourself, complete the following procedure.

▶   **To create a custom console**

Add the Event Viewer snap-in to the console

1. Click **Start**, click **Run**, type **MMC**, and then click **OK**.
2. On the **Console** menu, click **Add/Remove Snap-in**, and then click **Add**.
3. In the **Snap-in** column, double-click **Event Viewer**.
4. Click **Local computer: (the computer this console is running on)**, and then click **Finish**.
5. In the **Add Standalone Snap-in** dialog box, click **Close**.
6. In the **Add/Remove Snap-in** dialog box, click **OK**.

Hide unnecessary columns

7. In the console scope pane, click the **Event Viewer** node, and then select the **Application** node. The result pane displays the Application log file.
8. On the **View** menu, click **Choose Columns**.
9. In the **Displayed columns** list, select **Category,** and click **Remove**. Do the same for **User** and **Computer**, and then click **OK**.

Hide the console tree, toolbars, menus, and other elements

10. On the **View** menu, click **Customize**.
11. Clear all the check boxes, and then click **OK**.

Specify the console title and icon

12. On the **Console** menu, click **Options**.
13. In the first text box, type **My Custom Console**, and then click **Change Icon**.
14. In the **File name** text box, type **%SystemRoot%\system32\SHELL32.dll**, and then click **OK**.
15. Select the icon shown in Figure 11.2, and then click **OK**.

Design Guidelines

Figure 11.2   Change Icon dialog box

Specify the mode and save

16. In the **Console mode** drop-down list, select **User mode—limited access, single window**, and then click **OK**.

17. On the **Console** menu, click **Save As**.

18. In the **Save in** drop-down list, select **Desktop**; in the **File name** text box, type **My Custom Console**; and then click **Save**.

When you reopen the **My Custom Console** file, it should look similar to the console in Figure 11.3.

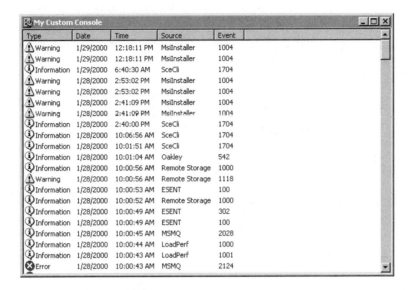

Figure 11.3   Stripped-down Event Viewer

The console shown in Figure 11.3 has a number of shortcomings. In the "My Custom Console with Taskpads" section later in this chapter, the shortcomings are enumerated and addressed using taskpads.

Add/Remove Snap-in Dialog Box

To add items to the console tree, use the **Add/Remove Snap-in** command on the **Console** menu of the MMC main menu bar. The **Add/Remove Snap-in** dialog box shown in Figure 11.4 enables you to add and remove snap-ins and other items from the current console. By default, these items appear under the **Console Root**.

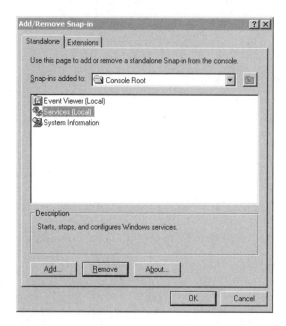

Figure 11.4   Add/Remove Snap-in dialog box

The **Add Standalone Snap-in** dialog box shown in Figure 11.5 displays a list of available snap-ins and other items, such as folders for organizing the namespace. If desired, you can add multiple instances of the same snap-in to a console. For computers running Windows 2000 that are members of a domain, this list includes both locally-installed snap-ins and snap-ins published in the Active Directory directory service. For snap-ins that are available in Active Directory, but not yet installed locally, **Not Installed** appears in the **Vendor** column. For more information about publishing snap-ins in Active Directory, see Chapter 5, "Deploying Snap-ins."

Figure 11.5   Add Standalone Snap-in dialog box

Some stand-alone snap-ins, such as Computer Management, are extended by other snap-ins. After you add a stand-alone snap-in to the console, you can click the **Extensions** tab in the **Add/Remove Snap-in** dialog box shown in Figure 11.6 to view the list of extension snap-ins and whether or not the extension snap-ins are loaded by MMC.

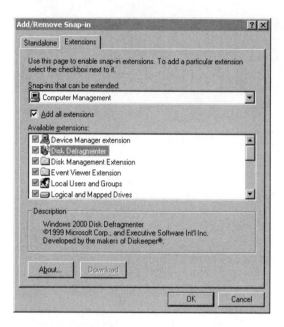

Figure 11.6   Add/Remove Snap-in dialog box, Extensions page

When the **Add all extensions** check box is selected, which is the default, MMC automatically loads all extension snap-ins. When a new extension snap-in is installed, MMC automatically loads the new extension as well.

When the **Add all extensions** check box is cleared, MMC loads only the extension snap-ins checked in the **Available extensions** list. In other words, if the check box next to the name of the extension snap-in is selected, MMC loads it; otherwise, the extension snap-in is not loaded. When a new extension snap-in is installed, its corresponding check box defaults to cleared. New extension snap-ins are not loaded by MMC until the user explicitly selects the check box next to the extension's name.

After an extension snap-in is enabled, it is displayed in the **Snap-ins that can be extended** drop-down list along with the stand-alone snap-ins. This means that the extension snap-in also has extensions that you can enable.

Like stand-alone snap-ins, an administrator can also publish extension snap-ins in Active Directory. Extension snap-ins available to a user from Active Directory appear in the list of available extension snap-ins with any locally installed extension snap-ins, except that they are followed by (**not installed**). You must specifically download extension snap-ins from the directory service to make them available in a console. Thus, to download all extensions for a given item, do not select the **Add all extensions** check box on the **Extensions** tab of the **Add/Remove Snap-in** dialog box. Instead, clear this check box and select the check boxes next to each extension that you want to download, and then click **Download**.

Customize View Dialog Box

You can control whether to hide or display many of the graphical user interface elements of a console by using the **Customize View** dialog box, available in MMC. On the Action menu bar, click **View**, and then click **Customize**. The **Customize View** dialog box is shown in Figure 11.7. As you select or clear the check boxes in this dialog box, you can view the console to confirm that the changes you made are what you expected.

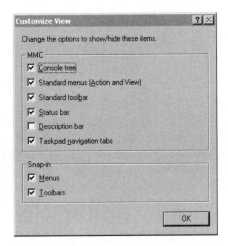

Figure 11.7   Customize View dialog box

Each of the check box labels in Figure 11.7 is called out in Figure 11.8 so that you can see exactly which graphical user interface elements are affected. Note that there is no snap-in menu in Figure 11.8; this is because we do not recommend using snap-in menus. For more information about snap-in menus, see Chapter 7, "Menus."

Design Guidelines

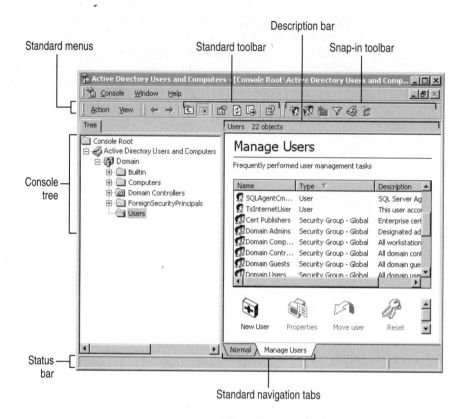

Figure 11.8   Active Directory with callouts from Customize View dialog box

In addition, note that if you clear the **Standard menus (Action and View)** check box and close the **Customize View** dialog box, you cannot gain access to commands on the **Action** and **View** menus, including the **Customize** command. For this reason, the **Customize View** menu item is also available on the system menu (also known as the Control menu). As shown in Figure 11.9, you can access the system menu by clicking the icon in the upper-left corner of the child window. If the console file was saved in **User mode–limited access, single window**, click the icon in the upper-left corner of the primary window.

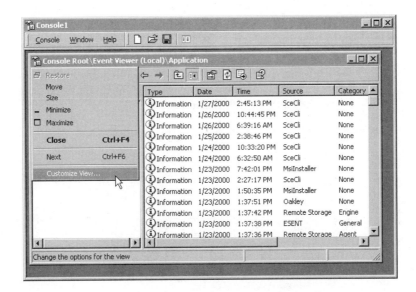

Figure 11.9   System menu with Customize View menu item

The **Console tree** option hides or displays the contents of the console tree. If a Favorite has been created, the **Favorites** tab is always independent of this setting. To hide both the console tree and **Favorites** (the entire left pane), you can click the **Show/Hide Console Tree/Favorites** button on the MMC common commands toolbar. For more information about snap-in menus, see Chapter 7, "Menus," and for more information about toolbars, see Chapter 8, "Toolbars."

Design Guidelines

Options Dialog Box

You can use the **Options** dialog box, shown in Figure 11.10, to change the title and icon of an MMC console, set the default console mode, and configure additional access options. To display the MMC **Options** dialog box, click **Console**, and then click **Options**.

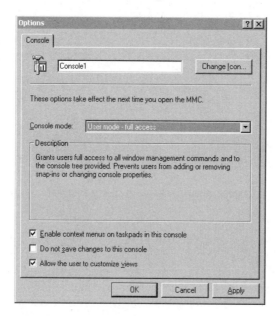

Figure 11.10   Options dialog box

Icon and Title

To change the default icon for a console, in the **Options** dialog box, click **Change Icon**, and then browse to a file containing icons. As shown in Figure 11.11, the new icon appears in the console title bar and in the title bar of any child windows. It also appears as the default icon in the Windows **Start** menu and on any desktop shortcut that you create to the console.

If you do not have your own file of icons, many files, such as snap-in .dll files, contain icons that you can use. In addition, on computers running Microsoft Windows NT and Windows 2000, Shell32.dll contains a variety of generic and useful icons.

To change the title for a console, type a new title in the text box to the right of the icon. As shown in Figure 11.11, this title appears in the console title bar. When saving your custom console, the file name and the title should be kept the same.

Figure 11.11   Customized console title and icon

Console Modes

You can assign a console one of two general access modes: *author* mode or *user* mode. User mode is available in three different forms. Below is a brief description of each mode:

Author mode
Enables full customization of the MMC console, including the ability to add or remove snap-ins, create new windows, create Favorites and taskpads, and access to all the options of the **Customize View** and **Options** dialog boxes. Users creating a custom console file for themselves or others typically use this mode. The resulting console is usually saved in one of the following user modes.

User mode-full access
The same as author mode, except that users cannot add or remove snap-ins, change console options, create Favorites, or create taskpads.

User mode-limited access, multiple windows
Provides access to only those parts of the console tree that were visible when the console file was saved. Users can create new windows, but cannot close any existing windows.

User mode-limited access, single window
Provides access to only those parts of the console tree that were visible when the console file was saved. Users cannot create new windows. Most of the console files in Windows 2000 are saved in this mode.

By selecting one of the user mode options, authoring features that a user might not need are eliminated. For instance, if you assign the **User mode-full access** option to a console, all window-management commands and full access to the console tree are provided, but a user is prevented from changing the basic functionality of the console.

Design Guidelines

Opening Consoles in Author Mode

Once a console file has been saved in user mode, there are two ways to open it in author mode again. Start MMC, click **Console**, click **Open,** and then select the console file you want to open. Additionally, from within Microsoft Windows Explorer or on the **Start** menu, select the console file or a shortcut to the console file, and then right-click to view the context menu. Next, as shown in Figure 11.12, click **Author**. MMC opens the console file in author mode.

Figure 11.12   Opening a console file in author mode

Additional Access Options

There are three other check boxes in the **Options** dialog box that you can select or clear to determine the behavior of a console. These options are only available for consoles saved in user mode.

Enable context menus on taskpads in this console

Select this check box to display the context menu when an object is right-clicked in the List view (see Figure 11.28). Conversely, if this check box is cleared, context menus are not displayed. The user is limited to the commands (tasks) you placed on the taskpad. For an explanation of context menus, see Chapter 7, "Menus." For more information about taskpads, see "Taskpads" later in this chapter.

Do not save changes to this console

By default, user customizations, such as which columns are visible and in which order, are automatically saved in the console file. Selecting this check box instructs MMC to discard all such customizations when the console is closed. You should use this setting for cases where many users share the same console file.

Allow the user to customize views

When this check box is selected, users can customize their console by using the **Customize View** dialog box. Clearing this check box disables the **Customize** menu item on the **View** menu and the **Customize View** menu item on the system menu. This prevents users from gaining access to the **Customize View** dialog box.

Modify Columns Dialog Box

You can use the **Modify Columns** dialog box, shown in Figure 11.13, to hide or display columns, or to change the order in which they appear in the result pane.

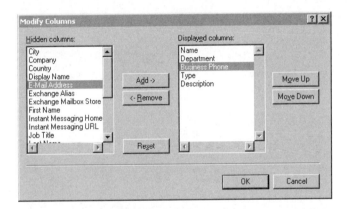

Figure 11.13   Modify Columns dialog box

To open this dialog box, select the node in the console tree for which you want to configure columns, click **View**, and then click **Choose Columns**. The **Choose Columns** menu item appears only when the result pane is in Detail view. If the Standard List view is in one of the other modes (List, Large Icons, or Small Icons), or if the snap-in supports only a Custom view for the selected node, the **Choose Columns** menu item is hidden.

Snap-in designers are encouraged to include columns for all of the major properties. Users can decide which properties are important to them and display the corresponding columns.

Console Tree and Navigation

You can simplify navigation in a console using a variety of methods, including renaming the console root, using the **New Window from Here** command, using **Favorites**, and creating a link between taskpads. All but the last method are discussed in this section. Taskpads are described in a later section of this chapter.

Renaming the Console Root

By default, the top node in a new MMC console is labeled **Console Root**. However, you can rename this node to something more meaningful to your users or your organization. An example of when you might do this is shown in Figure 11.14. The console contains three related snap-ins, and **Console Root** was renamed to reflect the function of the console as a whole. To rename **Console Root**, right-click **Console Root**, click **Rename**, and type the new name.

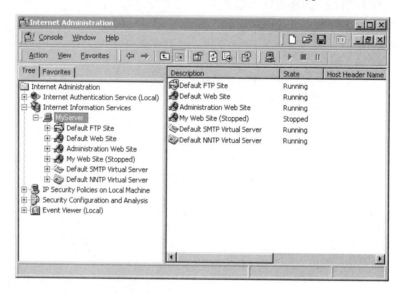

Figure 11.14   Custom console with renamed console root node

New Window from Here

You can create a new window from any point in the console tree, thereby hiding the nodes above. You might do this, for example, to eliminate the unnecessary **Console Root** node in a console that contains just one stand-alone snap-in. The next three figures illustrate the steps required to use the **New Window from Here** command.

As you can see in Figure 11.15, the Active Directory Users and Computers snap-in is already loaded in the console. To create a new window rooted at the top-level node of this snap-in, right-click the **Active Directory Users and Computers** node, and then click **New Window from Here**.

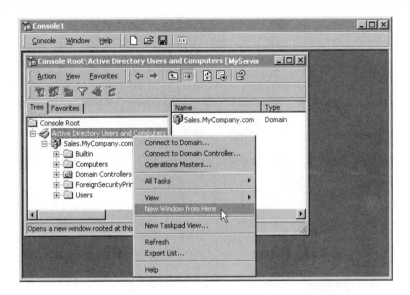

Figure 11.15   Selecting the New Window from Here command

As shown in Figure 11.16, the new window rooted on the **Active Directory Users and Computers** node appears in front of the original window.

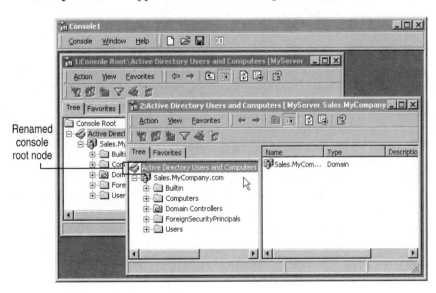

Figure 11.16   New window appears in front of original window

The next step is to close the original window by selecting it and clicking the **Close** button in the upper-right corner of the window. Finally, maximize the new window by clicking the **Maximize** button in the upper-right corner. Figure 11.17 shows the final results.

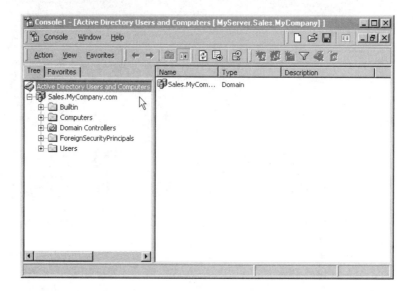

Figure 11.17   New window maximized, old window closed

You can right-click any node and click **New Window from Here** to create a new console window that displays the selected node and its children. When using a console configured in this way, users lose access to the functionality of nodes higher up in the console tree that have been hidden. This is a good way to restrict users to certain nodes.

However, this feature should be used with caution because you might inadvertently disable features that you thought were a function of the console, but were actually governed by a particular node in the console. For example, the top-level node of the Event Viewer snap-in enables a user to redirect the Event Viewer to another computer. A user cannot perform this action from any node below the top-level node. If you rooted the new window on the **Application** log node, users would only be able to view the event logs of the current computer. They would be unable to retarget another computer.

Favorites

The Favorites list is located on the **Favorites** tab and is displayed in the left pane. Since browsing to find objects in a large and complex namespace can sometimes be slow and cumbersome, you can use just the Favorites list to quickly gain access to the nodes you want. In addition, you can add shortcuts to nodes or tools that you use often or that are buried several levels deep in the console tree. You can also create a console with specific Favorites for key locations in the namespace, and then hide the console tree.

The **Favorites** tab appears automatically if you have already added an item to the Favorites list in a console and you open the console in author mode or in user mode. Favorites can only be added while in author mode. MMC Favorites are specific to MMC and are not available to other applications such as Internet Explorer. The converse is also true.

The **Favorites** menu, as shown in Figure 11.18, contains two items, **Add to Favorites** and **Organize Favorites**. To create a new Favorite, select a node in the console tree, and then on the **Favorites** menu, click **Add to Favorites**.

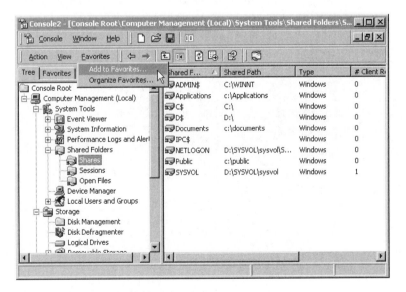

Figure 11.18   Favorites menu

After clicking **Add to Favorites**, you are prompted by the dialog box shown in Figure 11.19 to enter the name of the Favorite and the folder in which it is to be stored. The **Name** text box defaults to the name of the currently selected node.

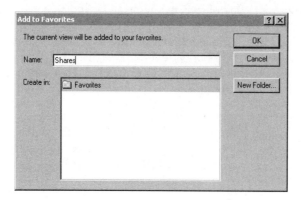

Figure 11.19   Add to Favorites dialog box

After you have added a few favorites, on the **Favorites** menu, click **Organize Favorites**. The **Organize Favorites** dialog box appears, as shown in Figure 11.20. Use this dialog box to manage your Favorites.

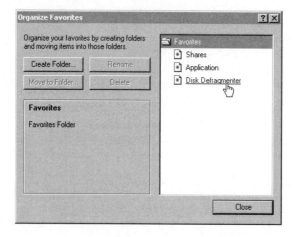

Figure 11.20   Organize Favorites dialog box

After you have created and arranged a few Favorites to your liking, you can view them by clicking the **Favorites** tab, as shown in Figure 11.21.

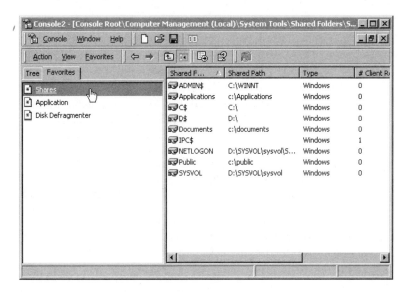

Figure 11.21   Favorites tab

Clicking an item in the Favorites list triggers the same result as selecting the target node directly in the console tree. Again, Favorites can be used to limit a user's view to only the nodes and commands that are directly relevant to his or her job function. Users can use the Favorites list to quickly gain access to just the nodes they want without having to browse the console tree.

Taskpads

Taskpads are configurable pages containing views of the result pane, as well as shortcuts to commands and programs both inside and outside a given console. You can use these shortcuts to perform tasks such as starting wizards, opening property pages, performing menu commands, running command-line programs, and opening Web pages. You can customize a taskpad view to contain all the tasks a given user might need. In addition, you can create multiple taskpad views in a console so that you can group similar or related tasks.

A taskpad view can make it easier for novice users to perform their jobs. For instance, you can add applicable tasks to a taskpad view, and then hide the console tree. This enables users to begin using tools before they are familiar with the location of particular items in the console tree or operating system.

You can also use taskpad views to make complex tasks easier. For example, if a user must frequently perform a task that involves multiple snap-ins and other tools, you can present tasks in a single location that open or run the necessary dialog boxes, property pages, command lines, and scripts.

Taskpad views are created using two wizards offered by MMC. The following section presents several examples of taskpads.

Taskpad Design Gallery

The next set of figures shows how taskpads can be used to address several common administrative scenarios, such as Getting Started, Regular Maintenance, and Troubleshooting.

When an application or service is installed, there are often post-installation tasks that must be performed. As shown in Figure 11.22, a Getting Started taskpad could be used to introduce users to the application and guide them through the post-installation steps.

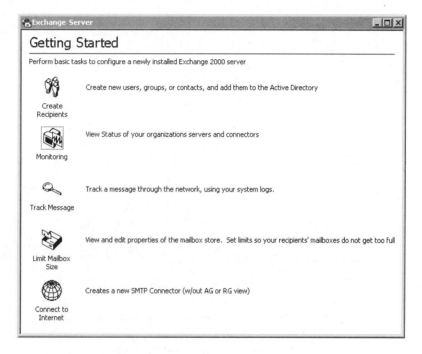

Figure 11.22   Example of a Getting Started taskpad

After the application or service is completely installed, the user may have to perform regular operational tasks, such as monitoring or backing up the server. A taskpad could be used to create a convenient list of frequently performed tasks, as shown in Figure 11.23.

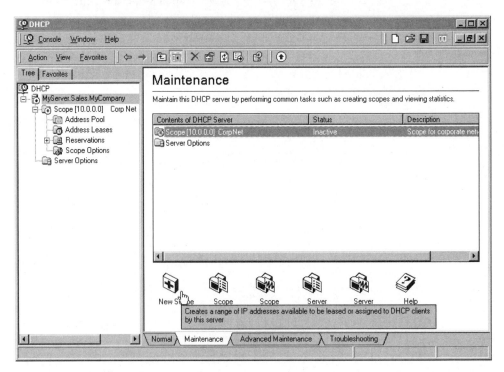

Figure 11.23   Example of a Maintenance taskpad

Some maintenance tasks are performed less frequently or are more advanced. As shown in Figure 11.24, a taskpad could be used to help the user discover and understand the more advanced maintenance tasks.

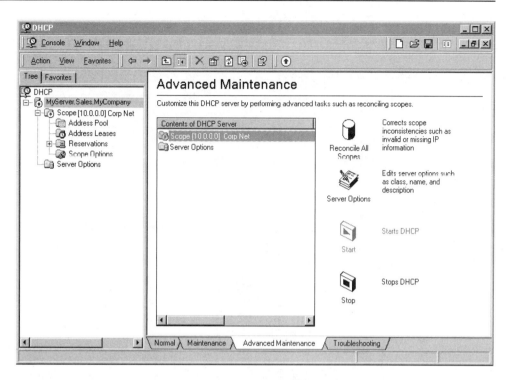

Figure 11.24   Example of an Advanced Maintenance taskpad

On occasion, an application or service begins to act oddly. As shown in Figure 11.25, a taskpad can help the administrator quickly find the right tools to discover, isolate, and correct the problem. Each of the tasks in this example is either a shortcut to a command-line program or to an online Help file. Taskpads are a convenient mechanism for consolidating tasks, tools, and Help information into one simple and easy-to-use user interface.

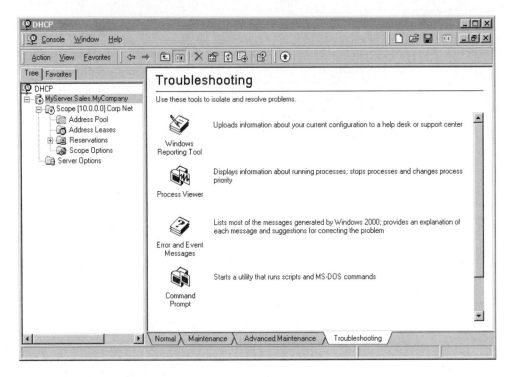

Figure 11.25   Example of a Troubleshooting taskpad

My Custom Console with Taskpads

Earlier in this chapter, Figure 11.3 illustrated how some of customization capabilities of MMC can be used to create a stripped-down Event Viewer snap-in. As implemented, there are several shortcomings with this console. Without explanatory text, context is missing. It is unclear which log is being displayed in the result pane. Task discovery is impaired because users must right-click one of the events in order to discover which commands are available.

Taskpads, as shown in Figure 11.26, can be used to address these limitations. By configuring the taskpad as illustrated in this figure, the type of log displayed is easily apparent, and the most frequently used commands are more easily discovered. The taskpad also offers a mechanism for accessing the system log file.

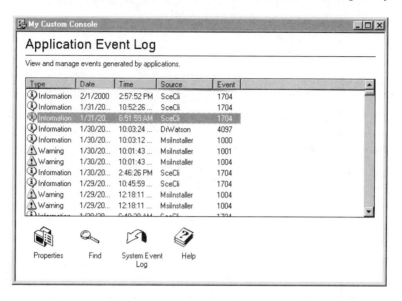

Figure 11.26   Example of a simplified Event Viewer using taskpads

The rest of this chapter describes the MMC wizards used to create taskpads. After reading the next few sections, you will be able to easily create a taskpad like the one shown in Figure 11.26.

Taskpad Elements

The previous section included a number of examples explaining how taskpads can be used. This section describes the elements of a taskpad and provides tips and techniques for creating effective taskpads.

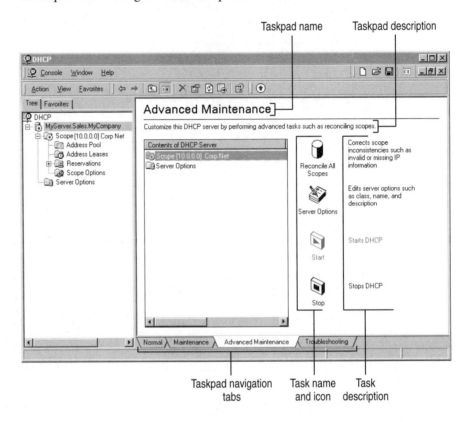

Figure 11.27   Taskpad anatomy

Taskpad Name

The taskpad name is prominently displayed at the top of the taskpad as well as in the *navigation tabs* at the bottom of each taskpad. Since a taskpad is a collection of related or similar tasks, choose a name that best represents the group of tasks as a whole. Names such as "Getting Started," "Frequent Operations," and "Troubleshooting" make it easy for users to quickly identify and locate specific tasks. Ensure that the name is 35 characters or less, including spaces. The default taskpad name is derived from the node name. If the node name includes dynamic information, such as a computer name, be sure to remove it from the taskpad name.

Taskpad Description

This element supplements the taskpad name in describing the purpose of the taskpad.

Task Name and Icon

Tasks can be created from three sources: menu commands, shell commands, or Favorites. If a task is created from a menu command, the task name defaults to the same name as the menu command. If context menus on taskpads are enabled (which is the default), the task name and the command on the context menu should be kept the same. If context menus on taskpads are disabled, you can name the task appropriately.

If the task starts a program or script, specify a task name that is familiar to the user, such as **Command Prompt**, instead of a cryptic filename such as **CMD.EXE**.

As shown in Figure 11.40, the New Task Wizard provides a large selection of icons. Select an icon that best symbolizes the purpose of the task. For common commands such as Properties, the New Task Wizard offers a default icon. For a complete table of icons and suggestions for their use, see Appendix B, "Taskpad Wizard Icons."

Task Description

When creating the taskpad, you should specify how task descriptions are displayed. They can be shown as InfoTips (as shown in Figure 11.23) or they can be displayed on the right side of the task name and icon (as shown in Figure 11.24). If a task is created from a menu command, the task description defaults to the same text shown in the status bar when the menu command is selected.

Taskpad Navigation Tabs

The taskpad navigation tabs shown in Figure 11.27 look and behave similar to the sheet tabs in Microsoft Excel. They enable a user to switch between different taskpad views. The taskpad title appears at the top of the taskpad in a large font and is repeated in a taskpad navigation tab. After the first taskpad view is created, two taskpad navigation tabs appear, one marked "Normal" and the other with the name of the taskpad view just created. The taskpad navigation tab marked "Normal" shows the result pane view offered by the snap-in. Tasks cannot be added to this taskpad view.

Design Guidelines

If you have a large number of taskpad views or if the taskpad names are very long, it is possible for one of the taskpad navigation tabs to be truncated or hidden. Unlike Excel, MMC does not offer a way to scroll through taskpad navigation tabs. Be sure that all of your taskpad navigation tabs are visible when the console is maximized in 800x600 screen resolution.

List Layout Styles

The list view displayed within the taskpad is the same list view normally displayed by the primary snap-in. In the New Taskpad View wizard, you select a style for the result pane that allows you to add a vertical or horizontal list view to the taskpad. You can also configure the size of the list to display. To take best advantage of the available space, experiment with the different list view sizes and orientations to determine which is best for the taskpad you are creating.

Vertical List

Figure 11.24 shows the vertical list style. Use this style for lists with few columns. This style is especially effective when you want the task descriptions shown on the taskpad instead of in InfoTips. You should limit the number of tasks to four or five to prevent the tasks from wrapping and so that users won't have to scroll to find tasks.

Horizontal List

Figure 11.23 shows the horizontal list style. Use this style for lists with multiple columns. When using this style, use InfoTip task descriptions.

No List

You can also choose not to display a list view, as illustrated in Figure 11.25.

Taskpads and Context Menus

When creating taskpads, consider if the user should be able to gain access to the context menus by right-clicking one of the items in the list. By default, as shown in Figure 11.28, context menus are enabled. If context menus are disabled, the user is limited to the specific tasks provided on the taskpad.

To change this setting, view the MMC **Options** dialog box by clicking **Console**, and then clicking **Options**. This setting is global and applies to all the taskpads in a console file. For more information about setting MMC options, see "Options Dialog Box" earlier in this chapter.

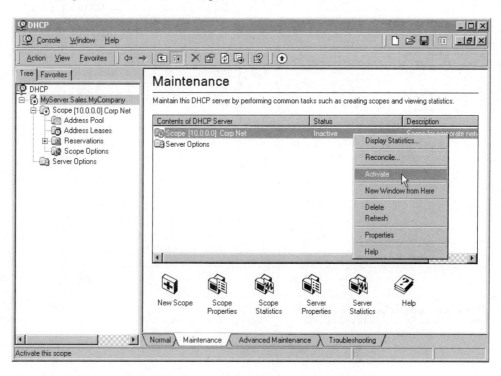

Figure 11.28   Example of using a context menu within a taskpad

Screen Display Size

While many Windows users currently use 800x600-resolution displays, if you want to reach the maximum number of users, you should target a 640x480 display. New installations of Windows 2000 Server default to 640x480. You can use Table 11.1 to determine how many tasks fit for a given layout and screen resolution. Some combinations of layout and screen resolution allow for a large number of tasks. The usability of a taskpad decreases if a user has to sort through more than 15 tasks or scroll to find tasks.

Table 11.1   Screen Resolution and Taskpad Contents

Screen resolution	Taskpad name	Taskpad description	Vertical list with task description			Horizontal list with task description as InfoTip			No list	
			Large	Medium	Small	Large	Medium	Small	InfoTip	Task text
640x480	30 characters or less	60 characters or 10 words	Text does not fit	3 tasks fit	3 tasks fit	5 tasks fit	10 tasks fit	15 tasks fit	15 tasks fit	3 tasks fit
800x600	30 characters or less – more fit but don't go larger	77 characters or 14 words	Text does not fit	5 tasks fit	5 tasks fit	7 tasks fit	14 tasks fit	28 tasks fit	35 tasks fit	5 tasks fit
1024x768	30 characters or less – more fit but don't go larger	85 characters or 20 words	7 tasks fit	7 tasks fit	7 tasks fit	10 tasks fit	20 tasks fit	30 tasks fit	50 tasks fit	7 tasks fit

Creating Taskpads

You can create taskpads by first using the New Taskpad View Wizard to create and configure a taskpad view, and then using the New Task Wizard to add individual tasks to the taskpad view. To use these wizards, you must have opened a console in author mode, and the console must contain at least one snap-in. The following two sections describe the pages of these wizards.

New Taskpad View Wizard

You can use the New Taskpad View Wizard to create a taskpad, configure the taskpad name, and select the layout style. You can set this wizard to automatically start the New Task Wizard when you finish creating a taskpad, or you can gain access to the New Task Wizard later by clicking the **Action** menu, clicking **Edit Taskpad View,** clicking the **Tasks** tab, and then clicking **New.**

To begin creating a taskpad, select a node in the console tree for which you want to configure a taskpad. Next, click the **Action** menu, and then click **New Taskpad View** to display the wizard Welcome page shown in Figure 11.29.

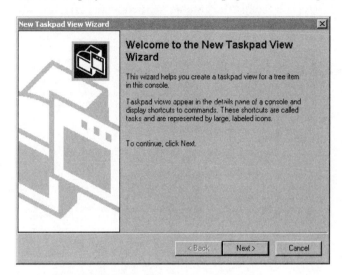

Figure 11.29   New Taskpad View Wizard Welcome page

Clicking **Next** displays the Taskpad Display page shown in Figure 11.30.

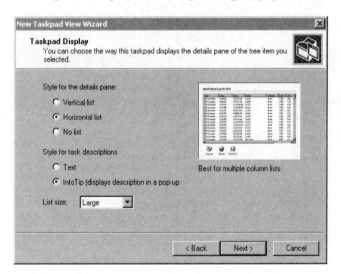

Figure 11.30   Taskpad Display page

On this page, you can choose whether or not to display a list in the taskpad, how it appears if displayed, and how to display text for task descriptions. You can click the different options to determine the style of the list view, task descriptions, and task size, and look at the graphic to preview the effect of your choices.

Clicking **Next** displays the Taskpad Target page shown in Figure 11.31.

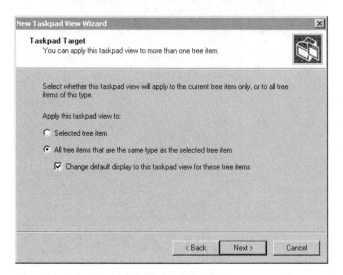

Figure 11.31   Taskpad Target page

You must provide the context for the taskpad. If you want a unique taskpad for a given node, on the Taskpad Target page, click **Selected tree item**. If you click **All tree items that are the same type as the selected tree item**, all nodes of the console tree with the same globally unique identifier (GUID) display the same taskpad. If you choose this option and want the taskpad to be the default view for the selected node, select the **Change default display to this taskpad view for these tree items** check box.

Note MMC determines the type of the target node by using the node type (a Windows standard COM GUID) identifier provided by the snap-in that created the node. For more information about node types, see Chapter 17, "Building the Basic Snap-in Framework." All nodes with the same node type are treated the same way. For this reason, it is important when writing a snap-in to:

- Use the same node type for nodes that belong to the same class.

- Do not use the same node type for nodes that are demonstrably different. For instance, all event log nodes can reasonably have the same node type, but the two nodes Users and Groups should each be of a different node type.

Clicking **Next** displays the Name and Description page shown in Figure 11.32.

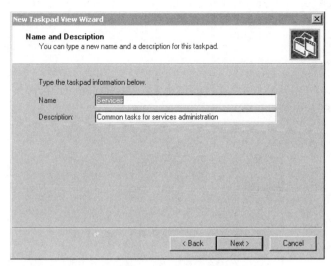

Figure 11.32   Name and Description page

Use this page to enter a name and description for the taskpad. The name appears at the top of the taskpad. If you add a description, it appears below the name as shown in Figure 11.27.

Clicking **Next** displays the wizard Completion page shown in Figure 11.33.

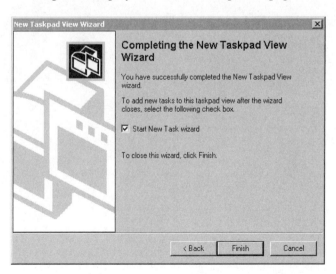

Figure 11.33   New Taskpad View Wizard Completion page

Clicking **Finish** completes the New Taskpad View Wizard. By default, the **Start New Task wizard** check box is selected, and MMC starts the New Task Wizard (see the next section).

New Task Wizard

The New Task Wizard is used to add tasks to the taskpad. It starts with the Welcome page shown in Figure 11.34.

Figure 11.34   New Task Wizard Welcome page

Clicking **Next** displays the Command Type page shown in Figure 11.35.

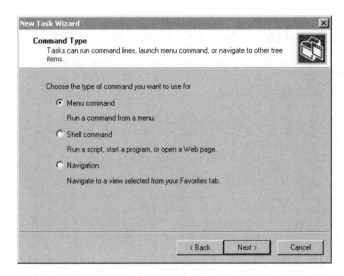

Figure 11.35   Command Type page

You can use this page to add menu commands, shell commands, or navigation to the taskpad. The process of creating tasks is different for each choice, as described in the following paragraphs.

Menu Command

Click the **Menu command** option button on the Command Type page to display the Shortcut Menu Command page shown in Figure 11.36.

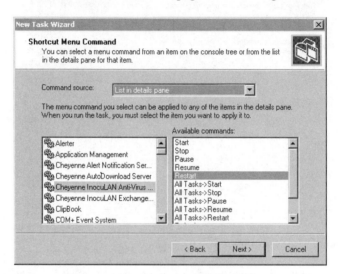

Figure 11.36   Shortcut Menu Command page

In the **Command source** drop-down box, click **List in details pane** to choose commands associated with the objects for the currently selected node, or click **Tree item task** to choose commands that come from other nodes in the console tree. Under **Available commands**, you must select a command.

Clicking **Next** displays the Name and Description page shown in Figure 11.39.

Shell Command

Click the **Shell command** option button on the Command Type page to display the Enter Commands and Parameters page shown in Figure 11.37.

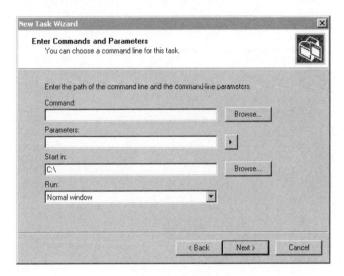

Figure 11.37   Enter Commands and Parameters page

You can use this page in the wizard to enter a program or script with parameters, specify the path to the program, and specify the size of the window in which to run the program. To enter the path of a program in the **Command** text box, either type the path or click **Browse** to find the path. Enter any parameters you want to use to open the program in **Parameters**. Click the arrow to select a column of the details list view to use as a parameter for the command entered in the **Command** text box. To enter the path in which to start the program entered in the **Command** text box, click the **Browse** button to the right of **Start in**. In **Run**, click the window size in which to run the program.

Clicking **Next** displays the Name and Description page shown in Figure 11.39.

Navigation

Clicking the **Navigation** option button on the Command Type page displays the Navigation Task page shown in Figure 11.38.

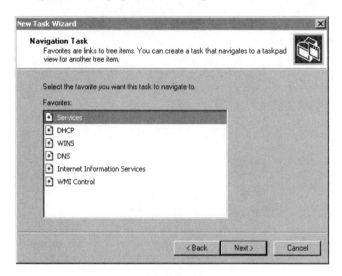

Figure 11.38   Navigation Task page

Note To use this option, you must have already added the favorite. For more information, see "Favorites" earlier in this chapter.

Click an entry in the **Favorites** list box, and then click **Next** to display the Name and Description page shown in Figure 11.39. If the Name and Description page's text boxes are empty, you must type text in the **Task name** text box. Typing text in the **Description** text box is optional.

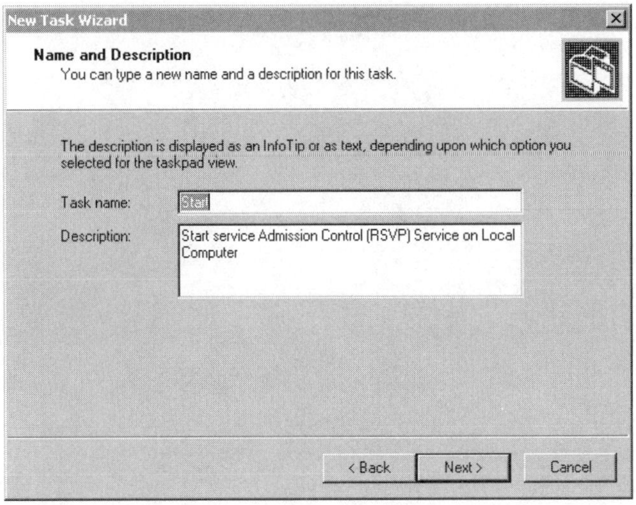

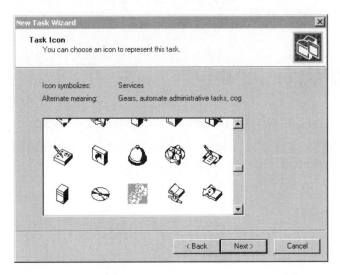

Figure 11.39   Name and Description page

Clicking **Next** displays the Task Icon page shown in Figure 11.40.

Figure 11.40   Task Icon page

You can either accept the default icon or select another icon that you want to appear on the taskpad. If there is no default for your task, see Appendix B, "Taskpad Wizard Icons," for suggestions on the icon to use for your task.

Clicking **Next** displays the wizard Completion page shown in Figure 11.41.

Figure 11.41   New Task Wizard Completion page

If you want to add more tasks to the taskpad, select **Run this wizard again**. If you are finished adding tasks, simply click **Finish** to complete the wizard and display the new taskpad in the result pane.

Taskpad Coding References

For more information about creating a snap-in taskpad using C++, see Chapter 20, "Using Different Result Pane View Types."

For more information about creating a snap-in taskpad using Microsoft Visual Basic, see Chapter 34, "Developing Snap-ins."

Designing Exchange

This section outlines how the Microsoft Exchange 2000 Server team used the guidelines described above to design and create taskpads for Exchange.

As part of the planning for Microsoft Exchange 2000 Server, several scenarios were developed for the use of taskpads. The design group laid out the following principal goals to guide the taskpad development:

- Provide a way to accomplish the tasks that a new administrator needs to do to get started.
- Provide a simple navigation model to do the 10 to 15 tasks that administrators do 80 percent of the time.
- Provide an Advanced option as a mechanism leading to the next 10 to 15 most frequently performed administrative tasks.

At the top level of the Exchange taskpads, the design group wanted to meet the following design goals:

- Exchange is the top node; no console tree is shown.
- Each taskpad links to all other taskpads.
- Some of the taskpads are called from nodes where there are few applicable tasks (such as servers and routing groups). These taskpads contain pointers to other taskpads and function as a link in the navigation model.

While considering these goals, the group identified one critical question: Does a taskpad also apply to nodes that an administrator adds, as long as these nodes are of the same type as the node under which the taskpad was originally created? The consensus was that such additions should work as long as they applied only to a node of the original type.

Using these design goals, the group set out to create a Getting Started taskpad, which would provide access to the following tasks:

- Set up a connector
- Run a migration wizard
- Add a user account
- Set up a recipient account
- Apply message delivery restrictions
- Perform address list management
- Perform public folder management

In addition, the taskpad should provide access to Exchange Help and to the Exchange Web site.

The initial Exchange 2000 Server taskpad is shown in Figure 11.42.

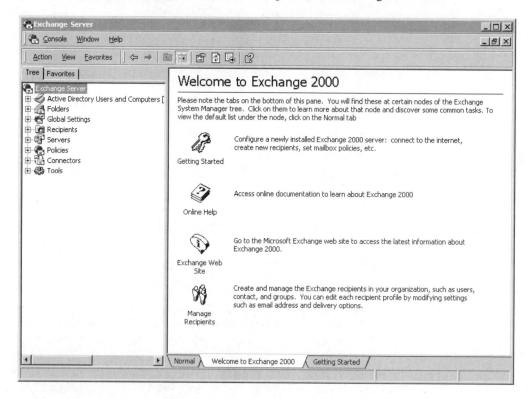

Figure 11.42   Exchange 2000 Getting Started taskpad

Although the intent of the design team was not to show the console tree (scope pane), it is included in Figures 11.42 and 11.43 to provide context for the taskpad.

Comparing the taskpad in Figure 11.42 with the goals stated at the beginning of this section, it appears to meet all three goals. The Getting Started taskpad helps new administrators get up and running quickly and easily, the Manage Recipients task channels advanced tasks to other taskpads, and the overall structure of the taskpad addresses the navigation goal.

As to the contents matching the original design, there are links to each task identified in the original list.

Because Active Directory already provides a node for managing users, the Exchange group opted to extend that node, rather than to create a new user management structure. They wanted to include these tasks:

- Enable mail
- Enable a mailbox
- Disable mail
- Delete a user
- Move a user

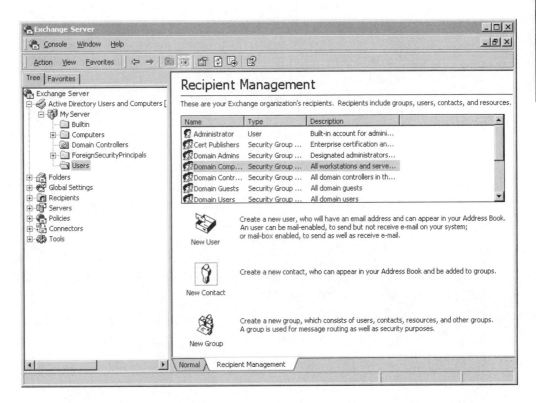

Figure 11.43   Exchange taskpad built on the Active Directory Users and Computers node

The taskpad in Figure 11.43 is from the Users node of the Active Directory Users and Computers snap-in. Extending this snap-in saved considerable development time and made user management easier by placing all the functionality in one place. A taskpad was added to make frequently performed tasks easy to discover and access.

Console and Taskpad Design Review

This section offers a review of the information in this chapter.

- Design your administration tool as a collection of small, dual-mode snap-ins. This makes it easier for your users to create user-specific custom consoles and easier for other developers to extend your snap-ins as well as to include one of your snap-ins as a part of their administration tool.

- When designing your snap-ins keep in mind that users can use the customization capabilities of MMC to create custom consoles either for personal use or for delegation.

- Create custom consoles for different types of users. Include only the functionality they need to get their job or task done.

- Be sure to implement columns for all of the important or useful properties. Users can use the **Modify Columns** dialog box to choose the columns they want to display.

- If you have only one stand-alone snap-in in a console, use **New Window from Here** to hide the **Console Root** node. If you have multiple stand-alone snap-ins in a console, rename **Console Root** to something meaningful and relevant.

- If you have important or frequently accessed nodes buried deep within a namespace, create some Favorites as a convenience to the user.

- Use taskpads for task discovery, getting started, alternative navigation, task integration, user customization, and task delegation.

- If you need to include a large number of tasks on a taskpad, consider creating two or more taskpads.

CHAPTER 12

Wizards

A *wizard* automates a task by taking the user through a step-by-step process. Since wizards were introduced in the Windows environment, they have been widely used, sometimes with great effect and sometimes not. In this chapter you will find guidelines for creating effective wizards. Note that snap-in wizards are created in the Wizard97 for Windows style.

Wizards should be provided as one way to accomplish tasks that are complex and sequential. A wizard should not be the only way to accomplish a task, however, because experienced users might feel slowed down by using the wizard. You shouldn't expect a wizard to teach users the snap-in's user interface (UI), because a wizard typically hides the UI from the user.

Wizards can be used for configuration, a task often done immediately after installation. In these cases, consider making the snap-in wizard able to respond to answer files. Answer files read information from .ini files. See the Microsoft Platform SDK for more information.

Planning a Wizard

Wizard design entails planning the sequential steps that walk the user through a specific task, designing the actual wizard pages, choosing the appropriate content for the wizard pages, and navigating within the wizard.

The first stage of planning a wizard involves evaluating the task and the potential users of the wizard. You can break the task up into several smaller wizards that lead from one to another. You can provide separate paths through the wizard for different levels of users, much like many install programs do. For smaller, less complex tasks, a single, self-contained wizard works well. Note that if your task can be done in a single window, you should use a dialog box or similar device instead of a wizard to complete the task.

Avoid a design that relies on secondary windows. You can confuse novice users if you ask them to leave the wizard for part of a task and then expect them to return to the wizard to complete the task.

Plan each page of the wizard to complete just one task. If two successive pages have similar content, spell out the differences for the user.

Create your wizard with a *Welcome page* and a *Completion page*. Pages between the Welcome and Completion pages are called *interior pages*.

Wizard Page Content

The content of the Welcome and Completion pages differs from each other and from the interior wizard pages.

Welcome Page Content

✓ The Welcome page should only contain the overview information for the wizard. If the wizard requires prior knowledge or setup, make sure the overview includes that information. On the Welcome page use language that is appropriate for the intended audience. For example, do not use technical jargon in a wizard intended for novice users.

Title the page, "Welcome to the *Wizard Name* Wizard." Use book title capitalization and no ending punctuation. Use a short paragraph or a bulleted list to explain the task that the wizard helps the user to complete. End the Welcome page text with "To continue, click Next."

Interior Page Content

✓ Place a title and a subtitle in the header area as shown in Figure 12.1. The subtitle, a complete sentence, should describe the task to be accomplished on the current page. If the purpose of the page is self-evident, use the subtitle to provide additional information, define a term used on the page, or ask a question that helps clarify the purpose of the page.

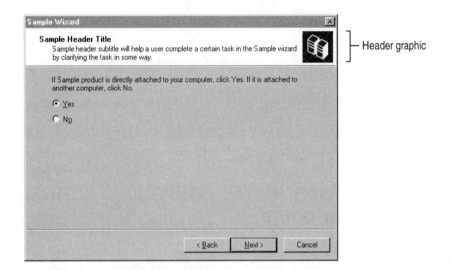

Figure 12.1   Interior page content

✓ Provide **Back**, **Next**, and **Cancel** buttons on each interior page. This also means you should not under any circumstances advance pages automatically. Automatic page advancement can leave users with the impression that they have done something wrong and have no way of fixing it.

Have each page complete only one action, and include on the page only those controls required by the action. Keep each page visually simple, and provide enough information on the page so that the user doesn't need online Help. Avoid forcing users to discover the proper sequence of actions; for instance, don't expect the user to select an object, drag it to a different list control, and then click a specified button.

Design Guidelines

If you need to use a control with functionality that hides some information, like a drop-down menu, include instructions on how to use the control. This prevents users from becoming confused by their inability to access some critical piece of information. If you show UI elements in static artwork, make it visually clear that the items are not active (see Figure 12.2 for an example that might be confusing). Users can easily assume that the UI is functional and they will try to interact with it, causing a great deal of frustration.

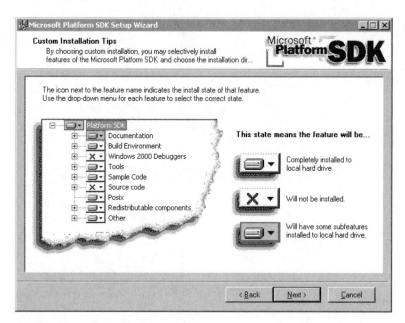

Figure 12.2   Inactive items on screen

Completion Page Content

Title this page, "Completing the *Wizard Name* Wizard." Use book title capitalization and no ending punctuation. End the Completion page text with "To close this wizard, click Finish."

✓ Use the Completion page to tell the user that the wizard was completed successfully or unsuccessfully. If the wizard was successful, summarize the actions performed. If the wizard was unsuccessful use this page to state the reasons why, if possible. Make the **Finish** button available only on this page.

If you include an optional action to be performed after the wizard closes, include a check box before the last line of the Completion page with one of the following text selections:

- When I click Finish, perform *action* for the first time.
- Perform *action* when this wizard closes.
- Begin *action* when this wizard closes.

On this page you can also offer the user the opportunity to access advanced properties in a properties page upon clicking **Finish**.

Physical Page Design

General page layout guidelines for wizard pages are illustrated in Figures 12.3 and 12.4. The layout measurements are provided in dialog units (dlus). The dialog units were calculated with MS Sans Serif 8-point font as the system default with the computer set to display small fonts.

Dialog units are used by C++ programmers. Each figure is followed by a table converting the measurements from dlus to twips, which are the units used by Visual Basic programmers. For more information about twips, see "Creating Display-Independent Property Pages" in Chapter 35. For more information about dialog units, see *Microsoft Windows User Experience*.

Design Guidelines

Font Sizes and Styles

For the Welcome and Completion pages, use Verdana Bold 12-point font for the title text. The title font name ("Verdana") and size (12) should be loaded from the resource file so that localizers can change it. Use MS Shell Dlg font for descriptive text on all pages.

For the interior pages, use MS Sans Bold for the title in the header section and MS Shell Dlg for the subtitle and for the text in the body of the page. In general, do not use bold text in the body of wizard pages.

Welcome and Completion Page Layout

When building a wizard using the Wizard97 common controls, for the Welcome and Completion pages use the dialog unit measurements indicated by the outer lines (dlus: 317w x 193h) in Figure 12.3. The controls automatically add 14 dlus to the right side. Shown in the figure are the measurements for text box X and Y coordinates.

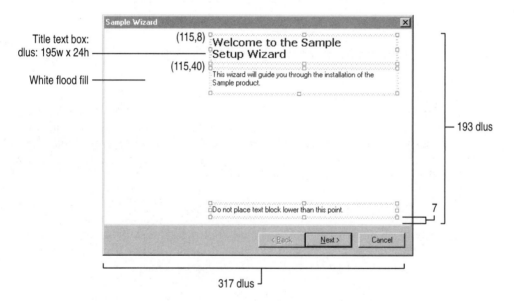

Figure 12.3   Welcome or Completion page layout in dialog units

Table 12.1   Visual Basic Dimensions for Welcome and Completion Pages

dlus	Small font twips	Large font twips
7	160	160
8	180	180
24	580	580
40	960	960
115	2780	2760
169	4100	4040
195	4740	4680
317	7720	7600

Interior Page Layout

When building a wizard using the Wizard97 common controls, for the interior pages use the dialog unit measurements indicated by the outer lines (dlus: 317w x 143h) in Figure 12.4. The controls automatically add 7 dlus to all four sides.

Design Guidelines

The common controls for Wizard97 automatically create the header sections of the interior wizard pages.

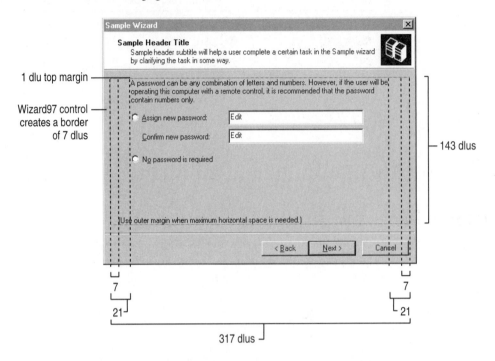

Figure 12.4   Interior page layout in dialog units

Table 12.2   Visual Basic Dimensions for Interior Page Layout

dlus	Small font twips	Large font twips
1	1	1
7	160	160
21	500	500
143	3480	3420
317	7720	7600

Margins and Indents

Margins in the Welcome and Completion pages should follow the specifications given in Figure 12.3. In the interior wizard pages, the margins and indents can vary depending on the content of the page, as shown in Figures 12.5 and 12.6.

Wide Margins

Only use the outer margin when the page contains particularly wide content, such as side-by-side list boxes. For layout measurements see Figure 12.4.

Figure 12.5   Use of outer margin in wizard page body

Indenting for Clarity

As a rule, indenting beyond the normal margins is not necessary. However, indenting can be used to visually separate similar groups of objects on a page, such as when there are more than two items on the page. Indenting is done in increments of 10 dlus (240 small font twips, 240 large font twips).

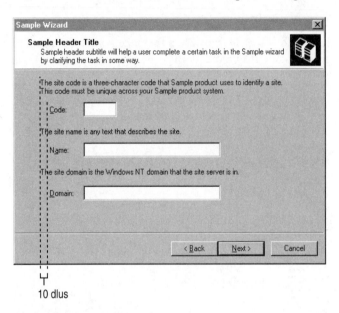

10 dlus

Figure 12.6   Indenting for clarity

Paragraph Spacing

There should be 7 dialog units (dlus) between paragraphs.

▶ **To calculate the vertical distance between paragraphs**

1. Start with the vertical dialog unit coordinate of the upper-left corner of the first paragraph text box.

2. To this number, add 8 dlus for each line of text in that paragraph.

3. Add 7 dlus for the space between paragraphs.

This will give you the vertical location of the text box for the second paragraph. Figure 12.7 shows paragraph spacing.

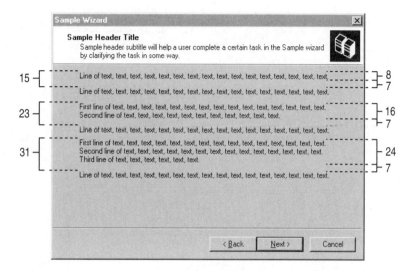

Figure 12.7   Correct paragraph spacing

Table 12.3   Visual Basic Dimensions for Paragraph Spacing

dlus	Small font twips	Large font twips
7	160	160
8	180	180
15	360	360
16	380	380
23	540	540
24	580	580
31	740	740

Design Guidelines

Spacing of Controls with Text

Figures 12.8, 12.9, and 12.10 show recommendations for the vertical layout and spacing of edit boxes, list boxes, and option buttons in relation to lines of text. The measurements noted in these figures show either vertical or horizontal placement of text and controls as measured in dialog units.

Figure 12.8   Relation of stacked edit boxes and text

Figure 12.9   Relation of text, list boxes, and edit boxes

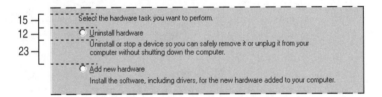

Figure 12.10   Relation of text and option buttons

Table 12.4   Visual Basic Dimensions for Relation of Text and Various Boxes

dlus	Small font twips	Large font twips
3	60	60
4	80	80
7	160	160
10	240	240
12	280	280

Table 12.4   (*continued*)

dlus	Small font twips	Large font twips
15	360	360
16	380	380
18	420	420
23	540	540

Wizard Page Art

This section details the art for the Welcome and Completion pages and for the interior wizard pages.

Welcome and Completion Page Art

The art on the Welcome page should also appear on the Completion page. The wizard art relies on a symbol design to convey a specific message. This can be accomplished in two ways:

- In the first method, the primary symbol image is used twice: within the square bounding box and again in the watermark background behind the square (see Figure 12.11).

- The second method employs two different symbol images to convey a specific message, and gives the user a better visual representation of the purpose of the wizard. In Figure 12.12, for example, the plus sign image in the square illustrates the action of "add" and the watermark background image illustrates the main subject, a printer.

The specified measurements for the overall wizard art area are larger than the area depicted in Figure 12.14 to allow for optimum display when the wizard is viewed in large fonts mode.

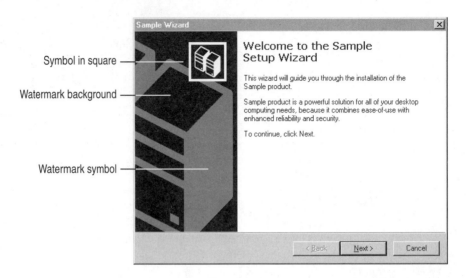

Figure 12.11   Wizard art for Welcome page and Completion page: using a single symbol image

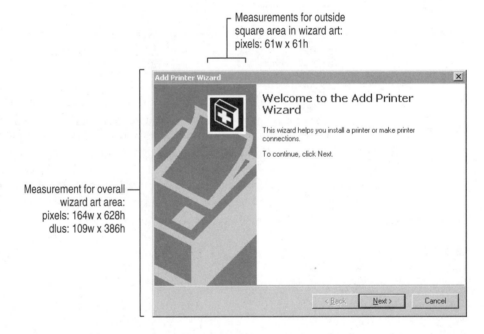

Figure 12.12   Wizard art for Welcome page and Completion page: using two symbol images

Interior Page Art

The same header graphic should appear in the right corner of all interior page header sections. Figure 12.13 shows a sample interior page.

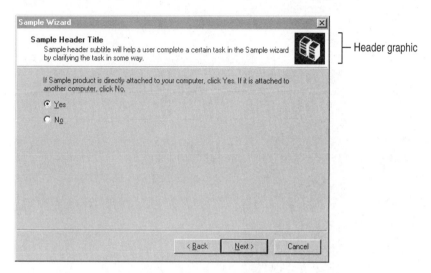

Figure 12.13   Interior page design

Wizard Design Gallery

The main purpose of any wizard should be to enable a user to perform a specific task with as little difficulty as possible. The user interface design for each wizard page should support that purpose by presenting one step per page, with the instructions for carrying out that step as clear and concise as possible.

The following examples represent a variety of page designs frequently encountered in wizards.

Welcome Pages: Appropriate Usage

Figures 12.14, 12.15, and 12.16 show Welcome page designs that introduce the user to the task of a wizard and supply any other pertinent information necessary for completing the task.

Figure 12.14   Welcome page design

The Welcome page design in Figure 12.14 illustrates the following:

- The name of the wizard appears in the title bar.

- "Welcome to the *Wizard Name* Wizard" appears as the title within the page.

- The wizard's task is stated.

- General pertinent information is stated.

- "To continue, click Next." is stated.

Figure 12.15   Welcome page design

The Welcome page design in Figure 12.15 illustrates the following additional or alternative options:

- The task of the wizard is presented as a detailed list. Bullet points are used for clarification. (Small bullet points can be created using the letter "h" in the Marlett font.)
- Important information for successful wizard completion is stated. The yellow alert icon is added for emphasis.

Figure 12.16   Welcome page design

The Welcome page design in Figure 12.16 illustrates the following additional or alternative options:

- Important information for successful wizard completion is stated.

- The option is given to not show the Welcome page in the future. This option can be implemented by the use of the check box and text shown in Figure 12.16. However, only use such an option for wizards that users access for administrative-type tasks or on a frequent basis.

Completion Pages: Appropriate Usage

The Completion page reinforces that the user has successfully completed all the steps of the wizard. It can also provide further closure of the wizard task by summarizing what was accomplished and, in certain cases, by stating what should be done next. Figures 12.17, 12.18, and 12.20 illustrate various Completion pages, and Figure 12.19 illustrates a related page.

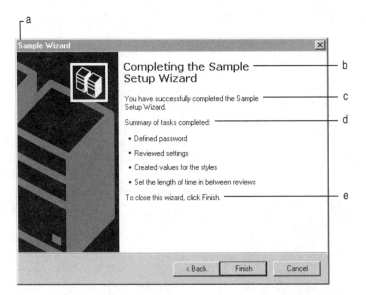

Figure 12.17   Completion page design

The Completion page design in Figure 12.17 illustrates the following:

- The name of the wizard appears in the title bar.

- "Completing the *Wizard Name* Wizard" appears as the title within the page.

- The notification that the wizard has been successfully completed.

- A brief list is presented of either the tasks the user completed while in the wizard or the tasks the user will complete upon clicking **Finish** and closing the wizard. If a longer list is needed than what is shown in Figure 12.17, place it in a scrolling list box. However, since the space available is limited, reserve the Completion page for a wizard closure that is as simple as possible. Crowding the Completion page, or any wizard page, with text reduces space needed for localization in some languages. Therefore, when longer lists or list boxes are necessary for summation put them on an interior wizard page preceding the Completion page.

- "To close this wizard, click Finish." is stated when tasks have been completed while in the wizard.

Figure 12.18   Completion page design

The Completion page design in Figure 12.18 illustrates the following additional or alternative options:

- Details of how to complete a process that was started in the wizard are given. The yellow alert icon is added for emphasis. In this example, after a user clicks **Finish** and the wizard closes, a standard progress dialog box with a progress bar will appear and remain on the screen until the process is completed. However, the user interface described in Figures 12.19 and 12.20 is preferable for any process lasting for more than a few minutes.

- The statement that in addition to the wizard closing, another action will take place when the user clicks **Finish**.

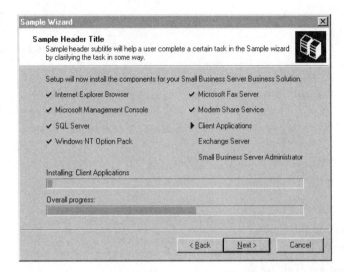

Figure 12.19   Summary page prior to Completion page

Figure 12.19 is an example of a page that can directly precede the wizard Completion page. It gives the user enhanced feedback on the final task that will take place as a result of the wizard, without having to exit the wizard first. After the process is completed, the wizard Completion page can follow to provide closure to the entire wizard task (see Figure 12.20).

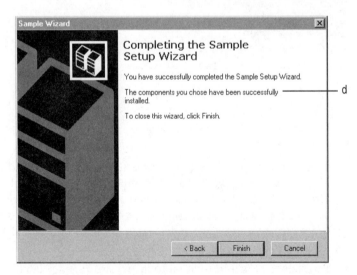

Figure 12.20   Completion page design

The Completion page design in Figure 12.20 illustrates the following additional or alternative options:

- Some specific element of functionality that the wizard has provided can be stated.

Interior Pages: Scenarios

Figures 12.21, 12.22, and 12.23 illustrate some common user interface issues specific to wizard design. However, most interior page wizard designs follow common Win32 user interface design style guidelines.

Displaying Secondary Windows

It is possible for inexperienced users to be confused by the addition of secondary windows. Figure 12.21 illustrates a situation where a user might click **Next** expecting to proceed to the following page and will instead remain on the first page looking at a secondary dialog box. Therefore, it is recommended that the content of the secondary dialog box be placed in a following wizard page, as in Figure 12.22.

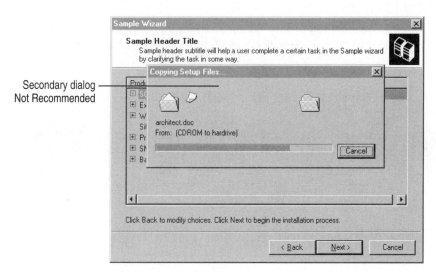

Figure 12.21   Incorrect use of secondary dialog box

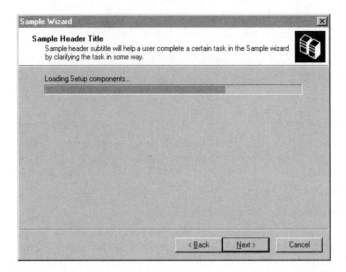

Figure 12.22   Secondary dialog box correctly incorporated as a wizard page

Using Alert Icons

To draw special attention to very important information, either the information bubble symbol or the yellow warning symbol can be added before text.

Figure 12.23 illustrates that:

- The information bubble icon can emphasize important yet not crucial information.
- The yellow warning icon can emphasize information vital to either the success of the task or the consequences of the actions performed on the wizard page.

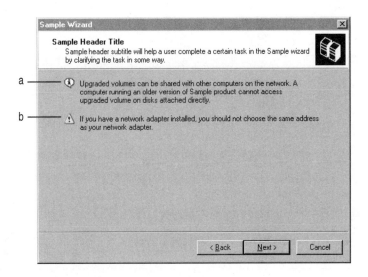

Figure 12.23   Alert icons

Wizard Coding References

If you are creating a snap-in using C++, see Chapter 23, "Adding Property Pages and Wizard Pages," for additional information about wizards.

If you are creating a snap-in using Visual Basic, see "Configuration Wizards" and "Initiating Property Sheet and Wizard Displays Programmatically" in Chapter 34, "Developing Snap-ins," for additional information about wizards.

Wizard Design Review

This section offers a capsule review of the information in this chapter. The design features denoted with a check mark in this list and in the chapter text are likely to become logo requirements.

- Provide step-by-step instructions.
- Put the overview information on the Welcome page, by itself.
- Limit each screen to one step. Minimize the number of controls and required actions on each screen.
- Do not advance screens automatically.
- State the purpose of each page in the page's header.
- Make the **Finish** button available only when the task is ready to be completed.

- Avoid a wizard design that requires the user to leave the wizard to complete a task.
- Consider advanced user needs when contemplating having a wizard as the only UI.
- Be careful not to automate too much of the process.
- Use caution when providing multiple access points for a wizard.
- When providing a list of wizards, make sure users can compare the options easily.
- Avoid context-sensitive wizards. Instead, prompt the user to choose.
- Ensure that the default state and behavior of all controls makes sense to users.
- Make all information visible. When this is impossible, include instructions for using view port controls.
- Avoid using secondary windows.
- Test textual descriptions with users to make sure they are clear.
- Use technical jargon only when necessary. Explain technical terms when they are used.
- Whenever possible, include Help text in the main body of the wizard rather than on a separate subscreen.
- Include navigation hints for novices.
- When showing UI elements in static artwork, make it visually clear that the items are not active.

CHAPTER 13

Dialog Boxes and Message Boxes

Dialog boxes and message boxes are secondary windows that appear in Windows applications, including MMC.

Use a dialog box when a user needs to supply information that is not a property of an object. For instance, in the Services snap-in, a dialog box is used to identify the targeted computer. Another case where you can use a dialog box is when information is required to restore an application to a consistent state.

Use a message box to warn the user of the consequences of an irreversible action, or to display an error message when a user action has caused an error.

Dialog Boxes

Use a dialog box to obtain information from a user. Limit the use of dialog boxes to situations when additional information is required to complete a command or when it is important to prevent any further interaction with the snap-in until a condition is satisfied.

Dialog Box Size

✓ Base the height of a dialog box on the size of its controls, but do not exceed 263 dialog units (dlus). A dialog box with a height greater than 263 dlus will not be fully visible on a 640x480-resolution monitor. For the width of the dialog box, use one of the standard Windows 2000 property page widths (252, 227, or 212 dlus). Do not exceed 263 dlus, the maximum recommended width for all secondary windows.

Figure 13.1 shows the three possible widths for dialog boxes, and Table 13.1 shows the dlu measurements converted to twips for Visual Basic programmers.

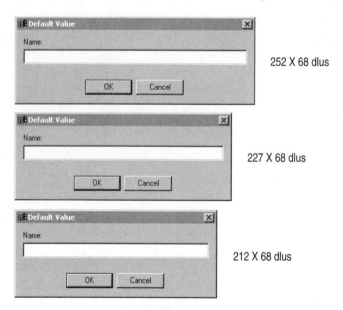

Figure 13.1   Dialog box widths

Table 13.1   Visual Basic Dimensions for Dialog Box Width

dlus	Small font twips	Large font twips
212	5160	5080
227	5520	5440
252	6120	6040
263	6400	6300

Dialog Box Elements

Always include on the title bar a Close (**X**) button and, if context-sensitive Help is supported, a "What's This" (**?**) button. Reflect in the dialog box title the name of the command that started the dialog box.

Most dialog boxes should include the **OK** and **Cancel** buttons. Use **OK** to accept the values in the dialog box and close it. Use **Cancel** to close the box, ignoring any changes made in the box. Set **OK** as the default. When there is a need for overview Help for the dialog box, include a **Help** button after the **Cancel** button. The Help invoked by this button should not repeat the control-by-control Help of the **?** button.

In some cases, you can change the **Cancel** button to a **Close** button dependent on some action of the user. In those cases, warn the user that the action about to be taken is not reversible.

In general, do not use icons in dialog boxes, except for the **About** dialog box. In that box, use a 32x32-pixel version of your product icon in the upper-left corner of the box. Icons are also used in message boxes, which are discussed in the next section.

For further information about creating dialog boxes, see *Microsoft Windows User Experience* Chapter 9, "Secondary Windows," and Chapter 14, "Visual Design."

Message Boxes

A message box is a secondary window that displays a message about a particular situation or condition. It is recommended that you use MMC-provided message box functions so you do not have to be concerned about sizing the message box or placing elements in it.

Because message boxes are disruptive, try to avoid using them. If you do use a message box, only display it when the application that generated it is active. Otherwise, it may not be clear to the user which application started the message. The system highlights the Windows taskbar button for an inactive application to alert the user that some action is required.

Message Box Design

Base the height of a message box on the number of lines of text that it contains, but do not exceed 263 dlus, because then it will not be fully visible on screens set at 640x480 resolution. Base the width of a message box on one of the three standard property page widths (212, 227, or 252 dlus). Do not use widths greater than 263 dlus, the maximum recommended width for all secondary windows.

Message Box Graphics

Most message boxes include a graphic that visually tells the user what kind of information the box contains. Table 13.2 shows the graphics most commonly used.

Table 13.2   **Message Types and Associated Symbols**

Symbol	Message type	Description
ⓘ	Information	Provides information about the results of a command. Offers no user choices; the user acknowledges the message by clicking **OK**.
⚠	Warning	Alerts the user to a condition or situation that requires the user's decision and input before proceeding, such as an impending action with potentially destructive irreversible consequences. The message can be in the form of a question—for example, "Save changes to MyReport?"
✕	Critical	Informs the user of a serious problem that requires intervention or correction before work can continue.

Place the alert symbol at the (7,7) dlu (or (160,160) for both small font and large font twips) coordinates as shown in Figure 13.2.

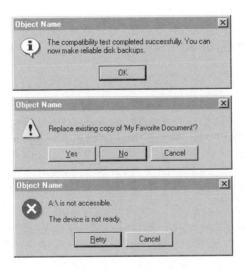

Figure 13.2   Alert symbols in message boxes

Earlier versions of Windows included a question mark message symbol. This message symbol was used for cautionary messages that were phrased as a question. Do not use the question mark (?) symbol in snap-in message boxes; it is reserved for Help.

Message boxes that do not require the user to make any choices, but do require an acknowledgment, should include an **OK** button centered under the text. If the box requires user action, include buttons such as **Yes**, **No**, and **Cancel**.

Design Guidelines

Snap-in Messages

Prior to MMC 1.2, snap-in message boxes were the same as Windows message boxes. Windows message boxes are *modal* and do not always provide a context for the message displayed. MMC 1.2 introduced snap-in message boxes that display the message in the result pane of the selected node, thereby making the message context clear.

Snap-in message boxes are not disruptive and persist, whereas Windows message boxes must be addressed and disappear after you close them. In an early Windows 2000 version of the Computer Management snap-in, you got several Windows message boxes if you tried to retarget the snap-in to an unavailable computer, because each extension snap-in displayed a message when it tried to connect to the computer and failed. After snap-in messages were introduced, this behavior was changed to display a single message in the result pane when you selected a node.

There are three types of messages: information, warning, and error. Figure 13.3 shows a sample information message and Figure 13.4 shows a sample warning message.

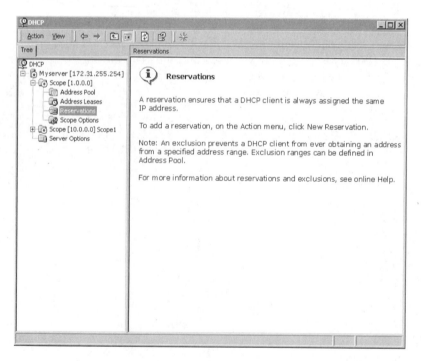

Figure 13.3   Information message in result pane

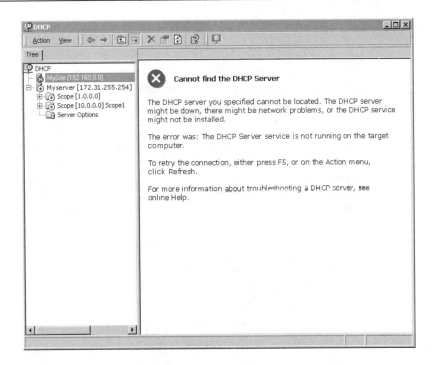

Figure 13.4   Error message in result pane

Use a 32x32-pixel icon in the message and 10 pt Tahoma black text throughout with the exception of the text to the right of the icon that is the message title. For the message title use 10 pt Tahoma bold black text. Make sure to include a description of why the message appears. If it is a warning or error message, provide a way to remedy the situation and if possible where to turn for more information.

Progress Message Boxes

MMC provides a progress message box (usually called a "progress bar") in the middle of the status bar. You should use this progress bar to provide a visual representation of the progress of a particular process. It automatically disappears when the process is complete.

The MMC progress bar has some advantages over Windows message box progress bars. Because the MMC progress bar is in the status bar, you always have a context for the process that is in progress. It also permits you to move to other MMC console windows and continue working, checking the progress bar as often as you like.

If a property page in your snap-in initiates a process that takes a significant amount of time, you may need to start a progress bar for that process to keep users informed of its status.

Message Box Text

Lines of text in message boxes should be short enough to read and understand easily. Many typographic references suggest that an optimal line length for reading is around 44 characters, and that when the line length is greater than 60 characters, the reader finds it difficult to track the sentence and tends to lose the context.

In the case of a single, one-line sentence, center the text vertically with the alert symbol, at the (35,12) dlu (or (840,280) for both small font and large font twips) coordinates. In all other cases, vertically align the first text control with the top of the symbol, placing it at the (35,7) dlu (or (840,160) for both small font and large font twips) coordinates. Figure 13.5 illustrates text placement.

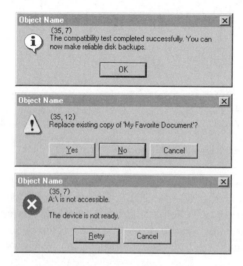

Figure 13.5   Text placement in message boxes

✓   The message text should be clear, concise, and written in terms that the user understands. Do not use technical terms or jargon. Try not to exceed two or three lines.

In the title bar, use the object name if the message is associated with a specific object; otherwise use the snap-in name as the title. Be sure to include a close button on the title bar.

For further information about composing message text and creating message boxes, see *Microsoft Windows User Experience* Chapter 9, "Secondary Windows." Also see "IConsole2" in the "MMC Interfaces and Methods" section of the MMC COM Reference in the MMC SDK on the companion CD-ROM.

Dialog Box and Message Box Design Review

This section offers a capsule review of the information in this chapter. The design features denoted with a check mark in this list and in the chapter text are likely to become logo requirements.

- For dialog box widths, use only 252, 227, or 212 dlus.
- Base the height of a dialog box on the size of its controls, but do not exceed 263 dlus.
- Write clear, concise message text for message boxes.
- Do not use technical terms or jargon in message text.

- Avoid having one dialog box start another in what becomes a chain of dialog boxes. Such chains are hard to use and often cause the user to lose focus on the current task.
- Avoid large blocks of text in dialog boxes. If such text is necessary, it may point to a problem in the UI or a need for more Help.
- Keep message text to three lines or fewer.

CHAPTER 14

Accessibility and Localization

Accessibility and localization are two areas of software development that deserve close attention. Accessibility means making your software and documentation usable by a wide range of users, including those with disabilities. Localization means making it easy to accommodate differences in language and culture, in both the software and the documentation.

This chapter provides a quick overview of both topics. For more in-depth treatment, see Chapter 15, "Special Design Considerations," in *Microsoft Windows User Experience*.

Accessibility

Creating software that is accessible to people with disabilities is not difficult, but retrofitting for accessibility is harder. In the planning and design stage, incorporate the guidelines in this section to create the best possible product for all your users.

There are many different types of disabilities, but they can be broadly categorized as follows:

Visual
> There are three general types of visual disabilities: slightly reduced visual acuity, total blindness, and colorblindness. Make sure your software supports larger text and graphics as well as speech and Braille utilities, and do not use color alone to convey information.

Hearing
> Users with hearing loss cannot use auditory output to communicate information. If you use auditory output to convey information, also include visual output to convey the same information.

Physical movement
> Some users have difficulty or are unable to move a mouse or press two keys at once. The best way to support these users is to support all your basic operations by using both simple keyboard and mouse interfaces. This will also help beginning users who may not be familiar with a computer interface.

Speech or language
> Spell-check and grammar utilities can help children, users with dyslexia, and non-native speakers of the supported languages. Screen readers are available for the blind, those with visual impairments, and those with reading impairments.

Cognitive
> People with cognitive disabilities such as perceptual differences and memory impairments can be aided by the use of icons and graphics to illustrate objects and choices. It can also be helpful to provide ways to customize the menus and dialog boxes or to hide graphics.

Seizure disorders
> Some users are sensitive to visual information that alternates its visual appearance or flashes at particular rates. Base the rate of change on a customizable interface that can be turned off.

A Quick Check for Accessibility

You can quickly test your software for accessibility with some tools that are part of the operating system and with others that are available in the Microsoft Active Accessibility SDK (MSAASDK), which is on the companion CD-ROM. For a full review, see *Microsoft Windows Guidelines for Accessible Software Design* at http://www.microsoft.com/enable/dev/guidelines/software.htm.

The remainder of this section presents questions and tests that illustrate a high-level evaluation of the accessibility of some product features. This example does not cover all of the items you should check for in a thorough product evaluation.

Feature:
Keyboard access

Question:
Can everything that can be done with the mouse also be done with the keyboard alone?

Test:
Unplug the mouse and navigate the UI for each feature using only the keyboard. Ensure that all functionality is achievable.

Feature:
Exposing keyboard/focus location

Question:
Can I visually see the focus indicator as I tab around the UI?

Are elements sending focus events so that accessibility aids can track the focus location?

Test:
Run Magnifier (click **Start**, point to **Programs**, point to **Accessories**, point to **Accessibility**, and click **Magnifier**). Then navigate the UI using both keyboard tabbing and mouse actions. Ensure that all navigation is tracked properly in Magnifier.

Debugging/More information:
Use tools installed with MSAASDK: http://www.microsoft.com/enable.

Use the AccEvent tool to determine if focus events are being sent, and are in the proper order.

Feature:
Exposing screen elements (including name, state, role, location, value)

Question:
Are all screen elements systematically exposed?

Test:

Run Inspect (shown in Figure 14.1), and separately use both the mouse and the keyboard alone to reach each element. Ensure that the information presented in the **Name**, **State**, **Role**, **Location**, and **Value** fields is meaningful to the user for each object in the UI.

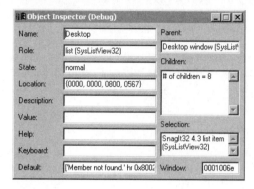

Figure 14.1   Inspect screen

Debugging/More information:

Inspect is installed with the MSAASDK.

Feature:

High contrast

Question:

Do all elements respond to color and font size changes?

Test:

In Control Panel, double-click the **Display** icon, click the **Appearance** tab, and then in the **Scheme** drop-down list box choose **High Contrast Black (extra large)**. Navigate through all UI elements ensuring that the color and font changes are reflected. Also, ensure that images or patterns drawn behind text are omitted.

Debugging/More information:

Specific settings are required for menus, dialog boxes, and other standard UI elements when high contrast is set. See the MSAASDK for details.

Feature:

Documentation

Question:

Is there a useful Help topic on Accessibility?

Test:

Run Help and search for "accessibility" and/or "disability."

Debugging/More information:

For more information, see http://www.microsoft.com/enable/.

Feature:

Show sounds

Question:

Do areas that use sound to convey information work with the Show Sounds feature?

Test:

In Control Panel, double-click the **Accessibility Options** icon and then click the **Sound** tab. Turn on "ShowSounds." Navigate to areas where sound is used to convey information and ensure that visual information is displayed with ShowSounds on.

Debugging/More information:

When the "show sounds as text" setting is enabled, the application must present all information visually instead of by sound alone.

Using sound as the sole means of conveying information is strongly discouraged (even if "show sounds as text" is not enabled).

Feature:

Adjustable timings

Question:

Can the user adjust or turn off all timing settings? (Examples are time-outs and blink rate.)

Test:

Ensure that areas with timing issues can be adjusted or turned off.

Feature:

System metrics

Question:

Do all areas support system metrics for size, timing, and appearance?

Test:

Work area—bring up the UI for the area in which you are testing, then open Magnifier (click **Start**, point to **Programs**, point to **Accessories**, point to **Accessibility**, and click **Magnifier**). Ensure that your UI doesn't overlap the Magnifier, either under or on top, and that your UI resizes with the rest of the desktop.

Colors, sizes, and fonts—In Control Panel, double-click the **Display** icon, click the **Appearance** tab, and then in the **Scheme** drop-down list box choose **High Contrast Test**. Ensure that all areas reflect the change.

Font size—In Control Panel, double-click the **Display** icon, click the **Settings** tab, and click **Advanced**. In the **Font Size** drop-down list box, choose **Other**. In the **Custom Font Size** dialog box, scale fonts to a larger size. Ensure that all areas reflect the change.

Design Guidelines

Feature:

Adjustable fonts

Question:

Can the user choose font names, styles, colors, and sizes for all text?

Test:

If the application is not responding to Control Panel, Display, and Appearance settings, then the application must have another method to change these settings.

Debugging/More information:

Set the system to a scheme with large fonts and color changes, such as **High Contrast Black (extra large)**, and check for resizing and color changes. These settings are queried using the **GetSysColor**, **GetSystemMetrics**, and **SystemParametersInfo** functions.

For the work area, run Magnifier (click **Start**, point to **Programs**, point to **Accessories**, point to **Accessibility**, and click **Magnifier**). Make sure that the windows in the application adjust to the new work area size. If you resize Magnifier to take up more of the screen, the windows should readjust to meet the new resized work area.

Feature:

Descriptions

Question:

Does the application provide textual descriptions for all complex images that convey information?

Does the application provide synchronized audio or textual description for informative videos and animation?

Test:

Identify and examine areas where images are used to convey information. Ensure that text is available to describe these visual elements.

Debugging/More information:

To get the work area of a monitor other than the primary display monitor, call the **GetMonitorInfo** function by using Active Accessibility, or the HTML LONGDESC attributes.

Localization

Localization may seem like an odd name for what many developers have known as translation (to another language). Localization encompasses more than simply translating the material (although the translation itself involves much work). It involves planning UI elements with translation in mind, not using culturally biased concepts (for instance, "in a New York minute") that might be meaningless in another language, and preparing samples, templates, and the like with an eye to the world market. This section applies to both snap-ins and saved console files.

Text

When planning the text in your snap-in, remember that its meaning and its size can be changed in the translation process. Three broad areas need to be addressed concerning text.

Meaning

Be careful not to use idiomatic language in the user interface or any of the documentation. Idioms can vary even within a language, let alone between languages. For instance, "pop" on the U.S. West Coast means a soft drink and "soda" on the East Coast also means a soft drink. You can often tell which coast someone grew up on by which term they use.

Terms and graphics that are culturally biased should also be avoided. For instance, a graphic of a U.S. rural mailbox might be meaningless to users in some European countries.

Effects of Translation

Translation can expand text by as much as 30 percent and for certain languages even more. As stated throughout the "Design Guidelines" section of this book, plan the space around and between UI elements to accommodate the effects of translation.

Interface Text

As you plan your snap-in, make provisions to ease the translation process. Store user interface text as resources in your application's resource file rather than including it in the source code of the snap-in. Remember to translate the menu comments that your snap-in stores in the system registry for file types.

Graphics

Although graphics tend to be universally understood, cultural bias can make some images unusable. For instance, the symbol of a wand for a wizard might work in some cultures and not in others. The one palm meaning "stop" at U.S. crosswalks is offensive in some cultures. Try to use neutral images.

Character Sets

Some countries require support for different character sets (code pages). Use the system-provided standard interfaces for supporting multiple character sets and sort tables. Keep these points in mind:

- Do not assume the character set is U.S. ANSI; it could be one of a wide variety of character sets.
- Use the system functions for supporting font selection.
- Always save the character set with font names in documents. If you use the system's rich text control, it will automatically handle preserving the correct font and character set.

Formats

The format for dates, time, money, measurements, and telephone numbers can change dramatically between countries. The set of country-related formats is referred to as a *locale*. Windows provides a standard way to find out the default format for a given locale. For more information see "International Features" in the "Base Services" section of the Platform SDK.

PART 3

Snap-in Help

This part contains information about the design and creation of Help for snap-ins. It differs in content from Part 2, which strictly dealt with designing snap-in user interface elements. Help is available for MMC and for snap-ins from the **Help** menu on the MMC Console main menu. Context-sensitive Help is available from context menus and can be created for property pages as needed.

Part 3 includes information about the type of Help to implement for each available Help entry point. The different Help entry points frequently have different design considerations which are noted in the text.

Detailed Help compiler settings are provided for Microsoft's HTML Help Workshop; these can be generalized for other HTML Help creation products.

An MMC snap-in can have both HTML Help files and context-sensitive Help. Note that it is assumed that readers of this chapter are familiar with a set of tools that can be used to create HTML Help and context-sensitive Help.

C H A P T E R   1 5

Creating Online Help

✓ When a user opens Help from a console that contains snap-ins, MMC creates a combined table of contents that displays Help for the loaded snap-ins as well as Help for MMC features. To make this possible, each snap-in must specify a compiled HTML Help file (.chm) that uses a binary table of contents. Then, if the user clicks the **Help** menu on the main menu bar of the MMC window, the menu has a single command, **Help Topics**, that displays the combined table of contents.

Figure 15.1 shows the MMC Help menu.

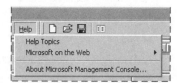

Figure 15.1   MMC Help menu

Snap-in Help

Consider a snap-in with the name "Snap-in" that specifies Snap-in.chm for HTML Help. To access the snap-in's Help, a user could click **Help**, and then click **Help Topics** to display the HTML Help file shown in Figure 15.2.

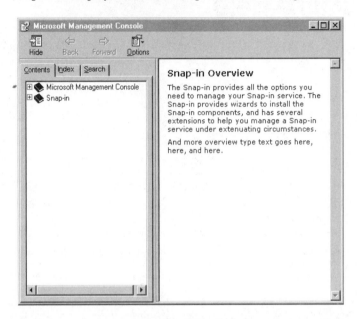

Figure 15.2   Sample MMC Help file

The Help for the main window of MMC is always listed first in the table of contents. Underneath this are books for each snap-in added to the current console. Snap-ins that have not specified a Help file do not appear in this list.

MMC can include a single Help file in its combined table of contents for each stand-alone or extension snap-in. Snap-in-specific Help should be documented in the snap-in's Help file.

Types of Help Topics

MMC uses three types of Help: conceptual, procedural, and context-sensitive. You have several choices regarding how you implement Help for your snap-in.

Conceptual Help

A conceptual topic provides background or overview information on an aspect or feature of the snap-in. Conceptual topics are primarily paragraphs of text, but can also provide links to other conceptual topics or procedures. Headings in conceptual topics should be hierarchical (that is, start with H1 and use headings in order).

Procedural Help

Procedural topics list the steps needed to accomplish a task. Keep ancillary text in notes at the end of the topic.

Context-Sensitive Help

Context-sensitive Help provides information about controls in the console tree, dialog boxes, or other screen elements.

Context-Sensitive Help for the Console Tree

For a console, context-sensitive Help involves hooking up appropriate topics from your .chm file for items in the console tree.

Context-Sensitive Help for Dialog Boxes

You can use either HTML Help or Microsoft Windows Help technology to create context-sensitive Help. HTML Help supports unformatted paragraphs only.

- **"What's This?" Help.** This is the standard context-sensitive Help used for Windows components. When a user clicks the "?" Help button and drags it to an item in a dialog box, a pop-up window appears with information about that item.

- **Help button.** Some dialog boxes have a **Help** button. If you use HTML Help, this displays the HTML Help window and a topic that describes the dialog box and provides links to appropriate procedures. For property pages with a **Help** button, do not duplicate the "What's This?" Help content. Instead, provide overview material about the contents of the property page.

> **Note** MMC version 1.1 does not allow the "**?**" Help button to be hidden. If you are using this version of MMC and **Help** buttons, you can display the same content for both "What's This?" Help and the **Help** button. An alternative is to write a default topic for all "What's This?" Help entry points that directs users to click the **Help** button.

Table 15.1 summarizes the preceding information and identifies the type of Help (conceptual and procedural, or context-sensitive) for each entry point.

Table 15.1   Help Format and Type

Entry point from open console or property page	Help format	Type of Help topics
Help on system menu	HTML Help	Conceptual and procedural
Help topics on **Help** menu	HTML Help	Conceptual and procedural
Help button on a property page (optional)	HTML Help	Conceptual and procedural
Help on **Action** menu	HTML Help	Conceptual and procedural
Right-click an item in the console tree and click **Help**	HTML Help	Context-sensitive
Right-click an item in the result pane and click **Help**	HTML Help	Context-sensitive
Icon	HTML Help	Conceptual and procedural
F1 from a console	HTML Help	Context-sensitive
F1 from a property page	Windows Help	Context-sensitive
"What's This?" question mark	Windows Help	Context-sensitive

Style Issues

This section addresses style conventions for MMC Help. Remember that because Help is for end users, some of the terms (such as "result pane") used throughout this book are not appropriate for the Help files.

Contents

In general, you should document procedures that are snap-in-specific variations of general MMC procedures, but you should not document MMC-specific procedures or MMC-specific UI elements. This is redundant to the MMC documentation. Note the following examples of what to document and what not to document:

- Do describe what a snap-in displays in a description bar, but do not tell how to display the description bar (which is an MMC task).
- Do not tell how to add a snap-in or extension snap-in, but if your snap-in or extension snap-in requires critical configuration steps during addition, you might include the steps for adding the snap-in along with the critical steps for configuring it.

Table of Contents

Each snap-in Help file to be merged in the MMC combined table of contents must incorporate an .hhc (table of contents) file. This .hhc file must contain a *single* primary book (the snap-in's top node). It can also contain secondary books and topics. More details about each of these elements are presented in the following table.

Table 15.2   Table of Contents

Element	Guidelines
Primary book	Label it with the name of the tool.
	Link it to an overview topic.
	Include navigational links to books and topics that follow.
Secondary books	Do not overuse; minimize the levels users have to click down.
	Include navigational links to books and topics that follow.
Topics	Group by subject or function if applicable.

Snap-in Help

In the Help file for MMC, all books have navigational links to books and pages that follow. Some books have additional content. In addition, the Help file for MMC conforms to the following structure guidelines. To be consistent with the MMC Help, you should follow this structure:

Component (primary book)

> How To (secondary book)
>
> Concepts (secondary book)
>
> > Introduction to *component*
> >
> > Understanding *component*
> >
> > Using *component*
>
> Troubleshooting (secondary book)

In "Concepts," all pages begin with an <H1> heading. The "Introduction to *component*" section is a high-level overview that describes what the component is and why a user might want to install it. The "Understanding *component*" section provides the conceptual framework necessary for intelligent overall use of the component. The "Using *component*" section contains conceptual information that relates to specific tasks as opposed to the component as a whole.

For more information on integrating your Help files with your snap-in see Chapter 18, "Adding About Information and HTML Help Support."

Use of Terms

The following terms have specific meanings when used in the context of MMC and snap-ins. Be sure to use them correctly and consistently in your Help files.

- **Console.** Use this term when referring to the tool hosted in the main MMC window. Do not use this term to refer to particular snap-ins or other tools that are assembled in a console. A console is bounded by the MMC window and includes any child windows. Each console has one *console tree* and each child window displays a *view* of the tree. Refer to a child window by its title or by what it displays. Refer to the main window by the name of the console. Refer to the child windows as *console windows* or, preferably, by description or task.

- **Console root.** Use this term when referring to the first or top-level item for all MMC consoles. All additions to the console tree appear under this item. It is written "console root" (lowercase) except when referring to the specific item called Console Root (initial capitals) that appears by default in a new console. You should rename Console Root to a name that describes the objects in the snap-in's namespace.

- **Console tree.** Use this term when referring to the left pane of an MMC console. It is written "console tree" (lowercase) unless referring to the command on the **Action** menu, which should be written Console Tree (initial capitals). Do not refer to the panes by their position, for example, do not use *left*, *right*, *middle*, *upper*, or *lower*. In addition, do not refer to the left pane as the *scope pane* in the Help file.

- **Details pane.** Use this term when referring to the right pane of an MMC console. If possible, refer to what is displayed in this pane rather than to the pane itself. Do not refer to the panes by their position, for example, do not use *left*, *right*, *middle*, *upper,* or *lower*. In addition, do not refer to the right pane as the *result pane* in the Help file.

- **Item.** Use this term when referring to specific content in the console tree. Do not use the terms *node* or *namespace*. If possible, refer to the actual name of the item in the tree unless you must use an explicit term. To direct users to an item, you should write out the entire path to the item.

- **Snap-in.** Use this term when writing about using snap-ins or extension snap-ins to create or modify MMC consoles. Do not use this term to refer to the console itself. It is written "snap-in" (lowercase) except when referring to a UI command (for example, **Add/Remove Snap-in**).

Creating Compiled Help Files

In this section you will find information on creating Help files, compiling Help files, and creating a table of contents for snap-in Help files. For coding details see Chapter 18, "Adding About Information and HTML Help Support."

Help Entry Points

A user can open Help from nine different points in MMC:

- The system menu (upper-left corner)
- The **Help** menu on the main menu bar
- The **Action** menu on a console
- Right-click an item in the console tree
- Right-click an item in the result pane
- The icon on the console toolbar
- F1 from a console
- F1 from a property page
- The "What's This?" Help button in a dialog box

The following table shows the expected behavior for Help when it is opened from each of these points.

Table 15.3   Help Entry Points

Entry point from open console or property page	Behavior when Help is opened
Help on system menu	Right pane displays MMC overview.
Help topics on **Help** menu	Right pane displays MMC overview.
Help button on a property page (optional)	Right pane displays an appropriate topic for the property page.
Help on **Action** menu	Right pane displays snap-in overview.
Right-click an item in the console tree and click **Help**	Right pane displays a snap-in-appropriate topic for the highlighted item.
Right-click an item in the result pane and click **Help**	Right pane displays a snap-in-appropriate topic for the highlighted item.
Icon	Right pane displays snap-in overview.

Entry point from open console or property page	Behavior when Help is opened
F1 from a console	Right pane displays a snap-in-appropriate topic for the highlighted item in the console tree.
F1 from a property page	Opens context-sensitive Help pop-up window for the highlighted field or control.
"What's This?" question mark	Opens context-sensitive Help pop-up window for the highlighted field or control.

Compiling MMC Help Files

A compiled HTML Help system is made up of the following files:

- **Table of contents file (.hhc).** Settings for the table of contents are not configurable when using a binary table of contents (as is used for MMC HTML Help files).

- **Index file (.hhk).** When you create the index file, remember that this index might be merged with the indexes for Help files for other snap-ins. Thus, you should follow standard indexing conventions.

- **Project file (.hhp).** You must compile your snap-in Help file using a binary table of contents. To set this value in your .hhp file using HTML Help Workshop, click **Change project options**, click the **Compiler** tab, and then select **Create a binary TOC**.

- **HTML files.** These files contain the contents of the compiled Help file.

- **Graphics files (optional).** You can add illustrations to your Help pages in the form of graphics files.

The .hhc, .hhk, .html, .hhp, and graphics files are compiled to create a .chm file. This section contains more information about these files and system requirements for MMC snap-in Help.

All HTML Help files for MMC snap-ins should use the same window definition settings in their .hhp files as the Help file that documents core MMC features (Mmc.chm). You can modify window definition settings in HTML Help Workshop by clicking **Add/Modify window definitions**. If you do not use the same settings as the Mmc.chm file, your files might not be displayed.

The following figures show project file settings, as viewed using HTML Help Workshop. Many fields in the figures that follow contain a variable in the form <variable>. Replace <tool name> with a value appropriate for your snap-in, such as *monitor* for the **Title** field in Figure 15.3. The following steps illustrate the settings required to create snap-in Help files; you can create these Help files with the tools of your choice.

Snap-in Help

Click **Change project options**, and then click the **General** tab.

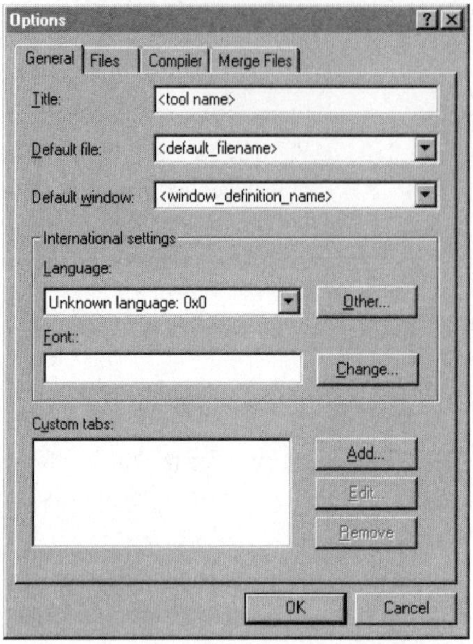

Figure 15.3   **HTML Help Workshop Options dialog box, General tab**

Note The window definition specified in **Default window** is defined in the **Window Types** dialog box accessed by clicking **Add/Modify window definitions**, and then clicking the **General** tab.

Note You should select a language under **Language**.

Click **Change project options**, and then click the **Files** tab.

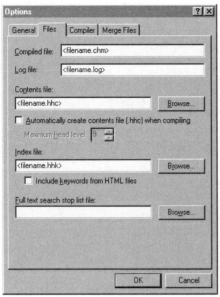

Figure 15.4   HTML Help Workshop Options dialog box, Files tab

Note   You *must* fill in the file name for **Contents file** for the table of contents to be displayed in the combined table of contents.

Click **Change project options**, and then click the **Compiler** tab.

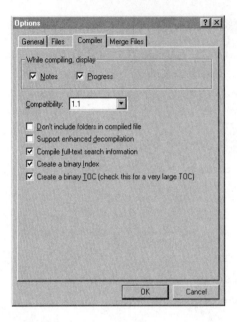

Figure 15.5   HTML Help Workshop Options dialog box, Compiler tab

Note   You *must* select **Create a binary TOC** for this file to be merged with the Help for MMC.

Click **Add/Modify window definitions**, and then click the **General** tab.

Figure 15.6   HTML Help Workshop Window Types dialog box, General tab

Snap-in Help

Click **Add/Modify window definitions**, and then click the **Buttons** tab.

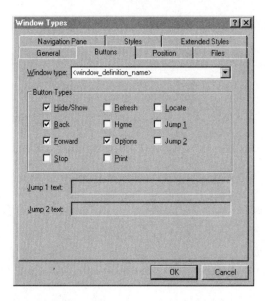

Figure 15.7   HTML Help Workshop Window Types dialog box, Buttons tab

Click **Add/Modify window definitions**, and then click the **Position** tab.

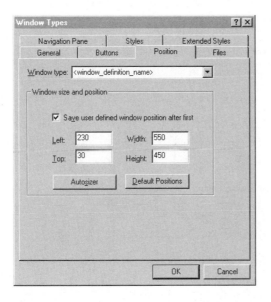

Figure 15.8   HTML Help Workshop Window Types dialog box, Position tab

Click **Add/Modify window definitions**, and then click the **Files** tab.

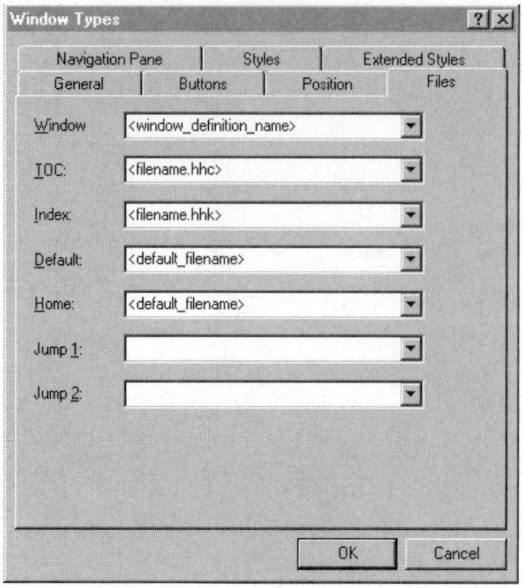

Figure 15.9   HTML Help Workshop Window Types dialog box, Files tab

Click **Add/Modify window definitions**, and then click the **Navigation Pane** tab.

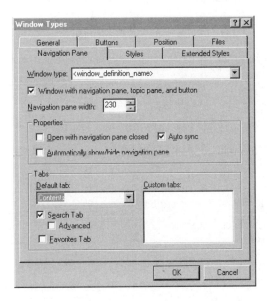

Figure 15.10   HTML Help Workshop Window Types dialog box, Navigation Pane tab

Online Help Design Review

This section offers a capsule review of the information in this chapter. The design features denoted with a check mark in this list and in the chapter text are likely to become logo requirements.

- You must use HTML Help to create a .chm file, so that the .chm file will merge with the rest of MMC Help.
- The .chm file must have a binary table of contents.
- Create a single top node, so that it is clear what tool the Help is referring to.

- Create conceptual and procedural HTML Help that will be rolled into the MMC console Help table of contents.
- Use either HTML Help or Microsoft Windows Help technology to create context-sensitive Help.
- Document snap-in-specific functionality, not MMC functionality.
- A snap-in's Help style should be consistent with the MMC console Help file's style.

Building Snap-ins with C++

The MMC SDK in its entirety is on the CD-ROM included with this book. The MMC COM SDK, which is used to create snap-ins with the C++ language, is part of the MMC SDK. Part 4 contains the MMC COM Programmer's Guide. The top-level topics in the MMC COM Reference and a discussion of the C++ sample snap-ins appear here as well. The SDK contains the source code for all the samples referenced in this book.

Note that the MMC SDK is part of the Microsoft Platform SDK. The MMC SDK on the companion CD-ROM is part of a special build of the Windows 2000 release of the Platform SDK. For information about updates for the Platform SDK, see http://msdn.microsoft.com/library.

CHAPTER 16

MMC COM Programmer's Guide Overview

The Microsoft Management Console (MMC) COM SDK provides a framework for writing COM-based snap-ins for managing applications. Because MMC is a framework, you need to do more than just read through the documentation of the various interfaces and methods to learn how to write your own snap-ins. You need to understand the MMC framework.

The MMC COM Programmer's Guide is an integral part of the MMC COM SDK documentation. In it, you will find conceptual information and programming guidelines that cover the MMC framework in detail.

The MMC COM Programmer's Guide is just one of three main sections that make up the MMC COM SDK. The remaining two sections are:

- MMC COM Reference
- MMC C++ Sample Snap-ins

This overview covers many of the basic concepts that you need to be aware of to use the MMC framework effectively. Some of the topics cover MMC concepts in detail; other topics present information at a higher level and point to more detailed information found elsewhere in the MMC SDK documentation.

The concepts covered in this section are referred to many times in the rest of the MMC SDK documentation. Therefore, it's a good idea to spend some time reading this section before going on.

C++ Snap-ins

This section covers the following topics:

- MMC-Related COM Interfaces
- Snap-in Namespace
- Clipboard Formats
- Data Objects and MMC
- Cookies
- Handles
- MMC Notification Messages
- Snap-in Modes and Required Interfaces
- **Add/Remove Snap-in** Dialog Box

MMC-Related COM Interfaces

The MMC SDK provides a number of COM interfaces for use in developing snap-ins. Snap-ins implement some of these interfaces and expose them to MMC. MMC implements the remaining interfaces and exposes them to snap-ins to use. As a result, much of the functionality you are likely to want for your snap-in is already available to you.

MMC creates instances of your snap-in as needed and calls the methods of the interfaces that your snap-in exposes. In turn, your snap-in can call the methods of the interfaces that MMC exposes, thereby incorporating features such as toolbars, context menus, and property sheets.

MMC implements the following interfaces:

IColumnData (new in MMC 1.2)

IConsole2

IConsoleNameSpace2

IConsoleVerb

IContextMenuCallback

IContextMenuProvider

*MMC implements the following interfaces: **(continued)***

IControlbar

IDisplayHelp

IHeaderCtrl2 (new in MMC 1.2)

IImageList

IMenuButton

IPropertySheetCallback

IPropertySheetProvider

IRequiredExtensions

IResultData

IToolbar

Snap-ins implement the following interfaces:

IComponent

IComponentData

IEnumTASK

IExtendContextMenu

IExtendControlbar

IExtendPropertySheet2

IExtendTaskPad

IRequiredExtensions

IResultDataCompare

IResultDataCompareEx (new in MMC 1.2)

IResultOwnerData

ISnapinAbout

ISnapinHelp2

Depending on the features you want, you may not need to use or implement all of these interfaces in your snap-in. Other sections of this overview refer to these interfaces and their methods frequently, so familiarizing yourself with them now may be helpful.

C++ Snap-ins

Ensuring Compatibility Between MMC Versions

It is important to understand that MMC's contract to compatibility from release to release is its COM interfaces. As long as a snap-in uses the MMC COM interfaces as documented in the MMC SDK documentation, it will remain compatible from one version to the next. A snap-in *must not* make assumptions about the internal implementation details of MMC, because these are subject to change. A snap-in that makes such assumptions for a particular version of MMC is likely to break in subsequent versions of MMC.

Detecting the MMC Version Number

Snap-ins built using one version of the MMC SDK might behave unpredictably if loaded in an earlier version of MMC. For example, a snap-in that uses an MMC 1.2 interface (for example, **IColumnData**) will not work properly if the user loads the snap-in in an MMC 1.1 console.

To ensure compatibility between snap-ins and the version of an MMC console in which they are loaded, snap-ins should implement a mechanism for detecting MMC version numbers. Although there is currently no MMC interface that allows a snap-in to determine the MMC version it is running under, there is a fairly straightforward workaround for achieving the same goal.

Basically, snap-ins can query for MMC interfaces introduced in different MMC versions to identify version numbers. For example, if a snap-in queries for the **IColumnData** interface and the query is successful (the **QueryInterface** call returns S_OK), then the snap-in knows that it is loaded in an MMC 1.2 or later console.

Depending on whether a snap-in is a primary snap-in or an extension snap-in, the details of how it detects the MMC version number differ.

For Primary Snap-ins

For detecting MMC version numbers, primary snap-ins must use either the **IConsole** interface pointer passed into their **IComponent::Initialize** implementation, or the **IUnknown** interface pointer passed into their **IComponentData::Initialize** implementation. Only these two interfaces can be used to query for the new MMC 1.2 interfaces.

The following sample implementation of a global function detects the MMC version number:

```
MMC_VERSION GetMMCVersion(IConsole *pConsole)
{

  HRESULT hr1;
  HRESULT hr2;
  MMC_VERSION mmcVersion;

  hr1 = pConsole->QueryInterface(IID_IConsole2,
        (void **)&m_ipConsole2);
  hr2 = pConsole->QueryInterface(IID_IColumnData,
        (void **)&m_ipColumnData);

  if (S_OK == hr1 && S_OK == hr2)
      mmcVersion = MMC12;
  else
  {
  if (S_OK == hr1 && S_OK != hr2)
      mmcVersion = MMC11;
  else
      mmcVersion = MMC10;
  }

  return mmcVersion;
}
```

The variable **mmcVersion** is an enumeration of type **MMC_VERSION**.

```
enum MMC_VERSION {MMC10 = 0, MMC11 = 1, MMC12 = 2};
```

The **IConsole** interface pointer passed into the **GetMMCVersion** function is the same one that is passed into the snap-in's **IComponent::Initialize** implementation.

Note that neither the **GetMMCVersion** function nor the **MMC_VERSION** enumeration in the preceding sample will work to identify an MMC version later than version 1.2. However, you can still use the function to identify whether the version number is 1.2 or later. That is, if the function determines that the version number is neither 1.0 nor 1.1, then it must be 1.2 or later.

C++ Snap-ins

For Extension Snap-ins

Not all types of extension snap-ins need to implement **IComponentData** or **IComponent**, so the workaround for primary snap-ins does not work for them. The following statements apply to extension snap-ins:

- For extension snap-ins, there is no difference in functionality between MMC versions 1.1 and 1.2, so there is no need for an extension snap-in to detect whether it is loaded in an MMC 1.2 or later console.

- Currently, there is no way for a non-namespace extension snap-in to detect the version of the MMC console in which it is loaded.

- Namespace extension snap-ins receive calls to their **IComponentData::Initialize** and **IComponent::Initialize** implementations, so they can use the same technique as primary snap-ins to detect MMC version numbers.

Snap-in Namespace

Snap-ins and the objects they manage are represented in the scope pane as nodes on a tree control. These nodes can be divided into three types:

- Built-in nodes
- Static nodes
- Enumerated nodes

Built-in nodes include folders, HTML pages, and ActiveX controls (OCXs). MMC implements built-in nodes and they do not interact directly with your snap-in. The other types of nodes, static and enumerated, offer viewing mechanisms: details view, custom HTML page, custom ActiveX control (OCX), or taskpad.

A node's most important property is its node type. This is a globally unique identifier (GUID) that describes the node's overall type; for example, whether it is a user, a machine, a domain entry in a Domain Name System (DNS) database, or something else. A node type is defined by the individual snap-in rather than by MMC and it is a GUID only because GUIDs ensure that name collisions do not occur. GUIDs in this context have no COM significance, although you generate them using Guidgen.exe just as you do other GUIDs. This procedure is documented in the Microsoft Platform SDK.

Nodes and IComponentData

The **IComponentData** interface is closely associated with the functionality of the nodes displayed in the scope pane. A snap-in's **IComponentData** object adds items to the scope pane when it receives an MMCN_EXPAND notification from the console through its **Notify** method.

While nodes themselves are maintained by MMC after their creation, **IComponentData** handles notifications sent to it through its **Notify** method whenever the user performs an action on a particular node.

Snap-ins implement **IComponentData** as COM cocreatable class objects. When the user loads a snap-in in an MMC console, MMC creates an instance of the snap-in by cocreating its **IComponentData** class object. There is only one instance of **IComponentData** per instance of a stand-alone snap-in or namespace extension snap-in.

MMC Static Nodes

A *static node* is a node in the MMC namespace that is present as long as the snap-in that provides it is loaded. Snap-ins must implement the **IComponentData** interface to have static nodes in the tree. The first time a static node is accessed in an MMC console, MMC calls **CoCreateInstance** to create an instance of the snap-in COM server that owns the static node in that console. Each static node in each console is associated with a different instance of a snap-in.

Only stand-alone snap-ins can have static nodes. Extension snap-ins can extend the static nodes of other snap-ins, but they never provide their own static nodes in any console in which they are loaded.

Stand-alone snap-ins use static nodes to store their setup configuration and relative placement in the console. The static node is inserted when the snap-in is loaded in a console. The console itself inserts the static node in the scope pane. This differs from *enumerated nodes*, which snap-ins insert themselves.

A static node has a cookie value of NULL. The snap-in must be prepared to receive notifications on a NULL cookie just like any other node.

C++ Snap-ins

When a stand-alone snap-in is loaded in a console file, MMC requests a data object for the snap-in's static node and then calls its **IDataObject::GetDataHere** method with the CCF_DISPLAY_NAME clipboard format to retrieve the static node's display name. MMC requests the display name when the static node is first displayed in the **Standalone** tab of the **Add/Remove Snap-in** dialog box and when the static node is first added to the scope pane. After the initial creation of the static node, a snap-in must use the **IConsoleNameSpace2::SetItem** method to change the static node's name.

Cookies, data objects, and clipboard formats are discussed in detail later on in this overview.

MMC Enumerated Nodes

Every static node in each multiple-document interface (MDI) child (view) can have its own subtree of enumerated nodes. These enumerated nodes are not persisted by MMC to the .msc (console) file; rather, the snap-in rebuilds them in each view as needed. The children of enumerated nodes are always other enumerated nodes, never static or built-in nodes.

When the user selects or expands the static node in the scope pane, the snap-in's implementation of **IComponentData** is notified and can insert enumerated nodes as children of that static node. Similarly, the same **IComponentData** interface is notified when one of those enumerated children is selected or expanded. That is, the same **IComponentData** interface is associated with the static node and all of its enumerated children belonging to the snap-in that owns the static node, in all views.

If there is more than one MDI child viewing a static node, the node will appear the same in each MDI child.

IComponent and the Result Pane

An instance of the **IComponent** interface is associated with each MDI child window of a snap-in. Several instances of **IComponent** are possible for each instance of **IComponentData** (one per view, plus others used by MMC).

Every snap-in that inserts items in the result pane must implement the **IComponent** interface. Similar to the **IComponentData** interface, it is one of the console's interfaces to the snap-in and is closely associated with the functionality of the items displayed in the result pane.

However, this does not imply that **IComponent** is the "result pane" interface and that **IComponentData** is the "scope pane" interface. Many actions performed on nodes in the scope pane are handled by **IComponent**. For example, when the user selects a node in the scope pane of a view, MMC sends the MMCN_SELECT notification to the snap-in's **IComponent** implementation associated with that view.

All **IComponent** instances of a snap-in are created through **IComponentData::CreateComponent**, and *not* through **CoCreateInstance**. Thus, it is possible for **IComponentData** to be aware of all **IComponent** instances that it creates by holding pointers to them and deleting the pointers when **IComponent::Destroy** is called. In addition, an **IComponent** instance can hold a pointer to the **IComponentData** instance that created it. This makes it easy, for example, for a snap-in to pass information from the document side to all views without having to call **IConsole2::UpdateAllViews**.

Scope and Result Items

From now on, we'll use the term *item* to describe all objects directly inserted by snap-ins in either the scope pane or the result pane. Snap-ins insert *scope items* and *result items* using the MMC interface methods **IConsoleNameSpace2::InsertItem** and **IResultData::InsertItem**, respectively. We use the term "item" instead of "node" in the MMC documentation because many interface methods in the MMC SDK use "item" to refer to either a scope item or a result item.

Note that snap-ins insert scope items in the scope pane, but the items can appear in either the scope pane or the result pane. Result items can only appear in the result pane. Finally, the term *static node* will continue to be used to refer to the stand-alone snap-in "root" scope item inserted by the console when the snap-in is loaded.

C++ Snap-ins

Clipboard Formats

Every node type requires one or more clipboard formats that a data object for any node of that node type must support. For example, the node type for a user might require that the object supports clipboard formats that provide the domain in which the user is located, and the distinguished name of the user. With a few exceptions the snap-in, and not MMC, defines these clipboard formats and the format of the data they return.

All clipboard formats supported by snap-ins (stand-alone or extension) must be registered. You can do this by using the Win32 **RegisterClipboardFormat** function, which is documented in the Microsoft Platform SDK.

Snap-ins must include support for the following four clipboard formats in all data objects that they provide to MMC as a result of calls to **IComponentData::QueryDataObject** or **IComponent::QueryDataObject**:

CCF_NODETYPE

CCF_SZNODETYPE

CCF_DISPLAY_NAME

CCF_SNAPIN_CLASSID

MMC uses the CCF_NODETYPE and CCF_SZNODETYPE formats to request the node type GUID of the currently selected scope or result item in class identifier (CLSID) and string form, respectively. Note that support for these two formats does not imply that MMC treats items differently according to node type; instead, an item's node type provides a way to determine which other snap-ins extend that item. For example, when a snap-in registers itself as extending the property sheets of objects generated by other snap-ins, it actually extends the property sheets for scope or result items of one or more specific node types.

The CCF_DISPLAY_NAME format is used to request the display name of a stand-alone snap-in's static node. Finally, CCF_SNAPIN_CLASSID is used to retrieve the snap-in's CLSID. For more information about CLSIDs and related topics, see the Platform SDK.

In most cases, MMC uses **IDataObject::GetDataHere** to specify the format of the requested data and the storage medium for the data. For example, MMC determines the node type by calling **IDataObject::GetDataHere** on the data object for a specified scope or result item, using the CCF_NODETYPE clipboard format.

Data Objects and MMC

Data transfer within MMC is accomplished using the COM interface **IDataObject**, which snap-ins implement. The actual data is shared in clipboard formats. The **IDataObject** interface includes methods that enable data to be transferred and notifications to be generated when data changes.

MMC uses the **IDataObject::GetDataHere** and **IDataObject::GetData** methods to get data from scope and result items. The **IDataObject** interface and its methods are documented in the Microsoft Platform SDK.

All data that is transferred resides in global memory, so the **TYMED** identifier of the **STGMEDIUM** structure passed to a data object in the **IDataObject::GetDataHere** method is always an HGLOBAL.

MMC frequently requests snap-ins to provide data objects by calling their **IComponentData::QueryDataObject** or **IComponent::QueryDataObject** method. For this reason, snap-in developers should ensure that this is an efficient operation.

One technique for improving efficiency is to implement a pool of data objects that can be used more than once to fulfill common MMC data requests. These data objects exist for the lifetime of a snap-in instance. Whenever MMC requests data that can be provided by one of these data objects, the snap-in supplies that data object to MMC and increments its reference count. This technique is based on the fact that data objects are COM objects; MMC simply releases its interface to a data object after it is no longer needed.

C++ Snap-ins

The following sequence diagram written in the Unified Modeling Language illustrates the general method by which MMC requests a data object from a snap-in. In the diagram, MMC calls the data object's **GetDataHere** method to request data in a specific clipboard format.

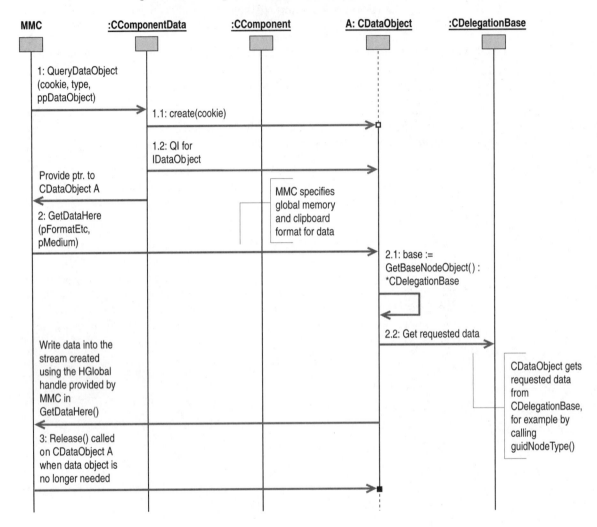

In the scenario depicted in the diagram, MMC calls the **QueryDataObject** method of **CComponentData**, which implements the MMC interface **IComponentData**. One of the arguments of **QueryDataObject** is the cookie value of the node for which MMC is requesting data. **CComponentData** creates a data object and passes the cookie to it. MMC then calls the **GetDataHere** method of the data object and specifies the required clipboard format in which the data object should render the requested data. The data object in the diagram delegates the data rendering to a delegation base. This is the preferred implementation in the MMC C++ Sample Snap-ins distributed with the MMC SDK. For information on how the delegation base is used, see "Samples Object Model" in Chapter 31.

The data object then writes the requested data back into the stream created by using the *HGlobal* handle provided to it by MMC in **GetDataHere**. After using the data and at an appropriate time, MMC releases the interface pointer to the data object with a call to the object's **Release** method.

Special Data Objects

In certain circumstances, the data object that MMC passes to the snap-in during a notification is a special type of data object instead of a pointer to an actual **IDataObject** object.

To determine whether the data object is a special data object, the snap-in can use the **IS_SPECIAL_DATAOBJECT** macro. A return value of TRUE indicates that the data object is a special data object. Based on the return value, the snap-in can then handle the notification message appropriately.

The special data object can take three values: DOBJ_NULL, DOBJ_CUSTOMOCX, and DOBJ_CUSTOMWEB.

The DOBJ_NULL value indicates that MMC does not require a data object for the notification message being sent. Examples of notification messages for which the LPDATAOBJECT is set to DOBJ_NULL include MMCN_FILTER_CHANGE and MMCN_FILTERBTN_CLICK.

The DOBJ_CUSTOMOCX value indicates that the result pane contains an OCX control. The DOBJ_CUSTOMWEB value indicates that the result pane contains a Web page.

C++ Snap-ins

MMC can pass DOBJ_CUSTOMOCX or DOBJ_CUSTOMWEB as the data object in the following methods with the following notifications:

- **IExtendControlbar::ControlbarNotify**
  - MMCN_BTN_CLICK
- **IComponent::Notify**
  - MMCN_BTN_CLICK with param set to MMC_VERB_PROPERTIES
  - MMCN_DELETE
  - MMCN_PASTE
  - MMCN_PRINT
  - MMCN_REFRESH

Cookies

Cookies are pointer-sized identifiers within an instance of a snap-in and are associated with a particular scope or result item. When inserting an item in the scope or result pane, a snap-in passes to MMC the value that will be used as the item's cookie value. The value is solely determined by the snap-in. MMC does not care whether the cookie is a pointer, an index, a hash, or any other type of reference. However, most snap-ins will use as cookies pointers to the internal C++ or COM objects that represent these items. When MMC needs a data object for a particular item, it uses the item's cookie value to uniquely identify the item.

NULL (0) is a special cookie value. MMC uses this cookie value to refer to the static node of a stand-alone snap-in. Because a stand-alone snap-in does not explicitly add the static node, MMC passes a NULL cookie value instead. A stand-alone snap-in should be able to handle NULL whenever MMC passes it a cookie value.

MMC passes the cookie of an item only to the snap-in that created that item. Extension snap-ins get a data object rather than a cookie. Most notifications also specify a data object rather than a cookie—even those notifications that are sent to the snap-in that inserted the item.

Because MMC usually identifies items with data objects rather than with cookies, most snap-in developers implement a clipboard format that quickly retrieves the cookie from the data object. It is important that this clipboard format not be published or used by extension snap-ins, because the internal structure that the cookie points to is subject to change. Instead, the snap-in being extended should publish other clipboard formats that provide the necessary information in a cleaner fashion.

Cookies and Inserting Items

Snap-ins insert items into the scope or result pane using the **IResultData::InsertItem** or **IConsoleNameSpace2::InsertItem** method. The cookie value of the inserted item is stored in the **lParam** member of the **SCOPEDATAITEM** structure (for scope items) or **RESULTDATAITEM** structure (for result items).

After an item is successfully inserted, MMC calls **IComponentData::GetDisplayInfo** or **IComponent:GetDisplayInfo**, depending on which object inserted the item. The snap-in can then cast the **lParam** (cookie) back into the reference for the selected item and retrieve the display name, image index, or other information that can be displayed in the result pane's columns.

As previously mentioned, MMC often requests data objects from snap-ins by calling the **IComponentData::QueryDataObject** or **IComponent::QueryDataObject** method. In the call to **QueryDataObject**, MMC also passes the cookie value of the item for which MMC requires data. If the requested data object is created to notify a snap-in of a user action on a particular scope or result item, MMC forwards the data object back to the snap-in, along with the appropriate notification message. The only way that the snap-in can properly identify the affected item is by means of the cookie value that is passed into the call to the **QueryDataObject** method.

It is therefore very important that any implementation of **IDataObject** stores the cookie value of the item for which MMC is requesting a data object. To see a sample implementation of this, see "Working with **IDataObject**" in Chapter 17.

Special Cookie Values

In certain situations, the **MMC_COOKIE** value that MMC passes in a call to the snap-in's **IComponent::QueryDataObject** method is a special type of cookie.

To determine if the cookie value is that of a special cookie, the snap-in can use the **IS_SPECIAL_COOKIE** macro. A return value of TRUE indicates that the cookie value is that of a special cookie type. The snap-in can then handle the data object appropriately based on the specific value of the cookie.

The special cookie can take two values: MMC_MULTI_SELECT_COOKIE and MMC_WINDOW_COOKIE. These values are reserved by MMC and should never be used by snap-ins to identify any scope or result items that they insert. These values are defined in the mmc.idl file.

C++ Snap-ins

The MMC_MULTI_SELECT_COOKIE value is used during multiselection. MMC passes this value to the snap-in to request a pointer to a multiselection data object. For details about multiselection data objects, see "Multiselection" in Chapter 25.

The MMC_WINDOW_COOKIE value is used for windows created programmatically in calls to the **IConsole2::NewWindow** method and with the *lOptions* parameter set to MMC_NW_OPTION_CUSTOMTITLE. MMC passes the value to request a pointer to the data object that supplies the string representing the snap-in's static node in the title bar.

Handles

When a scope item is inserted into the scope pane, MMC creates a *handle*, or *HSCOPEITEM*, that uniquely identifies the inserted item. For all items other than the static node, MMC returns the item's HSCOPEITEM after the snap-in successfully inserts the item in the scope pane using **IConsoleNameSpace2::InsertItem**.

In the case of the static node, MMC itself inserts it into the snap-in's namespace. MMC then passes the static node's HSCOPEITEM to the snap-in as the *param* parameter in the MMCN_EXPAND notification.

MMC also returns to the snap-in a handle for each inserted result item. This handle, called an *HRESULTITEM*, is returned after the snap-in successfully inserts the result item using **IResultData::InsertItem**.

A scope item's handle is valid for as long as the item is present in the snap-in's scope pane. Furthermore, a scope item's handle is the same in all views (MDI child windows). A result item's handle is only valid for as long as the item is displayed in a result pane. When the result pane is torn down, MMC destroys all handles to any of the result items that were displayed in the result pane.

A snap-in needs an item's handle in order to manipulate it using the methods of the **IConsoleNameSpace2**, **IConsole2**, and **IResultData** interfaces. Therefore, the snap-in should store the item's handle after successfully inserting it into the scope pane or result pane. In the case of result items, snap-ins can also acquire a result item's handle by calling the **IResultData::FindItemByLParam** method, which allows a snap-in to find a result item based on the snap-in-defined **lParam** value (cookie value).

Cookies vs. Handles

Cookies and handles both refer to inserted scope or result items. However, it's important to keep in mind the following differences between the two:

- An inserted item's cookie value is determined solely by the snap-in that inserts the item. The snap-in specifies the item's cookie value in the **lParam** member of the **SCOPEDATAITEM** or **RESULTDATAITEM** structure it must fill when inserting the item. MMC caches this value and uses it to uniquely identify the item in calls made to the snap-in's **IComponentData::QueryDataObject** or **IComponent::QueryDataObject** implementation.

- MMC creates an inserted item's handle and returns it to the snap-in after the item is successfully inserted. Snap-ins must specify an item's handle when attempting to manipulate the item using the methods of the **IConsoleNameSpace2**, **IConsole2**, or **IResultData** interface.

MMC Notification Messages

MMC notifications are generated by events caused by user input. MMC can send notification messages to the snap-in's **IComponentData::Notify**, **IComponent::Notify**, or **IExtendControlbar::ControlbarNotify** methods, depending on the notification.

Generally, notification messages generated because of user input in the scope pane are sent to the snap-in's **IComponentData** implementation. Notification messages generated from user actions in the result pane are sent to the **IComponent** instance that corresponds to the current view (MDI child window).

MMC calls the snap-in's **IExtendControlbar::ControlbarNotify** method when users initiate actions related to the toolbar.

For a list of all MMC notifications, see "MMC Notifications" in the MMC COM Reference section of the MMC SDK.

Depending on the notification type, MMC might include a pointer to a data object from the snap-in for the currently selected item in the scope or result pane. MMC requests the data object from the snap-in when the user selects the item and then returns the data object to the snap-in to provide the context information the snap-in needs to handle the notification message generated by a user action. This context information includes the cookie value of the affected item, whether the item is a scope or result item, and whether the item is selected or deselected.

Note that snap-ins are encouraged to implement default notification handlers for all MMC notifications and to return a value of S_FALSE for any notifications that they do not explicitly handle. This instructs MMC to perform a default operation for the particular notification.

C++ Snap-ins

Furthermore, when using a snap-in code base built for one version of MMC in a newer version of MMC, snap-in developers should ensure that their snap-ins implement default notification handlers for any new notifications available in the newer version. Otherwise, snap-ins may behave unexpectedly in the newer version. An example of this is the behavior of the **Modify Columns** dialog box, which allows users to customize list view columns. If user customizations are made, MMC sends the snap-in the MMCN_COLUMNS_CHANGED notification, which is introduced in MMC 1.2. For the customizations to take effect, the snap-in *must* return S_FALSE (or S_OK) in its MMCN_COLUMNS_CHANGED notification handler. If the notification is not handled, MMC will discard the user customizations.

Snap-in Modes and Required Interfaces

As previously mentioned, the following snap-in modes are possible:

- Stand-alone
- Extension
- Dual-mode

This section briefly discusses the MMC interfaces required to support each of these modes of operation.

Stand-alone Snap-ins

Stand-alone snap-ins must implement the **IComponentData** interface. Additional interfaces must also be implemented, depending on the type of functionality you want the stand-alone snap-in to have. These requirements are described in detail in the sections of the Programmer's Guide that cover adding features such as different result pane views, toolbars, and property pages.

Snap-in developers are also encouraged to implement the **ISnapinAbout** interface in their stand-alone snap-ins.

Stand-alone snap-ins that add to their namespace node types that are extended by extension snap-ins have additional requirements. For details, see "Requirements for Primary Snap-ins" in Chapter 24.

Extension Snap-ins

An extension snap-in can support any or all of the following extension types:

- Namespace extension
- Context menu extension
- Toolbar extension
- Menu button extension
- Property page extension
- Taskpad extension

Namespace extensions add scope items to a primary snap-in's scope pane. Namespace extensions must implement the **IComponentData** interface. Non-namespace extensions—context menu, toolbar, menu button, property page, and taskpad extensions—do not add scope items to a primary snap-in's scope pane, and consequently they do not need to implement **IComponentData**.

Context menu extensions implement **IExtendContextMenu**; toolbar and menu button extensions implement **IControlbar**. Property page extensions implement **IExtendPropertySheet2**. Finally, taskpad extensions implement the **IExtendTaskpad** interface.

For detailed information about interface and other requirements for extension snap-ins, see Chapter 24, "Working with Extension Snap-ins."

Dual-Mode Snap-ins

Dual-mode snap-ins must implement the interfaces needed by both stand-alone and extension snap-ins—that is, they must implement the **IComponentData** interface for stand-alone behavior and the appropriate interfaces necessary to support the desired extension behavior.

C++ Snap-ins

Add/Remove Snap-in Dialog Box

The **Add/Remove Snap-in** dialog box allows authors of saved console files to identify available snap-ins and add and remove snap-ins. The dialog box is available only for saved console files in Author mode.

The console identifies snap-ins by the information you make available through the system registry. This is explained in "MMC Registry Entries" in the MMC COM Reference section of the MMC SDK.

The **Add/Remove Snap-in** dialog box presents a list of available snap-in components. The dialog box relies on complete and accurate entries in the system registry. Accordingly, snap-ins should be self-registering and should complete this task as part of the installation sequence.

Snap-in developers are encouraged to implement the **ISnapinAbout** interface to provide MMC with a snap-in's About information. This information is *only* displayed in the **Add/Remove Snap-in** dialog box.

When a snap-in is added using the **Add/Remove Snap-in** dialog box, the console requests the snap-in to optionally display a configuration wizard for gathering settings during the insertion process. This is done by calling the snap-in's **IComponentData::QueryDataObject** method with CCT_SNAPIN_MANAGER as the value for the *types* parameter.

C H A P T E R   1 7

Building the Basic Snap-in Framework

This section discusses how to build a bare-bones snap-in in C++. To do so, you'll need to implement two MMC interfaces and two COM interfaces and write registration and unregistration code for the snap-in.

The two MMC-defined COM interfaces you need to implement are:

- **IComponentData**
- **IComponent**

The two standard COM interfaces you need to implement are:

- **IDataObject**
- **IClassFactory**

Note that this section does not cover how to add items to a snap-in's scope pane or result pane. Refer to Chapter 19, "Working with the Scope Pane" and Chapter 20, "Using Different Result Pane View Types" for this information.

While reading this section, you'll see frequent references to the Simple sample snap-in provided with the MMC SDK. To see other samples that are available, see Chapter 31, "Sample Organization and Structure."

C++ Snap-ins

Working with Key Interfaces

This section covers the following topics:

- Working with **IComponentData**
- Working with **IComponent**
- Working with **IDataObject**
- Working with **IConsole**

Working with IComponentData

This section discusses how to implement the **IComponentData** interface.

Cocreating an IComponentData Object

A snap-in is an in-process server DLL, and the instance of MMC that loads it is its client. For a discussion of how in-process servers are loaded into a caller's process space, refer to the Microsoft Developer Network (MSDN) Library. For a discussion of registering snap-ins, see "Registering and Unregistering a Snap-in" later in this chapter.

For this example, assume that the **CreateInstance** method of the snap-in's **IClassFactory** implementation is called and that the snap-in creates an instance of the **IComponentData** interface in response. As a result, the console now has a pointer to the snap-in's **IComponentData** implementation.

Here is the constructor for the **IComponentData** implementation, **CComponentData**, in the Simple snap-in sample:

```
CComponentData::CComponentData()
: m_cref(0), m_ipConsoleNameSpace(NULL), m_ipConsole(NULL)
{
  OBJECT_CREATED
  m_pStaticNode = new CStaticNode;
}
```

In the constructor, the **CComponentData** object's reference count is initialized to zero. **CComponentData** caches pointers to the console's **IConsoleNameSpace** and **IConsole** interfaces; these pointers are set during the initialization of **CComponentData** in its **Initialize** method.

OBJECT_CREATED is a macro that is defined as follows:

```
#define OBJECT_CREATED InterlockedIncrement(
(long *)&g_uObjects);
```

The *g_uObjects* global variable keeps a global count of the number of snap-in-provided interfaces that MMC is holding at any moment during the lifetime of the snap-in instance.

The constructor also creates an instance of the **CStaticNode** object, which is the snap-in object in the Simple snap-in sample that represents the snap-in's static node.

CStaticNode inherits from **CDelegationBase**. **CDelegationBase** is used in all the sample snap-ins to handle MMC requests to **IComponentData** and **IComponent** objects. For details about **CDelegationBase**, refer to "Samples Object Model" in Chapter 31.break

Initializing an IComponentData Object

MMC initializes a snap-in by calling the **Initialize** method of the **IComponentData** object. During initialization, **IComponentData** should query the console for its **IConsoleNamespace** and **IConsole** interfaces using the console's **IUnknown** interface pointer that is passed into the call to **Initialize**. The snap-in should then cache the returned pointers and use them for calling **IConsoleNamespace** and **IConsole** interface methods.

Initialization is also the correct time for a snap-in to add a strip of icons to the image list using the **IImageList::ImageListSetStrip** method. For an example of how this is done, see the Nodes sample in Chapter 31.

Creating an IComponent Object

When the **CreateComponent** method of the **IComponentData** object is called, the snap-in can create an instance of the **IComponent** interface. Typically, the newly created **IComponent** object caches a pointer to its parent **IComponentData** object in its constructor.

Note that MMC calls **CreateComponent** each time a new view (a new MDI child window) is created; thus each view is associated with a different **IComponent** object.

C++ Snap-ins

Sending Notifications to the IComponentData Object

The console calls the **Notify** method to notify the snap-in of an event that occurs, for example, when the user clicks the mouse.

Querying the IComponentData Object for a Data Object

MMC calls the snap-in's implementation of the **QueryDataObject** method to request a data object for a specific cookie, including the static folder (NULL cookie). The data object type is taken from the **DATA_OBJECT_TYPES** enumeration and determines the context in which MMC requests the data object. A CCT_SCOPE flag is set to indicate that the data object is for the scope pane. CCT_RESULT is set to indicate that it is for the result pane, and CCT_SNAPIN_MANAGER indicates that the **Add/Remove Snap-in** dialog box is being used. CCT_UNINITIALIZED indicates that the data object has an invalid type. Given context information, the snap-in can determine the context in which a data object is requested.

Getting Display Information

The **GetDisplayInfo** method retrieves display information for a namespace item in the scope pane.

Destroying the Object

The **Destroy** method releases all interfaces to the console, such as **IConsole** and **IConsoleNamespace2**. You should be aware that MMC remains in a state in which everything can be queried during the call to **Destroy** so the snap-in can get information from the console. On return from **Destroy**, however, data integrity cannot be guaranteed.

Comparing Data Objects

The **CompareObjects** method provides a way for a snap-in component to compare two data objects and determine whether they refer to the same physical object. This method is used, for example, to detect duplicate property sheets.

Working with IComponent

Among the **IComponent** methods, the **Initialize** method provides an entry point for the snap-in by allowing **QueryInterface** calls to **IConsole**. The console calls the **Notify** method to notify the snap-in component that an event has occurred as a result of a user action. The **Destroy** method releases all interfaces to the console such as **IConsole**.

The **QueryDataObject** method returns a pointer to an **IDataObject** that provides further information about the item specified by the *cookie* parameter. The *type* parameter indicates the context in which the data object is required. A value of CCT_SCOPE or CCT_SNAPIN_MANAGER indicates that the data object is for a scope item. A value of CCT_SNAPIN_MANAGER further indicates that the Snap-in Manager has requested the data object. A value of CCT_RESULT indicates that the cookie is that of a result item.

The **GetResultViewType** method determines the type of view in the result pane (for example, default list view, ActiveX control (OCX), URL path). The **GetDisplayInfo** method retrieves display information for a result item. The **CompareObjects** method provides a way for a snap-in component to compare two result items.

Working with IDataObject

For an overview of how data objects are used in MMC, see "Data Objects and MMC" in Chapter 16.

The MMC C++ sample snap-ins share a common implementation of **IDataObject**. The majority of samples implement only the **IDataObject::GetDataHere** method.

Here is the implementation of the constructor for the **IDataObject** implementation in the MMC C++ samples:

```
CDataObject::CDataObject(MMC_COOKIE cookie,
                         DATA_OBJECT_TYPES context)
  : m_lCookie(cookie), m_context(context), m_cref(0)
{
}
```

The data object stores the cookie value of the item for which the data object is being requested. MMC passes the item's cookie value in calls to the snap-in's **IComponentData::QueryDataObject** and **IComponent::QueryDataObject** implementations. When MMC requests information about the item from the snap-in (for example, by calling the data object's **GetDataHere** method), the snap-in examines the stored cookie value to determine the item in question.

There are special situations in which the *cookie* parameter passed into **IComponent::QueryDataObject** is not the cookie value of a scope or result item inserted by the snap-in. For details about these *special cookies*, see "Special Cookie Values" in Chapter 16.

C++ Snap-ins

Working with IConsole

Every instance of a snap-in that exists in the scope pane is unique, and the methods of the **IConsole** interface preserve that uniqueness. You use the **SetHeader** and **SetToolbar** methods to associate the **IHeaderCtrl2** and **IToolbar** interfaces with the snap-in's instance of **IConsole** and to provide column headers and toolbars associated with the result pane. You can use the **QueryResultView** method to get a pointer to an **IUnknown** interface to the result pane control only if your view is a custom OCX. This is the way to get the pointer to the OCX's **IDispatch** interface, which is documented in the Microsoft Platform SDK.

The **QueryScopeImageList** and **QueryResultImageList** methods allow you to get interface pointers to the image lists that the console provides for inserting icons in the scope and result panes. The **QueryConsoleVerb** method allows the snap-in to incorporate the functionality of standard verbs such as cut, copy, and paste, while the **SelectScopeItem** method is used to programmatically select a scope item in the scope pane. The **UpdateAllViews** method generates a notification to update one or more views because the content has changed. You can obtain a handle to the main frame window by using the **GetMainWindow** method. The remaining **IConsole** method is **MessageBox**, which the snap-in uses to provide information to the user.

The **IConsole2** interface is a newer version of the **IConsole** interface and is introduced in MMC version 1.1. **IConsole2** contains all the methods of **IConsole**, as well as three additional ones. The **Expand** method enables the snap-in to expand or collapse an item in the scope pane. The **IsTaskpadViewPreferred** method determines whether the user prefers taskpad views by default. Finally, the **SetStatusText** method enables the snap-in to change the text in the status bar.

A pointer to the **IConsole2** interface is passed to the snap-in through **IComponent::Initialize** and **IComponentData::Initialize**. Each **IComponent** or **IComponentData** object gets its own private **IConsole2** interface pointer.

When using the **IConsole2** interface for manipulating the result pane and result items, you should use the **IConsole2** interface pointer passed to the snap-in's **IComponent** implementation that owns the view. When using **IConsole2** for manipulating the scope pane and scope items, use the **IConsole2** interface pointer passed to the snap-in's **IComponentData** implementation.

Registering and Unregistering a Snap-in

Snap-ins are implemented as COM in-process server DLLs and must register themselves appropriately in the MMC registry area.

The following list describes all the places in the registry where a snap-in must register itself. Note that *{CLSID}*, *{snapinCLSID}*, and *{nodetypeGUID}* all denote string representations of the specified CLSIDs and GUIDs. The strings must begin with an open brace ({) and end with a close brace (}).

- The CLSID of the snap-in must be registered under the **HKEY_CLASSES_ROOT\CLSID** key in the *{CLSID}* subkey as an in-process server DLL. The snap-in must also register a threading model for its CLSID. The snap-in can specify either ThreadingModel = "Apartment" or ThreadingModel = "Both" for the threading model. Note that snap-in developers who are unsure of the requirements imposed by specifying ThreadingModel = "Both" should specify an apartment threading model.

  For details about the **HKEY_CLASSES_ROOT\CLSID** key, see the "CLSID Key" topic in the Microsoft Platform SDK.

- The CLSID of the snap-in must also be registered under the **HKEY_LOCAL_MACHINE\Software\Microsoft\MMC\SnapIns** key. The **SnapIns** key has the following form:

```
HKEY_LOCAL_MACHINE\Software\Microsoft\MMC\SnapIns\
    {snapinCLSID}
        NameString REG_SZ "SnapinDisplayName"
        About REG_SZ "{SnapinAboutCLSID}"
        StandAlone
        NodeTypes
            {nodetypeGUID}
```

- The *{snapinCLSID}* key specifies the string representation of the snap-in's CLSID. The string must begin with an open brace and end with a close brace.

- The **NameString** named value specifies the name of the snap-in displayed in the **Add/Remove Snap-in** dialog box. If this value is not set, the snap-in appears in the **Add/Remove Snap-in** dialog box with no name.

- The **About** named value specifies the string representation of the CLSID of the cocreatable object that is created using the **CoCreateInstance** COM function to get an interface pointer to **ISnapInAbout**. The string must begin with an open brace and end with a close brace. The **ISnapInAbout** object is created when MMC displays the icon and description for the snap-in in the **Add/Remove Snap-in** dialog box. If your snap-in does not implement **ISnapinAbout** or if the **About** value is not set, no description is displayed and a generic folder icon is displayed in the **Add/Remove Snap-in** dialog box. For details about implementing the **ISnapinAbout** interface, see "Adding About Information" in Chapter 18.

C++ Snap-ins

- The presence of the **StandAlone** key indicates that the snap-in is a stand-alone snap-in. If the snap-in is a stand-alone snap-in, add the **StandAlone** key. The snap-in can then be added to the namespace as a stand-alone snap-in in the **Standalone** tab of the **Add/Remove Snap-in** dialog box. Note that a stand-alone snap-in can also be an extension snap-in (that is, it can extend other snap-ins). If the snap-in is also an extension snap-in, it must be registered for the node types it extends. For details, see "Registration Requirements for Extension Snap-ins" in Chapter 24.

  If the snap-in is an extension snap-in only, do not add the **StandAlone** key. If the **StandAlone** key is not present, the snap-in cannot be added in the **Standalone** tab. An extension snap-in can extend other snap-ins in the **Extensions** tab. As stated in the previous paragraph, the extension snap-in must be registered as an extension for the node type that it extends in order for it to appear as an available extension for a stand-alone snap-in.

- The **NodeTypes** key contains subkeys that represent the snap-in's own node types. Each node type is represented as a subkey that is the GUID of the node type. All node types (that is, all node types for the snap-in specified by {*snapinCLSID*}) that can be extended should be added as subkeys in this key. If the snap-in is stand-alone, the node type for the snap-in's static node can also be added if you want other snap-ins to extend the static node.

  MMC uses the subkeys in this key to find the node types for the snap-in and then uses that list of node types to get the extensions for those node types. That set of extension snap-ins is displayed as available extensions for the snap-in in the **Extensions** tab of the **Add/Remove Snap-in** dialog box.

- The {*nodetypeGUID*} named value specifies the string representation of the GUID of the node type. The string must begin with an open brace and end with a close brace.

  In addition, all extension snap-ins for a particular node type must be registered under the **HKEY_LOCAL_MACHINE\Software\Microsoft\MMC\NodeTypes**{*node typeGUID}* key. For details, see "Registration Requirements for Extension Snap-ins" in Chapter 24.

For general information about the registry, see "Registry" and related sections in the Platform SDK.

Sample Code

All snap-ins must implement the following COM API functions:

- DllRegisterServer
- DllUnregisterServer
- DllGetClassObject
- DllCanUnloadNow

In addition, snap-ins must implement the **IClassFactory** interface.

This section contains code samples for the **DllRegisterServer** and **DllGetClassObject** functions, and an example of the **IClassFactory::CreateInstance** method. Note that unregistration and unloading code is omitted in this section. For a complete discussion of the four functions listed above and the **IClassFactory** interface, see "COM Server Responsibilities" and related sections in the Platform SDK.

The code samples are taken from the Extens sample that accompanies the MMC SDK. The Extens sample is discussed here because it also contains code for registering extendable node types.

C++ Snap-ins

DllRegisterServer Implementation

```
STDAPI DllRegisterServer()
{
  HRESULT hr = SELFREG_E_CLASS;
  _TCHAR szName[256];
  _TCHAR szSnapInName[256];

  LoadString(g_hinst, IDS_NAME, szName,
              sizeof(szName)/sizeof(szName[0]));
  LoadString(g_hinst, IDS_SNAPINNAME, szSnapInName,
              sizeof(szSnapInName)/sizeof(szSnapInName[0]));

  _TCHAR szAboutName[256];

  LoadString(g_hinst, IDS_ABOUTNAME, szAboutName,
              sizeof(szAboutName)/sizeof(szAboutName[0]));

  // register our CoClasses
  hr = RegisterServer(g_hinst, CLSID_CComponentData, szName);

  if SUCCEEDED(hr)
      hr = RegisterServer(g_hinst,
      CLSID_CSnapinAbout,
      szAboutName);

  // place the registry information for SnapIns
  if SUCCEEDED(hr)
      hr = RegisterSnapin(CLSID_CComponentData, szSnapInName,
                          CLSID_CSnapinAbout);

  return hr;
}
```

IDS_NAME, IDS_SNAPINNAME, and IDS_ABOUTNAME are resource identifiers that specify the human-readable names that appear with the entries in the registry.

The **DllRegisterServer** function registers two coclasses, **CLSID_CComponentData** and **CLSID_CSnapinAbout**. The **CLSID_CComponentData** coclass exposes the snap-in's **IComponentData** interface. The **CLSID_CSnapinAbout** coclass exposes the snap-in's **ISnapinAbout** interface. Both coclasses are registered in the **RegisterServer** function, which creates entries under the **HKEY_CLASSES_ROOT\CLSID** key for both of them.

```
HRESULT RegisterServer(HMODULE hModule, // DLL module handle
                       const CLSID& clsid,  // Class ID
                       const _TCHAR* szFriendlyName)  // IDs
{
  // Get server location.
  _TCHAR szModule[512] ;
  DWORD dwResult =
      ::GetModuleFileName(hModule,
      szModule,
      sizeof(szModule)/sizeof(_TCHAR)) ;

  assert(dwResult != 0) ;

  // Get CLSID
  LPOLESTR wszCLSID = NULL ;
  HRESULT hr = StringFromCLSID(clsid, &wszCLSID) ;

  assert(SUCCEEDED(hr)) ;

  MAKE_TSTRPTR_FROMWIDE(pszCLSID, wszCLSID);

  // Build the key CLSID\\{...}
  _TCHAR szKey[64];
  _tcscpy(szKey, _T("CLSID\\"));
  _tcscat(szKey, pszCLSID);

  // Add the CLSID to the registry.
  setKeyAndValue(szKey, NULL, szFriendlyName);

  // Add the server filename subkey under the CLSID key.
  setKeyAndValue(szKey, _T("InprocServer32"), szModule);

  // set the threading model
  _tcscat(szKey, _T("\\InprocServer32"));
  setValue(szKey, _T("ThreadingModel"), _T("Apartment"));

  // Free memory.
  CoTaskMemFree(wszCLSID);

  return S_OK;
}
```

The **setKeyAndValue** function is a helper function that sets the given key and its value. The **setValue** helper function sets the value of the given named value. Notice that the **RegisterServer** function sets the apartment threading model for the snap-in cocreatable class object that it registers. As previously stated, all snap-ins must register a threading model.

After **RegisterServer** returns, **DllRegisterServer** calls the **RegisterSnapin** function, which creates entries under the **HKEY_LOCAL_MACHINE\Software\Microsoft\MMC\SnapIns** key.

```
HRESULT RegisterSnapin(const CLSID& clsid, // Class ID
      const _TCHAR* szNameString,  // NameString
      const CLSID& clsidAbout)      // Class Id for About class

{
  // Get CLSID
  LPOLESTR wszCLSID = NULL ;
  LPOLESTR wszAboutCLSID = NULL;
  LPOLESTR wszExtendCLSID = NULL;
  NODESTRUCT *pNode;

  HRESULT hr = StringFromCLSID(clsid, &wszCLSID);

  if (IID_NULL != clsidAbout)
      hr = StringFromCLSID(clsidAbout, &wszAboutCLSID);

  MAKE_TSTRPTR_FROMWIDE(pszCLSID, wszCLSID);
  MAKE_TSTRPTR_FROMWIDE(pszAboutCLSID, wszAboutCLSID);

  // Add the CLSID to the registry.
  setSnapInKeyAndValue(pszCLSID, NULL, _T("NameString"),
                      szNameString) ;
  setSnapInKeyAndValue(pszCLSID, _T("StandAlone"), NULL, NULL);
  if (IID_NULL != clsidAbout)
      setSnapInKeyAndValue(pszCLSID, NULL, _T("About"),
                          pszAboutCLSID);

  // register the node types in g_Nodes as extendable nodes
  for (pNode = &(g_Nodes[0]);*pNode->szDescription;pNode++)
  {
      hr = StringFromCLSID(pNode->GUID, &wszExtendCLSID);
      MAKE_TSTRPTR_FROMWIDE(pszExtendCLSID, wszExtendCLSID);
      setSnapInExtensionNode(pszCLSID, pszExtendCLSID, pNode->
                            szDescription);
      CoTaskMemFree(wszExtendCLSID);
  }

  // Free memory.
  CoTaskMemFree(wszCLSID) ;
  if (IID_NULL != clsidAbout)
      CoTaskMemFree(wszAboutCLSID);

  return S_OK ;
}
```

The **RegisterSnapin** function uses the **setSnapInKeyAndValue** helper function to register the *{snapinCLSID}* key under the **HKEY_LOCAL_MACHINE\Software\Microsoft\MMC\SnapIns** key and to add subkeys and named values under the *{snapinCLSID}* key. Notice that the snap-in also registers its extendable node types. The **RegisterSnapin** function uses the **setSnapInExtensionNode** helper function to register the CLSIDs of its extendable node types under the **HKEY_LOCAL_MACHINE\Software\Microsoft\MMC\SnapIns***{snapinCLS ID}***\NodeTypes** subkey. The snap-in specifies the list of extendable node types in the **g_Nodes** array, which is an array of **NODESTRUCT** structures. Each element of the array specifies a different extendable node type's GUID and a description of the node type.

```
NODESTRUCT g_Nodes[] =
{
  { 0x2974380d, 0x4c4b, 0x11d2, { 0x89, 0xd8, 0x0, 0x0, 0x21, 0x47,
    0x31, 0x28 }, _T("People-powered Vehicles Node")},
  { 0x29743811, 0x4c4b, 0x11d2, { 0x89, 0xd8, 0x0, 0x0, 0x21, 0x47,
    0x31, 0x28 }, _T("Rocket Node")},
  { 0x2974380f, 0x4c4b, 0x11d2, { 0x89, 0xd8, 0x0, 0x0, 0x21, 0x47,
    0x31, 0x28 }, _T("Sky-based Vehicle Node")},
  {NULL, NULL}
};

struct NODESTRUCT
{
  GUID    GUID;
  _TCHAR  szDescription[256];
};
```

After the **DllRegisterServer** function returns, the Extens sample contains registry information under three different keys. Two of the keys are created for the snap-in coclass that exposes the **IComponentData** interface, and the third key is created for the snap-in coclass that exposes the **ISnapinAbout** interface.

C++ Snap-ins

Here are the registry entries for the snap-in coclass that exposes the
IComponentData interface:

```
HKEY_CLASSES_ROOT\CLSID\
  {AEA15790-A656-11D2-992F-000000000000}\
    InprocServer32 = REG_SZ  "<path to 32-bit inproc server>"
    ThreadingModel = REG_SZ "Apartment"

HKEY_LOCAL_MACHINE\SOFTWARE\Microsoft\MMC\SnapIns\
  {AEA15790-A656-11D2-992F-000000000000}\
    About = REG_SZ  "{AEA15792-A656-11D2-992F-000000000000}"
    NameString = REG_SZ "Sample D1 - Extendable Snapin"
    About = REG_SZ  "{AEA15792-A656-11D2-992F-000000000000}"
    NameString = REG_SZ "Sample D1 - Extendable Snapin"
    NodeTypes\
      {2974380D-4C4B-11D2-89D8-000021473128}\
        (Default) = REG_SZ "People-powered Vehicles Node"
      {29743811-4C4B-11D2-89D8-000021473128}\
        (Default) = REG_SZ "Rocket Node"
      {2974380F-4C4B-11d2-89D8-000021473128}\
        (Default) = REG_SZ "Sky-based Vehicle Node"
```

Here is the registry entry for the snap-in coclass that exposes the **ISnapinAbout**
interface:

```
HKEY_CLASSES_ROOT\CLSID\
  {AEA15792-A656-11D2-992F-000000000000
    InprocServer32 = REG_SZ  "<path to 32-bit inproc server>"
    ThreadingModel = REG_SZ "Apartment"
```

DllGetClassObject Implementation

The DllGetClassObject exported function is called by COM when MMC attempts to cocreate the class object referred to by CLSID_CComponentData and CLSID_CSnapinAbout. MMC gets the CLSID of this class object from the value specified under the HKEY_LOCAL_MACHINE\SOFTWARE\Microsoft\MMC\SnapIns\{*snapinCLSID*} subkey.

```
STDAPI DllGetClassObject(REFCLSID rclsid, REFIID riid,
                         LPVOID *ppvObj)
{
  if ((rclsid != CLSID_CComponentData) &&
      (rclsid != CLSID_CSnapinAbout))
      return CLASS_E_CLASSNOTAVAILABLE;

  if (!ppvObj)
      return E_FAIL;

  *ppvObj = NULL;

  // We can only hand out IUnknown and IClassFactory pointers.
  // Fail if they ask for anything else.
  if (!IsEqualIID(riid, IID_IUnknown) &&
      !IsEqualIID(riid, IID_IClassFactory))
      return E_NOINTERFACE;

  CClassFactory *pFactory = NULL;

  // make the factory passing in the creation function for
  // the type of object they want
  if (rclsid == CLSID_CComponentData)
      pFactory = new CClassFactory(CClassFactory::COMPONENT);
  else if (rclsid == CLSID_CSnapinAbout)
      pFactory = new CClassFactory(CClassFactory::ABOUT);

  if (NULL == pFactory)
      return E_OUTOFMEMORY;

  HRESULT hr = pFactory->QueryInterface(riid, ppvObj);

  return hr;
}
```

COMPONENT and ABOUT are values taken from the **FACTORY_TYPE** enumeration type defined by the snap-in:

```
enum FACTORY_TYPE {COMPONENT = 0, ABOUT = 1};
```

Depending on the class object being cocreated, the extension snap-in initializes the **m_factoryType** member variable of the **CClassFactory** object created in **DllGetClassObject** accordingly.

This value then determines the type of interface returned by the snap-in to MMC in the call to the snap-in's **IClassFactory::CreateInstance** implementation:

```
STDMETHODIMP CClassFactory::CreateInstance(LPUNKNOWN pUnkOuter,
                                REFIID riid, LPVOID * ppvObj)
{
  HRESULT  hr;
  void* pObj;

  if (!ppvObj)
      return E_FAIL;

  *ppvObj = NULL;

  // Our object does does not support aggregation, so we need to
  // fail if they ask us to do aggregation.
  if (pUnkOuter)
  return CLASS_E_NOAGGREGATION;

  if (COMPONENT == m_factoryType) {
      pObj = new CComponentData();
  } else {
      pObj = new CSnapinAbout();
  }

  if (!pObj)
      return E_OUTOFMEMORY;

  // QueryInterface will do the AddRef() for us, so we do not
  // do it in this function
  hr = ((LPUNKNOWN)pObj)->QueryInterface(riid, ppvObj);

  if (FAILED(hr))
      delete pObj;

  return hr;
}
```

C H A P T E R   1 8

Adding About Information and HTML Help Support

This section covers the following topics:

- Adding About Information
- Adding HTML Help Support

Adding About Information

The standard method for providing version and provider information within most applications that run on Windows platforms is the **About** menu selection item. MMC supports snap-in applications in providing this type of information. The information is displayed on a property page and is made available by using the **ISnapinAbout** interface.

A snap-in's About information is only displayed in the **Add/Remove Snap-in** dialog box. Note that this information is *not* available to the user of a console file. Only the authors of saved console files can access the snap-in's About information.

MMC also calls the snap-in's **ISnapinAbout** implementation to obtain custom folder images for the snap-in's static node. If a snap-in does not implement **ISnapinAbout**, MMC uses default folder images instead. Note that snap-ins can also programmatically specify the static node's folder images when the static node is selected and the snap-in receives an MMCN_EXPAND notification message. However, implementing **ISnapinAbout** is the recommended method for specifying the static folder images.

Methods belonging to **ISnapinAbout** include **GetSnapinDescription**, which provides text for the snap-in's description box. **GetProvider** handles the name of the provider, and **GetSnapinVersion** obtains the snap-in's version number. **GetSnapinImage** gets the main icon for the **About** property page, and **GetStaticFolderImage** gets the static folder images for the scope and result panes.

C++ Snap-ins

▶ **To add About information**

In the following, note that *{CLSID}* and *{snapinCLSID}* denote string representations of the specified CLSIDs. The strings must begin with an open brace ({) and end with a close brace (}).

1. Implement the **ISnapinAbout** interface in the snap-in.

2. Use a cocreatable COM object other than the snap-in's primary object (the one that exposes the snap-in's **IComponentData** interface) to expose the **ISnapinAbout** interface. This is so that, for performance reasons, MMC does not need to cocreate the entire snap-in to access its About information.

3. Register the CLSID of this cocreatable object under the **HKEY_CLASSES_ROOT\CLSID** key in the *{CLSID}* subkey as an in-process server DLL. Also register an apartment threading model for the cocreatable object. This allows the snap-in's **ISnapinAbout** interface to be marshaled by COM to MMC.

   For details about the **HKEY_CLASSES_ROOT\CLSID** key, see "CLSID Key" in the Microsoft Platform SDK. For example code, see "Registering and Unregistering a Snap-in" in Chapter 17.

4. Also register the CLSID of the cocreatable object under the **HKEY_LOCAL_MACHINE\Software\Microsoft\MMC\SnapIns***{snapinCLSID}* key. Note that the *{snapinCLSID}* key is the string representation of the snap-in's CLSID. In the **About** named value of the *{snapinCLSID}* key, specify the string representation of the CLSID of the cocreatable object. For details about the **SnapIns** key, see "Registering and Unregistering a Snap-in" in Chapter 17.

Sample Code

The following code samples show implementations of the **ISnapinAbout** interface methods. All samples are taken from the About sample snap-in that accompanies the MMC SDK. The About sample demonstrates how to add About information to a snap-in.

Note that all sample code assumes Unicode compilation.

GetSnapinDescription Implementation

```
STDMETHODIMP CSnapinAbout::GetSnapinDescription(
                    /* [out] */ LPOLESTR *lpDescription)
{
  _TCHAR szDesc[MAX_PATH];

  LoadString(g_hinst, IDS_SNAPINDESC, szDesc,
            sizeof(szDesc)/sizeof(szDesc[0]));

  return AllocOleStr(lpDescription, szDesc);
}
```

In the sample, **CSnapinAbout** is an instance of the **ISnapinAbout** interface. IDS_SNAPINDESC is a resource ID that specifies the description string.

GetProvider and GetSnapinVersion Implementations

```
STDMETHODIMP CSnapinAbout::GetProvider(
                    /* [out] */ LPOLESTR *lpName)
{
  return AllocOleStr(lpName, _T("Copyright © 1998 Microsoft
                    Corporation"));;
}

STDMETHODIMP CSnapinAbout::GetSnapinVersion(
                    /* [out] */ LPOLESTR *lpVersion)
{
  return AllocOleStr(lpVersion, _T("1.0"));;
}
```

AllocOleStr is a snap-in-defined method that allocates memory using the Win32 API function **CoTaskMemAlloc** and copies the specified string into it.

C++ Snap-ins

GetSnapinImage and GetStaticFolderImage Implementations

MMC calls the snap-in's **ISnapinAbout::GetSnapinImage** method to get the snap-in's icon for the **Add/Remove Snap-in** dialog box. MMC calls the **ISnapinAbout::GetStaticFolderImage** method to obtain the folder images for the snap-in's static node. MMC uses default static folder images and icons for snap-ins that do not implement **ISnapinAbout**.

```
STDMETHODIMP CSnapinAbout::GetSnapinImage(
                        /* [out] */ HICON *hAppIcon)
{
  *hAppIcon = m_hAppIcon;

  if (*hAppIcon == NULL)
      return E_FAIL;
  else
      return S_OK;
}


STDMETHODIMP CSnapinAbout::GetStaticFolderImage(
                        /* [out] */ HBITMAP *hSmallImage,
                        /* [out] */ HBITMAP *hSmallImageOpen,
                        /* [out] */ HBITMAP *hLargeImage,
                        /* [out] */ COLORREF *cMask)
{
  *hSmallImage = m_hSmallImage;
  *hLargeImage = m_hLargeImage;

  *hSmallImageOpen = m_hSmallImageOpen;

  *cMask = RGB(0, 128, 128);

  if (*hSmallImage == NULL || *hLargeImage == NULL ||
      *hSmallImageOpen == NULL)
      return E_FAIL;
  else
      return S_OK;
}
```

The About information icon and bitmaps are created from the snap-in's icon resources in the constructor for **CSnapinAbout**.

```
CSnapinAbout::CSnapinAbout()
: m_cref(0)
{
  OBJECT_CREATED

  m_hSmallImage =      (HBITMAP)LoadImage(g_hinst,
                       MAKEINTRESOURCE(IDB_SMBMP),
                       IMAGE_BITMAP, 16,
                       16, LR_LOADTRANSPARENT);

  m_hLargeImage =      (HBITMAP)LoadImage(g_hinst,
                       MAKEINTRESOURCE(IDB_LGBMP),
                       IMAGE_BITMAP, 32,
                       32, LR_LOADTRANSPARENT);

  m_hSmallImageOpen = (HBITMAP)LoadImage(g_hinst,
                       MAKEINTRESOURCE(IDB_SMOPEN),
                       IMAGE_BITMAP, 16,
                       16, LR_LOADTRANSPARENT);

  m_hAppIcon = LoadIcon(g_hinst, MAKEINTRESOURCE(IDI_ICON1));
}
```

OBJECT_CREATED is a snap-in-defined macro that increments the **CSnapinAbout** object's reference count.

Note that MMC does not require the snap-in to specify the icon's color mask in **GetSnapinImage**. For bitmaps, MMC requires a specific background color so it can generate a transparency mask. Icons, however, have built-in transparency so MMC does not require a specific background color.

Also, MMC makes copies of the returned icon and bitmaps. The snap-in can free the originals when the **ISnapinAbout** interface is released.

Adding HTML Help Support

This feature is introduced in MMC 1.1.

MMC uses HTML Help as its Help system. For each console file (.msc), snap-ins can provide their own compiled HTML Help files (.chm) that MMC combines into a single HTML Help collection file. A collection file is unique to each console file because different console files usually contain different snap-ins and, therefore, require different sets of Help files depending on the snap-ins that have been added.

This means that there is a single table of contents, index, and search engine containing the HTML Help topics for all snap-ins that have been added to the console file. When a user clicks **Help Topics** on the main console window's **Help** menu, MMC opens the merged HTML Help collection file that includes HTML Help files for all snap-ins in the current console file.

Note that for MMC to merge a snap-in's compiled HTML file into a collection file, the snap-in's file must be compiled with a binary table of contents (TOC). If using HTML Help Workshop, set the **Create a binary TOC** option to compile the file with a binary TOC.

For information about HTML Help authoring, see http://msdn.microsoft.com/workshop/c-frame.htm#/workshop/author/htmlhelp/.

MMC provides a number of interfaces and other language constructs for adding HTML Help support to snap-ins. MMC uses a snap-in's implementation of the **ISnapinHelp2** interface to request the name and location of the snap-in's compiled HTML Help file. The **GetHelpTopic** method enables the snap-in to add its compiled HTML Help file to the MMC Help collection file. The **GetLinkedTopics** method allows the snap-in to specify the names and locations of any HTML Help files that are linked to the snap-in's Help file (specified in the **GetHelpTopic** method).

The **IDisplayHelp** interface allows a snap-in to display a specific HTML Help topic within the collection file. By using the **ShowTopic** method (or the **MMCPropertyHelp** function in property pages), a snap-in can open any topic in any HTML Help file within the collection file. The snap-in must specify the compiled HTML Help file name and the topic file name. Note that **MMCPropertyHelp** should be used in property pages, which usually execute in a different thread than the snap-in.

The MMCN_CONTEXTHELP notification message is sent when the user requests Help about a selected item by pressing the F1 key or clicking the **Help** button. A snap-in responds to MMCN_CONTEXTHELP and displays a Help topic for the particular context by calling the **IDisplayHelp::ShowTopic** method, or by calling **MMCPropertyHelp** in the case of property pages.

The user can invoke Help in the following ways:

- Clicking **Help Topics** on the **Help** menu
- Pressing F1 or right-clicking the **Help** button for context-sensitive Help
- Clicking the **Help** button in a property page owned by the snap-in

When Help is invoked, MMC opens the single Help collection file (.col) that it builds and maintains for the current console file. MMC then calls the **IComponentData::QueryInterface** implementation of the owner of the item that is currently selected in the console (scope or result item) to query for the **ISnapinHelp2** interface.

ISnapinHelp2 is implemented by the snap-in's primary object, which is the object instantiated from the snap-in's CLSID when the snap-in is loaded. For primary snap-ins and namespace extensions, this will be the same object that implements the **IComponentData** interface.

When MMC requires the **ISnapinHelp2** interface, it creates a new instance of the snap-in's primary object and queries it for the interface. This instance of the primary object is only used for **ISnapinHelp2**; MMC releases the instance when it no longer needs the interface.

Snap-in authors should make sure that their snap-in's primary object can function properly in this scenario. For primary snap-ins or namespace extensions, a common error is for the primary object to free resources in its destructor that were acquired in calls to their **IComponentData::Initialize** implementation. Those resources should instead be freed in the **IComponentData::Destroy** method.

If the snap-in (either primary or extension) returns an **ISnapinHelp2** interface pointer, MMC knows that the snap-in provides the location of its HTML Help file. That is, it implements the **ISnapinHelp2::GetHelpTopic** method.

If the query fails for any reason, MMC places a "Help on <your snap-in name>" item on the **Help** menu. If the user clicks this menu item, MMC sends the MMCN_SNAPINHELP notification to the snap-in's **IComponent** implementation. The snap-in should respond by displaying whatever Help information it has.

MMC's support for the MMCN_SNAPINHELP notification predates its support for the **ISnapinHelp** interface. Before **ISnapinHelp**, each snap-in had to provide its own Help system and the MMCN_SNAPINHELP notification told it when to display the Help. Snap-ins are now strongly encouraged to support the **ISnapinHelp** (or **ISnapinHelp2**) interface for displaying Help topics (in HTML Help format).

C++ Snap-ins

If a snap-in provides an HTML Help file and MMC hasn't already called the snap-in's **ISnapinHelp2::GetHelpTopic** method to request the name and location of the file, it calls the method. It then adds the HTML Help file to the collection file.

MMC caches the name and location of each HTML Help file and stores this information in the collection file. MMC deletes the collection file whenever the console file is closed and rebuilds it the first time a user requests Help after opening a console file. After the collection file is built MMC continues to use it until the user adds or removes a snap-in, turns an extension on or off, or closes the console file.

When building the collection file MMC gets HTML Help files from all snap-in types that have been added to the console plus all of their static extensions that have been enabled by the user and all of their extensions that can only be enabled dynamically.

Note that dynamic extensions will always have their HTML Help files added to the collection file, regardless of whether they are instantiated in a console file. Because a snap-in can enable a dynamic extension at any time, MMC does not wait for a dynamic extension to be loaded before including its HTML Help file in the collection file.

To rebuild the collection file, MMC first queries for the **ISnapinHelp2** interface of each snap-in and extension in the set. It then calls the **ISnapinHelp2::GetHelpTopic** method of each snap-in that provides an HTML Help file. Finally, MMC merges all the HTML Help files into the collection file for the console.

Adding HTML Help Support: Interfaces

HTML Help requires the implementation or use of the following interfaces and methods:

- **ISnapinHelp2**

  ISnapinHelp2::GetHelpTopic

  ISnapinHelp2::GetLinkedTopics
- **IDisplayHelp**

  IDisplayHelp::ShowTopic

Other Constructs

MMC sends the following notification in response to the user's request for context-sensitive (F1) Help:

- MMCN_CONTEXTHELP

The following function enables you to call an HTML Help topic from a property sheet:

- **MMCPropertyHelp**

MMC sends the following notification in response to the user's request for Help to snap-ins that do not provide HTML Help by implementing **ISnapinHelp2**:

- MMCN_SNAPINHELP

Note that snap-ins are strongly encouraged to provide HTML Help.

C++ Snap-ins

Adding HTML Help Support: Implementation Details

▶   **To add HTML Help support**

1. Implement the **ISnapinHelp2** interface. Note that the snap-in's primary object, the one registered with the snap-in's class ID (CLSID), should expose this interface.

   In the snap-in's implementation of the **GetHelpTopic** method, specify the address of the null-terminated Unicode string that contains the path of the compiled Help file (.chm) for the snap-in.

   Note that for MMC to merge a snap-in's HTML Help file into the HTML Help collection file for the current console, the Help file must be compiled with the **Create a binary TOC** check box selected. This creates a binary contents file for the Help file.

2. If the snap-in's HTML Help file links to other Help files, implement the **ISnapinHelp2::GetLinkedTopics** method to specify the names and locations of these files.

3. Handle the MMCN_CONTEXTHELP notification, which is sent when the user requests Help about a selected item by pressing the F1 key or clicking the **Help** button. In the notification handler for MMCN_CONTEXTHELP, call the **IDisplayHelp::ShowTopic** method to display the Help topic for the particular context. For Help topics displayed for property pages, call **MMCPropertyHelp** instead.

Sample Code

The code shows sample implementations of the **ISnapinHelp2::GetHelpTopic** method and the notification handler for the MMCN_CONTEXTHELP notification message. All sample implementations are taken from the Help sample snap-in that accompanies the MMC SDK.

Note that all sample code assumes Unicode compilation.

ISnapinHelp2::GetHelpTopic Implementation

The **ISnapinHelp2** interface is implemented by the snap-in's **IComponentData** implementation.

```
HRESULT CComponentData::GetHelpTopic(
                    /* [out] */ LPOLESTR *lpCompiledHelpFile)
{
  *lpCompiledHelpFile = static_cast<LPOLESTR>(CoTaskMemAlloc(
                    (_tcslen(m_HelpFile) + 1) * sizeof(_TCHAR)));

  _tcscpy(*lpCompiledHelpFile, m_HelpFile);

  return S_OK;
}
```

The **CComponentData** object's member variable **m_HelpFile** specifies the HTML Help file for the snap-in. The variable is set in the object's constructor:

```
CComponentData::CComponentData()
: m_cref(0), m_ipConsoleNameSpace(NULL), m_ipConsole(NULL)
{
  OBJECT_CREATED

  m_pStaticNode = new CStaticNode;

  GetWindowsDirectory(m_HelpFile, sizeof(m_HelpFile));

  _tcscat(m_HelpFile, _T("\\HELP\\"));

  LoadString(g_hinst, IDS_HELPFILE,
          &m_HelpFile[_tcslen(m_HelpFile)],
          MAX_PATH - _tcslen(m_HelpFile));
}
```

IDS_HELPFILE is the local string resource that specifies the name of the HTML Help file. As you can see in the constructor, the Help file is located in the HELP subdirectory of the Windows directory. This is the standard Windows Help directory (%winnt%\help).

MMCN_CONTEXTHELP Notification Handler Implementation

The **CStaticNode::OnShowContextHelp** method handles MMCN_CONTEXTHELP in the Help sample. **CStaticNode** is the snap-in object representing the sample snap-in's static node.

```
HRESULT CStaticNode::OnShowContextHelp(IDisplayHelp *pDisplayHelp,
                                       LPOLESTR helpFile)
{
  _TCHAR topicName[MAX_PATH];

  _tcscpy(topicName, helpFile);

  // we should read this from a resource file
  _tcscat(topicName, _T("::/default.htm"));

  LPOLESTR pszTopic = static_cast<LPOLESTR>(CoTaskMemAlloc(
                          (_tcslen(topicName) + 1) * sizeof(_TCHAR)));

  _tcscpy(pszTopic, topicName);

  return pDisplayHelp->ShowTopic(pszTopic);
}
```

The **IDisplayHelp** interface allows the snap-in to display a specific HTML Help topic within MMC's collection file for the current console file. The snap-in obtains a pointer to this interface by calling **QueryInterface** on the **IConsole2** interface.

C H A P T E R   1 9

Working with the Scope Pane

This section discusses how the features associated with a snap-in's scope pane are implemented.

MMC defines several interfaces and other language constructs that a snap-in can use to work with the scope pane.

The **IConsoleNamespace2** interface enables snap-ins to manipulate items in the scope pane. **InsertItem** and **DeleteItem** insert or remove single items from the scope pane. You can set or retrieve single items by using the **SetItem** and **GetItem** methods. **GetChildItem**, **GetNextItem**, and **GetParentItem** walk the tree's items. The **Expand** method allows a snap-in to expand an item in the namespace without visibly expanding the item in the scope pane. Finally, **AddExtension** allows a snap-in to add an extension snap-in that dynamically extends the namespace of a selected item.

The **IConsole2** interface also contains a number of methods that snap-ins can use for working with scope items. The **Expand** method enables a snap-in to expand or collapse an item in the scope pane. The **SelectScopeItem** method allows a snap-in to force the selection of a specified item, and the **NewWindow** method allows the snap-in to programmatically create a new multiple-document interface (MDI) child window rooted at the specified item.

When the user selects a snap-in's scope item in the scope pane for the first time, the snap-in receives an MMCN_EXPAND notification. If the selected item has any child items, the snap-in responds to the notification by inserting the child items. The **SCOPEDATAITEM** structure is used for specifying each item's information, such as the snap-in object that corresponds to the item, whether the item also has child items to insert, and where the item should be inserted relative to its parent item.

After filling the **SCOPEDATAITEM** structure for each child item of the selected item, the snap-in inserts the items into the scope pane using the **IConsoleNamespace2::InsertItem** method. When **InsertItem** returns (with S_OK), the **ID** member of the **SCOPEDATAITEM** structure contains the HSCOPEITEM of the newly inserted item. MMC uses an item's HSCOPEITEM to uniquely identify the item.

MMC calls the snap-in's **IComponentData::GetDisplayInfo** method if it requires information to display a specific item in the scope pane; for example, a snap-in does not explicitly specify the display name of items (when filling the **SCOPEDATAITEM** structure) before inserting them in the scope pane. MMC then must rely on the snap-in to provide this information during calls to its **GetDisplayInfo** method.

On certain occasions, MMC may send the snap-in an MMCN_EXPANDSYNC notification to inform it that a specific scope item needs to be expanded synchronously; for example, when a console file is reloaded with an item expanded, the snap-in receives the notification so that it can insert any child items of the expanded item.

Note that MMC gives namespace extensions the opportunity to insert their own child items to scope items inserted by a primary snap-in. For details, see "Extending a Primary Snap-in's Namespace" in Chapter 24.

Working with the Scope Pane: Interfaces

The MMC SDK specifies several interfaces and other language constructs for working with the scope pane. The following interfaces and methods are available for working with scope items:

- **IComponentData**

    GetDisplayInfo
- **IConsoleNamespace2**

    InsertItem

    DeleteItem

    SetItem

    GetItem

    GetChildItem

    GetNextItem

    GetParentItem

    Expand

    AddExtension
- **IConsole2**

    Expand

    SelectScopeItem

    NewWindow

Other Constructs

The following notifications are available for working with scope items:

- MMCN_EXPAND
- MMCN_EXPANDSYNC
- MMCN_PRELOAD
- MMCN_REMOVE_CHILDREN

The following structures are available for working with scope items:

- **SCOPEDATAITEM**
- **MMC_EXPANDSYNC_STRUCT**

C++ Snap-ins

Working with the Scope Pane: Implementation Details

The following procedure applies to primary snap-ins that insert their own items into the scope pane. For details about how extension snap-ins can add items to the scope pane of a primary snap-in, see "Extending a Primary Snap-in's Namespace" in Chapter 24.

▶ **To insert items in the scope pane**

1. Determine the tree structure of the snap-in's scope pane; that is, how many child items the snap-in's root node (the static node) inserts, and whether these items have child items. Associate a snap-in object with each item in the scope pane, and determine a method for instantiating these objects. For an example of this, see the Nodes sample that accompanies the MMC SDK.

   Also, determine the node type GUID for each item in the scope pane. You can use the uuidgen.exe tool for generating GUIDs. To see how node type GUIDs are used in the Nodes sample, see "Setting the Node Type of a Scope or Result Item" in Chapter 31.

   For general information about nodes, see "Snap-in Namespace" in Chapter 16.

2. Handle the MMCN_EXPAND notification message, which MMC sends to the snap-in's **IComponentData** implementation when a scope item is selected for the first time in the scope pane. In response to the notification, the snap-in should do the following:

   - If the selected item has child items, the snap-in must fill a **SCOPEDATAITEM** structure for each child item and then insert the item in the scope pane by calling the **IConsoleNamespace2::InsertItem** method with a pointer to the address of the **SCOPEDATAITEM** structure. When **InsertItem** returns (with S_OK), the **ID** member of the **SCOPEDATAITEM** structure contains the HSCOPEITEM of the newly inserted item. Snap-ins should store the HSCOPEITEM of each inserted item and use it to later manipulate the item using the methods of the **IConsole2** and **IConsoleNameSpace2** interfaces.

Note that when filling a **SCOPEDATAITEM** structure for a child item, the snap-in can also specify whether that child item has child items of its own. If it does not have any child items, the snap-in should set the **cChildren** member of the structure to 0. This instructs MMC to hide the plus (+) sign when inserting the child item. If conditions change and the inserted child item has child items at a later time, the snap-in can modify the **cChildren** member by using **IConsoleNameSpace2::SetItem**.

- If the selected item does not have any child items, the snap-in must return S_FALSE.

3. Implement the **IComponentData::GetDisplayInfo** method. When inserting a scope item or a result item into MMC, the display name *must* be set to MMC_CALLBACK. After the snap-in returns from the MMCN_EXPAND notification handler, MMC calls **GetDisplayInfo** once for each inserted item in the scope pane (for which **SCOPEDATAITEM.displayname** = MMC_CALLBACK) to request the item's display name.

4. If necessary, handle the MMCN_EXPANDSYNC notification.

Sample Code

The following code shows sample implementations of a notification handler for the MMCN_EXPAND notification message and the **IComponentData::GetDisplayInfo** method. All sample implementations are taken from the Nodes sample snap-in that accompanies the MMC SDK.

Note that all sample code assumes Unicode compilation.

MMCN_EXPAND Notification Handler Implementation

The following method handles the MMCN_EXPAND notification message sent by MMC to the **IComponentData** interface in the Nodes sample snap-in when the "Future Vehicles" scope item is selected.

C++ Snap-ins

In the sample, **CComponentData** implements the **IComponentData** interface. The **CComponentData::Notify** method delegates the handling of the MMCN_EXPAND notification message to the snap-in object that represents the selected item. In the case of the "People-powered Vehicles" item, the notification message is handled by the snap-in's **CPeoplePoweredVehicle::OnExpand** method:

```
HRESULT CPeoplePoweredVehicle::OnExpand(
                            IConsoleNameSpace *pConsoleNameSpace,
                            IConsole *pConsole, HSCOPEITEM parent)
{
  SCOPEDATAITEM sdi;

  if (!bExpanded) {
      // create the child nodes, then expand them
      for (int n = 0; n < NUMBER_OF_CHILDREN; n++) {
          ZeroMemory(&sdi, sizeof(SCOPEDATAITEM) );
          sdi.mask = SDI_STR    |   // Displayname is valid
              SDI_PARAM         |   // lParam is valid
              SDI_IMAGE         |   // nImage is valid
              SDI_OPENIMAGE     |   // nOpenImage is valid
              SDI_PARENT        |   // relativeID is valid
              SDI_CHILDREN;         // cChildren is valid

          sdi.relativeID  = (HSCOPEITEM)parent;
          sdi.nImage      = children[n]->GetBitmapIndex();
          sdi.nOpenImage  = INDEX_OPENFOLDER;
          sdi.displayname = MMC_CALLBACK;
          sdi.lParam      = (LPARAM)children[n]; // The cookie
          sdi.cChildren   = 0;

          HRESULT hr = pConsoleNameSpace->InsertItem( &sdi );

          _ASSERT( SUCCEEDED(hr) );
      }
  }

  return S_OK;
}
```

IComponentData::GetDisplayInfo Implementation

```
HRESULT CComponentData::GetDisplayInfo( /* [out][in] */
                          SCOPEDATAITEM *pScopeDataItem)
{
  HRESULT hr = S_FALSE;

  // if they are asking for the SDI_STR we have one of those to give
  if (pScopeDataItem->lParam)
  {
      CDelegationBase *base = (CDelegationBase *)pScopeDataItem->
                              lParam;
      if (pScopeDataItem->mask & SDI_STR)
      {
          pScopeDataItem->displayname = const_cast<_TCHAR *>(base->
                                      GetDisplayName());
      }
      if (pScopeDataItem->mask & SDI_IMAGE)
      {
          pScopeDataItem->nImage = base->GetBitmapIndex();
      }
  }

  return hr;
}
```

Working with the Scope Pane: Additional Topics

This section covers the following topics:

- Programmatic Expansion of Scope Items
- Programmatic New Window Creation
- Status Bar Text

These features are available in MMC version 1.1 and later.

C++ Snap-ins

Programmatic Expansion of Scope Items

This feature is introduced in MMC version 1.1.

MMC specifies two **Expand** methods that allow you to programmatically expand a scope item.

The **IConsole2::Expand** method enables the snap-in to expand or collapse an item in the scope pane of a particular view. This method is the programmatic equivalent of the user clicking the plus or minus sign to expand or collapse an item in the scope pane. Note that each MDI window within the console represents a different view.

The **IConsoleNamespace2::Expand** method enables the snap-in to expand an item in the namespace without visibly expanding it in the scope pane. Use this method to expand a specified item for the purpose of inserting the child items beneath that item. The method does not expand the item in any views.

Programmatic New Window Creation

This feature is introduced in MMC version 1.1.

The **NewWindow** method is available in both the **IConsole** and **IConsole2** interfaces. This method enables a snap-in to open a new MDI window with a specified scope item as the root node. This is the programmatic equivalent of the **New Window From Here** command on the **View** context menu. The method also supports options for displaying the title bar text, the standard toolbars, and the scope pane. It also allows you to specify whether to persist the new window to the .msc file.

Status Bar Text

This feature is introduced in MMC version 1.1.

MMC allows a snap-in to change the text in the status bar of each MDI child window (view).

In MMC 1.1 and later, each view has a status bar. In addition, the **Status Bar** menu item is added to the **View** menu of each child window and its context menu.

The **IConsole2::SetStatusText** method enables a snap-in to change the text in the status bar.

CHAPTER 20

Using Different Result Pane View Types

MMC supports four types of result pane views:

- Standard result list view (usually called list view)
- Taskpad view
- Custom OCX view
- Custom Web page

The data displayed in a result pane is accessed by means of the snap-in's **IComponent** interface. When the user selects a scope item, the corresponding result data is displayed in the result pane. For a particular scope item, the snap-in can display one of the four types of result pane views.

List Views

The default result pane view type is a list view. A list view displays a collection of items, each consisting of an icon and a label, and provides several ways to display and arrange the items. For example, additional information about each item can be displayed in columns to the right of the icon and label.

A list view can have one of the following view type modes:

- Large icon
- Small icon
- List
- Detail
- Filtered

MMC implements list views using a list view control. The control supports the preceding view type modes, and the user can choose a mode by selecting a scope item and clicking **View** on the context menu. Note that snap-ins can programmatically set all view type modes.

For details about list views, see "Using List Views" later in this chapter.

Taskpad Views

A taskpad is a graphical way of presenting actions that can be performed on a selected item in the scope pane.

There are two types of taskpads: *snap-in taskpads* and *console taskpads*. Snap-in taskpads were introduced in MMC version 1.1 and are largely replaced by console taskpads in version 1.2. Console taskpads offer many advantages in terms of ease of creation, performance, display consistency, and ability of the user to customize console taskpads. In MMC 1.2, you should generally use console taskpads.

Snap-in Taskpad

A snap-in taskpad is implemented as a view on the selected scope item in the scope pane, and that view is represented as a dynamic HTML (DHTML) page in the result pane. The taskpad DHTML page lists actions that can be performed on the selected scope item. Each action is represented as a *task*, which consists of an image, a label, a description, and a mechanism for telling the snap-in to perform the associated action.

There are three types of snap-in taskpads:

Standard

MMC provides a default taskpad that displays the taskpad title and tasks.

Standard list view

MMC provides a list view taskpad (*listpad*) that has three elements: the taskpad title, a list control displaying items that can be selected, and tasks that perform actions on the selected items.

Custom

Your snap-in can provide its own DHTML page that displays tasks to perform as well as other elements.

If a particular scope item has a taskpad view, it is the responsibility of the snap-in that inserted the scope item to provide the user with a mechanism for accessing the taskpad. One solution is to add a menu item to the scope item's **View** context submenu. Note also that the snap-in can choose to display a taskpad for a scope item by default, so that the user automatically sees a taskpad view when the item is selected.

For details about implementing snap-in taskpads, see "Using Taskpads" later in this chapter.

C++ Snap-ins

Console Taskpad

Console taskpads are introduced in MMC 1.2. The user can use a console taskpad to run tasks such as starting wizards, opening property pages, performing menu commands, running command lines, and opening Web pages.

Console taskpads are implemented by MMC. That is, MMC takes care of setting up a console taskpad for a particular scope item.

To create a console taskpad, the user selects a scope item and then clicks the **New Taskpad View** context menu item. Next MMC asks the user, through the New Taskpad View wizard and the New Task wizard, for the information that it needs to create the console taskpad. The user can choose as tasks either menu commands, shell commands, or navigation shortcuts.

The menu commands that the user can choose from are the *same* context menu items that are present in the context menu of the selected scope item. MMC gets these menu commands from snap-ins in exactly the same way that it gets context menu items. That is; there is a one-to-one relationship between a menu command and a context menu item.

When the user chooses a menu command as a task and later clicks that task in the console taskpad, MMC forwards the user's action to the snap-in that added the menu item (menu command) associated with the selected task.

For details about console taskpads, see the MMC HTML Help file that can be invoked from within an MMC console.

Custom OCX Views

OCX controls, also known as ActiveX controls, are components (or objects) you can insert into a Web page or other application to reuse packaged functionality that someone else programmed. For more information about OCX controls, refer to the Microsoft Platform SDK.

A snap-in can launch an OCX control in the result pane of an MMC console.

For details about OCX views, see "Using Custom OCX Controls" later in this chapter.

Custom Web Pages

The result pane of an MMC console can host HTML pages that are located either locally on the computer with MMC, or on an external Web server.

For details about custom Web pages, see "Using Custom Web Pages" later in this chapter.

Using List Views

The default result pane view type is a list view. A list view displays a collection of items, each consisting of an icon and a label, and provides several ways to display and arrange the items. For example, additional information about each item can be displayed in columns to the right of the icon and label.

MMC implements list views using a list view control. The control supports a number of view type modes, and the user can choose a mode by selecting a scope item and clicking **View** on the context menu. Note that snap-ins can programmatically set all view type modes.

Many of the features associated with list views are provided by MMC interfaces. For example, **IResultData** allows snap-ins to manipulate items and the view style associated with the list view. **IResultData** methods include **InsertItem** and **DeleteItem**, which are used by snap-ins to insert or delete single items in the result pane. **DeleteAllRsltItems** allows deletion of all items in the pane. Snap-ins can find items or subitems by using **FindItemByLParam**. Single items can be set or retrieved using **SetItem** and **GetItem**. The next item can be retrieved by using **GetNextItem**. The view mode can be set or retrieved by using **SetViewMode** and **GetViewMode**. The state of a particular item can be modified with **ModifyItemState** and the result pane's view style can be set with **ModifyViewStyle**. Snap-ins can sort all items in the result pane with **Sort** and, after changing an item being displayed, update the item using **UpdateItem**. The text for the result pane's description bar can be set by using **SetDescBarText**.

The **IConsoleVerb** interface allows snap-ins to enable standard verbs including cut, copy, paste, delete, properties, rename, refresh, and print. **SetVerbState** enables a snap-in to set a given verb's button state, while **GetVerbState** is used to retrieve a verb's button state. The **SetDefaultVerb** and **GetDefaultVerb** methods allow a snap-in to set and retrieve the default action on an object.

IHeaderCtrl2 methods manipulate the number of columns and their text labels for the list view. With **InsertColumn**, a snap-in can add a column to a list view; with **DeleteColumn** it can remove one. You can set the width of a column with **SetColumnWidth** and retrieve the current width with **GetColumnWidth**. The **SetColumnText** method is available to set text in a specified column, and **GetColumnText** is available to retrieve current text.

Other **IHeaderCtrl2** methods include **SetChangeTimeOut**, **SetColumnFilter**, and **GetColumnFilter**. These methods provide support for users to filter list views based on filters set on each column in the result view.

C++ Snap-ins

The **IColumnData** interface allows snap-ins to access column configuration data that MMC persists in memory when the user customizes list view columns. Specifically, the user can:

- Change the width of a column.
- Reorder columns.
- Hide or display columns.
- Sort columns.

GetColumnConfigData allows a snap-in to retrieve the current width, order, and hidden status of a set of columns in a list view. **SetColumnConfigData** allows the snap-in to set this information. The **GetColumnSortData** and **SetColumnSortData** methods allow a snap-in to retrieve and set the sorted column and sorting direction for a column set.

With the **IImageList** interface, the snap-in can insert images to be used as icons for items in the result pane. **ImageListSetIcon** is used to set an icon in an image list, and **ImageListSetStrip** allows a snap-in to set a strip of icons in an image list.

A snap-in adds support for virtual lists by implementing the **IResultOwnerData** interface. For details, see "Owner Data/Virtual Lists" later in this chapter.

The **RESULTDATAITEM** structure is used frequently to accomplish much of the work associated with the result pane.

Using List Views: Interfaces

The MMC SDK specifies a number of interfaces and other language constructs for working with list views. The following interfaces are available:

- IColumnData
- IConsoleVerb
- IHeaderCtrl2
- IImageList
- IResultData
- IResultDataCompare
- IResultDataCompareEx
- IResultOwnerData (for virtual list views)

For details about these interfaces, see "Using List Views" and refer to their detailed descriptions in the MMC COM Reference section of the MMC SDK.

Other Constructs

The MMC SDK specifies a number of notifications for working with list views. Here is a list of the most common notifications. For a complete listing of all notifications, see "MMC Notifications" in the MMC COM Reference section of the MMC SDK.

- MMCN_ADD_IMAGES
- MMCN_COLUMN_CLICK
- MMCN_RENAME
- MMCN_RESTORE_VIEW
- MMCN_SELECT
- MMCN_SHOW
- MMCN_VIEW_CHANGE

The following enumeration types are the most common types used with list views. For a complete listing of all enumeration types, see "MMC Enumerations" in the MMC COM Reference section of the MMC SDK.

- **MMC_BUTTON_STATE**
- **MMC_CONSOLE_VERB**
- **MMC_FILTER_CHANGE_CODE**
- **MMC_FILTER_TYPE**
- **MMC_NOTIFY_TYPE**
- **MMC_RESULT_VIEW_STYLE**

The following structures are the most common ones used with list views. See "MMC Structures" in the MMC COM Reference section of the MMC SDK for a complete listing.

- **MMC_RESTORE_VIEW**
- **RESULTDATAITEM**

C++ Snap-ins

Using List Views: Implementation Details

▶ **To implement a list view**

1. Implement the **IComponent::GetResultViewType** method. The *ppViewType* parameter specifies the view type. For standard list views, the value of the parameter should be NULL, indicating that MMC should display the default view type (list view). Specify the view options with the *pViewOptions* parameter. Use the MMC_VIEW_OPTIONS_NONE option to specify no view options.

   Alternatively, if **IComponent::GetResultViewType** returns S_FALSE, MMC will automatically set the view type to list view and the view options to MMC_VIEW_OPTIONS_NONE.

2. Handle the MMCN_ADD_IMAGES notification message, which MMC sends to the snap-in's **IComponent** implementation to request images for the result pane.

3. Handle the MMCN_SHOW notification message, which MMC sends to the snap-in's **IComponent** implementation to indicate that the result pane has the focus. In response to the notification, the snap-in should do the following things:

   - If necessary, obtain interface pointers to the **IHeaderCtrl2** and **IResultData** interfaces by querying the **IConsole2** interface for them. Make sure to use the **IConsole2** interface associated with the snap-in's **IComponent** implementation, and not with its **IComponentData** implementation.

   - Add columns to the result pane using the **IHeaderCtrl2::InsertColumn** method.

- Enumerate the result data items for the result pane using the **IResultData::InsertItem** method.

- If necessary, set the view mode and view style for the list view using **IResultData::SetViewMode** and **IResultData::ModifyViewStyle**, respectively. One of the view modes you can set is filtered view. For details about this mode, see "Adding Filtered Views" later in this chapter.

4. Implement the **IComponent::GetDisplayInfo** method. After the snap-in returns from the MMCN_SHOW notification handler, MMC calls its **IComponent::GetDisplayInfo** implementation once for each item in the result pane to request the item's display information.

5. Handle the MMCN_SELECT notification message, which MMC sends after MMCN_SHOW to indicate which item in the scope pane is currently selected. In the notification handler, the snap-in has the opportunity to update the standard verbs for the scope item. See Chapter 25, "Enabling MMC Standard Verbs," for details.

   MMCN_SELECT is also sent when a result item is selected, at which time the snap-in can update the standard verbs for the selected item in the result pane.

Sample Code

The following code shows sample implementations of a notification handler for the MMCN_SHOW notification message and the **IComponent::GetDisplayInfo** method. All sample implementations are taken from the Nodes sample snap-in that accompanies the MMC SDK.

Note that all sample code assumes Unicode compilation.

MMCN_SHOW Notification Handler Implementation

The following method handles the MMCN_SHOW notification message sent by MMC to **IComponent** in the Nodes sample snap-in when the "Future Vehicles" scope item is selected.

C++ Snap-ins

In the sample, **CComponent** is an instance of the **IComponent** interface. The **CComponent::Notify** method delegates the handling of the MMCN_SHOW notification message to the actual snap-in object that represents the selected item. In the case of the "Future Vehicles" item, the notification message is handled in the snap-in's **CSpaceVehicle::OnShow** method.

```
HRESULT CSpaceVehicle::OnShow(IConsole *pConsole, BOOL bShow,
                         HSCOPEITEM scopeitem)
{
    HRESULT       hr = S_OK;

    IHeaderCtrl *pHeaderCtrl = NULL;
    IResultData *pResultData = NULL;

    if (bShow) {
        hr = pConsole->QueryInterface(IID_IHeaderCtrl,
                         (void **)&pHeaderCtrl);
        _ASSERT( SUCCEEDED(hr) );

        hr = pConsole->QueryInterface(IID_IResultData,
                         (void **)&pResultData);
        _ASSERT( SUCCEEDED(hr) );

        // Set the column headers in the results pane
        hr = pHeaderCtrl->InsertColumn( 0, _T("Rocket Class"), 0,
            MMCLV_AUTO );
        _ASSERT( S_OK == hr );
        hr = pHeaderCtrl->InsertColumn( 1, _T("Rocket Weight"), 0,
            MMCLV_AUTO );
        _ASSERT( S_OK == hr );
        hr = pHeaderCtrl->InsertColumn( 2, _T("Rocket Height"), 0,
            MMCLV_AUTO );
        _ASSERT( S_OK == hr );
        hr = pHeaderCtrl->InsertColumn( 3, _T("Rocket Payload"),
            0, MMCLV_AUTO );
        _ASSERT( S_OK == hr );
        hr = pHeaderCtrl->InsertColumn( 4, _T("Status"), 0,
            MMCLV_AUTO );
        _ASSERT( S_OK == hr );
```

```
        // insert items here
        RESULTDATAITEM rdi;

        hr = pResultData->DeleteAllRsltItems();
        _ASSERT( SUCCEEDED(hr) );

        if (!bExpanded)
        {
            // create the child nodes, then expand them
            for (int n = 0; n < NUMBER_OF_CHILDREN; n++)
            {
                ZeroMemory(&rdi, sizeof(RESULTDATAITEM) );
                rdi.mask =  RDI_STR     |    // Displayname is valid
                            RDI_IMAGE   |
                            RDI_PARAM;       // nImage is valid

                rdi.nImage      = children[n]->GetBitmapIndex();
                rdi.str         = MMC_CALLBACK;
                rdi.nCol        = 0;
                rdi.lParam      = (LPARAM)children[n];

                hr = pResultData->InsertItem( &rdi );

                _ASSERT( SUCCEEDED(hr) );
            }
        }

        pHeaderCtrl->Release();
        pResultData->Release();
    }

    return hr;
}
```

IComponent::GetDisplayInfo Implementation

MMC calls **IComponent::GetDisplayInfo** to request the display name and icon for each list view item in the result pane.

```
STDMETHODIMP CComponent::GetDisplayInfo(
                /* [out][in] */ RESULTDATAITEM *pResultDataItem)
{
  HRESULT hr = S_OK;
  CDelegationBase *base = NULL;

  // if they are asking for the RDI_STR we have one of those to give

  if (pResultDataItem->lParam)
  {
      base = (CDelegationBase *)pResultDataItem->lParam;
      if (pResultDataItem->mask & RDI_STR)
      {
          pResultDataItem->str = const_cast<_TCHAR *>(base->
          GetDisplayName(pResultDataItem->nCol));
      }
      if (pResultDataItem->mask & RDI_IMAGE)
      {
          pResultDataItem->nImage = base->GetBitmapIndex();
      }
  } else
  {
      m_pLastNode->GetChildColumnInfo(pResultDataItem);
  }

  return hr;
}
```

Owner Data/Virtual Lists

Virtual list views, also known as *owner data*, appear to the user as any other list view but the underlying code to populate them is optimized for large data sets. List views that contain more than several hundred items generally achieve significant performance improvement as virtual lists. The decision to use a virtual list view should be based on the cost of fetching the data as well as the volume of data. In the case of a remote database query with a huge result set a virtual list view would be an obvious choice. In other less clear-cut circumstances the snap-in developer should try both list view types before making a final choice.

A virtual list view control maintains very little item state information itself. Except for the item selection and focus information, all item information must be managed by the snap-in. MMC requests item information from the snap-in by calling the snap-in's **IComponent::GetDisplayInfo** implementation.

A snap-in adds support for virtual lists by implementing the **IResultOwnerData** interface. MMC calls the snap-in's **FindItem** implementation to find the next item in a virtual list matching a user-specified string. The **SortItems** method sorts the items of a virtual list. MMC calls the snap-in's implementation of this method when the user clicks the header item of a virtual list or when the snap-in calls **IResultData::Sort**.

Because a virtual list control is intended for large data sets, it is recommended that you cache requested item data to improve retrieval performance. The list view provides a cache-hinting mechanism to assist in optimizing the cache. MMC calls the **CacheHint** method when it is about to request display information by successfully calling the snap-in's **IComponent::GetDisplayInfo** method for a range of items in a virtual list. **CacheHint** allows the snap-in to collect the information ahead of time in cases where an optimization can be made.

The **IResultData** interface handles virtual lists as well. Because of the nature of virtual lists, not all methods apply and some methods have limited functionality. The primary difference in handling virtual lists it that because MMC does not maintain any storage for virtual items, it does not provide item IDs. Instead virtual list items are identified by their list position (index).

C++ Snap-ins

Virtual list views are implemented in much the same way as standard list views, with a few notable differences.

▶ **To implement a virtual list view**

1. Implement the **IComponent::GetResultViewType** method. The *ppViewType* parameter specifies the view type. For standard list views, the value of the parameter should be NULL, indicating that MMC should display the default view type (list view). Specify the view options with the *pViewOptions* parameter. Use the MMC_VIEW_OPTIONS_OWNERDATALIST option to specify a virtual list view.

2. Follow all instructions except for step 1 in "Using List Views: Implementation Details" earlier in this chapter.

3. Implement the **IResultOwnerData** interface. If necessary, develop a mechanism for caching the requested items in the virtual list view to improve performance. Implement the **CacheHint** method for optimizing retrievals.

Exporting List Views to a File

This feature is introduced in MMC 1.2.

The data displayed in all standard list views can be exported to a text file. When the user clicks the **Export List** context menu item while a scope item with a list view is selected, the visible columns in the list view are exported to a text file in the order in which they appear in the view.

This feature is supported directly by MMC, so there is no development impact for snap-ins.

Dynamically Updating List Views

You might want to implement a list view with items whose status changes over time and which should be dynamically updated to reflect the changes.

For example, suppose your snap-in displays a list view that shows the real-time status of resources that it manages. The snap-in should dynamically update the list view as the resource status values change.

Note that snap-ins are not allowed to call any MMC interfaces from a thread other than the main thread, so snap-ins must use thread-safe techniques to perform the updates.

Adding Filtered Views

A filtered view is an MMC standard list view. MMC allows users to filter a list view in the result pane of a scope item based on filters set on each list view column. Filtered views can be set as an option on standard (nonvirtual) list views or on virtual list views. Filtered views cannot be set for custom views (views implemented by an OCX control or a Web page).

When the user clicks the **Filtered** menu item (or the snap-in programmatically sets the view mode to filtered view), MMC turns on the filtered view and sends the snap-in an MMCN_FILTER_CHANGE notification, indicating that filtering has been enabled. MMC takes care of creating the filter header controls on each column of the result list. Each filter header control has a text box (for the filter value) and a filter button that enables the user to change the filter operator.

After the view mode has been set to filtered view, the snap-in is responsible for hiding or adding items in the result list based on the filter values and filter operators set on the columns. Note that the filter value is the value that the snap-in compares with the values in that column to determine whether an item should be added or removed in the list. The filter operator is the comparison operator that is used to compare the filter value against the column value of each item. The filter operators supported are determined by the snap-in.

The snap-in should update the filtered result view (based on the column filters) in the snap-in's notification handler for MMCN_FILTER_CHANGE when the *arg* value is MFCC_VALUE_CHANGE.

The snap-in is also responsible for the menu that enables the user to change the filter operator. The user clicks the filter button on the header control to force MMC to send an MMCN_FILTERBTN_CLICK notification to the snap-in. The snap-in must handle the MMCN_FILTERBTN_CLICK notification and display a menu that enables the user to change the filter operator.

Note that the filtered view mode does not affect the sort settings on the result list.

C++ Snap-ins

Adding Filtered Views: Interfaces

MMC provides snap-in developers with the following interface and methods for working with filtered views:

- **IHeaderCtrl2**

    IHeaderCtrl2::SetColumnFilter

    IHeaderCtrl2::GetColumnFilter

    IHeaderCtrl2::SetChangeTimeOut

Other Constructs

MMC defines the following notifications for working with filtered views:

- MMCN_FILTER_CHANGE
- MMCN_FILTERBTN_CLICK

Furthermore, MMC defines the following additional constructs to be used for working with filtered views:

- **MMC_FILTER_TYPE** enumeration
- **MMC_FILTER_CHANGE_CODE** enumeration
- **MMC_FILTERDATA** structure

Adding Filtered Views: Implementation Details

▶ **To implement a filtered view**

1. Notify MMC that the snap-in supports filtered view by setting the MMC_VIEW_OPTIONS_FILTERED flag in the *pViewOptions* parameter returned by **IComponent::GetResultViewType**.

    A **Filtered** menu item is added to the **View** menu when the snap-in notifies MMC that it supports filtered view.

2. Turn on filtered view. There are two ways to do this:

    - The user can click **Filtered** on the **View** menu.
    - The snap-in can programmatically set the view mode to filtered view by calling **IResultData::SetViewMode** with MMCLV_VIEWSTYLE_FILTERED passed in the *lViewMode* parameter.

    When the user clicks the **Filtered** menu item or the snap-in programmatically sets the view mode to filtered view, MMC turns on the filtered view and sends the snap-in an MMCN_FILTER_CHANGE notification, indicating that filtering has been enabled.

MMC takes care of creating the filter header controls on each column of the result view. Each filter header control has a text box (for the filter value) and a filter button that enables the user to change the filter operator.

3. Handle the MMCN_FILTER_CHANGE notification in the **IComponent::Notify** method.

    MMC calls **IComponent::Notify** with MMCN_FILTER_CHANGE as the *event* parameter when filtering has been enabled or disabled, or when a filter value has changed. The *arg* parameter is a value of enumerated type **MMC_FILTER_CHANGE_CODE** that specifies the type of change.

    Here are the values for **MMC_FILTER_CHANGE_CODE** and how the snap-in should handle them:

    MFCC_ENABLE

    > Indicates that filtered view was turned on.

    > If this is the first time the snap-in has switched to filtered view, the snap-in can initialize its column filters and filtering mechanisms here. The snap-in can use the **IHeaderCtrl2::SetColumnFilter** method to set the filter value and its maximum character length for each column. It can use the **IHeaderCtrl2::SetChangeTimeOut** method to set the filter change notification time-out. This time-out value is applied to all columns in the filtered list. The snap-in could also set the default filter operator for each column at this point. Note that the snap-in is responsible for storing, setting, and enabling the user to change the filter operator on each column.

    > Note that if the snap-in does not call **IHeaderCtrl2::SetColumnFilter** to set the filter data for a column, MMC sets the filter type to string filter and specifies no default value for the filter.

    > If a filtered view has been restored after switching to another view type or another scope item, the snap-in can either restore the last filtered view state or reinitialize the filters.

    MFCC_DISABLE

    > Indicates that filtered view was turned off.

    > The snap-in can store the current filter settings so that it can restore them when the filtered view is enabled again.

    MFCC_VALUE_CHANGE

    > Indicates that the filter value for a column in a result view list has changed. The *param* parameter of the **IComponent::Notify** method contains the column ID.

    > The snap-in can apply the filter for the specified column here. The snap-in must implement its own mechanism to filter the result list (see the next step).

MMC sends this notification in the following cases:

- If the user edits a column filter and either presses ENTER to apply the filter or switches to another column.

- If text has been typed and the filter change interval elapses with no further keystrokes. The filter change interval can be set using **IHeaderCtrl2::SetChangeTimeOut**.

- If the snap-in returns S_OK in response to an MMCN_FILTERBTN_CLICK notification.

4. Implement one or more methods to filter the result list.

The snap-in is responsible for hiding or adding items in the result list based on the filter values and filter operators set on the columns. Note that the filter value of a column is the value that the snap-in compares with the values in that column to determine whether an item should be added or removed in the list. The filter operator is the comparison operator that is used to compare the filter value against the column value of each item. The filter operators supported are determined by the snap-in.

The snap-in uses **IHeaderCtrl2::GetColumnFilter** to get the filter value set on the specified column. The snap-in is responsible for setting, storing, and maintaining the filter operator for each column. The snap-in can implement a method that completely rebuilds the result list by removing all items and re-adding them appropriately, or the snap-in can manipulate the existing items in the result list.

5. Handle the MMCN_FILTERBTN_CLICK notification in the **IComponent::Notify** method.

MMC calls **IComponent::Notify** with MMCN_FILTERBTN_CLICK as the *event* parameter when the user clicks the filter button in a filter header control. The *arg* parameter is the column ID of the column whose filter button was clicked.

The snap-in is responsible for the user interface that enables the user to change the filter operator. Usually, a menu is a sufficient user interface to make filter operator changes.

Therefore, the snap-in must handle the MMCN_FILTERBTN_CLICK notification by presenting some user interface to enable the user to specify a new filter operator. The *param* value points to the coordinates of the filter button. The snap-in can use those coordinates to calculate the placement of the user interface used to change the filter operator.

After the snap-in has handled the filter operator changes, it can return S_OK to generate an MMCN_FILTER_CHANGE notification with *arg* set to MFCC_VALUE_CHANGE and *param* set to the column ID.

Using Column Persistence

This feature is introduced in MMC 1.2.

Starting with version 1.2, MMC persists column customization and sorting parameters as the user moves between scope items in the scope pane. This allows a user to customize a list view, select another scope item in the scope pane, and then return to the original scope item with the customizations preserved. MMC will also save the customizations in the .msc file when the user saves the console and then restore them when the file is loaded.

The following column customization features are available:

- **Persistence of column widths.** MMC automatically persists user changes made to column widths.

- **Reordering of columns.** Users can change the order of columns in a list view.

- **Column visibility in list view.** Users can choose which columns to display in a list view.

- **Sorted column and sort direction information.** Users can select a column and choose to sort it in either ascending or descending order. The default sort is based on string comparison. Note that MMC does not support multicolumn sorting.

MMC also allows users to export a list view to a text file. Only visible columns are exported, in the order in which they appear in the list view.

MMC automatically persists in memory all user column customizations. This persisted information is known collectively as "column configuration data."

Column Set and Column Set ID

A *column set* is a set of columns inserted in the result pane by a snap-in when the user selects a scope item in the snap-in. When the user selects a different scope item in that snap-in, the same or a different column set may be shown by the snap-in.

MMC requires that every scope item specify a *column set ID* for the column set it inserts. MMC uses the ID of a column set to identify its persisted column configuration within each view. If the snap-in does not explicitly supply one then MMC uses the scope item's node type GUID. This means that if the snap-in has multiple scope items of the same node type in the scope pane, and it does not explicitly set an ID, then the user's customization will be propagated across the different list views. Snap-ins can change the ID by using the CCF_COLUMN_SET_ID clipboard format.

Column Persistence and Multiple Views

MMC persists column configuration data per column set *per view* per snap-in instance. As a result, the same column set ID can be used in multiple views, and all column sets with the same ID can be operated on independently. MMC will preserve each column set's data separately on a per-view basis.

As an example of this, suppose two views are open in a console. Each view shows the column set of the same scope item. Any user customizations to a column set in one of the views is then limited to that column set in that view, even if both column sets have the same ID.

Supporting CCF_COLUMN_SET_ID

Snap-ins should support CCF_COLUMN_SET_ID in the following situations:

- Some snap-ins might have the same set of columns for more than one node type. If such a snap-in wants MMC to propagate changes to the column set for all of these node types, it must implement the CCF_COLUMN_SET_ID clipboard format and return the same column set ID for all the node types. This allows a user to select one scope item, change some column configuration settings, and then see settings preserved in the result panes of different node types in the scope pane.

- A single scope item might have different column sets in its result pane. For instance, a snap-in might elect to display different sets of columns, depending on its state. In this case, the snap-in should implement CCF_COLUMN_SET_ID for each column set, taking care to specify a unique column set ID for each column set.

- Some snap-ins (for example, Event Viewer in Windows 2000) might have scope items of the same node type, but with different column sets (for example, System Log, Application Log, and Security Log). To distinguish these column sets from each other and to make sure that changes are not propagated to all scope items of the same node type, the snap-in should implement CCF_COLUMN_SET_ID to uniquely identify each column set.

How Snap-ins Affect Column Persistence

MMC allows the user to hide columns or make columns visible in the list view using the **Modify Columns** dialog box. If the user makes any column setting changes while the list view is displayed, MMC sends an MMCN_COLUMNS_CHANGED notification message to the snap-in. The notification tells the snap-in which columns in the list view are visible. The snap-in can return either S_OK or S_FALSE in its MMCN_COLUMNS_CHANGED notification handler to accept the user changes. If the snap-in rejects the changes, it should return E_UNEXPECTED instead and display a message box indicating why the user changes were rejected.

MMC also allows snap-ins to access the column configuration data that it persists in memory. This is because situations can arise in which snap-ins need to be aware of and react to user changes made to column configurations. For example, a snap-in may not want to fetch data for columns that are hidden in order to improve performance. Snap-ins may also need to modify persisted column configuration data.

MMC allows snap-ins to access column configuration data using the **IColumnData** interface. The **GetColumnConfigData** and **SetColumnConfigData** methods allow a snap-in to retrieve and set the current width, order, and hidden status of each column in a column set that is stored in memory by MMC. The **GetColumnSortData** method allows a snap-in to retrieve from memory the sorted column and sorting direction for a column set, while the **SetColumnSortData** method allows a snap-in to set this same information.

C++ Snap-ins

Using Column Persistence: Interfaces

MMC provides snap-in developers with the following interface for working with column persistence:

- **IColumnData**

Other Constructs

MMC defines the following notification and clipboard format for working with column persistence:

- MMCN_COLUMNS_CHANGED notification
- CCF_COLUMN_SET_ID clipboard format

MMC defines four structures to be used for accessing column configuration data:

- **MMC_COLUMN_DATA**
- **MMC_COLUMN_SET_DATA**
- **MMC_SORT_DATA**
- **MMC_SORT_SET_DATA**

MMC also defines the following structure for use with the MMCN_COLUMNS_CHANGED notification:

- **MMC_VISIBLE_COLUMNS**

Using Column Persistence: Implementation Details

This section covers both how to add snap-in support for the CCF_COLUMN_SET_ID clipboard format and how to access column configuration data using the **IColumnData** interface.

▶ **To add snap-in support for CCF_COLUMN_SET_ID**

1. Add the CCF_COLUMN_SET_ID clipboard format to the snap-in's **IDataObject** implementation. Usually, **IDataObject** has its supported clipboard formats as static members. If so, add the CCF_COLUMN_SET_ID format as a member:

   ```
   static UINT s_cfColumnSetID;
   ```

2. Register the CCF_COLUMN_SET_ID format and assign the registered format to the static member in the **IDataObject** implementation's constructor:

   ```
   s_cfColumnSetID = RegisterClipboardFormat
   (W2T(CCF_COLUMN_SET_ID));
   ```

3. Include support for the CCF_COLUMN_SET_ID format in the snap-in's implementation of the **IDataObject::GetData** method. See the "Sample Code" section for a sample implementation of the method.

▶ **To access column configuration data using IColumnData**

Before using the **IColumnData** interface, you should read "Using **IColumnData**" and "**IHeaderCtrl2** and Column Persistence" later in this chapter.

1. The **IColumnData** interface can be queried from the **IConsole** passed into **IComponent::Initialize** during the component's creation.

2. To retrieve and set the current width, order, and hidden status of columns in a column set, use the **GetColumnConfigData** and **SetColumnConfigData** methods. To retrieve and set the sorted column and sorting direction for columns in a column set, use the **GetColumnSortData** and **SetColumnSortData** methods.

3. When calling any of the **IColumnData** methods, fill an **SColumnSetID** structure to specify the ID of the column set on which the particular action is performed. If the snap-in does not support the CCF_COLUMN_SET_ID clipboard format, the column set ID is the node type GUID of the scope item that owns the list view. If the clipboard format is supported, the ID of the column set is the same one supplied to MMC in the snap-in's **IDataObject::GetData** implementation.

Sample Code

The following sample code shows how a snap-in can add support for
CCF_COLUMN_SET_ID:

```
// Handle CCF_COLUMN_SET_ID in IDataObject::GetData
if (cf == s_cfColumnSetID)
{
  BYTE    byData[256] = {0};
  SColumnSetID* pData = reinterpret_cast<SColumnSetID*>(byData);
  LPTSTR pszText =NULL;

  switch (m_pFolder->GetType())
  {
      // Set ID with a GUID.
      case TYPE_1:
          pData->cBytes = sizeof(cColumnIDForType1Folder);
          ::CopyMemory(pData->id, &cColumnIDForType1Folder,
                      pData->cBytes);
          break;

      // Set ID with a string.
      case TYPE_2:
          pszText = _T("___Column ID for Type2 node___");
          _tcscpy ((LPTSTR) pData->id, pszText);
          pData->cBytes = _tcslen ((LPTSTR) pData->id) *
                          sizeof (TCHAR);
          break;

      default:
          return (E_FAIL);
          break;
  }
  // Calculate the size of SColumnSetID.
  int cb = pData->cBytes + sizeof (SColumnSetID);

  lpMedium->tymed = TYMED_HGLOBAL;
  lpMedium->hGlobal = ::GlobalAlloc(GMEM_SHARE|GMEM_MOVEABLE, cb);
  if (lpMedium->hGlobal == NULL)
     return STG_E_MEDIUMFULL;

  BYTE* pb = reinterpret_cast<BYTE*>
              (::GlobalLock(lpMedium->hGlobal));
  CopyMemory(pb, pData, cb);
  ::GlobalUnlock(lpMedium->hGlobal);

  return S_OK;
}
```

Using Column Persistence: Advanced Topics

This section covers advanced topics about column persistence. The first topic, "How Column Configuration Data Is Used," discusses how MMC uses column configuration data in a variety of scenarios. The remaining two topics, "Using **IColumnData**" and "**IHeaderCtrl2** and Column Persistence," discuss material relevant to snap-in developers who want to access and perhaps modify column configuration data persisted by MMC.

How Column Configuration Data Is Used

This section covers how column configuration data is used by snap-ins and MMC.

Customizing a List View

When the user customizes a list view, column configuration data is used as follows:

1. A snap-in is added to a console.

2. One of its scope items is selected.

3. The snap-in populates a list view and uses **IHeaderCtrl2** to add some columns to the result pane.

4. The user customizes the list view, for example, by using the **Modify Columns** dialog box to change column order or visible/hidden status. MMC persists the new column configuration data based on either the column set ID or the node type GUID, depending on whether the snap-in supports CCF_COLUMN_SET_ID.

5. If there is any change in the visible/hidden status of a column, MMC sends the snap-in an MMCN_COLUMNS_CHANGED notification, indicating which columns in the column set are now visible. The snap-in handles the notification by fetching data for visible columns. Note that a snap-in can choose to update only the data of the visible columns, for instance, when there is concern about the performance impact of populating data in hidden columns.

    Also, the snap-in can reject any user customizations by returning E_UNEXPECTED in its MMCN_COLUMNS_CHANGED notification handler. In this case, the snap-in is responsible for informing the user why it is refusing the changes, for example, by means of a message box.

6. MMC applies the new column configuration data to the result pane. Assume column A was previously hidden and now is made visible by the user. When displaying visible columns in the result pane, MMC calls the **IComponent::GetDisplayInfo** method to get data for column A. Because the snap-in already has fetched data for the column (in the last step), the snap-in is ready to present the data when the method is called.

C++ Snap-ins

Applying Persisted Data to a List View

After customizing a list view or saving and reloading a console file, persisted column configuration data is applied to the list view of a selected scope item as follows:

1. MMC calls **IComponentData::QueryDataObject** to request a data object for the list view of the selected scope item. MMC then calls the data object's **GetData** method to request the column set ID in CCF_COLUMN_SET_ID format.

2. If the snap-in does not support CCF_COLUMN_SET_ID, MMC calls **IComponentData::QueryDataObject** to request a data object for the selected scope item and then queries it for the item's node type GUID.

3. MMC maintains a navigational history of the result pane. For each scope item in the history, MMC stores the view type and view options specified by **IComponent::GetResultViewType** when the result pane was originally displayed during the course of the current console session.

   - MMC notifies the snap-in with MMCN_RESTORE_VIEW with the stored view type and view options (which include the parameters of **IComponent::GetResultViewType**).

   - If the snap-in accepts the MMCN_RESTORE_VIEW notification (by handling the notification and returning S_OK in the handler), MMC sets the view; otherwise it calls the snap-in's **IComponent::GetResultViewType** method.

4. If MMC has column configuration data for the column set ID (or node type GUID) returned by the snap-in, the following things happen:

   - MMC sends the MMCN_SHOW notification to the snap-in.

   - The snap-in inserts columns.

   - As soon as the snap-in has inserted all its columns (and before inserting the list view items) MMC checks to make sure that the number of inserted columns matches the number of columns it has persisted along with the column configuration data.

     If the numbers match, MMC rearranges the columns using the persisted column configuration data (width, order, hidden status, and so on).

     If the numbers don't match, this means that the snap-in has added or deleted columns from the column set without persisting this new data. MMC doesn't apply the column configuration data and throws it away instead. For more details, see "**IHeaderCtrl2** and Column Persistence" later in this chapter.

5. If MMC does not have column configuration data for the column set ID (or node type GUID) returned by the snap-in, this means that the list view is still in its original state. That is, its column configuration data has not been changed by either the user or the snap-in since it was first displayed. In this case, MMC still calls **IComponent::GetResultViewType**, which it normally does when the user selects an item in the scope pane.

6. The snap-in inserts list view items and returns from MMCN_SHOW.

7. MMC uses the sort data to sort on the specified columns.

Saving and Reloading a Console File

During the saving and reloading of a console file, column configuration data is used as follows:

1. After customizing a list view, the user saves the console. MMC requests a data object for the scope item and calls the data object's **IDataObject::GetData** method with the CCF_COLUMN_SET_ID format. The snap-in provides the ID of the column set in the result pane.

    If the snap-in does not support CCF_COLUMN_SET_ID, MMC calls **IComponentData::QueryDataObject** to request a data object for the selected scope item and then queries it for the item's node type GUID.

2. The console is closed. The selection of the scope item is preserved when the console file is saved.

3. The console file is reloaded.

4. MMC loads all column configuration data for the snap-in into its own internal data structures.

5. The tree in the scope pane is expanded down to the scope item that was selected when the console file was saved, and the scope item is selected.

6. MMC begins applying the persisted data to the list view of the selected scope item.

C++ Snap-ins

Using IColumnData

MMC allows snap-ins to access the column configuration data of a column set using the **IColumnData** interface. This section covers how and when snap-in developers can use the interface.

The **IColumnData** interface can be used in any of the following situations:

- When handling an MMCN_EXPAND notification, a snap-in can use the methods of **IColumnData** to examine persisted column configuration data for the selected scope item's list view and to modify it if required. Also, if the snap-in initiates data fetching in this event, it can optimize by checking which columns will be visible.

- The snap-in receives an MMCN_COLUMNS_CHANGED notification when the user changes the visible status of any column in the column set. Note that MMCN_COLUMNS_CHANGED provides information about the columns of the column set that *will* be visible after the snap-in returns with S_OK or S_FALSE. If the snap-in calls **IColumnData::GetColumnConfigData** before returning from its MMCN_COLUMNS_CHANGED notification handler (with S_OK or S_FALSE), it will receive the current column settings.

The *param* parameter of the MMCN_COLUMNS_CHANGED notification tells the snap-in which columns are going to be visible due to the user changes. The snap-in can reject the changes by returning E_UNEXPECTED in its MMCN_COLUMNS_CHANGED notification handler. In this case, the snap-in is responsible for informing the user why it is refusing the changes, for example, by means of a message box.

MMC applies persisted data to a list view during the snap-in's handling of the MMCN_SHOW notification message. MMC applies the data during MMCN_SHOW because it is during this event that the snap-in sets up the list view columns in the result pane.

- When receiving an MMCN_SHOW notification with the *arg* parameter set to TRUE (indicating that the snap-in should set up the result pane), the snap-in can view or modify the configuration data *before* inserting columns. It can, for example, use the **IColumnData::GetColumnConfigData** method to see which columns in the column set are visible. Then, to optimize populating list view columns, the snap-in can choose to fetch data for and display only visible columns in the list view.

The snap-in can also modify (and persist) configuration data using **IColumnData::SetColumnConfigData** or **IColumnData::SetColumnSortData**.

Note that MMC applies the persisted column configuration data for the column set *immediately after* the snap-in has inserted the first item into the list view (using **IResultData::InsertItem**). MMC assumes at this point that the snap-in has completed adding its columns. If the snap-in needs to either view or modify configuration data that MMC will apply to the column set, it must do so before inserting the first list view item.

- Before the snap-in receives an MMCN_SHOW notification with the *arg* parameter set to FALSE (indicating that the result pane is being torn down and possibly replaced), MMC has already persisted any user customizations made to the list view (such as which columns are visible or hidden).

  When the snap-in receives MMCN_SHOW (with *arg*=FALSE), it can choose to modify the persisted data. MMC then applies the (newly) persisted data to the column set the next time the user selects its item. The persisted data is also applied to all column sets with the same ID, so if the user selects a different item with the same column set ID, MMC will also apply the persisted data to it.

  Note that the snap-in can undo some or all of the user customizations made to the list view.

- Currently, when handling an MMCN_SHOW notification, if a snap-in inserts result items asynchronously (the columns are inserted by the notification handler, but items are inserted in the list view later) then it cannot sort the items. In this case, the snap-in can use the methods of **IColumnData** to get the persisted sort data and then perform the sorting at a later time.

- A snap-in can add or remove columns in a column set using the methods of **IHeaderCtrl2**. See the following topic, "**IHeaderCtrl2** and Column Persistence," for information on how this relates to column persistence.

- Only user-initiated changes are persisted in memory automatically by MMC. The snap-in must use **IColumnData** to persist in memory any changes that it initiates. Examples of snap-in-initiated changes include changing the visibility status of a column during its insertion (with **IHeaderCtrl2::InsertColumn**) and modifying the width of a column (with **IHeaderCtrl2::SetColumnWidth**).

- Note that the **IColumnData** interface is not designed to be an alternative to the **IHeaderCtrl2** interface. Snap-ins should use **IHeaderCtrl2** as much as possible, because it allows the user to see any snap-in changes to a list view immediately. **IColumnData** should only be used in situations for which **IHeaderCtrl2** is not designed.

C++ Snap-ins

IHeaderCtrl2 and Column Persistence

The **IHeaderCtrl2** interface contains three methods that can be used to modify the column configuration data of a scope item's column set:

- **IHeaderCtrl2::InsertColumn**
- **IHeaderCtrl2::DeleteColumn**
- **IHeaderCtrl2::SetColumnWidth**

MMC does not persist in memory any changes made to a column set due to the action of **IHeaderCtrl2::InsertColumn**, **IHeaderCtrl2::DeleteColumn**, or **IHeaderCtrl2::SetColumnWidth**, so snap-ins are solely responsible for updating persisted column configuration data after using these methods.

Consider the following scenarios:

- **Scenario 1:** Suppose the user selects a scope item and doesn't customize its list view. The snap-in also makes no changes to the column set. The user selects a different item and then reselects the original item. In this case, the user will see the original list view that was displayed when the item was first selected.

- **Scenario 2:** Suppose the user selects a scope item for which MMC persists column configuration data. The user doesn't customize its list view. The snap-in doesn't make any changes either. The user then selects a different item. The user then reselects the original item. In the meantime, the data source for the original item has changed in some way, and as a result, the snap-in inserts an extra column into the list view of the original item using **IHeaderCtrl2::InsertColumn**. When applying the persisted data to the list view, MMC notices that the number of new columns does not match the number of columns persisted in memory. As a result, MMC throws away the persisted data and does not apply it to the column set.

In Scenario 2, the snap-in does not persist the new column configuration data after calling **IHeaderCtrl2::InsertColumn**, and consequently MMC ignores the outdated data persisted in memory when the list view is displayed.

To avoid this situation, snap-ins should always make sure that the persisted column configuration data for a particular column set is up-to-date. Here are a number of strategies that snap-ins can use to guarantee this:

- Immediately after making changes to a column set using the **IHeaderCtrl2** interface, snap-ins can call **IColumnData::SetColumnConfigData** to update the column set's persisted column configuration data.

- If a snap-in knows that a scope item's column set can change because of differences in the data source version or other data source properties, the snap-in can assign a different column set ID for each server version. This guarantees that column configuration data for each server version is stored separately.

  Then, when MMC asks for the column set ID for displaying the item's list view, the snap-in can apply the appropriate ID corresponding to the current server version.

- When handling an MMCN_EXPAND notification, a snap-in can use the methods of **IColumnData** to examine persisted column configuration data for the selected scope item's list view and modify it if required.

- See "Using **IColumnData**" earlier in this chapter for more suggestions.

C++ Snap-ins

Using Taskpads

For an overview of taskpads, see the beginning of this chapter. This section discusses how to implement snap-in taskpads.

Snap-in taskpads are introduced in MMC 1.1. In MMC 1.2, you should generally use console taskpads rather than snap-in taskpads. This section discusses how to implement snap-in taskpads in snap-ins that need to be backward compatible. Note that in the discussion the term "taskpad" is used in place of "snap-in taskpad."

The MMC SDK specifies a number of interfaces and other constructs for working with taskpads. MMC calls the snap-in's implementation of **IComponent::GetResultViewType** to display the result pane for a particular scope item. The snap-in uses the method to provide MMC with the address of a string containing the resource path to the taskpad template or HTML file and a group name that identifies the taskpad.

The **IExtendTaskPad** interface enables the snap-in to set up a taskpad and receive notifications from the taskpad. When the taskpad DHTML page is loaded, the **MMCCtrl** control on that page calls methods in MMC. In turn, MMC attempts to get the **IExtendTaskPad** interface from the **IComponent** object and calls the methods required to provide the **MMCCtrl** control with the data needed to render the taskpad's general elements: title text, banner image, and background image.

If the taskpad is a list view taskpad, MMC calls **IExtendTaskPad::GetListPadInfo** to get the title text for the list control, text for an optional button, and the command ID passed to **IExtendTaskPad::TaskNotify** when the button is clicked.

MMC calls the **IExtendTaskPad::EnumTasks** method to get a pointer to the **IEnumTASK** interface of an object that specifies the tasks the snap-in wants to add to the taskpad.

The **IEnumTASK::Next** method enables MMC to retrieve the next task in the snap-in's list of tasks. MMC calls this method until it returns S_FALSE to indicate there are no more tasks for the snap-in to add to the taskpad. The **IEnumTASK::Reset** method enables MMC to reset the enumeration to the beginning of the snap-in's task list.

MMC calls the **IExtendTaskPad::TaskNotify** method to notify the snap-in when the user clicks a task or a list view button. The list view button applies only to list view taskpads.

The **IEnumTASK::Skip** and **IEnumTASK::Clone** methods are included in the MMC SDK for completeness, but are not used by MMC. Snap-ins can simply return E_NOTIMPL in their implementation of these two methods.

Using Taskpads: Interfaces

Taskpads require the implementation of the following interfaces and methods:

- **IComponent**

    IComponent::GetResultViewType

- **IExtendTaskPad**

    IExtendTaskPad::EnumTasks

    IExtendTaskPad::GetBackground

    IExtendTaskPad::GetDescriptiveText

    IExtendTaskPad::GetListPadInfo

    IExtendTaskPad::GetTitle

    IExtendTaskPad::TaskNotify

- **IEnumTASK**

    IEnumTASK::Next

    IEnumTASK::Reset

Other Constructs

Taskpads use the following structures:

- **MMC_LISTPAD_INFO**
- **MMC_TASK**
- **MMC_TASK_DISPLAY_BITMAP**
- **MMC_TASK_DISPLAY_OBJECT**
- **MMC_TASK_DISPLAY_SYMBOL**

Taskpads use the following enumerated types:

- **MMC_ACTION_TYPE**
- **MMC_TASK_DISPLAY_TYPE**

Taskpads use the following notification:

- MMCN_LISTPAD

C++ Snap-ins

MMC Taskpad Controls and Objects

MMC has the following ActiveX controls that are used on taskpad HTML pages:

ListPad control
Displays a list view control that contains items from an **IResultData** result list. Used on list view taskpads only.

MMCCtrl control
Gets the taskpad configuration information (text, graphics, tasks) from the snap-in and communicates data back to the snap-in.

SysColorCtrl control
Is used on a taskpad DHTML page to get system color settings that can be applied to the taskpad. The control also has methods to derive colors based on one or more specified colors.

Taskpads also use the following objects (which are created by methods in the **MMCCtrl** control):

MMCDisplayObject object
Specifies the type of image and all the data required to use that image to display a task or the background on a taskpad.

MMCListPadInfo object
Represents a label and a button for the **ListPad** control to be added to the taskpad page. Should be used on list view taskpads only.

MMCTask object
Represents a task to be added to the taskpad.

Using Taskpads: Implementation Details

▶ **To implement a standard taskpad**

1. Implement a mechanism for storing the selected view type (standard list view or taskpad). This allows a standard list view or the appropriate taskpad to be loaded when MMC calls **IComponent::GetResultViewType** to display the result pane for your snap-in.

   The simplest way is to create a member variable in your **IComponent** object. In the **CComponent** class below, the **m_ViewType** member stores the view type:

```
// CComponent
class CComponent :
    public IComponent,
    public IExtendContextMenu,
    public IExtendTaskPad

{
public:
    CComponent()
    {
        //Default to standard view
        m_ViewType=0;
    }
    ~CComponent();

public:
    //store the view type: standard or taskpad
    long m_ViewType;
};
```

2. If your snap-in has taskpads as well as list and/or custom views for a particular scope item, the snap-in should by default display a taskpad for the item when it is selected. If the item has more than one taskpad view, the snap-in should display the default taskpad or whatever taskpad the snap-in determines to be appropriate. On subsequent visits to that item (using the **Back** and **Forward** buttons), the view type last selected by the user will be displayed (see "MMCN_RESTORE_VIEW" in the MMC COM Reference section of the MMC SDK for details).

3. Implement access to the taskpads. There are three ways to do this:

- Add one or more taskpad menu items to the **View** menu. You can add a single menu item to use it as an additional view type option on an item in the scope pane. You can use multiple menu items if you want access to specific taskpads, or if an item has multiple taskpads.

  Note that MMC calls the **IExtendContextMenu::AddMenuItems** method implemented by the **IComponent** that owns the view to allow it to add items to the **View** menu.

- Add tasks that link to other taskpads.

- Use only taskpad views.

4. If your snap-in uses context menus to switch to taskpad view, or if a taskpad task links to a taskpad on another item, the snap-in must set the view type member to the appropriate taskpad and then call the **IConsole2::SelectScopeItem** method. This forces a call to **IComponent::GetResultViewType** to load the appropriate taskpad.

5. Handle selection of a taskpad in **IComponent::GetResultViewType**.

   For a taskpad view that uses MMC's taskpad templates, *ppViewType* should point to the address of a string containing the resource path to the taskpad template and a group name that identifies the taskpad. Note that MMC passes the group name in calls to **IExtendTaskPad** methods to enable the snap-in to identify the particular taskpad that is being displayed (this is important if the snap-in has multiple taskpads).

   The string should have the following form:

   res://*filepath*/*template*#*groupname*

   where *filepath* is the full path to the MMC executable (Mmc.exe), *template* is the file name of the template that is stored as a resource within the file specified by *filepath*, and *groupname* is the name that identifies the taskpad.

   MMC supplies the following HTML files as templates:

Resource file	Description
Default.htm	Template for standard taskpad.
Listpad.htm	Template for "vertical" list view taskpad.
Horizontal.htm	Template for "horizontal" list view taskpad.

For example, the following string specifies that Mmc.exe has a path of c:/winnt/system32/mmc.exe, the standard taskpad is displayed (default.htm), and the group name is tpad1:

```
res://c:\\winnt\\system32\\mmc.exe/default.htm#tpad1
```

For a taskpad view that uses a custom HTML page, *ppViewType* should point to the address of a string containing the resource path to the custom taskpad's HTML file and a group name that identifies the taskpad. The string has the same form as the string for an MMC taskpad template—except the *filepath* should specify the path to the snap-in's DLL that stores the custom HTML page as a resource.

The following code fragment could be added to the **GetResultViewType** method to load the standard MMC taskpad with a group name of CMTP1 when the view type is set to IDM_TASKPAD1 and taskpad view is selected:

(Note that this code fragment assumes Unicode compilation. Also note that the Taskpads sample snap-in that accompanies the MMC SDK is both Unicode- and ANSI-compliant.)

```
if( IDM_TASKPAD == m_ViewType )
{
    *pViewOptions = MMC_VIEW_OPTIONS_NONE;
    *ppViewType = CreateResourcePath( NULL,
                    L"default.htm#CMPT1" );
    if( NULL == *ppViewType )
        return E_OUTOFMEMORY;

    return S_OK;
}
```

The **CreateResourcePath** method is defined as follows:

```
LPOLESTR CreateResourcePath(HINSTANCE hInst,
                            LPOLESTR szResource)
{
    WCHAR szBuffer[MAX_PATH];
    ZeroMemory( szBuffer, sizeof(szBuffer) );
    wcscpy( szBuffer, L"res://" );
    WCHAR* szTemp = szBuffer + wcslen( szBuffer );
    ::GetModuleFileNameW( hInst, szTemp,
                          sizeof(szBuffer) - wcslen(szBuffer) );
    wcscat( szBuffer, L"/" );
    wcscat( szBuffer, szResource );
    LONG nBufferSize = (wcslen(szBuffer) + 1) * sizeof(WCHAR);
    LPOLESTR szOutBuffer = (LPOLESTR)CoTaskMemAlloc(
                            nBufferSize );
    if( NULL == szOutBuffer )
        return (LPOLESTR)NULL;

    wcscpy( szOutBuffer, szBuffer );
    return szOutBuffer;
} //end CreateResoucePath()
```

6. Implement the **IExtendTaskPad** interface on your snap-in's **IComponent** object.

If your snap-in owns the item displaying the taskpad, **IExtendTaskPad** is used by MMC to set up the taskpad, to get a pointer to the **IEnumTASK** interface, and to send notifications from the taskpad to your snap-in.

If the taskpad is a list view taskpad, MMC calls **IExtendTaskPad::GetListPadInfo** to get the title text for the list control, text for an optional button, and the command ID passed to **IExtendTaskPad::TaskNotify** when the button is clicked.

MMC calls the **IExtendTaskPad::EnumTasks** method to get a pointer to the **IEnumTASK** interface of an object that specifies the tasks your snap-in wants to add to the taskpad. If a taskpad extension snap-in has been added to your snap-in, MMC gets a pointer to the **IExtendTaskPad** interface on that snap-in and calls the **IExtendTaskPad::EnumTasks** method to get a pointer to the **IEnumTASK** interface for that snap-in.

MMC calls the **IExtendTaskPad::TaskNotify** method to notify the snap-in when a task or a list view button has been clicked. The list view button applies only to list view taskpads—it is the optional button specified in the **IExtendTaskPad::GetListPadInfo** method. The command ID for the specific task or list view button is passed as a **VARIANT**.

7. Implement the **IEnumTASK** interface. MMC calls methods on this interface to get the tasks for the taskpad.

MMC calls the **IEnumTASK::Next** method to iterate the tasks. Each task is returned as an **MMC_TASK** structure.

8. If the taskpad is a list view taskpad, handle the MMCN_LISTPAD notification in **IComponent::Notify**.

When a list view taskpad is displayed, MMC clears the items in the result pane, attaches the list control used in the taskpad, and sends this notification with the *arg* set to TRUE. The snap-in must handle this notification by populating the list with items using the **IResultData** or **IResultOwnerData** interfaces.

When the view is switched from the list view taskpad to another view, MMC sends this notification with the *arg* set to FALSE. When the snap-in handles this notification, it can free any resources used to populate the list.

Console Taskpads

Console taskpads are introduced in MMC 1.2. The user can use a console taskpad to run tasks such as starting wizards, opening property pages, performing menu commands, running command lines, and opening Web pages.

Generally in MMC 1.2, there is little reason for choosing snap-in taskpads over console taskpads. Console taskpads offer many advantages in terms of ease of creation, performance, display consistency, and ability of the user to customize console taskpads.

Console taskpads are implemented by MMC. That is, MMC takes care of setting up a console taskpad for a particular scope item. To create a console taskpad, the user selects a scope item and then clicks the **New Taskpad View** context menu item. Next MMC asks the user, through the New Taskpad View wizard and the New Task wizard, for the information that it needs to create the console taskpad. The user can choose as tasks either menu commands, shell commands, or navigation shortcuts.

The menu commands that the user can choose from are the *same* context menu items that are present in the context menu of the selected scope item. MMC gets these menu commands from snap-ins in exactly the same way that it gets context menu items. That is, there is a one-to-one relationship between a menu command and a context menu item.

When the user chooses a menu command as a task and later clicks that task in the console taskpad, MMC forwards the user's action to the snap-in that added the menu item (menu command) associated with the selected task.

For details about console taskpads, see the MMC HTML Help file that can be invoked from within an MMC console.

C++ Snap-ins

Using Custom OCX Controls

This section covers how you can add functionality to your snap-in that enables it to launch a custom OCX control.

A snap-in can launch an OCX control in the result pane of an MMC console. The OCX control runs in the same thread as the snap-in, so snap-in developers only need to deal with threading issues if their OCX controls are multithreaded.

Note that custom OCX controls should be used sparingly, because they cannot be extended by other snap-ins. Snap-ins should instead use list views where possible.

The MMC SDK specifies two interface methods and a number of other constructs for working with custom OCX controls. MMC calls the snap-in's implementation of **IComponent::GetResultViewType** to display the result pane for a particular scope item. The snap-in uses the method to indicate to MMC that an OCX view should be launched and provides MMC with the CLSID of the OCX control. The snap-in can also specify whether a single instance of the OCX control should be cached and reused each time the scope item is selected, or whether MMC should instead destroy the cached OCX control and create a new custom control each time the item is selected. This is done using the MMC_VIEW_OPTIONS_CREATENEW option.

The second method, **IConsole2::QueryResultView**, can be used to query for the OCX control's **IUnknown** interface pointer. The snap-in can also acquire this pointer in a number of other ways, for example while handling the MMCN_INITOCX notification message.

MMC sends the snap-in an MMCN_INITOCX notification message with an interface pointer to the custom OCX control's **IUnknown** interface. The snap-in can use the pointer to perform any initialization of the OCX control before it is displayed in the result pane.

MMC sends the snap-in an MMCN_SHOW notification upon deselection of the result pane with the OCX view. The *arg* parameter of the notification is set to FALSE, indicating that the OCX view is going out of focus. At this time, the snap-in can do any necessary clean-up, such as ensuring that the OCX control is properly destroyed.

Using Custom OCX Controls: Interfaces

MMC provides snap-in developers with the following interface methods for working with OCX controls:

- **IComponent::GetResultViewType**
- **IConsole2::QueryResultView**

Other Constructs

MMC defines the following additional constructs for working with OCX controls:

- MMCN_INITOCX notification
- MMCN_BTN_CLICK notification
- MMCN_RESTORE_VIEW notification
- MMC_VIEW_OPTIONS_CREATENEW view option (see **IComponent::GetResultViewType**)
- **IS_SPECIAL_DATAOBJECT** macro

Using Custom OCX Controls: Implementation Details

▶   **To launch a custom OCX control in the result pane**

1. Implement a mechanism for storing the selected view type (for example, standard list view or OCX view) and the user's view preference. This allows a standard list view or the OCX view to be loaded when MMC calls **IComponent::GetResultViewType** to display the result pane for a particular scope item in your snap-in.

2. Handle selection of the OCX view in the **IComponent::GetResultViewType** method.

   For a custom view provided by an OLE custom control (OCX), the *ppViewType* parameter should point to the address of a string containing the string representation of the custom control's CLSID. The string must begin with an open brace ({) and end with a close brace (}). **GetResultViewType** expects a CLSID for the OCX control when the first character of the string is a brace. Note that the snap-in must allocate the string with the **CoTaskMemAlloc** Win32 API function.

   The following string represents the **Calendar** control and could be returned in the *ppViewType* parameter to display the **Calendar** control in the result view pane:

   {8E27C92B-1264-101C-8A2F-040224009C02}

MMC allows a single instance of each OCX type per snap-in instance per view. If the MMC_VIEW_OPTIONS_CREATENEW option is selected for the *pViewOptions* parameter, MMC will destroy the cached OCX control and create a new one every time an item requests the OCX view. Otherwise, MMC will display the cached OCX control instance for any of the snap-in's items that request this OCX view.

3. Handle the MMCN_SHOW notification message sent to the snap-in's **IComponent::Notify** implementation. In particular, keep the following things in mind:

- Your snap-in can interact with the OCX control placed in the result pane. To do so, during MMCN_SHOW, call **IConsole2::QueryResultView** to query for the OCX control object's **IUnknown** interface pointer.

- During MMCN_SHOW, the snap-in should cache the cookie (of the scope item) passed in the call to **IComponent::Notify** in the *lpDataObject* argument. The snap-in needs the cookie to identify the correct scope item when MMC sends it an MMCN_SELECT or MMCN_DESELECTALL notification message with a special data object (DOBJ_CUSTOMOCX or DOBJ_CUSTOMWEB).

- For snap-ins that have a custom result pane (OCX or Web), MMC sends the MMCN_SELECT or MMCN_DESELECTALL notification with a special data object when the result pane is selected or deselected. The only way for snap-ins to identify the corresponding scope item is to use the cookie cached during MMCN_SHOW.

- Note that, to make sure that the data object is DOBJ_CUSTOMOCX (for OCX views), the snap-in should check the data object using the **IS_SPECIAL_DATAOBJECT** macro before dereferencing it.

- Upon deselection of the result pane with the OCX view, the *arg* parameter of MMCN_SHOW is set to FALSE, indicating that the OCX view is going out of focus. At this time, the snap-in can do any necessary clean-up.

4. MMC sends the snap-in's **IComponent** implementation an MMCN_INITOCX notification message when its OCX control is initialized for the first time. During MMCN_INITOCX, the snap-in can perform any initialization procedures required by the OCX control.

The *param* parameter passed in the call to **IComponent::Notify** (with MMCN_INITOCX) contains the same **IUnknown** interface pointer obtainable by calling **IConsole2::QueryResultView** during the handling of the MMCN_SHOW notification.

5. If necessary, implement a mechanism by which the OCX control can communicate with the snap-in. One method is for the snap-in to expose a COM interface that the OCX control can call. Note that the OCX control runs in the same thread as the snap-in, so you only need to deal with threading issues if the OCX control is multithreaded.

6. If necessary, handle the MMCN_RESTORE_VIEW notification message. The notification is sent to the snap-in's **IComponent::Notify** method when the result pane for a scope item must be restored by the snap-in after the user has navigated the view history using the **Back** or **Forward** buttons.

   By handling the notification, the snap-in can find out what the view type and view options were the last time the result pane was displayed. This is particularly important if, for example, the **IComponent** associated with the corresponding scope item supports multiple view types. Say the result pane supports two view types: list view and OCX view. The default view type is list view. The user selects another scope item and then presses the **Back** button to return to the same item. The user expects the OCX view, but the snap-in's default behavior is to display the list view. By looking at the MMCN_RESTORE_VIEW notification, the snap-in can find out what the view type and the view options were the last time the result pane was displayed and perform the necessary steps to return the result pane to its previous state.

7. If the snap-in adds items to the **Action** menu when the OCX view is displayed in the result pane, MMC calls the **IExtendContextMenu::AddMenuItems** method of the corresponding **IComponent** implementation with a special data object for the OCX view. To make sure that the data object is DOBJ_CUSTOMOCX (for OCX views), the snap-in should check the data object using the **IS_SPECIAL_DATAOBJECT** macro before dereferencing it. Furthermore, using the cookie cached during MMCN_SHOW in step 3, the snap-in can identify the scope item corresponding to the OCX view and then add menu items accordingly.

8. If necessary, handle the MMCN_BTN_CLICK notification. For an OCX view for which the MMC_VERB_PROPERTIES verb is enabled, when the user clicks the **Properties** button on the console toolbar, MMC sends the snap-in an MMCN_BTN_CLICK notification message. The notification's param argument contains the MMC_VERB_PROPERTIES enumerator value, and its lpDataObject argument contains a special data object (DOBJ_CUSTOMOCX). If needed, the snap-in can identify the scope item that corresponds to the OCX view by using the cookie it cached during MMCN_SHOW as described in step 3 above.

C++ Snap-ins

Sample Code

The code shows sample implementations of the
IComponent::GetResultViewType method. All sample implementations are
taken from the ActiveX sample snap-in that accompanies the MMC SDK.

Note that all sample code assumes Unicode compilation.

IComponent::GetResultViewType Implementation

In the following sample code, only the OCX view type is supported by the
IComponent::GetResultViewType implementation associated with the
particular scope item.

In the ActiveX sample, **CComponent** is an instance of the **IComponent** interface.
The **CComponent::GetResultViewType** method delegates the handling of the
method to the actual snap-in object that represents the selected item. In the case of
the "People-powered Vehicles" item, the method is handled by in the snap-in's
CPerson::GetResultViewType method.

```
HRESULT CPerson::GetResultViewType(LPOLESTR *ppViewType,
                   long *pViewOptions)
{
  // for vb component
  // LPOLESTR lpOleStr;
  // HRESULT hr = StringFromCLSID(CLSID_VBComponent, &lpOleStr);
  // *ppViewType = lpOleStr;

  // for atl component
  LPOLESTR lpOleStr = _T("{9A12FB62-C754-11D2-952C-00C04FB92EC2}");
  *ppViewType = static_cast<LPOLESTR>(CoTaskMemAlloc(
                 (_tcslen(lpOleStr) + 1) * sizeof(_TCHAR)));
  _tcscpy(*ppViewType, lpOleStr);

  if (m_id % 2)
  {
      // create new control
      *pViewOptions = MMC_VIEW_OPTIONS_CREATENEW;
  } else
  {
      // share control
      *pViewOptions = MMC_VIEW_OPTIONS_NONE;
  }

  return S_OK;
}
```

Using the MMC Message OCX Control

This feature is introduced in MMC 1.2.

MMC provides a message OCX control that snap-ins can use for displaying messages in the result pane. The message OCX control optimizes the performance of snap-in error and warning messages and is therefore the recommended way for a snap-in to display such messages.

Snap-ins can also display messages using a modal message box. However, snap-ins should only use modal message boxes in response to a context menu action, or to alert the user of some error condition that is serious enough to warrant their use.

For messages that need only be displayed when a snap-in is selected, the best choice is to use the MMC message OCX control. The OCX control is displayed in the result pane of a snap-in, so the snap-in can only display a message using the control when it has the focus.

Typically, the message OCX should be used to inform the user of any problems the snap-in encounters when enumerating and displaying items in the result pane of the selected scope item.

The **IMessageView** interface allows snap-ins to interact with the message OCX control. Its methods can be used to set the text and icon of the error message displayed by the OCX control.

C++ Snap-ins

▶ **To use the MMC message OCX control**

1. If a snap-in wants to display a message (error message or other) for a particular scope item, it should call **IConsole2::SelectScopeItem** to select the item and force a call to its **IComponent::GetResultViewType** method.

2. Handle selection of the OCX view in the **IComponent::GetResultViewType** method.

   For the MMC message OCX control, the *ppViewType* parameter should be computed with the following:

   ```
   StringFromCLSID (CLSID_MessageView, ppViewType);
   ```

   The **StringFromCLSID** function allocates the buffer and formats the string in the correct manner needed by **GetResultViewType**.

3. Handle the MMCN_SHOW notification message sent to the snap-in's **IComponent::Notify** implementation. To obtain the message OCX control's **IUnknown** interface pointer, call **IConsole2::QueryResultView** and query for the **IMessageView** interface.

   Using the OCX control's **IUnknown** interface pointer, call the methods of the **IMessageView** interface to modify the text and icon of the message. Note that the snap-in can delete the text strings and icon immediately after the calls are made to **IMessageView** methods.

   Upon deselection of the result pane, the *arg* parameter of MMCN_SHOW is set to FALSE, indicating that the OCX view is being torn down. At this time, the snap-in can do any necessary clean-up.

Using Custom Web Pages

The result pane of an MMC console can host HTML pages that are located either locally on the computer with MMC or on an external Web server.

It's very easy to launch a custom Web page in a snap-in. This section discusses everything you need to do in the snap-in to make it happen.

▶ **To launch a custom Web page**

1. Implement a mechanism for storing the selected view type (for example, standard list view or Web view) and the user's view preference. This allows a standard list view or the Web view to be loaded when MMC calls **IComponent::GetResultViewType** to display the result pane for a particular scope item in your snap-in.

2. Handle selection of the Web view in the **IComponent::GetResultViewType** method.

   For a custom view provided by a Web page, *ppViewType* should point to the address of a string containing the URL for the page. The following string represents the URL for the Microsoft Web site and could be returned in the *ppViewType* parameter to display the Web site in the result view pane:

   ```
   www.microsoft.com
   ```

3. Handle the MMCN_SHOW notification message sent to the snap-in's **IComponent::Notify** implementation. In particular, keep the following things in mind:

   - During MMCN_SHOW, the snap-in should cache the cookie (of the scope item) passed in the call to **IComponent::Notify** in the *lpDataObject* argument. The snap-in needs the cookie to identify the correct scope item when MMC sends it an MMCN_SELECT or MMCN_DESELECTALL notification message with a special data object (DOBJ_CUSTOMOCX or DOBJ_CUSTOMWEB).

     For snap-ins that have a custom result pane (OCX or Web), MMC sends the MMCN_SELECT or MMCN_DESELECTALL notification with a special data object when the result pane is selected or deselected. The only way for snap-ins to identify the corresponding scope item is to use the cookie cached during MMCN_SHOW.

     Note that, to make sure that the data object is DOBJ_CUSTOMWEB (for Web views), the snap-in should check the data object using the **IS_SPECIAL_DATAOBJECT** macro before dereferencing it.

   - Upon deselection of the result pane with the Web view, the *arg* parameter of MMCN_SHOW is set to FALSE, indicating that the view is going out of focus. At this time, the snap-in can do any necessary clean-up.

C++ Snap-ins

4. If necessary, handle the MMCN_RESTORE_VIEW notification message. The notification is sent to the snap-in's **IComponent::Notify** method when the result pane for a scope item must be restored by the snap-in after the user has navigated the view history using the **Back** or **Forward** buttons.

By handling the notification, the snap-in can find out what the view type and view options were the last time the result pane was displayed. This is particularly important if, for example, the **IComponent** associated with the corresponding scope item supports multiple view types. Say the result pane supports two view types: list view and Web view. The default view type is list view. The user selects another scope item and then presses the **Back** button to return to the same item. The user expects the Web view, but the snap-in's default behavior is to display the list view. By looking at the MMCN_RESTORE_VIEW notification, the snap-in can find out what the view type and the view options were the last time the result pane was displayed and perform the necessary steps to return the result pane to its previous state.

5. If the snap-in adds items to the **Action** menu when the Web view is displayed in the result pane, MMC calls the **IExtendContextMenu::AddMenuItems** method of the corresponding **IComponent** implementation with a special data object for the Web view. To make sure that the data object is DOBJ_CUSTOMWEB (for Web views), the snap-in should check the data object using the **IS_SPECIAL_DATAOBJECT** macro before dereferencing it. The snap-in can then determine what is selected on the Web view and add menu items accordingly.

C H A P T E R   2 1

Working with Context Menus

MMC generates default context menus for the items in the scope and result panes, and snap-ins can extend these default context menus by providing context menu items of their own. The default context menus contain items, for example, for the **New** and **All Tasks** menus. These default menus are integral to the usability of the console, because they provide lists of the methods (or tasks) that can be invoked on a given item or a list of the objects that can be created within a given container.

Snap-ins add their own items to the default context menus by implementing the **IExtendContextMenu** interface. The snap-in's implementation of **IExtendContextMenu** calls methods in **IContextMenuCallback**, which is implemented by MMC. Some snap-ins also call methods in **IContextMenuProvider** (also implemented by MMC) when they need to build a context menu from scratch.

IContextMenuCallback is a callback mechanism that has one method, **AddItem**, for adding single items to a context menu. MMC provides the snap-in with an instance of **IContextMenuCallback** when one is needed. Snap-ins should not call **QueryInterface** for an instance of **IContextMenuCallback**, nor should they keep the instance of **IContextMenuCallback** beyond the scope in which it is provided.

The **IExtendContextMenu** interface is implemented by the snap-in and allows items to be added using the callback mechanism just mentioned. MMC calls the **IExtendContextMenu::AddMenuItems** method to give the extension an opportunity to add menu items. The snap-in typically calls the **IContextMenuCallback::AddItem** method zero or more times to add items to the context menu. MMC calls the **IExtendContextMenu::Command** method if the user selects an item added by the snap-in in the **AddMenuItems** method call.

C++ Snap-ins

Most snap-ins do not need to use the **IContextMenuProvider** interface. This interface allows snap-ins to add extensible context menus to result pane views other than the default list view. For example, if the view is an OCX, the snap-in itself can create the context menu using the Win32 API. However, using Win32 does not allow other snap-ins to extend this context menu as they can on other items. Instead, the OCX should call **QueryInterface** for a pointer to the **IContextMenuProvider** interface, and generate the context menu using its COM methods. This context menu can then be extended by other snap-ins. Incidentally, **IContextMenuProvider** derives from **IContextMenuCallback**, so it implicitly contains the **IContextMenuCallback::AddItem** method.

IContextMenuProvider methods include **EmptyMenuList**, which clears the context menu, and **ShowContextMenu**, which displays the menu. Its two remaining methods, **AddPrimaryExtensionItems** and **AddThirdPartyExtensionItems**, give other snap-ins the opportunity to extend the context menu.

The snap-in that has added an item to the scope or result pane is always considered to "extend" the item's context menu. MMC always calls its implementation of the **IExtendContextMenu::AddMenuItems** method if that snap-in implements the **IExtendContextMenu** interface. Snap-ins that wish to extend the context menus of items that they did not add must explicitly register themselves as being context menu extensions for items (scope or result) of that particular node type. For details, see "Extending a Primary Snap-in's Context Menu" in Chapter 24.

When a snap-in adds a menu item, it must specify an insertion point in the context menu where that item should be located. The default context menus created by MMC contain a set of insertion points where snap-ins can add items. To maintain consistency, snap-ins can only add items at these predefined insertion points. Snap-ins creating context menus from scratch using the **IContextMenuProvider** interface must provide these insertion points to allow other extensions to add items to their context menus.

The **CONTEXTMENUITEM** structure provides a variety of flags that can be set to manage MMC context menus, even when they are nested deeply and items are to be inserted in specific positions on the menu. MMC enforces menu integrity.

Working with Context Menus: Interfaces

MMC provides snap-in developers with the following interfaces for working with context menus:

- **IExtendContextMenu**
- **IContextMenuCallback**
- **IContextMenuProvider**

Other Constructs

The following additional construct is also used for working with context menus:

- **CONTEXTMENUITEM** structure

Working with Context Menus: Implementation Details

▶ **To add context menu items using IExtendContextMenu**

1. Implement the **IExtendContextMenu** interface and its two methods, **AddMenuItems** and **Command**.

   If you want to add context menu items to the context menu of a scope item, the snap-in's **IComponentData** implementation should implement and expose the **IExtendContextMenu** interface.

   If you want to add context menu items to the context menu of a result item, the snap-in's **IComponent** implementation responsible for that result item and its result pane should implement and expose the **IExtendContextMenu** interface.

   Also, if the user selects a scope item and then displays its context menu, MMC will give both the snap-in's **IComponentData** and **IComponent** (that owns the current view) implementations the opportunity to add menu items. MMC calls the **IExtendContextMenu::AddMenuItems** method implemented by the snap-in's **IComponent** to allow the snap-in to add menu items to the **View** menu. MMC calls the **IExtendContextMenu::AddMenuItems** method implemented by the snap-in's **IComponentData** to allow the snap-in to add menu items to all other menus. Only the snap-in's **IComponent** implementation can add items to the **View** menu.

C++ Snap-ins

If the user displays a scope item's context menu without first selecting the scope item, MMC will only give the snap-in's **IComponentData** implementation the opportunity to add menu items to all menus except the **View** menu. Consequently, the **View** menu only appears for a scope item if the user first selects an item.

2. In the snap-in's implementation of **AddMenuItems**:

- MMC specifies in the *pInsertionAllowed* parameter passed in the call to **AddMenuItems** the insertion points at which the snap-in can add context menu items. The snap-in should check the *pInsertionAllowed* flags for permission before attempting to add menu items at the MMC-defined insertion points. For example, a snap-in should not add menu items to CCM_INSERTIONPOINTID_PRIMARY_NEW or CCM_INSERTIONPOINTID_3RDPARTY_NEW unless the CCM_INSERTIONALLOWED_NEW flag is set.

  A primary snap-in is permitted to reset any of the insertion flags in its **AddMenuItems** method as a way of restricting the kinds of menu items that a third-party extension can add. For example, the primary snap-in can clear the CCM_INSERTIONALLOWED_NEW flag to prevent extensions from adding their own **New** menu items.

  The primary snap-in should not attempt to set bits in *pInsertionAllowed* that were originally cleared. This is because future versions of MMC may use bits that are not currently defined. Third-party extensions should not attempt to change *pInsertionAllowed* at all.

- For each item that the snap-in wants to add at an MMC-defined insertion point or at another insertion point determined by the snap-in, fill a **CONTEXTMENUITEM** structure. See the **CONTEXTMENUITEM** documentation in the MMC COM Reference section of the MMC SDK for details.

- For each item, add the item (its **CONTEXTMENUITEM** structure) to the context menu of the selected scope or result item by calling **AddItem** on the **IContextMenuCallback** interface passed in the *piCallback* parameter in the call to the snap-in's **IExtendContextMenu::AddMenuItems** method.

3. In the snap-in's implementation of **Command**:

- MMC calls **Command** with the same command identifier (**lCommandID**) that the snap-in assigned to the item in its **CONTEXTMENUITEM** structure when it added the item. The snap-in can process the command and then return S_OK.

- MMC reserves negative-valued command IDs for predefined menu command IDs that it sends to a snap-in's **Command** method. The –1 command ID is the MMCC_STANDARD_VIEW_SELECT enumerator value defined in Mmc.h. This is sent to **Command** when the user clicks a standard view command on the **View** menu (**Large**, **Small**, **List**, or **Detail**). This lets the snap-in know that the user is switching away from a custom view (OCX, HTML). After getting an MMCC_STANDARD_VIEW_SELECT command, the snap-in should request a standard view the next time its **IComponent::GetResultViewType** method is called and not request a custom view until one of its custom view menu items is selected. If the snap-in only uses standard views or only uses custom views, it can ignore the MMCC_STANDARD_VIEW_SELECT command.

Sample Code

The following code samples show implementations of the **IExtendContextMenu::AddMenuItems** and **IExtendContextMenu::Command** methods. All samples are taken from the CMenu sample snap-in that accompanies the MMC SDK. The CMenu sample demonstrates how to add items to the default context menus implemented by MMC.

Note that all sample code assumes Unicode compilation.

C++ Snap-ins

IComponent::AddMenuItems Implementation

```
HRESULT CComponent::AddMenuItems(
/* [in] */       LPDATAOBJECT piDataObject,
/* [in] */       LPCONTEXTMENUCALLBACK piCallback,
/* [out][in] */ long *pInsertionAllowed)
{
  CDelegationBase *base = GetOurDataObject(piDataObject)->
                          GetBaseNodeObject();
  return base->OnAddMenuItems(piCallback, pInsertionAllowed);
}
```

In the sample, **CComponent** is an instance of the **IComponent** interface. The **CComponent::AddMenuItems** method delegates the addition of the context menu items to the actual snap-in object that represents the selected scope or result item. In the case of the "Future Vehicles" item, the context menu items are added in the snap-in's **CSpaceVehicle::OnAddMenuItems** method:

```
HRESULT CSpaceVehicle::OnAddMenuItems(
                    IContextMenuCallback *pContextMenuCallback,
                    long *pInsertionsAllowed)
{
  HRESULT hr = S_OK;
  CONTEXTMENUITEM menuItemsNew[] =
  {
      {_T("Space based"), _T("Add a new space based vehicle"),
      IDM_NEW_SPACE, CCM_INSERTIONPOINTID_PRIMARY_NEW, 0,
      CCM_SPECIAL_DEFAULT_ITEM},
      {NULL, NULL, 0, 0, 0 }
  };

  // Loop through and add each of the menu items
  if (*pInsertionsAllowed & CCM_INSERTIONALLOWED_NEW)
  {
      for (LPCONTEXTMENUITEM m = menuItemsNew; m->strName; m++)
      {
          hr = pContextMenuCallback->AddItem(m);
          if (FAILED(hr))
          break;
      }
  }
  return hr;
}
```

IComponent::Command Implementation

```
HRESULT CComponentData::Command(
/* [in] */ long lCommandID,
/* [in] */ LPDATAOBJECT piDataObject)
{
  CDelegationBase *base = GetOurDataObject(piDataObject)->
                          GetBaseNodeObject();
  return base->OnMenuCommand(m_ipConsole, lCommandID);
}
```

As was the case for **CComponent::AddMenuItems**, the
CComponent::Command method delegates the processing of the context menu
item selection to the object that represents the selected scope or result item. In the
case of the "Future Vehicles" item, this object is **CSpaceVehicle**, and it processes
the item selection in its **OnAddMenuItems** method:

```
HRESULT CSpaceVehicle::OnMenuCommand(IConsole *pConsole,
                                     long lCommandID)
{
  switch (lCommandID)
  {
  case IDM_NEW_SPACE:
      pConsole->MessageBox(_T("Create a new space vehicle"),
          _T("Menu Command"), MB_YESNO|MB_ICONQUESTION, NULL);
      break;
  }

  return S_OK;
}
```

C++ Snap-ins

CHAPTER 22

Working with Toolbars and Menu Buttons

MMC makes it easy to use toolbars and menu buttons—two of the most frequently included features in today's applications. There are several interfaces related to these features, beginning with **IControlbar**. This interface allows for creating and manipulating a control bar to hold toolbars and other controls. This interface's methods include **Create**, which is used to create and return the requested control—either a toolbar or a drop-down menu. The other **IControlbar** methods are **Attach**, which associates a control with the control bar, and **Detach**, which breaks that association. You should also use these methods to display or hide a toolbar or menu button.

The **IExtendControlbar** interface allows a snap-in to add toolbars and menu buttons by using a callback interface, and has two methods. The first is **SetControlBar**, which gets a pointer to the **IControlbar** interface implemented by the console. The second method, **ControlbarNotify**, is the mechanism that allows the snap-in to respond to user actions such as mouse-button clicks. When the user causes an event, MMC sends a notification message to the snap-in. All notifications applicable to toolbars and menu buttons are listed in the documentation of the **ControlbarNotify** method in the MMC COM Reference section of the MMC SDK.

The **IToolbar** interface is implemented by the console. It allows your snap-in to perform a variety of actions related to toolbars, including creating them, adding items to them, extending them, and displaying them. The **AddBitmap** method allows you to add images to the toolbar, and the **AddButtons** method provides a way to add an array of buttons to the toolbar. To add a single button, you can use the **InsertButton** method; to remove one, you can use the **DeleteButton** method. Finally, you can get an attribute of a button by using the **GetButtonState** method and set an attribute with the **SetButtonState** method.

C++ Snap-ins

The **IMenuButton** interface is also implemented by the console. The interface enables a snap-in to add menu buttons to the console's menu bar. MMC provides one menu bar per view; when a snap-in has the focus you can add one or more menu buttons for the view to this bar. These buttons are always added by appending them to the buttons already in the menu bar.

The **IMenuButton** interface has three methods. These methods allow you to add and set the attributes and states of menu buttons. The **AddButton** method enables you to add a button to the MMC menu bar for a particular view. The **SetButton** method can then be used to set the text attributes of a button in the menu bar. Finally, the **SetButtonState** method enables you to change the state of a menu button.

The last interface you have to consider when working with toolbars is **IConsoleVerb**. The verbs—which include cut, copy, paste, print, and others you would expect to see—are listed in the **MMC_CONSOLE_VERB** enumeration. You can determine the state of a verb by using the **GetVerbState** method; you can set the state with the **SetVerbState** method.

An extension snap-in can add toolbar buttons and menu buttons for node types that it does not own (that is, node types added by a primary snap-in). MMC always calls an extension snap-in's implementation of the **IExtendControlbar::SetControlBar** method if that snap-in implements the **IExtendControlbar** interface. The extension snap-in can use the **IControlbar** interface passed to it in **SetControlBar** to attach a toolbar or menu button control to a primary snap-in's control bar and then add buttons and manipulate them using the **IToolbar** or **IMenuButton** interface.

Note that the extension snap-in manipulates a primary snap-in's control bar in the same way that the primary snap-in does. That is, programmatically the extension "owns" the control, so it need not consider any other snap-ins when dealing with issues such as the index values of bitmaps placed on the toolbar, or the command ID of items placed in a menu button. The only requirement for the extension snap-in is that it explicitly register itself as being a toolbar extension for items (scope or result) of the particular node type it wants to extend. For details, see "Extending a Primary Snap-in's Control Bar" in Chapter 24.

Working with Toolbars and Menu Buttons: Interfaces

MMC provides snap-in developers with the following interfaces for working with toolbars and menu buttons:

- **IExtendControlbar**
- **IControlbar**
- **IToolbar**
- **IMenuButton**

Other Constructs

The following additional constructs are also used for working with toolbars and menu buttons:

- MMCN_BTN_CLICK notification
- MMCN_MENU_BTNCLICK notification
- MMCN_SELECT notification
- MMCN_DESELECT_ALL notification
- **MMCBUTTON** structure
- **MENUBUTTONDATA** structure
- **MMC_CONSOLE_VERB** enumeration

Working with Toolbars: Implementation Details

▶ **To add toolbars using IExtendControlBar**

1. Implement the **IExtendControlbar** interface and its two methods, **SetControlBar** and **ControlbarNotify**.

   The snap-in's **IComponent** implementation should implement and expose the **IExtendControlBar** interface.

2. In the snap-in's implementation of **SetControlBar**:

   - Cache the **IControlBar** interface pointer that is passed into **SetControlBar**. Use this interface pointer to call the **IControlBar** methods.

   - Call **IControlBar::Create** with the *nType* parameter set to TOOLBAR to create a new toolbar. The *pExtendControlbar* parameter specifies the snap-in's **IExtendControlbar** interface associated with the control. The *ppUnknown* parameter will hold a pointer to the address of the **IUnknown** interface of the new toolbar control. Use this pointer to call the methods of the **IToolbar** interface associated with the new toolbar control.

C++ Snap-ins

- Add bitmaps by calling **IToolbar::AddBitmap**. Call this method only once to add all the toolbar bitmaps at one time.

- Fill an **MMCBUTTON** structure for each toolbar button that the snap-in adds and then add the buttons by calling **IToolbar::AddButtons** to add an array of buttons or **IToolbar::InsertButton** to add a single button.

3. In the snap-in's implementation of **ControlbarNotify**, handle the toolbar-specific notification messages that MMC sends during calls to the **ControlbarNotify** method. There are three such notifications: MMCN_BTN_CLICK, MMCN_SELECT, and MMCN_DESELECT_ALL.

- The MMCN_SELECT notification message is sent to the snap-in's **ControlbarNotify** method when an item is selected or deselected in either the scope pane or result pane. The snap-in can respond to this notification by attaching its toolbar to the toolbar control (using **IControlbar::Attach**) during selection of an item and then detaching the toolbar (using **IControlbar::Detach**) during deselection of that item.

- The MMCN_BTN_CLICK notification message is sent to the snap-in's **ControlbarNotify** implementation when a user clicks one of the snap-in's toolbar buttons. MMC sends this notification with the same command identifier (**idCommand**) that the snap-in assigned to the button in its **MMCBUTTON** structure when it added the button. The snap-in can process the command and then return S_OK.

4. Implement a mechanism for setting the attributes of the toolbar buttons using the **IToolbar::SetButtonState** method.

Sample Code

The following code samples show implementations of the **IExtendControlBar::SetControlBar** and **IExtendControlBar::ControlbarNotify** methods. All samples are taken from the Toolbar sample snap-in that accompanies the MMC SDK. The Toolbar sample demonstrates how to add a toolbar to a snap-in.

Note that all sample code assumes Unicode compilation.

IExtendControlBar::SetControlBar Implementation

```
HRESULT CComponent::SetControlbar(
                  /* [in] */ LPCONTROLBAR pControlbar)
{
  HRESULT hr = S_OK;

  // if we've got a cached toolbar, release it
  if (m_ipToolbar) {
      m_ipToolbar->Release();
      m_ipToolbar = NULL;
  }

  // if we've got a cached control bar, release it
  if (m_ipControlBar) {
      m_ipControlBar->Release();
      m_ipControlBar = NULL;
  }

  //
  // Install new pieces if necessary
  //

  // if a new one came in, cache and AddRef
  if (pControlbar) {
      m_ipControlBar = pControlbar;
      m_ipControlBar->AddRef();

      hr = m_ipControlBar->Create(TOOLBAR,  // type of control
          dynamic_cast<IExtendControlbar *>(this),
          reinterpret_cast<IUnknown **>(&m_ipToolbar));

      _ASSERT(SUCCEEDED(hr));

      // The IControlbar::Create AddRefs the toolbar object it
      // created so no need to do any addref on the interface.

      // add the bitmap to the toolbar
      HBITMAP hbmp = LoadBitmap(g_hinst,
                    MAKEINTRESOURCE(IDR_TOOLBAR1));
      hr = m_ipToolbar->AddBitmap(3, hbmp, 16, 16,
                    RGB(0, 128, 128)); // NOTE, hardcoded value 3
      _ASSERT(SUCCEEDED(hr));

      // Add the buttons to the toolbar
      hr = m_ipToolbar->AddButtons(ARRAYLEN(SnapinButtons1),
                                    SnapinButtons1);

      _ASSERT(SUCCEEDED(hr));
  }

  return hr;
}
```

C++ Snap-ins

In the sample, **CComponent** is an instance of the **IComponent** interface. **SnapinButtons1** is an array of **MMCBUTTON** structures that specify the properties of the toolbar buttons that the Toolbar sample adds.

```
static MMCBUTTON SnapinButtons1[] =
{
  { 0, ID_BUTTONSTART, TBSTATE_ENABLED, TBSTYLE_GROUP,
  L"Start Vehicle", L"Start Vehicle" },
  { 1, ID_BUTTONPAUSE, TBSTATE_ENABLED, TBSTYLE_GROUP,
      L"Pause Vehicle", L"Pause Vehicle"},
  { 2, ID_BUTTONSTOP,  TBSTATE_ENABLED, TBSTYLE_GROUP,
      L"Stop Vehicle",  L"Stop Vehicle" },
};
```

The ID_BUTTONSTART, ID_BUTTONPAUSE, and ID_BUTTONSTOP values specify the resource IDs defined by the snap-in for the toolbar's three buttons.

IExtendControlBar::ControlbarNotify Implementation

```
HRESULT CComponent::ControlbarNotify(
                    /* [in] */ MMC_NOTIFY_TYPE event,
                    /* [in] */ LPARAM arg,
                    /* [in] */ LPARAM param)
{
  HRESULT hr = S_OK;

  if (event == MMCN_SELECT)
  {
      BOOL bScope = (BOOL) LOWORD(arg);
      BOOL bSelect = (BOOL) HIWORD(arg);

      CDelegationBase *base =
          GetOurDataObject(reinterpret_cast<IDataObject *>(param))->
          GetBaseNodeObject();
      hr = base->OnSetToolbar(m_ipControlBar, m_ipToolbar, bScope,
                              bSelect);
  }
  else if (event == MMCN_BTN_CLICK)
  {
      CDelegationBase *base =
          GetOurDataObject(reinterpret_cast<IDataObject *>(arg))->
          GetBaseNodeObject();
      hr = base->OnToolbarCommand(m_ipConsole, (int)param);
  }

  return hr;
}
```

This sample implementation of the **ControlbarNotify** method handles the MMCN_SELECT and MMCN_BTN_CLICK notifications. The **CComponent::ControlbarNotify** method delegates the handling of the notification messages to the actual snap-in object that represents the selected scope or result item.

For example, when the user selects the "Future Vehicles" scope item in the scope pane and then a "Vehicle" result item in its result pane, the snap-in attaches its toolbar to the toolbar control. This is done in the **CRocket::OnSetToolbar** method, where **CRocket** is the snap-in object that represents the selected "Vehicle" result item.

```
HRESULT CRocket::OnSetToolbar(IControlbar *pControlbar,
                             IToolbar *pToolbar, BOOL bScope,
                             BOOL bSelect)
{
  HRESULT hr = S_OK;

  if (bSelect) {
      // Always make sure the toolbar is attached
      hr = pControlbar->Attach(TOOLBAR, pToolbar);
  } else {
      // Always make sure the toolbar is detached
      hr = pControlbar->Detach(pToolbar);
  }

  return hr;
}
```

The same method on the same object is called when the selected "Vehicle" result item is deselected.

C++ Snap-ins

The **CComponent::ControlbarNotify** method also delegates the handling of the MMCN_BTN_CLICK notification message to the snap-in object that represents the selected scope or result item. For example, MMC sends this message when the user selects a "Vehicle" result item (a **CRocket** object) and then clicks one of the toolbar buttons.

```
HRESULT CRocket::OnToolbarCommand(IConsole *pConsole, int commandID)
{
  _TCHAR szVehicle[128];

  switch (commandID)
  {
  case ID_BUTTONSTART:
      iStatus = RUNNING;
      break;

  case ID_BUTTONPAUSE:
      iStatus = PAUSED;
      break;

  case ID_BUTTONSTOP:
      iStatus = STOPPED;
      break;
  }

  wsprintf(szVehicle, _T("Vehicle %s has been %s"), szName,
      (long)commandID == ID_BUTTONSTART ? _T("started") :
      (long)commandID == ID_BUTTONPAUSE ? _T("paused") :
      (long)commandID == ID_BUTTONSTOP ? _T("stopped") :
      _T("!!!unknown command!!!"));
  int ret = 0;
  MAKE_WIDEPTR_FROMTSTR_ALLOC(wszVehicle, szVehicle);
  pConsole->MessageBox(wszVehicle, L"Vehicle command",
                    MB_OK | MB_ICONINFORMATION, &ret);

  return S_OK;
}
```

Each **CRocket** object stores its status (RUNNING, PAUSED, or STOPPED) in its **iStatus** member variable.

Calling IToolbar::SetButtonState

The Toolbar sample sets the attributes of its toolbar buttons in its
MMCN_SELECT notification handler during the selection of a "Vehicle" result
item. As usual, the handling of the notification is delegated to the **CRocket** object
that represents the selected result item:

```
HRESULT CRocket::OnSelect(CComponent *pComponent, IConsole *pConsole,
                          BOOL bScope, BOOL bSelect)
{
  if (bSelect) {
      switch (iStatus)
      {
      case RUNNING:
          pComponent->getToolbar()->SetButtonState(ID_BUTTONSTART,
                          BUTTONPRESSED, TRUE);
      pComponent->getToolbar()->SetButtonState(ID_BUTTONSTART,
                          ENABLED, FALSE);
      pComponent->getToolbar()->SetButtonState(ID_BUTTONPAUSE,
                          BUTTONPRESSED, FALSE);
          pComponent->getToolbar()->SetButtonState(ID_BUTTONPAUSE,
                          ENABLED, TRUE);
          pComponent->getToolbar()->SetButtonState(ID_BUTTONSTOP,
                          BUTTONPRESSED, FALSE);
          pComponent->getToolbar()->SetButtonState(ID_BUTTONSTOP,
                          ENABLED, TRUE);
          break;

      case PAUSED:
          //snap-in code omitted here
          break;

      case STOPPED:
          //snap-in code omitted here
          break;
      }
  }

  return S_OK;
}
```

Working with Menu Buttons: Implementation Details

▶ **To add menu buttons using IExtendControlBar**

1. Implement the **IExtendControlbar** interface and its two methods, **SetControlBar** and **ControlbarNotify**.

   The snap-in's **IComponent** implementation should implement and expose the **IExtendControlBar** interface.

2. In the snap-in's implementation of **SetControlBar**:

   - Cache the **IControlBar** interface pointer that is passed into **SetControlBar**. Use this interface pointer to call the **IControlBar** methods.

   - Call **IControlBar::Create** with the *nType* parameter set to MENUBUTTON to create a new menu button. The *pExtendControlbar* parameter specifies the snap-in's **IExtendControlbar** interface associated with the control. The *ppUnknown* parameter will hold a pointer to the address of the **IUnknown** interface of the menu button control. Use this pointer to call the methods of the **IMenuButton** interface associated with the new control.

   - Add the menu button by calling **IMenuButton::AddButton**. The *idCommand* parameter specifies a snap-in-defined value that uniquely identifies the menu button to be added. The *lpButtonText* and *lpTooltipText* parameters point to the values of the button text and tooltip text, respectively.

3. In the snap-in's implementation of **ControlbarNotify**, handle the menu button-specific notification messages that MMC sends during calls to the **ControlbarNotify** method. There are three such notifications: MMCN_MENU_BTNCLICK, MMCN_SELECT, and MMCN_DESELECT_ALL.

- The MMCN_SELECT notification message is sent to the snap-in's **ControlbarNotify** method when an item is selected or deselected in either the scope pane or result pane. The snap-in can respond to this notification by attaching its menu button to the control (using **IControlbar::Attach**) and enabling the menu button (using **IControlbar::SetButtonState**) during selection of an item. During deselection of the the item, the snap-in can once again call **IControlbar::SetButtonState**, this time to disable the menu button and make it hidden.

- The MMCN_MENU_BTNCLICK notification message is sent to the snap-in's **ControlbarNotify** implementation when a user clicks one of the snap-in's menu buttons. MMC sends this notification with a **MENUBUTTONDATA** structure that holds the same command identifier (**idCommand**) that the snap-in specified for the button when it added the button using **IMenuButton::AddButton**. The snap-in can process the command and then return S_OK.

4. Implement a mechanism for setting the attributes of the menu buttons using the **IMenuButton::SetButtonState** method.

Sample Code

The following code samples show implementations of the **IExtendControlBar::SetControlBar** and **IExtendControlBar::ControlbarNotify** methods. All samples are taken from the MenuBtn sample snap-in that accompanies the MMC SDK. The MenuBtn sample demonstrates how to add a menu button to a snap-in.

Note that all sample code assumes Unicode compilation.

C++ Snap-ins

IExtendControlBar::SetControlBar Implementation

```cpp
HRESULT CComponent::SetControlbar(
                    /* [in] */ LPCONTROLBAR pControlbar)
{
  HRESULT hr = S_OK;

  //
  //  Clean up
  //

  // if we've got a cached control bar, release it
  if (m_ipControlBar) {
      m_ipControlBar->Release();
      m_ipControlBar = NULL;
  }

  // if we've got a cached menubutton, release it
  if (m_ipMenuButton) {
      m_ipMenuButton->Release();
      m_ipMenuButton = NULL;
  }

  //
  // Install new pieces if necessary
  //

  // if a new one came in, cache and AddRef
  if (pControlbar) {
      m_ipControlBar = pControlbar;
      m_ipControlBar->AddRef();

      // add our menu button
      hr = m_ipControlBar->Create(MENUBUTTON,  // type of control
          dynamic_cast<IExtendControlbar *>(this),
          reinterpret_cast<IUnknown **>(&m_ipMenuButton));

          _ASSERT(SUCCEEDED(hr));

      // The IControlbar::Create AddRefs the menu button object it
      // created so no need to do any addref on the interface.

      hr = m_ipMenuButton->AddButton(IDR_STATE_MENU, L"Vehicle
                          Status", L"Change vehicle state");
      _ASSERT(SUCCEEDED(hr));
  }

  return hr;
}
```

In the sample, **CComponent** is an instance of the **IComponent** interface. IDR_STATE_MENU is a snap-in resource that defines the menu button layout.

IExtendControlBar::ControlbarNotify Implementation

```
{
  HRESULT hr = S_OK;

  if (event == MMCN_SELECT)
  {
      CDelegationBase *base =
          GetOurDataObject(reinterpret_cast<IDataObject *>(param))->
          GetBaseNodeObject();

          hr = base->SetMenuState(m_ipControlBar, m_ipMenuButton,
                  (BOOL) LOWORD(arg), (BOOL)HIWORD(arg));
  }
  else if (event == MMCN_MENU_BTNCLICK)
  {
      CDelegationBase *base =
          GetOurDataObject(reinterpret_cast<IDataObject *>(arg))->
          GetBaseNodeObject();

      hr = base->OnSetMenuButton(m_ipConsole,
              (MENUBUTTONDATA *)param);
  }

  return hr;
}
```

This sample implementation of the **ControlbarNotify** method handles the MMCN_SELECT and MMCN_MENU_BTNCLICK notifications. The **CComponent::ControlbarNotify** method delegates the handling of the notification messages to the actual snap-in object that represents the selected scope or result item.

C++ Snap-ins

For example, when the user selects the "Future Vehicles" scope item in the scope pane and then a "Vehicle" result item in its result pane, the snap-in attaches its menu button to the toolbar control and then sets the button's state to visible and enabled. This is done in the **CRocket::SetMenuState** method, where **CRocket** is the snap-in object that represents the selected "Vehicle" result item.

```
HRESULT CRocket::SetMenuState(IControlbar *pControlbar,
                             IMenuButton *pMenuButton,
                             BOOL bScope,
                             BOOL bSelect)
{
  HRESULT hr = S_OK;

  if (bSelect)
  {
      // Always make sure the menuButton is attached
      hr = pControlbar->Attach(MENUBUTTON, pMenuButton);

      hr = pMenuButton->SetButtonState(IDR_STATE_MENU, HIDDEN,
          FALSE);
      hr = pMenuButton->SetButtonState(IDR_STATE_MENU, ENABLED,
          TRUE);
  }
  else if (!bSelect)
  {
      hr = pMenuButton->SetButtonState(IDR_STATE_MENU, ENABLED,
          FALSE);
      hr = pMenuButton->SetButtonState(IDR_STATE_MENU, HIDDEN,
          TRUE);
  }

  return hr;
}
```

The same method on the same object is called when the selected "Vehicle" result item is deselected.

The **CComponent::ControlbarNotify** method also delegates the handling of the MMCN_MENU_BTNCLICK notification message to the snap-in object that represents the selected scope or result item. For example, MMC sends this message when the user selects a "Vehicle" result item (a **CRocket** object) and then clicks the menu button.

```
HRESULT CRocket::OnSetMenuButton(IConsole *pConsole,
                                 MENUBUTTONDATA *pmbd)
{
  HMENU hMenu = GetMenu(pmbd->idCommand);
  HRESULT hr = S_FALSE;
  HWND  hWnd;

  if (hMenu)
  {
      hr = pConsole->GetMainWindow(&hWnd);

      if (SUCCEEDED(hr))
      {
          LONG ret = TrackPopupMenuEx(hMenu, TPM_NONOTIFY |
                     TPM_RETURNCMD, pmbd->x,
                     pmbd->y, hWnd, NULL);

          if (ret != 0) { // !cancelled
              hr = OnMenuButtonCommand(pConsole, pmbd->idCommand,
                   ret);
          }
      }

      DestroyMenu(hMenu);
  }

  return hr;
}
```

The method first calls **GetMenu**, a snap-in-defined function that loads the snap-in's menu resource and calls the Win32 API function **EnableMenuItem** to specify the attributes of the menu button's items.

```
HMENU CRocket::GetMenu(int nMenuId)
{
  HMENU hResMenu = LoadMenu(g_hinst, MAKEINTRESOURCE(nMenuId));
  HMENU hMenu = GetSubMenu(hResMenu,0);

  if (IDR_STATE_MENU == nMenuId) {
      switch (iStatus)
      {
      case RUNNING:
          EnableMenuItem(hMenu, ID_COMMAND_START, MF_BYCOMMAND |
          MF_GRAYED);
          EnableMenuItem(hMenu, ID_COMMAND_PAUSE, MF_BYCOMMAND |
          MF_ENABLED);
          EnableMenuItem(hMenu, ID_COMMAND_STOP, MF_BYCOMMAND |
          MF_ENABLED);
          break;

      case PAUSED:
          //sample code removed here
          break;

      case STOPPED:
          //sample code removed here
          break;
      }
  } else {
      // some other menu, set state accordingly
  }

  return hMenu;
}
```

The ID_COMMAND_START, ID_COMMAND_PAUSE, and ID_COMMAND_STOP values specify the resource IDs defined by the snap-in for the menu button's three items.

Returning to the **CRocket::OnSetMenuButton** method, we see that it then calls the MMC interface method **IConsole2::GetMainWindow** to get a handle to the console's main frame window. It then passes this handle in a call to another Win32 API function, **TrackPopupMenuEx**; this function displays the menu button on the main frame window at the positions indicated by the **x** and **y** members of the **MENUBUTTONDATA** structure passed into **CRocket::OnSetMenuButton**. The **TrackPopupMenuEx** function also tracks the selection of items on the menu button and returns the command ID of the user's selection. The **CRocket** object than processes this selection in its **OnMenuButtonCommand** method:

```
HRESULT CRocket::OnMenuButtonCommand(IConsole *pConsole, int nMenuId,
                                     long lCommandID)
{
  _TCHAR szVehicle[128];

  if (IDR_STATE_MENU == nMenuId) {
      switch (lCommandID) {
      case ID_COMMAND_START:
          iStatus = RUNNING;
          break;

      case ID_COMMAND_PAUSE:
          iStatus = PAUSED;
          break;

      case ID_COMMAND_STOP:
          iStatus = STOPPED;
          break;
      }

      wsprintf(szVehicle, _T("Vehicle %s has been %s"), szName,
               (long)iStatus == RUNNING ? _T("started") :
               (long)iStatus == PAUSED ? _T("paused") :
               (long)iStatus == STOPPED ? _T("stopped") :
               _T("!!!unknown command!!!"));

      int ret = 0;
      MAKE_WIDEPTR_FROMTSTR(pszVehicle, szVehicle);
      pConsole->MessageBox(pszVehicle, L"Vehicle command",
                           MB_OK | MB_ICONINFORMATION, &ret);
  }

  return S_OK;
}
```

Each **CRocket** object stores its status (RUNNING, PAUSED, or STOPPED) in its **iStatus** member variable.

CHAPTER 23

Adding Property Pages and Wizard Pages

A *property sheet* is a window that allows the user to view and edit the properties of an item. A property sheet contains one or more overlapping child windows called *property pages*, each containing control windows for setting a group of related properties. For example, a page can contain the controls for setting the font properties of an item, including the type style, point size, color, and so on. Each page has a tab that the user can click to bring the page to the foreground of the property sheet. To learn how to add property pages to a snap-in, see "Adding Property Pages."

There is also a special type of property sheet called a *wizard*. Wizards are designed to present pages one at a time in a sequence that is controlled by the application. Instead of selecting from a group of pages by clicking a tab, users move forward and backward through the sequence, one page at a time, by clicking **Next** or **Back** buttons located at the bottom of the wizard. To learn how to add wizard pages to a snap-in, see "Adding Wizard Pages" later in this chapter.

C++ Snap-ins

Adding Property Pages

For more details about property sheets in general, see the Microsoft Platform SDK documentation. This section assumes that you have a thorough understanding of implementing property sheets and property pages using the Platform SDK. The rest of the discussion focuses on adding property pages to a snap-in using the interfaces and other constructs provided in the MMC SDK.

The MMC SDK defines three main interfaces for working with property pages. Two of these interfaces—**IPropertySheetProvider** and **IPropertySheetCallback**—are implemented by MMC and are used to create and maintain property sheet objects. The third interface, **IExtendPropertySheet2**, is implemented by the snap-in.

The **IPropertySheetProvider** interface implements Win32 property sheets as COM objects. This interface includes five methods:

- **CreatePropertySheet** creates a property sheet frame.
- **FindPropertySheet** determines whether a property sheet already exists.
- **AddPrimaryPages** collects pages from a primary snap-in.
- **AddExtensionPages** collects pages from extension snap-ins.
- **Show** displays a specific property sheet frame.

MMC uses its own **IPropertySheetProvider** implementation when it initiates the display of the property sheet—for instance, when the user activates the properties verb on an item. If the snap-in wishes to display property sheets at other times, it should call directly into MMC's **IPropertySheetProvider**. In both cases, the **IPropertySheetProvider** methods call into the snap-in's **IExtendPropertySheet** implementation and supply an **IPropertySheetCallback** interface pointer so that the snap-in can add property pages.

The **IPropertySheetCallback** interface contains two methods. **AddPage** allows a snap-in to add a single page to the MMC-owned property sheet of a scope or result item. **RemovePage** allows a snap-in to remove a page.

Snap-ins must also use **IPropertySheetProvider** to add a feature that has a property sheet as a user interface, but identifies the sheet as something else. An example of this is the **Select Computer** dialog box. This dialog box appears in the Event Viewer snap-in when the user selects the Event Viewer node and clicks the **Connect to another computer** context menu item.

A property sheet is associated with each scope item or result item for which the MMC_VERB_PROPERTIES verb is enabled. Snap-ins can enable this and all MMC verbs by calling the **IConsoleVerb::SetVerbState** method.

Note that MMC owns all property sheets, regardless of whether they are created by the snap-in using **IPropertySheetProvider** or used by the snap-in using **IPropertySheetCallback**. Snap-ins own property pages that they add to property sheets, but the property sheet objects themselves are created, maintained, and destroyed by MMC. Note also that each property sheet is modeless and is created in its own thread.

To add property pages that appear when the user activates the properties verb, snap-ins must implement the **IExtendPropertySheet2** interface. The **CreatePropertyPages** method is used to define the properties of one or more property pages using the **PROPSHEETPAGE** structure. The standard size for a property page in an MMC console is 252 dialog units horizontally and 218 dialog units vertically. The property pages are created using the **CreatePropertySheetPage** function and then added to the property sheet of an item using the **AddPage** method.

Snap-ins must also implement the **QueryPagesFor** method. MMC calls this method to verify that a property page exists for a particular scope or result item when the user clicks the **Properties** context menu item.

When an item's properties have changed, a snap-in uses the **MMCPropertyChangeNotify** function to notify its **IComponent** or **IComponentData** interface of the change. When a property sheet is destroyed, the snap-in must call the **MMCFreeNotifyHandle** function.

Primary snap-ins that add node types that can be extended by property page extensions must enable the MMC_VERB_PROPERTIES verb for the extendable items. For details about enabling standard verbs, see Chapter 25, "Enabling MMC Standard Verbs."

Primary snap-ins that do not add property pages of their own must still implement **IExtendPropertySheet2** and return S_OK in their implementation of the **IExtendPropertySheet2** methods.

C++ Snap-ins

Adding Property Pages: Interfaces

MMC provides snap-in developers with the following interfaces for working with property pages:

- **IExtendPropertySheet2**
- **IPropertySheetProvider**
- **IPropertySheetCallback**

Other Constructs

The following additional constructs are also used for working with property pages:

- MMCN_PROPERTY_CHANGE notification
- **PROPSHEETPAGE** structure
- **CreatePropertySheetPage** API function
- **MMCFreeNotifyHandle** function
- **MMCPropertyChangeNotify** function
- **MMCPropertyHelp** function
- **MMCPropPageCallback** function

Adding Property Pages: Implementation Details

The procedures outlined in this section assume that you want to create and add property pages to a property sheet that MMC creates and maintains for you. This requires that you implement the **IExtendPropertySheet2** interface and use the **IPropertySheetCallback** interface. You are not required to use the **IPropertySheetProvider** interface. If you are not sure whether or not you need to create your own property sheet, see "Using **IPropertySheetProvider**" later in this chapter before continuing.

▶ **To add a property page**

1. Determine whether you want to implement the property page for a scope item or for a result item. Then, depending on your choice, make sure that the snap-in's **IComponentData** or correct **IComponent** implementation implements the **IExtendPropertySheet2** interface.

2. Implement the **IExtendPropertySheet2::CreatePropertyPages** method in the appropriate **IComponentData** or **IComponent** implementation to add property pages.

   In the implementation of **CreatePropertyPages**:

   - Define one or more property pages by filling the **PROPSHEETPAGE** structure for each of the property pages with information about the page. Note that the standard size for a property page in an MMC console is 252 dialog units horizontally and 218 dialog units vertically.

   - For each **PROPSHEETPAGE** structure, call the API function **CreatePropertySheetPage** to create a property sheet page. The function returns a handle to the HPROPSHEETPAGE type that uniquely identifies the page.

   - Using the pointer to the **IPropertySheetCallback** interface passed to the snap-in in the call to the **CreatePropertyPages** method, call the **IPropertySheetCallback::AddPage** method to add each property page to the MMC-provided property sheet.

3. Implement a dialog box procedure for each property page. The **pfnDlgProc** member of each property page's **PROPSHEETPAGE** structure should be set to the address of this procedure.

4. Implement the **IExtendPropertySheet2::QueryPagesFor** method. MMC calls this method when the user selects a scope or result item and clicks the **Properties** context menu item. If this method returns S_OK, MMC then calls the snap-in's implementation of the **IExtendPropertySheet2::CreatePropertyPages** method.

5. Use the **IConsoleVerb::SetVerbState** method to enable the MMC_VERB_PROPERTIES enumerator value of the **MMC_CONSOLE_VERB** enumeration. The snap-in should call **SetVerbState** in the handler for the MMCN_SELECT notification sent to the corresponding **IComponentData** or **IComponent** object. This notification is sent to the snap-in when the user selects the scope item or result item for which you are implementing the property page.

6. The snap-in should call the **MMCPropertyChangeNotify** function if the user can change any page properties. As a result of this method call, an MMCN_PROPERTY_CHANGE notification is sent to the corresponding **IComponentData** or **IComponent** object. The snap-in should be prepared to handle this notification.

C++ Snap-ins

Sample Code

The following code shows sample implementations of **IExtendPropertySheet2** methods. All samples are taken from the PropPage sample snap-in that accompanies the MMC SDK. The PropPage sample demonstrates how to add property pages using the **IExtendPropertySheet2** interface. The sample snap-in displays a property sheet and adds pages to it when the user activates the properties verb of one of the "Rocket" items in the result pane of the "Future Vehicles" scope item.

Note that all sample code assumes Unicode compilation.

IExtendPropertySheet2::QueryPagesFor Implementation

```
HRESULT CComponent::QueryPagesFor(
    LPDATAOBJECT lpDataObject  // pointer to the data object)
{
  CDelegationBase *base = GetOurDataObject(lpIDataObject)->
                          GetBaseNodeObject();

  return base->QueryPagesFor();
}
```

In the sample, **CComponent** is an instance of the **IComponent** interface; it also implements **IExtendPropertySheet2**. The **CComponent** object delegates all behavior with respect to property pages to the actual snap-in object that represents the selected scope or result item. In the case of a "Rocket" result item, the snap-in object is **CRocket**. Here is how it handles the call to the snap-in's **IExtendPropertySheet2::QueryPagesFor** implementation:

```
HRESULT CRocket::QueryPagesFor()
{
  return S_OK;
}
```

IExtendPropertySheet2::CreatePropertyPages Implementation

```
HRESULT CComponent::CreatePropertyPages(
         /* [in] */ LPPROPERTYSHEETCALLBACK lpProvider,
         /* [in] */ LONG_PTR handle,
         /* [in] */ LPDATAOBJECT lpIDataObject)
{
  CDelegationBase *base = GetOurDataObject(lpIDataObject)->
                          GetBaseNodeObject();

  return base->CreatePropertyPages(lpProvider, handle);
}
```

The creation of the property pages is delegated to the selected **CRocket** object:

```
HRESULT CRocket::CreatePropertyPages(IPropertySheetCallback
                  *lpProvider, LONG_PTR handle)
{
  PROPSHEETPAGE psp;
  HPROPSHEETPAGE hPage = NULL;

  psp.dwSize = sizeof(PROPSHEETPAGE);
  psp.dwFlags = PSP_DEFAULT | PSP_USETITLE | PSP_USEICONID |
                PSP_HASHELP;
  psp.hInstance = g_hinst;
  psp.pszTemplate = MAKEINTRESOURCE(IDD_PROPPAGE_LARGE);
  psp.pfnDlgProc = DialogProc;
  psp.lParam = reinterpret_cast<LPARAM>(this);
  psp.pszTitle = MAKEINTRESOURCE(IDS_PST_ROCKET);
  psp.pszIcon = MAKEINTRESOURCE(IDI_PSI_ROCKET);

  hPage = CreatePropertySheetPage(&psp);
  _ASSERT(hPage);

  return lpProvider->AddPage(hPage);
}
```

C++ Snap-ins

IExtendPropertySheet2::GetWatermarks Implementation

```
HRESULT CComponent::GetWatermarks(
                /* [in]  */ LPDATAOBJECT lpIDataObject,
                /* [out] */ HBITMAP *lphWatermark,
                /* [out] */ HBITMAP *lphHeader,
                /* [out] */ HPALETTE *lphPalette,
                /* [out] */ BOOL *bStretch)
{
  CDelegationBase *base = GetOurDataObject(lpIDataObject)->
                          GetBaseNodeObject();

  return base->GetWatermarks(lphWatermark, lphHeader, lphPalette,
          bStretch);
}
```

Property sheets do not support watermarks:

```
HRESULT CRocket::GetWatermarks(HBITMAP *lphWatermark,
                HBITMAP *lphHeader,
                HPALETTE *lphPalette,
                BOOL *bStretch)
{
  return S_FALSE;
}
```

Note that MMC does not call the the snap-in's
IExtendPropertySheet2::GetWatermarks method when property pages are
added to a property sheet. The method is only called for wizards. The
implementation is shown here for the sake of completeness.

Adding Wizard Pages

This feature is introduced in MMC 1.1.

A *wizard* is a special type of property sheet. Wizards are designed to present pages one at a time in a sequence that is controlled by the application. Instead of selecting from a group of pages by clicking a tab, users move forward and backward through the sequence, one page at a time, by clicking **Next** or **Back** buttons located at the bottom of the wizard.

MMC allows a snap-in to add either standard wizard pages or Wizard97 pages. Wizard97 pages have a different style than standard wizard pages. Note that snap-ins are strongly encouraged to use the Wizard97 style for all wizards they create in order to have a consistent style throughout MMC.

For details about wizard pages in general, see the Microsoft Platform SDK documentation. This section assumes that you have a thorough understanding of implementing property sheets and property pages, including wizard pages, using the Platform SDK. The rest of the discussion focuses on adding wizard pages to a snap-in using the interfaces and other constructs provided in the MMC SDK.

The MMC interfaces used for adding wizard pages are the same as those used for adding property pages. The **IPropertySheetProvider** and **IPropertySheetCallback** interfaces are implemented by MMC and are used to create and maintain property sheet objects. The **IExtendPropertySheet2** interface is implemented by the snap-in.

For MMC to create the property sheet with wizard controls (a wizard), the snap-in itself must create the wizard using the **IPropertySheetProvider** interface and its **CreatePropertySheet** method. The snap-in can also specify in the method call that the wizard use the Wizard97 style.

In addition to the **CreatePropertySheet** method, the **IPropertySheetProvider** interface includes four other methods:

- **FindPropertySheet** determines whether a property sheet already exists for a particular scope or result item.
- **AddPrimaryPages** collects pages from a primary snap-in.
- **AddExtensionPages** collects pages from extension snap-ins.
- **Show** displays a specific property sheet frame.

C++ Snap-ins

To define wizard pages with watermarks and header bitmaps, snap-ins must implement the **IExtendPropertySheet2** interface. The **CreatePropertyPages** method is used to define the properties of one or more wizard pages using the **PROPSHEETPAGE** structure. The **GetWatermarks** method is used to specify the watermark and header bitmaps for the wizard. MMC calls the **QueryPagesFor** method to verify that a wizard page exists for a particular scope or result item when the user clicks the **Properties** context menu item.

Wizard pages are created using the **CreatePropertySheetPage** API function and then added to the wizard using the **AddPage** and the **IPropertySheetProvider::AddPrimaryPages** methods.

When wizard properties have changed, a snap-in uses the **MMCPropertyChangeNotify** function to notify its **IComponent** or **IComponentData** interface of the change. When a wizard is destroyed, the snap-in must call the **MMCFreeNotifyHandle** function.

Adding Wizard Pages: Interfaces

Snap-in developers use the same interfaces and other language constructs for adding both property pages and wizard pages. See "Adding Property Pages: Interfaces" earlier in this chapter for a complete list.

Adding Wizard Pages: Implementation Details

The procedures outlined in this section assume that you want to create and add wizard pages to your snap-in. To add standard property pages, see "Adding Property Pages: Implementation Details" earlier in this chapter.

▶ **To add wizard pages**

1. Implement a procedure, say a function called **InvokeWizardSheet**, that is called when the user performs an action that causes the snap-in to invoke the wizard.

2. In **InvokeWizardSheet**, call the **IPropertySheetProvider::CreatePropertySheet** method to create a wizard. Make sure that the *type* parameter passed in the call is set to FALSE (for wizard).

3. In **InvokeWizardSheet**, call the **IPropertySheetProvider::AddPrimaryPages** method, passing the snap-in's **IComponentData** or **IComponent** interface as the first parameter.

   In MMC's **AddPrimaryPages** implementation, MMC calls back to the snap-in's **IExtendPropertySheet2::CreatePropertyPages** method.

4. In **InvokeWizardSheet**, call **IPropertySheetProvider::Show** to display the wizard.

5. Implement the **IExtendPropertySheet2::CreatePropertyPages** method in the appropriate **IComponentData** or **IComponent** implementation to add pages to the wizard.

   In the implementation of **CreatePropertyPages**:

   - Define one or more wizard pages by filling the **PROPSHEETPAGE** structure for each of the pages with information about the page. Note that the standard size for a property page in an MMC console is 252 dialog units horizontally and 218 dialog units vertically.

   - For each **PROPSHEETPAGE** structure, call the API function **CreatePropertySheetPage** to create a page. The function returns a handle to the HPROPSHEETPAGE type that uniquely identifies the page.

   - Using the pointer to the **IPropertySheetCallback** interface passed to the snap-in in the call to the **CreatePropertyPages** method, call the **IPropertySheetCallback::AddPage** method to add each page to the wizard.

6. Implement a dialog box procedure for each page. The **pfnDlgProc** member of each page's **PROPSHEETPAGE** structure should be set to the address of this procedure.

7. The snap-in should call the **MMCPropertyChangeNotify** function if the user has changed any wizard properties. As a result of this method call, an MMCN_PROPERTY_CHANGE notification is sent to the appropriate **IComponent** object. The snap-in should be prepared to handle this notification.

C++ Snap-ins

▶ **To add wizard pages with the Wizard97 style**

To add wizard pages with the Wizard97 style, follow the previous procedure for adding wizard pages. In addition to the steps in that procedure:

1. In the call to the **IPropertySheetProvider::CreatePropertySheet** method, set the *dwOptions* parameter to MMC_PSO_NEWWIZARDTYPE. This specifies the Wizard97 style.

2. Implement the **IExtendPropertySheet2::GetWatermarks** method to specify the watermark and header bitmaps for the wizard.

3. By setting the **pszHeaderTitle** and **pszHeaderSubTitle** members of the **PROPSHEETPAGE** structure, you can specify the header title and subtitle text for interior Wizard97 pages.

▶ **To add Wizard97-style pages without watermarks and header bitmaps**

To add Wizard97-style pages without watermarks and header bitmaps, follow the instructions in "To add wizard pages with the Wizard97 style." In the snap-in's implementation of **IExtendPropertySheet2::GetWatermarks**, return a success code (for example, S_OK or S_FALSE) without providing any bitmaps.

Note that if **GetWatermarks** is not implemented or returns a failure code, MMC reverts the wizard requested by the snap-in in the call to **IPropertySheetProvider::CreatePropertySheet** to the non-Wizard97 style. This is to maintain compatibility with MMC 1.1.

Sample Code

The following code shows a sample implementation of an **InvokeWizard97Sheet** function for creating a Wizard97 page with watermark and header bitmaps.

A sample implementation of the **IExtendPropertySheet2::GetWatermarks** method is also shown below. For a sample implementation of the other **IExtendPropertySheet2** methods, see the Sample Code section of "Adding Property Pages: Implementation Details" earlier in this chapter.

Note that all sample code assumes Unicode compilation.

InvokeWizard97Sheet Function Implementation

```
HRESULT
InvokeWizard97Sheet (
  IPropertySheetProvider *pPrshtProvider,
  LPCWSTR wszTitle,
  LONG lCookie,
  LPDATAOBJECT pDataObject,
  IExtendPropertySheet2 *pPrimary, //IExtendPropertySheet2 interface
                                   //on the calling CComponentData
  USHORT usStartingPage)
{
  HRESULT hr = S_OK;

  // Because we pass NULL for the second arg, the first is not
  //allowed to be null.
  _ASSERT(NULL != lCookie);

  hr = pPrshtProvider->CreatePropertySheet(
                          wszTitle,
                          FALSE, // for wizard
                          lCookie,
                          pDataObject,
                          MMC_PSO_NEWWIZARDTYPE // for Wizard97 style
                          );
  if (S_OK == hr)
     return S_FALSE;

  hr = pPrshtProvider->AddPrimaryPages(pPrimary, TRUE, NULL, TRUE);

  if (S_OK == hr)
     return S_FALSE;

  hr = pPrshtProvider->Show(NULL, usStartingPage);

  if (S_FALSE == hr) // recover from a failed Show
  {
     pPrshtProvider->Show(-1,0); // frees wizard resources
                                 // held by MMC
     DeletePageHandles(usStartingPage); // snap-in defined function
                                        // to delete page handles
                                        // held by the snap-in
     return S_FALSE;
  }
  return hr;
}
```

C++ Snap-ins

IExtendPropertySheet2::GetWatermarks Implementation

The following sample code shows how the **IExtendPropertySheet2::GetWatermarks** method can be implemented. In this implementation, IDB_BANNER and IDB_WATERMARK are resource IDs that specify the header and watermark bitmaps, respectively.

```
STDMETHODIMP CComponentData::GetWatermarks(
                LPDATAOBJECT lpIDataObject,
                HBITMAP* lphWatermark,
                HBITMAP* lphHeader,
                HPALETTE* lphPalette,
                BOOL* pbStretch)
{
  *lphHeader = LoadBitmap(g_hinst, MAKEINTRESOURCE(IDB_BANNER));
  *lphWatermark = LoadBitmap(g_hinst,
                  MAKEINTRESOURCE(IDB_WATERMARK));
  *pbStretch = TRUE; // force the watermark bitmap to stretch

  return S_OK;
}
```

Adding Watermarks to Wizard97 Pages

This feature is introduced in MMC 1.1.

By implementing **IExtendPropertySheet2::GetWatermarks**, you can specify the bitmaps used for the watermark on Welcome and Completion pages and the header on interior pages.

By setting the **pszHeaderTitle** and **pszHeaderSubTitle** members of the **PROPSHEETPAGE** structure, you can specify the header title and subtitle text for interior wizard pages.

Using IPropertySheetProvider

This section summarizes the information about the **IPropertySheetProvider** interface that was presented in the preceding sections.

You should use the **IPropertySheetProvider** interface in your snap-in in any of the following situations:

- The snap-in adds wizard pages. In this case, the snap-in must use the **IPropertySheetProvider** interface to create a wizard, add wizard pages to it, and then display it. The only exception to this rule is the configuration wizard that MMC launches when a snap-in is inserted through the **Add/Remove Snap-in** dialog box.

- You want to add a feature that has a property sheet as a user interface element, but the sheet is identified as something else. An example of this is the **Select Computer** dialog box, which appears in the Event Viewer snap-in when the user selects the Event Viewer node and clicks the **Connect to another computer** context menu item.

Snap-ins that do not use the **IPropertySheetProvider** interface use another interface, **IPropertySheetCallback**, to add property pages to a property sheet created and maintained by MMC.

Choosing Between IPropertySheetProvider and IExtendPropertySheet2

The **IPropertySheetProvider** interface is implemented by MMC, and snap-ins call methods on the interface to perform specific actions, such as creating a property sheet. Snap-ins that add property pages can choose to either create their own property sheet, or use MMC's property sheet implementation. To create their own property sheet and then add pages to it, snap-ins must use the **IPropertySheetProvider** interface. To use MMC's property sheet and add pages to it, snap-ins must implement the **IExtendPropertySheet2** interface. The steps outlined in "Adding Property Pages: Implementation Details" earlier in this chapter show how to use MMC's property sheet and how to implement **IExtendPropertySheet2**.

- Snap-ins that use the **IPropertySheetProvider** interface directly must call the **IPropertySheetProvider::AddExtensionPages** method to allow extensions to add their own property pages.

- Extension snap-ins must implement the **IExtendPropertySheet2** interface. MMC passes to them the **IPropertySheetCallback** interface that they must use for adding property pages to a primary snap-in's property sheet.

- Snap-ins that add wizard pages must use the **IPropertySheetProvider** interface. This is because the only way that a snap-in can specify a wizard is by calling the **IPropertySheetProvider::CreatePropertySheet** method with the *type* parameter set to FALSE (for wizard). In the call to **CreatePropertySheet**, snap-ins can optionally set the the *dwOptions* parameter to MMC_PSO_NEWWIZARDTYPE to specify that the wizard pages have the Wizard97 style.

  The steps outlined in "Adding Wizard Pages: Implementation Details" earlier in this chapter show how to add wizard pages.

CHAPTER 24

Working with Extension Snap-ins

Extension snap-ins extend the functionality of other snap-ins, but they are not directly added to a console like stand-alone snap-ins. Extension snap-ins can add context menu items, property pages, toolbar buttons, taskpad tasks, and items to the namespace of the extended snap-in (also called the *primary snap-in*).

Primary snap-ins can themselves extend the functionality of other snap-ins. That is, the same snap-in code base can create a primary snap-in instance and an extension snap-in instance.

An extension snap-in is loaded only when the snap-in it extends is loaded and the feature it extends is used. For example, when the user displays a context menu in a stand-alone snap-in, MMC builds the context menu, prompts the stand-alone snap-in to add its items, and then prompts the extension snap-in to add its items. After all snap-ins have added their items, MMC displays the context menu and then forwards the menu click to the snap-in that owns the item.

An extension snap-in can extend only the node types that a stand-alone snap-in indicates as being extendable. The extension snap-in declares itself as a subordinate to the extendable node types, and then for each occurrence of those node types in the console, the console automatically adds the related snap-in extensions below it.

It is important to understand that a node type can represent a scope item, a standard list view result item, or a virtual list view result item added by the primary snap-in. Consult the documentation for the primary snap-in to determine what the node type represents and the format of its exported data.

C++ Snap-ins

There are three types of extension snap-ins; the difference between the various types depends on how they are added and removed:

- *Required extensions* are extension snap-ins that are automatically added to the primary snap-in when the primary snap-in is loaded. Required extensions are added to all instances of the primary snap-in. Required extensions cannot be removed programmatically or through the **Add/Remove Snap-in** dialog box.

- *Dynamic extensions* are extension snap-ins that are added to a scope item or result item programmatically at run time. A snap-in can dynamically add any type of extension to its own items. When an extension snap-in dynamically extends an item of a primary snap-in, the extension snap-in extends only the specific instance of the item. Other items of that node type are not affected. Dynamically adding an extension is not the same as adding an extension to a snap-in through the **Add/Remove Snap-in** dialog box. By using the **Add/Remove Snap-in** dialog box to add an extension to a snap-in, the extension is added to all instances of snap-ins of that type. If you want all instances of your snap-in to be extended by one or more snap-ins, the snap-in should implement required extensions. As just suggested, you cannot add or remove dynamic extensions through the **Add/Remove Snap-in** dialog box.

- Extension snap-ins that are neither required extensions nor dynamic extensions can be added or removed through the **Add/Remove Snap-in** dialog box. A list of available extensions is presented in the **Add/Remove Snap-in** dialog box of the primary snap-in that is loaded in the current console.

Flow of Information to Extension Snap-ins

Extension snap-ins receive context information through data objects, which are passed to extensions when the user selects a scope or result item of a node type that they extend. When the user selects the item in the primary snap-in, MMC requests a data object from the primary snap-in. MMC then passes the data object to the extension snap-in as a parameter in the method call that notifies the extension of the user action. The particular method that is called depends on the context. For example, context menu extensions receive data objects in calls to their **IExtendContextMenu::AddMenuItems** and **IExtendContextMenu::Command** implementations.

When requesting a data object from the primary snap-in, MMC specifies the cookie value of the selected scope or result item in the *cookie* parameter in the call to the **QueryDataObject** method. Recall that the cookie value of an item is simply a unique identifier for the item that the snap-in-supplies. For the extension snap-in to extract the correct context information from the data object it receives, a primary snap-in's implementation of **IDataObject** must store the cookie value of the item for which MMC is requesting a data object. The primary snap-in should then publish and support special clipboard formats that extensions can use for requesting context information. Primary snap-ins can also publish clipboard formats that allow bidirectional information exchange between the primary snap-in and extensions.

MMC places no restrictions on how data exchange using the **IDataObject** interface is accomplished. Following are two common methods that primary snap-ins can use:

- Implementing the **IDataObject::GetDataHere** method in data objects requested by MMC and passed on to extensions. Extension snap-ins are then responsible for allocating and freeing the storage medium in the method call, and for defining the format, medium, and target device to use when passing the data.

- Exposing a private interface on the data object. Extensions can then query the data object passed to them from MMC for the private interface and call methods on the interface to exchange information.

How MMC Loads an Extension Snap-in

When the user selects a scope or result item in the namespace of a primary snap-in, MMC checks to see if the node type of the selected item is extendable. If it is extendable, MMC looks in the registry under the **MMC\NodeTypes\{*nodetypeGUID*}\Extensions\{*extensionType}* subkey for the CLSIDs of all extensions that extend the particular node type. The {*nodetypeGUID*} key represents the node type GUID of the node type that is being extended, and {*extensionType*} represents the type of extension.

MMC then loads the extension snap-ins that extend the selected item and queries them for the interface that implements the extension features. For example, context menu extensions must implement the **IExtendContextMenu** interface, and MMC queries the extension snap-in for this interface when a node type it extends is selected. MMC uses the returned interface pointers to call methods on the extensions and to notify them of user actions.

Generally, MMC releases interfaces on extension snap-ins when their user interface is dismissed; for example, a context menu extension is released after the context menu is dismissed. The only exceptions to this are namespace extensions and taskpad extensions (that support the **IComponentData** interface). MMC retains their interfaces for the duration of the current MMC session.

Dynamic extensions and required extensions work differently. You can read about them in detail in "Adding Dynamic Extensions" and "Adding Required Extensions" later in this chapter.

Requirements for Primary Snap-ins

Primary snap-ins have the following requirements:

- Primary snap-ins must register the node type GUIDs of their extendable node types under the **HKEY_LOCAL_MACHINE\Software\Microsoft\MMC\SnapIns** *{snapinCLSID}***NodeTypes** key. The *{snapinCLSID}* key is the name for a snap-in's key and is the string representation of the snap-in's CLSID. For details about the **SnapIns** key, see "Registering and Unregistering a Snap-in" in Chapter 17.

  MMC uses the values in the **NodeTypes** key to find the node types for the snap-in and then uses that list of node types to get the extensions for those node types. That set of extension snap-ins is displayed as the available extensions for the snap-in on the **Extensions** tab of the **Add/Remove Snap-in** dialog box.

- Primary snap-ins must publish any clipboard formats that extension snap-ins need to be able to exchange data with them. Primary snap-in developers should also make information available about the data structures that must be used with the published clipboard formats.

- Primary snap-ins with node types that are extended by property page extensions must implement the **IExtendPropertySheet2** interface and enable the properties verb, even if they do not add any property pages themselves. For details, see "Extending a Primary Snap-in's Property Sheet" later in this chapter.

Primary snap-ins that also support required or dynamic extensions have additional requirements. For details about required extensions, see "Adding Required Extensions" later in this chapter. For details about adding support for dynamic extensions, see "Adding Dynamic Extensions" later in this chapter.

Requirements for Extension Snap-ins

Extension snap-ins are COM in-process DLLs that implement and expose MMC interfaces such as **IExtendContextMenu** and **IExtendControlbar**.

Extension snap-ins have three requirements:

- Extension snap-ins must implement the appropriate MMC interfaces and handle the MMC notifications that are sent in response to user actions.

- Extension snap-ins must register themselves in several places in the registry. This is discussed in detail in "Registration Requirements for Extension Snap-ins" later in this chapter.

- Extension snap-ins must be aware of and support the clipboard formats published by any primary snap-ins whose node types they extend.

C++ Snap-ins

Implementing MMC Interfaces in Extension Snap-ins

An extension snap-in can support any or all of the following extension types:

- Namespace extension
- Context menu extension
- Toolbar extension
- Menu button extension
- Property page extension
- Taskpad extension

Namespace extensions add scope items to a primary snap-in's scope pane. Namespace extensions must implement **IComponentData**. Non-namespace extensions—context menu, toolbar, menu button, property page, and taskpad extensions—do not add scope items to a primary snap-in's scope pane, and consequently they do not need to implement **IComponentData**.

Context menu extensions must implement **IExtendContextMenu**, toolbar and menu button extensions implement **IControlbar**, property page extensions implement **IExtendPropertySheet2**, and taskpad extensions implement **IExtendTaskpad**.

Details about writing extensions are provided in the following sections later in this chapter:

- "Extending a Primary Snap-in's Namespace"
- "Extending a Primary Snap-in's Context Menu"
- "Extending a Primary Snap-in's Control Bar"
- "Extending a Primary Snap-in's Property Sheet"
- "Extending a Primary Snap-in's Taskpad"

Registration Requirements for Extension Snap-ins

In addition to registering its class ID (CLSID) under the **HKEY_CLASSES_ROOT\CLSID** key as an in-process server DLL, an extension snap-in also must register its CLSID in two additional places in the registry:

- All snap-ins, including extensions, must be registered under the **HKEY_LOCAL_MACHINE\Software\Microsoft\MMC\SnapIns** key in the *{snapinCLSID}* key. The *{snapinCLSID}* key is the name for a snap-in's key and is the string representation of the snap-in's CLSID.

  Note that when registering an extension snap-in under the **SnapIns** key, the **StandAlone** key *must not* be added. The presence of the **StandAlone** key is used only to indicate that a snap-in is a stand-alone snap-in.

  For details about the **SnapIns** key, see "**SnapIns** Key" in the MMC COM Reference section of the MMC SDK. For details about registering snap-ins, see "Registering and Unregistering a Snap-in" in Chapter 17.

- The CLSID of the extension snap-in must also be registered under the **HKEY_LOCAL_MACHINE\Software\Microsoft\MMC\NodeTypes** key.

The **NodeTypes** key has the following form:

```
HKEY_LOCAL_MACHINE\Software\Microsoft\MMC\NodeTypes\
    {nodetypeGUID}
        Extensions
            NameSpace
                {extensionsnapinCLSID}
            ContextMenu
                {extensionsnapinCLSID}
            ToolBar
                {extensionsnapinCLSID}
            PropertySheet
                {extensionsnapinCLSID}
            Task
                {extensionsnapinCLSID}
        Dynamic Extensions
            {extensionsnapinCLSID}
```

- The *{nodetypeGUID}* key specifies the string representation of the GUID of the node type that is being extended. The string must begin with an open brace ({) and end with a close brace (}). There must also be a corresponding *{nodetypeGUID}* value in the primary snap-in's **HKEY_LOCAL_MACHINE\Software\Microsoft\MMC\SnapIns** *{snapinCLSID}***NodeTypes** key, where *{snapinCLSID}* is the string representation of the snap-in's CLSID.

C++ Snap-ins

- The **Extensions** key contains subkeys and values that list the snap-ins registered to extend the node type specified by {*nodetypeGUID*}. The extensions are grouped by extension type. There are five types: NameSpace, ContextMenu, ToolBar, PropertySheet, and Task. An extension snap-in must add its CLSID as a value in the appropriate extension type key for each type of extension it adds.

    - The **NameSpace** key contains values that represent the CLSIDs of snap-ins that can extend the namespace of items with this node type.

    - The **ContextMenu** key contains values that represent the CLSIDs of snap-ins that can extend the context menu of items with this node type.

    - The **ToolBar** key contains values that represent the CLSIDs of snap-ins that can extend the toolbar of items with this node type.

    - The **PropertySheet** key contains values that represent the CLSIDs of snap-ins that can extend the property sheet of items with this node type.

    - The **Task** key contains values that represent the CLSIDs of snap-ins that can extend the taskpad of items with this node type.

- The {*extensionsnapinCLSID*} key specifies the string representation of the CLSID of an extension snap-in. The string must begin with an open brace and end with a close brace.

- The **Dynamic Extensions** key contains values that represent the CLSIDs of snap-ins that should act only as dynamic extensions to this node type. Snap-ins listed in this key are not displayed on the **Extensions** tab of the **Add/Remove Snap-in** dialog box. Dynamic extensions are extension snap-ins that are added to a scope or result item programmatically at run time.

    Note that dynamic extensions must be registered under the **Dynamic Extensions** key *and* under the particular subkey of the **Extensions** key. MMC needs the registration under the **Extensions** key to determine the extension type of a particular dynamic extension.

MMC uses the CLSID of an extension snap-in to cocreate the snap-in's class object and to request the snap-in interface that implements a specific extension type. An extension snap-in can support a number of different extension types, and it is recommended that you register different CLSIDs for the snap-in under the **HKEY_LOCAL_MACHINE\Software\Microsoft\MMC\NodeTypes\ {*nodetypeGUID*}\Extensions\{*extensionType*}** subkey—one for each extension type that the snap-in supports. This enables the snap-in to detect the correct context when its **DllGetClassObject** method is called. The *rclsid* parameter in the function call is the same CLSID that MMC finds under the **HKEY_LOCAL_MACHINE\Software\Microsoft\MMC\NodeTypes\ {*nodetypeGUID*}\Extensions\{*extensionType*}** subkey. The *riid* parameter specifies the requested interface (usually **IClassFactory**). If the *rclsid* parameter is different for each extension type, snap-ins can detect which interface is requested during a call to **DllGetClassObject**.

If you register a different CLSID for each extension type the snap-in supports, make sure you also register each CLSID as an in-process server DLL under the **HKEY_CLASSES_ROOT\CLSID** key.

Sample Code

The code samples in this section contain the registration and class factory code necessary for an extension snap-in that extends the context menu of another (primary) snap-in. Although the samples are specific to context menu extensions, you can easily modify them to handle other extension types.

The code samples are taken from the CMenuExt sample that accompanies the MMC SDK. Note that unregistration and unloading code is omitted in this discussion.

Note that all sample code assumes Unicode compilation.

DllRegisterServer Implementation

```
STDAPI DllRegisterServer()
{
  HRESULT hr = SELFREG_E_CLASS;

  _TCHAR szName[256];
  _TCHAR szSnapInName[256];

  LoadString(g_hinst, IDS_NAME, szName,
             sizeof(szName)/sizeof(szName[0]));
  LoadString(g_hinst, IDS_SNAPINNAME, szSnapInName,
             sizeof(szSnapInName)/sizeof(szSnapInName[0]));

  _TCHAR szAboutName[256];

  LoadString(g_hinst, IDS_ABOUTNAME, szAboutName,
             sizeof(szAboutName)/sizeof(szAboutName[0]));


  // register our CoClasses
  hr = RegisterServer(g_hinst, CLSID_CContextMenuExtension, szName);

  if SUCCEEDED(hr)
      hr = RegisterServer(g_hinst, CLSID_CSnapinAbout, szAboutName);

  // place the registry information for SnapIns
  if SUCCEEDED(hr)
      hr = RegisterSnapin(CLSID_CContextMenuExtension, szSnapInName,
                          CLSID_CSnapinAbout);

  return hr;
}
```

C++ Snap-ins

IDS_NAME, IDS_SNAPINNAME, and IDS_ABOUTNAME are resource identifiers that specify the human-readable names appearing with the entries in the registry.

The **DllRegisterServer** function registers two coclasses: **CLSID_CContextMenuExtension** and **CLSID_CSnapinAbout**. The **CLSID_CSnapinAbout** coclass is a cocreatable class object that exposes the **ISnapinAbout** interface that MMC uses to retrieve About information for the snap-in. The **CLSID_CContextMenuExtension** coclass exposes the snap-in's **IExtendContextMenu** interface to MMC. Both coclasses are registered in the **RegisterServer** function, which creates entries under the **HKEY_CLASSES_ROOT\CLSID** key for both of them.

The **RegisterServer** function does not contain code specific to registering an extension snap-in, so this topic does not contain a detailed explanation of that function. The following example focuses on the **RegisterSnapin** function, which creates entries specific to extension snap-ins under the **HKEY_LOCAL_MACHINE\Software\Microsoft\MMC\SnapIns** key and the **HKEY_LOCAL_MACHINE\Software\Microsoft\MMC\NodeTypes** {*nodetypeGUID*}**\Extensions\ContextMenu** subkey.

```cpp
HRESULT RegisterSnapin(const CLSID& clsid,          // Class ID
                       const _TCHAR* szNameString,  // NameString
                       const CLSID& clsidAbout,     // About Class ID
                       const BOOL fSupportExtensions)
{
  // Get CLSID
  LPOLESTR wszCLSID = NULL ;
  LPOLESTR wszAboutCLSID = NULL;
  LPOLESTR wszExtendCLSID = NULL;
  LPOLESTR wszNodeCLSID = NULL;
  EXTENDER_NODE *pNodeExtension;
  _TCHAR szKeyBuf[1024] ;
  HKEY hKey;


  HRESULT hr = StringFromCLSID(clsid, &wszCLSID) ;

  if (IID_NULL != clsidAbout)
      hr = StringFromCLSID(clsidAbout, &wszAboutCLSID);

  MAKE_TSTRPTR_FROMWIDE(pszCLSID, wszCLSID);
  MAKE_TSTRPTR_FROMWIDE(pszAboutCLSID, wszAboutCLSID);
```

```
// Add the CLSID to the registry.
setSnapInKeyAndValue(pszCLSID, NULL, _T("NameString"),
                        szNameString) ;
if (IID_NULL != clsidAbout)
    setSnapInKeyAndValue(pszCLSID, NULL, _T("About"),
                        pszAboutCLSID);

if (fSupportExtensions)
{
    // Build the key NodeType
    setSnapInKeyAndValue(pszCLSID, _T("NodeTypes"), NULL, NULL);

    _TCHAR szKey[64] ;
    _tcscpy(szKey, pszCLSID) ;
    _tcscat(szKey, _T("\\NodeTypes")) ;
    setSnapInKeyAndValue(szKey, pszCLSID, NULL, NULL);
}

// register each of the node extensions
for (pNodeExtension = &(_NodeExtensions[0]);*pNodeExtension->
    szDescription;pNodeExtension++)
{
    hr = StringFromCLSID(pNodeExtension->guidNode,
                        &wszExtendCLSID);
    MAKE_TSTRPTR_FROMWIDE(pszExtendCLSID, wszExtendCLSID);
    _tcscpy(szKeyBuf,
            _T("SOFTWARE\\Microsoft\\MMC\\NodeTypes\\"));
    _tcscat(szKeyBuf, pszExtendCLSID);

    switch (pNodeExtension->eType)
    {
    case ContextMenuExtension:
        _tcscat(szKeyBuf, _T("\\Extensions\\ContextMenu"));
        break;
    default:
        break;
    }

    // Create and open key and subkey.
    long lResult = RegCreateKeyEx(HKEY_LOCAL_MACHINE ,szKeyBuf,
                                0, NULL,
                                REG_OPTION_NON_VOLATILE,
                                KEY_ALL_ACCESS, NULL,
                                &hKey, NULL) ;

    if (lResult != ERROR_SUCCESS)
    {
        return FALSE ;
    }
```

C++ Snap-ins

```
        hr = StringFromCLSID(pNodeExtension->guidExtension,
                             &wszNodeCLSID);
        assert(SUCCEEDED(hr));

        MAKE_TSTRPTR_FROMWIDE(pszNodeCLSID, wszNodeCLSID);
        // Set the Value.
        if (pNodeExtension->szDescription != NULL)
        {
            RegSetValueEx(hKey, pszNodeCLSID, 0, REG_SZ,
                          (BYTE *)pNodeExtension->szDescription,
                          (_tcslen(pNodeExtension->
                          szDescription)+1)*sizeof(_TCHAR)) ;
        }

        RegCloseKey(hKey) ;

        CoTaskMemFree(wszExtendCLSID);
        CoTaskMemFree(wszNodeCLSID);
    }

    // Free memory.
    CoTaskMemFree(wszCLSID) ;
    if (IID_NULL != clsidAbout)
        CoTaskMemFree(wszAboutCLSID);

    return S_OK ;
}
```

The **setSnapInKeyAndValue** function is a helper function that sets the given key and its value under the **HKEY_LOCAL_MACHINE\Software\Microsoft\MMC\SnapIns** key.

The **fSupportExtensions** Boolean value specifies whether the extension snap-in also has extendable node types. This value is FALSE in the case of the CMenuExt sample.

The entry for the snap-in under the **HKEY_LOCAL_MACHINE\Software\Microsoft\MMC\NodeTypes\ {*nodetypeGUID*}\Extensions\ContextMenu** subkey is built in the block of code that begins with the following:

```
    // register each of the node extensions
    for (pNodeExtension = &(_NodeExtensions[0]);
                       *pNodeExtension->szDescription;
                       pNodeExtension++)
```

The block of code ends with the following:

```
    CoTaskMemFree(wszNodeCLSID);
}
// Free memory.
```

Here is what the entry looks like after it is built:

```
HKEY_LOCAL_MACHINE\SOFTWARE\Microsoft\MMC\NodeTypes\
   {2974380D-4C4B-11D2-89D8-000021473128}\
       Extensions\
           ContextMenu
               {CE0F5BF0-ABFB-11D2-993A-0080C76878BF}  =
               REG_SZ "Extension to the People-powered Node
               ↪ Context Menu"
```

The *nodetypeGUID* is the value of the node type GUID of the "People-powered Vehicle" item. This item is added to the scope pane of many of the C++ sample snap-ins that accompany the MMC SDK, such as the Extens sample.

The value under the **ContextMenu** key represents the CLSID of the CMenuExt sample. The CMenuExt sample extends items of node type *nodetypeGUID* in the Extens sample.

Returning to the code block, the **_NodeExtensions** array is an array of **EXTENDER_NODE** structures; it lists all the node types that the extension snap-in extends:

```
EXTENDER_NODE _NodeExtensions[] =
{
  {ContextMenuExtension,
      {0x2974380d, 0x4c4b, 0x11d2, { 0x89, 0xd8, 0x0, 0x0, 0x21,
      0x47, 0x31, 0x28}},
      {0xce0f5bf0, 0xabfb, 0x11d2, {0x99, 0x3a, 0x0, 0x80, 0xc7,
      0x68, 0x78, 0xbf}},
      _T("Extension to the People-powered Node Context Menu")
  },
  {DummyExtension,
      NULL,
      NULL,
      NULL
  }
};
```

C++ Snap-ins

The **EXTENDER_NODE** structure is defined as follows:

```
struct EXTENDER_NODE
{
  EXTENSION_TYPE  eType;
  GUID            guidNode;
  GUID            guidExtension;
  _TCHAR          szDescription[256];
};
```

EXTENSION_TYPE is an enumeration type that lists all possible types of extensions, as follows:

```
enum EXTENSION_TYPE
{
  NameSpaceExtension,
  ContextMenuExtension,
  ToolBarExtension,
  PropertySheetExtension,
  TaskExtension,
  DynamicExtension,
  DummyExtension
};
```

To summarize, the **RegisterSnapin** function registers the extension snap-in as only one type of extension: a context menu extension. You can easily modify this by adding additional elements to the **_NodeExtensions** array—one for each additional node type that the extension snap-in extends—and then modifying the **RegisterSnapin** function accordingly.

The **guidNode** member of the **_NodeExtensions[0]** array specifies the node type GUID of the "People-powered Vehicle" item, and the **guidExtension** member of the same array element specifies the CLSID of the extension snap-in (CMenuExt).

DllGetClassObject Implementation

COM calls the **DllGetClassObject** exported function when MMC attempts to cocreate the class object referred to by **CLSID_CContextMenuExtension**. MMC gets the CLSID of this class object from the value specified under the **HKEY_LOCAL_MACHINE\Software\Microsoft\MMC\NodeTypes\ {*nodetypeGUID*}\Extensions\ContextMenu** subkey.

```
STDAPI DllGetClassObject(REFCLSID rclsid, REFIID riid, LPVOID *ppvObj)
{
  if ((rclsid != CLSID_CContextMenuExtension) &&
      (rclsid != CLSID_CSnapinAbout))
      return CLASS_E_CLASSNOTAVAILABLE;


  if (!ppvObj)
      return E_FAIL;

  *ppvObj = NULL;

  // We can only hand out IUnknown and IClassFactory pointers.
  // Fail if they ask for anything else.
  if (!IsEqualIID(riid, IID_IUnknown) &&
      !IsEqualIID(riid, IID_IClassFactory))
      return E_NOINTERFACE;

  CClassFactory *pFactory = NULL;

  // make the factory passing in the creation function for the type
  // of object they want
  if (rclsid == CLSID_CContextMenuExtension)
      pFactory = new CClassFactory(CClassFactory::CONTEXTEXTENSION);
  else if (rclsid == CLSID_CSnapinAbout)
      pFactory = new CClassFactory(CClassFactory::ABOUT);

  if (NULL == pFactory)
      return E_OUTOFMEMORY;

  HRESULT hr = pFactory->QueryInterface(riid, ppvObj);

  return hr;
}
```

The values CONTEXTEXTENSION and ABOUT are taken from the **FACTORY_TYPE** enumeration type that the snap-in defines:

```
enum FACTORY_TYPE {CONTEXTEXTENSION = 0, ABOUT = 1};
```

C++ Snap-ins

Depending on the class object being cocreated, the extension snap-in initializes the **m_factoryType** member variable of the **CClassFactory** object created in **DllGetClassObject** accordingly.

This value determines the type of interface the snap-in returns to MMC in the call to the snap-in's **IClassFactory::CreateInstance** implementation:

```
STDMETHODIMP CClassFactory::CreateInstance(LPUNKNOWN pUnkOuter,
                                 REFIID riid, LPVOID * ppvObj)
{
  HRESULT  hr;
  void* pObj;

  if (!ppvObj)
      return E_FAIL;

  *ppvObj = NULL;

  // Our object does does not support aggregation, so we need to
  // fail if they ask us to do aggregation.
  if (pUnkOuter)
      return CLASS_E_NOAGGREGATION;

  if (CONTEXTEXTENSION == m_factoryType) {
      pObj = new CContextMenuExtension();
  } else {
      pObj = new CSnapinAbout();
  }

  if (!pObj)
      return E_OUTOFMEMORY;

  // QueryInterface will do the AddRef() for us, so we do not
  // do it in this function
  hr = ((LPUNKNOWN)pObj)->QueryInterface(riid, ppvObj);

  if (FAILED(hr))
      delete pObj;

  return hr;
}
```

If MMC requests the extension snap-in's **IExtendContextMenu** implementation, the snap-in returns a pointer to a new **CContextMenuExtension**, which implements the requested interface, in **ppvObj**.

Extending a Primary Snap-in's Namespace

This section discusses the steps necessary for an extension snap-in to extend the namespace of a primary snap-in. For general information about working with extension snap-ins, see the beginning of this chapter.

A primary snap-in registers the extendable node types it adds to its namespace. An extension snap-in can extend the namespace of a primary snap-in's node type by adding the appropriate registration code and then implementing the **IComponentData** interface.

When the user selects a scope item in a primary snap-in that is extended by a namespace extension, MMC requests the extension's **IComponentData** interface and calls **IComponentData::Initialize** to initialize the extension's **IComponentData** object (unless it is already initialized). Like a primary snap-in, a namespace extension can add scope items and enumerate the result pane of any items it adds. When the user selects a scope or result item that a namespace extension has added, MMC uses the extension's **IComponentData** or **IComponent** implementation to notify the extension of notification messages and to request data objects.

A namespace extension owns any scope or result items that it adds. Therefore, it can extend its own items by adding context menu items, property pages, toolbars, and other features, just like any other snap-in.

Also, any scope or result items added by a namespace extension can also be extended by other extension snap-ins. The namespace extension then behaves like a primary snap-in, so it must register the node type GUIDs of its extendable node types and publish any clipboard formats that other extension snap-ins require for extracting context information.

It is important to note that MMC cocreates one instance of a namespace extension for each primary snap-in instance that it extends. This namespace extension instance extends all nodes of the appropriate node type that appear under that instance of the primary snap-in.

C++ Snap-ins

▶   **To extend a primary snap-in's namespace**

In the following procedure, note that *{CLSID}*, *{snapinCLSID}*, and *{nodetypeGUID}* all denote string representations of the specified CLSIDs and GUIDs. The strings must begin with an open brace ({) and end with a close brace (}).

1. The CLSID of each snap-in (extension or stand-alone) must be registered under the **HKEY_CLASSES_ROOT\CLSID** key in the *{CLSID}* subkey as an in-process server DLL. The snap-in must also register a threading model for the snap-in CLSID. An apartment threading model is recommended.

    For details about the **HKEY_CLASSES_ROOT\CLSID** key, see the "**CLSID** Key" topic in the Microsoft Platform SDK. For example code, see "Registering and Unregistering a Snap-in" in Chapter 17.

2. All snap-ins must be registered under the **HKEY_LOCAL_MACHINE\Software\Microsoft\MMC\SnapIns** key in the *{snapinCLSID}* key. Also, if the namespace extension adds scope or result items that can be extended by other extension snap-ins, add the node type GUIDs of the extendable node types under the **HKEY_LOCAL_MACHINE\Software\Microsoft\MMC\SnapIns\ *{snapinCLSID}*\NodeTypes** key.

    For details about the **SnapIns** key, see "Registering and Unregistering a Snap-in" in Chapter 17.

3. Register the CLSID of the extension snap-in under the **HKEY_LOCAL_MACHINE\Software\Microsoft\MMC\NodeTypes\ *{nodetypeGUID}*\Extensions\Namespace** subkey, where *nodetypeGUID* is the GUID of the node type whose namespace is being extended. For details about the **NodeTypes** key, see "Registration Requirements for Extension Snap-ins" earlier in this chapter.

4. Implement the **IComponentData** interface as you would for adding scope items to the scope pane of a primary snap-in. See "Working with the Scope Pane: Implementation Details" in Chapter 19 for instructions.

5. The namespace extension's **IComponentData::Notify** method will receive an MMCN_EXPAND notification message the first time the user selects a primary snap-in's scope item that is extended by the namespace extension. For the namespace extension to know that it is being asked to add its own items underneath the primary snap-in's scope item, you will need to implement a mechanism for seeing if the currently selected scope item belongs to the primary snap-in or the namespace extension. See the Sample Code section for a sample implementation.

6. If any of the scope items added by the namespace extension also have result pane views, you will need to implement the **IComponent** interface as well. See Chapter 20, "Using Different Result Pane View Types," for information about the various view types available.

7. Also implement the **IDataObject** interface. MMC will request data objects from the extension snap-in when one of the scope or result items it adds is selected by the user.

8. If the namespace extension extends its own items by adding context menu items, toolbars, menu buttons, or property pages, implement the required interfaces. See Chapter 22, "Working with Toolbars and Menu Buttons," and Chapter 23, "Adding Property Pages and Wizard Pages," for details.

Sample Code

The code samples in this section cover two issues:

- Registering a namespace extension snap-in
- Implementing **IComponentData::Notify**

All code samples are taken from the documentation of the NameExt sample that accompanies the MMC SDK.

Note that all sample code assumes Unicode compilation.

Namespace Extension Registration Code

The following is a sample registry entry for the **NodeTypes** key for a node type with a Namespace extension.

```
HKEY_LOCAL_MACHINE\SOFTWARE\Microsoft\MMC\NodeTypes\
   {2974380F-4C4B-11d2-89D8-000021473128}\
      Extensions\
         Namespace
            {64026453-6A22-11d3-9154-00C04F65B3F9}  =
            REG_SZ "Namespace Extension to the Sky-based Vehicle
                     node"
```

The *nodetypeGUID* is the value of the node type GUID of the "Sky-based Vehicle" scope item; this item is added to the scope pane of many of the C++ sample snap-ins that accompany the MMC SDK, for example, the Extens sample.

The value under the **Namespace** key represents the CLSID of the NameExt sample. The NameExt sample extends scope items of node type *nodetypeGUID* in the Extens sample.

In the NameExt sample, the **RegisterSnapin** function called by the extension snap-in's **DllRegisterServer** function contains the code for adding the extension's CLSID to the **NodeTypes** key for a node type that is being extended. This code is very similar to that in the CMenuExt sample and is documented in "Registration Requirements for Extension Snap-ins" earlier in this chapter.

C++ Snap-ins

The only difference between the implementation of the **RegisterSnapin** function in the CMenuExt and NameExt samples is in the switch statement found in the function:

```
switch (pNodeExtension->eType)
{
case NameSpaceExtension:
  _tcscat(szKeyBuf, _T("\\Extensions\\Namespace"));
  break;
default:
  break;
}
```

As you can see, the switch statement in the NameExt sample has been modified to only consider the case where the extension type can be NameSpaceExtension. Recall that **pNodeExtension** points to the **_NodeExtensions** array that lists all the node types that the extension snap-in extends:

```
EXTENDER_NODE _NodeExtensions[] =
{
  {NameSpaceExtension,
      {0x2974380f, 0x4c4b, 0x11d2, { 0x89, 0xd8, 0x0, 0x0, 0x21,
      0x47, 0x31, 0x28 } },
      {0x64026453, 0x6a22, 0x11d3, {0x91, 0x54, 0x0, 0xc0, 0x4f,
      0x65, 0xb3, 0xf9} },
      _T("Namespace Extension to the Sky-based Vehicle node")},
  {DummyExtension,
      NULL,
      NULL,
      NULL}
}
```

The NameExt sample is only a namespace extension, so the **_NodeExtensions** array only has one element (of type **EXTENDER_NODE** structure).

IComponentData::Notify Implementation

The NameExt sample uses the data object passed into **IComponentData::Notify** to determine the node type GUID of the currently selected scope item. If this value matches the node type GUID of the scope item that the NameExt sample extends, then the extension snap-in adds its own items as child items of the selected scope item. If the value doesn't match, the extension is being asked to add child items to one of its own scope items.

The following code sample taken from the NameExt sample uses this technique.
Note that **CComponentData** implements the **IComponentData** interface.

```
HRESULT CComponentData::Notify(
                        /* [in] */ LPDATAOBJECT lpDataObject,
                        /* [in] */ MMC_NOTIFY_TYPE event,
                        /* [in] */ LPARAM arg,
                        /* [in] */ LPARAM param)
{

  HRESULT hr = S_FALSE;

  if (NULL == lpDataObject)
      return hr;

  switch (event)
  {
  case MMCN_EXPAND:

      GUID myGuid;
      GUID* pGUID= &myGuid;
      // extract GUID of the the currently selected node type from
      // the data object
      hr = ExtractObjectTypeGUID(lpDataObject, pGUID);
      _ASSERT( S_OK == hr );

      /* compare node type GUIDs of currently selected node and the
         node type we want to extend. If they are are equal,
         currently selected node is the type we want to extend, so
         we add our items underneath it. */

      if (IsEqualGUID(*pGUID, getPrimaryNodeType()))
          OnExpand(m_ipConsoleNameSpace, m_ipConsole,
                  (HSCOPEITEM)param);

      else
      // currently selected node is one of ours instead
      {
          CDelegationBase *base = GetOurDataObject(lpDataObject)->
                                  GetBaseNodeObject();
          hr = base->OnExpand(m_ipConsoleNameSpace, m_ipConsole,
                  (HSCOPEITEM)param);
      }

      break;
  }
  return hr;
}
```

C++ Snap-ins

The **ExtractObjectTypeGUID** function returns the node type GUID of the currently selected scope item. The **getPrimaryNodeType** function returns the GUID of the node type that the extension snap-in extends. If the values returned by the two functions match, the scope item belongs to a primary snap-in. The extension snap-in then adds its own items underneath it.

If the node type GUIDs differ, the currently selected scope item belongs to the extension snap-in.

Extending a Primary Snap-in's Context Menu

This section discusses the specific steps necessary for an extension snap-in to extend the context menu of a node type owned by a primary snap-in. To read about working with extension snap-ins in general, see the beginning of this chapter.

A primary snap-in registers the extendable node types that it adds to its namespace. An extension snap-in can extend the context menu of a primary snap-in's node type by adding the appropriate registration code and then implementing the **IExtendContextMenu** interface.

▶   **To extend a primary snap-in's context menu**

In the following procedure, note that *{CLSID}*, *{snapinCLSID}* and *{nodetypeGUID}* all denote string representations of the specified CLSIDs and GUIDs. The strings must begin with an open brace ({) and end with a close brace (}).

1. The CLSID of each snap-in (extension or stand-alone) must be registered under the **HKEY_CLASSES_ROOT\CLSID** key in the *{CLSID}* subkey as an in-process server DLL. The snap-in must also register a threading model for the snap-in CLSID. An apartment threading model is recommended.

   For details about the **HKEY_CLASSES_ROOT\CLSID** key, see the "**CLSID** Key" topic in the Microsoft Platform SDK. For example code, see "Registering and Unregistering a Snap-in" in Chapter 17.

2. All snap-ins must be registered under the **HKEY_LOCAL_MACHINE\Software\Microsoft\MMC\SnapIns** key in the *{snapinCLSID}* key. For details about the **SnapIns** key, see "Registering and Unregistering a Snap-in" in Chapter 17.

3. Register the CLSID of the extension snap-in under the **HKEY_LOCAL_MACHINE\Software\Microsoft\MMC\NodeTypes\{*nodetypeGUID*}\Extensions\ContextMenu** subkey, where *nodetypeGUID* is the node type GUID of the node type whose context menu is being extended. For details about the **NodeTypes** key, see "Registration Requirements for Extension Snap-ins" earlier in this chapter.

4. Implement the **IExtendContextMenu** interface as you would for adding items to the context menu of a primary snap-in. See "Working with Context Menus: Implementation Details" in Chapter 21 for instructions.

Sample Code

For a detailed discussion of registering context menu extensions, see the Sample Code section in "Registration Requirements for Extension Snap-ins" earlier in this chapter.

For sample implementations of the **IExtendContextMenu** interface methods, see "Working with Context Menus: Implementation Details" in Chapter 21. For a more detailed look at context menu extensions, see the documentation of the CMenuExt sample that accompanies the MMC SDK.

The following is a sample registry entry for the **NodeTypes** key for a node type with a ContextMenu extension:

```
HKEY_LOCAL_MACHINE\SOFTWARE\Microsoft\MMC\NodeTypes\
  {2974380D-4C4B-11D2-89D8-000021473128}\
     Extensions\
        ContextMenu
           {CE0F5BF0-ABFB-11D2-993A-0080C76878BF}  =
           REG_SZ "Extension to the People-powered Node
                     Context Menu"
```

The *nodetypeGUID* is the value of the node type GUID of the "People-powered Vehicle" item; this item is added to the scope pane of many of the C++ sample snap-ins that accompany the MMC SDK, for example, the Extens sample.

The value under the **ContextMenu** key represents the CLSID of the CMenuExt sample. The CMenuExt sample extends scope items of node type *nodetypeGUID* in the Extens sample.

In the CMenuExt sample, the **RegisterSnapin** function called by the extension snap-in's **DllRegisterServer** function contains the code for adding the extension's CLSID to the **NodeTypes** key for a node type that is being extended. This code is documented in detail in "Registration Requirements for Extension Snap-ins" earlier in this chapter.

C++ Snap-ins

Extending a Primary Snap-in's Control Bar

This section discusses the specific steps necessary for an extension snap-in to extend the control bar of an extendable node type owned by a primary snap-in. To read about working with extension snap-ins in general, see the beginning of this chapter.

A primary snap-in registers the extendable node types that it adds to its namespace. An extension snap-in can extend the control bar of a primary snap-in's node type by adding the appropriate registration code and then implementing the **IExtendControlBar** interface. The snap-in can then associate either a toolbar or menu button with the control bar and add items accordingly.

▶   **To extend a primary snap-in's control bar**

In the following procedure, note that *{CLSID}*, *{snapinCLSID}*, and *{nodetypeGUID}* all denote string representations of the specified CLSIDs and GUIDs. The strings must begin with an open brace ({) and end with a close brace (}).

1. The CLSID of each snap-in (extension or stand-alone) must be registered under the **HKEY_CLASSES_ROOT\CLSID** key in the *{CLSID}* subkey as an in-process server DLL. The snap-in must also register a threading model for the snap-in CLSID. An apartment threading model is recommended.

   For details about the **HKEY_CLASSES_ROOT\CLSID** key, see the "**CLSID** Key" topic in the Microsoft Platform SDK. For example code, see "Registering and Unregistering a Snap-in" in Chapter 17.

2. All snap-ins must be registered under the **HKEY_LOCAL_MACHINE\Software\Microsoft\MMC\SnapIns** key in the *{snapinCLSID}* key. For details about the **SnapIns** key, see "Registering and Unregistering a Snap-in" in Chapter 17.

3. Register the CLSID of the extension snap-in under the **HKEY_LOCAL_MACHINE\Software\Microsoft\MMC\NodeTypes\ {nodetypeGUID}\Extensions\ToolBar** subkey, where *nodetypeGUID* is the node type GUID of the node type whose control bar is being extended. For details about the **NodeTypes** key, see "Registration Requirements for Extension Snap-ins" earlier in this chapter.

4. Implement the **IExtendControlBar** interface as you would for adding a toolbar or menu button to the control bar of a primary snap-in. See "Working with Toolbars: Implementation Details" or "Working with Menu Buttons: Implementation Details" in Chapter 22 for instructions.

Sample Code

The code samples in this section are for the registration code necessary for an extension snap-in that extends another (primary) snap-in's control bar. While the samples are specific to control bar extensions (toolbar or menu button), they can easily be modified to handle other extension types.

For sample implementations of the **IExtendControlBar** interface methods, see "Working with Toolbars: Implementation Details" or "Working with Menu Buttons: Implementation Details" in Chapter 22. For a more detailed look at control bar extensions, see the documentation of the TBarExt sample that accompanies the MMC SDK.

The following is a sample registry entry for the **NodeTypes** key for a node type with a Toolbar extension:

```
HKEY_LOCAL_MACHINE\SOFTWARE\Microsoft\MMC\NodeTypes\
   {29743811-4C4B-11D2-89D8-000021473128}\
      Extensions\
         Toolbar
            {20E42DD2-5CCF-11D3-9147-00C04F65B3F9}  =
            REG_SZ "Extension to the Vehicle Node Toolbar"
```

The *nodetypeGUID* is the value of the node type GUID of the "Vehicle" result item; this item is added to the result pane of many of the C++ sample snap-ins that accompany the MMC SDK, for example, the Extens sample.

The value under the **Toolbar** key represents the CLSID of the TBarExt sample. The TBarExt sample extends result items of node type *nodetypeGUID* in the Extens sample.

In the TBarExt sample, the **RegisterSnapin** function called by the extension snap-in's **DllRegisterServer** function contains the code for adding the extension's CLSID to the **NodeTypes** key for a node type that is being extended. This code is very similar to that in the CMenuExt sample and is documented in "Registration Requirements for Extension Snap-ins" earlier in this chapter.

C++ Snap-ins

The only difference between the implementation of the **RegisterSnapin** function in the CMenuExt and TBarExt samples is in the switch statement found in the function:

```
switch (pNodeExtension->eType)
{
case ToolBarExtension:
  _tcscat(szKeyBuf, _T("\\Extensions\\ToolBar"));
  break;
case ContextMenuExtension:
  _tcscat(szKeyBuf, _T("\\Extensions\\ContextMenu"));
  break;
default:
  break;
}
```

As you can see, the switch statement in the TBarExt sample has been modified to include the case where the extension type can be ToolBarExtension. Recall that **pNodeExtension** points to the **_NodeExtensions** array that lists all the node types that the extension snap-in extends:

```
EXTENDER_NODE _NodeExtensions[] =
{
  {ToolBarExtension,
      {0x29743811, 0x4c4b, 0x11d2, { 0x89, 0xd8, 0x0, 0x0, 0x21,
      0x47, 0x31, 0x28}},
      {0x20e42dd2, 0x5ccf, 0x11d3, {0x91, 0x47, 0x0, 0xc0, 0x4f,
      0x65, 0xb3, 0xf9}},
      _T("Extension to the Vehicle Node Toolbar")},

  {DummyExtension,
      NULL,
      NULL,
      NULL}
};
```

The TBarExt sample is only a toolbar extension, so the **_NodeExtensions** array only has one element (of type **EXTENDER_NODE** structure).

Finally, note that both toolbar and menu button extensions register themselves in the same way. The only difference between these two extension types is in how they implement the methods of the **IExtendControlbar** interface.

Extending a Primary Snap-in's Property Sheet

This section discusses the specific steps necessary for an extension snap-in to extend the property sheet of an extendable node type owned by a primary snap-in. To read about working with extension snap-ins in general, see the beginning of this chapter.

A primary snap-in registers the extendable node types that it adds to its namespace. An extension snap-in can extend the property sheet of a primary snap-in's node type by adding the appropriate registration code and then implementing the **IExtendPropertySheet2** interface.

Primary snap-ins that add node types that can be extended by property page extensions must enable the MMC_VERB_PROPERTIES verb for the extendable items. For details about enabling standard verbs, see Chapter 25, "Enabling MMC Standard Verbs." Primary snap-ins that do not add property pages of their own must still implement **IExtendPropertySheet2** and return S_OK in their implementation of the **IExtendPropertySheet2** methods.

A primary snap-in that uses **IPropertySheetProvider** to display a property sheet must explicitly enable extension snap-ins to add extension pages by calling **IPropertySheetProvider::AddExtensionPages**.

▶ **To extend a primary snap-in's property sheet**

In the following procedure, note that *{CLSID}*, *{snapinCLSID}*, and *{nodetypeGUID}* all denote string representations of the specified CLSIDs and GUIDs. The strings must begin with an open brace ({) and end with a close brace (}).

1. The CLSID of each snap-in (extension or stand-alone) must be registered under the **HKEY_CLASSES_ROOT\CLSID** key in the *{CLSID}* subkey as an in-process server DLL. The snap-in must also register a threading model for the snap-in CLSID. An apartment threading model is recommended.

   For details about the **HKEY_CLASSES_ROOT\CLSID** key, see the "**CLSID** Key" topic in the Microsoft Platform SDK. For example code, see "Registering and Unregistering a Snap-in" in Chapter 17.

2. All snap-ins must be registered under the **HKEY_LOCAL_MACHINE\Software\Microsoft\MMC\SnapIns** key in the *{snapinCLSID}* key. For details about the **SnapIns** key, see "Registering and Unregistering a Snap-in" in Chapter 17.

3. Register the CLSID of the extension snap-in under the **HKEY_LOCAL_MACHINE\Software\Microsoft\MMC\NodeTypes\ {*nodetypeGUID*}\Extensions\PropertySheet** subkey, where *nodetypeGUID* is the node type GUID of the node type whose property sheet is being extended. For details about the **NodeTypes** key, see "Registration Requirements for Extension Snap-ins" earlier in this chapter.

4. Implement the **IExtendPropertySheet2::CreatePropertyPages** method to add property pages.

   In the implementation of **CreatePropertyPages**:

   - Define one or more property pages by filling the **PROPSHEETPAGE** structure for each of the property pages with information about the page. Note that the standard size for a property page in an MMC console is 252 dialog units horizontally and 218 dialog units vertically.

   - For each **PROPSHEETPAGE** structure, call the API function **CreatePropertySheetPage** to create a property sheet page. The function returns a handle to the HPROPSHEETPAGE type that uniquely identifies the page.

   - Using the pointer to the **IPropertySheetCallback** interface passed to the snap-in in the call to the **CreatePropertyPages** method, call the **IPropertySheetCallback::AddPage** method to add each property page to the MMC-provided property sheet.

5. Implement a dialog box procedure for each property page. The **pfnDlgProc** member of each property page's **PROPSHEETPAGE** structure should be set to the address of this procedure.

6. Implement the **IExtendPropertySheet2::QueryPagesFor** method. MMC calls this method when the user selects a scope or result item and clicks the **Properties** context menu item. If this method returns S_OK, MMC then calls the snap-in's implementation of the **IExtendPropertySheet2::CreatePropertyPages** method.

Sample Code

The code samples in this section are for the registration code necessary for an extension snap-in that extends another (primary) snap-in's property sheet. While the samples are specific to property sheet extensions, they can easily be modified to handle other extension types.

For sample implementations of the **IExtendPropertySheet2** interface methods, see "Adding Property Pages: Implementation Details" in Chapter 23. For a more detailed look at property sheet extensions, see the documentation of the PPgeExt sample that accompanies the MMC SDK.

The following is a sample registry entry for the **NodeTypes** key for a node type with a property sheet extension:

```
HKEY_LOCAL_MACHINE\SOFTWARE\Microsoft\MMC\NodeTypes\
  {29743811-4C4B-11D2-89D8-000021473128}\
      Extensions\
          PropertySheet
              {CFCDC9F3-C50E-11D2-952B-00C04FB92EC2}  =
              REG_SZ "Extension to the Rocket Node"
```

The *nodetypeGUID* is the value of the node type GUID of the "Rocket" result item; this item is added to the result pane of many of the C++ sample snap-ins that accompany the MMC SDK, for example, the Extens sample.

The value under the **PropertySheet** key represents the CLSID of the PPgeExt sample. The PPgeExt sample extends result items of node type *nodetypeGUID* in the Extens sample.

In the PPgeExt sample, the **RegisterSnapin** function called by the extension snap-in's **DllRegisterServer** function contains the code for adding the extension's CLSID to the **NodeTypes** key for a node type that is being extended. This code is very similar to that in the CMenuExt sample and is documented in "Registration Requirements for Extension Snap-ins" earlier in this chapter.

The only difference between the implementation of the **RegisterSnapin** function in the CMenuExt and PPgeExt samples is in the switch statement found in the function:

```
switch (pNodeExtension->eType)
{
case NameSpaceExtension:
  _tcscat(szKeyBuf, _T("\\Extensions\\NameSpace"));
  break;
case ContextMenuExtension:
  tcscat(szKeyBuf, _T("\\Extensions\\ContextMenu"));
  break;
case ToolBarExtension:
  _tcscat(szKeyBuf, _T("\\Extensions\\ToolBar"));
  break;
case PropertySheetExtension:
  _tcscat(szKeyBuf, _T("\\Extensions\\PropertySheet"));
  break;
case TaskExtension:
  _tcscat(szKeyBuf, _T("\\Extensions\\Task"));
  break;
case DynamicExtension:
  _tcscat(szKeyBuf, _T("\\Dynamic Extensions"));
default:
  break;
}
```

C++ Snap-ins

As you can see, the switch statement in the PPgeExt is a generic statement that accounts for all extension types. The PPgeExt sample is only a property page extension, as can be seen upon examination of the **_NodeExtensions** array. Recall that **pNodeExtension** points to the **_NodeExtensions** array that lists all the node types that the extension snap-in extends:

```
EXTENDER_NODE _NodeExtensions[] =
{
  {PropertySheetExtension,
      {0x29743811, 0x4c4b, 0x11d2, { 0x89, 0xd8, 0x0, 0x0, 0x21,
      0x47, 0x31, 0x28}},
      {0xcfcdc9f3, 0xc50e, 0x11d2, {0x95, 0x2b, 0x0, 0xc0, 0x4f,
      0xb9, 0x2e, 0xc2}},
      _T("Extension to the Rocket Node")}},
  {DummyExtension,
      NULL,
      NULL,
      NULL}
};
```

The PPgeExt sample is only a property page extension, so the **_NodeExtensions** array only has one element (of type **EXTENDER_NODE** structure).

Extending a Primary Snap-in's Taskpad

This section discusses the specific steps necessary for an extension snap-in to extend the taskpad of an extendable node type owned by a primary snap-in. To read about working with extension snap-ins in general, see the beginning of this chapter.

A primary snap-in registers the extendable node types that it adds to its namespace. An extension snap-in can extend the taskpad of a primary snap-in's node type by adding the appropriate registration code and then implementing the **IExtendTaskPad** and **IEnumTASK** interfaces. The snap-in extends a node type's taskpad by adding additional tasks to it.

A taskpad extension can optionally support **IComponentData**. If it does, it gains two features of namespace extensions:

- Once created, the taskpad extension remains loaded for the duration of the MMC session.
- The taskpad extension can persist data in the console file by implementing **IPersistStream**. See Chapter 26, "Snap-in Persistence Model," for more information.

Note that if the extension snap-in wants to create its own taskpad, rather than use a primary snap-in's taskpad, it should be a namespace extension instead. As a namespace extension, it can add a scope item to a primary snap-in's scope pane and create a taskpad view for that item. For details about namespace extensions, see "Extending a Primary Snap-in's Namespace" earlier in this chapter.

C++ Snap-ins

▶   **To extend a primary snap-in's taskpad**

In the following procedure, note that *{CLSID}*, *{snapinCLSID}*, and *{nodetypeGUID}* all denote string representations of the specified CLSIDs and GUIDs. The strings must begin with an open brace ({) and end with a close brace (}).

1. The CLSID of each snap-in (extension or stand-alone) must be registered under the **HKEY_CLASSES_ROOT\CLSID** key in the *{CLSID}* subkey as an in-process server DLL. The snap-in must also register a threading model for the snap-in CLSID. An apartment threading model is recommended.

    For details about the **HKEY_CLASSES_ROOT\CLSID** key, see the "**CLSID** Key" topic in the Microsoft Platform SDK. For example code, see "Registering and Unregistering a Snap-in" in Chapter 17.

2. All snap-ins must be registered under the **HKEY_LOCAL_MACHINE\Software\Microsoft\MMC\SnapIns** key in the *{snapinCLSID}* key. For details about the **SnapIns** key, see "Registering and Unregistering a Snap-in" in Chapter 17.

3. Register the CLSID of the extension snap-in under the **HKEY_LOCAL_MACHINE\Software\Microsoft\MMC\NodeTypes\ {*nodetypeGUID*}\Extensions\Task** subkey, where *nodetypeGUID* is the node type GUID of the node type whose taskpad is being extended. For details about the **NodeTypes** key, see "Registration Requirements for Extension Snap-ins" earlier in this chapter.

4. Implement the **IExtendTaskPad** and **IEnumTASK** interfaces. The only **IExtendTaskPad** interface methods you must implement are **EnumTasks** and **TaskNotify**. All other methods can return E_NOTIMPL. The extension's **EnumTasks** implementation is used by MMC to get a pointer to the extension's **IEnumTASK** interface. The **TaskNotify** method is used for sending notifications from the taskpad to the extension when one of the extension's tasks is clicked. Note that the primary snap-in that owns the scope item that is displaying the taskpad is responsible for loading the taskpad template and setting up the taskpad through its own **IExtendTaskPad** methods.

5. If the taskpad extension persists data in the console file, the snap-in must implement **IComponentData**. As a result of implementing **IComponentData**, once loaded, the taskpad extension remains loaded for the duration of the current MMC session. Also, the extension's cocreatable class object is responsible for exposing the snap-in's **IComponentData** and **IExtendTaskPad** interfaces.

Sample Code

The following is a sample registry entry for the **NodeTypes** key for a node type with a taskpad extension:

```
HKEY_LOCAL_MACHINE\SOFTWARE\Microsoft\MMC\NodeTypes\
    {29743811-4C4B-11D2-89D8-000000000000}\
        Extensions\
            Task
                {20E42DD2-5CCF-11D3-9147-000000000000} =
                REG_SZ "Extension to the Taskpad node's taskpad"
```

The *nodetypeGUID* is the value of the node type GUID of the node whose taskpad is extended by the extension snap-in. The value under the **Task** key represents the CLSID of the extension snap-in.

Note that the GUIDs in the preceding sample are dummy values and should not be used in actual snap-ins.

Adding Dynamic Extensions

This feature is introduced in MMC 1.1.

Dynamic extensions are extension snap-ins that are added to a scope or result item programmatically at run time. A snap-in can dynamically add any type of extension to any of its own items.

A primary snap-in can add known extension snap-ins on a *per-item* basis to items that it (the primary snap-in) owns. For example, if a primary snap-in has a namespace extension that adds an item to its namespace, the primary snap-in cannot dynamically extend the item provided by the namespace extension because the snap-in does not own that item.

When a primary snap-in dynamically extends one of its items, the extension snap-in extends only the specific instance of the item. Other items of that node type are not affected. Dynamically adding an extension is not the same as using the **Add/Remove Snap-in** dialog box to add an extension to a snap-in. By using the dialog box to add an extension to a primary snap-in, the extension is added to all instances of snap-ins of that type. If you want all instances of your snap-in to be automatically extended by one or more extension snap-ins, the snap-in should implement required extensions. For more information about required extensions, see "Adding Required Extensions" later in this chapter.

When adding a dynamic extension, the primary snap-in must know the CLSID of the extension snap-ins that can extend it. To prevent extension snap-ins from indiscriminately extending all snap-ins or extending snap-ins inappropriately, MMC forces primary snap-ins to specify the extension snap-ins by their CLSIDs.

In addition to registering its class ID (CLSID) under the **HKEY_CLASSES_ROOT\CLSID** key as an in-process server DLL, a dynamic extension snap-in also must register its CLSID in three additional places in the registry:

- All extension snap-ins, including dynamic extensions, must be registered under the **HKEY_LOCAL_MACHINE\Software\Microsoft\MMC\SnapIns** key in the *{snapinCLSID}* key. The *{snapinCLSID}* key is the name for a snap-in's key and is the string representation of the snap-in's CLSID. For details about the **SnapIns** key, see "**SnapIns** Key" in the MMC COM Reference section of the MMC SDK. For details about registering snap-ins, see "Registering and Unregistering a Snap-in" in Chapter 17.

- All extension snap-ins, including dynamic extensions, must also be registered under the **HKEY_LOCAL_MACHINE\Software\Microsoft\MMC\NodeTypes\ *{nodetypeGUID}*\Extensions** key, where the *{nodetypeGUID}* key specifies the string representation of the GUID of the node type that is being extended, and the **Extensions** key contains subkeys and values that list the snap-ins that are registered to extend the node type specified by *{nodetypeGUID}*.

- Extension snap-ins that can only be loaded as dynamic extensions must be registered under the **HKEY_LOCAL_MACHINE\Software\Microsoft\MMC\NodeTypes\ *{nodetypeGUID}*\Dynamic Extensions** key. The **Dynamic Extensions** key contains values that represent the CLSIDs of snap-ins that should act only as dynamic extensions to the node type specified by *{nodetypeGUID}*.

    Snap-ins listed under the **Dynamic Extensions** key are not displayed on the **Extensions** tab of the **Add/Remove Snap-in** dialog box.

For details about the **NodeTypes** key, see "Registration Requirements for Extension Snap-ins" earlier in this chapter.

To dynamically extend the namespace of a primary snap-in, use **IConsoleNameSpace2::AddExtension**. For other types of extensions (context menus, toolbars, property sheets, taskpads), add the CCF_MMC_DYNAMIC_EXTENSIONS clipboard format to the **IDataObject** implementation for the items you want to extend. The CCF_MMC_DYNAMIC_EXTENSIONS format uses the **SMMCDynamicExtensions** structure, which contains the CLSIDs of the snap-ins that you want to add to an item.

Dynamic extensions apply only to the current session and are not persisted in the console file. For namespace extensions, dynamic extensions persist only for the lifetime of the scope item specified by the *hItem* parameter of **IConsoleNameSpace2::AddExtension**. Non-namespace dynamic extensions are not persisted beyond a single use. Each time a context menu, property sheet, or snap-in toolbar is displayed, MMC looks at the **IDataObject** for the selected item to get the active dynamic extensions.

If you want to allow future extension snap-ins to dynamically extend your snap-in, you can do one of the following:

- If you want to be able to add your own dynamic extensions to the snap-in, you can reserve CLSIDs that can be used by your extensions in the future. Note that MMC will ignore non-namespace extension snap-ins that are not properly registered. For namespace extensions, **IConsoleNameSpace2::AddExtension** returns E_INVALIDARG if the CLSID is not registered as a namespace extension.

- If you want to enable other snap-in developers to create extensions that can be dynamically added to your snap-in, your snap-in can read the list of extensions to add dynamically from the registry or from an initialization file and extension snap-ins can add themselves there.

For general information about registering extension snap-ins, see "Registration Requirements for Extension Snap-ins" earlier in this chapter.

C++ Snap-ins

Adding Dynamic Extensions: Interfaces

Dynamic namespace extensions require the use of the following interface and method:

- **IConsoleNameSpace2**

    IConsoleNameSpace2::AddExtension

Other Constructs

Non-namespace dynamic extensions (context menu, property sheet, toolbar, taskpad) must support the following clipboard format in their **IDataObject** implementation:

- CCF_MMC_DYNAMIC_EXTENSIONS

The clipboard format uses the following structure:

- **SMMCDynamicExtensions**

Dynamic Namespace Extensions

This feature is introduced in MMC 1.1.

A snap-in can dynamically add namespace extensions to any of its own scope items. To dynamically extend one of your snap-in's scope items, the snap-in simply calls the **IConsoleNameSpace2::AddExtension** method. Note that the **AddExtension** method only works for items that are directly owned by the snap-in making the **AddExtension** call.

In addition, **AddExtension** adds the extension (specified by the CLSID specified in the *lpClsid* parameter) to a particular instance of a scope item (which is specified by the *hItem* parameter). It does not affect other scope items of that node type.

A common place to add dynamic namespace extensions is in the MMCN_EXPAND notification handler of the snap-in's **IComponentData** object.

Note that the extension snap-in must be a namespace extension. In addition, the MMC registry entries for the primary snap-in and the extension snap-in must be set correctly. For details on setting MMC registry entries for namespace extensions, see "Extending a Primary Snap-in's Namespace" earlier in this chapter.

As with all namespace extensions, the extension snap-in must be able to handle the data object of the scope item being extended in the primary snap-in. To interact with a primary snap-in, an extension snap-in must understand the primary snap-in's clipboard formats.

Dynamic Non-Namespace Extensions

This feature is introduced in MMC 1.1.

Using the CCF_MMC_DYNAMIC_EXTENSIONS clipboard format, a snap-in can also add any of the following types of extensions to its own scope or result items:

- Context menus
- Toolbars
- Property sheets
- Taskpads

For these types of extensions, add the clipboard format CCF_MMC_DYNAMIC_EXTENSIONS to the snap-in's **IDataObject** implementation for the items you want to extend. The CCF_MMC_DYNAMIC_EXTENSIONS format uses the **SMMCDynamicExtensions** structure. This structure specifies the extension snap-ins you want to extend the item represented by the **IDataObject** object.

Note that the MMC registry entries for the primary snap-in and the extension snap-in must be set correctly. For details on setting MMC registry entries for namespace extensions, see "Registration Requirements for Extension Snap-ins" earlier in this chapter.

The following steps describe how to implement dynamic extensions for non-namespace extensions:

▶ **To implement dynamic extensions for non-namespace extensions**

1. Add the CCF_MMC_DYNAMIC_EXTENSIONS clipboard format to the snap-in's **IDataObject** implementation.

   Usually, **IDataObject** has its supported clipboard formats as static members. If so, add the CCF_MMC_DYNAMIC_EXTENSIONS format as a member:

   ```
   static UINT s_cfDynamicExtensions;
   ```

   Register the CCF_MMC_DYNAMIC_EXTENSIONS format and assign the registered format to the static member in the **IDataObject** implementation's constructor:

   ```
   s_cfDynamicExtensions = RegisterClipboardFormat
                   (W2T(CCF_MMC_DYNAMIC_EXTENSIONS));
   ```

2. Handle the CCF_MMC_DYNAMIC_EXTENSIONS format in the
    IDataObject::GetData method.

The following example handles the CCF_MMC_DYNAMIC_EXTENSIONS
format and returns an **SMMCDynamicExtensions** structure that contains an
array of two GUIDs that are the CLSIDs of the two extension snap-ins
(CLSID_Snapin1 and CLSID_Snapin2) that will extend the item:

```
if (cf == s_cfDynamicExtensions)
{
    UINT cGuids = 2;
    UINT size = sizeof(SMMCDynamicExtensions) +
                (cGuids-1) * sizeof(GUID);

    lpMedium->hGlobal = ::GlobalAlloc(GPTR, size);

    if (!lpMedium->hGlobal)
        return E_OUTOFMEMORY;

    SMMCDynamicExtensions* pdata =
                reinterpret_cast<SMMCDynamicExtensions*>
                (lpMedium->hGlobal);
    pdata->count = cGuids;
    int i=0;
    pdata->guid[i++] = CLSID_Snapin1;
    pdata->guid[i++] = CLSID_Snapin2;
    return S_OK;
}
```

Just before MMC needs to use an extensible feature (that is, just before creating
and displaying a context menu, property sheet, toolbar, or taskpad), MMC calls
IDataObject::GetData on the data object for the selected item and asks for
dynamic extensions to add through the CCF_MMC_DYNAMIC_EXTENSIONS
clipboard format. Based on the CLSIDs passed in the
SMMCDynamicExtensions structure, MMC attempts to add the specified
extensions to the extensible feature. If an extension is unavailable or unregistered,
MMC skips that extension and continues to the next CLSID passed in the
structure.

Adding Required Extensions

Required extensions are extension snap-ins that are automatically added to the primary snap-in when the primary snap-in is loaded. By implementing the **IRequiredExtensions** interface, a snap-in specifies the list of required extensions that MMC should load when that snap-in is loaded.

Required extensions are added to all instances of the primary snap-in. In addition, required extensions cannot be removed programmatically or through the **Add/Remove Snap-in** dialog box.

Required extensions are persisted in the console file, but at each session the snap-in is queried for the list. Only required extensions specified by the latest query are used.

The snap-in can specify that all registered extension snap-ins should be added by implementing the **IRequiredExtensions::EnableAllExtensions** method. The snap-in can specify a specific list of registered extension snap-ins to be added by implementing the **IRequiredExtensions::GetFirstExtension** and **IRequiredExtensions::GetNextExtension** methods.

C++ Snap-ins

C H A P T E R   2 5

Enabling MMC Standard Verbs

A primary snap-in has the opportunity to enable MMC standard verbs for scope or result items when its **IComponent::Notify** method is called with the MMCN_SELECT notification message. Note that MMC standard verbs are not to be confused with context menu items that snap-ins can add to the context menus of their scope and result items. For details about context menus, see Chapter 21, "Working with Context Menus."

The **MMC_CONSOLE_VERB** enumeration defines the command identifiers available for standard verbs. The following verbs are allowed:

- MMC_VERB_NONE
- MMC_VERB_OPEN
- MMC_VERB_COPY
- MMC_VERB_PASTE
- MMC_VERB_DELETE
- MMC_VERB_PROPERTIES
- MMC_VERB_RENAME
- MMC_VERB_REFRESH
- MMC_VERB_PRINT
- MMC_VERB_CUT

When a standard verb is enabled for an item and the user selects it, MMC calls the snap-in's **IComponent::Notify** method with the appropriate notification message. See the **MMC_CONSOLE_VERB** documentation in the MMC COM Reference section of the MMC SDK for details.

C++ Snap-ins

Note that MMC does not send a notification message in the case of the MMC_VERB_PROPERTIES, MMC_VERB_COPY, and MMC_VERB_CUT verbs. When the MMC_VERB_PROPERTIES verb is enabled and the user selects it, MMC calls the **IExtendPropertySheet2::CreatePropertyPages** method of all snap-ins (primary and extension) that add property pages for the selected item. Note that primary snap-ins are responsible for enabling the MMC_VERB_PROPERTIES verb. Extension snap-ins cannot do this, because they do not own the item for which the verb is enabled.

When the MMC_VERB_COPY or MMC_VERB_CUT verb is enabled and the user selects it, MMC calls the snap-in's **IComponentData::QueryDataObject** or **IComponent::QueryDataObject** implementation to request a data object for the selected item.

The MMC_VERB_CUT, MMC_VERB_COPY, and MMC_VERB_PASTE verbs must all be enabled in snap-ins that support cut/copy/paste operations. Note that snap-ins that support cut/copy/paste operations also automatically support drag-and-drop operations as well—no extra coding is required. For details, see "Drag and Drop" later in this chapter.

As mentioned above, snap-ins enable standard verbs in their MMCN_SELECT notification handler. In the notification handler, snap-ins should call **IConsole2::QueryConsoleVerb** to request a pointer to MMC's **IConsoleVerb** interface implementation. Using the returned interface pointer, snap-ins can then call the **IConsoleVerb::SetVerbState** method to enable the standard verbs, one call per standard verb. Snap-ins can also call the **SetDefaultVerb** method to set the default verb for an item. The default verb is indicated in bold type in the item's context menu.

Some of the standard verbs have associated toolbar buttons. For example, when the MMC_VERB_DELETE verb is enabled for an item, MMC displays a toolbar button when the item is selected. The user can then either click the toolbar button or click the **Delete** context menu item to delete the item.

Enabling MMC Standard Verbs: Implementation Details

▶ **To enable standard verbs**

1. Handle the MMCN_SELECT notification message, which MMC sends to indicate which item in the scope pane is currently selected.

2. In the notification handler, call **IConsole2::QueryConsoleVerb** to request a pointer to MMC's **IConsoleVerb** interface implementation.

3. Use the returned interface pointer to call **IConsoleVerb::SetVerbState**, once for each standard verb that you want to enable for the selected item. Also call other **IConsoleVerb** verbs as necessary.

Sample Code

The following sample code shows how to enable standard verbs in the notification handler for the MMCN_SELECT notification message:

```
HRESULT CRocket::OnSelect(IConsole *pConsole, BOOL bScope,
                          BOOL bSelect)
{
  HRESULT hr;

  // enable rename, refresh, delete and properties verbs
  IConsoleVerb *pConsoleVerb;

  hr = pConsole->QueryConsoleVerb(&pConsoleVerb);
  _ASSERT(SUCCEEDED(hr));

  if ( SUCCEEDED(hr) )
  {
      hr = pConsoleVerb->SetVerbState(MMC_VERB_RENAME, ENABLED, TRUE);
      hr = pConsoleVerb->SetVerbState(MMC_VERB_REFRESH, ENABLED,
          TRUE);
      hr = pConsoleVerb->SetVerbState(MMC_VERB_DELETE, ENABLED, TRUE);
      hr = pConsoleVerb->SetVerbState(MMC_VERB_PROPERTIES, ENABLED,
          TRUE);

      //also set MMC_VERB_PROPERTIES as the default verb
      hr = pConsoleVerb->SetDefaultVerb(MMC_VERB_PROPERTIES);
      pConsoleVerb->Release();
  }
  else
      hr = S_FALSE;

  return hr;
}
```

C++ Snap-ins

Drag and Drop

Drag-and-drop operations work automatically in snap-ins that implement the cut, copy, and paste standard verbs. This section discusses how to implement these verbs and what the various responsibilities of the source and destination of a drag-and-drop operation are.

To read about how to enable MMC standard verbs, see the preceding topics in this chapter.

The following drag-and-drop operations are possible in MMC:

- Items (scope and result items) from one result pane can be dragged and dropped into another result pane or into the scope item that owns the result pane.

- A scope item in the scope pane can be dragged and dropped into another scope item.

Drag and drop operations also apply in multiple views, or even in multiple snap-ins. You can, for example, select a scope or result item in one view of one snap-in, drag it into another snap-in's result pane, and drop it. Of course, you can achieve the same results by cutting or copying the source scope or result item and then pasting it in the destination scope item or its result pane.

Note that drag-and-drop operations on snap-in static nodes are not allowed. You cannot, for example, add two snap-ins to a console, select the console root to display the static nodes of the two snap-ins in the result pane, and select one of the static nodes and then drag and drop it in the other static node in the scope pane.

How Drag and Drop Works in MMC

To understand drag and drop, you really need to understand how the cut, copy, paste, and delete verbs work in a drag-and-drop operation. Basically, the mechanism of cutting or copying a scope or result item and pasting it in another scope item or its result pane works in the following way:

1. The user selects the source scope or result item (henceforth the "source item") and either cuts or copies it. If the source item is cut, its icon is grayed out, indicating that the item will be cut after a successful paste. MMC calls the **IComponent::QueryDataObject** method of the source snap-in's current view and requests a data object for the cut or copied source item.

2. The user then selects the destination scope item or a result item in its result pane (henceforth "destination item"). MMC then calls the **IComponent::Notify** method of the destination snap-in's current view with the MMCN_QUERY_PASTE notification. The *lpDataObject* parameter passed in the method call contains the data object for the destination item, and the *arg* parameter contains the data object for the source item.

3. If the source item can be pasted in the destination item, the destination snap-in's MMCN_QUERY_PASTE notification handler returns S_OK. Otherwise, it returns S_FALSE. Also, note that the user is allowed to paste the source item in the destination item *only* if the snap-in returns S_OK in its MMCN_QUERY_PASTE notification handler. Otherwise, MMC disables the paste verb for the destination item.

4. If the destination snap-in accepts the paste, MMC then calls the **IComponent::Notify** method of the destination's current view with the MMCN_PASTE notification. Again, the *lpDataObject* parameter contains the destination item's data object, and the *arg* parameter contains the source item's data object. The *param* parameter is an out parameter that will hold a data object for the source item after a successful paste. This is so the source snap-in can know which item to delete after a successful paste.

5. The destination snap-in performs the paste operation and returns S_OK in its MMCN_PASTE notification handler for the destination item. The destination snap-in must also specify a data object for the successfully pasted source item in the *param* parameter. This data object is in turn forwarded to the source snap-in through the MMCN_CUTORMOVE notification. If the operation is a copy operation as opposed to a cut operation, the destination snap-in need not fill the *param* parameter.

6. In a cut operation, MMC then calls the **IComponent::Notify** method of the source snap-in's current view with the MMCN_CUTORMOVE notification. The *arg* parameter passed in the method call contains the data object for the cut source item. The source snap-in handles the notification and then returns S_OK.

   Note that MMC does not delete a source item that has been cut by the user. If the user cuts a result item from a result pane, and the result pane is still visible after the cut, the snap-in should call **IResultData::DeleteItem** to remove the cut item. For a cut scope item, the snap-in should call **IConsoleNameSpace2::DeleteItem** to delete the scope item from the scope pane.

C++ Snap-ins

Drag and Drop: Implementation Details

The following procedure describes how to implement drag-and-drop functionality in your snap-in. Note that only single-selection drag and drop is discussed here. Multiselection drag and drop is implemented in essentially the same way as described here. However, there are some differences, and these are discussed in detail in the "Multiselection" section later in this chapter.

▶ **To implement single-selection drag and drop**

1. Enable the cut, copy, and paste standard verbs. The source scope or result item (henceforth the "source item") enables the cut and copy verbs, and the destination scope or result item (henceforth the "destination item") should enable the paste verb. See the beginning of this chapter for details.

2. Handle the MMCN_QUERY_PASTE, MMCN_PASTE, and MMCN_CUTORMOVE notifications. All notifications are sent to the snap-in's **IComponent::Notify** implementation. The following steps discuss which snap-in (the source or the destination) is responsible for handling which notification.

3. In the destination snap-in, handle the MMCN_QUERY_PASTE and MMCN_PASTE notifications.

   • MMC sends the MMCN_QUERY_PASTE notification if there is a data object available to paste. The destination snap-in should examine the data object and return S_OK if the object can be pasted or S_FALSE if the object cannot be pasted. If the data object can be pasted, MMC enables the paste verb for the destination item.

   • The MMCN_PASTE notification is sent when the user attempts to paste the source item in the destination item. After a successful paste, for cut/paste operations, the destination snap-in must specify a data object for the successfully pasted scope or result item in the *param* parameter (sent through MMCN_PASTE). This data object is forwarded to the source snap-in through the MMCN_CUTORMOVE notification.

4. In the source snap-in, handle the MMCN_CUTORMOVE notification. MMC sends this notification after a successful paste in a cut/copy operation. The *arg* parameter passed through the notification contains the data object for the cut source item.

   Note that MMC does not delete a source item that has been cut by the user. If the user cuts a result item from a result pane, and the result pane is still visible after the cut, the snap-in should call **IResultData::DeleteItem** to remove the cut item. For a cut scope item, the snap-in should call **IConsoleNameSpace2::DeleteItem** to delete the scope item from the scope pane.

Sample Code

The following code samples show notification handlers for the
MMCN_QUERY_PASTE, MMCN_PASTE, and MMCN_CUTORMOVE
notifications.

All samples are taken from the CutCopy sample snap-in that accompanies the
MMC SDK. The CutCopy sample demonstrates how to implement drag and drop
in a single snap-in. In the sample, either a "Rocket" result item or a "Space
Station" scope item can be the source of drag-and drop-operations, and "Space
Station" scope items are the destination.

Note that all sample code assumes Unicode compilation.

IComponent::Notify Implementation

One of the trickiest aspects of implementing drag and drop is to properly
implement the snap-in's **IComponent::Notify** method. Here is how this method is
implemented in the CutCopy sample. Note that the following code sample only
shows cases in which MMCN_QUERY_PASTE, MMCN_PASTE, or
MMCN_CUTORMOVE is sent. See the CutCopy sample for the entire
implementation of **IComponent::Notify**.

Note that in all cases, **base** is defined as follows unless otherwise noted:

```
CDelegationBase *base =
            GetOurDataObject( lpDataObject )->GetBaseNodeObject();
```

In the MMC C++ sample snap-ins, all snap-in objects that are inserted in either
the scope or result pane are derived from the **CDelegationBase** base class. For
details about how **CDelegationBase** is used in SDK samples, see "Samples
Object Model" in Chapter 31.

Case MMCN_QUERY_PASTE

Let's start with the MMCN_QUERY_PASTE case:

```
case MMCN_QUERY_PASTE:
{
  CDataObject *pPastedDO = GetOurDataObject((IDataObject *)arg);
  if (pPastedDO != NULL)
  {
      CDelegationBase *pasted = pPastedDO->GetBaseNodeObject();
          if (pasted != NULL)
          {
              hr = base->OnQueryPaste(pasted);
          }
  }
}

break;
```

C++ Snap-ins

The *lpDataObject* parameter in the method call contains a data object for the destination scope item. The *arg* parameter in the method call contains a data object for the source scope or result item. MMC requests a data object for the source item when the user selects the item and then either cuts or copies it. The destination snap-in determines in its **CSpaceStation::OnQueryPaste** method whether or not the data object in the *arg* parameter can be pasted in the destination scope item. **CSpaceStation** objects represent the "Space Station" scope items in the sample.

```
HRESULT CSpaceStation::OnQueryPaste(CDelegationBase *pPasted)
{
        CRocket *pRocket = dynamic_cast<CRocket *>(pPasted);

        if (NULL == pRocket)
        {
            // See if this is CSpaceStation.
            CSpaceStation* pSpaceStn =
                    dynamic_cast<CSpaceStation*>(pPasted);
            if ( (NULL != pSpaceStn) &&
                (pSpaceStn != this) )
            {
                return S_OK;
            }
            return S_FALSE;
        }

        if (pRocket->m_pSpaceStation != this)
                for (int n = 0; n < MAX_CHILDREN; n++)
                {
                    if (NULL == children[n])
                    {
                        return S_OK;
                    }
                }

        return S_FALSE;
}
```

Case MMCN_PASTE

Let's now look at the MMCN_PASTE case:

```
case MMCN_PASTE:
{
    CDataObject *pPastedDO = GetOurDataObject((IDataObject *)arg);
    if (pPastedDO != NULL)
    {
        CDelegationBase *pasted = pPastedDO->GetBaseNodeObject();

        if (pasted != NULL)
        {
            hr = base->OnPaste(m_ipConsole, m_pParent, pasted);

            if (SUCCEEDED(hr))
            {
                // Determine if the item to be pasted is scope or
                // result item.
                CRocket* pRocket = dynamic_cast<CRocket*>(pasted);
                BOOL bResult = pRocket ? TRUE : FALSE;
                //Rocket item is a result item.

                CDataObject *pObj = new
                    CDataObject((MMC_COOKIE)pasted, bResult ?
                    CCT_RESULT : CCT_SCOPE);

                if (!pObj)
                    return E_OUTOFMEMORY;

                pObj->QueryInterface(IID_IDataObject,
                                        (void **)param);

                //Code for updating all views omitted here.
                //See CutCopy sample for complete code.
            }
        }
    }

    break;
}
```

The *lpDataObject* parameter in the method call contains a data object for the destination scope item. The *arg* parameter in the method call contains a data object for the source scope or result item. If the source item is to be cut after the paste operation, the destination snap-in must specify a data object for the successfully pasted item in the *param* parameter (sent through MMCN_PASTE). This data object is forwarded to the source snap-in through the MMCN_CUTORMOVE notification.

C++ Snap-ins

The snap-in performs the paste operation in its **CSpaceStation::OnPaste** method:

```
HRESULT CSpaceStation::OnPaste(IConsole *pConsole,
        CComponentData *pComponentData, CDelegationBase *pPasted)
{
    CRocket *pRocket = dynamic_cast<CRocket *>(pPasted);

    HRESULT hr = S_OK;

    if (NULL == pRocket)
    {
        // See if this is CSpaceStation, if so paste it into this
        // item.
        CSpaceStation* pSpaceStn =
                    dynamic_cast<CSpaceStation*>(pPasted);
        if ( (NULL != pSpaceStn) && (pSpaceStn != this) )
        {
            CSpaceStation* pNewStation = new CSpaceStation();

            SCOPEDATAITEM sdi;
            ZeroMemory(&sdi, sizeof(SCOPEDATAITEM) );
            sdi.mask = SDI_STR|         // Displayname is valid
                       SDI_PARAM   |    // lParam is valid
                       SDI_IMAGE   |    // nImage is valid
                       SDI_OPENIMAGE |  // nOpenImage is valid
                       SDI_PARENT  |
                       SDI_CHILDREN;

            sdi.relativeID  = (HSCOPEITEM)GetHandle();
            sdi.nImage      = pNewStation->GetBitmapIndex();
            sdi.nOpenImage  = INDEX_OPENFOLDER;
            sdi.displayname = MMC_CALLBACK;
            sdi.lParam      = (LPARAM)pNewStation; // The cookie
            sdi.cChildren   = 0;
            hr = pComponentData->GetConsoleNameSpace()->
                            InsertItem( &sdi );
            _ASSERT( SUCCEEDED(hr) );
            pNewStation->SetHandle((HANDLE)sdi.ID);
```

```
        }

        //increment count of child space stations
        m_cChildSpaceStations++;

        return hr;
    }

    if (pRocket->m_pSpaceStation == this)
            return S_FALSE;

    //Create a new CRocket for the destination CSpaceStation
    CRocket *myRocket = new CRocket(pRocket->m_pSpaceStation,
        pRocket->szName, pRocket->nId, pRocket->lWeight,
        pRocket->lHeight, pRocket->lPayload);

    for (int n = 0; n < MAX_CHILDREN; n++) {
        if (NULL == children[n])
        {
            // put it here

            children[n] = myRocket;
            children[n]->isDeleted = FALSE;
            children[n]->nId = n;
            children[n]->m_pSpaceStation = this;

            return S_OK;
        }
    }

    return S_FALSE;
}
```

Each "Rocket" result item is represented by an underlying **CRocket** snap-in object.

Case MMCN_CUTORMOVE

Finally, the MMCN_CUTORMOVE case:

```
if (MMCN_CUTORMOVE == event && pLastPasteQuery != NULL)
{
    //arg contains the data object of the cut object
    //we get its CDelegationBase and then cast it
    //to its proper type.
    CDelegationBase *base = GetOurDataObject( (LPDATAOBJECT)arg )->
                            GetBaseNodeObject();
    CRocket *pRocket = dynamic_cast<CRocket *>(base);

    if (NULL == pRocket)
    {// The cut item is a scope item. Delete it.
        CSpaceStation* pSpaceStn =
            dynamic_cast<CSpaceStation*>(base);
        if (NULL != pSpaceStn)
        {
            hr = pSpaceStn->OnDeleteScopeItem(m_pParent->
                            GetConsoleNameSpace());
            return hr;
        }
    }

    //The cut item is a result item. Set its isDeleted member to
    //TRUE. This tells the source scope item that the object no
    //longer needs to be inserted in its result pane
    pRocket->setDeletedStatus(TRUE);

    //Code for updating all views omitted here.
    //See CutCopy sample for complete code.

    return S_OK;
}
```

MMC sends this notification to the source snap-in after a successful paste in a cut/copy operation. The *arg* parameter in the method call contains the data object for the cut result item.

As previously stated, MMC does not delete the cut scope or result item; it is up to the source snap-in to do this.

In the CutCopy sample, a simple Boolean flag is used to determine which "Rocket" result items have been cut and therefore no longer need to be inserted. The sample sets this flag in its MMCN_CUTORMOVE handler by calling the **CRocket::setDeletedStatus** method. Recall that **CRocket** objects represent "Rocket" result items.

For cut scope items, the snap-in calls the **CSpaceStation::OnDeleteScopeItem**. This function uses the **IConsoleNamespace2::DeleteItem** function to delete the scope item from the scope pane. See the CutCopy sample for the code of the **OnDeleteScopeItem** function.

Multiselection

Multiselection is allowed only in the result pane. By default, multiselection is disabled in the list view. To enable multiselection, set the MMC_VIEW_OPTIONS_MULTISELECT flag in the *ViewOptions* parameter during calls to the snap-in's **IComponent::GetResultViewType** implementation.

What happens on multiselection depends on the items that are selected in the result pane. There are two possible scenarios:

- Scope or result items owned by a single snap-in are selected.
- Scope items owned by multiple snap-ins are selected.

Multiselection and Items Owned by a Single Snap-in

Multiselection for items owned by a single snap-in works in the following way:

1. In a list view for which multiselection is enabled, the user selects one scope or result item and then selects another one.

2. Upon selection of the next item, MMC calls the current view's **IComponent::QueryDataObject** implementation. The *cookie* parameter passed into the call contains the value of the MMC_MULTI_SELECT_COOKIE special cookie, indicating to the snap-in that MMC is requesting a special, snap-in-defined *multiselection data object*.

   Note that, in general, snap-ins can use the **IS_SPECIAL_COOKIE** macro to determine whether or not the value contained in the *cookie* parameter refers to a special cookie.

3. The snap-in creates the multiselection data object identifying the items currently selected in the result pane, and returns it to MMC. The snap-in should call **IResultData::GetNextItem** with **RESULTDATAITEM.nState =** LVIS_SELECTED to get all its selected items.

   The multiselection data object provided by the snap-in must also provide the list of node type GUIDs of all its currently selected items. This is done by supporting the CCF_OBJECT_TYPES_IN_MULTI_SELECT clipboard format in the multiselection data object's **IDataObject::GetData** implementation. The data format used with the clipboard format is an **SMMCObjectTypes** structure. MMC uses this structure to determine the extension snap-ins that extend any of the seleced items.

4. MMC calls the snap-in's **IComponent::Notify** implementation for the current view with the MMCN_SELECT notification to indicate that items are selected in the result pane. The *lpDataObject* parameter contains the multiselection data object created by the snap-in.

5. The snap-in examines the multiselection data object and enables verbs for the selected items. Note that the snap-in only needs to explicitly enable verbs for any one of the selected items. MMC then sets the verbs for the other items. See "Multiselection and Standard Verbs" later in this chapter for information about verb behavior during multiselection.

6. MMC then calls the **GetData** method of the multiselection data object with the CCF_OBJECT_TYPES_IN_MULTI_SELECT clipboard format to request a list of the node type GUIDs of all the currently selected items. The snap-in uses the **SMMCObjectTypes** structure for providing the requested information. MMC uses CCF_OBJECT_TYPES_IN_MULTI_SELECT to determine which extension snap-ins extend any of the selected items.

7. MMC then finds which extensions can extend *all* of the selected items and creates them when the appropriate extension feature is needed, for example, when the user displays a selected item's context menu.

8. Control now returns to the user. If the user selects another item as part of the multiselection, MMC releases its interface to the multiselection data object and requests a new one. Steps 2 through 6 in this process are then repeated.

   If the user instead operates on the multiselection by, for example, activating one of the enabled verbs, what happens next depends on the performed operation. See "User Operations during Multiselection" later in this chapter for details.

9. After the multiselection operation is completed, MMC releases its interface to the multiselection data object.

Scope Items Owned by Multiple Snap-ins

Scope items owned (inserted) by multiple snap-ins can be part of a multiselection. In this case, multiselection works in essentially the same way as it does in the case when all items are owned by a single snap-in, with the following differences:

- MMC calls the **IComponent::QueryDataObject** implementation (with *cookie* == MMC_MULTI_SELECT_COOKIE) of the primary snap-in and each namespace extension that owns any of the selected items to request a multiselection data object. Consequently, all namespace extensions whose items are allowed to be part of a multiselection must implement **IComponent**.

  Note that, in the call to **IResultData::GetNextItem** with **RESULTDATAITEM.nState** = LVIS_SELECTED, MMC will only return items that the calling snap-in owns, skipping over the items owned by other snap-ins. Therefore, each snap-in involved in a multiselection provides a multiselection data object identifying only *its* items currently selected in the result pane.

- During some multiselection operations (for example, paste operations) MMC creates a composite data object consisting of an array of multiselection data objects provided by all the snap-ins involved in a multiselection. This composite data object is forwarded to snap-ins, which can then use the CCF_MULTI_SELECT_SNAPINS clipboard format for extracting the array of multiselection data objects. The data format used with the clipboard format is the **SMMCDataObjects** structure.

Multiselection and Standard Verbs

For multiselection, verbs behave as follows:

- Open, rename, and refresh are disabled by default.
- Copy, paste, and delete are inclusive. That is, if one of the selected items can be copied, then copy is enabled. The same is true for the paste and delete verbs.
- Property and print are exclusive and are applicable only when items from a single snap-in are selected. Their state depends on the snap-in.

User Operations During Multiselection

MMC allows the following user operations on multiply selected items:

- Activation of any of the allowed verbs, by using either context menus or the corresponding toolbar buttons.
- Selection of any context menu items, placed either by the primary snap-in or by any of its extensions. Note, however, that MMC only gives extension snap-ins that extend *all* the selected items an opportunity to add their extensions.
- Drag-and-drop operations.

Data Objects Sent During Multiselection Operations

The following table lists the types of data objects that can be sent to snap-ins in response to user operations that involve multiselection items.-

Notification or interface method	Data object sent
MMCN_BTN_CLICK	Provided by MMC. Array of snap-in-provided multiselection data objects.
MMCN_CUTORMOVE	Provided by the destination snap-in. Data object with the list of successfully pasted items.
MMCN_DELETE	Multiselection data object. Provided by snap-in.
MMCN_QUERY_PASTE	Provided by MMC. Array of snap-in-provided multiselection data objects.
MMCN_PASTE	Multiselection data object. Provided by snap-in.
MMCN_PRINT	Multiselection data object. Provided by snap-in.
MMCN_SELECT	Multiselection data object. Provided by snap-in.
IExtendContextMenu methods	Provided by MMC. Array of snap-in-provided multiselection data objects.
IExtendPropertySheet2 methods	Provided by MMC. Array of snap-in-provided multiselection data objects.

C++ Snap-ins

Multiselection and Drag and Drop Operations

The "Drag and Drop" section earlier in this chapter discusses how to support drag-and-drop functionality in a snap-in. However, the discussion and procedures outlined in that section only discuss drag and drop for operations involving a single selected item. Snap-ins that allow drag-and-drop operations on multiple items need to be aware of the following additional issues:

1. The procedure outlined in the following topic, "Multiselection: Implementation Details," must be implemented in all source snap-ins that allow items inserted by them to be part of a multiselection.

2. During the MMCN_QUERY_PASTE notification message, MMC provides a composite data object that contains an array of multiselection data objects. The multiselection data objects are provided by the source snap-ins (primary or extension) that own items in the multiselection. Note that each source snap-in is responsible for defining the format of the multiselection data object that it provides.

    The destination snap-in can use the CCF_MMC_MULTISELECT_DATAOBJECT clipboard format to determine whether or not the data object it receives during MMCN_QUERY_PASTE is a composite data object.

    If the data object is a composite data object, the destination snap-in must use the CCF_MULTI_SELECT_SNAPINS clipboard format for extracting the array of multiselection data objects from it. The data format used with the clipboard format is the **SMMCDataObjects** structure.

    The destination snap-in can examine as many of the multiselection data objects as it needs to in determining whether or not to accept the paste.

3. If the destination accepts the paste operation, MMC sends it an MMCN_PASTE notification message, once for *each* multiselection data object. The *lpDataObject* parameter contains the pointer to a multiselection data object.

    If objects that are being pasted need to be deleted at the source as a result of a previous cut or move operation, then the *param* parameter contains a pointer to an **IDataObject** interface. If the paste is successful, the destination snap-in should return a data object with the list of successfully pasted items, which in turn will be passed to each source snap-in for the MMCN_CUTORMOVE notification.

    The format to communicate the list of items successfully pasted should be defined by each source snap-in. The most straightforward mechanism is for the destination snap-in to manipulate the multiselection data object in a manner defined by each source snap-in, increment the data object's reference count, and then return it in the *param* parameter.

Note that the *param* for MMCN_PASTE will be 0 if it does not involve a previous cut or move operation.

4. After a successful cut or move operation, each source snap-in will receive the MMCN_CUTORMOVE notification message. The *lpDataObject* parameter contains the data object returned by the destination snap-in after a successful paste. The source snap-in must examine the data object for the list of the successfully pasted items and perform whatever actions it deems necessary on the items.

If the mechanism suggested in step 3 is followed by the destination snap-in, each source snap-in will receive back its own multiselection data object in the MMCN_CUTORMOVE notification message.

Multiselection: Implementation Details

▶ **To implement multiselection for items in a result pane list view**

1. In the snap-in's **IComponent::GetResultViewType** implementation, set the *pViewOptions* parameter passed in the method call to MMC_VIEW_OPTIONS_MULTISELECT. This enables multiselection. Note that multiselection can be enabled on a per-list-view basis.

2. In the snap-in's **IComponent::QueryDataObject** implementation, handle the case when the MMC_MULTI_SELECT_COOKIE special cookie is passed in the method call. MMC uses this special cookie to indicate to the snap-in that MMC is requesting a special, snap-in-defined multiselection data object.

Snap-ins can use the **IS_SPECIAL_COOKIE** macro to determine whether or not the value contained in the method call's *cookie* parameter refers to a special cookie.

3. Create the multiselection data object when the **IComponent::QueryDataObject** implementation is called with the MMC_MULTI_SELECT_COOKIE special cookie. Follow these guidelines when creating the data object:

   - The multiselection data object should define some data structure that identifies the items currently selected in the result pane. A simple solution is to define an array of cookies whose elements are the cookie values of the currently selected items. The data object can then provide access to the array's data either by defining a custom clipboard format or through a public member function.

   To query MMC for the currently selected items that it owns, the snap-in should call **IResultData::GetNextItem**. Set the **mask**, **nIndex**, and **nState** members of the **RESULTDATAITEM** structure passed in the method call. To retrieve only selected items, the value of the **nState** member should be LVIS_SELECTED.

- The multiselection data object must also provide the list of node type GUIDs of all its currently selected items. This is done by supporting the CCF_OBJECT_TYPES_IN_MULTI_SELECT clipboard format in the multiselection data object's **IDataObject::GetData** implementation. The data format used with the clipboard format is an **SMMCObjectTypes** structure. MMC uses this structure to determine the extension snap-ins that extend any of the selected items.

- The multiselection data object should have some way of identifying itself as a "nonstandard" data object. This is so that the snap-in can properly handle subsequent notification messages that pass the multiselection data object. One simple method is to create a member variable of type MMC_COOKIE, say **m_lCookie**, and set its value to MMC_MULTI_SELECT_COOKIE. Note that, in general, all data objects created by the snap-in in response to calls to **QueryDataObject** should store the *cookie* parameter passed in the call. For more information about cookies, see "Cookies" in Chapter 16.

4. MMC forwards the multiselection data object to the snap-in's **IComponent::Notify** implementation along with the MMCN_SELECT notification message. This gives the snap-in the opportunity to enable verbs for its selected items. Note that the snap-in only needs to explicitly enable verbs for any one of the selected items. MMC then sets the verbs for the other items.

5. Implement the **IDataObject::GetData** method and handle the case in which MMC calls the method on the multiselection data object with the CCF_OBJECT_TYPES_IN_MULTI_SELECT clipboard format to request a list of the node type GUIDs of all the currently selected items. The snap-in should provide the requested information using the **SMMCObjectTypes** structure.

6. If necessary, handle the case where the snap-in can receive an MMC-provided composite data object in calls to its **IExtendContextMenu** or **IExtendPropertySheet2** methods. The composite data object contains an array of multiselection data objects. The multiselection data objects are provided by the source snap-ins (primary or extension) that own items in the multiselection. Note that each source snap-in is responsible for defining the format of the multiselection data object that it provides.

The snap-in can use the CCF_MMC_MULTISELECT_DATAOBJECT clipboard format to determine whether or not a data object passed to it is a composite data object.

If the data object is a composite data object, the snap-in must use the CCF_MULTI_SELECT_SNAPINS clipboard format for extracting the array of multiselection data objects from it. The data format used with the clipboard format is the **SMMCDataObjects** structure.

Sample Code

The following code samples demonstrate how to:

- Create a multiselection data object.
- Support the CCF_OBJECT_TYPES_IN_MULTI_SELECT clipboard format.
- Handle the MMCN_SELECT notification during multiselection.

All samples are taken from the MultiSel sample snap-in that accompanies the MMC SDK. The MultiSel sample demonstrates how to add multiselection functionality in a snap-in.

Note that all sample code assumes Unicode compilation.

Creating a Multiselection Data Object

The snap-in creates a multiselection data object during the call to its **IComponent::QueryDataObject** implementation when the *cookie* parameter contains the MMC_MULTI_SELECT_COOKIE value. Here is how the MultiSel sample creates the data object during the method call to its **IComponent::QueryDataObject** implementation:

```
//Use The IS_SPECIAL_COOKIE macro to see if cookie is a special cookie
if ( IS_SPECIAL_COOKIE (cookie) )
{
     if ( MMC_MULTI_SELECT_COOKIE == cookie)
     {
         pObj = new CDataObject(cookie, type);
         if (!pObj)
             return E_OUTOFMEMORY;

         //create the multiselection data object
         hr = GetCurrentSelections(pObj);
         _ASSERT( SUCCEEDED(hr) );

         hr = pObj->QueryInterface(IID_IDataObject,
                    (void **)ppDataObject);
         _ASSERT( SUCCEEDED(hr) );

         return hr;
     }
}
```

The multiselection data object's **m_lCookie** member variable is set to the value of MMC_MULTI_SELECT_COOKIE. We'll see how this value is used in the code samples that follow.

C++ Snap-ins

The MultiSel sample dynamically creates an array of cookies that will hold the cookie values of all the items selected in the current result pane. The array is created in the multiselection data object's constructor:

```
CDataObject::CDataObject(MMC_COOKIE cookie, DATA_OBJECT_TYPES context)
: m_lCookie(cookie), m_context(context), m_cref(0)
{
    // Do the following if the data object is a
    // multiselection data object

    if ( MMC_MULTI_SELECT_COOKIE == m_lCookie )
    {
        pCookies = new MMC_COOKIE[MAX_COOKIES];
        for (int n = 0; n < MAX_COOKIES; n++)
        {
            pCookies[n] = NULL;
        }
    }
}
```

The *pCookies* member variable is declared in the class declaration of the snap-in's **IDataObject** implementation, **CDataObject**:

```
MMC_COOKIE* pCookies;
```

Returning to the snap-in's **IComponent::QueryDataObject** implementation, the **GetCurrentSelections** method is a public member function of the snap-in's **IComponent** implementation. It fills the multiselection data object's array of cookies with the cookie values of the currently selected items.

The implementation of the **GetCurrentSelections** method is omitted here. To see how the method is implemented, refer to the MultiSel sample code.

Supporting the CCF_OBJECT_TYPES_IN_MULTI_SELECT Clipboard Format

The CCF_OBJECT_TYPES_IN_MULTI_SELECT clipboard format is supported in the multiselection data object's **GetData** method. The method is implemented in the following way in the MultiSel sample:

```
HRESULT CDataObject::GetData (LPFORMATETC lpFormatetcIn,
        LPSTGMEDIUM lpMedium)
{
    HRESULT hr = S_FALSE;
    const   CLIPFORMAT cf = lpFormatetcIn->cfFormat;
    CDelegationBase *base = GetBaseNodeObject();
```

```
    if (cf == s_cfMultiSelect)
    {
        // MMC requires support for this format to load any
        // extensions that extend the selected result items

        BYTE byData[256] = {0};
        SMMCObjectTypes* pData =
            reinterpret_cast<SMMCObjectTypes*>(byData);

        //We need the node type GUID of the selected items.
        //from CRocket::thisGuid
        GUID guid = { 0x29743811, 0x4c4b, 0x11d2,
                        { 0x89, 0xd8, 0x0, 0x0, 0x21, 0x47,
                          0x31, 0x28 }
                    };

        //Enter data required for the SMMCObjectTypes structure
        //count specifies the number of unique node types in the
        //multiselection. Here, all CRocket items are of the same
        //node type, so count == 1.
        pData->count = 1;
        pData->guid[0] = guid;

        // Calculate the size of SMMCObjectTypes.
        int cb = sizeof(GUID)*(pData->count) +
                    sizeof (SMMCObjectTypes);

        //Fill out parameters
        lpMedium->tymed = TYMED_HGLOBAL;
        lpMedium->hGlobal = ::GlobalAlloc(GMEM_SHARE|GMEM_MOVEABLE,
                                cb);
        if (lpMedium->hGlobal == NULL)
            return STG_E_MEDIUMFULL;

        BYTE* pb = reinterpret_cast<BYTE*>(::GlobalLock(
                                        lpMedium->hGlobal));
        CopyMemory(pb, pData, cb);
        ::GlobalUnlock(lpMedium->hGlobal);

        hr = S_OK;
    }
    return hr;
}
```

The required data format for the CCF_OBJECT_TYPES_IN_MULTI_SELECT clipboard format is the **SMMCObjectTypes** structure.

Handling the MMCN_SELECT Notification During Multiselection

MMC sends the MMCN_SELECT notification message during multiselection to allow the snap-in to enable the standard verbs for the multiselection operation. Here is how the MultiSel sample handles the notification message in its **IComponent::Notify** implementation:

```
case MMCN_SELECT:
    //check for multiselection
    if ( MMC_MULTI_SELECT_COOKIE == GetOurDataObject(lpDataObject)->
                                        GetCookie() )
    {
        if ( (BOOL)LOWORD(arg) == 0 && (BOOL)HIWORD(arg) == 1 )
        {
            //We need the cookie of any of the multiselection items
            //to enable the delete verb for all the items.
            MMC_COOKIE ourCookie = GetOurDataObject(lpDataObject)->
                                        GetMultiSelectCookie(0);

            base = reinterpret_cast<CDelegationBase *>(ourCookie);
            hr = base->OnSelect(m_ipConsole, (BOOL)LOWORD(arg),
                (BOOL)HIWORD(arg));
        }
        return hr;
    }
    else
        hr = base->OnSelect(m_ipConsole, (BOOL)LOWORD(arg),
            (BOOL)HIWORD(arg));
    break;
```

The **GetOurDataObject** function is a global function defined by all sample snap-ins for working with data objects and clipboard formats. For details about the method, see "Samples Object Model" in Chapter 31.

The **GetMultiSelectCookie** function is a public member function of the multiselection data object used for retrieving cookie values from its array of multiselection cookies. Here is the function's definition:

```
MMC_COOKIE GetMultiSelectCookie(int n) { return pCookies[n]; }
```

As previously stated, when the snap-in receives the MMCN_SELECT notification with a multiselection data object, it only needs to enable verbs for any one of the selected items in the result pane. MMC takes care of propagating the settings to the other selected items.

CHAPTER 26

Snap-in Persistence Model

One of the strengths of MMC is that it allows each snap-in to persist private configuration data in the console file. Snap-ins can persist their data by implementing either the **IPersistStreamInit**, the **IPersistStream**, or the **IPersistStorage** interface. All of these interfaces are provided as part of COM and are documented in the Microsoft Platform SDK.

MMC will always query a snap-in for **IPersistStream**. If it doesn't receive an **IPersistStream** interface pointer, it will query for **IPersistStreamInit**, then for **IPersistStorage**. Snap-ins that don't persist their data should simply return with an appropriate error code when MMC queries them for any of these interfaces.

Snap-ins are encouraged to implement either the **IPersistStream** or **IPersistStreamInit** interface to persist their data. Both interfaces are lightweight and easy to implement. In contrast, the **IPersistStorage** interface requires the implementation of many features not needed by snap-ins that simply want to persist their data.

Note that MMC supports both **IComponentData** and **IComponent** persistence. The snap-in's **IComponentData** object should persist view-independent data for each of its scope items. Each **IComponent** object should persist any view-specific data it requires to re-create its own view.

For snap-ins that support persistence, MMC calls the **Load** and **Save** methods whenever a user action initiates a console file load or save. Most often this occurs when a file is loaded, or when the user clicks **Save** or **Save As** on the **File** menu. The snap-in should be sure to accurately implement the **IsDirty** method.

Note that extension snap-ins in general cannot persist their data. The only exceptions to this rule are namespace and taskpad extensions. Namespace extensions must always implement **IComponentData**. Taskpad extensions that support persistence must also implement **IComponentData**. Namespace extensions can support **IComponentData** and **IComponent** persistence. Taskpad extensions can only support **IComponentData** persistence.

C++ Snap-ins

CHAPTER 27

MMC and WMI

Windows Management Instrumentation (WMI) is Microsoft's implementation of Web-Based Enterprise Management (WBEM), an industry initiative to develop a standard technology for accessing management information in an enterprise environment. WMI uses the industry-standard Common Information Model (CIM) to represent systems, applications, networks, devices, and other managed objects in an enterprise environment.

C++ Snap-ins

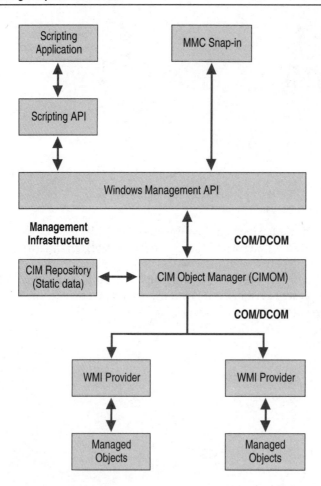

Figure 27.1   WMI Architecture

The architecture of the WMI technology consists of the following components:

1. **Management infrastructure**—the WMI Service and the CIM Repository. The WMI Service coordinates requests for management data between client applications and the sources of the data. The CIM Repository typically holds *static* management data that does not regularly change, such as class definitions. Dynamic management data is retrieved on demand from the data source through a provider.

2. **Managed objects**—any part of the enterprise network from a small piece of hardware such as a disk drive to a large software application such as a database system. These managed objects are *modeled* using the Common Information Model (CIM).

3. **Providers**—components that supply *dynamic* management data about managed objects, handle object-specific requests, or generate WMI events. Providers communicate with the WMI Service using a COM-based API and are normally written using the C or C++ programming language.

4. **Management applications**—client applications that use WMI information to monitor, configure, and control managed objects, measure performance, or perform a variety of other administrative tasks. These applications include stand-alone applications, ActiveX controls, scripts, and MMC snap-ins. Applications can be written in any programming language that can communicate with the WMI Service using one of these WMI-supported APIs:

   - COM-based API for C/C++
   - Scripting API for Visual Basic, DHTML, ASP, WSH, and so on

Third-party developers can place information, including static data, in the CIM Repository by using the Managed Object Format (MOF) language and its compiler, MOFComp.exe, or one of the standard WMI APIs.

WMI currently ships several dynamic providers for Microsoft operating system components including Win32 objects, SNMP data, registry entries, WMI Security, Active Directory, Windows Driver Model (WDM), Windows Installer, Windows NT Event Log, and performance counters.

MMC snap-ins can be used to display any information that is available through WMI. MMC easily integrates with WMI to display WMI information. This is demonstrated in the WMI sample that is provided with the MMC SDK. The sample demonstrates how a snap-in can connect to WMI, retrieve and display information, and receive WMI event notifications when the information changes. This particular sample accesses static information stored in the WMI Repository to simplify the example. In most cases, snap-ins and other management applications will retrieve dynamic data supplied by a WMI provider. It should be noted that whether data is static or dynamic, there is no difference in the way the management application requests it from WMI.

C++ Snap-ins

For detailed information about WMI, refer to the Windows Management Instrumentation topic and related topics in the Microsoft Platform SDK documentation. Note that the complete WMI SDK documentation can also be downloaded from the following Web site:

http://msdn.microsoft.com/developer/sdk/wmisdk/default.asp

The rest of this section discusses information specific to accessing WMI data from within a snap-in.

Accessing WMI Data

To access WMI data, snap-ins must first connect to a WMI namespace on a particular host machine. All snap-in communication with the desired namespace is then performed using an **IWbemServices** object bound to the namespace.

It is important to note that a *WMI* namespace is different from an *MMC* namespace. A WMI namespace is a logical grouping of WMI classes and instances in the WMI Repository, and controls their scope and visibility. An MMC namespace refers to the hierarchical organization of snap-ins and nodes in an MMC console.

To simplify the connection process, snap-ins can use the **IWbemLocator** interface. This interface provides only one method, **ConnectServer**, which allows WMI clients (snap-ins) to obtain a COM pointer to an **IWbemServices** object bound to the desired namespace on the desired target machine.

To use **IWbemLocator**, snap-ins must create an instance of the **IWbemLocator** interface that is in-process. The **IWbemLocator** interface pointer returned by **CoCreateInstance** gives snap-ins access to the namespace hierarchy managed by the WMI Repository.

Asynchronous Event Notification and Security Issues

WMI can generate two types of events: temporary and permanent. Criteria for both types of events are described using the WQL query language, which is an SQL subset. The following table summarizes the differences between the two types of WMI events.

Temporary	Permanent
Only delivered if the event consumer is running.	Uses COM/DCOM to load the event consumer if it's not already loaded.
Registered by calling **IWbemServices::ExecNotification QueryAsync**.	Registered by adding various "registration" instances to WMI as detailed in the "Event Notification" topic in the WMI section of the Platform SDK.
Events received by your implemention of **IWbemObjectSink**.	Events received by your implementation of **IWbemUnboundObjectSink**.
Event delivery cancelled by calling **IWbemServices::CancelAsyncCall** or exiting the application.	Event delivery cancelled by deleting the above "registration" instances.

The WMI sample demonstrates temporary events and is provided with the MMC SDK. An event is registered by calling **IWbemServices::ExecNotificationQueryAsync**. This method describes the desired events using the WQL query language and includes a pointer to the **IWbemObjectSink** object that will receive the event notifications. When an action satisfies the criteria of the WQL query, WMI sends an event notification to the snap-in by calling the **IWbemObjectSink** object's **Indicate** method.

Because snap-ins run in MMC's process space as in-process server DLLs, they do not own the process token associated with MMC's process space and should not make changes to it. Because of this, DCOM security rules make it difficult for snap-ins to accept event notifications from WMI.

To circumvent this problem, snap-ins need to tell DCOM that they will accept events from an unauthenticated user (of MMC's process space). This is done by using the **IUnsecuredApartment** interface. This interface creates a dedicated process for hosting the snap-in's **IWbemObjectSink** implementation. The **IUnsecuredApartment** interface contains a method, **CreateObjectStub**, which can be used to create an "event forwarder" to assist in receiving method calls from WMI. This function binds an unsecured object sink to a local object sink so that DCOM security will not prevent asynchronous calls from WMI resulting from an asynchronous method call such as **IWbemServices::ExecNotificationQueryAsync**. The unsecured object sink is then used in the asynchronous methods of the **IWbemServices** interface.

C++ Snap-ins

Threading Issues and Accessing WMI Data

To prevent their user interface from being blocked, snap-ins might choose to create a background thread for connecting to WMI. Note that snap-ins that obtain **IWbemServices or IEnumWbemClassObject** pointers in a background thread must marshal it into their main thread or any other dialog's thread.

MMC and WMI: Implementation Details

The procedures outlined in this section describe how to connect to a WMI namespace, retrieve and display information, and receive asynchronous event notifications when the underlying data in the namespace changes.

Note that this discussion does not cover how to implement WMI-related interfaces and methods. For information related to WMI, refer to the Windows Management Instrumentation topic and related topics in the Platform SDK documentation.

▶ **To connect to a WMI namespace**

1. Connect to the desired WMI namespace on the desired host machine. To simplify the connection process, you can use the **IWbemLocator** interface and its **ConnectServer** method. This method allows WMI client applications (snap-ins) to obtain a pointer to an **IWbemServices** object bound to the desired namespace on the desired target machine.

2. To use the **IWbemLocator** interface:

   - Use the COM API function **CoCreateInstance** to cocreate an instance of the **IWbemLocator** interface in-process. **CoCreateInstance** returns an **IWbemLocator** interface pointer, which you can use to call the **ConnectServer** method.

   - Call the **ConnectServer** method to specify the WMI namespace that the snap-in connects to. The method returns a pointer to an **IWbemServices** object bound to the desired namespace. This is the "services pointer" that the snap-in uses to access WMI services for the namespace.

▶ **To retrieve information from WMI**

Most information in WMI is represented as instances of a particular WMI class. The class is the definition of what an object looks like, while the instance is an actual occurance of the class containing specific properties. It is possible to enumerate all instances of a given class, request a subset of the instances that match the criteria of a query, or retrieve a specific instance based on a unique set of key values.

1. In order to enumerate all instances of a known class, call **CreateInstanceEnum** on the snap-in's **IWbemServices** pointer. The **CreateInstanceEnum** method returns an **IEnumWbemClassObject** pointer.

2. Call the **Next** method on this **IEnumWbemClassObject** pointer to get each successive **IWbemClassObject** pointer.

3. For smarter filtering, call the **ExecQuery** method on the **IWbemServices** pointer, which allows you to use WQL, a subset of the SQL query language, to narrow down the results of the query to the items of interest.

4. To retrieve a specific instance of a class, call the **GetObject** method on the **IWbemServices** pointer, which retrieves that desired instance directly using the keys specified.

5. Use the various methods of **IWbemClassObject** to retrieve property, method, and qualifier information as desired.

▶ **To invoke a WMI method**

Methods are actions or operations that can be executed against a class or instances of a class. Most methods are defined to operate on an instance of a class. An example of this would be a "compress" method that can be run on instances of a data file class instance. When run, the method would attempt to use a compression algorithm to reduce the size of the file stored on the system.

1. Prepare the input and output parameters by calling the **GetMethod** method on the **IWbemClassObject** pointer. The input parameter is an **IWbemClassObject** populated with the required properties. It is not necessary to retrieve the output parameter object before invoking the method. The method will populate the output class as needed. Note that **GetMethod** must be called on a CIM Class Definition type of **IWbemClassObject**; not on a CIM Instance type.

2. Use the appropriate methods on **IWbemClassObject** to fill in the input parameter's properties.

3. Call **ExecMethod** on the **IWbemServices** pointer to invoke the method.

4. Examine the error codes from **ExecMethod** itself and the output parameter's properties as appropriate for the particular method.

C++ Snap-ins

▶ **To receive asynchronous event notifications**

The steps outlined in this procedure deal with the fact that WMI events are received on a WMI-owned thread. By using a snap-in-defined window message, the snap-in can transfer flow control to the main MMC thread where MMC interfaces can be called in response to the WMI event. Note that MMC-defined COM interfaces cannot be marshaled. The WMI sample provided with the MMC SDK uses this technique.

1. Implement the WMI interface **IWbemObjectSink**.

2. For security reasons (see "Asynchronous Event Notification and Security Issues" earlier in this chapter) snap-ins must use the **IUnsecuredApartment** interface to bind the snap-in's local object sink (an instance of its **IWbemObjectSink** implementation) to an unsecured object sink that receives the event notifications. The **IUnsecuredApartment** interface contains the **CreateObjectStub** method, which the snap-in can use to create the unsecured object sink.

3. Using the **IWbemServices** services pointer obtained in the call to **IWbemLocator::ConnectServer**, call the **IWbemServices::ExecNotificationQueryAsync** method to register for "temporary" WMI events of interest. In the call to **ExecNotificationQueryAsync**, make sure that the *pResponseHandler* parameter contains a pointer to the unsecured object sink created in the call to **IUnsecuredApartment::CreateObjectStub**.

   As registered events become available, WMI calls the **Indicate** method on the **IWbemObjectSink** object supplied in the call to **ExecNotificationQueryAsync**.

4. Handle calls to the snap-in's **IWbemObjectSink::Indicate** method.

Sample Code

The WMI sample provided with the MMC SDK demonstrates how a snap-in can connect to a WMI namespace, display WMI information, and receive asynchronous event notifications when WMI information changes.

To keep the sample simple and consistent with other MMC SDK samples, the WMI Repository is used like a conventional database—simply storing and retrieving information as static data. A more common scenario is for client applications to access *dynamic* WMI information about managed objects.

Note that WMI also provides the **IWbemStatusCodeText** interface, which is generally useful for translating HRESULT error codes to human-readable text. This includes non-WMI HRESULT codes. This is demonstrated in the **CBicycleFolder::ErrorString** function in the WMI sample.

C H A P T E R   2 8

MFC and Snap-in Development

You can use Microsoft Foundation Classes (MFC) in your snap-in code.
However, snap-ins that use the MFC library can make no assumptions other than
those provided by the MMC COM interfaces. The only connection between a
snap-in and MMC are the COM interfaces that the snap-in exposes to MMC.

Snap-in DLLs can be either statically or dynamically linked to MFC libraries.
When statically linking to MFC, follow the guidelines for using
AFX_MANAGE_STATE that are available on the MSDN library.

MFC and Property Pages

MFC must have the correct module state set from exported functions or COM interfaces. This includes calls made from the operating system to the module. For exported functions or COM interfaces, this is done by adding the **AFX_MANAGE_STATE** macro at the beginning of all exported functions in snap-in DLLs that dynamically link to MFC:

```
AFX_MANAGE_STATE(AfxGetStaticModuleState( ))
```

For an operating system call, MFC does this automatically. Because MMC's property sheet is not an MFC **CPropertySheet** object, the operating system call due to the callback is in the wrong module state. As a result, you need to make sure that the module state is correctly set during the page creation. This is the purpose of the **MMCPropPageCallback** function declared in the Mmc.idl file. After the module state has been set, the only **AFX_MANAGE_STATE** calls that need to be made are those exposed by the COM interfaces implemented by the snap-in (for example **IExtendPropertySheet2::CreatePropertyPages**).

The **MMCPropPageCallback** function is declared as follows:

```
STDAPI MMCPropPageCallback(
  void * vpsp,  // pointer to PROPSHEETPAGE structure
);
```

The *vpsp* argument is the pointer to a Windows **PROPSHEETPAGE** structure. By default, MFC specifies its own callback function in the **pfnCallback** member of the structure. Therefore, for each page you create derived from the MFC class **CPropertyPage**, you must call **MMCPropPageCallback** with a pointer to the page's callback.

Note that **MMCPropPageCallback** should not be called by snap-ins that statically link MFC libraries. A call to this function by such a snap-in will not link correctly.

For each page derived from **CPropertyPage**, call **MMCPropPageCallback** with a pointer to the page's callback, following these guidelines:

- All pages for a particular property sheet must use the same callback pointer.
- If you replace MFC's callback with your own, your callback must call MFC's callback.
- You must call this function with each **CPropertyPage** derived class.

The following code sample shows how both the **AFX_MANAGE_STATE** macro and the **MMCPropPageCallback** function can be used in a snap-in's **IExtendPropertyPropertySheet2::CreatePropertyPages** implementation:

```
STDMETHODIMP CPropertySheet::CreatePropertyPages(
        LPPROPERTYSHEETCALLBACK lpProvider, long handle,
        LPDATAOBJECT lpIDataObject)
{
    AFX_MANAGE_STATE(AfxGetStaticModuleState());

    ASSERT(lpIDataObject != NULL);

    CPropertyPage* pBasePage;

    // Create the property page. CExtPage1 is a CPropertyPage.
    CExtPage1* pPage = new CExtPage1();

    //pPage->m_hConsoleHandle = handle;
    pBasePage = pPage;

    // Object gets deleted when the page is destroyed
    ASSERT(lpProvider != NULL);

    HRESULT hr = MMCPropPageCallback(&pBasePage->m_psp);
    if (SUCCEEDED(hr))
    {
        HPROPSHEETPAGE hPage = CreatePropertySheetPage(
                               &pBasePage->m_psp);
        if (hPage == NULL)
            return E_UNEXPECTED;

            lpProvider->AddPage(hPage);
    }

    return hr;
}
```

Displaying OCX Controls on Property Pages

If you have property pages that use MFC to display an OCX control, Windows will fail to create the page because it does not know how to create the OCX control. As a result, you need to create the OCX control manually. Additionally, your control will be ignored by the dialog manager for TAB key operation.

CHAPTER 29

Distributing Your Snap-in

This section covers the following integration topics related to installing and administering snap-ins:

- Microsoft Installer Integration
- Policy Integration

Microsoft Installer Integration

Microsoft Windows Installer (MSI) provides the ability to load a snap-in installation into the Microsoft Directory Service and have it be downloaded automatically when the user tries to open a console file that references that snap-in.

Snap-in users can distribute a saved console file to recipients who may not have installed all the snap-ins referenced in the console file. When a user performs an action that requires a snap-in that is not locally installed, MMC's integration with MSI makes it possible for the snap-in to be downloaded automatically and installed on the user's local machine.

MMC's integration with MSI also makes it possible to add to the current console snap-ins that are not locally installed. MMC uses the Vendor column in the **Add Standalone Snap-in** dialog box to indicate whether a stand-alone snap-in is locally installed. If the snap-in is not locally installed, the words "Not Installed" appear in the column. The snap-in is downloaded automatically and installed when the user adds it.

Users can use the **Add/Remove Snap-in** dialog box to explicitly enable or disable individual extension snap-ins. When the user enables an extension snap-in that is not locally installed, a **Download** button is enabled in the dialog box. When the user clicks the button, the extension snap-in is downloaded and locally installed.

C++ Snap-ins

For a snap-in to be automatically downloaded and installed, an *installation package* must be created for that snap-in. An installation package contains all the information that MSI requires to install or uninstall an application or product and to run the setup user interface (if there is one). Each installation package includes an .msi file, which contains an installation database, a summary information stream, and data streams for various parts of the installation. The .msi file can also contain one or more transforms, internal source files, and external source files or cabinet files required by the installation.

How to create installation packages is discussed in detail in the MSI documentation, which is available in the Microsoft Platform SDK. The rest of this section covers the MMC-specific details about creating MSI packages for snap-ins.

During the creation of an MSI package, the PublishComponent table must be filled. The PublishComponent table has a number of fields; one of these fields, **ComponentID**, is critical to creating MSI packages for snap-ins.

The **ComponentID** field specifies the string GUID that represents the category of components being grouped together. MSI installs and removes an application or product from a user's system in pieces referred to as *components*. Components are collections of resources that are always installed or removed from a user's system together. A resource can be a file, registry key, shortcut, or anything else that can be installed. Every component is assigned a unique component code GUID.

In the case of MMC, the value of the **ComponentID** field depends on the type of snap-in—stand-alone or extension—for which the MSI package is being created. The following procedure specifies what the value of this field should be.

▶ **To create an MSI package for a snap-in**

1. Follow the instructions given in the MSI documentation available in the Platform SDK for creating MSI packages for Windows applications.

2. Fill the **ComponentID** field of the PublishComponent table, according to the following rules:

   - If you are creating an MSI package for a stand-alone snap-in, the value of this field must be the following string:

     "{374F2F70-060F-11D2-B9A8-0060977B1D78}"

     This string represents the GUID generated by MSI for MMC.

   - If you are creating an MSI package for an extension snap-in, the value of this field must be the string representation of the CLSID of the snap-in that is being extended. If the extension snap-in extends more than one snap-in, a different MSI package is required for each snap-in that is extended.

Enabling the "Download Missing COM Components" Policy

For snap-ins missing on a system to be installed automatically, the administrator of that system must enable the "Download missing COM components" policy. The default setting of this policy is "Not configured," meaning that automatic downloads are disabled.

Administrators can use the Group Policy snap-in to edit policies. To change the setting of the "Download missing COM components" policy, go to either the **User Configuration** or **Computer Configuration** node of the Group Policy snap-in, depending on whether the policy should be set at the User or the Computer level. The policy setting is available in the result pane of the **Administrative Templates/System** subnode.

Note that there are potential unintended side effects to enabling the "Download missing COM components" policy. For more information about Group Policy, see the Group Policy documentation in the Platform SDK.

Policy Integration

In Windows 2000, group policies are intended to allow administrators to determine access to tools and functionality on a group basis, for either computers or users. For MMC, administrators may wish to prevent a specific group from accessing specified snap-in functionality.

Group Policy, as it relates to MMC and snap-ins, can accomplish the following:

- **Restrict author mode.** Administrators can specify that author mode is restricted for any group.
- **Restrict access to specified snap-ins.** Administrators can restrict access to a specified list of snap-ins.
- **Grant access to a list of permitted snap-ins.** Administrators can grant access to a specified list of snap-ins. Snap-ins not included in the list have restricted access.

Note that policies regarding MMC and snap-ins are applicable to individual users and groups of users. The policies cannot be applied to computers.

For details about Group Policy, see the Group Policy documentation, which is available in the Microsoft Platform SDK. The rest of this section discusses the features that snap-ins must provide for administrators to apply Group Policy to them.

C++ Snap-ins

Snap-ins and Group Policy

Group policies are administered using the the Group Policy snap-in. The Group Policy snap-in obtains registry-based policy settings from an administrative template (.adm) file. An .adm file defines the property page the Group Policy snap-in will display to allow an administrator to manage its settings. The file also indicates the registry location where the settings are stored.

Each snap-in that can be administered with the Group Policy snap-in must provide an .adm file. The .adm file should display for the administrator two check boxes that allow the snap-in to be placed on either a "permitted" list or a "restricted" list. The list a snap-in is on is determined by a value of the *Restrict_Run* named Boolean value at the following registry location:

```
HKEY_CURRENT_USER\SOFTWARE\Policies\Microsoft\MMC\{snapin GUID}
```

The *{snapin GUID}* key is the string representation of the snap-in's CLSID. The following table lists the different values that the *Restrict_Run* named value can take:

Value of *Restrict_Run*	Description
Value not present	Behavior is unrestricted.
0	The snap-in is placed on the "permitted" list.
1	The snap-in is placed on the "restricted" list.

The following is a sample .adm file for a snap-in:

```
CLASS USER

CATEGORY !!MMC
  CATEGORY !!MMC_EventVwr
      POLICY !!MMC_Permit_EventVwr
          KEYNAME
              Software\policies\Microsoft\MMC\Permitted\
              {394C052E-B830-11D0-9A86-00C04FD8DBF7}\
          Explain !!MMC_Permit_EventVwr_Explain
          VALUENAME Event_Viewer_Extension
          VALUEON "1"
      END POLICY
      POLICY !!MMC_Restrict_EventVwr
          KEYNAME
              Software\policies\Microsoft\MMC\Restricted\
              {394C052E-B830-11D0-9A86-00C04FD8DBF7}\
          Explain !!MMC_Restrict_EventVwr_Explain
          VALUENAME Event_Viewer_Extension
          VALUEON "1"
      END POLICY
  END CATEGORY
END CATEGORY

[strings]
MMC="MMC"
MMC_EventVwr="Event Viewer"
MMC_Permit_EventVwr="Permit the event viewer snapin"
MMC_Permit_EventVwr_Explain="When this checkbox is enabled, the
user(s) effected by this policy will be allowed to use the event
viewer snapin unless it has been explicitly restricted."
MMC_Restrict_EventVwr="Restrict the event viewer snapin"
MMC_Restrict_EventVwr_Explain="When this checkbox is enabled, the
user(s) effected by this policy will be prevented from using the event
viewer snapin. A restrictive policy will take precedence over a
permissive policy."
```

C++ Snap-ins

C H A P T E R   3 0

MMC COM Reference

This chapter presents an overview of COM interfaces implemented by MMC and by snap-ins. Detailed descriptions of the interfaces and their methods, and of other programming constructs used to create snap-ins, appear in the MMC COM Reference section of the MMC SDK on the companion CD-ROM.

MMC Interfaces and Methods

MMC interfaces and their methods are arranged according to who implements them—MMC or snap-ins. The methods are provided in vtable order on the page describing each interface.

COM Interfaces Implemented by MMC

- **IColumnData**—The **IColumnData** interface allows a snap-in to set and retrieve the persisted view data of list view columns to use for column customization. It provides methods for programmatically providing the same functionality that MMC provides in the **Modify Columns** dialog box. In addition, the **IColumnData** interface provides methods for setting and retrieving the sorted column and sort direction of a particular column set.

- **IConsole2**—The **IConsole2** interface enables communication with the console.

- **IConsoleNameSpace2**—The **IConsoleNameSpace2** interface enables snap-ins to enumerate dynamic subcontainers in the scope pane. The particular snap-in determines what qualifies as a subcontainer. For example, a snap-in that features a domain object might enumerate individual groups or organizations within the domain.

- **IConsoleVerb**—The **IConsoleVerb** interface allows snap-ins to enable standard verbs including cut, copy, paste, delete, properties, rename, refresh, and print. Whenever an item is selected, the snap-in can update the state of these verbs.

- **IContextMenuCallback**—The **IContextMenuCallback** interface is used to add menu items to a context menu.

- **IContextMenuProvider**—The **IContextMenuProvider** interface implements methods that create new context menus, for the purpose of adding items to those menus, to enable extensions to extend those menus, and to display the resultant context menus.

- **IControlbar**—The **IControlbar** interface provides a way to create toolbars and other controls.

- **IDisplayHelp**—The **IDisplayHelp** interface enables a snap-in to display a specific HTML Help topic within the merged MMC HTML Help collection file for the console.

- **IHeaderCtrl2**—The **IHeaderCtrl2** interface enables the manipulation of columns and indicates the kind of information that is to be presented in the result pane of the console.

- **IImageList**—The **IImageList** interface enables the snap-in to insert images to be used as icons for items in the result or scope pane of the console.

- **IMenuButton**—The **IMenuButton** interface enables the snap-in to add and manage menu buttons.

- **IMessageView**—The **IMessageView** interface provides support for specifying the text and icons for error messages displayed using the MMC message OCX control. MMC provides a message OCX control that snap-ins can use for displaying error messages in the result pane.

- **IPropertySheetCallback**—The **IPropertySheetCallback** interface is used by a snap-in to add its property pages to a property sheet.

- **IPropertySheetProvider**—The **IPropertySheetProvider** interface implements Win32 property sheets as COM objects. Snap-ins can use the **IPropertySheetProvider** interface for adding wizard pages to a snap-in. **IPropertySheetProvider** is also used when a snap-in adds a feature that has a property sheet as the user interface but identifies it as something else.

- **IRequiredExtensions**—The **IRequiredExtensions** interface enables a snap-in to add some or all of the extension snap-ins that extend it.

- **IResultData**—The **IResultData** interface enables a snap-in to add, remove, find, and modify items associated with the result pane. It also enables the manipulation of the view style of the result pane.

- **IStringTable**—The **IStringTable** interface privides a means of storing string data with a snap-in. A string table is created in the console file as needed for each snap-in by MMC.

- **IToolbar**—The **IToolbar** interface is used to create new toolbars, to add items to them, to extend the toolbars, and to display the resultant new toolbars.

COM Interfaces Implemented by the Snap-in

- **IComponent**—The **IComponent** interface enables MMC to communicate with snap-ins. Similar to the **IComponentData** interface, **IComponent** is typically implemented at the view level and is closely associated with items being displayed in the result pane.

- **IComponentData**—The **IComponentData** interface enables MMC to communicate with snap-ins. Similar to the **IComponent** interface, **IComponentData** is typically implemented at the document level and is closely associated with items (folders) being displayed in the scope pane.

- **IEnumTASK**—The **IEnumTASK** interface enables a snap-in to enumerate the tasks to add to a task pad.

- **IExtendContextMenu**—The **IExtendContextMenu** interface enables snap-ins to add items to an existing context menu.

- **IExtendControlbar**—The **IExtendControlbar** interface enables a snap-in to add control bars to the console. This provides a way to improve the functionality and appearance of your snap-in by adding toolbars or other user interface enhancements.

- **IExtendPropertySheet2**—The **IExtendPropertySheet2** interface enables a snap-in to add pages to the property sheet of an item.

- **IExtendTaskpad**—The **IExtendTaskpad** interface enables a snap-in to set up a taskpad and receive notifications from the taskpad.

- **IResultDataCompare**—The **IResultDataCompare** interface allows primary snap-ins to compare result items that are displayed in a sorted order in the result pane.

- **IResultDataCompareEx**—The **IResultDataCompareEx** interface allows primary snap-ins to compare both scope and result items that are displayed in a sorted order in the result pane.

- **IResultOwnerData**—The **IResultOwnerData** interface allows snap-ins to use virtual lists.

- **ISnapinAbout**—The **ISnapinAbout** interface enables the console to get copyright and version information from a snap-in. The console also uses this interface to obtain images for the static folder from the snap-in.

- **ISnapinHelp2**—The **ISnapinHelp2** interface enables the console to get the location of a snap-in's compiled HTML Help file. The console merges the HTML Help files of all snap-ins with the MMC console HTML Help collection file.

C++ Snap-ins

IColumnData

The **IColumnData** interface is introduced in MMC 1.2.

The **IColumnData** interface allows a snap-in to set and retrieve the persisted view data of list view columns to use for column customization. For details about when to use the **IColumnData** interface, see "Using **IColumnData**" in Chapter 20.

The interface provides methods for programmatically providing the same functionality that MMC provides in the **Modify Columns** dialog box. In addition, the **IColumnData** interface provides methods for setting and retrieving the sorted column and sort direction of a particular column set.

All data set and retrieved by the methods of the **IColumnData** interface is persisted by MMC in memory, and not in a stream or storage medium. This data is persisted to an .msc console file only when the user chooses the **Save** menu command.

MMC persists column data (also called column configuration data) per column set (using a column set's ID) per view per snap-in instance. Within each view, each column set ID references its own column configuration data. The snap-in can use the **IColumnData** interface pertaining to the particular view to access the column configuration data of that view.

For details about column customization, see "Using Column Persistence" in Chapter 20.

The **IColumnData** interface can be queried from the **IConsole** passed into **IComponent::Initialize** during the component's creation.

When to Implement

Do not implement this interface. It is implemented by MMC.

When to Use

Use **IColumnData** whenever your snap-in needs to access the persisted view data of its list view columns. Note that the interface can affect the display of list views.

Methods in Vtable Order

IUnknown methods	Description
QueryInterface	Returns pointers to supported interfaces.
AddRef	Increments reference count.
Release	Decrements reference count.

IColumnData methods	Description
SetColumnConfigData	Sets the width, order, and hidden status of columns in a column set.
GetColumnConfigData	Retrieves the width, order, and hidden status of columns in a column set.
SetColumnSortData	Sets the sorting direction for columns in a column set.
GetColumnSortData	Retrieves the sorting direction for columns in a column set.

IComponent

The **IComponent** interface enables MMC to communicate with snap-ins. Similar to the **IComponentData** interface, **IComponent** is typically implemented at the view level and is closely associated with items being displayed in the result pane.

When to Implement

Implement the **IComponent** interface in your in-process server DLL to communicate with the console, which displays the result pane and enumerates the items it contains.

All snap-ins that add result items to the namespace implement this interface. They should also implement **IComponentData**.

When to Use

IComponent enumerates result items. It also provides display information for scope items when they appear in the result pane.

Extension snap-ins that do not extend the namespace (but extend other features like context menus, toolbars, and so on) need not implement **IComponent**.

Methods in Vtable Order

IUnknown methods	Description
QueryInterface	Returns pointers to supported interfaces.
AddRef	Increments reference count.
Release	Decrements reference count.

IComponent methods	Description
Initialize	Provides an entry point to the console.
Notify	Called by the console to notify the snap-in of actions taken by a user.
Destroy	Releases all references to the console.
QueryDataObject	Returns a data object that can be used to retrieve context information for the specified cookie.

C++ Snap-ins

IComponent methods	Description
GetResultViewType	Determines what the result pane view should be.
GetDisplayInfo	Retrieves display information about an item in the result pane.
CompareObjects	Enables a snap-in to compare two data objects acquired through **QueryDataObject**. Note that data objects can be acquired from two different instances of **IComponent**.

IComponentData

The **IComponentData** interface enables MMC to communicate with snap-ins. Similar to the **IComponent** interface, **IComponentData** is typically implemented at the document level and is closely associated with items (folders) being displayed in the scope pane.

When to Implement

Implement **IComponentData** in your in-process server DLL to communicate with the console's Node Manager. It enumerates a snap-in's dynamic scope items (also called folders). It also displays information for the scope items.

When to Use

The **IComponentData** interface is required for any snap-in that enumerates items in the master namespace (scope pane). **IComponentData** is also required for persistence. See Chapter 26, "Snap-in Persistence Model," for details about persistence.

Generally, extension snap-ins that do not extend the namespace (but extend other features like context menus, toolbars, and so on) need not implement this interface. The only exception to this is in the case of persisted data, for which **IComponentData** is required. Only namespace and taskpad extensions can have persisted data

Methods in Vtable Order

IUnknown methods	Description
QueryInterface	Returns pointers to supported interfaces.
AddRef	Increments reference count.
Release	Decrements reference count.

IComponentData methods	Description
Initialize	Provides an entry point to the console.
CreateComponent	Creates a component that will be associated with this **IComponentData**.
Notify	Called by the console to notify the snap-in of actions taken by a user.

IComponentData methods	Description
Destroy	Releases all references to the console.
QueryDataObject	Returns a data object that can be used to retrieve context information for the specified cookie.
GetDisplayInfo	Retrieves display information about an item in the scope pane.
CompareObjects	Enables a snap-in to compare two data objects acquired through **QueryDataObject**. Note that data objects can be acquired from two different instances of **IComponentData**.

IConsole2

The **IConsole2** interface is introduced in MMC 1.1.

The **IConsole2** interface enables communication with the console. **IConsole2** is a new version of the **IConsole** interface for MMC 1.1. **IConsole2** is the same as **IConsole** with addition of the following methods:

- **IConsole2::Expand**
- **IConsole2::IsTaskpadViewPreferred**
- **IConsole2::SetStatusText**

When to Implement

Do not implement **IConsole2**. It is implemented by the console's Node Manager. A pointer to the **IConsole2** interface is passed to the snap-in through **IComponent::Initialize** and **IComponentData::Initialize**. Each **IComponent** and **IComponentData** gets its own private **IConsole2** interface pointer.

When to Use

This interface enables snap-ins to communicate with the console.

When using **IConsole2** for manipulating the result pane and result items, use the **IConsole2** interface pointer passed to the snap-in's **IComponent** implementation that owns the view.

When using **IConsole2** for manipulating the scope pane and scope items, use the **IConsole2** interface pointer passed to snap-in's **IComponentData** implementation.

Methods in Vtable Order

IUnknown methods	Description
QueryInterface	Returns pointers to supported interfaces.
AddRef	Increments reference count.
Release	Decrements reference count.

C++ Snap-ins

IConsole2 methods	Description
SetHeader	Used by instances of **IComponent** only. Sets the header interface to be used for this **IComponent**.
SetToolbar	Used by instances of **IComponent** only. Sets the toolbar interface to be used for this **IComponent**.
QueryResultView	Queries **IConsole** for the result view object's **IUnknown** interface pointer.
QueryScopeImageList	Queries the console-provided scope pane's image list.
QueryResultImageList	Queries the console-provided result pane's image list.
UpdateAllViews	Generates a notification to update views because of content change.
MessageBox	Displays a message box.
QueryConsoleVerb	Query for the **IConsoleVerb** interface.
SelectScopeItem	Selects the given scope item.
GetMainWindow	Returns a handle to the main frame window.
NewWindow	Creates a new window rooted at the specified scope item.
Expand	Enables the snap-in to expand or collapse an item in the scope pane.
IsTaskpadViewPreferred	Determines whether the user prefers taskpad views by default.
SetStatusText	Enables the snap-in to change the text in the status bar.

IConsoleNameSpace2

The **IConsoleNameSpace2** interface is introduced in MMC 1.1.

The **IConsoleNameSpace2** interface enables snap-ins to enumerate dynamic subcontainers in the scope pane. The particular snap-in determines what qualifies as a subcontainer. For example, a snap-in that features a domain object might enumerate individual groups or organizations within the domain.

The snap-in can query for a pointer to the **IConsoleNameSpace2** interface during a call to its **IComponentData::Initialize** method.

| When to Implement | Do not implement **IConsoleNameSpace2**. It is implemented by the console's Node Manager. |

| When to Use | A snap-in uses **IConsoleNameSpace2** to add or delete items associated with the scope pane. A snap-in can also expand items. |

Methods in Vtable Order

IUnknown methods	Description
QueryInterface	Returns pointers to supported interfaces.
AddRef	Increments reference count.
Release	Decrements reference count.

IConsoleNameSpace2 methods	Description
InsertItem	Enables the snap-in to insert a single item into the scope pane.
DeleteItem	Enables the snap-in to delete a single item from the scope pane.
SetItem	Enables the snap-in to set the attributes of a single scope pane item.
GetItem	Enables the snap-in to get the attributes of a single scope pane item.
GetChildItem	Enables the snap-in to get the handle to the first child item.
GetNextItem	Enables the snap-in to get the handle to the next item.
GetParentItem	Enables the snap-in to get the handle to the parent item.
Expand	Enables the snap-in to expand an item in the namespace without visibly expanding the item in the scope pane.
AddExtension	Enables the snap-in to add a dynamic namespace extension to a selected item.

C++ Snap-ins

IConsoleVerb

The **IConsoleVerb** interface allows snap-ins to enable standard verbs including cut, copy, paste, delete, properties, rename, refresh, and print. Whenever an item is selected, the snap-in can update the state of these verbs.

When to Implement

Do not implement this interface. It is implemented by MMC's Node Manager.

When to Use

Use **IConsoleVerb** whenever a snap-in can be enhanced by providing users with the ability to perform the standard actions noted above. They can be enabled, disabled, or hidden based on the currently selected item.

Methods in Vtable Order

IUnknown methods	Description
QueryInterface	Returns pointers to supported interfaces.
AddRef	Increments reference count.
Release	Decrements reference count.

IConsoleVerb methods	Description
GetVerbState	Gets the state of a verb.
SetVerbState	Sets the state of a verb.
SetDefaultVerb	Sets the default verb.
GetDefaultVerb	Gets the default verb.

IContextMenuCallback

The **IContextMenuCallback** interface is used to add menu items to a context menu.

When to Implement

Do not implement this interface. It is implemented by MMC 's Node Manager.

When to Use

There are two situations in which you use **IContextMenuCallback**. The first is during a call to **IExtendContextMenu::AddMenuItems** (implemented by the snap-in). Use **IContextMenuCallback::AddItem** to add items to the context menu for an item you own in the result list view, in the scope pane, or for an item you are extending as a third-party context menu extension. If one of the items you add is selected, you are notified by **IExtendContextMenu::Command**.

The second situation in which you use this interface is when you create a context menu using **IContextMenuProvider**. In that case, you call **IContextMenuCallback::AddItem** after calling **IContextMenuProvider::EmptyMenuList** and before calling **IContextMenuProvider::ShowContextMenu**.

Methods in Vtable Order

IUnknown methods	Description
QueryInterface	Returns pointers to supported interfaces.
AddRef	Increments reference count.
Release	Decrements reference count.

IContextMenuCallback method	Description
AddItem	Adds one item to the context menu.

C++ Snap-ins

IContextMenuProvider

The **IContextMenuProvider** interface implements methods that create new context menus, for the purpose of adding items to those menus, to enable extensions to extend those menus, and to display the resultant context menus.

When to Implement

Do not implement this interface. It is implemented by MMC's Node Manager. The **IContextMenuProvider** interface can be queried from the **IConsole** interface passed to the snap-in through **IComponent::Initialize** and **IComponentData::Initialize**. Depending on whether the **IConsole** interface belongs to the snap-in's **IComponent** or **IComponentData** implementation, the **IContextMenuProvider** can be used for creating context menus in the result pane or scope pane, respectively.

Note that the snap-in can cache the **IContextMenuProvider** interface pointer for a given pane (scope or result) and reuse it each time it needs to create a context menu in that pane.

When to Use

Most snap-ins do not need to use the **IContextMenuProvider** interface. This interface allows snap-ins to add extensible context menus to result pane views other than the default list view. For example, if the view is an OCX, the snap-in can create the context menu itself using the Win32 API. However, using Win32 does not allow other snap-ins to extend this context menu as they can on other items. Instead, the OCX should call **QueryInterface** for a pointer to the **IContextMenuProvider** interface, and generate the context menu using its COM methods. This context menu can then be extended by other snap-ins.

Methods in Vtable Order

Note that **IContextMenuProvider** is derived from **IContextMenuCallback** so you can call the methods of **IContextMenuCallback** on an instance of **IContextMenuProvider**.

IUnknown methods	Description
QueryInterface	Returns pointers to supported interfaces.
AddRef	Increments reference count.
Release	Decrements reference count.

IContextMenuProvider methods	Description
EmptyMenuList	Clears the context menu.
AddPrimaryExtensionItems	Enables a specified snap-in to extend the context menu.
AddThirdPartyExtensionItems	Enables all snap-ins that have registered as third-party context menu extensions for this node type to extend the context menu.
ShowContextMenu	Displays the context menu.

IControlbar

The **IControlbar** interface provides a way to create toolbars and other controls.

When to Implement

Do not implement this interface. It is implemented by MMC.

When to Use

Use **IControlbar** whenever toolbars or other controls will enhance your snap-in's user interface.

Methods in Vtable Order

IUnknown methods	Description
QueryInterface	Returns pointers to supported interfaces.
AddRef	Increments reference count.
Release	Decrements reference count.

IControlbar methods	Description
Create	Creates and returns a control.
Attach	Associates a control with a control bar.
Detach	Removes a control from a control bar.

C++ Snap-ins

IDisplayHelp

The **IDisplayHelp** interface is introduced in MMC version 1.1.

The **IDisplayHelp** interface enables a snap-in to display a specific HTML Help topic within the merged MMC HTML Help file. If the snap-in implemented **ISnapinHelp2::GetHelpTopic**, MMC merges the snap-in's compiled HTML Help file (.chm) into the MMC HTML Help collection file.

When to Implement

Do not implement this interface. It is implemented by MMC.

When to Use

Use **IDisplayHelp** whenever your snap-in needs to display an HTML Help topic from the merged MMC HTML Help collection file.

The snap-in can get a pointer to this interface by calling **QueryInterface** on the **IConsole2** interface.

Methods in Vtable Order

IUnknown methods	Description
QueryInterface	Returns pointers to supported interfaces.
AddRef	Increments reference count.
Release	Decrements reference count.

IDisplayHelp method	Description
ShowTopic	Displays the specified HTML Help topic in the merged MMC HTML Help file.

IEnumTASK

The **IEnumTASK** interface is introduced in MMC 1.1.

The **IEnumTASK** interface enables a snap-in component to enumerate the tasks to add to a taskpad.

When to Implement

Implement this interface in your in-process server DLL to add one or more tasks to a taskpad. You must also implement the **IExtendTaskPad** interface. For more information, see "Using Taskpads" in Chapter 20.

When to Use

Only MMC calls this interface.

MMC calls the **IExtendTaskPad::EnumTasks** method to get a pointer to the **IEnumTASK** interface of an object that specifies the tasks your snap-in wants to add to the taskpad. If a taskpad extension snap-in has been added to your snap-in, MMC gets a pointer to the **IExtendTaskPad** interface on that snap-in and calls the **IExtendTaskPad::EnumTasks** method to get a pointer to the **IEnumTASK** interface for that snap-in.

Methods in Vtable Order

IUnknown methods	Description
QueryInterface	Returns pointers to supported interfaces.
AddRef	Increments reference count.
Release	Decrements reference count.

IEnumTASK methods	Description
Next	Enables MMC to retrieve the next task in the snap-in's list of tasks.
Skip	Not used by MMC. Skips the specified number of tasks.
Reset	Enables MMC to reset the enumeration to the beginning of the list.
Clone	Not used by MMC. Creates a new **IEnumTASK** object that has the same state as this **IEnumTASK** object.

C++ Snap-ins

IExtendContextMenu

The **IExtendContextMenu** interface enables a snap-in to add items to an existing context menu. This is how extensions add menu items to the context menus for the objects that they insert into the scope pane or list view result pane. This interface is also the means by which third-party context menu extensions add items to the context menus of node types that they extend.

When a user right-clicks items that belong to a snap-in and are also in the scope pane or list view result pane, MMC generates a default context menu. The snap-in that added the item is offered an opportunity to extend the context menu as a primary extension. MMC then offers all registered and enabled extensions the opportunity to add additional menu items.

When to Implement

Implement this interface as part of your in-process server DLL whenever the capability to extend a snap-in component's context menus is required.

When to Use

Only MMC calls this interface.

Methods in Vtable Order

IUnknown methods	Description
QueryInterface	Returns pointers to supported interfaces.
AddRef	Increments reference count.
Release	Decrements reference count.

IExtendContextMenu methods	Description
AddMenuItems	Enables the extension to add menu items.
Command	Indicates that an extension item on a context menu was selected.

IExtendControlbar

The **IExtendControlbar** interface enables an extension to add control bars to the console. This provides a way to improve the functionality and appearance of your snap-in by adding toolbars or other user interface enhancements.

When to Implement

Implement **IExtendControlbar** as part of your in-process server DLL when you want to add control bars.

When to Use

Only MMC calls this interface.

Methods in Vtable Order	**IUnknown methods**	**Description**
	QueryInterface	Returns pointers to supported interfaces.
	AddRef	Increments reference count.
	Release	Decrements reference count.

IExtendControlbar methods	**Description**
SetControlbar	Attaches or detaches the control bar.
ControlbarNotify	Specifies notifications resulting from user actions.

IExtendPropertySheet2

The **IExtendPropertySheet2** interface is introduced in MMC 1.1.

The **IExtendPropertySheet2** interface enables a snap-in component to add pages to the property sheet of an item.

IExtendPropertySheet2 is a new version of the **IExtendPropertySheet** interface for MMC 1.1. **IExtendPropertySheet2** is exactly the same as **IExtendPropertySheet** with addition of the following method:

- **IExtendPropertySheet2::GetWatermarks**

When to Implement

Implement this interface in your in-process server DLL to add property pages for a snap-in component. **QueryInterface** is called on the primary snap-in object and the console then calls **IExtendPropertySheet2::QueryPagesFor**. If the snap-in responds with S_OK, the console calls **IExtendPropertySheet2::CreatePropertyPages**, which gives the snap-in an opportunity to add its pages. Finally, the console creates the sheet to display the pages. If the snap-in returns S_FALSE, no property sheet is created for the object.

IExtendPropertySheet2::GetWatermarks was added for MMC version 1.1 so that a snap-in can supply the watermark and header bitmap for the Wizard97 style.

Note that each property sheet is created in its own thread. If any COM interface pointer is passed from the **IComponent** interface to the property page, this pointer must be marshaled. For more information, see "Processes and Threads" in the Microsoft Platform SDK and the Apartment Model discussion in the COM specification. The size of the property page is determined by the primary snap-in. If you are extending a property sheet for an object that does not belong to your snap-in, the dialog box templates you use should conform to the dimensions established by the primary snap-in.

C++ Snap-ins

When to Use   This interface can be used to add information about the properties of an object whenever you consider it appropriate. It may also be useful to know that property pages can also be implemented using either the Win32 API or a class library such as the MFC Library.

Methods in Vtable Order

IUnknown methods	Description
QueryInterface	Returns pointers to supported interfaces.
AddRef	Increments reference count.
Release	Decrements reference count.

IExtendPropertySheet2 methods	Description
CreatePropertyPages	Adds pages to a property sheet.
QueryPagesFor	Determines whether the object needs pages.
GetWatermarks	Gets the watermark and header bitmap for the Wizard97 style.

IExtendTaskPad

The **IExtendTaskPad** interface is introduced in MMC 1.1.

The **IExtendTaskPad** interface enables a snap-in component to set up a taskpad and receive notifications from the taskpad.

When to Implement   Implement this interface in your in-process server DLL to add one or more taskpads to a snap-in component.

If you implement the **IExtendTaskPad** interface to display one or more taskpads for your snap-in's scope items, you must implement this interface in the **IComponent** object. For information about implementing **IExtendTaskPad** for taskpad extension snap-ins, see "Using Taskpads" in Chapter 20.

You must also implement the **IEnumTASK** interface to specify the tasks you want to add to a taskpad.

If your snap-in owns the scope item displaying the taskpad, **IExtendTaskPad** is used by MMC to set up the taskpad, to get a pointer to the **IEnumTASK** interface, and to send notifications from the taskpad to your snap-in. To display the task in taskpads for your snap-in's items, you must also load the taskpad by specifying the taskpad template in **IComponent::GetResultViewType**.

If your snap-in is a taskpad extension, **IExtendTaskPad** is used by MMC to get a pointer to the **IEnumTASK** interface and to send notifications from the taskpad to your snap-in. Note that the snap-in that owns the scope item that is displaying the taskpad is responsible for loading the taskpad template and setting up the taskpad through its own **IExtendTaskPad** methods.

For more information, see "Using Taskpads" in Chapter 20.

When to Use

Only MMC calls this interface.

When the taskpad DHTML page is loaded, the **MMCCtrl** control on that page calls methods in MMC. In turn, MMC attempts to get the **IExtendTaskPad** from the **IComponent** object and calls the methods required to provide the **MMCCtrl** control with the data needed to render the taskpad's general elements: title text, banner image, and background image. If MMC cannot get a pointer to the **IExtendTaskPad** interface on your snap-in, the taskpad is not displayed.

If the taskpad is a list view taskpad, MMC calls **IExtendTaskPad::GetListPadInfo** to get the title text for the list control, text for an optional button, and the command ID passed to **IExtendTaskPad::TaskNotify** when the button is clicked.

MMC calls the **IExtendTaskPad::EnumTasks** method to get a pointer to the **IEnumTASK** interface of an object that specifies the tasks your snap-in wants to add to the taskpad. If a taskpad extension snap-in has been added to your snap-in, MMC gets a pointer to the **IExtendTaskPad** interface on that snap-in and calls the **IExtendTaskPad::EnumTasks** method to get a pointer to the **IEnumTASK** interface for that snap-in.

MMC calls the **IExtendTaskPad::TaskNotify** method to notify the snap-in when a task or a list view button has been clicked. The list view button applies only to list view taskpads—it is the optional button specified in the **IExtendTaskPad::GetListPadInfo** method.The command ID for the specific task or list view button is passed as a **VARIANT**.

Methods in Vtable Order

IUnknown methods	Description
QueryInterface	Returns pointers to supported interfaces.
AddRef	Increments reference count.
Release	Decrements reference count.

C++ Snap-ins

IExtendTaskPad methods	Description
TaskNotify	Enables MMC to notify the snap-in when a task is clicked. If the taskpad is a list view taskpad, MMC also calls **TaskNotify** when a list view button is clicked.
EnumTasks	Enables MMC to get a pointer to the **IEnumTASK** interface of the object that contains the snap-in's tasks.
GetTitle	Enables MMC to get the taskpad's title text.
GetDescriptiveText	Enables MMC to get the taskpad's descriptive text, which is displayed beneath the title.
GetBackground	Enables MMC to get the taskpad's background image.
GetListPadInfo	Used for list view taskpads only. Enables MMC to get the title text for the list control, text for an optional button, and the command ID passed to **IExtendTaskPad::TaskNotify** when the button is clicked.

IHeaderCtrl2

The **IHeaderCtrl2** interface is introduced in MMC 1.2.

The **IHeaderCtrl2** interface enables the manipulation of columns and indicates the kind of information that is to be presented in the result view pane of the console.

IHeaderCtrl2 is a new version of the **IHeaderCtrl** interface for MMC 1.2. **IHeaderCtrl2** is the same as **IHeaderCtrl** with addition of the following methods:

- **IHeaderCtrl2::SetChangeTimeOut**
- **IHeaderCtrl2::SetColumnFilter**
- **IHeaderCtrl2::GetColumnFilter**

These methods provide support for users to filter list views based on filters set on each column in the result view. Note that a return value of E_NOTIMPL by any one of these methods indicates that list view filtering is not available in the version of MMC in which the snap-in is loaded.

The **IHeaderCtrl2** interface can be queried from the **IConsole** interface passed into **IComponent::Initialize** during the component's creation.

When to Implement

Do not implement **IHeaderCtrl2**. It is implemented by the console's Node Manager.

When to Use

Use **IHeaderCtrl2** to add or remove columns, change column titles or widths, enable list view filtering, set and get the filter value on a specified column, and to set the time-out interval for filter change notifications.

Methods in Vtable Order

IUnknown methods	Description
QueryInterface	Returns pointers to supported interfaces.
AddRef	Increments reference count.
Release	Decrements reference count.

IHeaderCtrl2 methods	Description
InsertColumn	Adds a column to a default result view.
DeleteColumn	Removes a column from a default result view..
SetColumnText	Sets the text in a specified column.
GetColumnText	Retrieves the text from a specified column.
SetColumnWidth	Sets the width of a specified column.
GetColumnWidth	Retrieves the width of a specified column.
SetChangeTimeOut	Sets the time-out for filter change notification.
SetColumnFilter	Sets filter data.
GetColumnFilter	Gets filter data.

C++ Snap-ins

IImageList

The **IImageList** interface enables the user to insert images to be used as icons for items in the result or scope pane of the console. When an image is inserted, an index is passed in and associated with the image. Any time the image is to be used, the user can refer to it by the index that he or she assigned.

Note that because the image list is shared among many components, the user-specified index is a "virtual" index that gets mapped internally to the actual index.

When to Implement

Do not implement the **IImageList** interface. It is implemented by MMC. The snap-in can call the **IConsole2::QueryScopeImageList** method to get an **IImageList** interface pointer.

When to Use

Use the **IImageList** interface whenever a snap-in component will benefit from the ability to insert images that can be used as icons.

The scope pane and the result pane (if it is the default list view) each have an image list. The snap-in should add the specified images of items to be displayed prior to adding the items themselves to either of the panes. The images for the scope pane are added only once, whereas the images for the result pane are added every time the snap-in gets a SHOW(TRUE) notification message.

Methods in Vtable Order

IUnknown methods	Description
QueryInterface	Returns pointers to supported interfaces.
AddRef	Increments reference count.
Release	Decrements reference count.

IImageList methods	Description
ImageListSetIcon	Sets an icon in the image list.
ImageListSetStrip	Sets a strip of icons in the image list.

IMenuButton

The **IMenuButton** interface enables the user to add and manage menu buttons for a snap-in. MMC provides one menu bar per view; when a snap-in has the focus you can add one or more menu buttons for the view to this bar. These buttons are always added by appending them to the buttons already in the menu bar.

When to Implement

Do not implement the **IMenuButton** interface. It is implemented by MMC.

When to Use

You should use the **IMenuButton** interface whenever your snap-in requires—or can benefit from having—one or more additional menu buttons in the MMC menu bar for the particular view. To access the **IMenuButton** interface your snap-in must implement the **IExtendControlbar** interface. When MMC invokes your **IExtendControlbar::SetControlbar** method it passes an **IControlbar** interface. You can create an **IMenuButton** interface by calling the **IControlbar::Create** method.

Methods in Vtable Order

IUnknown methods	Description
QueryInterface	Returns pointers to supported interfaces.
AddRef	Increments reference count.
Release	Decrements reference count.

ImenuButton methods	Description
AddButton	Adds a button to the menu bar.
SetButton	Sets the attributes of a menu bar button.
SetButtonState	Sets the state of a menu bar button.

C++ Snap-ins

IMessageView

The **IMessageView** interface is introduced in MMC 1.2.

The **IMessageView** interface provides support for specifying the text and icons for error messages displayed using the MMC message OCX control. For details on using the control, see "Using the MMC Message OCX Control" in Chapter 20.

When to Implement

Do not implement the **IMessageView** interface. It is implemented by MMC.

When to Use

You should use this interface in your snap-in if you intend to use the MMC message OCX control for displaying error messages. The message OCX control optimizes the performance of snap-in error and warning messages and is therefore the recommended way for a snap-in to display such messages.

To obtain the message OCX control's **IUnknown** interface pointer, call **IConsole2::QueryResultView** and query for the **IMessageView** interface in the snap-in's MMCN_SHOW notification handler that is sent to the snap-in when the result pane with the OCX view has the focus.

Methods in Vtable Order

IUnknown methods	Description
QueryInterface	Returns pointers to supported interfaces.
AddRef	Increments reference count.
Release	Decrements reference count.

IMessageView methods	Description
SetTitleText	Changes the title for the result pane message.
SetBodyText	Changes the text for the result pane message.
SetIcon	Changes the icon for the result pane message.
Clear	Clears the title, text, and icon of the result pane message.

IPropertySheetCallback

The **IPropertySheetCallback** interface is a COM-based interface used by a snap-in to add its property pages to a property sheet.

When to Implement

Do not implement this interface. It is implemented by MMC's Node Manager.

When to Use

A pointer to this interface is passed in when **IExtendPropertySheet2::CreatePropertyPages** is called so the snap-in can add or remove property pages.

Methods in Vtable Order

IUnknown methods	Description
QueryInterface	Returns pointers to supported interfaces.
AddRef	Increments reference count.
Release	Decrements reference count.

IPropertySheetCallback methods	Description
AddPage	Enables the snap-in to add a page to a property sheet.
RemovePage	Enables the snap-in to remove a page from a property sheet.

C++ Snap-ins

IPropertySheetProvider

The **IPropertySheetProvider** interface implements Win32 property sheets as COM objects. A property sheet object contains the code necessary for handling modeless operation and determining which other snap-ins are extending the node type. The size of the property sheet is set by the primary snap-in and extensions are forced to accept that size.

When to Implement

Do not implement this interface. It is implemented by MMC's Node Manager. The **IPropertySheetProvider** interface can be queried from the **IConsole** interface passed to the snap-in through **IComponent::Initialize** and **IComponentData::Initialize**.

When to Use

MMC uses its own **IPropertySheetProvider** implementation when it initiates the display of the property sheet, as for instance when the user activates the properties verb on an item. If the snap-in wishes to display property sheets at other times, it should call directly into MMC's **IPropertySheetProvider**. In both cases, the **IPropertySheetProvider** methods call into the snap-in's **IExtendPropertySheet** implementation and supply an **IPropertySheetCallback** interface pointer so that the snap-in can add property pages.

Snap-ins must also use **IPropertySheetProvider** to add a feature that has a property sheet as a user interface, but identifies the sheet as something else. An example of this is the **Select Computer** dialog box. This dialog box appears in the Event Viewer snap-in when the user selects the Event Viewer node and clicks the **Connect to another computer** context menu item.

For MMC to create a property sheet with wizard controls (a wizard sheet), the snap-in must use the **IPropertySheetProvider** interface and its **CreatePropertySheet** method.

Methods in Vtable Order

IUnknown methods	Description
QueryInterface	Returns pointers to supported interfaces.
AddRef	Increments reference count.
Release	Decrements reference count.

IPropertySheetProvider methods	Description
CreatePropertySheet	Creates a property sheet frame.
FindPropertySheet	Determines whether a property sheet exists.
AddPrimaryPages	Collects property pages from the primary snap-in.
AddExtensionPages	Collects pages from one or more extension snap-ins.
Show	Displays a specific property sheet frame.

IRequiredExtensions

The **IRequiredExtensions** interface is introduced in MMC 1.1.

The **IRequiredExtensions** interface enables a snap-in to add some or all of the extension snap-ins registered for your snap-in.

When to Implement

Implement **IRequiredExtensions** as part of your OLE in-process server DLL when you want MMC to add some or all of the extension snap-ins registered for your snap-in.

The **IRequiredExtensions** interface must be implemented in the **IComponentData** object.

When to Use

This interface is only called by MMC.

MMC calls these methods on the snap-in's **IComponentData** object. When MMC loads the snap-in, it calls the **IRequiredExtensions::EnableAllExtensions** method to check whether the snap-in wants all registered extensions added to the snap-in. If that method returns S_OK, all registered extensions are added. If the return is not S_OK, MMC checks whether the snap-in has a list of specific required snap-ins by calling **IRequiredExtensions::GetFirstExtension**. If the return is S_OK, MMC adds the first extension and calls **IRequiredExtensions::GetNextExtension** iteratively to get the rest of the required extensions and add them. When **IRequiredExtensions::GetNextExtension** returns a non-S_OK value, MMC has come to the end of the list and stops iterating the required extension list.

Methods in Vtable Order

IUnknown methods	Description
QueryInterface	Returns pointers to supported interfaces.
AddRef	Increments reference count.
Release	Decrements reference count.

C++ Snap-ins

IRequiredExtensions methods	Description
EnableAllExtensions	Enables all extensions.
GetFirstExtension	Gets first required extension.
GetNextExtension	Gets next required extension.

IResultData

The **IResultData** interface enables a user to add, remove, find, and modify items associated with the result view pane. It also enables the manipulation of the view style of the result view pane.

The **IResultData** interface was designed to give the impression that the result view pane would be used by only one component, but components should be aware that the result view pane can, in fact, be shared by several components. All item manipulations are performed through the use of an item ID assigned when the item is inserted. This ID is guaranteed to be both static and unique for the life of the item. When an item is deleted, the ID is freed and can be used by other new items in the list. You should never keep an item ID around after its associated item has been deleted.

The **IResultData** interface handles virtual (owner data) lists as well. Because of the nature of virtual lists, not all methods apply and some methods have limited functionality. These differences are detailed in the descriptions of individual methods. The primary difference in handling virtual lists it that because the console does not maintain any storage for virtual items, it does not provide item IDs. Instead virtual list items are identified by their list position (index).

When to Implement

Do not implement the **IResultData** interface. It is implemented by MMC's Node Manager.

When to Use

You can use **IResultData** to allow the user of your snap-in component to change items in the result view pane or to change the result pane's view style.

Methods in Vtable Order

IUnknown methods	Description
QueryInterface	Returns pointers to supported interfaces.
AddRef	Increments reference count.
Release	Decrements reference count.

IResultData methods	Description
InsertItem	Enables the snap-in to insert a single item.
DeleteItem	Enables the snap-in to delete a single item.
FindItemByLParam	Enables the snap-in to find an item or subitem based on a user-inserted value.
DeleteAllRsltItems	Enables the snap-in to delete all items.
SetItem	Enables the snap-in to set a single item.
GetItem	Enables the snap-in to retrieve a single item.
GetNextItem	Returns the *lParam* of the first item.
ModifyItemState	Enables the snap-in to modify the item's state.
ModifyViewStyle	Enables the snap-in to set the result view style.
SetViewMode	Enables the snap-in to set the result view mode.
GetViewMode	Enables the snap-in to retrieve the result view mode.
UpdateItem	Redraws an item in the result pane after it has been changed.
Sort	Sorts all result items.
SetDescBarText	Sets result view description bar text.
SetItemCount	Sets the number of items in a virtual list.

C++ Snap-ins

IResultDataCompare

The **IResultDataCompare** interface allows primary snap-ins to compare result items that are displayed in a sorted order in the result pane. MMC uses a primary snap-in's implementation of this interface for all results items. Scope items from either the primary snap-in or any extensions are left unsorted at the top of the list.

The **IResultDataCompare** interface differs from the **IResultDataCompareEx** interface. **IResultDataCompareEx** allows primary snap-ins to compare both scope and result items.

When to Implement

Implement **IResultDataCompare** in your snap-in when the built-in sort functionality provided by MMC is insufficient.

When to Use

The following events occur in sequence when the snap-in triggers a sorting operation:

1. The snap-in calls **IResultData::Sort**, which is implemented by MMC. There are no resources allocated for this call.

2. MMC determines if the snap-in has set the MMC_VIEW_OPTIONS_LEXICAL_SORT option for the result pane whose scope or result items are to be sorted. If the option is set, MMC lexically sorts first all scope items (including those inserted by extensions), followed by result items.

3. If the MMC_VIEW_OPTIONS_LEXICAL_SORT option is not set, MMC determines whether the snap-in implements **IResultDataCompareEx**. If it does, it allocates **RDCOMPARE** and two **RDCITEMHDR** structures. MMC then calls **IResultDataCompareEx::Compare**, passing the structures it allocated. Otherwise, skip steps 4 through 6.

4. The snap-in does the comparison, returning the result in *pnResult*.

5. MMC releases the structures allocated in step 3.

6. Steps 3 through 5 repeat zero or more times, once for each set of items in the result pane that are compared with each other.

7. If the snap-in does not implement **IResultDataCompareEx**, MMC determines if it implements **IResultDataCompare**. If the snap-in implements **IResultDataCompare**, MMC then calls **IResultDataCompare::Compare**. Otherwise, skip steps 8 and 9.

8. The snap-in does the comparison, returning the result in *pnResult*.

9. Steps 7 and 8 repeat zero or more times, once for each set of items in the result pane that are compared with each other.

10. If the snap-in does not implement **IResultDataCompare**, MMC will use its built-in sort functionality for performing the sorting operation.

11. **ResultData::Sort** returns.

Methods in Vtable Order

IUnknown methods	Description
QueryInterface	Returns pointers to supported interfaces.
AddRef	Increments reference count.
Release	Decrements reference count.

IResultDataCompare method	Description
Compare	Compares two cookies.

IResultDataCompareEx

The **IResultDataCompareEx** interface is introduced in MMC 1.2.

The **IResultDataCompareEx** interface allows primary snap-ins to compare both scope and result items that are displayed in a sorted order in the result pane. MMC uses a primary snap-in's implementation of this interface for all scope and result items. Any scope items inserted by extension snap-ins are left unsorted at the bottom of the list.

The **IResultDataCompareEx** interface differs from the **IResultDataCompare** interface. **IResultDataCompare** allows primary snap-ins to compare only result items. Scope items from either the primary snap-in or any extensions are left unsorted at the top of the list.

When to Implement

Implement **IResultDataCompareEx** in your snap-in when the built-in sort functionality provided by MMC is insufficient.

When to Use

The following events occur in sequence when the snap-in triggers a sorting operation:

1. The snap-in calls **IResultData::Sort**, which is implemented by MMC. There are no resources allocated for this call.

2. MMC determines if the snap-in has set the MMC_VIEW_OPTIONS_LEXICAL_SORT option for the result pane whose scope or result items are to be sorted. If the option is set, MMC lexically sorts first all scope items (including those inserted by extensions), followed by result items.

C++ Snap-ins

3. If the MMC_VIEW_OPTIONS_LEXICAL_SORT option is not set, MMC determines whether the snap-in implements **IResultDataCompareEx**. If it does, it allocates **RDCOMPARE** and two **RDITEMHDR** structures. MMC then calls **IResultDataCompareEx::Compare**, passing the structures it allocated. Otherwise, skip steps 4 through 6.

4. The snap-in does the comparison, returning the result in *pnResult*.

5. MMC releases the structures allocated in step 3.

6. Steps 3 through 5 repeat zero or more times, once for each set of items in the result pane that are compared with each other.

7. If the snap-in does not implement **IResultDataCompareEx**, MMC determines if it implements **IResultDataCompare**. If the snap-in implements **IResultDataCompare**, MMC then calls **IResultDataCompare::Compare**. Otherwise, skip steps 8 and 9.

8. The snap-in does the comparison, returning the result in *pnResult*.

9. Steps 7 and 8 repeat zero or more times, once for each set of items in the result pane that are compared with each other.

10. If the snap-in does not implement IResultDataCompare, MMC uses its built-in sort functionality for performing the sorting operation.

11. **IResultData::Sort** returns.

Methods in Vtable Order

IUnknown methods	Description
QueryInterface	Returns pointers to supported interfaces.
AddRef	Increments reference count.
Release	Decrements reference count.

IResultDataCompareEx method	Description
Compare	Compares two result view items.

IResultOwnerData

The **IResultOwnerData** interface supports the use of virtual lists, which are list view controls that have the LVS_OWNERDATA style set. The methods of this interface are applicable only to virtual lists.This is an optional interface and snap-ins can implement it for enhanced virtual list performance and functionality.

When to Implement Methods in Vtable Order

Implement this interface to support virtual lists.

IUnknown methods	Description
QueryInterface	Returns pointers to supported interfaces.
AddRef	Increments reference count.
Release	Decrements reference count.

IResultOwnerData methods	Description
FindItem	Finds result items matching the specified string.
CacheHint	Allows the snap-in to collect the display information for a range of items ahead of time in cases where an optimization can be made.
SortItems	Sorts the items in a virtual list.

C++ Snap-ins

ISnapinAbout

The **ISnapinAbout** interface enables the console to get copyright and version information from a snap-in. The console also uses this interface to obtain images for the static folder from the snap-in.

When to Implement

All snap-ins should implement this interface to provide the information that is typically found in an **About** property page. Default static folder images and icons are used for display if the **ISnapinAbout** interface is not implemented.

For efficiency, the **ISnapInAbout** interface is usually implemented by a separate cocreatable class object. The class ID of this class object must be provided as a value under the snap-in's MMC registry key. See "**SnapIns** Key" in the MMC COM Reference section of the MMC SDK for details. MMC will call **CoCreateInstance** to create an instance of the class object when it is needed.

MMC attempts to create About objects on a background thread to avoid blocking the UI thread. Snap-in authors are encouraged to design their **About** class object to use an apartment or free threading model to support this.

When to Use

This interface is used by MMC's Snap-in Manager.

Methods in Vtable Order

IUnknown methods	Description
QueryInterface	Returns pointers to supported interfaces.
AddRef	Increments reference count.
Release	Decrements reference count.

ISnapinAbout methods	Description
GetSnapinDescription	Obtains snap-in description box text.
GetProvider	Obtains the name of the snap-in provider.
GetSnapinVersion	Obtains the version number of the snap-in.
GetSnapinImage	Obtains the main icon for the **About** box.
GetStaticFolderImage	Obtains static folder images for both the scope and result panes.

ISnapinHelp2

The **ISnapinHelp2** interface is introduced in MMC 1.1.

The **ISnapinHelp2** interface allows snap-ins to add HTML Help support. **ISnapinHelp2** is a new version of the **ISnapinHelp** interface for MMC 1.1. **ISnapinHelp2** is the same as **ISnapinHelp** with the addition of the following method:

- **ISnapinHelp2::GetLinkedTopics**

When to Implement

Implement the **ISnapinHelp2** interface in the snap-in's primary object (the one instantiated from the snap-in's CLSID).

The **ISnapinHelp2::GetHelpTopic** method enables the snap-in to add its compiled HTML Help file to the MMC Help file.

To display specific topics within the merged MMC HTML Help file, the snap-in must use the **IDisplayHelp::ShowTopic** method—except in property sheets. Within a property sheet, the snap-in must call the **MMCPropertyHelp** function.

To specify the names and locations of other HTML Help files that the snap-in's HTML Help file links to, use the **ISnapinHelp2::GetLinkedTopics** method.

If your snap-in does not have an HTML Help file (.chm), then it should not implement this interface.

When to Use

When the user selects one of your snap-in's scope or result items and then clicks the **Help** menu, MMC calls the **QueryInterface** method of the snap-in's **IComponentData** implementation to get a pointer to the **ISnapinHelp2** interface.

If your snap-in supports the interface, MMC does not add a **Help** menu item specifically for your snap-in (for example, **Help on Event Viewer**) because the snap-in's HTML Help file is merged into the MMC HTML Help collection file.

If your snap-in does not support the interface, MMC adds a **Help** menu item for the snap-in. This is for backward compatibility with MMC 1.0 snap-ins. The snap-in is responsible for handling the MMCN_SNAPINHELP notification in its **IComponent::Notify** method when the user selects the snap-in's **Help** menu item.

C++ Snap-ins

When the following actions occur, MMC checks whether the snap-in has just been added. If so, MMC rebuilds the Help collection file:

- Snap-in calls **IDisplayHelp::ShowTopic**.
- Snap-in calls **MMCPropertyHelp**.
- User clicks the **Help** menu or the **Help** context menu item.

When MMC needs to rebuild the Help collection file, MMC calls **QueryInterface** for a pointer to the **ISnapinHelp2** interface and calls the **ISnapinHelp2::GetHelpTopic** method. MMC can call **CoCreateInstance** to create an instance of the object to get this interface. Or if MMC has already created an **IComponentData** object, MMC can call **QueryInterface** on that object for the **ISnapinHelp2** interface. For non-namespace extensions that do not have an **IComponentData** object, MMC always calls **CoCreateInstance** to create the object to get the **ISnapinHelp2** interface.

Methods in Vtable Order

IUnknown methods	Description
QueryInterface	Returns pointers to supported interfaces.
AddRef	Increments reference count.
Release	Decrements reference count.

ISnapinHelp2 methods	Description
GetHelpTopic	Merges the snap-in's HTML Help file into the MMC HTML Help file.
GetLinkedTopics	Allows the snap-in to specify the names and locations of any HTML Help files that are linked to the snap-in's Help file.

IStringTable

The **IStringTable** interface is introduced in MMC 1.1.

The **IStringTable** interface privides a means of storing string data with the snap-in. A string table is created in the console file as needed for each snap-in by MMC.

The **IStringTable** interface allows strings to be saved in the console file. Note that this interface is designed to work with specialized localization tools. Snap ins without access to these localization tools will not benefit from using this interface.

When to Implement

Do not implement this interface. It is implemented by MMC.

When to Use

Use **IStringTable** whenever you need persistant storage for strings. The interface can be queried from the **IConsole** passed into **IComponent::Initialize** or **IComponentData::Initialize** during the component's creation.

Strings are stored by snap-in, not by view, so any **IStringTable** interface returned by MMC can be used for accessing the snap-in's strings.

Methods in Vtable Order

IUnknown Methods	Description
QueryInterface	Returns pointers to supported interfaces.
AddRef	Increments reference count.
Release	Decrements reference count.

IStringTable Methods	Description
AddString	Adds a string to the snap-in's string table.
GetString	Retrieves a string from the snap-in's string table.
GetStringLength	Retrieves the length of a string from the snap-in's string table.
DeleteString	Removes a string from the snap-in's string table.
DeleteAllStrings	Removes all strings from the snap-in's string table.
FindString	Finds a string in the snap-in's string table.
Enumerate	Returns an enumerator into a snap-in's string table.

C++ Snap-ins

IToolbar

The **IToolbar** interface is used to create new toolbars, to add items to them, to extend the toolbars, and to display the resultant new toolbars. Each toolbar is created on its own band within the control bar.

When to Implement

Do not implement this interface. It is implemented by MMC.

When to Use

Use **IToolbar** whenever your snap-in will be enhanced by the presence of toolbars.

Methods in Vtable Order

IUnknown methods	Description
QueryInterface	Returns pointers to supported interfaces.
AddRef	Increments reference count.
Release	Decrements reference count.

IToolbar methods	Description
AddBitmap	Adds an image to the toolbar.
AddButtons	Adds an array of buttons to the toolbar.
InsertButton	Adds a single button to the toolbar.
DeleteButton	Removes a button from the toolbar.
GetButtonState	Gets an attribute of a button.
SetButtonState	Sets an attribute of a button.

C H A P T E R   3 1

C++ Sample Snap-ins

A number of sample snap-ins are provided with the MMC SDK. These samples are referred to extensively in the MMC SDK documentation. This chapter provides a detailed discussion of the samples.

All of the sample snap-ins discussed in this chapter share the following attributes:

- Each sample snap-in is designed to demonstrate the implementation of particular MMC interfaces independently of the other samples.
- The samples are implemented in C++ and use the Win32 API.
- COM interfaces are implemented directly without the use of the Active Template Library (ATL) framework.

Using tools such as WinDiff to view differences between the samples is highly recommended and will be very beneficial in understanding how specific MMC elements are implemented.

C++ Snap-ins

Sample Organization and Structure

The MMC C++ sample snap-ins are installed as part of the Microsoft Platform SDK. Currently this location has a path similar to the following. Here, it is assumed that D: is the Platform SDK installation drive:

```
D:\Platform SDK\Samples\SysMgmt\MMC\
```

The following table lists the available samples and provides a short description of each one.

Sample	Name	Description	MMC interfaces
A	Simple	Demonstrates absolute minimum requirements for implementing an MMC snap-in. Also covers snap-in registration and installation details.	**IComponent, IComponentData**
B	About	Shows how to add "About" information. Includes demonstration of how to add icons and copyright and provider information.	**ISnapinAbout**
C	Help	Demonstrates two different methods for displaying and integrating HTML Help in snap-ins. Covers how to add a snap-in-specific Help item to MMC's **Help** menu. Also shows how to integrate a snap-in's Help with MMC and with the Help of other snap-ins.	**ISnapinHelp2**
D	Nodes	Demonstrates how to add items to both the scope and result panes of a snap-in's user interface. Demonstrates a simple and extensible class hierarchy for adding items.	**IHeaderCtrl2, IResultData, IConsoleNamespace2**
D1	Extens	Demonstrates the few changes needed in Sample D to make snap-in-inserted items extendable. Highlights include changes to the base registration code and "publication" of node type IDs.	
E	CMenu	Demonstrates how to enable MMC context menu items and to add snap-in-defined context menu items.	**IExtendContextMenu**

Sample	Name	Description	MMC interfaces
F	MenuBtn	Demonstrates how to add menu buttons to a snap-in.	**IMenuButton, IExtendControlBar**
G	Toolbar	Demonstrates how to add toolbars to a snap-in.	**IToolBar, IExtendControlBar**
H	PropPage	There are several types of MMC property sheets. This sample shows how to implement property sheets using the Win32 property sheet model. **IExtendPropertySheet2** is for implementing context menu-driven user interface elements.	**IExtendPropertySheet2**
J	OpenServ	Demonstrates how to add a very specific property sheet that allows users to connect to a remote server during a snap-in's startup. Presents a standard that snap-ins should follow for the "connect to computer" user experience.	
K	Taskpads	Demonstrates how to add two basic taskpad types to a snap-in: taskpads that enumerate simple user tasks and custom taskpads. Custom taskpads give the snap-in developer more freedom in presenting tasks.	**IExtendTaskPad, IEnumTask**
L	ActiveX	Demonstrates how to launch a custom ActiveX control in the result pane of a snap-in.	MMCN_INITOCX notification, **IConsole2::Query ResultView**
N	NameExt	Demonstrates how to extend a primary snap-in's namespace using an extension snap-in.	**IComponent, IComponentData**
Q	CMenuExt	Demonstrates how to extend a primary snap-in's context menus using an extension snap-in.	**IExtendContextMenu**

C++ Snap-ins

Sample	Name	Description	MMC interfaces
R	PPgeExt	Demonstrates how to extend a primary snap-in's property sheets using an extension snap-in.	**IExtendPropertySheet2**
S	TBarExt	Demonstrates how to extend a primary snap-in's toolbar using an extension snap-in.	**IToolBar**, **IExtendControlBar**
W	Complete	Demonstrates a snap-in with a context menu, toolbar, and property page. All node types added by the snap-in are extendable. Also enables delete, refresh, and rename verbs and support for **IConsole2::UpdateAllViews**.	**IExtendContextMenu**, **IToolBar**, **IExtendControlBar**, **IConsoleVerb**, **IConsole2**
X	CutCopy	Demonstrates how to add cut/copy functionality in a snap-in.	MMCN_QUERY_ PASTE, MMCN_PASTE, MMCN_CUTORMOVE notifications
Y	MultiSel	Demonstrates how to add multiselection functionality in a snap-in.	MMC_MULTI_ SELECT_COOKIE special cookie, CCF_OBJECT_TYPES_ IN_MULTI_SELECT clipboard format
Z	WMI	Demonstrates how a snap-in binds to a WMI data store.	

Using the Samples

The following samples are base samples. You can use them to understand how to implement basic snap-in functionality.

- Simple
- About
- Help
- Nodes
- Extens

The following samples are "major" samples. Each of these samples is implemented on top of one of the five base samples.

- CMenu
- MenuBtn
- Toolbar
- PropPage
- OpenServ
- Taskpads
- ActiveX
- CutCopy
- Complete
- WMI

The following samples are extension samples. Each extension sample extends the Extens sample.

- CMenuExt
- PPgeExt
- NameExt
- TBarExt

Building the Samples

To build any of the MMC C++ sample snap-ins, the following environment is required:

- Microsoft Windows 2000, Windows NT 4.0, or Windows 98 operating system
- Microsoft Visual C++ 6.0; or properly installed C++ compiler, linker, and resource compiler that are compatible with Microsoft Visual C++ 6.0
- Microsoft Windows 2000 RC1 or later version of the Microsoft Platform SDK

It is usually wise to install the Platform SDK last. The Platform SDK provides .h (include) files and .lib (library) files needed for MMC and COM functionality coded in the samples.

The MMC C++ sample snap-ins assume an environment with the Platform SDK properly installed. However, releases of Microsoft Visual C++ after version 6.0 may also provide the Mmc.h include file and Mmc.lib library file needed for compilation. In such cases, installation of the Platform SDK may not be required to compile the samples.

Each sample directory has the necessary source files to build and run the sample. For convenient use in Microsoft Visual Studio, a project file is provided for each sample. This file has the .dsp extension. A Samples.dsw workspace file is also provided in the main directory so that you can view and compile all the samples at once from within Visual Studio.

▶ **To load the appropriate project for a sample from a command prompt**

1. Make sure that the directory containing the Msdev.exe executable file of your Visual Studio installation is in your system's path.

2. Run Visual Studio at the command prompt in the sample's directory as follows:

   ```
   MSDEV <MYSAMPLE>.DSP
   ```

You can also simply double-click the .dsp file in Windows Explorer to load a sample's workspace into Visual Studio. From within Visual Studio you can then browse the C++ classes of the sample source and generally perform the other edit-compile-debug operations.

Note that, as part of the Platform SDK, the compilation of these samples from within Visual Studio requires the proper setting of directory paths in Visual Studio.

► **To set the directory paths (assuming Visual Studio 6.0)**

1. Run Microsoft Visual Studio (Visual C++).

2. On the **Tools** menu, click **Options**.

3. In the **Options** dialog box, click the **Directories** tab.

4. In the **Show Directories For** drop-down list box, select "Executable files" and enter the Bin directory path for your installed Platform SDK (for example, D:\Platform SDK\Bin). Click the up arrow button to move this newly entered path so that it is the first entry in the "Directories" list.

5. In the **Show Directories For** drop-down list box, select "Include files" and enter the INCLUDE directory path for your installed Platform SDK (for example, D:\Platform SDK\Include). Click the up arrow button to move this newly entered path so that it is the first entry in the "Directories" list.

   Follow the same procedure for adding the INCLUDE\Win64\mfc and INCLUDE\Win64\crt directory paths to the list of include files. These paths can follow the INCLUDE directory path in the list. Note that INCLUDE refers to the directory path for your installed Platform SDK.

6. In the **Show Directories For** drop-down list box, select "Library files" and enter the Lib directory path for your installed Platform SDK (for example, D:\Platform SDK\Lib). Click the up arrow button to move this newly entered path so that it is the first entry in the "Directories" list.

7. In the **Options** dialog box, click **OK** to complete the settings.

From there you can use the editor, debugger, and project facilities to edit, compile, link, and debug.

Building ANSI or Unicode Versions of the Samples

All of the MMC C++ samples can be built in both ANSI and Unicode environments. When building a Unicode version of a sample, you should ensure that the proper preprocessor settings are entered in the project settings of the sample's .dsp project file.

► **To build a Unicode version of a sample**

1. Load the sample's .dsp project file in Microsoft Visual Studio (Visual C++).

2. On the **Tools** menu, click **Project**.

3. In the **Settings For** drop-down list box, select "Win32 Release" for a release build or "Win32 Debug" for a debug build.

4. In the **Project Settings** dialog box, click the **C/C++** tab.

5. In the **Preprocessor definitions** field, make sure that the UNICODE and _UNICODE definitions are included. If not, add them.

6. In the Project Settings dialog box, click OK to complete the settings.

C++ Snap-ins

Sample Snap-ins Discussion

This section covers in detail each of the C++ sample snap-ins. It also provides a brief discussion of the Unified Modeling Language (UML) that is used in the samples.

The MMC SDK comes with the following C++ sample snap-ins:

Sample A: Simple

Sample B: About

Sample C: Help

Sample D: Nodes

Sample D1: Extens

Sample E: CMenu

Sample F: MenuBtn

Sample G: Toolbar

Sample H: PropPage

Sample J: OpenServ

Sample K: Taskpads

Sample L: ActiveX

Sample N: NameExt

Sample Q: CMenuExt

Sample R: PpgeExt

Sample S: TBarExt

Sample W: Complete

Sample X: CutCopy

Sample Y: MultiSel

Sample Z: WMI

Note that the UML diagrams used in the samples discussion explain specific sample implementation details. They do not explain in general terms how MMC and snap-ins work.

Unified Modeling Language

The Unified Modeling Language (UML) is the industry-standard modeling language for specifying and documenting both data and processes in software systems. The UML was released in November 1997 by a consortium of companies led by Rational Software Corporation. For details about the UML, visit the Object Management Group's (OMG) Web site at http://www.omg.org.

The discussions of the sample snap-ins only treat those elements in the UML that are appropriate for modeling the sequence of interactions and collaborations between MMC and the objects of a snap-in.

Also, the UML diagrams used in the samples discussion explain specific sample implementation details. They do not explain in general terms how MMC and snap-ins work.

Objects and Other Elements

The UML specifies the following elements for displaying objects:

A :CDataObject

Object names are underlined and preceded with a colon (:). If several instances of a class need to be distinguished from each other, the object name will additionally be preceded with some unique identifier, such as the letter "A" in the preceding diagram.

In addition to class instances, the sequence diagrams used to document the MMC samples also contain the following types of elements:

MMC   **DLLGetClassObject (function)**

The first element is self-explanatory. The second element represents the standard COM-related function **DLLGetClassObject**.

Messages

Messages between objects are represented by a labeled arrow on a link line connecting the objects. A sequence number is added to show the sequential order of the messages. Here is an example of a message between two objects:

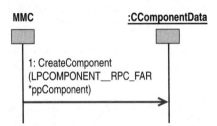

In this example, MMC is calling the **CreateComponent** method of the snap-in's **CComponentData** object. This is the first message in a sequence of messages. The argument and argument type are shown in parentheses.

Generally, a message from one object to another has the following syntax:

```
msgNumber : returnValue := Message(argType msgArg) :
   returnValueType
```

To save space, the *argType* parameter in a message's argument list can be omitted.

Occasionally, the text of a message is more descriptive in nature, as in the following example:

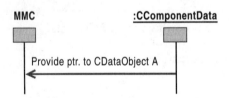

In this example, **CComponentData** provides MMC with a pointer to an instance of **CDataObject** in response to an MMC query for a data object. Notice that a sequence number is not shown. Generally, only messages that are explicit calls to the methods of an object have sequence numbers.

A message can be sent from an object to itself. The following example illustrates this:

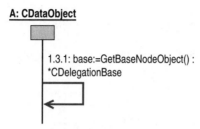

In this example, an instance of **CDataObject** is sending itself a **GetBaseNodeObject** message.

Two additional types of messages specified in the UML are the Create message and nesting messages.

The Create Message

The UML specifies a language-independent way of illustrating the creation of instances using the Create message. The following figure shows an example of this:

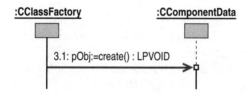

Like any other message, the Create message can also specify arguments to the constructor of the object being instantiated.

Notice the tip of the arrow linking the two objects. An arrowhead followed by a small white box is used to indicate the instantiation of an object. The later destruction of the object is indicated by an arrowhead followed by a small black box, as described in "Sequence Diagrams and Annotations."

C++ Snap-ins

Nesting Messages

When responding to a message, an object can send a sequence of messages to other objects. To indicate that these messages are "nested," the incoming message number is prefixed to the outgoing message number, as in the following example:

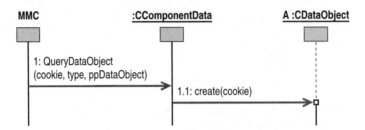

There are some situations where it suffices to know that a snap-in object responds to a message sent by MMC by sending messages to other objects. Details about the nested messages are irrelevant and may even distract the reader from understanding a particular sequence diagram.

The following element is used for such situations:

As is the case with all nested messages, the incoming message number is prefixed to the outgoing message number. However, the message syntax is not included in the message. The message arrow begins at the object that sends it and terminates midway between the sending object and the receiving object.

Sequence Diagrams and Annotations

A sequence diagram shows the order in which messages between objects are executed.

Time flows from top to bottom in a sequence diagram. A solid vertical line indicates an object that is active. A dashed vertical line indicates an object that is inactive. If an object is instantiated after the beginning of time as recorded in the diagram, then its creation is indicated by a Create message and a black arrow followed by a white box.

The lifetime of an object instantiated with a Create message is indicated by a solid vertical line that begins with the Create message and ends with a Release message, which is a standard COM method implemented by all COM interfaces. A black arrow followed by a black box is used with the Release message as a visual indicator of the object's destruction.

Note that this way of depicting object creation and destruction deviates from standard UML notation but was chosen to improve readability.

Finally, all sequence diagrams in the MMC documentation can contain annotations that add information to help in their interpretation. Annotations are indicated by a left bracket enclosing text.

The following figure illustrates everything we've discussed so far about the UML and its usage in the MMC documentation:

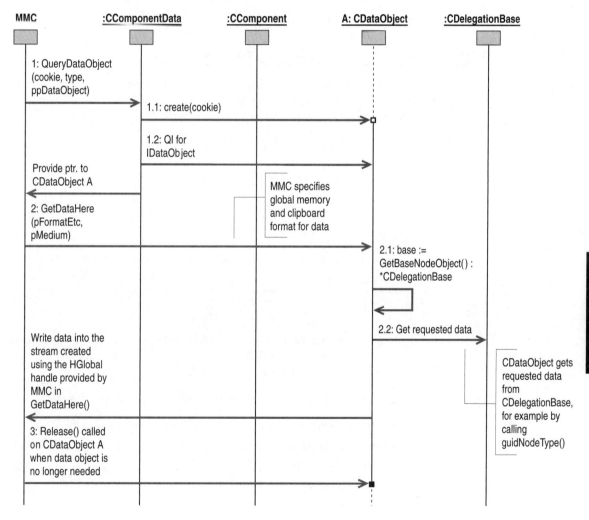

This figure is an important one and illustrates the general schema for how a snap-in should handle data requests from MMC. It's discussed in detail in "Data Objects and MMC" in Chapter 16, so here we'll only consider it in terms of its usage of the UML.

The first thing you'll notice is that five "objects" are depicted in the diagram. All of them except **CDataObject** are "alive" at time zero of this diagram and remain alive even after the end of the diagram. **CDataObject** has only a limited lifetime, which begins with its creation (black arrow with white box) in step 1.1 and ends with its destruction (black arrow with black box) in step 3.

In response to the **QueryDataObject** message in step 1, **CComponentData** calls two methods on **CDataObject**. The numbering of these messages indicates that they are "nested" within the incoming message to **CComponentData**.

There are two annotations in the diagram.

Special MMC Notation for QueryDataObject

MMC requests data objects from snap-ins all the time. If every data request in a particular scenario were depicted in a sequence diagram, the diagram would be very cluttered, making it difficult to extract any meaningful information.

To alleviate this problem, the following notation is used to illustrate data requests:

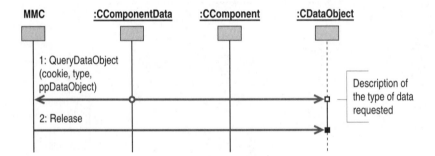

In the diagram, **CComponentData** is an implementation of the **IComponentData** interface, and **CComponent** is an **IComponent** interface implementation. **CDataObject** is an implementation of **IDataObject**.

Basically, it's important to know the following things about a data request:

- What are the parameters of the **QueryDataObject** message sent by MMC?
- Which object, **CComponentData** or **CComponent**, is receiving the request?
- What type of data is MMC requesting? Examples include the node type GUID of the selected scope item and the display name of the snap-in's static node.

All of this is indicated by the notation in step 1. The parameters are indicated in the message itself. A black circle placed on the intersection of **CComponentData**'s vertical line and the link line indicates that it is the receiving object of the message. The annotation indicates the type of data being requested. The black arrow followed by a white box indicates that a **CDataObject** is being created as a result of the message. The black arrow at the tail of the link line indicates that the sending object (MMC) receives data as a result of the query.

Samples Object Model

The C++ samples provided with the MMC SDK use a simple, delegation-based object model. The following figure illustrates this:

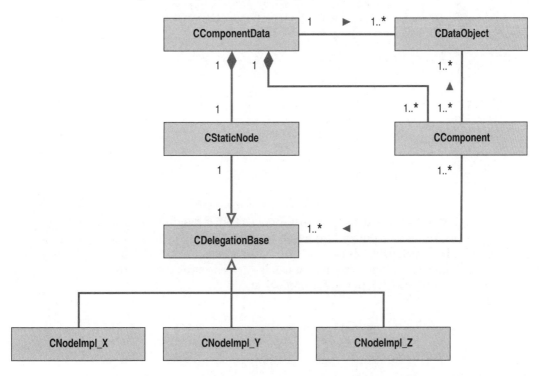

CComponentData, **CComponent**, and **CDataObject** are MMC/COM interface implementations of **IComponentData**, **IComponent**, and **IDataObject**, respectively. The other objects are defined by the snap-in. The **CStaticNode** object represents a stand-alone snap-in's static node. The **CNodeImpl_X**, **CNodeImpl_Y**, and **CNodeImpl_Z** objects represent either scope or result items that a snap-in inserts into its namespace.

C++ Snap-ins

As shown in the diagram, a **CComponentData** object aggregates a **CStaticNode** object—that is, the **CStaticNode** object only exists as long as the **CComponentData** object that aggregates it exists. The **CComponentData** object object can also aggregate one or more **CComponent** objects.

One or more **CDataObject** instances can be associated with the single **CComponentData** object. **CDataObject** instances can also be associated with **CComponent** objects. Both **CComponentData** and **CComponent** objects create instances of **CDataObject** in their **QueryDataObject** methods.

CComponentData delegates all static node behavior to **CStaticNode**. That is, for any **QueryDataObject** calls made by MMC that require data for the NULL cookie (which corresponds to the static node), the snap-in creates a data object whose cookie is a pointer to the **CStaticNode** object. The following code fragment taken from the implementation of **CComponent::QueryDataObject** in the Simple sample snap-in shows this:

```
STDMETHODIMP CComponent::QueryDataObject(MMC_COOKIE cookie,
                DATA_OBJECT_TYPES type, LPDATAOBJECT *ppDataObject)
{
  CDataObject *pObj = NULL;
  if (cookie == 0)
      pObj = new CDataObject((MMC_COOKIE)m_pComponentData->
              m_pStaticNode );
  else
      pObj = new CDataObject(cookie);
}
```

CStaticNode and all other snap-in objects that represent snap-in-inserted scope and result items inherit from **CDelegationBase**, another snap-in-defined object. **CDelegationBase** is the "delegation base" common to all of the sample snap-ins. It contains all the behavior for handling notifications sent to both **CComponentData** and **CComponent**.

The following code shows how MMC notification messages are delegated to the **CDelegationBase** base object:

```
HRESULT CComponentData::Notify(lpDataObject, event, arg, param)
{
  HRESULT hr;
  CDelegationBase *base = GetOurDataObject(lpDataObject)->
                            GetBaseNodeObject();
  switch (event)
  {
  case MMCN_EXPAND:
      hr = base->OnExpand(m_ipConsoleNameSpace, m_ipConsole,
                  (HSCOPEITEM)param);
      break;
  default:
      hr = S_FALSE;
      break;
  }
  return hr;
}
```

GetOurDataObject is a global function defined by all sample snap-ins for working with data objects and clipboard formats. Basically, it uses a snap-in-defined clipboard format called s_cfInternal for getting the **this** pointer of the data object passed to **CComponentData::Notify**. The **IDataObject** custom method **GetBaseNodeObject** (defined by the snap-in) returns the cookie value of the data object's base **CDelegationBase** object. The event that triggered the notification is then handled by the **CDelegationBase** object.

CDelegationBase also acts as a delegation base for other MMC requests and calls. For example, here is the implementation of **CComponent::GetResultViewType** in the Simple sample snap-in:

```
STDMETHODIMP CComponent::GetResultViewType( cookie,
                        LPOLESTR *ppViewType,long *pViewOptions)
{
  CDelegationBase *base = (CDelegationBase *)cookie;
  // Ask for default listview.
  if (base == NULL) {
      *pViewOptions = MMC_VIEW_OPTIONS_NONE;
      *ppViewType = NULL;
  }
  else
      return base->GetResultViewType(ppViewType, pViewOptions);
  return S_OK;
}
```

The actual method that performs the request is determined polymorphically at run time. This scheme works because all objects of items in the scope pane and result pane are instances of classes that inherit directly from the **CDelegationBase** class. The **CDelegationBase** base class defines default behaviors for all virtual functions that may or may not be overridden in derived classes.

Sample A: Simple

The Simple sample demonstrates the absolute minimum requirements for implementing an MMC snap-in.

This section uses sequence diagrams written in the Unified Modeling Language (UML) to show the object interactions relevant to understanding the sample.

Note that the UML diagrams used in describing this sample explain specific sample implementation details. They do not explain in general terms how MMC and snap-ins work.

Snap-in registration is not covered in this discussion. For details about registering snap-ins, see "Registering and Unregistering a Snap-in" in Chapter 17.

MMC snap-ins are COM in-process server DLLs. MMC is the client. For details about how in-process server DLLs are loaded by client applications, see "COM Clients and Servers" and related topics in the Microsoft Platform SDK documentation. The rest of this discussion covers how the Simple sample is loaded in an MMC console.

In this discussion, it is assumed that the snap-in is being added to an empty MMC console from the **Add/Remove Snap-in** dialog box. Let's take a look at how the sample's code is invoked.

The entry point into the sample code is the function **DLLGetClassObject**. MMC initiates this first event by calling **CoCreateInstance** to get the **IUnknown** interface of the snap-in. This causes COM to call **DllGetClassObject** in the snap-in's DLL. The **DllGetClassObject** creates the Class Factory (a **CClassFactory** object) and returns an **IClassFactory** interface to COM. Then COM calls **IClassFactory::CreateInstance**, which creates an object that implements **IComponentData** (this is the snap-in's cocreatable class object) and returns the snap-in's **IUnknown** to COM. This **IUnknown** is then forwarded to MMC.

The following sequence diagram describes the sequence of events starting with the invocation of **DLLGetClassObject** and ending with the creation of the snap-in's static node.

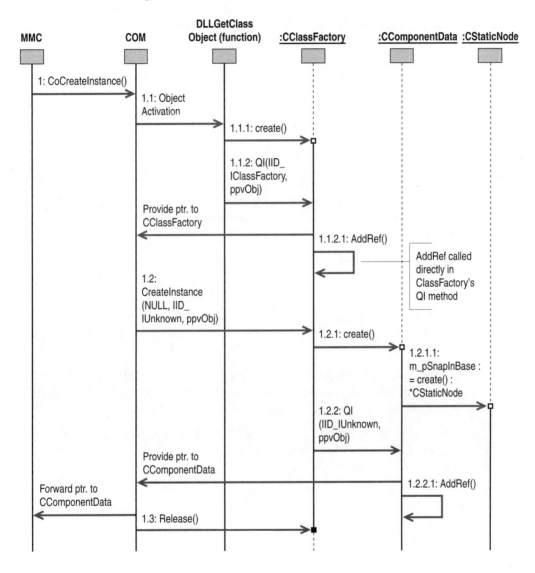

Using the **IClassFactory** pointer provided to it by the snap-in, COM invokes **CClassFactory**'s **CreateInstance** method to create a **CComponentData** object, which implements **IComponentData**. Remember that the **IComponentData** interface is the entry point into the snap-in, and that there is one instance of its implementation per snap-in instance. Here's the constructor of **CComponentData**:

```
CComponentData::CComponentData()
: m_cref(0), m_ipConsoleNameSpace(NULL), m_ipConsole(NULL)
{
  OBJECT_CREATED
  m_pStaticNode = new CStaticNode;
}
```

The pointers *m_ipConsoleNameSpace* and *m_ipConsole* point to the MMC console's **IConsoleNameSpace** and **IConsole** interfaces, respectively. As you will see later, **CComponentData** will cache these interface pointers during its initialization. Note that these interface pointers get released when the snap-in is destroyed.

OBJECT_CREATED is a macro that is defined as follows;

```
#define OBJECT_CREATED InterlockedIncrement((long *)&g_uObjects);
```

The *g_uObjects* global variable keeps a global count of the number of snap-in-provided interfaces that MMC is holding at any moment during the lifetime of the snap-in instance.

The constructor creates an instance of **CStaticNode**, which represents the root node (static node) of the snap-in. **CComponentData** caches an interface pointer to **CStaticNode** in its *m_pStaticNode* member variable.

After **CComponentData** is created, the **CClassFactory** object queries it for its **IUnknown** interface. The object returns the interface to COM, which then forwards the interface to MMC.

Initializing CComponentData and Displaying the Snap-in Root Node

The following sequence diagram describes the sequence of events that occur in order to initialize **CComponentData** and display the snap-in's root node (static node) in the scope pane.

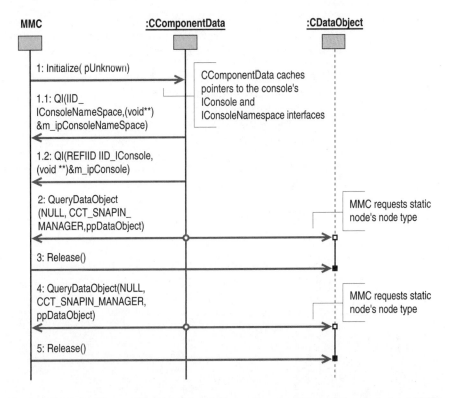

During initialization, **CComponentData** caches interface pointers to the MMC console's **IConsole** and **IConsoleNamespace** interfaces. Note that these interfaces are not used in this snap-in.

After **Initialize** returns, MMC displays the snap-in's static node in the scope pane. To do so, it calls the **QueryDataObject** method on **CComponentData** to get information about the snap-in's static node. Since MMC needs both the static node's node type and display name, it calls **QueryDataObject** twice. Each time, **CComponentData** creates an instance of **CDataObject** in response and provides MMC a pointer to it.

CDataObject registers all clipboard formats required by MMC in its constructor. The formats required by MMC to display the snap-in static node's node type and display name are s_cfNodeType and s_cfDisplayName, respectively.

CDataObject delegates the task of getting the actual requested data to the **CDelegationBase** delegation base. After receiving the requested data in the appropriate clipboard format and using it as needed, MMC destroys the data object. After getting the static node's display name, MMC displays the static node in the scope pane.

For details about data objects and how they are used in MMC, see "Data Objects and MMC" in Chapter 16.

Creating CComponent and Expanding the Snap-in Root Node

The display name of the snap-in's static node is "Sample A - Simple." Clicking the item in the scope pane triggers a series of interactions to create an instance of **CComponent** and to expand the static node. These interactions are shown in the next three sequence diagrams. The following sequence diagram shows the first few interactions:

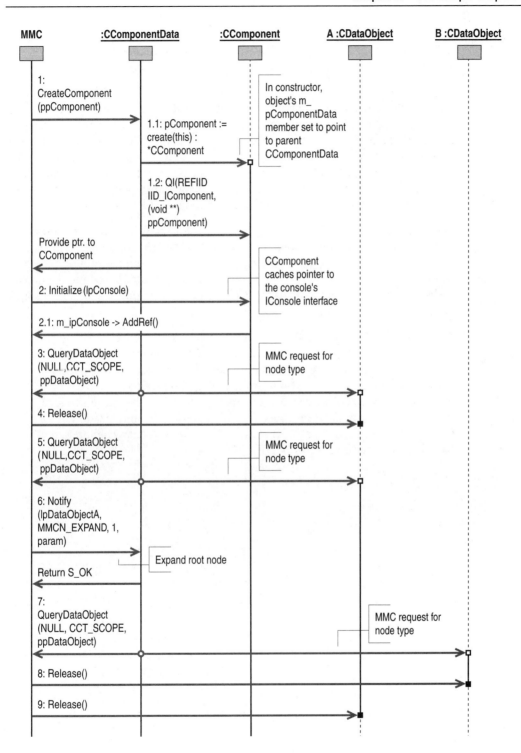

MMC   **:CComponentData**   **:CComponent**   **A :CDataObject**   **B :CDataObject**

1: CreateComponent (ppComponent)

1.1: pComponent := create(this) : *CComponent

In constructor, object's m_pComponentData member set to point to parent CComponentData

1.2: QI(REFIID IID_IComponent, (void **) ppComponent)

Provide ptr. to CComponent

CComponent caches pointer to the console's IConsole interface

2: Initialize (lpConsole)

2.1: m_ipConsole -> AddRef()

3: QueryDataObject (NULL, CCT_SCOPE, ppDataObject)

MMC request for node type

4: Release()

5: QueryDataObject (NULL, CCT_SCOPE, ppDataObject)

MMC request for node type

6: Notify (lpDataObjectA, MMCN_EXPAND, 1, param)

Expand root node

Return S_OK

7: QueryDataObject (NULL, CCT_SCOPE, ppDataObject)

MMC request for node type

8: Release()

9: Release()

C++ Snap-ins

In this and the following two sequence diagrams, you'll notice that MMC makes a number of calls to **CComponentData**'s **QueryDataObject** method to request data objects. For details about how data objects are used in MMC, see "Data Objects and MMC" in Chapter 16.

We won't be too concerned about exactly why MMC requests multiple data objects for apparently the same information. But generally, MMC will only keep a reference (interface pointer) to a data object around for as long as it needs it. As soon as the data object has fulfilled its purpose, MMC releases the interface. Note that MMC does not destroy the data object. This allows snap-ins to optimize the allocation of resources for data objects by implementing a pool of data objects that can be used more than once for fulfilling common MMC data requests.

Let's start at the top of the sequence diagram. MMC calls the **CreateComponent** method of **CComponentData** to create an instance of **CComponent**, which implements the **IComponent** interface. Recall that **CComponent** represents the console's result pane. During its creation and subsequent initialization, the object caches interface pointers to its parent **CComponentData** object and the console's **IConsole2** interface.

After calls to **CComponentData**'s **QueryDataObject** method, MMC tells the snap-in to expand the selected item by calling **CComponentData**'s **Notify** method with an MMCN_EXPAND notification. If the static node had any children to enumerate, the snap-in would call methods of the **IConsoleNamespace2** interface at this point. Recall that the snap-in cached a pointer to the **IConsoleNamespace2** interface during the initialization of **CComponentData**. But since the static node doesn't have any children, the **Notify** method simply returns S_OK.

The following sequence diagram shows the next few interactions:

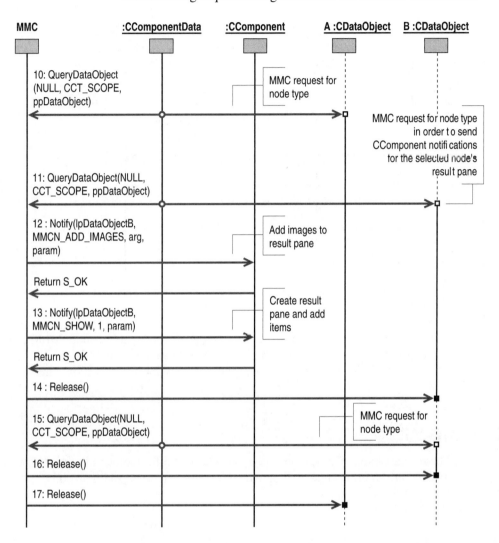

After further calls to **CComponentData**'s **QueryDataObject** method, MMC tells the snap-in to insert any images for the result pane of the static node by calling **CComponent**'s **Notify** method with an MMCN_ADD_IMAGES notification. Since there are no images to add, the notification is ignored. Similarly, the MMCN_SHOW notification sent next is also ignored.

The following sequence diagram shows the last few interactions:

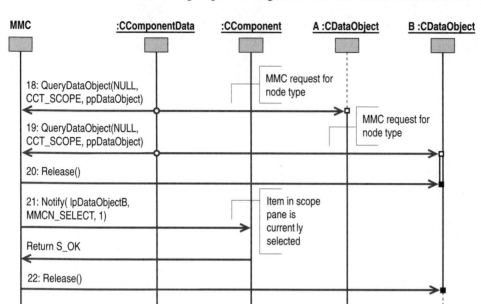

After further calls to **CComponentData**'s **QueryDataObject** method, MMC tells the snap-in to set the standard verbs for the result pane items by calling **CComponent**'s **Notify** method with an MMCN_SELECT notification. Since there are no items in the result pane, the notification is ignored.

Sample B: About

The About sample demonstrates how to add About information to snap-ins. For detailed information about adding About information, see "Adding About Information" in Chapter 18.

Sample C: Help

The Help sample demonstrates how to add HTML Help support to snap-ins. The sample shows how to integrate a snap-in's Help with MMC and with the Help of other snap-ins. The sample also shows how to implement context-sensitive (F1) Help in a snap-in.

This section uses a sequence diagram written in the Unified Modeling Language (UML) to show the object interactions relevant to understanding the demonstration.

Note that the UML diagrams used in describing this sample explain specific sample implementation details. They do not explain in general terms how MMC and snap-ins work.

Implementing Help

This section discusses how the Help sample implements the **ISnapinHelp2** interface to integrate the sample snap-in's Help with MMC. The sample also supports context-sensitive (F1) Help by using the **IDisplayHelp** interface.

In the sequence diagram that follows, we'll assume the following:

1. The user has just added the Help sample snap-in to an MMC console.
2. The user selects a scope item (say the snap-in's static node) and presses F1 for context-sensitive Help.

By assuming this scenario, you'll see what the snap-in needs to do to both support the **ISnapinHelp** (or **ISnapinHelp2**) interface and use the **IDisplayHelp** interface. In the discussion that follows, we'll also cover the other issues that come into play when this scenario doesn't apply.

Four objects are involved when the user invokes context-sensitive (F1) Help in the snap-in:

- MMC
- The snap-in's **CComponentData** implementation
- The snap-in's **CComponent** implementation
- The snap-in object representing the snap-in's static node

The following sequence diagram shows how these four objects interact.

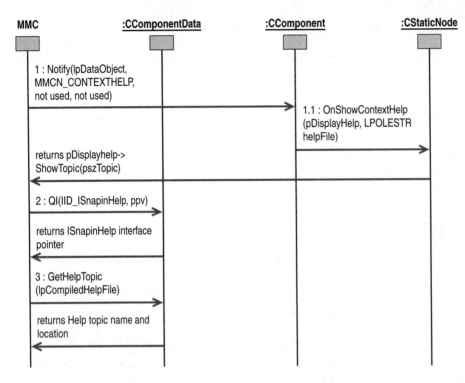

When the user presses the F1 key, MMC sends the **IComponent** associated with the static node an MMCN_CONTEXTHELP notification message. The **CStaticNode::OnShowContextHelp** method handles MMCN_CONTEXTHELP in the snap-in. **CStaticNode** is the snap-in object representing the static node.

Here is the the snap-in's implementation of the method:

```
HRESULT CStaticNode::OnShowContextHelp(IDisplayHelp *pDisplayHelp,
                        LPOLESTR helpFile)
{
  _TCHAR topicName[MAX_PATH];

  _tcscpy(topicName, helpFile);

  // we should read this from a resource file
  _tcscat(topicName,  _T("::/default.htm"));

  LPOLESTR pszTopic = static_cast<LPOLESTR>(CoTaskMemAlloc(
                        (_tcslen(topicName) + 1) * sizeof(_TCHAR)));

  _tcscpy(pszTopic, topicName);

  return pDisplayHelp->ShowTopic(pszTopic);
}
```

The sample uses the same topic (Default.htm) for all contexts, so it simply appends "::://default.htm" to the string representing the file name of the snap-in's HTML Help file. It then returns by calling **IDisplayHelp::ShowTopic** to request MMC to display the specified Help topic in the Help collection file for the current console file.

The **IDisplayHelp** interface allows the snap-in to display a specific HTML Help topic within MMC's collection file. The snap-in obtains a pointer to this interface by calling **QueryInterface** on the **IConsole2** interface.

Note that for property pages, the snap-in should call **MMCPropertyHelp** instead of **IDisplayHelp::ShowTopic**. Because an MMC property sheet typically runs on a separate thread, the property page cannot use the **IDisplayHelp** interface directly. Instead, the property page can call **MMCPropertyHelp** to achieve the same result. **MMCPropertyHelp** takes the same topic string parameter as **IDisplayHelp::ShowTopic** and handles marshaling the request to the main MMC thread.

Now that MMC has the name of the Help topic to display for the current context, it has to make sure that the snap-in can provide the topic. To do so, it queries the snap-in's **IComponentData** implementation for the **ISnapinHelp** (or **ISnapinHelp2**) interface. If the snap-in returns an interface pointer, MMC knows that the snap-in provides an HTML Help file. That is, it implements the **ISnapinHelp2::GetHelpTopic** method.

If the query fails for any reason, MMC places a "Help on <your snap-in name>" item on the **Help** menu. If the user selects this menu item, MMC sends the MMCN_SNAPINHELP notification to the snap-in's **IComponent**. The snap-in should respond by displaying whatever Help information it has for the context.

Note that snap-ins are strongly encouraged to support the **ISnapinHelp** (or **ISnapinHelp2**) interface. The MMCN_SNAPINHELP notification predates the **ISnapinHelp** interface. Before **ISnapinHelp**, each snap-in had to provide its own Help system and the MMCN_SNAPINHELP notification told it when to display the Help.

Because the snap-in does indeed return an **ISnapinHelp** interface pointer, MMC goes ahead and checks to see if it has already added the snap-in's HTML Help file to the collection file.

In this scenario, the snap-in was just added to the console, so its HTML Help file isn't part of the collection file for the console. Consequently, MMC calls the snap-in's implementation of the **ISnapinHelp2::GetHelpTopic** method to get the location of the Help file. Here is the method's implementation in the sample:

```
HRESULT CComponentData::GetHelpTopic(
                   /* [out] */ LPOLESTR *lpCompiledHelpFile)
{
  *lpCompiledHelpFile = static_cast<LPOLESTR>(CoTaskMemAlloc(
                   (_tcslen(m_HelpFile) + 1) * sizeof(_TCHAR)));

  _tcscpy(*lpCompiledHelpFile, m_HelpFile);

  return S_OK;
}
```

The **CComponentData** object's member variable **m_HelpFile** specifies the HTML Help file for the snap-in. The variable is set in the object's constructor:

```
CComponentData::CComponentData()
: m_cref(0), m_ipConsoleNameSpace(NULL), m_ipConsole(NULL)
{
  OBJECT_CREATED
  m_pStaticNode = new CStaticNode;

  GetWindowsDirectory(m_HelpFile, sizeof(m_HelpFile));
  _tcscat(m_HelpFile, _T("\\HELP\\"));
  LoadString(g_hinst,IDS_HELPFILE, &m_HelpFile[_tcslen(m_HelpFile)],
             MAX_PATH - _tcslen(m_HelpFile));
}
```

IDS_HELPFILE is the local string resource that specifies the name of the HTML Help file. As you can see in the constructor, the Help file is located in the HELP subdirectory of the Windows directory. This is the standard Windows Help directory (%winnt%\help). Note that you don't have to put your Help file in this directory. But if you do put it elsewhere, you must specify the full path name to the file in your snap-in's **ISnapinHelp2::GetHelpTopic** implementation.

If your snap-in implements the **ISnapinHelp2** interface, and not the older **ISnapinHelp** interface, MMC will call **ISnapinHelp2::GetLinkedTopics** after **ISnapinHelp2::GetHelpTopic** returns with S_OK. This gives the snap-in an opportunity to specify any additional HTML Help files that its own Help file links to.

The sample snap-in implements **ISnapinHelp**, so the call to **GetLinkedTopics** is never made.

MMC now has everything it needs to display the Help topic for the current context.

Sample D: Nodes

The Nodes sample demonstrates how to add items to both the scope and result panes of a snap-in's user interface. The sample uses a simple and extensible class hierarchy for adding items.

This section uses sequence diagrams written in the Unified Modeling Language (UML) to show the object interactions relevant to understanding the demonstration.

Note that the UML diagrams used in describing this sample explain specific sample implementation details. They do not explain in general terms how MMC and snap-ins work.

C++ Snap-ins

Setting the Node Type of a Scope or Result Item

This section discusses how the node types of the scope and result items inserted by the Nodes sample are set and used. For more general information about node types, see "Snap-in Namespace" in Chapter 16.

A scope or result item's node type is specified as a GUID (globally unique identifier). The node type is defined by the snap-in rather than by MMC and it is a GUID only because that is a dependable way to avoid name collisions. GUIDs in this context have no COM significance, although you generate them using uuidgen.exe just as you would other GUIDs. This procedure is documented in the Microsoft Platform SDK.

Here are the definitions for the node type GUIDs for some of the snap-in objects representing scope items in the Nodes sample:

```
const GUID CStaticNode::thisGuid = { 0x2974380c, 0x4c4b, 0x11d2,
            { 0x89, 0xd8, 0x0, 0x0, 0x21, 0x47, 0x31, 0x28 } };

const GUID CSpaceVehicle::thisGuid = { 0x29743810, 0x4c4b, 0x11d2,
            { 0x89, 0xd8, 0x0, 0x0, 0x21, 0x47, 0x31, 0x28 } };

const GUID CSkyBasedVehicle::thisGuid = { 0x2974380f, 0x4c4b, 0x11d2,
            { 0x89, 0xd8, 0x0, 0x0, 0x21, 0x47, 0x31, 0x28 } };
```

Each item (scope and result) implements a **getNodeType** public member function that is called when its node type is requested:

```
virtual const GUID & getNodeType() { return thisGuid; }
```

This function is called in the snap-in's **IDataObject::GetDataHere** implementation, which MMC calls with the CCF_NODETYPE format to request the selected item's node type:

```
HRESULT CDataObject::GetDataHere(
                FORMATETC *pFormatEtc,    // [in]
                STGMEDIUM *pMedium        // [out] )
{
  const   CLIPFORMAT cf = pFormatEtc->cfFormat;
  IStream *pStream = NULL;

  CDelegationBase *base = GetBaseNodeObject();

  HRESULT hr = CreateStreamOnHGlobal( pMedium->hGlobal, FALSE,
            &pStream );
  if ( FAILED(hr) )
      return hr;             // Minimal error checking

  hr = DV_E_FORMATETC;          // Unknown format
```

```
    if (cf == s_cfDisplayName) {
        //removed in this sample code
    }
    else if (cf == s_cfNodeType) {
        const GUID *pGUID = (const GUID *)&base->getNodeType();

        hr = pStream->Write(pGUID, sizeof(GUID), NULL);
    }
    else if (cf == s_cfSZNodeType) {
        //removed in this sample code
    }
    else if (cf == s_cfSnapinClsid) {
        //removed in this sample code
    }
    else if (cf == s_cfInternal) {
        //removed in this sample code
    }

    pStream->Release();

    return hr;
}
```

In the preceding function, the **GetBaseNodeObject** method (defined by the snap-in) returns the cookie value of the data object's base **CDelegationBase** object. For a description of how **CDelegationBase** is used in the MMC SDK samples, see "Samples Object Model" earlier in this chapter.

Adding Scope Items

When a snap-in adds scope items in the scope pane, it is really performing two separate actions:

- Creating Snap-in Objects for Scope Items
- Inserting Scope Items

The Nodes sample snap-in owns all the items that it adds; that is, none of the items are inserted by extension snap-ins. For an example of how extension snap-ins extend primary snap-ins, see the Extens sample snap-in.

Creating Snap-in Objects for Scope Items

The scope pane of the Nodes sample snap-in contains a number of different items. Each scope item is represented by a different snap-in object. In the sample, all objects are created after the creation of the snap-in's **IComponentData** implementation, **CComponentData**.

The following sequence diagram shows the order in which objects for scope items are created. This diagram applies both when the user adds the Nodes snap-in to an MMC console using the **Add/Remove Snap-in** dialog box and when the snap-in is loaded from an .msc file.

Note that this diagram does not give a detailed description of what happens when a snap-in is first loaded in a console and its **IComponentData** implementation is created and initialized. See the documentation of the Simple sample for this level of detail.

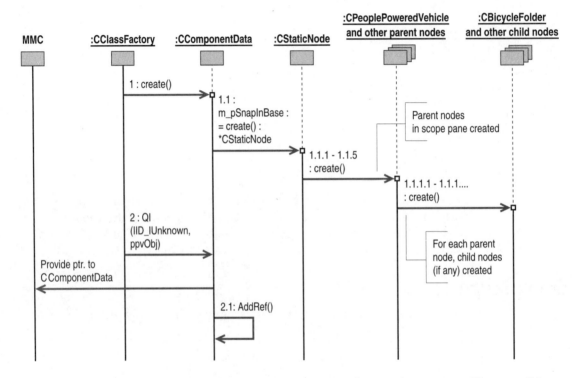

As the diagram suggests, the Nodes sample snap-in uses an easily extensible hierachical model for creating objects. We'll look at this model more closely in the discussion that follows.

Let's start by looking at the constructor of the snap-in's **IComponentData** implementation, **CComponentData**:

```
CComponentData::CComponentData()
: m_cref(0), m_ipConsoleNameSpace(NULL), m_ipConsole(NULL)
{
  OBJECT_CREATED
  m_pStaticNode = new CStaticNode;
}
```

The constructor creates an instance of **CStaticNode**, which represents the root node (static node) of the snap-in. **CComponentData** caches an interface pointer to **CStaticNode** in its *m_pStaticNode* member variable.

Here is **CStaticNode**'s constructor:

```
CStaticNode::CStaticNode()
{
  children[0] = new CPeoplePoweredVehicle;
  children[1] = new CLandBasedVehicle;
  children[2] = new CSkyBasedVehicle;
  children[3] = new CSpaceVehicle;
  children[4] = new CBackgroundFolder;
}
```

The constructor creates the five snap-in objects that represent the child items of the snap-in's static node. These items may or may not be parent items. If they are parent items, their children are instantiated in their constructors, as is the case for **CPeoplePoweredVehicle**:

```
CPeoplePoweredVehicle::CPeoplePoweredVehicle()
{
  children[0] = new CBicycleFolder;
  children[1] = new CSkateboardFolder;
  children[2] = new CIceSkateFolder;
}
```

If the items are not parent items, their constructors can be used, for example, to instantiate the objects (items) that are later inserted in their associated result pane views. For example, in the constructor for **CSpaceVehicle** (which represents the "Future Vehicles" scope item), the **CRocket** objects inserted into the result pane's list view are created:

```
CSpaceVehicle::CSpaceVehicle()
{
  for (int n = 0; n < NUMBER_OF_CHILDREN; n++)
  {
      children[n] = new CRocket(_T("Rocket"), n+1, 500000, 265,
                                75000);
  }
}
```

We won't go into detail about the result pane in this discussion. If you're interested, see "Implementing a List View in the Result Pane" later in this chapter to learn about how this particular list view is implemented in the Nodes sample.

This concludes the discussion on how snap-in objects for scope items. In the next section, "Inserting Scope Items," we'll see how the snap-in inserts these objects as items in the scope pane.

C++ Snap-ins

Inserting Scope Items

After creating snap-in objects for scope items, the snap-in still has to enumerate and insert the scope items before they can appear in the scope pane.

When a scope item is selected in the scope pane for the first time (either by the user or programmatically), MMC sends the snap-in's **IComponentData** implementation an MMCN_EXPAND notification message. The snap-in then has the opportunity to insert any child items into the scope pane.

The following sequence diagram shows how the MMCN_EXPAND notification is handled by the snap-in when the user selects the following three different items in order:

1. The snap-in's static node ("Sample D - Children")
2. "People-powered Vehicles"
3. "Sky-based Vehicles"

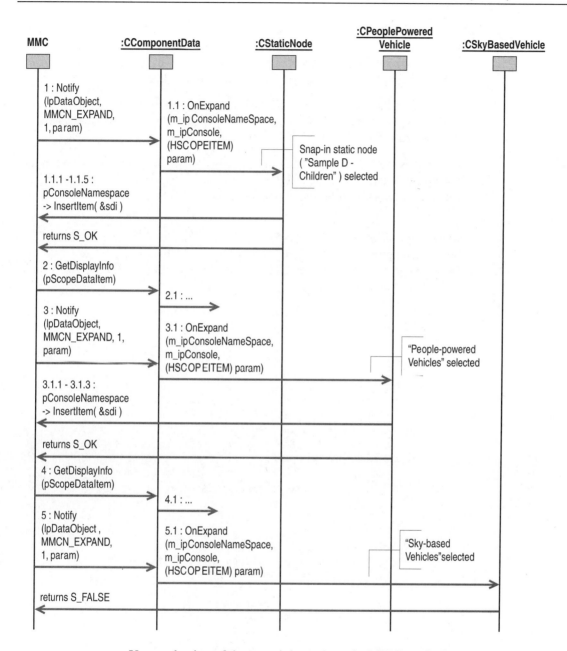

Upon selection of the snap-in's static node, MMC sends the snap-in an MMCN_EXPAND notification with *arg* set to 1 (to indicate that the item is being expanded) and *param* set to the HSCOPEITEM of the static node.

When an item is inserted into the scope pane, an HSCOPEITEM, which uniquely identifies the item, is associated with it. For all items other than the static node, MMC returns the item's HSCOPEITEM after the snap-in successfully inserts the item in the scope pane (using **IConsoleNameSpace2::InsertItem**).

In the case of the static node, MMC itself inserts it into the snap-in's namespace. MMC then passes the static node's HSCOPEITEM to the snap-in as the *param* parameter in the MMCN_EXPAND notification.

As already stated, an HSCOPEITEM uniquely identifies an individual item in the scope pane. Data objects can also be used by snap-ins to uniquely identify an item, but there is no MMC requirement that states that they must be used in this way.

Now that we've discussed the HSCOPEITEM parameter, let's see how the snap-in handles the MMCN_EXPAND notification. The **CStaticNode::OnExpand** method handles the notification for the snap-in's static node. Here is its implementation:

```
HRESULT CStaticNode::OnExpand(IConsoleNameSpace
➡ *pConsoleNameSpace, IConsole *pConsole, HSCOPEITEM parent)
{
  SCOPEDATAITEM sdi;

  if (!bExpanded) {
      // create the child nodes, then expand them
      for (int n = 0; n < NUMBER_OF_CHILDREN; n++) {
          ZeroMemory(&sdi, sizeof(SCOPEDATAITEM) );
          sdi.mask = SDI_STR    |    // Displayname is valid
              SDI_PARAM          |    // lParam is valid
              SDI_IMAGE          |    // nImage is valid
              SDI_OPENIMAGE      |    // nOpenImage is valid
              SDI_PARENT         |
              SDI_CHILDREN;

          sdi.relativeID  = (HSCOPEITEM)parent;
          sdi.nImage      = children[n]->GetBitmapIndex();
          sdi.nOpenImage  = INDEX_OPENFOLDER;
          sdi.displayname = MMC_CALLBACK;
          sdi.lParam      = (LPARAM)children[n];        // The cookie
          sdi.cChildren   = (n == 0);

          HRESULT hr = pConsoleNameSpace->InsertItem( &sdi );

          _ASSERT( SUCCEEDED(hr) );
      }
  }
  return S_OK;
}
```

In the method, the snap-in fills a **SCOPEDATAITEM** structure for each of its child items. The **mask** member of the structure specifies an array of flags indicating which other members of the structure contain valid data.

Notice that the **relativeID** member is the HSCOPEITEM of the item's parent. The snap-in should fill the **relativeID** member with an MMC-specified unique item identifier (HSCOPEITEM). An item is inserted in the scope pane at a position relative to the item specified by this member. The relative position is determined by the mask settings. The SDI_PARENT mask setting indicates that the item is to be inserted as the last child of the parent item. In the case of the static node, this means that each of its children will be successively inserted as the last child.

When an item is inserted in the scope pane using **IConsoleNameSpace2::InsertItem** (as is the case here), the **displayname** member must be set to MMC_CALLBACK. MMC then calls the snap-in's **IComponentData::GetDisplayInfo** method to request the display name for the item when it appears in the scope pane.

The **lParam** member specifies a 32-bit value to associate with the item. As already mentioned, MMC caches this value and uses it to uniquely identify the scope item. MMC then passes this item, which is also known as a cookie, as the first parameter in calls to the snap-in's **IComponentData::QueryDataObject** implementation.

The **cChildren** member specifies the number of enumerated child items that the current item inserts when it is expanded. In the sample snap-in, the static node's first child item ("People-powered Vehicles") enumerates child items of its own, so that's why **cChildren** is set to the value of the Boolean expression (n==0).

After filling in the **SCOPEDATAITEM** structure, the snap-in inserts the item into the scope pane using the **IConsoleNamespace2:InsertItem** method. When **InsertItem** returns (with S_OK), the **ID** member of the **SCOPEDATAITEM** structure contains the HSCOPEITEM of the newly inserted item. Note that snap-ins should store the HSCOPEITEM of each inserted item and use it to later manipulate the item using the methods of the **IConsole2** and **IConsoleNameSpace2** interfaces.

After inserting all the items, the **CStaticNode::OnExpand** method returns with S_OK and program control returns to the snap-in's **IComponentData::Notify** method.

After the snap-in returns from **IComponentData::Notify** with S_OK, MMC calls its **IComponentData::GetDisplayInfo** implementation once for each inserted item in the scope pane to request the item's display name. This is because the **displayname** member of the **SCOPEDATAITEM** structure created for the inserted item was set to MMC_CALLBACK, indicating to MMC that the SDI_STR item attribute is a callback attribute.

C++ Snap-ins

Because five child items were inserted underneath the static node, there are five successive calls to **IComponentData::GetDisplayInfo**. Here is the implementation of **IComponentData::GetDisplayInfo** from the sample:

```
HRESULT CComponentData::GetDisplayInfo(
                        /* [out][in] */ SCOPEDATAITEM
                  ➥ *pScopeDataItem)
{
  HRESULT hr = S_FALSE;

  // if they are asking for the SDI_STR we have one of those to give
  if (pScopeDataItem->lParam) {
      CDelegationBase *base = (CDelegationBase *)pScopeDataItem->
                              lParam;
      if (pScopeDataItem->mask & SDI_STR) {
          pScopeDataItem->displayname =
          const_cast<_TCHAR *>(base->GetDisplayName());
      }

      if (pScopeDataItem->mask & SDI_IMAGE) {
          pScopeDataItem->nImage = base->GetBitmapIndex();
      }
  }

  return hr;
}
```

The **SCOPEDATAITEM** structure passed into **GetDisplayInfo** identifies each item for which MMC requests display information. The **lParam** member holds the cookie value of the item. Recall that the snap-in sets this value in the **SCOPEDATAITEM** structure created for the item.

After the snap-in provides the item's display name and returns S_OK, the item is displayed in the scope pane. This process continues until all child items of the static node are displayed. MMC then waits for the next user action before sending any further notification messages to the snap-in.

The rest of the sequence diagram shows what happens when the user selects first the "People-powered Vehicles" item and then the "Sky-based Vehicles" item.

The "People-powered Vehicles" item also has child items. These items are enumerated and inserted in the scope pane in the same way that the static node's child items were. Then, the snap-in provides their display names when its **IComponentData::GetDisplayInfo** method is called.

Finally, the "Sky-based Vehicles" item has no child items, so the snap-in's MMCN_EXPAND notification handler for the item simply returns S_FALSE.

Implementing a List View in the Result Pane

This section discusses how the Nodes sample snap-in implements a list view in the result pane associated with one of the snap-in's scope items.

The Nodes snap-in also demonstrates how to implement a number of other result pane view types. Implementation details about these view types are not presented here. However, you're encouraged to read more about them in Chapter 20, "Using Different Result Pane View Types."

- The result pane associated with the "Sky-based Vehicles" item implements an MMC message OCX control. See "Using the MMC Message OCX Control" in Chapter 20 for details.

- The result pane associated with the "Ice Skates" item implements a virtual list view. See "Owner Data/Virtual Lists" in Chapter 20 for details.

Let's now return to list view implementation details. Three objects are involved in implementing a list view in the result pane of an MMC console:

- MMC
- The snap-in's IComponent implementation
- The snap-in object for the scope item corresponding to the result pane with the list view

The following sequence diagram shows how these three objects interact when a scope item is selected in the scope pane and a list view is created in its corresponding result pane. In the diagram, the **CDelegationBase** object is the delegation base (and base class) common to all snap-in objects for scope and result items in the snap-in. For details, see "Samples Object Model" earlier in this chapter.

C++ Snap-ins

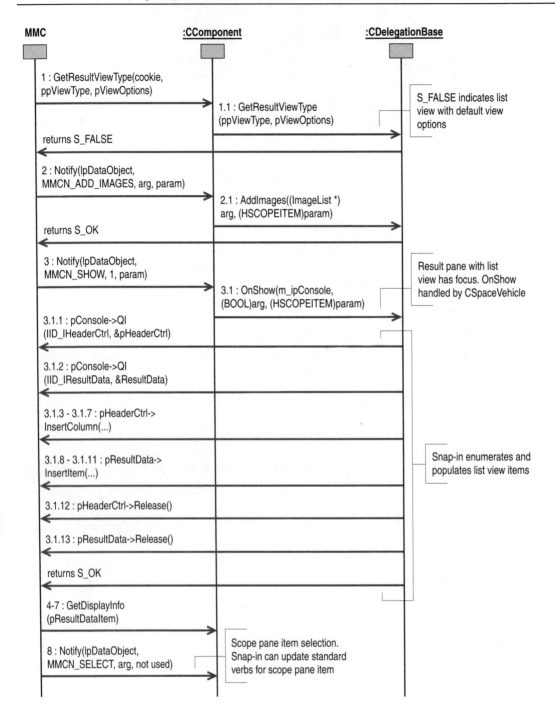

MMC   :CComponent   :CDelegationBase

1 : GetResultViewType(cookie,
ppViewType, pViewOptions)

1.1 : GetResultViewType
(ppViewType, pViewOptions)

S_FALSE indicates list
view with default view
options

returns S_FALSE

2 : Notify(lpDataObject,
MMCN_ADD_IMAGES, arg, param)

2.1 : AddImages((ImageList *)
arg, (HSCOPEITEM)param)

returns S_OK

3 : Notify(lpDataObject,
MMCN_SHOW, 1, param)

3.1 : OnShow(m_ipConsole,
(BOOL)arg, (HSCOPEITEM)param)

Result pane with list
view has focus. OnShow
handled by CSpaceVehicle

3.1.1 : pConsole->QI
(IID_IHeaderCtrl, &pHeaderCtrl)

3.1.2 : pConsole->QI
(IID_IResultData, &ResultData)

3.1.3 - 3.1.7 : pHeaderCtrl->
InsertColumn(...)

3.1.8 - 3.1.11 : pResultData->
InsertItem(...)

Snap-in enumerates and
populates list view items

3.1.12 : pHeaderCtrl->Release()

3.1.13 : pResultData->Release()

returns S_OK

4-7 : GetDisplayInfo
(pResultDataItem)

8 : Notify(lpDataObject,
MMCN_SELECT, arg, not used)

Scope pane item selection.
Snap-in can update standard
verbs for scope pane item

When the user selects the scope item entitled "Future Vehicles," MMC calls the **IComponent::GetResultViewType** method of the **IComponent** that is associated with the item. In the sample, the **IComponent** object does not directly implement the method, so the method's implementation in its base class object, **CDelegationBase**, is called instead. **GetResultViewType** returns S_FALSE, indicating to MMC that it should display a list view with default view options (none) in the result pane.

To specify nondefault view options for the list view, **GetResultViewType** must not return S_FALSE. Instead, it should set the value of the *ppViewType* parameter to NULL, indicating that MMC should display the default view type (list view). Then, it should specify the view options with the *pViewOptions* parameter. The MMC_VIEW_OPTIONS_NONE option specifies the default value (no view options).

Next, MMC sends an MMCN_ADD_IMAGES notification message. The snap-in handles the message by setting up a collection of images to be displayed in the result pane.

The next notification sent to the snap-in is MMCN_SHOW. MMC sends the notification to tell the snap-in that the result pane has the focus. This is a crucial notification, and the snap-in handles it by inserting columns into the list view and enumerating and populating the list view's items.

C++ Snap-ins

MMCN_SHOW is sent to the snap-in's **IComponent::Notify** implementation. The notification message is delegated to the snap-in object that represents the selected scope item, **CSpaceVehicle**. Here is the implementation of **CSpaceVehicle::OnShow** from the sample:

```
HRESULT CSpaceVehicle::OnShow(IConsole *pConsole, BOOL bShow,
➡ HSCOPEITEM scopeitem)
{
  HRESULT       hr = S_OK;

  IHeaderCtrl *pHeaderCtrl = NULL;
  IResultData *pResultData = NULL;

  if (bShow) {
      hr = pConsole->QueryInterface(IID_IHeaderCtrl,
          (void **)&pHeaderCtrl);
      _ASSERT( SUCCEEDED(hr) );

      hr = pConsole->QueryInterface(IID_IResultData,
          (void **)&pResultData);
      _ASSERT( SUCCEEDED(hr) );

      // Set the column headers in the results pane
      hr = pHeaderCtrl->InsertColumn( 0, _T("Rocket Class"), 0,
                                        MMCLV_AUTO );
      _ASSERT( S_OK == hr );
      hr = pHeaderCtrl->InsertColumn( 1, _T("Rocket Weight"), 0,
                                        MMCLV_AUTO );
      _ASSERT( S_OK == hr );
      hr = pHeaderCtrl->InsertColumn( 2, _T("Rocket Height"), 0,
                                        MMCLV_AUTO );
      _ASSERT( S_OK == hr );
      hr = pHeaderCtrl->InsertColumn( 3, _T("Rocket Payload"), 0,
                                        MMCLV_AUTO );
      _ASSERT( S_OK == hr );
      hr = pHeaderCtrl->InsertColumn( 4, _T("Status"), 0,
                                        MMCLV_AUTO );
      _ASSERT( S_OK == hr );

      // insert items here
      RESULTDATAITEM rdi;
```

```
        if (!bExpanded) {
            // create the child nodes, then expand them
            for (int n = 0; n < NUMBER_OF_CHILDREN; n++) {
                ZeroMemory(&rdi, sizeof(RESULTDATAITEM) );
                rdi.mask   = RDI_STR    |   // Displayname is valid
                             RDI_IMAGE  |
                             RDI_PARAM;     // nImage is valid
                rdi.nImage     = children[n]->GetBitmapIndex();
                rdi.str        = MMC_CALLBACK;
                rdi.nCol       = 0;
                rdi.lParam     = (LPARAM)children[n];

                hr = pResultData->InsertItem( &rdi );

                _ASSERT( SUCCEEDED(hr) );
            }
        }

        pHeaderCtrl->Release();
        pResultData->Release();
    }

    return hr;
}
```

In **CSpaceVehicle::OnShow**, the snap-in obtains interface pointers to the **IHeaderCtrl** and **IResultData** interfaces by querying MMC's **IConsole** interface for them. It's very important to note that the **IConsole** used here is the one passed to the snap-in's **IComponent** implementation during the call to the snap-in's **IComponent::Initialize** implementation. Both the snap-in's **IComponent** and **IComponentData** implementations are passed pointers to **IConsole**, but these are pointers to two different **IConsole** implementations. If the snap-in queries the wrong **IConsole**, all subsequent calls to **IHeaderCtrl** and **IResultData** methods will lead to unpredictable results.

Incidentally, the snap-in sample could have used the **IHeaderCtrl2** and **IConsole2** interfaces, which are newer versions of **IHeaderCtrl** and **IConsole**, respectively.

After inserting columns into the list view using the **IHeaderCtrl::InsertColumn** method, the snap-in fills a **RESULTDATAITEM** structure for each item (a **CRocket** object) in the list view and then calls **IResultData::InsertItem** to insert the item in the list view.

C++ Snap-ins

Notice that the **lParam** member of the structure is set to the address of the list view item's object. After the snap-in calls **InsertItem**, MMC caches the **lParam** member of the **RESULTDATAITEM** structure and gives the value back to the snap-in as a cookie when the item is selected. The same cached **lParam** value is passed to the snap-in when MMC calls its **IComponent::GetDisplayInfo** implementation (described below).

After the snap-in returns from **CSpaceVehicle::OnShow** with S_OK, MMC calls its **IComponent::GetDisplayInfo** implementation once for each data item in the result pane to request the item's display name. This is because the **str** member of the **RESULTDATAITEM** created for each inserted data item was set to MMC_CALLBACK, indicating to MMC that the RDI_STR item attribute is a callback attribute.

In the sample, there are 15 individual data items in the result pane for which MMC requests the display name (three **RESULTDATAITEM** structures multiplied by five columns). Here is the implementation of **IComponent::GetDisplayInfo** from the sample:

```
STDMETHODIMP CComponent::GetDisplayInfo(
                /* [out][in] */ RESULTDATAITEM *pResultDataItem)
{
  HRESULT hr = S_OK;
  CDelegationBase *base = NULL;

  // if they are asking for the RDI_STR we have one of those to give
  if (pResultDataItem->lParam)
  {
      base = (CDelegationBase *)pResultDataItem->lParam;

      if (pResultDataItem->mask & RDI_STR)
      {
          pResultDataItem->str = const_cast<_TCHAR *>(base->
          GetDisplayName(pResultDataItem->nCol));
      }

      if (pResultDataItem->mask & RDI_IMAGE)
      {
          pResultDataItem->nImage = base->GetBitmapIndex();
      }

  } else
  {
      m_pLastNode->GetChildColumnInfo(pResultDataItem);
  }

  return hr;
}
```

The **RESULTDATAITEM** structure passed into **GetDisplayInfo** identifies each data item for which MMC requests display information. The **lParam** member uniquely identifies the list view object associated with the data item, and the **ncol** member identifies the column for which the data item is being requested. The snap-in uses both pieces of information to provide the display name and data for each data item in the list view.

Finally, MMC sends the snap-in an MMCN_SELECT notification message to indicate which scope pane item is currently selected. At this point, the snap-in can respond to the notification by updating the standard verbs for the scope pane item. The same notification message is sent to the snap-in when the user selects one of the items in the result pane. In this case, the message indicates which result pane item (object) is selected, and the snap-in can update the standard verbs for that item.

Sample D1: Extens

The Extens sample is a sample of a primary snap-in whose functionality is extended by a number of different extension snap-ins. The following is a list of the MMC sample snap-ins that extend the Extens sample:

- CMenuExt
- PPgeExt
- NameExt
- TBarExt

The CMenuExt sample is a context menu extension. It adds a context menu item to the "People-powered Vehicle" scope item in the Extens sample when the user displays the scope item's context menu.

The PPgeExt sample is a property page extension that extends "Rocket" result items in the Extens sample by adding a property page when the user selects a "Rocket" item and clicks the **Properties** context menu item.

The NameExt sample is a namespace extension that extends the "Sky-based Vehicle" scope item by adding a child item of its own. The sample also creates it own list view and enumerates items in the list view.

The TBarExt sample is a toolbar extension that also extends "Rocket" result items in the Extens sample. TBarExt creates a toolbar control and adds toolbar buttons when the user selects the "Future Vehicles" scope item. The toolbar control is attached when the user selects a "Rocket" result item.

C++ Snap-ins

In order for the Extens sample to be extended by extension snap-ins, it must do the following things:

- The Extens sample must register the node type GUIDs of its extendable node types under the **HKEY_LOCAL_MACHINE\Software\Microsoft\MMC\SnapIns\ *{snapinCLSID}*\NodeTypes** key. The *{snapinCLSID}* key is the name for a snap-in's key and is the string representation of the snap-in's CLSID. For details about the **SnapIns** key, see "Registering and Unregistering a Snap-in" in Chapter 17.

    MMC uses the values in the **NodeTypes** key to find the node types for the snap-in and then uses that list of node types to get the extensions for those node types. That set of extension snap-ins is displayed as the available extensions for the snap-in on the **Extensions** tab of the **Add/Remove Snap-in** dialog box.

    Note that "Registering and Unregistering a Snap-in" uses sample code taken from the Extens sample to discuss how primary snap-ins register the node type GUIDs of their extendable node types.

- The Extens sample must publish any clipboard formats that extension snap-ins will need to exchange data with it. The Extens sample registers the four "standard" clipboard formats required of all MMC snap-ins:

    CCF_NODETYPE

    CCF_SZNODETYPE

    CCF_DISPLAY_NAME

    CCF_SNAPIN_CLASSID

In order for the extension snap-ins to extend the functionality of the Extens sample, they must do the following things:

- Extension snap-ins must implement the appropriate MMC interfaces and handle the various MMC notifications sent in response to user actions.

- Each extension snap-in must register its CLSID in the appropriate {nodetypeGUID} subkey of the HKEY_LOCAL_MACHINE\Software\Microsoft\MMC\NodeTypes key. The {nodetypeGUID} subkey specifies the string representation of the GUID of the node type that is being extended. For details about the NodeTypes key, see "Registration Requirements for Extension Snap-ins" in Chapter 24.

- Extension snap-ins must be aware of and support the clipboard formats published by any primary snap-ins whose node types they extend.

Details about writing extensions are provided in the following sections in Chapter 24:

- "Extending a Primary Snap-in's Namespace"
- "Extending a Primary Snap-in's Context Menu"
- "Extending a Primary Snap-in's Control Bar"
- "Extending a Primary Snap-in's Property Sheet"
- "Extending a Primary Snap-in's Taskpad"

Sample E: CMenu

The CMenu sample demonstrates how to enable MMC context menu items and how to add snap-in-defined context menu items. The sample implements the **IExtendContextMenu** interface and uses the **IContextMenuCallback** interface to add context menu items to MMC default context menus.

This section uses sequence diagrams written in the Unified Modeling Language (UML) to show the object interactions relevant to understanding the demonstration.

Note that the UML diagrams used in describing this sample explain specific sample implementation details. They do not explain in general terms how MMC and snap-ins work.

Adding Context Menu Items

The CMenu sample adds context menu items to a number of the MMC-defined default context menus. The following is a list of all the default context menus to which the sample adds its own items:

- The "Land-based Vehicles" item has an menu item in its New submenu.
- The "Sky-based Vehicles" item has an menu item in its New submenu.
- The "Future Vehicles" item has an menu item in its New submenu.
- Each result item in the result pane of the "Future Vehicles" scope item has three menu items in its All Tasks submenu.

Also, the **Action** menu at the top of an MMC console is the context menu for a given scope item or result item. When the snap-in adds items to a scope item's context menu or a result item's context menu, MMC automatically adds the same items (in the appropriate submenus) to the **Action** menu.

We'll see how the snap-in adds a context menu item to the **New** submenu of the "Future Vehicles" scope item. The following sequence diagram shows the objects that are involved and the interactions that they have with each other.

C++ Snap-ins

The diagram assumes that the user has selected the "Future Vehicles" scope item in the scope pane. Messages 1 through 2.1.1 are sent when the user right-clicks the item to open its context menu. Messages 3 through 3.1 are sent when the user clicks the **Spaced based** item in the **New** submenu.

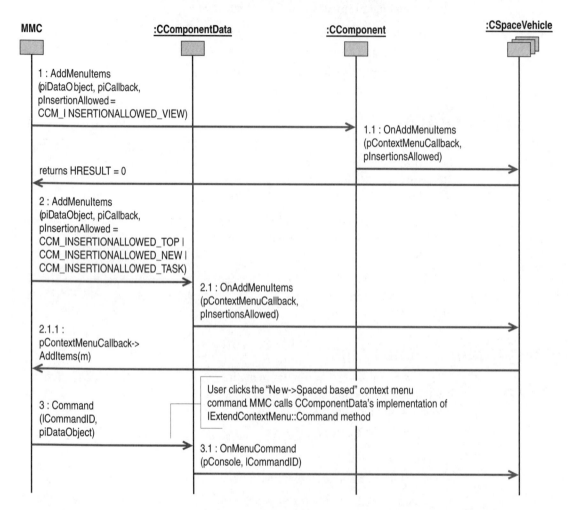

In the sample snap-in, when the user selects the "Future Vehicles" scope item and then right-clicks the scope item, MMC gives the snap-in the opportunity to add context menu items to the default context menus.

In the scenario depicted in the sequence diagram, MMC calls the **IExtendContextMenu::AddMenuItems** method implemented by **CComponent**, which is the snap-in's **IComponent** implementation. (MMC first queries **CComponent** for the **IExtendContextMenu** interface. If **CComponent** returns an interface pointer, MMC calls **AddMenuItems** on the interface.)

MMC calls **CComponent**'s implementation of **AddMenuItems** to allow the snap-in to add menu items to the **View** context submenu. MMC indicates this by setting the *pInsertionAllowed* parameter passed in the call to CCM_INSERTIONALLOWED_VIEW. This value means that only the CCM_INSERTIONALLOWED_VIEW bit is set and therefore allowed.

Because the user selected the "Future Vehicles" scope item in the scope pane before opening its context menu, MMC knows that the snap-in will be setting up the result pane associated with the selected scope item. Therefore it gives the snap-in the opportunity to add view-specific items to the context menu. All view-specific items are added to the **View** submenu. Since this submenu is related to items in the result pane, the call to **AddMenuItems** is made on the **IComponent** implementation responsible for setting up the result pane.

If the user right-clicks a scope item in the scope pane without first selecting it, or if the user selects a scope item in the result pane, MMC will not attempt to populate its context menu with a **View** submenu, and consequently MMC will not call **AddMenuItems** on the **IComponent** responsible for the scope item's result pane.

The **CComponent::AddMenuItems** method delegates the addition of the context menu items to the actual snap-in object that represents the selected scope or result item. In the case of the "Future Vehicles" item, the context menu items are added in the snap-in's **CSpaceVehicle::OnAddMenuItems** method:

```
HRESULT CSpaceVehicle::OnAddMenuItems(IContextMenuCallback
➥ *pContextMenuCallback, long *pInsertionsAllowed)
{
  HRESULT hr = S_OK;
  CONTEXTMENUITEM menuItemsNew[] =
  {
      { _T("Space based"), _T("Add a new space based vehicle"),
          IDM_NEW_SPACE, CCM_INSERTIONPOINTID_PRIMARY_NEW, 0,
          CCM_SPECIAL_DEFAULT_ITEM },
      { NULL, NULL, 0, 0, 0 }
  };

  // Loop through and add each of the menu items
  if (*pInsertionsAllowed & CCM_INSERTIONALLOWED_NEW)
  {
      for (LPCONTEXTMENUITEM m = menuItemsNew; m->strName; m++)
      {
          hr = pContextMenuCallback->AddItem(m);

          if (FAILED(hr))
              break;
      }
  }

  return hr;
}
```

In **CSpaceVehicle::OnAddMenuItems**, the snap-in fills a **CONTEXTMENUITEM** structure for each item to be inserted. The **lInsertionPointID** member indicates where the item should be inserted. Here, the value is CCM_INSERTIONPOINTID_PRIMARY_NEW, indicating that the snap-in wants to add items to the top of the **New** submenu. The **New** submenu is present for context menus in both the scope pane and the result pane. The CCM_SPECIAL_DEFAULT_ITEM flag specifies that the item should be the default menu item.

Before adding the **CONTEXTMENUITEM** structure, the snap-in checks to see if MMC is allowing it to insert the item into the desired location, namely if the CCM_INSERTIONALLOWED_NEW flag is set in the *pInsertionAllowed* parameter passed in the call to **CComponent::AddMenuItems**. However, as already discussed, the value of the *pInsertionAllowed* parameter is CCM_INSERTIONALLOWED_VIEW, so the snap-in returns from the method without inserting anything.

(Incidentally, the CCM_INSERTIONALLOWED_NEW insertion allowed flag is derived from the CCM_INSERTIONPOINTID_PRIMARY_NEW system insertion point ID. See the Mmc.idl file for details.)

After giving the snap-in's **IComponent** implementation the opportunity to add items to the **View** submenu, MMC now gives the snap-in's **IComponentData** implementation the chance to add items to the top of the context menu and to the **New** and **Task** submenus. After first querying the **IComponentData** implementation (**CComponentData**) for the **IExtendContextMenu** interface, MMC calls the **AddMenuItems** method on the interface with the *pInsertionAllowed* parameter set to CCM_INSERTIONALLOWED_TOP | CCM_INSERTIONALLOWED_NEW | CCM_INSERTIONALLOWED_TASK, indicating that these three bits are allowed.

The **CComponentData::AddMenuItems** method delegates the addition of the context menu items to **CSpaceVehicle::OnAddMenuItems**, which is the same snap-in object to which the **CComponent::AddMenuItems** method delegates the task of adding menu items (for the "Future Vehicles" scope item). Now, since the CCM_INSERTIONALLOWED_NEW bit is set in the *pInsertionAllowed* parameter, the snap-in can fill a **CONTEXTMENUITEM** structure for the menu item it wants to add ("Space based") and then add it to the context menu by calling **AddItem** on the **IContextMenuCallback** interface passed to **CComponentData::AddMenuItems** by MMC and internally passed on to **CSpaceVehicle::OnAddMenuItems**.

C++ Snap-ins

The last set of interactions depicted in the sequence diagram occur when the user chooses the **Space based** item on the **New** submenu. Since items on the **New** submenu are added by the snap-in's **IComponentData** implementation (**CComponentData**), MMC calls **CComponentData::Command** with the same command identifier (*lCommandID*) that the snap-in assigned to the item in its **CONTEXTMENUITEM** structure when it added the item.

```
HRESULT CComponentData::Command(
                        /* [in] */ long lCommandID,
                        /* [in] */ LPDATAOBJECT piDataObject)
{
 CDelegationBase *base = GetOurDataObject(piDataObject)->
                        GetBaseNodeObject();

  return base->OnMenuCommand(m_ipConsole, lCommandID);
}
```

As was the case for **CComponent::AddMenuItems**, the **CComponent::Command** method delegates the processing of the context menu item selection to the object that represents the selected scope or result item. In the case of the "Future Vehicles" item, this object is **CSpaceVehicle**, and it processes the item selection in its **OnAddMenuItems** method:

```
HRESULT CSpaceVehicle::OnMenuCommand(IConsole *pConsole, long
↪ lCommandID)
{
  switch (lCommandID)
  {
  case IDM_NEW_SPACE:
      pConsole->MessageBox(_T("Create a new space vehicle"),
              _T("Menu Command"), MB_YESNO|MB_ICONQUESTION, NULL);
      break;
  }

  return S_OK;
}
```

In this specific implementation of the **IExtendContextMenu::Command** method, the snap-in opens a message box indicating that the context menu item was selected.

Sample F: MenuBtn

The MenuBtn sample demonstrates how to add a menu button control and a menu button to a snap-in. The sample implements the **IExtendControlbar** interface to add a menu button control and then uses the **IExtendToolbar** interface to add the menu button.

The menu button control and menu button are created when the user selects the "Future Vehicles" scope item. The menu button is attached when the user selects a "Rocket" result item.

For detailed information about menu buttons, see Chapter 22, "Working with Toolbars and Menu Buttons."

Sample G: Toolbar

The Toolbar sample demonstrates how to add a toolbar control and toolbar buttons to a snap-in. The sample implements the **IExtendControlbar** interface to add a toolbar control and then uses the **IExtendToolbar** interface to add the snap-in bitmaps and toolbar buttons to the control.

This section uses sequence diagrams written in the Unified Modeling Language (UML) to show the object interactions relevant to understanding the demonstration.

Note that the UML diagrams used in describing this sample explain specific sample implementation details. They do not explain in general terms how MMC and snap-ins work.

C++ Snap-ins

Adding Toolbars

The Toolbar sample adds a toolbar and its bitmaps and buttons to the snap-in when the user selects one of the "Vehicle" result items in the result pane of the "Future Vehicles" scope item. The snap-in creates the toolbar control when its **IExtendControlbar::SetControlbar** method is called. Let's go through the exact sequence of toolbar-related actions that take place in the snap-in. These actions can be grouped into three major steps:

1. MMC queries the snap-in's **IComponent** implementation for an **IExtendControlbar** interface. If the snap-in returns an interface pointer, MMC knows that the snap-in supports toolbars and uses the pointer to call the snap-in's **IExtendControlbar** methods.

2. MMC calls the snap-in's **IExtendControlbar::SetControlbar** method to allow the snap-in to create a toolbar control and add bitmaps and buttons to it.

3. MMC calls the snap-in's **IExtendControlbar::ControlbarNotify** method to notify the snap-in that a scope or result item is selected, or that a toolbar button is clicked.

Let's look at steps 2 and 3 more closely.

The following sequence diagram depicts what happens in step 2 in detail.

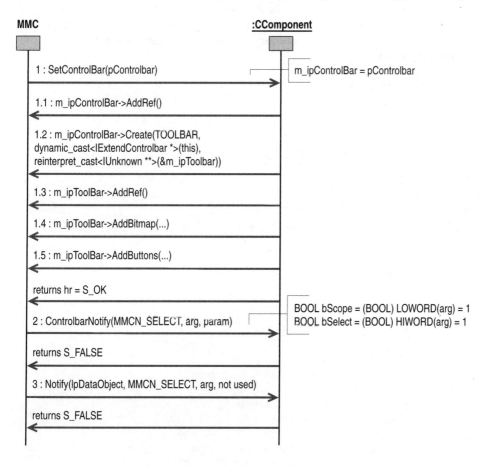

MMC

:CComponent

1 : SetControlBar(pControlbar)

m_ipControlBar = pControlbar

1.1 : m_ipControlBar->AddRef()

1.2 : m_ipControlBar->Create(TOOLBAR,
dynamic_cast<IExtendControlbar *>(this),
reinterpret_cast<IUnknown **>(&m_ipToolbar))

1.3 : m_ipToolBar->AddRef()

1.4 : m_ipToolBar->AddBitmap(...)

1.5 : m_ipToolBar->AddButtons(...)

returns hr = S_OK

BOOL bScope = (BOOL) LOWORD(arg) = 1
BOOL bSelect = (BOOL) HIWORD(arg) = 1

2 : ControlbarNotify(MMCN_SELECT, arg, param)

returns S_FALSE

3 : Notify(lpDataObject, MMCN_SELECT, arg, not used)

returns S_FALSE

When the user selects an arbitrary scope item, MMC calls the snap-in's
IExtendControlbar::SetControlbar method. In the sample, **CComponent** is an
instance of the **IComponent** interface and is the snap-in object that implements
and exposes the **IExtendControlbar** interface. Here is its implementation of
SetControlbar:

```
HRESULT CComponent::SetControlbar(
                    /* [in] */ LPCONTROLBAR pControlbar)
{
  HRESULT hr = S_OK;

  // if we've got a cached toolbar, release it
  if (m_ipToolbar) {
      m_ipToolbar->Release();
      m_ipToolbar = NULL;
  }
  // if we've got a cached control bar, release it
  if (m_ipControlBar) {
      m_ipControlBar->Release();
      m_ipControlBar = NULL;
  }

  //
  // Install new pieces if necessary
  //

  // if a new one came in, cache and AddRef
  if (pControlbar) {
      m_ipControlBar = pControlbar;
      m_ipControlBar->AddRef();

      hr = m_ipControlBar->Create(TOOLBAR,  // type of control
          dynamic_cast<IExtendControlbar *>(this),
          reinterpret_cast<IUnknown **>(&m_ipToolbar));

      _ASSERT(SUCCEEDED(hr));

      m_ipToolbar->AddRef();

      // add the bitmap to the toolbar
      HBITMAP hbmp = LoadBitmap(g_hinst,
                    MAKEINTRESOURCE(IDR_TOOLBAR1));
      hr = m_ipToolbar->AddBitmap(3, hbmp, 16, 16,
                    RGB(0, 128, 128)); //NOTE, hardcoded
                    ↪ value 3
```

```
    _ASSERT(SUCCEEDED(hr));

    // Add the buttons to the toolbar
    hr = m_ipToolbar->AddButtons(ARRAYLEN(SnapinButtons1),
                       SnapinButtons1);

    _ASSERT(SUCCEEDED(hr));
  }

  return hr;
}
```

After caching the incoming **IControlbar** pointer and incrementing its reference count, the snap-in creates a toolbar control by calling MMC's implementation of the **IControlbar::Create** method. In the method call, the *nType* parameter is set to TOOLBAR to create a new toolbar. The *pExtendControlbar* parameter specifies the snap-in's **IExtendControlbar** interface associated with the control. The *ppUnknown* parameter will hold a pointer to the address of the **IUnknown** interface of the new toolbar control. The snap-in then uses this pointer to call the methods of the **IToolbar** interface associated with the new toolbar control.

After calling **AddRef** on the received **IToolbar** interface pointer, the snap-in adds the toolbar bitmaps by calling **IToolbar::AddBitmap**. Note that the snap-in should only call this method once, during which time it should add all its toolbar bitmaps.

The snap-in then adds the toolbar buttons to the toolbar control by calling **IToolbar::AddButtons**. The **SnapinButtons1** array holds the **MMCBUTTON** structures that specify the properties of the toolbar buttons.

```
static MMCBUTTON SnapinButtons1[] =
{
  { 0, ID_BUTTONSTART, TBSTATE_ENABLED, TBSTYLE_GROUP, L"Start
      Vehicle", L"Start Vehicle" },
  { 1, ID_BUTTONPAUSE, TBSTATE_ENABLED, TBSTYLE_GROUP, L"Pause
      Vehicle", L"Pause Vehicle"},
  { 2, ID_BUTTONSTOP,  TBSTATE_ENABLED, TBSTYLE_GROUP, L"Stop
      Vehicle",  L"Stop Vehicle" },
};
```

After the method returns, MMC calls the **CComponent::ControlBarNotify** and **CComponent::Notify** methods to inform the snap-in that a scope item is selected in the scope pane. (Remember that **CComponent** implements the **IExtendControlbar** interface.)

C++ Snap-ins

The snap-in's **CComponent::Notify** method does not handle the
MMCN_SELECT notification message for the selected scope item, so it returns
S_FALSE. Likewise, the snap-in's **CComponent::ControlBarNotify** method
does not handle MMCN_SELECT for the selected scope item, so it also returns
S_FALSE. We'll see below how **CComponent::ControlBarNotify** handles
MMCN_SELECT when a "Vehicle" result item is selected.

We haven't yet looked at how the toolbar control is attached to the snap-in and
how the snap-in sets (and refreshes) the toolbar buttons and processes button
clicks. These actions are all depicted in the following sequence diagram, which
we will now discuss in detail.

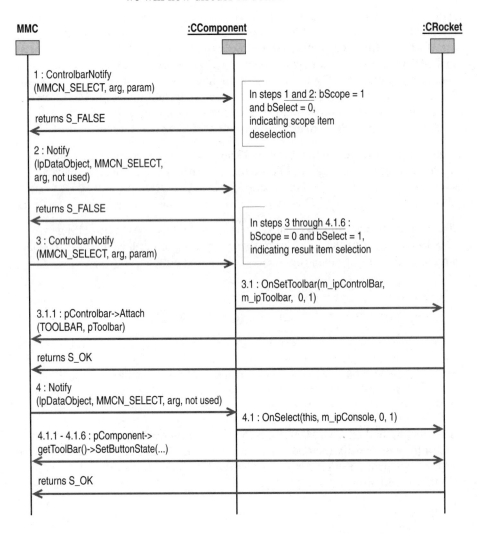

Note that the sequence diagram assumes that the user first selects a "Vehicle" result item in the result pane of the selected "Future Vehicles" scope item. Upon selection of a "Vehicle" result item, MMC calls **CComponent::ControlBarNotify** and **CComponent::Notify** to inform the snap-in of the deselection of the "Future Vehicles" scope item in the scope pane. Again, the snap-in does not handle the MMCN_SELECT notification message for the selected scope item, so both methods return S_FALSE.

MMC then again calls **CComponent::ControlBarNotify** and **CComponent::Notify**, this time to notify the snap-in of the selection of the "Vehicle" result item. The snap-in *does* handle MMCN_SELECT for all "Vehicle" result items. Let's first take a look at the "generic" **CComponent::ControlBarNotify** method that is called when any scope or result item is selected:

```
HRESULT CComponent::ControlbarNotify(
                    /* [in] */ MMC_NOTIFY_TYPE event,
                    /* [in] */ LPARAM arg,
                    /* [in] */ LPARAM param)
{
  HRESULT hr = S_OK;

  if (event == MMCN_SELECT)
  {
      BOOL bScope = (BOOL) LOWORD(arg);
      BOOL bSelect = (BOOL) HIWORD(arg);

      CDelegationBase *base =
          GetOurDataObject(reinterpret_cast<IDataObject *>(param))->
          GetBaseNodeObject();
      hr = base->OnSetToolbar(m_ipControlBar, m_ipToolbar, bScope,
                              bSelect);
  } else if (event == MMCN_BTN_CLICK)
  {
      CDelegationBase *base =
              GetOurDataObject(reinterpret_cast<IDataObject *>(arg))->
              GetBaseNodeObject();
      hr = base->OnToolbarCommand(m_ipConsole, (int)param);
  }

  return hr;
}
```

The **ControlbarNotify** implementation in the sample handles the MMCN_SELECT and MMCN_BTN_CLICK notifications. The **CComponent::ControlbarNotify** method delegates the handling of the notification messages to the actual snap-in object that represents the selected scope or result item. In the case of a "Vehicle" result item, this is a **CRocket** object.

```
HRESULT CRocket::OnSetToolbar(IControlbar *pControlbar, IToolbar
↳ *pToolbar, BOOL bScope, BOOL bSelect)
{
  HRESULT hr = S_OK;

  if (bSelect) {
      // Always make sure the toolbar is attached
      hr = pControlbar->Attach(TOOLBAR, pToolbar);
  } else {
      // Always make sure the toolbar is detached
      hr = pControlbar->Detach(pToolbar);
  }

  return hr;
}
```

As you can see, the sample uses the MMCN_SELECT notification passed in the call to **ControlbarNotify** to attach and detach the toolbar from the toolbar control.

Recall that MMC also calls **CComponent::Notify** with MMCN_SELECT to notify the snap-in of the selection of the "Vehicle" result item. As usual, the handling of the notification is delegated to the **CRocket** object that represents the selected result item:

```
HRESULT CRocket::OnSelect(CComponent *pComponent, IConsole
➥ *pConsole, BOOL bScope, BOOL bSelect)
{
  if (bSelect) {
      switch (iStatus)
      {
      case RUNNING:
          pComponent->getToolbar()-
          ➥ >SetButtonState(ID_BUTTONSTART,
                                      BUTTONPRESSED, TRUE);
          pComponent->getToolbar()-
          ➥ >SetButtonState(ID_BUTTONSTART,
                                      ENABLED, FALSE);
          pComponent->getToolbar()-
          ➥ >SetButtonState(ID_BUTTONPAUSE,
                                      BUTTONPRESSED, FALSE);
          pComponent->getToolbar()-
          ➥ >SetButtonState(ID_BUTTONPAUSE,
                                      ENABLED, TRUE);
          pComponent->getToolbar()->SetButtonState(ID_BUTTONSTOP,
                                      BUTTONPRESSED, FALSE);
          pComponent->getToolbar()->SetButtonState(ID_BUTTONSTOP,
                                      ENABLED, TRUE);
          break;

      case PAUSED:
          //snap-in code omitted here
          break;

      case STOPPED:
          //snap-in code omitted here
          break;
      }
  }

    return S_OK;
  }
```

Each **CRocket** object stores its status (RUNNING, PAUSED, OR STOPPED) in its **iStatus** member variable. The snap-in uses the current status of the selected **CRocket** object to set the attributes of its toolbar buttons, which it does by calling **IToolbar::SetButtonState**. (The sample caches the **IToolbar** interface pointer in its **CComponent** and retrieves the pointer with the **getToolBar** function.)

Let's finally take a look at how the snap-in processes the selection of one of the toolbar buttons. Suppose the "Vehicle" result item is selected and the user clicks one of the toolbar buttons. MMC again calls **CComponent::ControlBarNotify**, this time to inform the snap-in of an MMCN_BTN_CLICK event. The notification is handled by the **CRocket** object that represents the selected "Vehicle" result item:

```
HRESULT CRocket::OnToolbarCommand(IConsole *pConsole, int commandID)
{
  _TCHAR szVehicle[128];

  switch (commandID)
  {
  case ID_BUTTONSTART:
      iStatus = RUNNING;
      break;

  case ID_BUTTONPAUSE:
      iStatus = PAUSED;
      break;

  case ID_BUTTONSTOP:
      iStatus = STOPPED;
      break;
  }

  wsprintf(szVehicle, _T("Vehicle %s has been %s"), szName,
           (long)commandID == ID_BUTTONSTART ? _T("started") :
           (long)commandID == ID_BUTTONPAUSE ? _T("paused") :
           (long)commandID == ID_BUTTONSTOP ? _T("stopped") :
           _T("!!!unknown command!!!"));

  int ret = 0;
  MAKE_WIDEPTR_FROMTSTR_ALLOC(wszVehicle, szVehicle);
  pConsole->MessageBox(wszVehicle,
      L"Vehicle command", MB_OK | MB_ICONINFORMATION, &ret);

  return S_OK;
}
```

The snap-in changes the status of the **CRocket** object based on the button clicked by the user. Finally, an MMC message box is used to display a message to the user.

Sample H: PropPage

The PropPage sample demonstrates how to add a property page.

The "Rocket" result items in the sample enable the properties verb. Upon activation of the verb, a property page appears.

For detailed information about property pages, see Chapter 23, "Adding Property Pages and Wizard Pages."

Sample J: OpenServ

The OpenServ sample demonstrates how to add a wizard page when a snap-in is added to a console through the **Add/Remove Snap-in** dialog box. When a snap-in is added, MMC queries it for its **IExtendPropertySheet2** interface. If the snap-in implements the interface, MMC gives it the opportunity to display a wizard page for allowing the user to specify snap-in-defined configuration information.

The sample displays a **Connect to Server** dialog box when it is added to a console. The **Connect to Server** dialog box is the wizard page.

For detailed information about wizard pages, see Chapter 23, "Adding Property Pages and Wizard Pages."

C++ Snap-ins

Sample K: Taskpads

The Taskpads sample demonstrates how to add taskpads in a snap-in.

When the user selects either the "Bicycles" or "Ice Skates" scope items, the sample displays a vertical listpad in the result pane. A default taskpad is displayed in the result pane of the "Skateboard" scope item.

For detailed information about taskpads, see "Using Taskpads" in Chapter 20.

Sample L: ActiveX

The ActiveX sample demonstrates how to launch a custom OCX control from the result pane of an MMC console. This section uses a sequence diagram written in the Unified Modeling Language (UML) to show the object interactions relevant to understanding the demonstration.

Note that the UML diagrams used in describing this sample explain specific sample implementation details. They do not explain in general terms how MMC and snap-ins work.

Launching the Custom OCX Control

Three objects are involved in launching a custom OCX control in the result pane of an MMC console:

- MMC
- The snap-in's CComponent implementation
- The snap-in object for the scope item with an OCX view. Each child item of the "People-powered Vehicles" scope item display an OCX view.

The following sequence diagram shows how these three objects interact during the launching of an OCX control. In the diagram, the **CDelegationBase** object is the delegation base (and base class) common to all snap-in objects represents scope and result items. For details, see "Samples Object Model" earlier in this chapter.

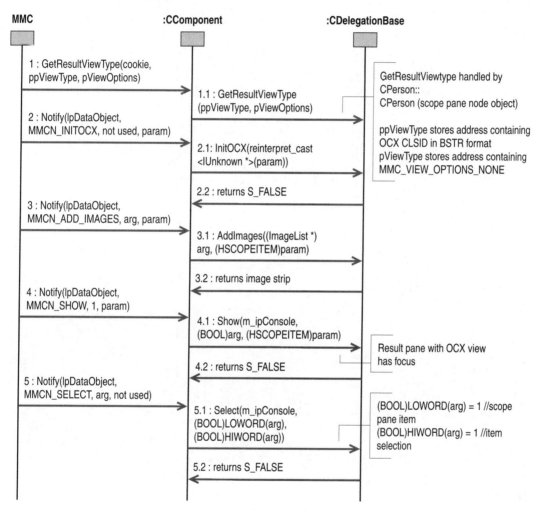

When the user selects one of the scope items with an OCX view, MMC calls the **GetResultViewType** method of the result pane's **IComponent**. The call is then delegated to the snap-in object representing the selected item. In the diagram, this results in a call to **CPerson::GetResultViewType**. Here is the method implementation in the sample:

```
HRESULT CPerson::GetResultViewType(LPOLESTR *ppViewType, long
↪ *pViewOptions)
{
  // for vb component
  // LPOLESTR lpOleStr;
  // HRESULT hr = StringFromCLSID(CLSID_VBComponent, &lpOleStr);
  // *ppViewType = lpOleStr;

  // for atl component
  LPOLESTR lpOleStr = _T("{9A12FB62-C754-11D2-952C-00C04FB92EC2}");
  *ppViewType = static_cast<LPOLESTR>(CoTaskMemAlloc(
                (_tcslen(lpOleStr) + 1) * sizeof(_TCHAR)));

  _tcscpy(*ppViewType, lpOleStr);

  if (m_id % 2) {
      // create new control
      *pViewOptions = MMC_VIEW_OPTIONS_CREATENEW;
  } else {
      // share control
      *pViewOptions = MMC_VIEW_OPTIONS_NONE;
  }

  return S_OK;
}
```

The *ppViewType* parameter is set to point to the address of a string containing the string representation of the custom control's CLSID. The string must begin with an open brace ({) and end with a close brace (}). Note that **GetResultViewType** expects a CLSID for the OCX control when the first character of the string is a brace.

MMC allows a single instance of each OCX type per snap-in instance per view. In **GetResultViewType**, you can either cache the OCX control for a particular scope item and reuse it each time the item is selected, or create a new OCX control each time. To create a new control each time the item is selected, use the MMC_VIEW_OPTIONS_CREATENEW option for the *pViewOptions* parameter. If the option is selected, MMC will destroy the cached OCX and create a new one every time a item requests the OCX view. Otherwise, MMC will display the cached OCX instance for any of the snap-in's items that request this OCX view.

After **GetResultViewType** returns with S_OK, MMC sends the snap-in a series of notification messages. The first, MMCN_INITOCX, allows the snap-in to perform any initialization procedures needed by the OCX control. The *param* parameter passed in the call to **IComponent::Notify** (with MMCN_INITOCX) contains a pointer to the custom OCX control's **IUnknown** interface. The snap-in can use this pointer during MMCN_INITOCX or any other time to communicate with the OCX control.

MMCN_INITOCX is not handled by the scope item, so the snap-in returns S_FALSE in **IComponent::Notify**.

Next, MMC sends the MMCN_ADD_IMAGES notification message. The snap-in handles the message by setting up a collection of images to be displayed in the result pane.

The next notification sent to the snap-in is MMCN_SHOW. Here, the snap-in has a second opportunity to obtain the OCX control object's **IUnknown** interface pointer. To do so, call **IConsole2::QueryResultView**.

Furthermore, during MMCN_SHOW, the snap-in can cache the cookie (of the scope item) passed in the call to **IComponent::Notify** in the *lpDataObject* argument. The snap-in needs the cookie to identify the correct scope item when MMC sends it an MMCN_SELECT or MMCN_DESELECTALL notification message with a special data object (DOBJ_CUSTOMOCX or DOBJ_CUSTOMWEB). MMC sends the notification with a special data object when the result pane is selected or deselected. The only way for a snap-in to identify the corresponding scope item is to use the cookie cached during MMCN_SHOW.

Finally, MMC sends the snap-in an MMCN_SELECT notification with the cookie of the selected scope item. The snap-in doesn't do anything special with this information, so it returns S_FALSE in **IComponent::Notify**.

The OCX control now appears in the result pane of the selected scope item.

C++ Snap-ins

Sample N: NameExt

The NameExt sample demonstrates how to create a namespace extension. The sample adds a scope item to the namespace of the Extens sample.

The NameExt sample extends the "Sky-based Vehicle" scope item of the Extens sample by adding a child item of its own. The sample also creates its own list view and inserts "Extension Space Vehicle" items in the list view.

The "Extension Planes" scope item also has a context menu item added by the extension. Each "Extension Space Vehicle" result item also has a context menu item added by the extension.

For detail information about namespace extensions, see "Extending a Primary Snap-in's Namespace" in Chapter 24.

Sample Q: CMenuExt

The CMenuExt sample demonstrates how to create a context menu extension. The sample adds a context menu item to the context menu of one of scope items of the Extens sample.

The extension's context menu item is added to the **New** context menu of the "People-powered Vehicles" scope item when the user selects the scope item.

For detailed information about context menu extensions, see "Extending a Primary Snap-in's Context Menu" in Chapter 24.

Sample R: PpgeExt

The PpgeExt sample demonstrates how to add an extension snap-in's property page to a property sheet displayed by a primary snap-in. The sample extends Extens sample.

The sample creates and adds its own property page when the user activates the properties verb on a "Rocket" result item. The Extens sample does not add any of its own property pages.

For detailed information about property page extensions, see "Extending a Primary Snap-in's Property Sheet" in Chapter 24.

Sample S: TBarExt

The TBarExt sample demonstrates how to create a toolbar extension. The sample extends the Extens sample.

TBarExt creates a toolbar control and adds toolbar buttons when the user selects the "Future Vehicles" scope item in the Extens sample. The toolbar control is attached when the user selects a "Rocket" result item.

For detailed information about toolbar extensions, see "Extending a Primary Snap-in's Control Bar" in Chapter 24.

Sample W: Complete

The Complete sample implements an array of features in a single sample. Specifically, the sample demonstrates the following:

- The sample implements the IExtendPropertySheet2, IExtendContextMenu, IExtendControlbar, and ISnapinAbout interfaces for adding property page, context menu, toolbar and About information functionality.

- The sample enables the delete, rename, refresh, and properties verbs for "Rocket" result items.

- The sample updates all open views when:

    - Any of the "Rocket" result item verbs are activated.

    - Any of the toolbar buttons are pressed

    - The user clicks the **New Future Vehicle** context menu item of the "Future Vehicles" scope item.

The **New Future Vehicle** context menu item is added to the **New** context menu of the "Future Vehicles" scope item.

The "Rocket" result items enable the properties verb. Upon activation of the verb, a property page appears.

The sample creates a toolbar control and adds buttons when the user selects the "Future Vehicles" scope item. The toolbar is attached when the user selects a "Rocket" result item.

C++ Snap-ins

Sample X: CutCopy

The CutCopy sample demonstrates how to add drag-and-drop functionality in a snap-in.

The sample enables the cut, copy, paste, and delete verbs for "Rocket" result items. Items can be cut/copied in the result pane of one "Space Station" scope item and pasted in the result pane of another "Space Station." The snap-in also supports cutting or copying a "Space Station" scope item and pasting it in another "Space Station" scope item.

Note that drag and drop works automatically in snap-ins that enable the cut, copy and paste verbs and handle the MMCN_QUERY_PASTE, MMCN_PASTE, and MMCN_CUTORMOVE notifications.

For detailed information about implementing drag and drop, see "Drag and Drop" in Chapter 25.

Note that the sample also demonstrates how to update all views when the user performs a drag-and-drop operation or changes the display name of "Rocket" result items.

Sample Y: MultiSel

The MultiSel sample demontrates how to add multiselection functionality in a snap-in.

Multiselection is allowed for all "Rocket" result items in the sample. To implement multiselection, the sample supports the CCF_OBJECT_TYPES_IN_MULTI_SELECT clipboard format and handles the case when it receives the MMC_MULTI_SELECT_COOKIE special cookie in its **IComponent::QueryDataObject** implementation.

The sample demonstrates multiselection in the context of deleting multiple result items in a result pane. Note that the sample also demonstrates how to update all views after the user deletes one or more result items.

For detailed information about implementing multiselection, see "Multiselection" in Chapter 25.

Sample Z: WMI

The WMI sample is an MMC stand-alone snap-in that shows you how to integrate WMI and MMC. The snap-in enumerates instances of the **Bicycle** class and displays them in the result pane. You can select an instance from the result pane and use the **Properties** dialog box to modify its property values. The sample also shows you how to use event notification in MMC to keep the displayed data current.

The WMI-related code for this sample is contained in the People.cpp and People.h files that are part of the WMI sample. The sample uses three classes: **CEventSink**, **CBicycleFolder**, and **CBicycle**. The **CEventSink** class is the sink that receives the asynchronous event notification calls. It contains the **Indicate** method that triggers a refresh of the **Bicycle** instance data when a new instance is created in the repository. The sink is created in **CBicycleFolder::RegisterEventSink**.

The **root\Vehicles** namespace is created by compiling the Vehicles.mof MOF file that is part of the WMI sample. To compile the Vehicles.mof file, first make sure that the WMI service is properly installed and running. Then, run the following command in a command prompt from within the WMI sample directory *before* loading the sample in an MMC console. Here we assume that that the WMI sample is located in the C:\Platform SDK\Samples\SysMgmt\MMC\WMI directory:

```
wmi_sample_dir:\>MOFComp Vehicles.mof
```

Note that the MOFComp.exe executable file is installed in the system32\wbem directory. For details about MOF files and the MOFComp compiler, see the "Managed Object Format (MOF) Language" topic and related topics in the WMI section of the Platform SDK documentation.

Also note that the WMI core components (including MOFComp.exe) are a standard part of the Microsoft Windows 2000 operating system, but not the Windows NT 4.0 or Windows 95/98 operating systems. The WMI core components for Windows NT 4.0 and Windows 95/98 can be downloaded from:

http://msdn.microsoft.com/developer/sdk/wmisdk/default.asp

The **CBicycleFolder** class represents the "Bicycle" scope item in the scope pane. **CBicycleFolder** is responsible for a majority of the work, such as connecting to WMI, registering for WMI event notification, enumerating the bicycle data, and listing the bicycle data in the results pane.

The sample connects to the **root\Vehicles** namespace on a background thread in **CBicycleFolder::ThreadProc** so that a potentially slow connection does not block the rest of the snap-in's user interface.

CBicycleFolder::ThreadProc implmentation

```
...
CoInitialize(NULL);

while(true)
{
    WaitForSingleObject(pThis->m_doWork, -1);

    switch(pThis->m_threadCmd)
    {
    case CT_CONNECT:
        {
            IWbemLocator *pLocator = 0;
            HRESULT hr;

            // Create an instance of the WbemLocator interface.
            hr = CoCreateInstance(CLSID_WbemLocator,
                NULL, CLSCTX_INPROC_SERVER,
                IID_IWbemLocator, (LPVOID *)&pLocator);
            if(SUCCEEDED(hr))
            {
                hr = pLocator->ConnectServer(L"root\\Vehicles",
                                            // Network
                            NULL,           // User
                            NULL,           // Password
                            NULL,           // Locale
                            0,              // Security Flags
                            NULL,           // Authority
                            NULL,           // Context
                            &pThis->m_realWMI);  // Namespace

                // tell the callback the result of the connection.
                if(pThis->m_connectHwnd)
                    PostMessage(pThis->m_connectHwnd,
                    WM_WMI_CONNECTED, hr, 0);
            }
        }
        break;
```

```
case CT_GET_PTR:
    if(pThis->m_realWMI != NULL)
    {
        hr = CoMarshalInterThreadInterfaceInStream(
            IID_IWbemServices,
            pThis->m_realWMI,
            &(pThis->m_pStream));
    }

    SetEvent(pThis->m_ptrReady);
    break;

case CT_EXIT:
    if(pThis->m_realWMI != NULL)
    {
        pThis->m_realWMI->Release();
        pThis->m_realWMI = 0;
    }
    SetEvent(pThis->m_ptrReady);
    return 0;
    break;

} //endswitch

} //endwhile(true)

return 0;
}
```

Once the connection is made, the background thread sends a
WM_WMI_CONNECTED message to **CBicycleFolder::WindowProc** so that
flow control switches back to MMC's main thread. This message handler calls
GetPtr to marshal the **IWbemServices** pointer so that it can be used in MMC's
main thread. This handler then uses the marshaled pointer to retrieve bicycle
information from WMI.

CBicycleFolder::WindowProc implementation

```
...
    switch (uMsg)    {
    case WM_WMI_CONNECTED:
        if(pThis != NULL)
        {
            IWbemServices *service = 0;
            HRESULT hr = pThis->GetPtr(&service);
            if(SUCCEEDED(hr))
            {
                pThis->RegisterEventSink(service);
                pThis->EnumChildren(service);

                // m_pResultData gets set when an onShow has happened.
                // If set, the user already wants
                // to see equipment but the connection was slower than
                // the UI. Catchup now.
                if(pThis->m_pResultData)
                    pThis->DisplayChildren();

                    // done with the marshaled service ptr.
                service->Release();
                service = 0;
            }
        }
        else
        {
            TCHAR errMsg[255] = {0};
            pThis->ErrorString((HRESULT)wParam, errMsg, 255);
            MessageBox(hwnd, errMsg, _T("WMI Snapin Sample"),
                        MB_OK|MB_ICONSTOP);
        }
        break;

...
    } //endswitch

    return DefWindowProc(hwnd, uMsg, wParam, lParam);
}
```

Note that MMC pointers cannot be marshaled to other threads or processes. Since this snap-in needs to simultaneously use MMC and WMI pointers, the WMI pointer is marshaled into MMC's main thread. Generally speaking, you must marshal **IWbemServices** and **IEnumWbemClassObject** pointers to use them is a thread other than the one in which they were created. It is not necessary to marshal other WMI COM pointers such as **IWbemClassObject**, since they are actually in-process.

In addition to the Connection request, the background thread also listens for a Get_Pointer request, which starts the marshaling process for the current **IWbemServices** object pointer when **CBicycleFolder::GetPtr** is called. This thread exists for the life of the node, because it holds the original **IWbemServices** pointer that must exist for the life of the marshaled pointers.

Once a WMI connection is established, the sample registers to receive temporary event notifications for **Bicycle** instances that are created. The sample uses **IWbemServices:ExecNotificationQueryAsync** to register for the event. The event registration occurs in **CBicycleFolder::RegisterEventSink**.

Because snap-ins are DLLs, the sample uses the **IUnsecuredApartment** interface to create a dedicated process for hosting its **IWbemObjectSink** implementation. For more details, see the "Security Considerations with Asynchronous Calls" topic in the WMI section of the Platform SDK documentation.

C++ Snap-ins

CBicycleFolder::RegisterEventSink implementation

```cpp
void CBicycleFolder::RegisterEventSink(IWbemServices *service)
{
  // allocate the sink if its not already allocated.
  if(m_pStubSink == 0)
  {
  CEventSink *pEventSink = 0;
      IUnknown* pStubUnk = 0;

      // create the 'real' sink.
      pEventSink = new CEventSink(m_connectHwnd);
      pEventSink->AddRef();

      // create an unsecapp object.
      CoCreateInstance(CLSID_UnsecuredApartment, NULL,
                       CLSCTX_LOCAL_SERVER, IID_IUnsecuredApartment,
                       (void**)&m_pUnsecApp);

      // give the 'real' sink to the unsecapp to manage.
      // Get a 'pStubUnk' in return.
      m_pUnsecApp->CreateObjectStub(pEventSink, &pStubUnk);

      // from that pUnk, get a wrapper to your original sink.
      pStubUnk->QueryInterface(IID_IWbemObjectSink,
                               (void **)&m_pStubSink);
      pStubUnk->Release();

      // release the 'real' sink cuz m_pStubSink "owns" it now.
      long ref = pEventSink->Release();
  }

  HRESULT hRes = S_OK;
  BSTR qLang = SysAllocString(L"WQL");
  BSTR query = SysAllocString(L"select * from
                              __InstanceCreationEvent where
                              TargetInstance isa \"Bicycle\"");
```

```
// execute the query. For *Async, the last parm is a sink object
// that will be sent the resultset instead of returning the normal
// enumerator object.
if(SUCCEEDED(hRes = service->ExecNotificationQueryAsync(qLang,
                            query, 0L, NULL, m_pStubSink)))
{
    OutputDebugString(_T("Executed filter query\n"));
}
else
{
    OutputDebugString(_l("ExecQuery() failed\n"));
}
//endif ExecQuery()

SysFreeString(qLang);
SysFreeString(query);
}
```

The sink's **Indicate** method sends a WM_REFRESH_EVENT message to the sample's window handler (WindowProc) when a new instance of **Bicycle** is created. This message handler marshals a **IWbemServices** pointer, empties the current enumeration of bicycles (in **CBicycleFolder::EmptyChildren**), creates a new enumeration that contains the new instance(in **CBicycleFolder::EnumChildren**), and displays the enumeration in the results pane (in **CBicycleFolder::DisplayChildren**).

CBicycleFolder::WindowProc implementation

```
...
    case WM_REFRESH_EVENT:
        if(pThis != NULL)
        {
            IWBemServices *service = 0;
            HRESULT hr = pThis->GetPtr(&service);
            if(SUCCEEDED(hr))
            {
                pThis->EmptyChildren();
                pThis->EnumChildren(service);
                pThis->DisplayChildren();

                // done with the marshaled service ptr.
                service->Release();
                service = 0;
            }
        }
        break;
...
```

To see WMI call the snap-in's **Indicate** method and to send the WM_REFRESH_EVENT message, compile the More.mof file, which is also part of the WMI sample, *after* displaying bicycles for the first time in the result pane:

```
wmi_sample_dir:\>MOFComp More.mof
```

After the above command successfully returns, a new bicycle instance is added to the **root\Vehicles** namespace, thus triggering a "refresh" event notification.

The **CBicycleFolder::EnumChildren** method calls **IWbemServices::CreateInstanceEnum** to create the list of bicycles. The sample traverses the enumeration using **IEnumWbemClassObject::Next** to create a simple array that is used later to fill the result pane. Keeping the bicycles in a backing store eliminates the need to re-enumerate the bicycles every time the bicycle folder is expanded.

CBicycleFolder::EnumChildren implementation

```
bool CBicycleFolder::EnumChildren(IWbemServices *service)
{
  IEnumWbemClassObject *pEnumBikes = NULL;
  HRESULT hr = S_OK;

  // get the list of bicycles...
  if(SUCCEEDED(hr = service->CreateInstanceEnum((bstr_t)L"Bicycle",
                           WBEM_FLAG_SHALLOW, NULL,
                    ➥ &pEnumBikes)))
        {
      // NOTE: pBike MUST be set to NULL for Next().
      IWbemClassObject *pBike = NULL;
      CBicycle *pBikeInst = 0;

      ULONG uReturned = 1;

      while((SUCCEEDED(hr = pEnumBikes->
            Next(-1, 1, &pBike, &uReturned))) &&
            (uReturned != 0))
      {
          // Add the bike...
          pBikeInst = new CBicycle(this, pBike);

          m_children.Add(pBikeInst);

          // Done with this object. pBikeInst "owns" it now.
          if(pBike)
          {
              pBike->Release();
```

```
                    // NOTE: pBike MUST be reset to NULL for Next().
                    pBike = NULL;
                }
            } // endwhile

            // Done with this enumerator.
            if (pEnumBikes)
            {
                pEnumBikes->Release();
                pEnumBikes = NULL;
            }
        } // endif CreateInstanceEnum()

    return SUCCEEDED(hr);
    }
```

The user can update a bicycle's properties by using the **Properties** dialog box.
The **CBicycle** class is responsible for creating the **Properties** dialog box and
updating the instance in WMI. When the user clicks **OK** or **Apply** in the
Properties dialog box, the PSN_APPLY message handler, found in
CBicycle::DialogProc, determines whether the property values were changed. If
the values changed, **CBicycle::PutProperty** calls **IWbemClassObject::Put** to
update the property values. After the in-process **IWbemClassObject** is updated
and any values changed, a new **IWbemServices** pointer is marshaled and
IWbemServices::PutInstance writes the updated instance in the WMI
Repository.

PSN_APPLY message handler implementation

```
...
    // if any property changed, write it back to WMI.
    if(changed)
    {
        IWbemServices *service = 0;
        // dialogs run in their own thread so use the marshaling
        // helper to get a useable IWbemServices ptr.
        // NOTE: IWbemClassObjects are in-proc so they DONT need to be
        // marshaled.
        if(SUCCEEDED(pBike->m_parent->GetPtr(&service)))
        {
            service->PutInstance(pBike->m_inst,
            WBEM_FLAG_CREATE_OR_UPDATE, 0, 0);
            service->Release();
            HRESULT hr = MMCPropertyChangeNotify(pBike->m_ppHandle,
                                                 (long)pBike);
        }
    }
```

PART 5

Building Snap-ins with Visual Basic

The Windows 2000 release of the Microsoft Platform SDK is the first release vehicle for the Microsoft Snap-in Designer for Visual Basic version 1.0. Part 5 provides an overview of the Snap-in Designer for Visual Basic and detailed coverage of how to use it to create snap-ins.

A discussion of several sample snap-ins also appears here. The complete code for all the samples is included in the MMC SDK, which resides on the CD-ROM. Part 5 also includes high-level topics from the "Using the Object Model" section which appears in its entirety on the CD-ROM.

CHAPTER 3 2

Snap-in Designer for Visual Basic

The Snap-in Designer for Visual Basic is a development tool that enables
Microsoft Management Console snap-ins to be written in Microsoft Visual Basic.
The following topics provide an overview of the designer's features and introduce
basic concepts.

Software Requirements

The following software is required to run the Snap-in Designer for Visual Basic:

- Microsoft Windows NT Workstation or Server version 4.0 with Service Pack 3
  or later, or Microsoft Windows 2000 beta 3 or later, or Microsoft Windows 95
  or Windows 98.

- Microsoft Visual Basic version 6.0 (no specific service pack required)

- Microsoft Management Console version 1.1 or later

What Is the Snap-in Designer?

The Snap-in Designer for Visual Basic is an ActiveX designer that allows a snap-in to be written entirely in Visual Basic. The designer supports 100% of MMC 1.1 and MMC 1.2 functionality, so a Visual Basic snap-in can do anything that can be done in a C++ snap-in. When the snap-in designer is installed, it is integrated into the Visual Basic integrated development environment (IDE) and it adds a new project type called "SnapIn."

The designer window is used to define most of the snap-in's user interface (UI) and run-time behavior. For behavior that can't be defined at design time, you write code for event handlers in the designer's code window. Examples of events are toolbar button clicks, menu clicks, snap-in loading, and so on. This is similar to using a Visual Basic form and writing code for events that occur throughout the form's life cycle and when the user interacts with its UI. Double-clicking any element in the designer window takes you to the relevant event handler in the code window.

The snap-in's code uses an object model defined by the designer that maps all of the UI elements in a snap-in. This is similar to a Visual Basic form in that the form object has its properties and events, and all of the controls on the form have their properties and events.

Snap-ins can be debugged in Visual Basic's source debugger and they can be compiled into DLLs. The Visual Basic Package and Deployment Wizard can be used to create a setup program for your snap-in.

The designer allows for rapid development of snap-ins and requires significantly less code than C++ snap-ins. Both development and test time are greatly reduced and the learning curve is much shorter for new snap-in programmers. Simple snap-ins such as menu extensions can be written with a tiny amount of MMC "plumbing" code. For example, the ComDetect sample snap-in that extends the FileExplorer sample's context menus contains 35 lines of code and only 8 of them pertain to interfacing with MMC. Much of the very complex code in C++ snap-ins has been vastly simplified so features such as multiple selection in list views require no more than a few lines of very easy coding.

What Is an ActiveX Designer?

An ActiveX designer is an in-process ActiveX object that extends the functionality of the Visual Basic IDE. Visual Basic 6.0 ships with numerous ActiveX designers such as the Data Environment Designer, the DHTML Page Designer, webclasses, and so on. Designers must be written in C++ and they consist of a design-time component and a run-time DLL. Visual Basic defines a special set of interfaces in addition to the standard ActiveX control interfaces that it uses to communicate with designers. These interfaces allow a designer to seamlessly integrate into the IDE and handle such things as saving and loading of the designer's state information, registration, debugging, and so on.

When a designer is installed it appears on the **Designers** tab in the **Components** dialog box from the **Project** menu. When a designer is added to a project it appears like any other project window such as a form or a **UserControl** object. The developer interacts with the designer window to enter as much information as possible to determine its run-time behavior. When the project is saved the designer saves its information into a .dsr file and a .dsx file. This is similar to the way a form saves its information into an .frm file and an .frx file.

When the project is compiled into a DLL, the designer stores all of the settings entered by the developer as well as registration information in the compiled DLL. Visual Basic also stores all of the compiled event handler code in the DLL. The DLL can be registered just like any ActiveX DLL by using Regsvr32.exe.

When the designer object is loaded at run time, (for example, when MMC loads your snap-in), the Visual Basic runtime is loaded and then it loads the designer's runtime DLL and gives it the information stored at design time. The designer runtime communicates with the containing application (Mmc.exe in the case of snap-ins) and uses the design-time information to answer most of the container's requests. When the designer runtime cannot answer a request or it needs to give the snap-in the opportunity to customize the response, it fires an event into the compiled Visual Basic code. The code you wrote for the event handler is run and will typically call back into the runtime using the object model or return a value that tells the runtime how to respond to the container. The snap-in designer runtime implements every method of every C++ interface defined by MMC. Calls into the object model either store information to be returned later to MMC or make calls to one of MMC's interfaces.

Starting a Snap-in Project

▶   **To start a snap-in project**

1. Start Visual Basic 6.0.

2. If the **New Project** dialog box is not open, on the **File** menu, click **New Project**. In the **New Project** dialog box select **SnapIn**.

3. Double-click **SnapIn1** in the Project window to open the designer.

You may notice that in addition to the snap-in designer, the project also contains a user control called **SnapInControl**. This user control does not contain any code or controls. It is used when adding property pages to your snap-in. Do not remove **SnapInControl** from your project. See "Property Pages" in Chapter 34 for more information.

The Designer Window

The designer window displays a tree view in which each node represents a set of properties related to some aspect of your snap-in. It is used to define the characteristics of your snap-in and also serves as documentation of the elements of your snap-in. Selecting any node shows the related properties in Visual Basic's property browser window (usually in the lower-right portion of the IDE). Most nodes have associated property sheets that can be invoked from the context menu or from the toolbar.

The structure of the tree view generally does not map to the nodes that your snap-in will add to MMC's scope pane. It is simply used as a visual tool to organize the properties of the snap-in.

The root node of the tree view displays the name of your snap-in. When a new snap-in project is started it displays **SnapIn1**. You should change **SnapIn1** to your snap-in's name immediately after starting the project.

The Extensions node always has an entry for your snap-in. Using the context menu you can specify which features of the console your snap-in implements (that is, which features of the console it extends). If your snap-in extends other snap-ins' node types, then they will also appear along with the features extended.

The Nodes section describes nodes that your snap-in will add to MMC's scope pane at run time. The Auto-Create section describes nodes that will automatically be added by the designer runtime. This section of the tree view does actually map to the appearance of the nodes in MMC's scope pane at run time. The Other section describes nodes that will be added programmatically by your snap-in (for example, in response to the user expanding an existing node). Any node can have result views and child nodes.

The Tools section contains entries for all of the image lists, menus, and toolbars used by your snap-in.

The Result Views section contains entries for every result view defined by your snap-in. Every result view that appears in the Nodes section also appears in the Result Views section.

Building a Snap-in Project

▶   **To build a snap-in project**

1. Start a snap-in project.

2. On the **File** menu, click **Make SnapIn.ocx**.

3. When prompted for the file name, change the extension to .dll. A snap-in project is derived from an ActiveX control project so Visual Basic suggests an .ocx extension. There is no requirement to change the extension to .dll, but snap-ins generally use .dll rather than .ocx.

4. After the DLL has been built, on the **Project** menu, click **Properties**.

5. Click the **Component** tab.

6. Select **Binary Compatibility**. This ensures that the snap-in will always use the same CLSID.

Deploying a Snap-in

A snap-in created in Visual Basic needs the following components on a target computer:

1. The DLL created by Visual Basic

2. The snap-in designer runtime (mssnapr.dll)

3. The Visual Basic 6.0 runtime

You can use the Visual Basic Package and Deployment Wizard to create a setup program for your snap-in. If you would like to manually deploy your snap-in on a computer that already has the Visual Basic 6.0 runtime installed, do the following:

1. Copy your snap-in's DLL to your target directory.

2. Copy mssnapr.dll to **\Program Files\Common Files\Microsoft Shared\SnapInDesigner**.

3. Use Regsvr32 to register both DLLs. The designer runtime (mssnapr.dll) must be registered *before* your snap-in's DLL. If it is not registered first then registration of your snap-in's DLL will fail.

Note that registering your snap-in's DLL adds all of the necessary entries to the MMC keys under **HKEY_LOCAL_MACHINE\Software\Microsoft\MMC**.

The Package and Deployment Wizard places the designer runtime in **\Program Files\Common Files\Microsoft Shared\SnapInDesigner**. If you create your own setup program you must install the designer runtime in the same directory. Failure to do this could cause installation problems for future versions of the designer.

▶ **When using the Package and Deployment Wizard you can also add a saved console file (.msc) to the package using the following steps:**

1. Start the Package and Deployment Wizard and proceed to the form entitled "Package and Deployment Wizard - Included Files" and click **Add**.

2. Select "All Files" in the **Files of type** drop-down list box.

3. Move to the saved console file (.msc), and click **Open** to add the file.

4. Proceed to the form entitled "Package and Deployment Wizard - Start Menu Items" and click **New Item**.

5. In the **Target** drop-down list box, click to select the .msc file.

6. In the **Name** text box, enter the name you want for your icon, and click **OK**.

7. Finish the Package and Deployment Wizard.

When the application is installed, the icon for the console file will be created in the **Programs** submenu of the **Start** menu.

Debugging a Snap-in

A snap-in can be debugged like any other Visual Basic project. Set your breakpoints and press F5 or click the run button on the toolbar. Visual Basic will prompt for the program to run for debugging. There are two options:

1. Click **Wait for components to be created**, click **OK**, and then start MMC manually. During subsequent debugging sessions Visual Basic will not prompt for these options. After pressing F5 you will only need to start MMC.

2. Click **Start program:** and enter the path to Mmc.exe. Visual Basic will start MMC when you close the dialog box. During subsequent debugging sessions Visual Basic will start MMC when you press F5. You can also save a console file (.msc) when running your snap-in and specify its name as a parameter following the Mmc.exe path. Subsequent debugging sessions will then start MMC with your snap-in loaded. To change the debugging settings click **Project**, click **Properties**, and then click the **Debugging** tab.

There are some caveats particular to snap-ins because while your snap-in is running within the Visual Basic IDE, MMC is running in a separate process. This can make things like selection events (for example, Views_Select or Views_UpdateControlbar) difficult to debug because new events are being fired while you step through the initial event. In general, it is advisable to remove the breakpoint and press F5 after stepping through one of these event handlers so that MMC has a chance to process the selection changes. If you do not remove the breakpoint you may find that it is hit repeatedly and you never have a chance to interact with MMC.

C H A P T E R   3 3

Common Development Tasks

The following topics describe the steps for some common development tasks using the designer, along with some sample event handler code.

Creating a Simple Snap-in with a URL Result View

1. Start a snap-in project.
2. In the tree view click SnapIn1/Nodes/Auto-Create/Static Node/Result Views.
3. Right-click, click **Add New Result View**, and then click **URL View**.
4. Click **URLView1**, right-click, and click **Properties**.
5. In the URL text box, type the URL of a Web page that your computer has access to (for example, http://www.microsoft.com) and click **OK**.
6. Click **SnapIn1** at the top of the designer's tree view, right-click, and click **Properties**. In the **Default Result View** combo box at the bottom of the property page click **URLView1**. Click **OK**.
7. On the **Project** menu, click **Properties** and click the **Debugging** tab. Select **Start Program** and type the path to Mmc.exe on your computer (for example, c:\winnt\system32\mmc.exe). Click **OK**.
8. Click the run button (right-facing triangle) or press F5.
9. When MMC starts, on the **Console** menu, click **Add/Remove Snap-in**.
10. Click **Add**.
11. On the list of snap-ins click **SnapIn1**, click **Add**, and then click **Close**.
12. Click OK.
13. Your snap-in should appear under the console root.
14. Click its static node and your selected Web page should appear in the result pane.
15. Close MMC.
16. Return to Visual Basic and click the stop button (square) or on the **Run** menu click **End**.

Visual Basic Snap-ins

Creating a Simple Snap-in with a List View

1. Start a snap-in project.

2. In the tree view click SnapIn1/Nodes/Auto-Create/Static Node/Result Views.

3. Right-click, click **Add New Result View**, and then click **ListView**.

4. Click **ListView1**, right-click, and click **Properties**.

5. Click the **Column Headers** tab.

6. Click **Insert Column**.

7. In the **Text** text box type **My Column 1**.

8. Click **Auto Width**.

9. In the **Key** text box type **Col1** and click **OK**. You have now defined a list view with one column.

10. On the **View** menu, click **Code** to open the code window.

11. In the left combo box click **ResultViews**.

12. In the right combo box click **Initialize**.

13. In the ResultViews_Initialize event handler, type:

```
ResultView.ListView.ListItems.Add 1, , "Item 1 Text"
➥ ResultView.ListView.ListItems(1).ListSubItems.
➥ Add 1, , "Column 1 Text"
```

This event handler is called when MMC is about to display the list view and the snap-in should populate it with display data. The preceding code added a single item to the list view. When the list view is in report mode it will display "Column 1 Text" in its one and only column. When the list view is in any other mode, it will display a single item with the text "Item 1 Text".

14. Click **SnapIn1** at the top of the tree view in the designer window. Right-click and click **Properties**.

15. In the **Default Result View** combo box click **ListView1**.

16. Change **Display Name** to **ListViewTest**. Click **OK**.

17. Press F5 or click the run button.

18. In MMC, on the **Console** menu, click **Add/Remove Snap-in**.

19. Click **Add**.

20. On the list of snap-ins click **ListViewTest**, click **Add**, and then click **Close**.

21. Click **OK**.

22. Your snap-in should appear under the console root.

23. Click its static node and the list view will appear with the single item. Use the **View** menu to switch between view modes.

Creating a Simple Snap-in with an OCX Result View

1. Start a snap-in project.

2. In the tree view click SnapIn1/Nodes/Auto-Create/Static Node/Result Views.

3. Right-click, click **Add New Result View**, and then click **OCX View**.

4. Click **OCXView1**, right-click, and click **Properties**.

5. In the **ProgID** text box, type the ProgID of an ActiveX control installed on your computer and click **OK**. For example, **MSComCtl2.MonthView.2** is the ProgID of the **MonthView** control that ships with Visual Basic 6.0.

6. Click **SnapIn1** at the top of the designer's tree view, right-click, and click **Properties**. In the **Default Result View** combo box at the bottom of the property page click **OCXView1**. Click **OK**.

7. On the **Project** menu, click **Properties** and click the **Debugging** tab. Select **Start Program** and type the path to Mmc.exe on your computer (for example, c:\winnt\system32\mmc.exe). Click **OK**.

8. Click the run button or press F5.

9. When MMC starts, on the **Console** menu, click **Add/Remove Snap-in**.

10. Click **Add**.

11. On the list of snap-ins click **SnapIn1**, click **Add**, and then click **Close**.

12. Click **OK**.

13. Your snap-in should appear under the console root.

14. Click its static node and your ActiveX control should appear in the result pane.

15. Close MMC.

16. Return to Visual Basic and click the stop button or on the **Run** menu click **End**.

Creating a Simple Snap-in with a Snap-in Taskpad Result View

1. Start a snap-in project.
2. In the tree view click SnapIn1/Nodes/Auto-Create/Static Node/Result Views.
3. Right-click, click **Add New Result View**, and then click **Taskpad**.
4. Click **Taskpad1**, right-click, and click **Properties**.
5. In the **Title** text box, type **My Taskpad Title**.
6. In the **Description** text box, type **My Taskpad Description**.
7. Click the **Tasks** tab and click **Insert Task**.
8. In the **Text** text box, type **My Task**.
9. In the **Help string** text box, type **My Help String**.
10. In the **Image Type** group box, click **Symbol**.
11. In the **Font family name** text box, type **GLYPH 100**.
12. In the **EOT file** text box, type **res://mmc.exe/glyph100.eot**.
13. In the **Symbol string** text box, type **4** and click **OK**.
14. Double click **Taskpad1** to go to the code window for the ResultViews_TaskClick event. Enter the following line of code:

```
ConsoleMsgBox "Task clicked: " & Task.Text
```

15. Click **SnapIn1** at the top of the designer's tree view, right-click, and click **Properties**. In the **Default Result View** combo box at the bottom of the property page click **Taskpad1**. Click **OK**.
16. On the **Project** menu, click **Properties** and click the **Debugging** tab. Select **Start Program** and type the path to Mmc.exe on your computer (for example, c:\winnt\system32\mmc.exe). Click **OK**.
17. Click the run button or press F5.
18. When MMC starts, on the **Console** menu, click **Add/Remove Snap-in**.
19. Click **Add**.
20. On the list of snap-ins click **SnapIn1**, click **Add**, and then click **Close**.
21. Click **OK**.

22. Your snap-in should appear under the console root.

23. Click its static node and your taskpad should appear in the result pane.

24. Hold the mouse over the task to see the Help string.

25. Click the task to see the message box displayed in the ResultViews_TaskClick event handler.

26. Close MMC.

27. Return to Visual Basic and click the stop button or on the **Run** menu click **End**.

Creating a Simple Snap-in with Multiple Nodes

1. Start a snap-in project.

2. In the tree view click SnapIn1/Nodes/Auto-Create/Static Node/Children. Right-click and click **Add Child Node**.

3. Click **Node1**, click **Children**, right-click, and click **Add Child Node**.

4. Click **SnapIn1** at the top of the tree view in the designer window. Right-click and click **Properties**.

5. Change **Display Name** to **Multi-Node Snap-in**. Click **OK**.

6. Press F5 or click the run button.

7. In MMC, on the **Console** menu, click **Add/Remove Snap-in**.

8. Click **Add**.

9. On the list of snap-ins click **Multi-Node Snap-in**, click **Add**, and then click **Close**.

10. Click **OK**.

11. Your snap-in should appear under the console root.

12. Expand the static node and then expand Node1.

Creating a Context Menu Extension Snap-in to Display FileExplorer File Names

1. Start a snap-in project.

2. Bring up the property sheet for the snap-in (root of the tree view).

3. Select **Extension**. Click **OK**.

4. Bring up the property sheet for the Extensions node (directly beneath the root of the tree view).

5. Select **lvExplorerFiles** and click **OK**. If **lvExplorerFiles** does not appear, then FileExplorer may not be registered. It can be registered using Regsvr32 or by reinstalling the snap-in designer.

6. Right-click the newly added lvExplorerFiles node. Click **Context Menus** and then click **Task**.

7. Right-click **Tools**, click **Menus** and click **Add Menu**.

8. Right-click the newly added **Menu1** and click **Add Menu**. While the cursor is still blinking, change the name to **DisplayFileName**.

9. In the property browser window, change the **Caption** property to **Display File Name**.

10. Double-click the lvExplorerFiles/Context Menus/Task node to go to the code for the event handler where extension task menu items are added.

11. Enter the following line of code to add your menu to MMC's task menu:

```
ContextMenu.AddMenu Menu1
```

12. In the left combo box in the code window, click **DisplayFileName**. The event handler for menu item selection is displayed. Add the following lines of code to extract the file name from FileExplorer's exported data and display it in a message box:

```
Dim FileName As String
➥ FileName = FormatData(Selection.DataObjects(1).GetData
➥ ("File"), 1, siString) MsgBox "The file name is: "
➥ & FileName, vbOKOnly, "Simple Extension"
```

13. Press F5 or click the run button.

14. In MMC, add FileExplorer to the console. Take all of the defaults in the configuration wizard.

15. In the console, expand FileExplorer until you reach a drive or folder containing files. In the result pane, right-click a file, click **All Tasks** and then click **Display File Name**. You will see the message box displayed in the Visual Basic IDE. In a snap-in that is compiled and run outside of the IDE the message box would display directly in MMC.

C H A P T E R   3 4

Developing Snap-ins

The following topics describe the various portions of the designer window, related coding tasks, and how to use them to create the features of a snap-in.

Defining the Snap-in Properties

The snap-in **Name** is used to identify the snap-in in Visual Basic code and in your project. (It is also used externally as the right portion of your snap-in's ProgID, but you should never need that for anything because registration is handled automatically.)

NodeTypeName is used to identify your snap-in's static node in its registry entry under **HKEY_LOCAL_MACHINE\Software\Microsoft\MMC\SnapIns**.

DisplayName appears in the console's **Add Standalone Snap-in** dialog box and will also appear as the text for your static node when it is displayed in the scope pane or in the result pane.

Provider, **Version**, and **Description** are used in the console's **About** box.

Default Result View is optional and specifies the name of a result view defined at design time that will be displayed by default for the static node if you do not change it dynamically in your code at run time.

Small Folders, **Small OpenFolders**, and **Large Folders** determine the images that will be used for scope items. If you do not want to use MMC's default images you must define three image lists for the snap-in. These image lists are used for your static node and for scope items when they appear in the scope pane. You must define corresponding images at the same index in each image list because you define only a single image index for the static node and for each scope item. If your scope items can also appear in a list view, then you must add the same images at the same indexes to the list view's image lists. An easy way of doing this is to use the same image lists for both the snap-in properties and the list view properties.

Visual Basic Snap-ins

A snap-in's static node is extensible by other snap-ins. When the user interacts with the static node other snap-ins can add child nodes, context menu items, property pages, toolbar and menu buttons, and taskpad tasks. The designer will add a key for the node in the registration database under **HKEY_LOCAL_MACHINE\SOFTWARE\Microsoft\MMC\NodeTypes**. Snap-in developers are strongly encouraged to make all of their node types extensible to allow for future enhancements. Extensibility is a key feature of the MMC architecture and to enable it requires no more than the registration database entry. Snap-ins can also attach data to the static node at run time to give extensions any extra information needed for their enhancements. For more information see "Developing Extension and Dual-Mode Snap-ins" in this chapter. Although it should rarely be needed, if a snap-in must disable extensibility, use the property browser to set **Extensible** to **False**.

Nodes

Nodes are the scope items added to the console's tree view. A stand-alone snap-in always has a static node that is created automatically when the snap-in is added to a console. The snap-in can choose to add children to the static node in response to the user's interaction with the UI or to changes in the underlying data managed by the snap-in.

Nodes can be defined at design time or at run time in your code. When you define a node at design time you must decide whether it will be created automatically or programmatically at run time. Nodes that appear in the Auto-Create section are created automatically as the user expands down from the static node.

The node name defined in the designer is the node's type name. The **ScopeItems.AddPredefined** method is used at run time to add a node using a design-time definition. Nodes can also be defined completely programmatically by using the **ScopeItems.Add** method. Both of these methods add the nodes to the scope pane and are typically called in the ScopeItems_Expand event.

It is possible to define a node at design time under **Nodes\Other** that has automatically created child nodes. **ScopeItems.AddPredefined** is called to add that node, and then the runtime automatically adds all of its auto-create children as the node and any of its descendants are subsequently expanded.

Nodes that are not auto-create can be grouped as desired under **Nodes\Other**. For example, suppose that whenever your snap-in creates NodeB it is always as a child of NodeA but neither node is auto-create. You can choose to place NodeB as a child of NodeA in the designer for organizational purposes only.

At run time, every node created by your snap-in has a **ScopeItem** object that is a member of the **ScopeItems** collection. A node defined at design time is essentially a template for a **ScopeItem** because it defines the initial values of the **ScopeItem**'s properties. A scope item can be displayed in MMC's tree view in the scope pane or it can be displayed in the result pane when its parent displays a list view. (Even the static node can appear in the result pane when MMC's "Console Root" node is selected in the scope pane.) When a scope item is displayed in its parent's list view in report mode, you must define the data that is displayed in the columns of the list view. To define column headers for a **ScopeItem**, display the properties for a node in the designer and click the **Column Headers** tab. The definitions are the same as for a list view. The column headers defined for a scope item must use the same keys as those of the list view in which they will appear.

All nodes are extensible by other snap-ins. When the user interacts with a node, other snap-ins can add child nodes, context menu items, property pages, toolbar and menu buttons, and taskpad tasks. The designer will add a key for the node in the registration database under **HKEY_LOCAL_MACHINE\SOFTWARE\Microsoft\MMC\NodeTypes**. Snap-in developers are strongly encouraged to make all of their node types extensible to allow for future enhancements. Extensibility is a key feature of the MMC architecture and to enable it requires no more than the registration database entry. Snap-ins can also attach data to a node at run time to give extensions any extra information needed for their enhancements. For more information see "Developing Extension and Dual-Mode Snap-ins" in this chapter. Although it should rarely be needed, if a snap-in must disable extensibility, use the property browser to set **Extensible** to **False**.

Image Lists

Image lists are very similar to the Visual Basic Common Controls **ImageList**. Image lists are added under **Tools\Image Lists**. Add your images and choose your mask color the same as you would for a Common Controls **ImageList**. After defining an image list, you can specify it in snap-in, list view, or toolbar properties.

Small bitmaps must be 16x16 pixels. Large bitmaps must be 32x32 pixels. An image list must always contain bitmaps of a single size. Toolbars use only small bitmaps.

Visual Basic Snap-ins

Result Views

The designer allows creating list views, OCX views, URL views, and taskpads. Message views can only be created at run time. Result views created at design time are known as *predefined result views*. You can create the result view directly under a node or in the general Result Views section at the bottom of the designer's tree view. The static node and any number of other nodes can use predefined views. You can also specify the use of a predefined view in your code at run time (see **GetResultViewInfo** in "ScopePaneItems" in Chapter 36).

All result view types can also be defined in code at run time although this is typically unnecessary for types other than the message view.

Result views can be created directly on a node or in the master Result Views section at the bottom of the designer tree view. When an existing result view is added to a node it is added as a reference and shared among the nodes. This means that regardless of where you invoke the result view's property sheet you will be accessing the same result view.

All result view properties include a check box indicating whether to add the result view to the console's **View** menu. If the check box is selected, two other fields are enabled for menu item text and corresponding status bar text. At run time, populating the **View** menu and switching between the result views is handled automatically.

List Views

List views, like image lists, are similar to the Visual Basic Common Controls **ListView**. Column headers and sorting are defined just as in the Common Controls **ListView** except that MMC has no column header icon. Two image lists are required for a list view: one for small icons and one for large icons. The small icons list must contain only 16x16 bitmaps. The large icons list must contain only 32x32 bitmaps. Unlike a Common Controls **ListItem**, a snap-in list item only has one index property for its icon. This means that the large and small images in each image list must correspond.

If your snap-in will display scope items in a list view, then you must also define the scope item images in the list view image lists. These images must be at the same indexes as in the snap-in image lists. As mentioned in "Defining the Snap-in Properties" earlier in this chapter, the scope items and the list view can share an image list.

At run time the snap-in has access to the list view's properties by using **ResultView.ListView**. Use the ResultViews_Initialize event to populate the list view.

All list views are extensible by other snap-ins. When the user interacts with a list item, other snap-ins can add context menu items, property pages, and toolbar and menu buttons. The designer will add a key for the list view's node type in the registration database under **HKEY_LOCAL_MACHINE\SOFTWARE\Microsoft\MMC\NodeTypes**. Snap-in developers are strongly encouraged to make all of their list views extensible to allow for future enhancements. Extensibility is a key feature of the MMC architecture and to enable it requires no more than the registration database entry. Snap-ins can also attach data to a list item at run time to give extensions any extra information needed for their enhancements. For more information see "Developing Extension and Dual-Mode Snap-ins" in this chapter. Although it should rarely be needed, if a snap-in must disable extensibility, use the property browser to set **Extensible** to **False**.

URL Views

A URL view requires only defining the URL that MMC will navigate to in the result pane.

A snap-in may need to use a file:// URL that references an HTML file in the snap-in DLL's directory or relative to that directory. For more information see "Using Relative URLs" in Chapter 35.

OCX Views

An OCX view requires defining the ProgID of the control that will be displayed in the result pane. In your code, you can access the control in **ResultView.Control** starting from the ResultViews_InitializeControl event and continuing until the result view is destroyed following the ResultViews_Terminate event.

Your snap-in can indicate to MMC whether to create a single instance of the control and cache it or to create a new instance of the control every time it is used. To change this setting, select the OCX view's node in the tree view and use the property browser to set the **AlwaysCreateNewOCX** property. Note that if **AlwaysCreateNewOCX=False** then the snap-in will receive the ResultViews_InitializeControl event only once when the control is created. For subsequent uses of the OCX view, the snap-in can access **ResultView.Control** starting from the ResultViews_Activate event.

Snap-in Taskpads

All aspects of a snap-in taskpad can be defined at design time. Taskpads require the use of bitmaps, GIF files, and font files in resources. These can be added to the project using the Visual Basic Resource Editor add-in. For custom taskpads, the HTML file should also be stored as a resource. See "Using Resources in Taskpads" in this chapter for more information.

One option particular to taskpads is a check box indicating whether the taskpad should be used in the case where the user has selected the console option "Show taskpad views by default" in MMC 1.1. (This option is not in MMC 1.2.) If a node has both taskpads and non-taskpads, it can specify a non-taskpad as its default result view. The non-taskpad will be displayed if the user has not set the console option. If the user has set the option then the taskpad will be displayed.

If the node has multiple taskpads defined, then one of them must have "Use when taskpad preferred" selected. When the user has set the console option, the runtime will choose this taskpad regardless of the node's default result view.

At run time the snap-in has access to the taskpad's properties by using **ResultView.Taskpad**. This object has a **Tasks** collection that defines the tasks. A snap-in can change a taskpad's properties at run time in the ResultViews_Initialize event.

A list view taskpad can be designated horizontal or vertical (the default) by selecting the taskpad in the designer and setting **ListpadStyle** in the property browser. **ListpadStyle** can also be set at run time in the ResultViews_Initialize event.

A snap-in can define a taskpad and decide at run time to display only a subset of its tasks. This can be controlled by setting the **Task.Visible** property in ResultViews_Initialize.

If a task is defined using the **Notify** option, then the ResultViews_TaskClick event is fired when the user clicks the task. For list view taskpads, the ResultViews_ListpadButtonClick event is fired when the user clicks the listpad button. If a custom taskpad uses **MMCCtrl.Notify** to call into the snap-in, the ResultViews_TaskNotify event is fired.

Using Resources in Taskpads

MMC requires that taskpads store bitmaps, GIF files, font files, and custom taskpad HTML files as resources within the snap-in's DLL. This can be done for Visual Basic snap-ins by using the Visual Basic Resource Editor add-in. An *add-in* is a program that can be activated from the Visual Basic IDE that has access to everything in your project. To activate the Resource Editor add-in click **Add-In Manager** on the **Add-Ins** menu. In the **Add-In Manager** dialog box click **VB 6 Resource Editor** and select **Loaded** or **Load on Startup**. In the project window right-click and click **Add/Resource File**. The Resource Editor will prompt for a file name and create a .res file that will become part of the project.

To use a bitmap in a taskpad, add it to your resource file and change the suggested resource ID to a meaningful name, for example, MyBitmap. To use the bitmap in the taskpad specify it as #2/MyBitmap. The #2 indicates that the resource is a bitmap.

To use a GIF, font file, or custom taskpad HTML file, add it as a custom resource. To specify the resource in taskpad properties use the prefix CUSTOM/. For example, to use a GIF added as a custom resource named MyGif, specify CUSTOM/MyGif.

Snap-ins can also use resources that are within Mmc.exe. For example, MMC has a symbol font called "Glyph 100" that can be used for task images defined by a symbol string. To specify an MMC resource use "res://mmc.exe/<*resource name*>". For example, to use the Glyph 100 font for a symbol string specify "res://mmc.exe/glyph100.eot". The designer runtime will determine the full path of Mmc.exe and expand the URL before it is returned to MMC.

Message Views

When running under MMC 1.2 snap-ins can also use message views. A message view is a simple ActiveX control supplied by MMC that displays an icon, a title, and some message text. This can be useful when a snap-in needs to display an error message or other simple textual information in response to the selection of a scope item in the scope pane. For example, if selecting a scope item causes a lengthy asynchronous operation to fetch the data for the result pane, the snap-in should display a message view explaining the situation. When the data finally arrives, if the same scope item is still selected, then the snap-in can change the result view and display the data.

To display a message view call **ScopePaneItem.DisplayMessageView** or handle the ScopePaneItems_GetResultViewInfo event and return **siMessageView**. Using either technique, a snap-in can change the message view's parameters before MMC displays them by handling the ResultViews_Activate event and accessing **ResultView.MessageView**. A message view's parameters can also be changed at any time while it is displayed in the result view. This can be useful in the scenario described above to display progress updates to the user.

Toolbars

Toolbars are similar to the Visual Basic Common Controls **Toolbar**. An image list must be defined and specified in the toolbar's general property page. Buttons are defined exactly as for a Common Controls **Toolbar**.

The toolbar is added to the console in the Views_SetControlbar event. An **MMCControlbar** object is passed to the event. Call the **Attach** method passing the toolbar.

The toolbar's state can be updated upon a selection change by handling the Views_UpdateControlbar event. This allows enabling/disabling/adding/removing buttons. Toolbars can also be changed in response to other events such as menu clicks. Toolbar button clicks are handled as for a Common Controls **Toolbar** in the *<ToolbarName>*_ButtonClick event.

Menu Buttons

Snap-ins are generally encouraged to use MMC's context menus, but they can also add menu buttons to the MMC control bar. Menu buttons are created the same way as the Visual Basic Common Controls **Toolbar**. You define a menu button by adding a button to a toolbar and giving it the **DropDown** style. The **ButtonMenu** objects that define the items on the menu button are specified at the bottom of the property page. A toolbar that contains **DropDown** buttons must contain only buttons of that style. This restriction, which does not occur in the Common Controls **Toolbar**, is due to the fact that MMC does not allow mixing toolbar buttons and menu buttons.

The menu button is added to the console in the Views_SetControlbar event. An **MMCControlbar** object is passed to the event. Call the **Attach** method passing the toolbar object that defines the menu button(s).

A menu button's state can be updated upon a selection change by handling the Views_UpdateControlbar event. This allows enabling/disabling/adding/removing menu buttons. When a menu button is clicked, the <*ToolbarName*>_ButtonDropDown event is fired. That event is used to enable/disable/add/remove individual menu items by manipulating the button's **ButtonMenus** collection. Following that event, the drop-down menu is displayed and, if the user clicks an item, the <*ToolbarName*>_ButtonMenuClick event is fired.

Menus

Menus are handled similarly to the way pop-up menus are created using the Visual Basic intrinsic menu control. The Visual Basic Menu Editor is not used for snap-ins. Instead, the menu definitions are done directly in the designer's tree view. To add a menu, right-click **Tools/Menus** and click **Add Menu** or click the menu button on the toolbar. This action creates a containing menu that will hold the items to be displayed at a given insertion point in MMC's context menu. The containing menu itself is not displayed at run time.

Right-click **Menu1** and click **Add Menu** or click the menu button on the toolbar. This action creates the first menu item. Menu nodes can be demoted/promoted and moved up or down using the arrows on the toolbar.

The **MMCMenu** object represents both containing menus and menu items. To set the properties for a menu item, select it in the tree view and use the property browser. In particular, you should set the **Caption** property to something meaningful. **Caption** determines the text that will be displayed in MMC's context menu. For more information see "MMCMenu" in Chapter 36.

To use a menu, you must write a line of code to add it to the context menu. There are several events that allow adding menus to the various insertion points for primary snap-ins:

- Views_AddTopMenuItems
- Views_AddTaskMenuItems
- Views_AddNewMenuItems
- Views_AddViewMenuItems

For extension snap-ins, the events are:

- ExtensionSnapIn_AddNewMenuItems
- ExtensionSnapIn_AddTaskMenuItems

These events are fired when MMC gives the snap-in the opportunity to add menu items to the corresponding insertion point in its context menu. For example, when the user right-clicks a scope item, MMC displays a context menu that includes a **New** submenu. The snap-in will receive the Views_AddNewMenuItems event to allow it to add items to that submenu.

In all the events, a **ContextMenu** object is passed. Call the **AddMenu** method to add the containing menu. As mentioned previously, the containing menu will not appear at run time but all of its contained items will be added to the insertion point. Note that the **ContextMenu** object can only be used during the event and the snap-in should not store a reference to it.

To handle a menu item click, in the code window, click the menu item name in the left combo box. The *<MenuName>*_Click event will be displayed in the code window. Alternatively, double-click the menu in the designer window and the *<MenuName>*_Click event will be displayed in the code window.

Alternatively, the event can be handled in the *<ContainingMenuName>*_Click event. In this case you must examine the *Index* parameter to determine which item was clicked.

At run time, menu items can be disabled/grayed/hidden/checked by changing the properties of the **MMCMenu** object before calling **ContextMenu.AddMenu**.

Items can be added to a menu at run time by calling **MMCMenu.Children.Add**. For dynamic menu items added to an existing menu, it is easiest to handle the click event on the containing menu. It is also possible to handle the event on the new menu item itself by declaring a module-level variable of type **MMCMenu** using **Dim WithEvents**. Assign the object returned from **MMCMenu.Children.Add** to this variable.

Submenus can be added to a menu at run time by calling
MMCMenu.Children.Add and then adding children to that new **MMCMenu**
object. To handle the events on the submenu use a module-level variable and **Dim
WithEvents** as described above.

A snap-in can define completely new menus in code by using **Dim WithEvents**
as described above and passing that **MMCMenu** object to **ContextMenu.Add**.
Menu items and submenus are added to the menu the same way as for menus
defined at design time.

Property Pages

Property pages are added to the project just as for a user control. On the **Project**
menu, click **Add Property Page**. The property page design and UI-handling code
are done exactly as for a user control. The only significant difference is that in the
PropertyPage_SelectionChanged event, **SelectedControls** contains the
ScopeItem(s) and/or **MMCListItem**(s) for which properties are being displayed.
The property page can store a reference to the **ScopeItem**(s) and/or
MMCListItem(s) in module-level variables to be used when the user interacts
with the property page.

For the property page to be registered, it must be associated with **SnapInControl**,
the user control that is part of every snap-in project. Open the control and in the
property browser select the **Property Pages** property and click the **...** button.
Select the check boxes for your property pages. Do not select any of the stock
property pages. If your project directory contains more than one snap-in, you must
change the name of the additional **SnapInControl** source files from SnapIn.ctl to
a name of your choice. Do not change the name of the control itself.

Primary snap-ins can enable the user to invoke properties for scope items and list
items by enabling the properties verb in the Views_Select event:

```
ConsoleVerbs(siProperties).Enabled = True
```

When the user invokes properties using the context menu, the toolbar, or
ALT+ENTER, the snap-in receives the Views_QueryPagesFor event. MMC fires
this event to ask whether the snap-in has property pages for the selected item(s). If
True is returned then the snap-in will receive the Views_CreatePropertyPages
event to allow it to add property pages to the property sheet that MMC is about to
display. This event has an *MMCPropertySheet* parameter that is used to add
property pages. Call **MMCPropertySheet.AddPage** for each property page you
wish to add. This object can only be used during the event and the snap-in should
not store a reference to it.

When the user activates another page, clicks **OK**, or clicks **Apply**, the property page receives the ApplyChanges event just as it would for an ActiveX control property page. This event handler serves the same purpose as it does in an ActiveX control for validating the user's input. If the input is not correct then the handler displays a message and sets **Changed=True** to prevent the property sheet from closing. The property page can inform the snap-in of property changes to the selected item(s) by calling **ScopeItem.PropertyChanged** or **MMCListItem.PropertyChanged** and passing a **Variant** containing any accompanying information the property page needs to communicate to the snap-in. These methods will generate the ScopeItems_PropertyChanged and ResultViews_PropertyChanged events. The **Variant** can contain any data type as long as any objects used support remotable interfaces because MMC runs the property page in a separate thread. Note that any object implemented by a Visual Basic class will be remotable.

After displaying a property page for a list item(s) the user may select a different scope item in the scope pane. When this happens, the list view that owns the list item(s) will be destroyed but the property page may be holding on to the orphaned **MMCListItem** object(s). For more information on handling this situation see "Handling Orphaned Property Pages" in Chapter 35.

Property pages can optionally implement an interface defined by the designer runtime called **IMMCPropertyPage**. This interface gives the property page access to extra functionality in MMC that is not part of a standard Visual Basic property page.

Before the page is displayed, **IMMCPropertyPage_GetDialogUnitSize** is called to allow the page to determine its size using dialog units. For more information see "Creating Display-Independent Property Pages" in Chapter 35.

The **IMMCPropertyPage_Initialize** method is called when the page is created following the PropertyPage_SelectionChanged event. It receives a reference to the **MMCPropertySheet** object and the optional *InitData* parameter passed to **MMCPropertySheet.AddPage**. This allows the snap-in to communicate to the property page any extra data other than what is contained in the selected objects. The property page can store the **MMCPropertySheet** object in a module-level variable and use it to dynamically add and remove pages, activate pages, change button states, and request a reboot after the sheet is closed. For more information see "**MMCPropertySheet**" in Chapter 36.

When the user clicks the **Help** button on the property sheet the runtime calls **IMMCPropertyPage_Help**. The property page can call the **MMCPropertyHelp** function (exported from Mssnapr.dll) to ask MMC to display its integrated Help.

When the user attempts to cancel the property sheet by pressing ESC, clicking **Cancel**, or clicking the **X** button in the upper-right corner, then **IMMCPropertyPage_QueryCancel** is called. The page uses this method to decide whether to allow the cancellation request. If it is allowed then **IMMCPropertyPage_Cancel** is called for ESC or **Cancel** and **IMMCPropertyPage_Close** is called for the **X** button.

To display a property sheet in response to an event other than Views_CreatePropertyPages use the **MMCPropertySheetProvider** object. See "Initiating Property Sheet and Wizard Displays Programmatically" in this chapter for more information.

Configuration Wizards

Configuration wizards consist of a series of property pages displayed within a wizard property sheet. The sheet has **Back**, **Next**, **Finish**, and **Help** buttons that can be enabled and disabled by the property pages. Because Visual Basic does not directly support Win32 wizard property sheets, the snap-in designer defines an interface called **IWizardPage** that must be implemented by every property page used within a wizard. Each property page must include the statement

```
Implements IWizardPage
```

at the top of the module. In the code window Visual Basic will add **IWizardPage** to the left combo box and all of its methods to the right combo box. The snap-in must implement each method but it does not necessarily have to write code in every one. The interface has methods that inform the property page of activation and button clicks. Using out parameters from **IWizardPage** methods, the property page can control the user's navigation among the pages. It can also determine whether to display a **Finish** button on each page and the text of that button. See "IWizardPage" in Chapter 36 for more information.

As with regular property pages, wizard property pages must be associated with **SnapInControl**.

Visual Basic Snap-ins

When a snap-in is selected in the console's **Add Standalone Snap-in** dialog box, it will receive the SnapIn_QueryConfigurationWizard event. If the snap-in returns **True** then it will receive the SnapIn_CreateConfigurationWizard event, in which it can add its property pages to the wizard by calling **MMCPropertySheet.AddWizardPage**. Unlike **MMCPropertySheet.AddPage**, this method takes an extra argument that is an object of the snap-in's choosing. This object will be available to the property pages as **SelectedControls(0)** in their PropertyPage_SelectionChanged event. When the user has completed the wizard, the snap-in will receive the SnapIn_ConfigurationComplete event. The snap-in-defined object passed to **MMCPropertySheet.AddWizardPage** is passed as a parameter to that event.

To display a wizard at any other time use the **MMCPropertySheetProvider** object. See "Initiating Property Sheet and Wizard Displays Programmatically" in this chapter for more information.

Initiating Property Sheet and Wizard Displays Programmatically

A primary snap-in can initiate the display of a property sheet or a wizard at any time by using the **MMCPropertySheetProvider** object. This object is available as a property of the current view and can be accessed using **CurrentView.PropertySheetProvider**. See "View" in Chapter 36 for more information.

MMCPropertySheetProvider.CreatePropertySheet creates a new property sheet. The new sheet can optionally omit the **Apply** button.

MMCPropertySheetProvider.AddPrimaryPages causes the snap-in's Views_QueryPagesFor and Views_CreatePropertyPages events to be called. The snap-in should respond just as it does for user-invoked property sheets. To create a property sheet, call **MMCPropertySheet.AddPage** for each page in Views_CreatePropertyPages. To create a wizard, call **MMCPropertySheet.AddWizardPage** for each page.

If the snap-in is creating a property sheet and would like extensions to add their pages then call **MMCPropertySheetProvider.AddExtensionPages**.

To display the property sheet or wizard call **MMCPropertySheetProvider.Show**.

Note Under MMC 1.1 **MMCPropertySheetProvider** cannot be used with the Visual Basic debugger.

For more information see "MMCPropertySheetProvider" in Chapter 36.

Adding Help to a Snap-in

Starting in MMC 1.1, snap-ins can merge their HTML Help (.chm) files with MMC's Help so that MMC can display a single integrated Help system. If your snap-in uses HTML Help then specify the name of the .chm file in the **SnapIn.HelpFile** property. This can be done at design time using the property browser window or at run time in SnapIn_Load. The file can be specified with the full path to be used at run time or with no path. If no path is specified then the .chm file should be installed in the same directory as the snap-in's DLL.

When users select a scope item or a list item they can request Help for the selection by using F1, the toolbar Help button, or the **Help** item on MMC's context menu. For a scope item the snap-in will receive the ScopeItems_Help event. For a list item the snap-in will receive ResultViews_Help. Both events receive the selected item. In a multiple-selection list view the snap-in will receive the first list item in the selection. The snap-in can display a topic in the merged Help by calling **DisplayHelpTopic** and specifying the topic to display. The topic is identified using the following format:

helpfilename::topicfilename

where *helpfilename* is the file name of the snap-in's HTML Help file (.chm) that MMC merged into the MMC HTML Help file (this is the file name only, not the path to the original HTML Help file), and *topicfilename* is the internal path to the topic file within the snap-in's .chm file. The author of the snap-in's HTML Help file determines whether there is an internal directory structure for the topic HTML files or if all topic HTML files are at the root of the .chm file. For example, the following code line shows how to display Help for a scope or result item:

```
ShowHelpTopic "myHelpFile.chm::topics/topic_1.htm"
```

Here, myHelpFile.chm is the file name of the HTML Help file, and topics/topic_1.htm is the internal path to the topic file for the item.

Note that merged Help will not work while running under the Visual Basic debugger.

If the .chm file has hyperlinks to other .chm files then these files can be specified in the property **SnapIn.LinkedTopics**. Topics should be specified as one or more strings separated by semicolons containing Help topics that have hyperlinks from the snap-in's main Help file. Setting this property tells MMC to merge those Help files along with the main file specified in **SnapIn.HelpFile**.

If the snap-in does not use a merged Help file, (that is, **SnapIn.HelpFile** is not set to the name of its .chm), then when the user requests Help the snap-in will receive the SnapIn_Help event. This event has no context information parameters such as the selected scope item. It is the snap-in's responsibility to display Help in response to this event. Snap-ins using an older WinHelp file might choose to display their Help in this manner. **DisplayHelpTopic** cannot be used because it can only display topics in the merged Help.

When the user clicks **Help** on the property sheet the property page can call the **MMCPropertyHelp** function (exported from Mssnapr.dll) to ask MMC to display a topic in the merged Help file. See "Property Pages" in this chapter for more information.

Developing Extension and Dual-Mode Snap-ins

Extension snap-ins extend the functionality of other snap-ins but they are not directly added to a console like stand-alone snap-ins. Extension snap-ins can add context menu items, property pages, toolbar buttons, taskpad tasks, and nodes to the namespace of the extended snap-in. An extension snap-in is only loaded when the snap-in it extends is loaded and the feature it extends is used. For example, when the user displays a context menu in a stand-alone snap-in, MMC builds the context menu, asks the stand-alone snap-in to add its items, and then asks the extension snap-in to add its items. After all snap-ins have added their items, MMC displays the context menu and then forwards the menu click to the snap-in that owns the item.

The sample snap-ins include examples of all the different extension types. FileViewer extends the toolbar, context menu, taskpad, and property pages of FileExplorer. ComDetect extends the context menu. DriveStats extends the namespace.

A dual-mode snap-in can be loaded both stand-alone and as an extension. The FileExplorer sample is an example of a dual-mode snap-in. It can be added to a console to run stand-alone or it can be added as an extension to **Computer Management\System Tools** on Microsoft Windows 2000.

To create an extension or dual-mode snap-in, display the snap-in properties (on the root of the designer's tree view), and choose the snap-in type. Close the snap-in properties and display properties for the Extensions node in the designer window. This will display a list of all the registered node types on your development computer. Select the node type(s) your snap-in will extend. If the snap-in you are extending is not registered on your computer you can add its node type to the list by clicking **Add**.

It is important to understand that a node type can represent either a scope item or a list item added by the extended snap-in. Consult the snap-in's documentation to determine what the node type represents and the format of its exported data.

After closing the **Extensions** property sheet the designer will add the chosen node types to the tree view. Select each node type and use the context menu or property browser to indicate which feature of the node type your snap-in will extend. The designer will add the features to its tree view. Double-click a feature to go to the event handler where your snap-in will add its extensions. To delete a feature or a node type, select it and use the DELETE key, the **Delete** item on the context menu, or the delete button on the toolbar.

All extension events are on the **ExtensionSnapIn** object. These events receive an **MMCDataObject** object (or a collection of **MMCDataObject** objects when multiple selection is enabled and multiple snap-ins are involved in the selection). This object gives the snap-in access to the data exported by the stand-alone snap-in. Visual Basic snap-ins can read any data exported by a C++ snap-in. The data is received by the extension snap-in as a **Byte** array. **MMCDataObject** has a method called **FormatData** that can assign a portion of a **Byte** array to Visual Basic data types. For more information see "MMCDataObject" in Chapter 36 and "Importing Data from C++ Snap-ins" in Chapter 35.

The ExtensionSnapIn_AddNewMenuItems and ExtensionSnapIn_AddTaskMenuItems events are used to add items to the **New** and **All Tasks** submenus of MMC's context menus. Define your menus as you would for a stand-alone snap-in and add them using **ContextMenu.AddMenu**. Click events are handled on the menu object as in a stand-alone snap-in.

ExtensionSnapIn_SetControlbar is used to add a toolbar to MMC when the extended node type is selected. Define your toolbar as you would for a stand-alone snap-in and call **Controlbar.Attach**. Both toolbars and menu buttons can be added. Click events are handled on the toolbar object as in a stand-alone snap-in.

ExtensionSnapIn_CreatePropertyPages is used to add a property page to the property sheet being displayed for the extended node type. Define your property page as you would for a stand-alone snap-in and call **MMCPropertySheet.AddPage**. In the PropertyPage_SelectionChanged event, **SelectedControls(0)** will contain the same **MMCDataObject** passed to **ExtensionSnapIn_CreatePropertyPages**. Extensions for multiple-selection property pages are not supported by MMC 1.1 or by MMC 1.2 prior to Windows 2000 RC2.

ExtensionSnapIn_AddTasks is used to add tasks to a taskpad being displayed by the extended node type. It receives the taskpad's group name and an empty **Tasks** collection. The extension snap-in adds tasks to the collection and then receives the ExtensionSnapIn_TaskClick event when the user clicks one of its tasks. The group name of a taskpad displayed by a Visual Basic snap-in is the taskpad's name in the designer window. This can also be defined at run time using the **Taskpad.Name** property.

ExtensionSnapIn_Expand is called when the extended node type is expanded in the scope pane. The extension can call **ScopeItems.AddPredefined** or **ScopeItems.Add** just as it does for a stand-alone snap-in to add its nodes as children of the extended node. When the user selects the extension's child nodes the events fired are the same as for a node added by a stand-alone snap-in.

In addition to the extension features, you must also decide whether your extension will be dynamic. The **Dynamic** property can be set in the Visual Basic property browser. A dynamic extension is not automatically loaded when the feature it extends is used. The extended snap-in must explicitly tell MMC to load the snap-in.

Stand-alone and dual-mode Visual Basic snap-ins can load dynamic extensions by accessing **ScopeItem.DynamicExtensions** or **MMCListItem.DynamicExtensions**. These properties are collections of **Extension** objects for every extension registered for the node type. The **Extension** object has properties that indicate which features are extended. It also has **Enabled** and **NameSpaceEnabled** properties that determine whether the dynamic extension will be loaded for namespace and non-namespace features.

Printing

A snap-in can allow the user to request printing for selected items by enabling the print verb in its Views_Select event handler. For more information see "Views" in Chapter 36.

When the print verb is enabled MMC displays a printer button on the toolbar and adds a **Print** item to its **Action** and context menus. When the user makes a selection and invokes print the snap-in receives the Views_Print event. The selected items are passed as a parameter to this event. It is then up to the snap-in to determine what and how to print.

C H A P T E R   3 5

Programming Techniques

The following topics discuss various techniques for implementing common snap-in features such as exchanging data with other snap-ins, drag/drop, and multiple selection.

Using Forms

A Visual Basic form is essentially a modal dialog box. (Forms can be modeless, but not within an ActiveX DLL such as a snap-in.) Snap-ins are generally discouraged from displaying modal dialog boxes because the MMC UI is shared. A modal dialog box locks out other snap-ins within the console that might require user interaction. The preferred technique is to use a property page without an **Apply** button. MMC's property page mechanism uses a separate thread so as not to lock out the console UI. A snap-in can display a property page at any time using the **MMCPropertySheetProvider** object. An example of this can be found in the DriveStats sample in ResultView_ListpadButtonClick.

There still may be times when a modal dialog box is necessary and a snap-in can use a form for this purpose. An example of using a form is in the FileExplorer sample when the user invokes "Run As" to run a file with a specified command line. See the subroutine **LaunchFileRunAs**.

See "Initiating Property Sheet and Wizard Displays Programmatically" in Chapter 34 for more information.

Changing the Mouse Cursor

Visual Basic UI code commonly changes the mouse cursor to an hourglass during lengthy operations by setting **Screen.MousePointer**. MMC does not provide a way for snap-ins to change the mouse cursor because the UI is shared and snap-ins should not lock out the user from interaction with other snap-ins in the console. Consequently, **Screen.MousePointer** does not work in Visual Basic snap-ins.

If your snap-in does have some lengthy operation to perform, it should be done in a property sheet if possible. By creating a property sheet programmatically using the **MMCPropertySheetProvider** object, the snap-in can simulate a modeless form with **OK** and **Cancel** buttons. MMC will run the property sheet in a separate thread and the page can change **Screen.MousePointer**.

See "Initiating Property Sheet and Wizard Displays Programmatically" in Chapter 34 for more information.

Asynchronous Population of Scope and Result Panes

Snap-ins may not always be able to populate the scope and result panes at the MMC-appointed times (when a scope item is expanded or when a list view is displayed). Snap-ins can retrieve their data from sources that fire events as data arrives (for example, the **Internet Transfer** control) or snap-ins can poll their data sources periodically. Snap-ins can call **ScopeItems.AddPredefined**, **ScopeItems.Add**, and **CurrentListview.ListItems.Add** during these events but the call must occur in the snap-in module. If the asynchronous event occurs in another module then the handler must call into a public method in the snap-in module that will add the items. The snap-in can pass a reference to itself to a public method in the data collection module where it can be stored in a module-level variable. The following code illustrates this technique. Assume that the snap-in has a class called **clsDataCol** that acquires the data asynchronously.

```
In the snap-in's module (for example, MySnapIn.dsr):

Private m_DataCol As clsDataCol

Private Sub SnapIn_Load
  Set m_DataCol = New clsDataCol
  m_DataCol.SetSnapIn Me
End Sub

Public Sub PopulateMMC(…)
  ' This method is called from clsDataCol when data arrives
  ScopeItems.AddPredefined(…)
End Sub

In the clsDataCol module (clsDataCol.cls):

Private m_MySnapIn As MySnapIn

Public Sub SetSnapIn(TheSnapIn As MySnapIn)
  Set m_MySnapIn = TheSnapIn
End Sub

Private Sub SomeEventHandler(…)
  ' Call into the snap-in so it can add a scope item
  m_MySnapIn.PopulateMMC …
End Sub
```

A snap-in can also fetch data using a separate thread or process. A separate data-fetching process can be written in Visual Basic. The data-fetching project should be an ActiveX EXE and it should have a class that raises events. For example, consider an ActiveX EXE project called **DataFetch** with a class called **Fetcher**. The class defines an event called SendDataToSnapIn:

```
Public Event SendDataToSnapIn(Data As Variant)
```

When the class receives the data and is ready to send it to the snap-in it fires the event:

```
Dim SomeData As Variant
… code that sets SomeData …
RaiseEvent SendDataToSnapIn(SomeData)
```

In the snap-in, reference the **DataFetch** type library using **References** on the **Project** menu. The snap-in declares a module-level variable holding a **Fetcher** object and creates an instance of the object in the SnapIn_Load event:

```
Dim WithEvents m_Fetcher As DataFetch.Fetcher

Private Sub SnapIn_Load
  Set m_Fetcher = New DataFetch.Fetcher
End Sub
```

Creating the object instance starts an instance of DataFetch.exe and returns a reference to the **Fetcher** object. Because the snap-in uses **Dim WithEvents** in its declaration, it must implement the events defined by the **Fetcher** object. When **Fetcher** calls **RaiseEvent**, the snap-in's event handler is called and it can populate the scope pane or result pane:

```
Private Sub m_Fetcher_SendDataToSnapIn(Data As Variant)
  ScopeItems.AddPredefined etc.
End Sub
```

Using a separate thread requires writing a COM object in C++. The COM object should have a default dual interface and define an event interface that is also dual. It must also support **IConnectionPointContainer** and **IConnectionPoint** to allow the snap-in to sink its events. The snap-in code is the same as for the out-of-process example described above. When the COM object is created by the snap-in, it will be created on the same thread as the snap-in. The COM object can create a separate thread to do the data fetching. The COM object can marshal the event sink interface using **CoMarshalInterThreadInterfaceInStream** and pass it to the data-fetching thread so that it can fire the events directly. Alternatively, the data-fetching thread can communicate with the COM object using any desired communication mechanism and the COM object can fire the events.

Coordinating Image Lists

The various image lists used by a snap-in can be simplified by using the same image lists for both the scope and result panes. A snap-in that displays list views must specify five image lists.

In the scope pane these are **SmallFolders**, **SmallOpenFolders**, and **LargeFolders**. These can be specified at design time in the snap-in property sheet (displayed for the root node of the designer tree view) or in the property browser. They can also be specified at run time in SnapIn_Initialize.

In the result pane, the image lists are **ResultView.ListView.Icons** and **ResultView.ListView.SmallIcons**. These can be specified at design time in the list view property sheet or at run time in ResultViews_Initialize.

A list item only uses the result pane image lists. A scope item uses the snap-in image lists when it appears in the scope pane and it uses the result pane image lists when it appears in the result pane.

The easiest technique for keeping images coordinated in both panes is to create three image lists: one each for small, small open, and large bitmaps. Put the scope item images at the beginning of each image list. In the small and large lists, add the list view images following the scope item images. By doing this, the scope item's **Folder** property that is used to specify its image key or index will reference the same image regardless of whether it appears in the scope pane or in the result pane.

Importing Data from C++ Snap-ins

Visual Basic snap-ins use **MMCDataObject.GetData** to import data from C++ snap-ins. The designer runtime uses the **IDataObject** interface to communicate with C++ snap-ins.

When a Visual Basic snap-in imports data from a C++ snap-in, the designer runtime will try both **IDataObject::GetData** and **IDataObject::GetDataHere** with TYMED_HGLOBAL and TYMED_ISTREAM. **MMCDataObject.GetData** has an optional parameter *MaximumLength*. If this parameter is passed in then the designer runtime will ask the extended snap-in for its data by calling **IDataObject::GetDataHere**(TYMED_HGLOBAL) with a buffer of the specified length. If the parameter is not passed the runtime will try various combinations of **IDataObject::GetData** and **IDataObject::GetDataHere** using TYMED_HGLOBAL and TYMED_ISTREAM.

The runtime will try ANSI clipboard format names on all systems and both Unicode and ANSI names on Windows NT and Windows 2000.

The **MMCDataObject.FormatData** method can convert portions of a byte stream from some common C++ data types to Visual Basic data types. The following table shows how to code these conversions. It assumes that the importing Visual Basic snap-in has executed the following code to assign the data to a local variable of type **Variant** and that the data type is at the first byte. When the data type is located later in the array, the second parameter to **FormatData** would specify the one-based index of that location.

```
Dim Data As Variant
Data = DataObject.GetData("SomeFormatName")
```

Exported data type from C++ snap-in	Import in Visual Basic snap-in

BYTE or **unsigned char**	```Dim Bytes As Bytes()```
	```Dim TheByte As Byte```
	```Bytes = Data```
	```TheByte = Bytes(1)```

short	```Dim i As Integer``` ```i = FormatData(Data, 1, siInteger)```
int	```Dim l as Long``` ```l = FormatData(Data, 1, siLong)```
long	```Dim l As Long``` ```l = FormatData(Data, 1, siLong)```
float	```Dim s As Single``` ```s = FormatData(Data, 1, siSingle)```
double	```Dim d As Double``` ```d = FormatData(Data, 1, siDouble)```
BOOL	```Dim b As Boolean``` ```b = FormatData(Data, 1, siCBoolean)```
DATE	```Dim d as Date``` ```d = FormatData(Data, 1, siDate)```
CY	```Dim c As Currency``` ```c = FormatData(Data, 1, siCurrency)```
Unicode string	```Dim s As String``` ```s = FormatData(Data, 1, siString)```

Multiple concatenated null-terminated Unicode strings with double null termination	```Dim Strings As String()```
	```Strings = FormatData(Data, 1,```
	```siMultiString)```

For more information see "MMCDataObject" in Chapter 36 and "Developing Extension and Dual-Mode Snap-ins" in Chapter 34.

Publishing and Interpreting Data Formats from a Visual Basic Snap-in

Snap-ins that have extensible node types must document their data formats so that other snap-ins will be able to interpret their exported data. Documentation should include both the interface methods and the format of the data.

Visual Basic snap-ins always use **MMCDataObject.GetData** regardless of whether the source snap-in is written in Visual Basic or in C++. When a Visual Basic snap-in imports data from another snap-in (regardless of the source), it receives a **Byte** array within a **Variant** that must be converted into Visual Basic data types. **MMCDataObject.FormatData** and **SnapIn.FormatData** perform these conversions. See "MMCDataObject" in Chapter 36 for more information.

A Visual Basic snap-in can also import data from itself. If it calls **MMCDataObject.GetData** within the same instance of itself (for example, during a drag/drop operation), it will receive the same **Variant** that is passed to **MMCDataObject.SetData** and it does not need to call **FormatData**. If a snap-in imports data from a different instance of itself (for example, dragging and dropping between consoles), then it must call **FormatData** to interpret the **Byte** array.

When a C++ snap-in imports data from a Visual Basic snap-in it can use **IDataObject::GetData** or **IDataObject::GetDataHere** with TYMED_HGLOBAL or TYMED_ISTREAM. The designer runtime registers all clipboard format names as both ANSI and Unicode names on Windows NT and Windows 2000 using the Win32 API functions **RegisterClipboardFormatA** and **RegisterClipboardFormatW**. Formats are registered as ANSI names on Windows 95 and Windows 98.

The following table shows data types used in the **Variant** passed to **MMCDataObject.SetData** and how Visual Basic and C++ snap-ins must interpret them. The table assumes that the importing Visual Basic snap-in has executed the following code to assign the data to a local variable of type **Variant**:

```
Dim Data As Variant
Data = DataObject.GetData("SomeFormatName")
```

Exported data type from Visual Basic snap-in	Import in Visual Basic snap-in	Import in C++ snap-in

Byte	`Dim Bytes As Bytes()`
	`Dim TheByte As Byte`
	`Bytes = Data`
	`TheByte = Bytes(1)`
		Read `sizeof(VARIANT.bVal)` into `VARIANT.bVal`.
		`VARIANT.vt = VT_UI1`.

Integer	`Dim i As Integer` `i = FormatData (Data, 1, siInteger)`	Read `sizeof(VARIANT.iVal)` into `VARIANT.iVal`. `VARIANT.vt = VT_I2`.
Long	`Dim l as Long` `l = FormatData (Data, 1, siLong)`	Read `sizeof(VARIANT.lVal)` into `VARIANT.lVal`. `VARIANT.vt = VT_I4`.
Single	`Dim s As Single` `s = FormatData (Data, 1, siSingle)`	Read `sizeof(VARIANT.fltVal)` into `VARIANT.fltVal`. `VARIANT.vt = VT_R4`.
Double	`Dim d As Double` `d = FormatData (Data, 1, siDouble)`	Read `sizeof(VARIANT.dblVal)` into `VARIANT.dblVal`. `VARIANT.vt = VT_R8`.
Boolean	`Dim b As Boolean` `b = FormatData (Data, 1, siBoolean)`	Read `sizeof(VARIANT.boolVal)` into `VARIANT.boolVal`. `VARIANT.vt = VT_BOOL`.
Date	`Dim d as Date` `d = FormatData (Data, 1, siDate)`	Read `sizeof(VARIANT.date)` into `VARIANT.date`. `VARIANT.vt = VT_DATE`.

Exported data type from Visual Basic snap-in	Import in Visual Basic snap-in	Import in C++ snap-in
Currency	`Dim c As Currency` `c = FormatData (Data, 1, siCurrency)`	Read sizeof(VARIANT.cyVal) into VARIANT.cyVal. VARIANT.vt = VT_CY.
String	`Dim s As String` `s = FormatData (Data, 1, siString)`	Read data as a null-terminated Unicode string.
Persisted Object	`Dim o As Object` `Set o = FormatData (Data, 1, siObject)`	Use TYMED_ISTREAM or use TYMED_GLOBAL and create stream on HGLOBAL. Use **ReadClassStm** to get CLSID. Call **CoCreateInstance** and then **IUnknown::QueryInterface**(IID_ IPersistStreamInit). Call **IPersistStreamInit::Load**().
Object Reference	`Dim o As Object` `Set o = FormatData (Data, 1, siObject Instance)`	Use TYMED_ISTREAM or use TYMED_GLOBAL and create stream on HGLOBAL. Use **ReadClassStm** to get CLSID. Call **CoUnmarshalInterface(IID_IUnknown)** and then **IUnknown::QueryInterface** for the desired interface.
Byte Array	`Dim Bytes As Bytes()` `Bytes = Data`	Data is **BYTE** array.
String Array	`Dim Strings As String()` `Strings = FormatData (Data, 1, siMulti String)`	Read data as concatenated null-terminated Unicode strings terminated by a double Unicode null character.

Establishing Two-Way Communication Between Primary and Extension Snap-ins

A common design technique is to use a primary snap-in with one or more extension snap-ins. For example, the Windows 2000 Computer Management snap-in is really a shell that houses numerous extension snap-ins that configure all the systems on a given machine. In a situation where the same organization writes both the primary and the extension snap-ins, it is often desirable to have two-way communication between the primary snap-in and its extensions. This can be done by creating a Visual Basic class in the primary snap-in and adding that class in **Project/References** of each extension snap-in. The primary snap-in should export a data format that holds an instance of the class. The following example exports an instance of MyClass in the data for a scope item:

```
Dim cls As New MyClass

cls.SomeProperty = SomeValue
ScopeItem.Data.SetData "MyClass Format", siObjectReference
```

The extension snap-in gets a reference to the object by using the **SnapIn.FormatData** or **MMCDataObject.FormatData** method. The following example assumes that the extension snap-in received the **MMCDataObject** in a parameter called *Data*:

```
Dim cls As MyClass
Dim v As Variant
v = Data.GetData("MyClass Format")
Set cls = FormatData(v, 1, siObjectInstance)
```

The extension snap-in can then access the methods and properties of the class.

If the primary and extension snap-ins need to asynchronously communicate then the class could also support events and both snap-ins can use **Dim WithEvents**. One snap-in can then call a method that will fire an event that is handled by the other snap-in. For more information on Visual Basic classes and using **WithEvents** see the Visual Basic documentation.

Visual Basic Snap-ins

Using Virtual List Views

Virtual list views appear to the user as any other list view but the underlying code to populate them is optimized for large data sets. List views that contain more than several hundred items generally achieve significant performance improvement as virtual lists. The decision to use a virtual list view should be based on the cost of fetching the data as well as the volume of data. In the case of a remote database query with a huge result set a virtual list view would be an obvious choice. In other less clear-cut circumstances the developer should try both list view types before making a final choice.

In a nonvirtual list view the snap-in typically populates the entire list view in the ResultViews_Initialize or ResultViews_Activate event by calling **MMCListItems.Add**. As the user scrolls through the list view the snap-in does not receive any further events.

In a virtual list view the snap-in typically calls **MMCListItems.SetItemCount** in the ResultViews_Activate event to tell MMC how many items are in the list view. This allows MMC to adjust the scroll bars and calculate the index of the displayed list items as the user navigates using the PAGEUP, PAGEDOWN, HOME, and END keys. **MMCListItems.SetItemCount** must be called before any columns are added to the list view. If the snap-in uses a predefined list view then it should call **MMCListItems.SetItemCount** in the ResultViews_Activate event because the designer runtime will add the columns to MMC when this event handler returns. If the snap-in is adding the columns in code then it should do so in the ResultViews_Initialize event and the snap-in should then call **MMCListItems.SetItemCount** in ResultViews_Activate.

When MMC needs to display data for a list view the snap-in receives the GetVirtualItemDisplayInfo event:

```
Private Sub ResultViews_GetVirtualItemDisplayInfo(ByVal
➥ ResultView As SnapInLib.ResultView, ByVal ListItem As
➥ SnapInLib.MMCListItem)
```

The **MMCListItem** object passed to this event is only used for the duration of the event. The snap-in must examine **ListItem.Index** to determine which item MMC has requested and then set **ListItem.Text**. If the list view might be changed to detail or filtered mode then the snap-in must also populate **ListItem.ListSubItems**. **ListItem.Icon** should also be set at this time.

GetVirtualItemDisplayInfo is fired as the user navigates through the list view. For example, if the user has sized the console such that the list view can display 25 items then when the result pane is created the snap-in will receive this event 25 times. If the user then presses the PAGEDOWN key the snap-in will receive the event another 25 times so that MMC can repopulate the window.

A snap-in can also change the properties of any currently displayed list item by simply referencing it in the **MMCListItems** collection as it would for a nonvirtual list view:

```
CurrentListView.ListItems(23).Text = "Some new text"
CurrentListView.ListItems(23).Update
```

The only difference is that the snap-in must always use a numeric index. Keys cannot be used to reference virtual list items because the items are not actually stored in the **MMCListItems** collection.

When MMC needs the exported data for a virtual list item the snap-in receives the GetVirtualItemData event:

```
Private Sub ResultViews_GetVirtualItemData(ByVal ResultView As
➥ SnapInLib.ResultView, ByVal ListItem As SnapInLib.MMCListItem)
```

This event allows the snap-in to set exported data for extensions in **MMCListItem.Data** and to enable dynamic extensions for the list item using **MMCListItem.DynamicExtensions**. If the snap-in needs to use **MMCListItem.Tag** it should set it in this event.

In virtual list views **MMCListItem.ID** is set to a string containing the index of the list item. If the snap-in needs to set this property it should do so in the GetVirtualItemData event. **MMCListItem.ID** is used by the runtime to determine whether two list items represent the same underlying data. For more information see "MMCListItem" in Chapter 36.

SortItems is called to inform the snap-in that list items will be fetched in sorted order on a particular column. MMC does not do anything for sorting a virtual list view other than firing this event. The snap-in will continue to receive GetVirtualItemDisplayInfo events as needed to repopulate the window but it must return the appropriate data according to the sorting criteria.

The CacheHint event is called to allow the snap-in to begin asynchronous fetching of data for list items that are likely to be displayed soon:

```
Private Sub ResultViews_CacheHint(ByVal ResultView As
➥ SnapInLib.ResultView, ByVal StartingIndex As Long, ByVal
➥ EndingIndex As Long)
```

Visual Basic Snap-ins

Typical usage of this event is to initiate the data fetch for the items from **StartingIndex** to **EndingIndex**. If the data arrives before it is needed then the snap-in can store it in locally until it is requested by MMC. If the user navigates to an area of the list view that is far from the prefetched data then the snap-in can discard it. The snap-in can monitor the user's navigation by examining **MMCListItem.Index** in the GetVirtualItemDisplayInfo event.

FindItem is called when the user searches for items by typing the initial letters:

```
Private Sub ResultViews_FindItem(ByVal ResultView As
⤷ SnapInLib.ResultView, ByVal Name As String, ByVal
⤷ StartingIndex As Long, ByVal Wrap As Boolean, ByVal
⤷ PartialName As Boolean, Found As Boolean, Index As Long)
```

The user is typing characters to navigate to an item based on the value of the list item's text (**MMCListItem.Text**). **Name** contains the characters the user has typed so far. **StartingIndex** indicates which item the search should begin from. **Wrap** indicates whether the snap-in should continue searching from the beginning if it has not found the item between **StartingIndex** and the end of the data set. **PartialName** indicates whether the snap-in should consider item text that begins with **Name** to be a match.

DeselectAll is called when the user deselects everything in the list view so that the snap-in can update console verbs and toolbars.

Note Unlike nonvirtual list views, MMC does not automatically add child scope items to a virtual list view. If the snap-in needs to display a child scope item in a virtual list view, it must simulate it by using the scope item's image and column data for a virtual list item.

Using Column Persistence

This feature is introduced in MMC 1.2. It is not available in MMC 1.1.

Starting with version 1.2, MMC persists column customization and sorting parameters as the user moves between scope items in the scope pane. This allows a user to customize a list view, select another node, and then return to the original node with the customizations preserved. MMC also saves the customizations in the .msc file when the user saves the console and then restores them when the file is loaded.

MMC requires that every scope item have an ID for identifying its persisted column configuration within each view. If the snap-in does not explicitly supply an ID then MMC uses the scope item's node type GUID. This means that if the snap-in has multiple scope items of the same node type in the scope pane, and it does not explicitly set an ID, then the user's customization will be propagated across the different list views. Snap-ins can change the ID by setting **ScopePaneItem.ColumnSetID**. This property is on **ScopePaneItem** rather than **ScopeItem** because it only applies to the display of the **ScopeItem** within a particular view.

Customization affects column visibility, column width, column order, sort order, sort column, and sort icon display. Customization properties are available from **View.ColumnSettings** and **View.SortSettings**.

View.ColumnSettings returns a collection of **ColumnSetting** objects. The **ColumnSetting** object has properties for width, visibility, and position.

ViewSortSettings returns a collection of **SortKey** objects. The **SortKey** object has properties for column number, sort order, and sort icon display. As of MMC 1.2, there can only be one sort key.

If the snap-in needs to persist additional information related to column or sort settings (for example, the columns of a customized multicolumn sort) it can use **ScopePaneItem.Tag** to hold this information. If the snap-in needs to persist this information in the .msc file it should implement the Views_WriteProperties and Views_ReadProperties events. Those events allow persisting data on a per-view basis.

When a snap-in sets properties on **ColumnSetting** and **SortKey** objects, no changes are made to the persisted column data. To change the persisted column data the snap-in must call **ColumnSettings.Persist** and/or **SortKeys.Persist**.

Snap-ins can examine the column persistence data in ScopeItems_Expand, ExtensionSnapIn_Expand, and ResultViews_Activate to determine whether data fetching can be optimized (for example, data for a hidden column need not be fetched). If the snap-in needs to make changes it can change the corresponding properties and call **ColumnSettings.Persist** and/or **SortKeys.Persist**.

Visual Basic Snap-ins

If the user makes any column setting changes while the list view is displayed the snap-in receives the ResultViews_ColumnsChanged event:

```
Private Sub ResultViews_ColumnsChanged(ByVal ResultView As
➥ SnapInLib.ResultView, ByVal Columns As Variant, Persist As
➥ Boolean)
```

The *Columns* parameter contains an array of column numbers of visible columns in the order set by the user. For example, if the list view had four columns and the user moved column 3 before column 2 and hid column 4, then the array would contain the numbers 1, 3, 2. If the snap-in returns **Persist=False** then the changes will not be persisted and they will only affect the current instance of the list view. In this case the snap-in should display a message box explaining why the user's changes will not be persisted.

If the snap-in needs to monitor sorting changes it should handle the ResultViews_ColumnClick event:

```
Private Sub ResultViews_ColumnClick(ByVal ResultView As
➥ SnapInLib.ResultView, ByVal ColumnNumber As Long, ByVal
➥ SortOrder As SnapInLib.SnapInSortOrderConstants)
```

ColumnNumber indicates the column clicked and *SortOrder* indicates in which direction MMC will do the sort.

Another opportunity to make changes is in ResultViews_Deactivate. In this event the snap-in can determine the user's configuration by examining the corresponding properties and then decide whether to make any changes. As in ResultViews_Activate, the snap-in must change the properties and then call **ColumnSettings.Persist** and/or **SortKeys.Persist** to persist the changes.

Using Column Filtering

This feature is introduced in MMC 1.2. It is not available in MMC 1.1.

In MMC 1.2 and later a list view can be displayed in filtered mode. The list view displays an edit control and a small button underneath each column header.

The typical user action is to type text into the edit control and press ENTER. The snap-in then receives the ResultViews_FilterChange event:

```
Private Sub ResultViews_FilterChange(ByVal ResultView As
➥ SnapInLib.ResultView, ByVal Column As
➥ SnapInLib.MMCColumnHeader, ByVal ChangeType As
➥ SnapInLib.SnapInFilterChangeTypeConstants)
```

ChangeType in this case will be set to **siValueChange**. MMC does nothing further in response to this user input. The snap-in can apply the new filtering criteria or ignore the input. If the user enters text and does not press ENTER then this event will be fired after a time-out specified in milliseconds by **MMCListView.FilterChangeTimeout**.

This event is also fired when the user switches in and out of filtered mode using the console's "View" mode. In those cases *ChangeType* will be set to **siEnable** or **siDisable**.

Filter values for a column are considered textual or numeric. The values can be read and written by a snap-in using the properties **MMCColumnHeader.TextFilter** and **MMCColumnHeader.NumericFilter**. **MMCColumnHeader.NumericFilter** is used to set a numeric filter value. The snap-in can also get its value to determine if the user has entered a numeric value in the column filter and examine that value. The **MMCColumnHeader.TextFilter** property serves the same function for text values. **MMCColumnHeader.TextFilterMaxLen** can be used to get and set the maximum length of text the user can enter. To prevent the user from entering a value, set **MMCColumnHeader.TextFilterMaxLen** to zero. If the filter value is blank then both properties return an empty **Variant**. To make the value empty set either property to an empty **Variant**.

If the user clicks the filter button the snap-in receives the ResultViews_FilterButtonClick event:

```
Private Sub ResultViews_FilterButtonClick(ByVal ResultView As
➥ SnapInLib.ResultView, ByVal Column As
➥ SnapInLib.MMCColumnHeader, ByVal Left As Long, ByVal Top As
➥ Long, ByVal Height As Long, ByVal Width As Long)
```

MMC also does nothing in response to this user input. The snap-in should display a pop-up menu using **View.PopupMenu** to allow the user to choose a filter operator. The coordinates passed to the ResultViews_FilterButtonClick event indicate the size and position of the filter button so that the snap-in can display the pop-up menu at the same location.

Implementing Multiple Selection

Multiple selection is possible in list views in which the snap-in has explicitly enabled this feature. It can be done at design time or at run time in the ResultViews_Initialize event by setting the list view's **MultiSelect** property.

Any event that has an *MMCClipboard* parameter can potentially involve multiple items in a list view with multiple selection enabled. The snap-in must simply iterate through **MMCClipboard.ScopeItems** and **MMCClipboard.ListItems** to determine which items are selected. No other action is needed on the part of the snap-in. Supporting multiple selection is only marginally more difficult than supporting single selection because the snap-in must iterate through these collections rather than examining only the first element. The added effort is trivial and snap-ins should support multiple selection wherever appropriate for their underlying data.

MMCClipboard also contains an **MMCDataObject** collection. If the selection occurred in a list view containing child scope items from multiple snap-ins then **MMCClipboard.DataObjects** will contain an element from each snap-in involved. This situation is not common but it could occur when a node is selected in the scope pane that has multiple namespace extensions and it is displaying a list view with multiple selection enabled.

As the user adds items to the selection the snap-in receives the Views_GetMultiSelectData event. This event is fired when the second item is selected and for every item thereafter. It allows the snap-in to export data specific to the multiple selection because the designer runtime cannot export the data attached to each item individually. For example, the FileExplorer sample handles this event by adding a "Folders" format and a "Files" format to the **MMCDataObject**. Each format contains a string array of the folder and file paths included in the selection. Note that the event handler does not need special logic to determine if the data object already contains data from an earlier invocation of the event—it should just set the data formats with the new data relevant to the selection. The designer runtime supplies a new **MMCDataObject** every time this event is fired.

Implementing Drag/Drop and Cut/Copy/Paste

Drag/drop and cut/copy/paste are implemented in a snap-in using MMC events rather than the standard Visual Basic mechanism. MMC simplifies these operations into a single set of events so if a snap-in supports drag/drop then it also supports cut/copy/paste. MMC consolidates everything into two possible operations: copy and move. The events involved are:

- Views_Select. The snap-in determines if cut, copy, and paste are permitted on the current selection.

- Views_QueryPaste. MMC asks the destination snap in whether it can accept a paste operation on a particular scope item.

- Views_Paste. The destination snap-in receives the pasted items. If the operation is a move then it returns information on which items it pasted.

- Views_Cut. Used only for a move operation. The source snap-in receives information telling it which items were pasted.

When the user makes a selection in either the scope pane or the result pane the snap-in receives the Views_Select event. The snap-in uses this event to examine the selection and then uses the **MMCConsoleVerbs** collection to determine the state of console verbs such as cut, copy, paste, delete, refresh, and so on. If the snap-in permits the user to cut or copy the selected item(s) then those verbs are enabled.

If the user starts a drag, clicks **Copy** or **Cut** on the context menu, or clicks the cut or copy toolbar button, then the snap-in does not receive any events. This is handled entirely by MMC.

When the user drags the selection over a scope item owned by the snap-in, or displays a context menu for that scope item, the snap-in receives the Views_QueryPaste event. If the snap-in returns **True** then the paste item appears on the context menu or the mouse cursor changes to the copy icon. As with any OLE drag operation, if the user presses the ALT key the drag cursor changes to the move icon.

If the user drops the selection with a copy cursor onto a scope item owned by the snap-in, or clicks **Paste** on the context menu for that scope item, the snap-in receives the Views_Paste event:

```
Private Sub Views_Paste(ByVal DestView As SnapInLib.View, ByVal
➥ SourceItems As SnapInLib.MMCClipboard, ByVal DestScopeItem As
➥ SnapInLib.ScopeItem, ByVal RetToSource As
➥ SnapInLib.MMCDataObject, ByVal Move As Boolean)
```

SourceItems contains the items being copied. *DestScopeItem* is the scope item to which the user would like to copy the items. *RetToSource* is not used in this case and *Move* is **False**.

The snap-in iterates through *SourceItems* and performs whatever operations are necessary on its underlying data to implement the copy into the containing scope item referenced by *DestScopeItem*. This completes the operation.

If the user drops the selection with a move cursor onto a scope item owned by the snap-in, or clicks **Paste** on the context menu for that scope item after cutting the source, then the snap-in also receives the Views_Paste event. In this case *Move* is **True**.

If the source and destination belong to the same instance of the same snap-in then *RetToSource* is not used. The snap-in must perform a copy operation on its underlying data and set **ScopeItem.Pasted=True** and **MMCListItem=True** for every item successfully copied. The snap-in will then receive the the Views_Cut event:

```
Private Sub Views_Cut(ByVal View As SnapInLib.View, ByVal
➥ ItemsPasted As SnapInLib.MMCClipboard, ByVal RetFromTarget As
➥ SnapInLib.MMCDataObject)
```

The contents of *ItemsPasted* are the same as that of *SourceItems* in the Views_Paste event. The snap-in must iterate through the items and examine **ScopeItem.Pasted** and **MMCListItem.Pasted** to determine which items were successfully copied to the destination and then delete them from the source.

For a move operation where the source and destination do not belong to the same instance of the same snap-in then *RetToSource* is used in the Views_Paste event. This is an **MMCDataObject** object and the snap-in must call **MMCDataObject.SetData** to return information to the source snap-in describing which items were successfully pasted. The format of this data is determined by the source snap-in. If you are moving items between instances of your own snap-in then you decide on the format. If your snap-in is accepting a paste from another snap-in then you must consult the source snap-in's documentation for information on how to format the data. For more information about exchanging data with other Visual Basic and C++ snap-ins see "Importing Data from C++ Snap-ins" and "Publishing and Interpreting Data Formats from a Visual Basic Snap-in" in this chapter.

When the cross-snap-in Views_Paste event completes then the source snap-in receives the Views_Cut event and uses *RetFromTarget* instead of examining **ScopeItem.Pasted** and **MMCListItem.Pasted**. *RetFromTarget* is the **MMCDataObject** used by the target snap-in in Views_Paste to communicate which items were successfully pasted. As mentioned above, the source snap-in determines the format of the data. In Views_Cut it should call **MMCDataObject.GetData**, examine the data, and delete the successfully pasted items from the source.

Handling Refresh

A snap-in can allow the user to request a refresh operation for selected items by enabling the refresh verb in its Views_Select event handler. For more information see "Views" in Chapter 36.

When the refresh verb is enabled MMC displays a refresh button on the toolbar, adds a **Refresh** item to its **Action** and context menus, and interprets the F5 key as a refresh request. When the user makes a selection and invokes refresh the snap-in receives the Views_Refresh event. The selected items are passed as a parameter to this event. It is then up to the snap-in to determine what and how to refresh.

Snap-ins typically enable refresh for single scope item selections in the scope pane. This is similar to how Windows Explorer allows the user to refresh the contents of a folder. To test for this condition use the following code in the Views_Select event:

```
Private Sub Views_Select(ByVal View As SnapInLib.View, ByVal
➥ Selection As SnapInLib.MMCClipboard, ByVal Selected As
➥ Boolean, ByVal ConsoleVerbs As SnapInLib.MMCConsoleVerbs)

If Selected And (Selection.SelectionType = siSingleScopeItem)
➥ Then
      If Not CurrentScopePaneItem Is Nothing Then
          If CurrentScopePaneItem.ScopeItem Is
          ➥ Selection.ScopeItems(1) Then
              ConsoleVerbs(siRefresh).Enabled = True
          End If
      End If
End If
```

The code first checks that something has been selected (as opposed to deselected). It also checks that the selection consists of a single scope item. If there is a scope item selected in the scope pane then **CurrentScopePaneItem** will have a reference to it. If the scope item referenced by **CurrentScopePaneItem** is the same as the selected scope item then the snap-in knows that it has been selected in the scope pane and it enables the refresh verb.

When the user invokes refresh the snap-in should do whatever is appropriate to refresh the displayed data. The typical response would be to empty the list view by calling **CurrentListView.ListItems.Clear** and then repopulate it. If the selected scope item has children then it may be necessary to remove them by calling **ScopeItem.RemoveChildren** and then repopulate the scope pane.

Visual Basic Snap-ins

History Navigation: Handling the Back and Forward Buttons

Snap-in developers do not need to write any code to handle history navigation within a console. The designer runtime takes care of restoring the appropriate result views. When the user clicks **Back** the snap-in will see the Views_Select event just as if the user had selected the previous node but there will be no ScopePaneItems_GetResultViewInfo or ScopePaneItems_GetResultView events because the user has already determined which result view should be displayed. Following Views_Select the snap-in will receive ResultViews_Initialize followed by ResultViews_Activate. If the result view was cached by specifying **Keep=True** in ResultViews_Deactivate, then the snap-in will only see ResultViews_Activate. For more information on caching result views see "ScopePaneItems" in Chapter 36.

Using Relative URLs

There are several situations in which a snap-in may need to specify a URL that references a location in the snap-in DLL's directory or relative to that directory:

- A URL result view that references an HTML file shipped with the snap-in.
- A URL result view that references an HTML file stored as a resource in the snap-in's DLL.
- A taskpad task added in code that references a bitmap or GIF file stored as a resource in the snap-in's DLL.

All of these situations require assembling the URL string with **App.Path** and the relative portion of the URL. **App** is a global object present in all Visual Basic applications that contains various properties of the execution environment. **App.Path** contains the path to the directory where the snap-in's DLL is installed.

▶ **To use a relative URL in a URL result view that references an HTML file installed in the same directory as the snap-in's DLL**

1. Do not define a URL result view in the designer.
2. Code the ScopePaneItems_GetResultViewInfo event handler as follows (assuming the node's name is "URLNode"):

```
Private Sub ScopePaneItems_GetResultViewInfo(_
ByVal ScopePaneItem As SnapInLib.ScopePaneItem, _
ViewType As SnapInLib._
SnapInResultViewTypeConstants, _
DisplayString As String)

   If ScopePaneItem.Name = "URLNode" Then
      ViewType = siURLView
      DisplayString = "file://" & App.Path & "\MyFile.htm"
   End If

End Sub
```

▶   **To use a relative URL in a URL result view that references an HTML file stored as a custom resource in the snap-in's DLL**

1. Do not define a URL result view in the designer.

2. Using the Visual Basic Resource Editor add-in, add a custom resource for the HTML file and change its ID to "MyResFile.htm". (For more information on using the Resource Editor add-in see "Using Resources in Taskpads" in Chapter 34.)

3. Code the ScopePaneItems_GetResultViewInfo event handler as follows (assuming the node's name is "URLNode"):

```
Private Sub ScopePaneItems_GetResultViewInfo(_
ByVal ScopePaneItem As SnapInLib.ScopePaneItem, _
ViewType As SnapInLib._
SnapInResultViewTypeConstants, _
DisplayString As String)

If ScopePaneItem.Name = "URLNode" Then
  ViewType = siURLView
  DisplayString = "res://" & App.Path & _
  ➡ "\MySnapIn.dll" & "/CUSTOM/MyResFile.htm"
  End If

End Sub
```

▶   **To use a relative URL for a taskpad task image that references a bitmap stored as a resource in the snap-in's DLL**

1. Define a Taskpad result view in the designer and make it the default result view for the node.

2. Using the Visual Basic Resource Editor add-in, add a bitmap resource and change its ID to "MyBitmap". (For more information on using the resource editor add-in see "Using Resources in Taskpads" in Chapter 34.)

3. Code the ResultViews_Initialize event handler as follows (assuming the node's name is "TaskpadNode"):

```
Private Sub ResultViews_Initialize(_
ByVal ResultView As SnapInLib.ResultView)
  If ResultView.ScopePaneItem.Name = "TaskpadNode" Then
      Dim t As Task
      Set t = ResultView.Taskpad.Tasks.Add
      t.ActionType = siNotify
      t.Text = "My Task"
      t.HelpString = "My Task HelpString"
      t.ImageType = siBitmap
      t.MouseOverImage = "res://" & App.Path & _
      ➡ "\MySnapIn.dll" & "/#2/MyBitmap"
  End If
End Sub
```

Localization

Visual Basic snap-ins can store all of their displayed strings in resources just as C++ snap-ins do. The Visual Basic Resource Editor add-in allows defining string resources. The Visual Basic function **LoadResString** is used to load the strings. Following are the various strings displayed at run time and the events in which they should be set:

- **SnapIn.DisplayName**, **SnapIn.Description**, **SnapIn.Provider**, **SnapIn.Version**—set in SnapIn_Initialize.

- **ScopeItem.ScopeNode.DisplayName**—set in ScopeItems_Initialize for auto-created ScopeItems or when calling **ScopeItems.Add** or **ScopeItems.AddPredefined**.

- **MMCColumnHeader.Text**—set in ResultViews_Initialize.

- **MMCListItem.Text** and **MMCListSubItem.Text**—set when the list item is added to the list view or in a virtual list view set in ResultViews_GetVirtualItemDisplayInfo.

- **MMCButton.Caption** and **MMCButtonMenu.Text**—set only for menu buttons in Views_SetControlbar or ExtensionSnapIn_SetControlbar.

- **MMCButton.TooltipText**—set only for toolbar buttons in Views_SetControlbar or ExtensionSnapIn_SetControlbar.

- **MMCMenu.Caption** and **MMCMenu.StatusBarText**—set in Views_AddNewMenuItems, Views_AddTopMenuItems, Views_AddTaskMenuItems, Views_AddViewMenuItems, ExtensionSnapIn_AddNewMenuItems, or ExtensionSnapIn_AddTaskMenuItems. Note that automatic view menu strings set in result view property pages at design time are not localized. Snap-ins that need to localize these strings must handle the view menu manually using Views_AddViewMenuItems and MMCMenu_Click to switch result views.

- **Taskpad.Title**, **Taskpad.DescriptiveText**, **Taskpad.ListpadTitle**, **Taskpad.ListpadButtonText**, **Task.Text**, **Task.HelpString**—set in ResultViews_Initialize.

For more information on localization of Visual Basic code see the topic "International Issues" in the Visual Basic documentation.

Visual Basic Snap-ins

Using Unicode Strings

Unicode strings can be used for any string in the snap-in object model. In particular, if a snap-in needs to display a multilingual list view it can set **MMCListView.UseFontLinking = True** and then set both **MMCListItem.Text** and **MMCListSubItem.Text** to Unicode strings. The strings can come from a database or other data source or they can be hard-coded using Visual Basic's **ChrW** function. For example, to set a string S to the first three characters of the Cyrillic character set use:

```
S = ChrW(&H400) & ChrW(&H401) & ChrW(&H402)
```

ScopeItem and ScopeNode: Making Sense of Name, Key, NodeTypeName, and DisplayName

Snap-in developers are often confused about the relationship between the following properties:

- **ScopeItem.Name**
- **ScopeItem.Key**
- **ScopeNode.NodeTypeName**
- **ScopeNode.NodeTypeGUID**
- **ScopeNode.DisplayName**

The following paragraphs describe each property and its relationship to the others.

ScopeItem.Name and **ScopeItem.Key** must always match. Early in the development of the snap-in designer there was a difference between the two, but their meanings have since merged. By the time the merge occurred, there were too many snap-ins in existence that might break if **ScopeItem.Name** were removed so it had to be kept.

ScopeItem.Key is simply the string that uniquely identifies the instance of the **ScopeItem** object within the **ScopeItems** collection, just like in any other Automation (formerly called OLE Automation) collection. If the snap-in changes **ScopeItem.Key** then it must change **ScopeItem.Name** to match (and vice-versa).

ScopeNode.DisplayName is the string displayed for the scope item in the scope pane and in the result pane when it is not in detail or filtered mode.

ScopeNode.NodeTypeName is the exported name for the node type that is used in the registration database under MMC's **NodeTypes** key. Think of it as a class name for a particular type of **ScopeItem**. Because node type names are not guaranteed to be unique among snap-ins, MMC also requires a node type GUID that is in **ScopeNode.NodeTypeGUID**. The designer generates this GUID but you can change it at run time.

When you define a node at design time, the name you give it in the designer is its node type name. When you call **ScopeItems.AddPredefined**, the first parameter is the node type name. A node defined at design time is really a template used to initialize the properties of the **ScopeItem** at run time. If you define a node completely in code by calling **ScopeItems.Add**, you must explicitly set **ScopeNode.NodeTypeName** and **ScopeNode.NodeTypeGUID**. Even if the scope item is not extensible, it is still important to set **ScopeNode.NodeTypeGUID** because MMC uses the GUID to preserve the selection of a scope item when it saves the console file (.msc). It also uses the GUID to preserve console taskpads that are created for the node.

Why is there a separate **ScopeNode** object? Why not make those properties part of **ScopeItem**? The answer is that **ScopeNode** represents a node in the scope pane regardless of ownership. That is why extension events like ExtensionSnapIn_Expand receive a **ScopeNode**. The **ScopeNode** is also used to navigate the scope tree using **ScopeNode.Parent**, **ScopeNode.Child**, and so on. **ScopeNode.Owned** tells you whether a node belongs to your snap-in. You can also index the **ScopeItems** collection with the **ScopeNode**; for example:

```
If SomeScopeNode.Owned Then
  Set MyScopeItem = ScopeItems(SomeScopeNode)
End If
```

Visual Basic Snap-ins

Creating Display-Independent Property Pages

A property page is generally developed on a single computer that always uses the same video adapter with the same resolution and font size. When the snap-in is distributed to customers it may run on a variety of video adapters, resolutions, and with small or large fonts. To ensure that a property page will always appear correctly regardless of video configuration the following steps should be taken:

1. Use the property page's default **ScaleMode** property value of **Twip**.

2. If developing with small fonts and implementing IMMCPropertyPage_**GetDialogUnitSize**, leave some extra space between the controls and the bottom of the page. This is needed because when the page is displayed on a computer with large fonts its height will be squeezed slightly.

3. If developing with large fonts and implementing **IMMCPropertyPage_GetDialogUnitSize**, leave some extra space between the controls and the right side of the page. This is needed because when the page is displayed on a computer with small fonts its width will be squeezed slightly.

4. Always test the page with both small and large fonts.

Twips are used for the **ScaleMode** property because they are a device-independent measurement that also has a very fine granularity. The word twip is a contraction of "twentieth of a point." A point is 1/72 of an inch so a twip is 1/1440 of an inch. When printing, a point is 1/72 of a physical inch but on the screen it represents 1/72 of a logical inch. The physical size of a logical inch is determined by the video configuration and it is calculated to allow smaller font sizes (for example, 8-point) to appear in a reasonable size on the screen. If an 8-point font were displayed on the screen using its physical size it would not be readable. The logical inch provides the needed magnification and also allows programs to calculate the size of their windows and controls using a device-independent measurement.

The MMC guidelines for property page sizes, control sizes, and control spacing are all given in dialog units. The dialog unit is also a device-independent measurement that is based on the average height and width of the characters in the font used in a dialog box. For vertical measurements, a dialog unit is 1/8 of the height of the characters in the dialog box's font. For horizontal measurements a dialog unit is 1/4 of the average width of the characters in the dialog box's font. While dialog units are not as granular as twips, they are sufficient for the layout of windows containing text and controls such as property pages.

Visual Basic does not use the dialog unit measurement, but the designer does allow a property page to specify its size in dialog units at run time. If a property page implements the **IMMCPropertyPage** interface, the designer runtime will call **IMMCPropertyPage_GetDialogUnitSize(Height, Width)**. If the property page does not have code in this method then the design-time size will be used.

To determine the size to use at design time, use the default **ScaleMode** of **Twip** and use the dialog-unit-to-twips calculator that is available from the context menu on the root node of the designer tree view.

As explained earlier, when moving from small fonts to large fonts, the height of a page measured in dialog units becomes slightly smaller and the width becomes slightly larger. This may seem counterintuitive, because one would expect that logical units should keep their proportions. Understanding how this happens requires some additional explanation. Continue reading only if you are interested in the theory.

Windows typically uses 96 pixels per logical inch for small fonts and 120 pixels per logical inch for large fonts. This means that a font in a given point size in small fonts must increase its physical size by 25 percent when moving to large fonts. Unfortunately, the system cannot always make such exact changes. For example, on a sample small-fonts system, the MS Sans Serif 8 font has a height of 13 pixels. When moving to large fonts, by adding 25 percent the size should change to 16.25 pixels. Video adapters do not allow addressing the screen in fractions of a pixel so the system rounds it down to 16 pixels.

Consider what happens to a measurement in dialog units such as MMC's recommended property page height of 218. A vertical dialog unit is 1/8 of the font height, so the height of a property page in logical inches on the sample small-fonts system is calculated as follows:

```
218 dlus ÷ 8 units/character = 27.25 characters
27.25 characters X 13 pixels/character = 354.25 pixels
354.25 pixels ÷ 96 pixels/logical inch = 3.69 logical inches
```

If we do the same calculation on a large-fonts system we find that the property page will actually be shorter in logical inches:

```
218 dlus ÷ 8 units/character = 27.25 characters
27.25 characters X 16 pixels/character = 440 pixels
440 pixels ÷ 120 pixels/logical inch = 3.66 logical inches
```

Because the property page size in a Visual Basic snap-in is measured in twips (1/1440 of a logical inch), the logical inch size will be the same regardless of the font size. For property pages coded in C++, the logical inch size will be slightly different on both systems. Using the preceding example, if there were no rounding errors, then when moving to large fonts, the 3.69 logical inches would be:

```
3.69 logical inches X 120 pixels/logical inch = 442.8 pixels
```

Now you can see that a property page specified in twips will be about 3 pixels higher than a property page specified in dialog units when moving to large fonts. (In practice, due to rounding, the pixel difference may be slightly higher.) If your property page implements **IMMCPropertyPage_GetDialogUnitSize** and it returns 218 for the height, then on a large-fonts system, it will be created slightly smaller than what was expected at design time because of the difference in calculations. This should generally not be a problem, but pages that have controls close to the bottom may need to be moved up to allow for the decreased height.

A similar problem occurs in the width calculations except that the page becomes too large when moving to large fonts. On the sample system, the average width of a character in the MS Sans Serif 8 font is 6 pixels. When moving to large fonts, adding 25 percent would require 7.5 pixels. The system rounds this up to 8 pixels. Because the font is too large, the size of the horizontal dialog unit increases more than it should and the width of the page increases. Because of this, pages designed on a large-fonts system should leave some extra room on the right side, because the width of the page will be squeezed when moving to small fonts.

For more information see "IMMCPropertyPage" in Chapter 36.

Displaying Property Pages to Edit Security Attributes

Snap-ins often need to allow the user to configure the security attributes of an object such as a file or a folder. In Windows 2000, the **CreateSecurityPage** Win32 API function can be used to create a property page that edits an access control list (ACL). Unfortunately, this convenient API is only available in C++. It can be used in a Visual Basic snap-in with a little help from a small COM object written in C++ and by calling **MMCPropertySheet.AddPageProvider** from within a property page.

The Visual Basic property page should implement the **IMMCPropertyPage** interface and in **IMMCPropertyPage_Initialize** it should call **MMCPropertySheet.AddPageProvider**. This method receives the CLSID of an object and returns a reference to the object and the HWND of the property sheet. For example, assuming that the COM object's class is called **PageProvider** and the snap-in project has referenced its object library in **Project/References**:

```
Const CLSIDPageProvider = "{2205DFD5-E441-4144-AEBF-08B38F19760A}"

Private Sub IMMCPropertyPage_Initialize(ByVal Data As Variant, _
          ByVal PropertySheet As SnapInLib.MMCPropertySheet)

    Dim Provider As PageProvider
    Dim hwndSheet As Long
    Set Provider=PropertySheet.AddPageProvider(CLSIDPageProvider
    ➡ ,_  hwndSheet)
```

The COM object must also implement a default interface that has methods
allowing the Visual Basic property page to manipulate it. For example, the
PageProvider object described above might be defined in its Interface Definition
Language (IDL) file as follows:

```
[
  uuid(CFD7BADA-5BDD-4CEA-B9C1-EEB55A431439),
  version(1.0),
  helpstring("SecurityObject 1.0 Type Library")
]
library SECURITYOBJECTLib
{
  importlib("stdole32.tlb");
  importlib("stdole2.tlb");

    [
        object,
        uuid(5BA90939-218F-417E-BDC8-A56F11ADFC2F),
        dual,
        helpstring("IPageProvider Interface"),
        pointer_default(unique)
    ]
    interface IPageProvider : IDispatch
    {
        [id(1),helpstring("Add the security page to the property
        ↪ sheet")]
        HRESULT AddSecurityPage(BSTR ServerName,
                                BSTR ObjectName,
                                BSTR PageTitle,
                                long hwndSheet);
    };

    [
        uuid(2205DFD5-E441-4144-AEBF-08B38F19760A),
        helpstring("PageProvider Class")
    ]
    coclass PageProvider
    {
        [default] interface IPageProvider;
    };
};
```

After creating the sample **PageProvider** object, the Visual Basic property page would call its **AddSecurityPage** method passing the parameters needed to call the **CreateSecurityPage** API function:

```
Provider.AddSecurityPage "SomeServerName", _
                              "C:\SomeFolder\SomeFile.ext", _
                              "Security", _
                              hwndSheet
```

The COM object's implementation of that method would then send a **PSM_ADDPAGE** message to the HWND of the property sheet. The following example assumes that the same object also implements the **ISecurityInformation** interface required by the **CreateSecurityPage** function:

```
STDMETHODIMP PageProvider::AddSecurityPage(BSTR ServerName,
                                           BSTR ObjectName,
                                           BSTR PageTitle,
                                           long hwndSheet)
{
        ... code to store the parameters ...

        HPROPSHEETPAGE hPage = ::CreateSecurityPage(
        ↪ static_cast<ISecurityInformation *>(this));
        if (NULL == hPage)
        {
            return HRESULT_FROM_WIN32(::GetLastError());
        }

        ::SendMessage((HWND)hwndSheet, PSM_ADDPAGE, 0, (LPARAM)hPage);

    return S_OK;
}
```

For more information see "MMCPropertySheet" and "IMMCPropertyPage" in Chapter 36.

Communicating Between Property Pages and Coordinating Apply Events

Snap-ins often display multiple property pages for a single object such as a scope item or a list item. Each page receives its PropertyPage_ApplyChanges event separately but the snap-in needs to defer its changes to the underlying object until all pages have processed this event. The situation is further complicated by the fact that a page receives this event both when the user selects another page and when the user clicks **OK** or **Apply**. This means that the last page displayed will receive two successive ApplyChanges events when the user clicks **OK** or **Apply**.

This situation can be handled by using a Visual Basic class that collects data from each page as the PropertyPage_ApplyChanges event is fired and changes the underlying data after all pages have reported. Here are the steps:

1. Create a class with methods or properties that hold the changes to the underlying data and a reference to that data.

2. In Views_CreatePropertyPages, create an instance of the class and pass it as the *InitData* parameter to **MMCPropertySheet.AddPage**.

3. Implement **IMMCPropertyPage** in each page and store a reference to the class in **IMMCPropertyPage_Initialize**.

4. In each page's PropertyPage_ApplyChanges event, if the user input is OK then set the changed properties on the class and call a method on the class to tell it that the page has applied changes (for example, MyClass.PageDone("General Page").

5. In MyClass.PageDone, track the callers and when the same page calls twice in succession, update the underlying object.

If any page doesn't call MyClass.PageDone, then the user did not visit the page.

A related issue is how property pages can communicate with each other. This can be done using the same class as described above or it can be enhanced by defining an interface and having each page implement it. The class can implement a method that takes a reference to that interface as a parameter; for example:

```
MyClass.Register(PageName As String, PageInterface As MyInterface)
```

In **IMMCPropertyPage_Initialize**, each page calls MyClass.Register("MyPageName", Me) and that method keeps arrays of the page names and the corresponding MyInterface references. The class can implement another method such as

```
MyClass.GetPage(PageName As String) As MyInterface
```

that looks up a page by name and returns a reference to its MyInterface implementation. That would allow any page to talk to any other page at any time.

Visual Basic Snap-ins

Creating Wizard97-Style Wizards

Visual Basic snap-ins cannot directly implement Wizard97-style wizards, but they can be simulated by using **Image** and **Shape** objects on the property page for the watermark and header. For wizards initiated programmatically using **MMCPropertySheetProvider.CreatePropertySheet**, the snap-in must specify the **siWizard97** style. For configuration wizards, MMC does this automatically, although a snap-in is not required to simulate a Wizard97-style wizard.

On the Welcome page, place an **Image** object on the left side of the page and set its **Picture** property to the watermark bitmap. In the page's PropertyPage_Paint event add code to stretch the **Image** to the height of the page at run time:

```
Private Sub PropertyPage_Paint()
PaintPicture PaintPicture imgWatermark.Picture, 0, 0, _
                                    imgWatermark.Width, Height
End Sub
```

Note that some bitmaps might not stretch perfectly. Some adjustment of the bitmap content may be necessary. Wizard97-style wizards should be tested on systems with both small and large fonts settings in **Control Panel/Display**. If the snap-in is to be deployed on both MMC 1.1 and MMC 1.2 then the wizard should be tested on both systems in both font sizes. On an MMC 1.1 system with Internet Explorer 4.0 installed, the bitmap will not be stretched. On an MMC 1.1 system with Internet Explorer 5, or on an MMC 1.2 system (that requires Internet Explorer 5), the bitmap will be stretched. The stretching occurs because Internet Explorer 5 installs a newer version of comctl32.dll that implements Win32 property sheets and wizards. This newer version sizes the wizard pages slightly larger than their design-time size.

On the interior pages, use a **Label** with a white background for both the header title and the subtitle text. For the header bitmap use a **PictureBox**. For the header background use a **Shape** control with a white background. The shape control is placed on top of the labels and the **PictureBox**. In the PropertyPage_Paint event call **Shape.Move** to stretch the **Shape** to the width of the property page at run time.

```
Private Sub PropertyPage_Paint()
    Shape1.Move 0, 0, Width
End Sub
```

For more information see "MMCPropertySheetProvider" in Chapter 36.

Why Doesn't a Right-Click in the Scope Pane Change the Current Selection?

If a **ScopeItem** is selected in the scope pane and the user right-clicks a different **ScopeItem**, the snap-in receives the Views_Select event but the new **ScopeItem** does not remain selected. After the user has dismissed the context menu, the selection returns to the original **ScopeItem**. This can be confusing because the Views_Select event might be interpreted to indicate that the right-clicked **ScopeItem** is about to display a result view and become **CurrentScopeItem**.

MMC uses the same behavior as the Windows Explorer for a right-click in the scope pane. This allows the user to perform a paste operation on a **ScopeItem** without having to select it and change the result pane. For example, the user has selected a folder and is using context menus to copy and paste various files to other folders. If every right-click on a folder changed the contents of the result pane, this would become a very tedious operation.

The snap-in can tell when a **ScopeItem** has been selected with a left-click when it gets the ScopePaneItems_GetResultViewInfo event. This event is fired when MMC asks the snap-in what type of result view to display for the **ScopeItem**.

Why Don't ScopeItems in a List View Display Text in Detail Mode?

When a **ScopeItem** that has child **ScopeItem** objects is selected in the scope pane and it displays a list view, MMC will automatically add the child **ScopeItem** objects to the list view. When the list view is not in detail or filtered mode, MMC uses **ScopeItem.ScopeNode.DisplayName** for the displayed text. When the list view is in detail or filtered mode, then MMC needs some way to determine the text to be displayed in the columns. This situation is sometimes difficult to understand because the parent **ScopeItem** defines the columns of the list view but the child **ScopeItem** objects must somehow define the text that will be displayed.

ScopeItem.ColumnHeaders contains the column definitions that are used when a **ScopeItem** appears in a list view in the result pane. **ScopeItem.ListSubItems** contains the strings that are displayed in the columns. **ScopeItem.SubItems** contains references to the same text as a string array rather than a collection of **MMCListSubItem** objects. **ScopeItem.ColumnHeaders** and **ScopeItem.ListSubItems** are used when the **ScopeItem**'s parent is selected in the scope pane and MMC displays its child **ScopeItem** objects in the result pane. The child **ScopeItem** must define columns that have keys matching one or more of the parent's list view columns. When the designer runtime receives a request for a column's text from MMC, it uses the parent list view's column key to reference the corresponding column in **ScopeItem.ColumnHeaders**. It then uses that header's index to reference the **MMCListSubItem**. The algorithm is as follows. Assume that MMC requests the text for the child **ScopeItem**'s column n:

```
Key = ParentListView.ColumnHeaders(n).Key
Header = ChildScopeItem.ColumnHeaders(Key)
Text = ChildScopeItem.ListSubItems(Header.Index)
```

The reason for matching keys rather than simply using the corresponding indexes is to allow a **ScopeItem** to appear in more than one list view. By using the keys, the snap-in can display only a subset of the **MMCListSubItem** objects in a particular list view. For more information see "ScopeItem," "MMCColumnHeaders," and "MMCListSubItems" in Chapter 36.

Handling Orphaned Property Pages

The following user scenarios require special handling for property pages displaying list item data:

1. Multiple properties invocations on the same list item
   - User opens a property sheet for a list item.
   - User returns to list view and requests properties again for the same list item.

2. Orphaned property pages
   - User opens a property sheet for a list item.
   - User selects a different scope item in the scope pane.
   - User reselects the original scope item in the scope pane.
   - User returns to list view and requests properties again for the same list item.

Case 2 is called an orphaned property page because the list view that owns the list item is destroyed when the user selects a different scope item. The existing property sheet will always be activated on the second request because MMC asks the designer runtime whether the list item in the open property sheet matches the list item for which the second properties invocation has occurred. In case 2, if the property page has stored a reference to the list item, then it is important to remember that the list view that owns that list item no longer exists. A new list view has replaced it and that list view contains a new list item representing the same underlying data. This is why the runtime needs the **MMCListItem.ID** property so that it can determine whether the two list items represent the same underlying data.

These are both important test cases and should be checked for your snap-in if you support property sheets for list items. In particular, you should check your property pages' behavior after the sheet has been orphaned. You can call **MMCListItem.PropertyChanged** in that situation but your ResultViews_PropertyChanged event handler will receive a *ResultView* parameter that is **Nothing**. This indicates to the snap-in that the result view has been destroyed since the user opened the sheet. If your event handler depends on the *ResultView* parameter then you must do the following check:

```
If Not ResultView Is Nothing Then
   ...code that uses ResultView...
End If
```

If your event handler needs to change existing list items' displayed text (**MMCListItem.Text** and **MMCListItem.ListSubItem(n).Text**), then it should enumerate the existing views and check whether a corresponding list item is being displayed. An example of this is:

```
Private Sub ResultViews_PropertyChanged(_
ByVal ResultView As SnapInLib.ResultView, _
ByVal ListItem As SnapInLib.MMCListItem, _
ByVal Data As Variant)

    On Error GoTo Trap

    Dim v As View
    Dim spi As ScopePaneItem
    Dim rv As ResultView
    Dim li As MMCListItem

    For Each v In Views
        For Each spi In v.ScopePaneItems
            For Each rv In spi.ResultViews
                On Error Resume Next
                Set li = rv.ListView.ListItems(Data)
                On Error GoTo Trap
                If Not li Is Nothing Then
                    li.Text = ListItem.Tag
                    li.Update
                End If
            Next rv
        Next spi
    Next v

    Exit Sub
Trap:
    DisplayError "ResultViews_PropertyChanged"
End Sub
```

The loop looks at every existing result view and checks whether it is displaying a list item for the data that has changed. In this example, the property page called **MMCListItem.PropertyChanged** and passed the index of the changed item as the *Data* parameter. The loop then uses the *Data* parameter to index the collection. In a more realistic situation a snap-in would likely use **MMCListItem.Key**. For example, the FileExplorer sample stores the full path of the file in **MMCListItem.Key** so it could use that to check whether a list item for that file is in each list view.

When testing this behavior you should also try it with multiple views. If you support multiple selection then you should test both single and multiple selections.

For more information see "MMCListItem" in Chapter 36.

CHAPTER 36

Using the Object Model

Understanding the designer object model is essential for writing all but the most trivial of snap-ins. The following sections describe each object, its usage, and its properties, methods, and events. It is strongly recommended that you also use the Visual Basic object browser. Press F2 to invoke it in the Visual Basic IDE.

The following diagram illustrates the main objects and their relationships. These are explained in detail in the following sections.

Designer Object Model

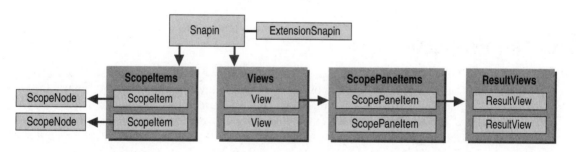

Collections

The object model makes extensive use of collections for objects that have an indeterminate number of instances at design time. For example, the **View** object represents a multiple-document interface (MDI) child window in the console. It is not possible to know how many windows the user will open at run time so a collection is used (**Views**). Objects are added and removed from the collection as the user opens and closes windows. All elements in collections have **Key** (string) and **Index** (numeric, one-based) properties that identify the object and its ordinal position within the collection. Most objects have a **Tag** property that is a **Variant** allowing the snap-in to associate extra data with the object.

When objects in a collection can generate events, those events are handled on the collection rather than on the object itself. For example, a user can interact with a view, so events are needed on the **View** object. If the number of views is known at design time then each one can have its own event handler much like controls on a form (for example, Button1_Click). Because the user can open any number of views, the events are fired on the **Views** collection and the individual **View** object is passed as a parameter to each event handler. This is similar to the use of control arrays on a form where there is one event handler that receives the index of the control that generated the event.

The Tag Property

Most objects in the snap-in object model have a **Variant** property called **Tag**. This is similar to the **Tag** property used in many Common Controls objects in standard Visual Basic applications. It can be used to store any data that the snap-in needs to associate with the object. **Tag** may contain something simple such as an **Integer** value or it may contain an object. If a snap-in needs to store more than a simple value, it should use a Visual Basic class with properties to hold the needed data.

SnapIn

The **SnapIn** object is the top-level object. It represents the snap-in itself and handles global information and events such as the snap-in name, version, and so on as well as console serialization. Properties of **Snap-in** are module-level variables and are accessible without a prefix; for example, **SnapIn.DisplayName** can be coded as **DisplayName**.

Name is used to identify the snap-in within the Visual Basic code and is similar to a class name.

DisplayName is used in the scope pane as the text for the static node and it also appears in the Snap-in Manager when a user is adding or removing a snap-in from the console.

NodeTypeName is used to identify the snap-in's static node in its registration database entries.

NodeTypeGUID is generated by the designer and it is also used to identify the snap-in's static node in its registration database entries.

Description is displayed in the Snap-in Manager after the snap-in is added and when the user requests to display About information.

Provider, **Version**, and **Icon** are displayed in the Snap-in Manager as part of the About information.

Type indicates whether the snap-in is stand-alone, an extension, or dual-mode.

RuntimeMode is used by dual-mode snap-ins at run time to determine whether they were loaded as a primary or extension snap-in.

SmallFolders, **SmallFoldersOpen**, and **LargeFolders** specify the image lists that are used for nodes added to the scope pane by the snap-in. They must all contain the corresponding images at the same indexes. **StaticFolder** specifies the index or key of the image used for the static node.

HelpFile specifies the name of an HTML Help file (.chm) that the snap-in will merge with MMC's Help. If the snap-in's Help file contains links to other Help files then **LinkedTopics** specifies a semicolon-delimited list of the additional .chm files. The **ShowHelpTopic** method can be used to display a specific topic in the merged Help file. The Help event is for snap-ins that do not use MMC's merged Help and instead display their own Help. See "Adding Help to a Snap-in" in Chapter 34 for more information.

MMCCommandLine contains the contents of the command line used to start Mmc.exe. Snap-ins can use command-line information to customize the use of a saved console file. When running under the Visual Basic debugger this property is not available in primary snap-ins prior to the SnapIn_Load event and it is not available at all in non-namespace extensions.

TaskpadViewPreferred indicates whether the user has set the corresponding console option in MMC 1.1.

RequiredExtensions is a collection that contains an **Extension** object representing all of the registered extensions for the snap-in. In the SnapIn_Initialize event the snap-in can set **Extension.Enabled** for each extension snap-in that must be loaded when the snap-in is loaded.

Preload can be set by a snap-in at run time to indicate that it should be loaded before its parent node is expanded the next time the console file is loaded. This can be useful in situations where a snap-in's static node has a dynamic display name (for example, contains the local computer name). If the snap-in is not preloaded then MMC will use the display name stored in the console file. A preloaded snap-in receives the Preload event in which it can set **DisplayName**.

The **SnapIn** object also has some properties that serve as shorthand to access frequently used objects within the hierarchy. These are **CurrentView**, **CurrentScopePaneItem**, **CurrentScopeItem**, **CurrentResultView**, and **CurrentListView**. The following table shows each of these properties and the corresponding full object path. Note that any of these properties can contain the value **Nothing** at any time depending on the state of the console. Always check the value before using the property (for example, If Not CurrentView Is Nothing Then ....).

Property	Shorthand for
CurrentView	Views.CurrentView
CurrentScopePaneItem	Views.CurrentView.ScopePaneItems.SelectedItem
CurrentScopeItem	Views.CurrentView.ScopePaneItems.SelectedItem. ScopeItem
CurrentResultView	Views.CurrentView.ScopePaneItems.SelectedItem. ResultView
CurrentListView	Views.CurrentView.ScopePaneItems.SelectedItem. ResultView.ListView

StringTable is a reference to an **MMCStringTable** object that allows a snap-in to store strings in the saved console file. For more information see "MMCStringTable" in this chapter.

The **ConsoleMsgBox** method is used by primary snap-ins to display message boxes instead of the standard Visual Basic **MsgBox** function. MMC displays the message box on behalf of the snap-in. Extension snap-ins must use **MsgBox**.

The **FormatData** method is used by extension snap-ins when importing data. It can convert a range within a **Byte** array to any Visual Basic data type.

The **Trace** method can be used when debugging a snap-in using other debuggers such as Microsoft Visual C++ or NTSD (NT Symbolic Debugger). It calls the Win32 API function **OutputDebugString**.

Snap-ins can write to and read from the console file (.msc) in the WriteProperties and ReadProperties events. These events work exactly as for **UserControl** and persistable Visual Basic classes using a **PropertyBag**. In addition to these events the snap-in also receives Views_WriteProperties and Views_ReadProperties events that allow storing view-specific data in the console file. For more information see "Views" in this chapter.

The Load and Unload events are fired for primary snap-ins when MMC adds the snap-in to the console and when it is removed. The Initialize and Terminate events are similar to Visual Basic classes and signal the creation and destruction of the snap-in. When the Snap-in Manager displays its **Add Standalone Snap-in** dialog box, the snap-in is created but it is not loaded. The snap-in will only receive the Initialize event in this case. When the user chooses the snap-in and it is loaded into the console then the snap-in will receive another Initialize event followed by the Load event. When a console file is loaded the snap-in also receives Initialize followed by Load.

When the user chooses to add a snap-in in the Snap-in Manager, the snap-in receives the QueryConfigurationWizard event. If the snap-in returns **True**, then it receives the CreateConfigurationWizard event in which it can add its pages to the property sheet. When the user completes the wizard the snap-in receives the ConfigurationComplete event. See "Configuration Wizards" in Chapter 34 for more information.

The major objects below **SnapIn** in the object hierarchy are actually properties of **SnapIn** (for example, **ExtensionSnapIn**, **ScopeItems**, **Views**). This allows the snap-in to handle events from those objects. This is analogous to the way controls are used with Visual Basic **Form** objects. For example, after adding a button, a **Form** has a new property called **Button1** and its events, such as Button1_Click, are handled in the **Form**'s module.

ExtensionSnapIn

The **ExtensionSnapIn** object encapsulates the set of events that apply to snap-ins that extend other snap-ins in ways such as adding menu items, property pages, toolbars, tasks, and extending their namespace. It has no properties or methods. For more information on writing extensions see "Developing Extension and Dual-Mode Snap-ins" in Chapter 34.

AddNewMenuItems and AddTaskMenuItems are called for context menu extensions when MMC is about to display a context menu for a node type extended by the snap-in. An extension snap-in can only add items to the **New** and **All Tasks** submenus. When the user selects an item added by a context menu extension the **MMCMenu** object's Click event is fired just as for a primary snap-in's context menus.

AddTasks is called for taskpad extensions when MMC is displaying a taskpad for the node type extended by the snap-in. The snap-in uses a **Tasks** collection to add its tasks. When the user clicks a task added by an extension, the snap-in receives the TaskClick event.

CreatePropertyPages is called for property page extensions when MMC is creating a property sheet for the node type extended by the snap-in. The snap-in uses the event to add its pages to the sheet as it would for a primary snap-in. Note that unlike a primary snap-in, an extension does not receive a QueryPagesFor event. MMC does not need this information because it is the primary snap-in's QueryPagesFor event that determines whether the user can invoke properties on the node. If the extension does not have property pages then it can simply return without adding anything.

SetControlbar is called for toolbar extensions to allow them to add their toolbars and menu buttons to MMC. UpdateControlbar is called when the selection changes so that the extension can enable and disable its buttons based on the selected item(s). Toolbar and menu button events are handled on the **Toolbar** object as they are in a primary snap-in.

Expand is called for a namespace extension when the node type it extends is expanding. ExpandSync is called in the same situation when a console file is loading to indicate that MMC would like the snap-in to add its child nodes immediately. If the snap-in cannot complete its namespace population synchronously then it can return **Handled=False**. It will then receive an Expand event in which it can initiate asynchronous scope tree population.

Collapse and CollapseSync are the counterparts to the expand events. They are not currently supported by MMC but may be in future versions.

These events will appear in the Visual Basic code as
`ExtensionSnapIn_<EventName>`.

ScopeItems

The **ScopeItems** collection represents the collection of all nodes added to the namespace by the snap-in. (This includes the snap-in's own namespace and that of any snap-ins it extends.) **ScopeItem** represents a single scope item. Its properties represent the aspects of a scope item that are independent of the view in which it appears. Nodes defined at design time can optionally be created by the designer runtime. These are known as "auto-create" nodes and they simply appear in the **ScopeItems** collection as their parent nodes are expanded. To create dynamic nodes at run time the snap-in adds an item to the collection. To remove an item from the namespace its **ScopeItem** is removed from the collection. All scope item events are on the collection. **ScopeItem** does not have any events. Each event has a parameter that is the **ScopeItem** object for which the event applies.

The **ScopeItems** collection also includes an element for the static node in primary snap-ins. It can be referenced using the special key "Static Node"; for example, **ScopeItems**("Static Node").

The **AddPredefined** method adds a node to the scope pane using a design-time definition from the Nodes section of the designer's tree view. The **Add** method is used to add a node to the scope pane using run-time definitions only.

The Initialize event is fired when a scope item is created. This is particularly useful for auto-create nodes because this event informs the snap-in that the node was created.

The Terminate event is fired when a scope item is destroyed. When MMC is closed all scope items are destroyed. This event gives the snap-in a chance to do any associated cleanup.

The Expand event is fired when a node is expanded in the scope pane. Snap-ins use this event to add children to the expanding node. The ExpandSync event is called in the same situation when a console file is loading to indicate that MMC would like the snap-in to add its child nodes immediately. If the snap-in cannot complete its namespace population synchronously then it can return **Handled=False**. It will then receive an Expand event in which it can initiate asynchronous scope tree population.

Collapse and CollapseSync are the counterparts to the expand events. They are not currently supported by MMC but may be in future versions.

The Rename event is called when the user requests to rename a scope item. It can only be called if the snap-in has enabled the rename verb during the previous Views_Select event when the scope item was selected. See "**Views**" for more information.

The PropertyChanged event is called when one of the snap-in's property pages calls **ScopeItem.PropertyChanged**. Snap-ins use this mechanism so that a property page (which MMC runs in a separate thread) can inform the snap-in of changes made to the scope item.

The Help event is called when the user requests Help while the scope item is selected. This event is only used if the snap-in is using a merged HTML Help file. See "Adding Help to a Snap-in" for more information.

When a primary snap-in is removed from the console all of its children are removed and the snap-in receives the RemoveChildren event. When the parent of a namespace extension's root node is removed then it also receives this event.

Syntax	ScopeItems As **ScopeItems**

Properties		
	Count	Returns a count of the **ScopeItem** objects in the collection.
	Item	Returns a **ScopeItem** object in the collection referenced by key, index, or **ScopeNode**.

Methods		
	Add	Adds a **ScopeItem** to the collection and a corresponding node to the scope pane.
	AddPreDefined	Adds a **ScopeItem** to the collection and a corresponding node to the scope pane based on a design-time definition.
	Remove	Removes a **ScopeItem** from the collection and its corresponding node from the scope pane.

Events

These events will appear in the Visual Basic code as `ScopeItems_<EventName>` because **ScopeItems** is the property of the **SnapIn** object that holds the one and only **ScopeItems** collection.

Collapse	Not called in current versions of MMC.
CollapseSync	Not called in current versions of MMC.
Expand	Allows the snap-in to add child nodes to the expanding node.
ExpandSync	Allows the snap-in to add child nodes to the expanding node when MMC requests synchronous scope pane population.
Help	Called when the user requests Help for a **ScopeItem**.
Initialize	Called when a **ScopeItem** is created.
PropertyChanged	Called when a property page calls **ScopeItem.PropertyChanged**.
RemoveChildren	Called when MMC is about to remove the children of a **ScopeItem**.
Rename	Called when the user performs a rename operation on a **ScopeItem**.
Terminate	Called when a **ScopeItem** is about to be destroyed.

ScopeItem

The **ScopeItem** object represents a node added to the namespace by the snap-in. There is only one instance of a **ScopeItem** for every node added to the namespace regardless of the number of views in which it appears.

The **Name** property is identical to the **Key** and it is used to identify the individual **ScopeItem** within the **ScopeItems** collection. If you change either of these properties then you must change the other to match it. For more information see "ScopeItem and ScopeNode: Making Sense of Name, Key, NodeTypeName, and DisplayName."

Folder contains the index or key of the image used for the **ScopeItem** in both the scope pane and list view image lists. Because there is only one **Folder** property, all image lists must contain the corresponding image at the same index or use the same key. See "Coordinating Image Lists" for more information on how to organize image list elements.

ScopeNode contains an object that encapsulates properties of the node that are available for all nodes regardless of ownership. It is used to navigate the namespace and also holds the scope item's display name. See "**ScopeNode**" for more information.

ColumnHeaders contains the column definitions that are used when a **ScopeItem** appears in a list view in the result pane. **ListSubItems** contains the strings that are displayed in the columns. **SubItems** contains references to the same text as a string array rather than as a collection of **MMCListSubItem** objects. **ColumnHeaders** and **ListSubItems** are used when the **ScopeItem** object's parent is selected in the scope pane and MMC displays its child **ScopeItems** in the result pane. If the user or the snap-in puts the list view into detail mode then the child scope items typically display some data in the columns. The parent's list view defines the columns. The child **ScopeItem** must define columns that have keys matching one or more of the parent's list view columns. When the designer runtime receives a request for a column's text from MMC, it uses the parent list view's column key to reference the corresponding column in **ScopeItem.ColumnHeaders**. It then uses that header's index to reference the **MMCListSubItem**. The algorithm is as follows. Assume that MMC requests the text for the child **ScopeItem**'s column n:

```
Key = ParentListView.ColumnHeaders(n).Key
Header = ChildScopeItem.ColumnHeaders(Key)
Text = ChildScopeItem.ListSubItems(Header.Index)
```

The reason for matching keys rather than simply using the corresponding indexes is to allow a **ScopeItem** to appear in more than one list view. By using the keys, the snap-in can display only a subset of the **ListSubItems** objects in a particular list view. For more information on column headers and list subitems see "**MMCColumnHeaders**" and "**MMCListSubItems**."

Data contains an **MMCDataObject** that contains the data exported by the **ScopeItem** to be used by extension snap-ins that extend its node type. See "**MMCDataObject**" for more information on how to set data for export. See "Developing Extension and Dual-Mode Snap-ins" for more information on extensions.

For extensible nodes defined at design time, the **ScopeItem**'s node type name is the same as its name in the Nodes section of the designer's tree view. The node type GUID is generated by the designer and the node is automatically registered under MMC's **NodeTypes** key.

DynamicExtensions contains a collection of **Extension** objects that encapsulate the properties of all dynamic extensions registered for the scope item's node type. A snap-in can load a dynamic extension for namespace or other features by setting **Extension.NamespaceEnabled=True** or **Extension.Enabled=True**. For more information on registered extensions see "**Extension**." This can be done when the scope item is created or in the specific feature event handler (for example, Views_AddNewMenuItems). The first time **DynamicExtensions** is accessed the designer runtime will read the registration database. If performance is a concern then the snap-in should defer enabling dynamic extensions until the feature event handler.

ScopeItem.SlowRetrieval indicates to MMC whether a **ScopeItem** can be displayed quickly when a saved console file is reloaded. If this property is **True** then MMC will not reselect a scope item when the .msc file is reloaded unless it is the target of a console taskpad. The same rule applies for persisting a view if the scope item is at the root of a view (regardless of whether it is selected).

The **Pasted** property is used in cut-and-paste operations within a single instance of a snap-in. If **True** it indicates that the item was successfully pasted. See "Implementing Drag/Drop and Cut/Copy/Paste" for more information.

The **PropertyChanged** method is used from a property page when it changes some aspect of the data represented by the **ScopeItem**. When the property page calls this method the snap-in receives the ScopeItems_PropertyChanged event.

The **RemoveChildren** method removes all of the scope item's children from the scope pane.

Syntax

ScopeItem As ScopeItem

Properties

ColumnHeaders	Columns for scope item's display data when scope item is displayed in result pane in report mode.
Data	Data exported by the **ScopeItem** for extension snap-ins.
DynamicExtensions	Collection of objects representing dynamic extensions registered for the scope item type.
Folder	Position in **SnapIn** image lists of image used for scope item in scope pane and result pane.
Index	Index of the **ScopeItem** in the **ScopeItems** collection.
Key	Key of the **ScopeItem** in the **ScopeItems** collection.
ListSubItems	**ListSubItem** objects for text displayed when scope item is displayed in result pane in report mode.
Name	Name of the **ScopeItem**. Must always match key.
NodeID	Unique nonlocalized ID used to identify a scope item so that it can be reselected when a console file is loaded.
Pasted	Set by the snap-in during a paste operation to indicate that the scope item was successfully pasted.
ScopeNode	**ScopeNode** object associated with this scope item.
SlowRetrieval	Indicates whether the data for the scope item can be retrieved quickly when the console file (.msc) is reloaded.
SubItems	Text displayed when scope item is displayed in result pane in report mode.
Tag	Holds any private snap-in data associated with the **ScopeItem**.

| Methods | **PropertyChanged** | Called from a property page to inform the snap-in of changes made in the property sheet. Causes ScopeItems_PropertyChanged event to be fired. |
| | **RemoveChildren** | Deletes all child nodes of the scope item. |

Events   This object has no events.

ScopeNode

The **ScopeNode** object represents a node in the console namespace. It contains the properties that are available for all nodes regardless of ownership. **ScopeItem** has a property that returns its associated **ScopeNode**. When navigating the namespace snap-ins move between **ScopeNode** objects.

The **Owned** property indicates whether a **ScopeNode** is owned by the snap-in. For an owned scope node, its **ScopeItem** can be retrieved by using the **ScopeNode** object as an index into the **ScopeItems** collection.

Navigation in the scope pane is done using the **Parent**, **Child**, **FirstSibling**, **Next**, and **LastSibling** properties. Each of these returns a **ScopeNode** for the adjacent node.

HasChildren can be set to to tell MMC whether the node will have any children added to it when it is expanded. If **HasChildren=False** then a plus sign (+) is not displayed to the left of the node in the scope pane. Getting **HasChildren** indicates whether the node currently has any child nodes. When a node is added programmatically using **ScopeItems.AddPredefined** or **ScopeItems.Add** an optional parameter can be used to specify whether the node will have children. **HasChildren** can also be set for a node at design time using the property browser.

ExpandedOnce indicates whether the node has ever been expanded.

DisplayName contains the text displayed for the scope item in the scope pane and in the result pane when it is not in detail mode.

For extensible nodes defined at design time the **ScopeItem**'s node type name is the same as its name in the Nodes section of the designer's tree view. The node type GUID is generated by the designer and the node is automatically registered under MMC's **NodeTypes** key. For nodes defined in code at run time the snap-in developer must manually register the node type. The developer must also choose a node type GUID in this case and set **NodeTypeName** and **NodeTypeGUID**.

Visual Basic Snap-ins

The **ExpandInTreeView** and **CollapseInTreeView** methods expand and collapse the node in the scope pane. These are UI operations only and will have no effect if the node has not been expanded in the namespace.

ExpandInNameSpace programmatically initiates the expansion of the node and will generate a ScopeItems_Expand event. It has no effect on the UI.

The **NewWindow** method allows a snap-in to create a new view. There are numerous options to determine the appearance of the view (for example, no toolbars, no scope pane, and so on) and the snap-in can determine its title bar text.

Syntax	**ScopeNode As ScopeNode**	

Properties	**Child**	Returns the **ScopeNode** that is the first child of the node.
	DisplayName	The name displayed in the console for the node.
	ExpandedOnce	Indicates whether the scope node has been expanded at least once.
	FirstSibling	Returns the **ScopeNode** that is the first sibling of the node.
	HasChildren	Setting this property determines whether a plus sign (+) is displayed next to the node in the MMC tree view. Getting this property returns a value indicating whether the node currently has any children.
	LastSibling	Returns the **ScopeNode** that is the last sibling of the node.
	Next	Returns the **ScopeNode** that is the next sibling of the node.
	NodeTypeGUID	GUID used to identify the type of node.
	NodeTypeName	Name used to identify the type of node.
	Owned	Indicates whether the node was created by the snap-in.
	Parent	Returns the **ScopeNode** that is the parent of the node.

Methods	**ExpandInNameSpace**	Expands the node in the namespace (but not in the tree view).

Events	This object has no events.	

Views

The **Views** collection is the collection of **View** objects representing the multiple-document interface (MDI) windows currently open in the console that contain nodes owned by the snap-in. The snap-in does not explicitly create **View** objects. Items are added to and removed from this collection in response to the user opening and closing windows in the console. Events on this collection handle MDI window life-cycle events such as activate/deactivate and minimize/maximize as well as many user interactions such as selection and cut/paste.

The **CurrentView** property returns the **View** object corresponding to the view that currently has focus. **SnapIn.CurrentView** is a shorthand reference to this property. This property can have the value **Nothing** if there is no current view (for example, while the snap-in is loading).

The Initialize event is fired when the view is created. This informs the snap-in that a new window has been opened. This can happen when the snap-in is first loaded into a console or when a saved console file (.msc) is loaded.

The Load event is fired after MMC has completed initialization of the new view. At this point the snap-in can check the MMC version using the **View** object's properties. See "View" in this chapter for more information.

The Terminate event is fired when a window is destroyed. A window is destroyed when the user closes it or closes MMC.

The Activate and Deactivate events are fired as the view gains and loses focus.

The WriteProperties event is fired when the user saves a console that includes the **View**. The snap-in can use this event to store view-specific data that will be needed when the console file is loaded. When MMC is restoring the view during console file load, the snap-in will receive the ReadProperties event. These events work exactly as for **UserControl** and persistable Visual Basic classes using a **PropertyBag**. Note that these events are fired in addition to the SnapIn_ReadProperties and SnapIn_WriteProperties events that are used for serialization of the snap-in's global serialization data in a console file. For more information see "SnapIn" in this chapter.

The Select event is fired whenever the user changes the selection in either the scope pane or the result pane. The selection is passed in an *MMCClipboard* parameter. This object contains collections of scope items, list items, and data objects for foreign nodes (added by namespace extensions). The event also receives an **MMCConsoleVerbs** collection that the snap-in uses to enable or disable the console verbs such as cut, copy, paste, print, refresh, rename, and delete. When a verb is enabled its toolbar button will appear and a corresponding item will appear on MMC's context menu if the user right-clicks the selected item(s).

When the user makes a multiple selection the snap-in receives the GetMultiSelectData event so that it can determine the data that will be exported for the selected items as a group. The data is used by extension snap-ins that support multiple selection.

The SetControlbar event is fired to allow the snap-in to add or remove toolbars and menu buttons from the console. An **MMCControlbar** object is passed as a parameter and its **Attach** and **Detach** methods are used to access the console's control bar.

The UpdateControlbar event is fired so that the snap-in can enable/disable and set the visibility of its toolbar and menu buttons.

The Refresh event is fired if the console enabled the refresh verb in the Select event and the user invoked refresh from the context menu, from the toolbar, or by pressing F5.

The Delete event is fired if the console enabled the delete verb in the Select event and the user invoked delete from the context menu, from the toolbar, or by pressing the DELETE key.

The Print event is fired if the console enabled the print verb in the Select event and the user invoked print from the context menu or the toolbar.

The QueryPaste event is fired if the console enabled the paste verb in the Select event and the user is dragging selected item(s) over a scope item or displays the context menu. If the snap-in returns **True** and the user completes the operation then the snap-in receives the Paste event. If the operation was a move (as opposed to a copy) then the snap-in receives the Cut event. See "Implementing Drag/Drop and Cut/Copy/Paste" in Chapter 35 for more information.

The QueryPagesFor event is fired if the console enabled the properties verb in the Select event and the user invoked properties from the context menu, from the toolbar, or by pressing ALT+ENTER. If the snap-in returns **True** then it receives the CreatePropertyPages event in which it can add its pages to the console's property sheet. See "Property Pages" in Chapter 34 for more information.

When the user displays a context menu the snap-in has the opportunity to add items to four different insertion points. There are four different events that correspond to each of these points. AddNewMenuItems is for MMC's **New** submenu. AddTaskMenuItems is for MMC's **All Tasks** submenu. AddTopMenuItems allows adding items to the top of the context menu. AddViewMenuItems is for MMC's **View** submenu. The new, task, and top insertion points are also used on MMC's **Action** menu button drop-down. The view insertion point is also used on MMC's **View** menu button drop-down.

The SpecialPropertiesClick event is fired when the result pane contains a non-list view (OCX, URL, or taskpad), and the result pane has focus, and the snap-in has enabled the properties verb, and the user clicks the properties button on the toolbar. It has a single *SnapInSelectionTypeConstants* parameter containing **siSpecialWeb** or **siSpecialOcx**. If the snap-in needs to display properties it can use **View.PropertySheetProvider**. If the snap-in is displaying an OCX view, then it can also pass **View.PropertySheetProvider** to the ActiveX control.

Syntax	**Views As Views**

Properties		
	Count	Count of **View** objects currently in the collection.
	CurrentView	Reference to the **View** object that represents the currently active view in the console. Can also be accessed as **SnapIn.CurrentView**.
	Item	Retrieves a **View** object from the collection references by index or key.

Methods   This collection has no methods.

Events   Events will appear in the Visual Basic code as `Views_<EventName>` because **Views** is the property of **SnapIn** that contains the collection.

Activate	Called when a view becomes the active view.
AddNewMenuItems	Called to allow the snap-in to add items to the **New** submenu of MMC's context menu.
AddTaskMenuItems	Called to allow the snap-in to add items to the **All Tasks** submenu of MMC's context menu.
AddTopMenuItems	Called to allow the snap-in to add items to the top of MMC's context menu.
AddViewMenuItems	Called to allow the snap-in to add items to MMC's **View** menu.
CreatePropertyPages	Called to allow a snap-in to add its page(s) to a property sheet.
Cut	Called after a user has completed a cut-and-paste operation.
Deactivate	Called when the active view is changed.
Delete	Called when the user invokes the delete verb by clicking the delete button, context menu item, or pressing the DELETE key.
GetMultiSelectData	Called when the user selects multiple items in the result pane to allow the snap-in to export data for the selection.

Events *(continued)*	Initialize	Called when a view is created.
	Load	Called when MMC has completed initialization of the view. MMC version number and services are available at this time.
	Maximize	The view has been maximized.
	Minimize	The view has been minimized.
	Paste	The user has invoked the paste verb by dropping, clicking the paste button, or clicking **Paste** on the context menu.
	Print	The user has invoked the print verb by clicking the print button or clicking **Print** on the context menu.
	QueryPagesFor	Asks the snap-in whether it has property pages to display for the selected item(s).
	QueryPaste	Called to ask the snap-in if the selected item(s) can accept a paste operation.
	ReadProperties	Called to allow the snap-in to read its view-specific serialization data from a saved console file (.msc).
	Refresh	The user has invoked the refresh verb by clicking the refresh button, pressing F5, or clicking **Refresh** on the context menu.
	Select	Called when the selection changes in a view.
	SetControlbar	Called to allow the snap-in to add its toolbars and menu buttons to the MMC control bar.
	SpecialPropertiesClick	Called when the result pane contains a taskpad, URL result view, or OCX result view, and the user clicks the properties button on the toolbar.
	Terminate	Called when a view is destroyed.
	UpdateControlbar	Called to allow the snap-in to update its toolbars and menu buttons according to the selected item(s).
	WriteProperties	Called to allow the snap-in to write its view-specific serialization data to a saved console file (.msc).

Visual Basic Snap-ins

View

The **View** object represents a single MDI child window in the console. All events for a view are fired on the **Views** collection.

The **MMCMajorVersion** and **MMCMinorVersion** properties allow primary snap-ins to determine the MMC version. They are available starting from the Views_Load event. Non-namespace extensions do not have access to the MMC version but as of MMC 1.2 there is no difference in available functionality between MMC 1.1 and MMC 1.2 for these extensions.

The **Caption** property is used when a new view is created programmatically using **ScopeNode.NewWindow**. It determines the text of the view's title bar.

PropertySheetProvider is an **MMCPropertySheetProvider** object that allows a snap-in to programmatically initiate the display of property sheets and wizards. See "Initiating Property Sheet and Wizard Displays Programmatically" in Chapter 34 for more information.

The **SelectScopeItem** method is used to select a scope item in the scope pane and optionally specify its result view. If the scope item does not appear in the view's scope pane then this method has no effect. This situation can occur if the user invokes **New Window from Here** on a node below the snap-in's static node or if the snap-in programmatically does the same using **ScopeNode.NewWindow**.

The **SetStatusBarText** method inserts text into the view's status bar in the lower-left corner. This method should only be called when a node added by the snap-in is currently selected in the scope pane. It cannot be used when the snap-in's static node is selected in the scope pane.

The status bar has three sections, which are delineated by the pipe character (|). For example, setting the text in the status bar to "Big| Bad| Wolf" places "Big" in the leftmost section of the status bar, "Bad" in the middle section, and "Wolf" in the rightmost section.

If more than three fields are delineated (that is, there are more than two pipes), then everything that would be placed in the fourth and higher fields is omitted.

In addition, the middle section is designed to function as a progress bar. This functionality is invoked by passing the percent (%) character as the first character, followed by a number between 0 and 100, into the middle section. Instead of text, this section then displays a progress bar that is zero to 100 percent complete. For example, passing "Done|%75" places "Done" in the left section and a progress bar 75 percent complete in the middle section.

If you want to display a string that begins with "%" in the middle section of the status bar, then begin the string with "%%". This causes the middle section to display text and removes the first "%". For example: "cheesy|%%poofs%" results in the left section containing "cheesy" and the middle section containing "%poofs%". If an invalid number or non-numeric text is entered in the middle section following a "%", then the middle section is empty. If a "%" is the only character in the section, then it will be shown as text.

The **PopupMenu** method is used only for column filtering. It allows the snap-in to display a menu defined at design time or in code as a pop-up menu at a specified location. For more information see "Using Column Filtering" in Chapter 35.

The **ScopePaneItems** property is a collection of **ScopePaneItem** objects representing the set of scope items owned by the snap-in that are currently in the view's scope pane. See "ScopePaneItems" in this chapter for more information.

Syntax	View As View

Properties

Caption	For primary snap-ins sets the title bar in a view created by calling **View.NewWindow(siCustomTitle, Caption)**.
ColumnSettings	Column persistence settings for the view. MMC 1.2 only.
Index	Ordinal position of the **View** in the **Views** collection.
Key	Key that uniquely identifies the **View** in the **Views** collection.
MMCMajorVersion	Returns the MMC major version number.
MMCMinorVersion	Returns the MMC minor version number.
Name	Name that uniquely identifies the **View** in the **Views** collection.
PropertySheetProvider	**MMCPropertySheetProvider** object that can be used to initiate property sheet and wizard displays programmatically.
ScopePaneItems	Collection of **ScopePaneItem** objects contained within the view.
SortSettings	Sort persistence settings for the view. MMC 1.2 only.
Tag	Holds any private snap-in data associated with the **View**.

Methods

CollapseInTreeView	Collapses a node in the view's scope pane.
ExpandInTreeView	Expands a node in the view's scope pane.
NewWindow	Creates a new view.
PopupMenu	Displays a pop-up menu. Used for column filtering.
SelectScopeItem	Selects a scope item in the view's scope pane.
SetStatusBarTest	Displays text in MMC status bar (at the bottom of the view window).

Events   This object has no events.

ScopePaneItems

The **ScopePaneItems** collection represents the collection of scope items created by the snap-in that are currently visible in the scope pane within a single **View**. **ScopePaneItem** represents an instance of **ScopeItem** in a scope pane and its properties pertain to the view-specific aspects of a scope item such as its current **ResultView**. All events are on the collection. To check whether a scope item is currently in the scope pane the **ScopeItem** object can be used as an index into the **ScopePaneItems** collection. Unfortunately, if the **ScopePaneItem** is not present, it does not mean that the **ScopeItem** is not in the scope pane because MMC does not always tell the snap-in which items are there. The designer runtime collects all available hints in order to populate **ScopePaneItems**. Snap-ins do not add or remove items from this collection. The only time a **ScopePaneItem** is guaranteed to be present is when a **ScopeItem** is selected in the scope pane and a result view is displayed for it in the result pane.

The **Parent** property contains a reference to the **View** object that owns the **ScopePaneItems** collection.

The **SelectedItem** property contains a reference to the **ScopePaneItem** for the currently selected scope item in the scope pane. **SnapIn.CurrentScopePaneItem** is a shorthand reference to this property. **SelectedItem** can be **Nothing** if there is no selection in the scope pane belonging to the snap-in.

The Initialize event is called when a **ScopePaneItem** is created. The Terminate event is called when it is destroyed.

The GetResultViewInfo event is called when the user selects the scope item in the scope pane. It allows the snap-in to determine what type of result view will be displayed. The designer runtime determines a default based on design-time definitions. If the node was defined at run time or if no default result view was chosen at design time, then the runtime defaults to a list view. The parameters contain the runtime's default and the snap-in can change them as needed. See "ScopePaneItem" in this chapter for more information on how to set the *DisplayString* parameter.

The GetResultView event is called when the snap-in is caching result views. Snap-ins can decide to cache a result view in the ResultViews_Deactivate event by returning **Keep=True**. Caching can be useful for a result view that is displayed often and requires significant time and/or processing to populate. If there are cached result views then the snap-in can handle this event and return the index of an existing result view in the **ScopePaneItem.ResultViews** collection. This event is only fired if the snap-in did not handle GetResultViewInfo or did not change any of the parameters in its handler.

Syntax	**ScopePaneItems As ScopePaneItems**	
Properties	Count	Count of **ScopePaneItem** objects in the collection.
	Item	Returns a **ScopePaneItem** object in the collection referenced by index or key.
	Parent	Returns the **View** object that owns the collection.
	SelectedItem	Returns the **ScopePaneItem** that represents the currently selected node in the scope pane of the owning view.

Methods   This collection has no methods.

Events   These events will appear in the Visual Basic code as
                 `ScopePaneItems_<EventName>`.

	GetResultView	If ScopePaneItems_GetResultViewInfo is not handled then this event is called to allow the snap-in to reuse an existing result view.
	GetResultViewInfo	Called to allow the snap-in to set the result view type and display string for the specified scope pane item.
	Initialize	Called when a **ScopePaneItem** object is created.
	Terminate	Called when a **ScopePaneItem** object is destroyed.

ScopePaneItem

The **ScopePaneItem** object encapsulates all of the properties of a scope item that are particular to an instance of the scope item within a view. The **Name** and **Key** properties always match those of the underlying **ScopeItem**.

Parent contains a reference to the owning **ScopePaneItems** collection.

ScopeItem contains a reference to the underlying **ScopeItem**.

DisplayString contains information specific to the currently displayed result view for the **ScopePaneItem**. **ResultViewType** is an enumeration that contains the current type of result view. The following table describes the contents of **DisplayString** for the different result view types.

Result view type	DisplayString contents
siURLView	URL navigated to in result pane.
siOCXView	ProgID of ActiveX control displayed in result pane.
siTaskpad, siListpad, siCustomTaskpad	res:// URL to path of taskpad template followed by "#" and then the group name. See the MMC SDK C++ documentation for **IComponent::GetResultViewType** (in Chapter 17) for details on this format.
siListView	Empty.
siMessageView	Empty.
siPreDefined	Name of result view in designer window.

ResultView contains a reference to the **ResultView** object for the current contents of the result pane.

ResultViews is a collection of all of the existing result views for the **ScopePaneItem**. Normally there is only one **ResultView** in this collection but if the snap-in chooses to cache result views in the ResultViews_Deactivate event then they are not removed from the collection and can be reused by handling ScopePaneItems_GetResultView. See "ScopePaneItems" in this chapter for more information.

HasListViews indicates whether the **ScopePaneItem** is displaying or can display result views in the result pane. If **HasListViews=True** then MMC will add the list view options (large, small, list, report, filtered) to its **View** menu. The default is **True**. If the snap-in needs to set this property to **False** it must do so in the ResultViews_Initialize event.

ColumnSetID is used for column persistence and identifies the instance of the **ScopeItem** in the scope pane. If not set then it defaults to the scope item's node type GUID in **ScopeItem.ScopeNode.NodeTypeGUID**. Using the default tells MMC that all nodes of this type, when selected in the scope pane and displaying a list view, will use the same column settings. If a snap-in needs to maintain individual column settings then it should set **ColumnSetID** to a unique value for each instance of the **ScopePaneItem** object for the node. The FileExplorer sample is an example of using the default setting. This allows users to customize column settings in one folder and then have them preserved as they navigate to other folders. This happens because all folders use the same node type. If FileExplorer wanted to preserve the settings on a per-folder basis then it would give each folder's **ScopePaneItem** a unique value for **ColumnSetID**.

The **DisplayNewResultView** method is used to change the contents of the result pane. Parameters are the result view type and the display string. The same effect can be achieved by setting **ResultViewType** and **DisplayString** and then reselecting the scope item using **View.SelectScopeItem**.

Visual Basic Snap-ins

DisplayMessageView displays a message view in the result pane and allows specifying all of its properties as parameters. This can also be done by using **DisplayNewResultView** and then setting the message view properties in ResultViews_Activate.

Syntax	ScopePaneItem As ScopePaneItem	

Properties		
ColumnSetID	Identifies a set of column and sort settings persisted by MMC.
DisplayString	Used in combination with **ResultViewType** to determine the type of result view displayed for the **ScopePaneItem**.
HasListViews	Indicates whether the scope pane item can display list views. Determines whether view menu options are enabled in the console.
Index	Index of the **ScopePaneItem** within its owning **ScopePaneItems** collection.
Key	Key of the **ScopePaneItem** within its owning **ScopePaneItems** collection.
Name	Name of the **ScopePaneItem**. Always the same as **Key**.
Parent	Returns the **ScopePaneItems** collection that owns the **ScopePaneItem**.
ResultView	A reference to the **ResultView** object representing the currently displayed result view for the **ScopePaneItem**.
ResultViews	The collection of **ResultViews** for the **ScopePaneItem**.
ResultViewType	Determines the type of result view displayed for the **ScopePaneItem**.
ScopeItem	Reference to the **ScopeItem** object that the **ScopePaneItem** represents in the scope pane of its view.
Tag	Can be used by the snap-in to associate data with the **ScopePaneItem**.

Methods		
DisplayMessageView	Displays a message view in the result pane.
DisplayNewResultView	Displays the specified result view in the result pane.

Events	This object has no events.	

ResultViews

The **ResultViews** collection represents the collection of result views displayed in the result pane by its owning **ScopePaneItem**. **ResultView** represents a single result view. The developer does not directly create result views—they are created by the designer runtime when needed. As with the other objects, all events are on the collection and each has a parameter that is the **ResultView** for which the event applies.

The Initialize event is called when a **ResultView** is created. If the result pane will contain a list view then the Initialize event is a good opportunity to populate the list view. For list views defined in code, column headers should be added at this time. This event is also used for setting list view properties such as **HideSelection**, **LexicalSort**, **MultiSelect**, **ShowChildScopeItems**, **Virtual**, and sorting properties if they were not set at design time. This event should also be used to hide columns if needed. If the result pane will contain a taskpad then tasks can be hidden at this time. If the result pane will contain an OCX view then **ResultView.AlwaysCreateNewOCX** can be set at this time to disable OCX caching. See "ResultView" in this chapter for more information on OCX caching.

The InitializeControl event is fired when an ActiveX control in an OCX view is created. The snap-in can access the control in **ResultView.Control**. If the control is cached then this event is received only once when the control is first created. If the result view is displayed again then **ResultView.Control** can be accessed starting in the ResultViews_Activate event.

The Activate event is called when the result view is about to be displayed. It can also be used for list view population. If a result view is cached, it will receive Activate when it is about to be reused. See "ScopePaneItems" in this chapter for more information on result view caching.

The Deactivate event is called when the result view is about to be removed from the result pane. If the snap-in needs to cache the result view it can return **Keep=True** from this event. If the snap-in needs to override the user's column customization or sort settings it should do so during this event. For more information see "Using Column Persistence" in Chapter 35.

Visual Basic Snap-ins

The Terminate event is called when the result view is destroyed.

The ListItemDblClick event is called when the user double-clicks a list item. ScopeItemDblClick is called when the user double-clicks a scope item in the result pane. Both events have a *DoDefault* parameter that if returned as **True** indicates to MMC to take the default action. If the event is not handled or *DoDefault* is not changed then the default action will occur. Default action for a scope item is to select it in the scope pane and expand it. Default action for a list item is the default verb. The default verb is open unless the snap-in changes it in the Views_Select event. Double-clicking a scope item in the scope pane does not fire an event because MMC always expands or collapses the node in response to this action.

The ColumnClick event is called when the user clicks a column header to initiate sorting. MMC begins the sort operation following this event.

The CompareItems event is called during a sort operation to allow the snap-in to do customized sorting (for example, comparing dates or other binary fields). If the snap-in does not handle this event or its handler does not return a result then the designer runtime does a case-insensitive comparison of the column text. In MMC 1.1 this event is only passed list items. This is because MMC 1.1 does not support sorting child scope items in the result pane. In MMC 1.2 CompareItems can receive any combination of both list items and scope items. This allows the snap-in to determine how child scope items will be sorted in the result pane.

The ColumnsChanged event is called when the user has customized the column settings using the **Choose Columns** dialog box from MMC's **View** menu. If the snap-in returns **Persist=True** (the default) then MMC will persist the user's changes. If the user selects another node in the scope pane with the same column set ID or returns to this node then the column settings will be preserved. See "ScopePaneItem" in this chapter for more information on setting the column set ID.

The ItemRename event is called if the snap-in enabled the rename verb in Views_Select and the user selected **Rename** from the context menu or used a slow double-click to initiate the rename operation.

The ItemViewChange event is called in every result view when the snap-in calls **MMCListItem.UpdateAllViews**. This is useful for operations like rename where the action occurs in one view but other views are potentially displaying the same list item. The snap-in should check whether it is displaying the same list item and update **MMCListItem.Text** and **MMCListItem.ListSubItems** accordingly.

The PropertyChanged event is called when a property page calls **MMCListItem.PropertyChanged** to inform the snap-in of changes made in the property sheet.

The FilterChange event is called for filtered list views when the user changes the filter value and the time-out designated by **MMCListView.FilterChangeTimeout** has elapsed. The snap-in can examine the new value in **MMCColumnHeader.TextFilter** or **MMCColumnHeader.NumericFilter**.

The FilterButtonClick event is fired when the user clicks the filter button. The snap-in should display a pop-up menu using **View.PopupMenu** to allow the user to change the filter criteria.

For virtual list views, a number of events are fired as MMC needs information to populate the list view. GetVirtualItemDisplayInfo is fired when MMC needs the list item and list subitem text. GetVirtualItemData is fired to allow the snap-in to set exported data for extensions in **MMCListItem.Data** and to enable dynamic extensions for the list item using **MMCListItem.DynamicExtensions**. SortItems is fired to inform the snap-in that list items will be fetched in sorted order on a particular column. CacheHint is fired to allow the snap-in to begin asynchronous fetching of data for list items that are likely to be displayed soon. FindItem is fired when the user searches for items by typing the initial letters. DeselectAll is fired when the user deselects everything in the list view so that the snap-in can update console verbs and toolbars.

The TaskClick event is fired when the user clicks a task in a taskpad. TaskNotify is fired when a custom taskpad calls **MMCCtrl.TaskNotify**. For more information on using **MMCCtrl** on a custom taskpad DHTML page see the MMC SDK documentation.

The ListpadButtonClick event is fired when the user clicks the button on a list view taskpad.

Visual Basic Snap-ins

Syntax	**ResultViews As ResultViews**	
Properties	Count	Count of **ResultView** objects in the collection.
	Item	References a **ResultView** object in the collection by index or key.

Methods   This object has no methods.

Events   These events will appear in the Visual Basic code as `ResultViews_<EventName>`.

Activate	Called when a result view is about to be shown in the result pane.
CacheHint	Virtual lists only. Called to allow the snap-in to start asynchronous caching of list items that will likely be displayed.
ColumnClick	Called when the user clicks a list view column header.
ColumnsChanged	Called when the user makes a change to the column configuration in a list view.
CompareItems	Nonvirtual lists only. Called during a sort operation to allow the snap-in to do custom comparison of items in the result pane.
Deactivate	Called when a result view is being removed from the result pane.
DeselectAll	Virtual lists only. Called when all items in the specified list view have been deselected.
FilterButtonClick	Called when the user clicks the filter button on the header control.
FilterChange	Called when the user has made a change to the filter value for a column.
FindItem	Virtual lists only. Called to find the ordinal index of an item by name.

Events	GetVirtualItemData	Virtual lists only. Called to allow the snap-in to initialize **MMCListItem.Data**.
(continued)	GetVirtualItemDisplayInfo	Virtual lists only. Called when the snap-in must initialize display properties for a list item.
	Help	Called when the user has requested Help for the specified result view item.
	Initialize	Called when a **ResultView** object is created.
	InitializeControl	Called when an ActiveX control is created in a result pane.
	ItemRename	Called when the user requests to rename the specified list item.
	ItemViewChange	Called when the result view needs to be refreshed in response to an **MMCListItem.UpdateAllViews**() call.
	ListItemDblClick	Called when the user double-clicks a list item.
	ListpadButtonClick	Called when the user has clicked the button on a snap-in list view taskpad.
	PropertyChanged	Called when a property page calls **MMCListItem.PropertyChanged** to inform the snap-in of changes made in the property sheet.
	ScopeItemDblClick	Called when the user double-clicks a scope item in the result pane.
	SortItems	Virtual lists only. Called to inform the snap-in that the list items will be fetched in sorted order.
	TaskClick	Called when the user has clicked a task on a snap-in taskpad.
	TaskNotify	Called from a custom taskpad when script has called **MMCCtrl.TaskNotify**.
	Terminate	Called when a **ResultView** object is about to be destroyed.

Visual Basic Snap-ins

ResultView

The **ResultView** object encapsulates the properties of the result pane. It contains objects that control the properties of the list view, taskpad, and message view.

The **Type** and **DisplayString** properties are read-only copies of the owning **ScopePaneItem**'s properties. See "ScopePaneItem" in this chapter for more information.

ScopePaneItem contains a reference to the **ScopePaneItem** that owns the **ResultView**.

The **Control** property contains a reference to the ActiveX control in the result pane when the **ResultView** is an OCX view. **Control** can be assigned to a variable of the control's type in order to make access to its properties and methods more efficient. For example:

```
Dim Ctl As MyControl
Set Ctl = ResultView.Control
Ctl.SomeProperty = SomeValue
```

AlwaysCreateNewOCX determines whether MMC will cache the ActiveX control in an OCX view. The default is **False** meaning that MMC will cache. If caching is not desirable then this property should be set to **True** in ResultViews_Initialize.

ListView is a reference to an **MMCListView** object that encapsulates the properties of the list view. It is used when the **ResultView** is a list view and also when it is a list view taskpad. See "MMCListView" in this chapter for more information.

Taskpad is a reference to a **Taskpad** object that encapsulates the properties of a snap-in taskpad. It is used when the **ResultView** is a taskpad or a list view taskpad. See "Taskpad" in this chapter for more information.

MessageView is a reference to an **MMCMessageView** object that encapsulates the properties of a message view. It is used when the **ResultView** is a message view. See "MMCMessageView" in this chapter for more information.

DefaultItemTypeGUID is used as the node type for list items in a list view. When a list item is created its **ItemTypeGUID** property is set from this value. For list views defined at design time it is generated by the designer. If the list view is extensible then the node type is registered under MMC's **NodeType** key in the registration database. For list views defined in code it is generated by the designer runtime. The snap-in can change **DefaultItemTypeGUID** and it can change **ItemTypeGUID** for individual list items, but in that case the developer is responsible for the registration database entries.

SetDescBarText inserts text into the result pane's description bar. The description is not visible by default. The user must request to make it visible using MMC's **View** menu in MMC 1.1 or using the **Customize** dialog box from the **View** menu in MMC 1.2.

Syntax

ResultView As ResultView

Properties

AlwaysCreateNewOCX	Determines whether an ActiveX control is cached.
Control	Gives the snap-in access to the ActiveX control in an OCX result view
DefaultItemTypeGUID	Default value assigned to **MMCListItem.ItemTypeGUID** for list items in a list view.
DisplayString	Together with **Type** indicates the type of result view.
Index	Index of the **ResultView** in its owning **ResultViews** collection.
Key	Key of the **ResultView** in its owning **ResultViews** collection.
ListView	**MMCListView** object used when result view contains a list view.
MessageView	**MMCMessageView** object used when result view contains a message view.
Name	For snap-in use to identify the **ResultView** object.
ScopePaneItem	**ScopePaneItem** object that owns the **ResultView** object.
Tag	For snap-in use to associate data with the **ResultView** object.
Taskpad	**Taskpad** object used when the result view contains a snap-in taskpad.
Type	Together with **DisplayString** indicates the type of result view.

Methods

SetDescBarText	Sets the text in MMC's description bar for the result view.

Events

This object has no events.

Visual Basic Snap-ins

MMCImageList

MMCImageList is similar to a Visual Basic Common Controls **ImageList** control and is used to hold images used in the scope pane, in the result pane, and in toolbars. Image lists can be created at design time or at run time using the **New** keyword. An image list created at design time becomes a module-level object in the snap-in at run time. It can be referenced by its design-time name, for example, **ImageList1.Tag = 1**.

Image lists can only contain bitmaps and all bitmaps in an image list must be the same size. Small bitmaps are 16x16 pixels and large bitmaps are 32x32 pixels.

MaskColor is used to determine which color pixel will be treated as transparent at run time. Pixels of this color will not be painted so that the underlying background will show through.

ListImages references an **MMCImages** collection containing the images.

MMCImages

MMCImages is a collection of **MMCImage** objects used by **MMCImageList**. It is a standard collection and the snap-in can both add and remove images at run time.

MMCImage

MMCImage represents a single bitmap. It uses a Visual Basic **StdPicture** object to hold the bitmap.

MMCListView

MMCListView defines the contents of a list view in the result pane and allows the snap-in to change its properties. It works very similarly to the Common Controls **ListView** object.

ColumnHeaders references an **MMCColumnHeaders** collection that defines the columns used when the list view is in report mode.

ListItems references an **MMCListItems** collection that defines the list items displayed in the list view. A snap-in can only add list items to a list view. Child scope items that appear for container nodes are added automatically by MMC. The list items can be initially populated in the ResultViews_Initialize or ResultViews_Activate event. List items can also be added or removed at any time following these events in response to UI interactions (for example, toolbar button click, context menu selection) or as asynchronously fetched data arrives. For more information on asynchronous list view population see "Asynchronous Population of Scope and Result Panes" in Chapter 35.

SelectedItems references an **MMCClipboard** object that contains the currently selected item(s) in the list view.

SetScopeItemState can be used to change the appearance and selection status of a scope item that appears in a list view because its parent node is selected in the scope pane. The **MMCListView.ListItems** collection does not contain elements that represent scope items because MMC automatically adds child scope items to a list view. A **ScopeItem** object represents a scope item and its properties determine the text displayed in either the scope pane or the result pane. This method allows programmatically selecting, highlighting, and so on a scope item when it is in the result pane. A snap-in can only determine whether a scope item appears in the list view by checking whether its parent node is the currently selected scope item (referenced by **SnapIn.CurrentScopeItem**).

View determines the view mode of the list view (large icons, small icons, list, detail, or filtered). Filtered views require MMC 1.2 or later.

Icons and **SmallIcons** reference **MMCImageList** objects that define the bitmaps displayed with the list items as well as the child scope items that appear in the list view. For more information on using image lists in list views and in the scope pane see "Coordinating Image Lists" in Chapter 35.

Visual Basic Snap-ins

MultiSelect determines whether the list view will support multiple selection. It can be set at design time or at run time in ResultViews_Initialize. Multiple selection is very easy to support in a Visual Basic snap-in because the **MMCClipboardObject** that contains the selected items simply uses list item and scope item collections that can be iterated. See "MMCClipboard" in this chapter for more information.

Virtual determines whether the list view will contain list items (nonvirtual) or whether the snap-in will respond to requests from MMC to supply list item data (virtual). This property can be set at design time or at run time in ResultViews_Initialize. Virtual list views are useful when the logical data set consists of a large number of list items and the snap-in does not want to prefetch the entire set. MMC does not automatically add child scope items to virtual list views so if the snap-in requires them, it must add fake scope items using list items that display the same data and respond similarly to selection and double-clicks. See "ResultViews" in this chapter for events that must be handled by virtual list views.

HideSelection determines whether the list view will support multiple selection. It can be set at design time or at run time in ResultViews_Initialize.

ShowChildScopeItems determines whether the list view will display child scope items. It requires MMC 1.2 or later. It can be set at design time or at run time in ResultViews_Initialize.

UseFontLinking determines whether strings used for list item and list subitem text will contain multiple languages. If **True** then the list view will determine which fonts it needs based on the language of the Unicode characters within the strings. For more information on using Unicode characters in list item text see "Using Unicode Strings" in Chapter 35.

There are numerous properties that relate to sorting. **SortOrder** determines whether sorting will be ascending or descending. **SortKey** determines the column on which the list view is sorted. **SortHeader** determines whether clicking a column header initiates a sort operation. The **Sorted** property determines whether the list view will be sorted. These can all be set at design time or at run time. Setting **Sorted=True** at run time will initiate a sort operation. During a sort operation the ResultViews_CompareItems event will be fired. If the snap-in does not handle that event then the designer runtime uses a case-insensitive string comparison.

MMC 1.2 added some additional sorting properties. **SortIcon** determines whether the up- and down-arrow icons will appear in the column headers when clicked by the user to initiate a sort. MMC sorts on a single column only but the snap-in can make comparisons based on multiple columns in the ResultViews_CompareItems event. In this case the snap-in can turn off the sort icon because it would falsely indicate to the user that the sort is on a single column. **SortIcon** can be set at design time or at run time in ResultViews_Initialize.

Also added in MMC 1.2 is **LexicalSort**. In MMC 1.1, scope items in the result pane are left unsorted and appear at the top of the list view. In MMC 1.2, if **LexicalSort=True** then the ResultViews_CompareItems event is not fired and MMC uses a lexical sort on the scope items followed by the list items. **LexicalSort** can be set at design time or at run time in ResultViews_Initialize.

FilterChangeTimeOut determines the interval between the time the user makes a filter value change and the firing of the ResultViews_FilterChange event. The time-out is used when the user makes a change but does not press ENTER. **FilterChangeTimeOut** requires MMC 1.2 or later. It can be set at design time or at run time. See "Using Column Filtering" in Chapter 35 for more information.

MMCColumnHeaders

MMCColumnHeaders is a collection of the **MMCColumnHeader** objects that define the columns displayed when a list view is in detail or filtered mode. Column headers can be defined at design time in the list view property sheet or at run time in the ResultViews_Initialize or ResultViews_Activate event. Virtual list views that define columns programmatically must do so in ResultViews_Initialize only.

The **ScopeItem** object also uses an **MMCColumnHeaders** collection to map the data it displays when it appears in a list view.

For more information see "MMCListView" and "ScopeItem" in this chapter.

MMCColumnHeader

MMCColumnHeader defines the properties of a single column displayed in a list view in detail or filtered mode.

Text is the text displayed in the column header. Text can be changed at any point during run time.

Width determines the column's width in pixels. It can also be set to **siColumnAutoWidth** to indicate that the width should match the length of the column's text. Width can be changed at any point during run time.

Alignment determines whether the column's text will be aligned left, right, or centered. It can only be specified at design time or when the column header is added by calling **MMCColumnHeaders.Add**. After the column has been added this property can only be used to examine the alignment.

Hidden determines whether the column will be visible. It must be set at run time in the ResultViews_Initialize or ResultViews_Activate event. Virtual list views must set it in ResultViews_Initialize only.

Visual Basic Snap-ins

In MMC 1.2 or later the list view can use column filtering. The filter value for a column can be numeric or textual. The **NumericFilter** property is used to set a numeric filter value. The snap-in can also get its value to determine if the user has entered a numeric value in the column filter and examine its value. The **TextFilter** property serves the same function for text values. If the filter value is blank then both properties return an empty **Variant**. To make the value empty set either property to an empty **Variant**.

MMCListItems

MMCListItems is a collection of the **MMCListItem** objects that define the contents of a list view. A list view's list items collection can be initially populated in the ResultViews_Initialize or ResultViews_Activate event. List items can also be added or removed at any time following these events in response to UI interactions (for example, toolbar button click, context menu selection) or as asynchronously fetched data arrives. For more information on asynchronous list view population see "Asynchronous Population of Scope and Result Panes" in Chapter 35.

In virtual list views, the collection is always empty but the snap-in can reference the properties of any virtual item by using an index (keys cannot be used). For more information see "Using Virtual List Views" in Chapter 35.

In addition to standard collection methods and properties, **MMCListItems** also has a **SetItemCount** method. For nonvirtual list views, calling this method asks MMC to preallocate memory for the specified number of items to improve performance. For virtual lists, this method tells MMC how many items exist in the list so that it can correctly paint the scroll bars and handle navigation using the END key. **SetItemCount** must be called in the ResultViews_Activate event.

MMCListItem

MMCListItem represents a single list item in a list view.

The **Text** property defines the text displayed for the list item when the list view is in large icon, small icon, or list mode.

The **ListSubItems** property references a collection of **MMCListSubItem** objects that define the text for the columns when the list view is in detail or filtered mode. The **SubItems** property is a string array that can be used as shorthand for referencing the **Text** property of each **MMCListSubItem**. For example, the following lines of code are equivalent:

```
ListSubItems(1).Text = "Some Text"
SubItems(1) = "Some Text"
```

Note that the snap-in must add items to the **MMCListSubItems** collection before they can be referenced using **SubItems**.

Icon contains the numeric index or string key of the image displayed with the list item. The index or key must be the same in the containing list view's **LargeIcons** and **Icons** image lists. For more information on using image lists see "Coordinating Image Lists" in Chapter 35.

Selected determines whether a list item is selected in the list view.

DropHilited determines whether a list item is highlighted as a drag/drop target.

Focused determines whether a list item is currently surrounded by a standard focus rectangle. Only one item has the focus, even in a multiple selection.

ItemTypeGUID contains the node type GUID for the list item. This defaults to the containing result view's **DefaultItemTypeGUID** property but can be changed by the snap-in at any time.

Data references an **MMCDataObject** containing the data exported by the snap-in for the list item. Snap-ins that extend the list item's node type use this data to determine their actions. For more information see "Developing Extension and Dual-Mode Snap-ins" in Chapter 34.

DynamicExtensions is a collection of **Extension** objects representing the set of dynamic extensions registered for the list item type. Dynamic extensions are only loaded for an instance of a list item if they are enabled by setting **Extension.Enabled=True**. This can be done when the list item is created or in the specific feature event handler (for example, Views_AddNewMenuItems). The first time **DynamicExtensions** is accessed the designer runtime will read the registration database. If performance is a concern then the snap-in should defer enabling dynamic extensions until the feature event handler.

ID is a string property that uniquely identifies a list item with the underlying data that it represents. Its default value is the same as **Key** in a nonvirtual list view. In a virtual list view its default value is the string representation of the list item's index. The designer runtime uses this property when comparing list items to determine whether they represent the same underlying data. This can happen after displaying a property page for a list item(s) when the user selects a different scope item in the scope pane. The list view that owns the list item(s) will be destroyed but the property page may be holding on to the orphaned **MMCListItem** object(s). For more information on handling this situation see "Handling Orphaned Property Pages" in Chapter 35.

MMCListSubItems

MMCListSubItems is a collection of **MMCListSubItem** objects used to define the text displayed in the columns of a list view in detail or filtered mode. Snap-ins do not create **MMCListSubItems** objects. They are added to the **MMCListView.ListSubItems** or **ScopeItem.ListSubItems** collections. **ScopeItem.ListSubItems** is only used when a **ScopeItem** appears in a list view.

The text of a list subitem can also be accessed using the string array referenced by **MMCListView.SubItems** or **ScopeItem.SubItems**. The advantage of using the **MMCListSubItems** collection is that the **MMCListSubItem** object has a **Tag** property that allows the snap-in to store extra information with the list subitem. This is useful when the snap-in needs to keep extra information on a per-column, per-row basis.

MMCListSubItem

MMCListSubItem defines the text displayed in a column of a list view in detail or filtered mode. The **Text** property holds the text displayed. The **Tag** property allows the snap-in to associate extra information with the list subitem.

MMCDataObjects

MMCDataObjects is a collection of **MMCDataObject** objects used to export data to and import data from other snap-ins. See "MMCDataObject" in this chapter for more information.

MMCDataObject

MMCDataObject is used to export data to and import data from other snap-ins. Every **ScopeItem** and every **MMCListItem** has a **Data** property that returns an **MMCDataObject** containing the data exported by that object.

MMCDataObject.SetData exports data from the snap-in. It takes a **Variant** containing the data and format name. The **Variant** can contain any simple type (**Integer**, **Long**, **String**, and so on), an object that supports persistence (such as a Visual Basic class), **Byte** arrays, and **String** arrays.

MMCDataObject.GetFormat checks to see whether a data format is available when importing data.

MMCDataObject.GetData retrieves the data for a specific format as a **Byte** array in a **Variant**.

The **FormatData** method can be used to interpret any subset of the **Byte** array as any simple data type, a persisted object, or multiple concatenated null-terminated Unicode strings.

MMCDataObject.ObjectTypes returns a **String** array containing the node type GUIDs of all the object types exported by the snap-in when multiselection is used.

Clear removes all data added by **SetData**.

For more information see "Importing Data from C++ Snap-ins" in Chapter 35 and "Developing Extension and Dual-Mode Snap-ins" in Chapter 34.

MMCClipboard

MMCClipboard is used to hold the user's selections in the result pane. It contains collections of **ScopeItems**, **MMCListItems**, and **MMCDataObjects**. It is very simple to use and makes supporting multiple selection just as easy as supporting single selection. The snap-in need only iterate through each of the collections to determine what is selected.

The **SelectionType** property is an enumeration that allows a snap-in to quickly determine the nature of the selection. It has the following values:

Value	Meaning
siSingleScopeItem	A single scope item owned by the snap-in.
siSingleListItem	A single list item owned by the snap-in.
siSingleForeign	A single item owned by another snap-in.
siMultiScopeItems	Multiple scope items owned by the snap-in.
siMultiListItems	Multiple list items owned by the snap-in.
siMultiMixed	List items and scope items owned by the snap-in.
siMultiForeign	Multiple items owned by other snap-ins.
siMultiMixedForeign	Multiple items. Some are owned by the snap-in and some by other snap-ins.
siSpecialWeb	The user has selected or deselected the result pane that currently contains a URL view or a taskpad view. Used for Views_Select, Views_UpdateControlbar, toolbar, and menu button events when the result pane contains a snap-in taskpad or a URL result view.
siSpecialOcx	The user has selected or deselected the result pane that currently contains an OCX view. Used for Views_Select, Views_UpdateControlbar, toolbar, and menu button events when the result pane contains an OCX result view.
siEmpty	There are no currently selected objects.

MMCMenus

MMCMenus is a collection of **MMCMenu** objects. It is used to hold the child menus of an **MMCMenu** object referenced from its **Children** property. See "MMCMenu" in this chapter and "Menus" in Chapter 34 for more information.

MMCMenu

MMCMenu is similar to the Visual Basic intrinsic menu control. It is used to represent a single item on a console context menu as well as a container of menu items added at a single insertion point (top, **View** menu, **All Tasks** menu, and **New** menu). Events are fired on the individual **MMCMenu** objects and on the containing **MMCMenu**. Menus can be defined at design time, at run time, or a combination of both (for example, adding children to a menu created at design time).

The **Name** property is used to identify the **MMCMenu** object in Visual Basic code. A menu created at design time becomes a module-level object in the snap-in at run time. It can be referenced by its design-time name, for example, **Menu1.Tag = 1**.

The **Index** property determines the menu's position both in the collection and when it is added to the insertion point in MMC's context menu. The **Key** property is for snap-in use to help further identify the menu.

Caption contains the text displayed in MMC's context menu.

StatusBarText contains the text displayed in the status bar when the menu is highlighted by the user.

Visible determines whether the menu is visible at run time.

Enabled determines whether the user can select the menu at run time.

Grayed determines whether the menu is dimmed and disabled at run time.

Checked determines whether the menu has a check mark displayed next to its caption.

MenuBreak indicates whether the menu item begins a new column.

MenuBarBreak indicates whether the menu item begins a new column with a separating vertical line.

There is no separator property because MMC does not permit snap-ins to add separator lines to its context menus. You may have seen some C++ snap-ins that do this, but it is against the MMC UI guidelines and is consequently not possible from a Visual Basic snap-in.

Children contains the collection of child menus contained by the menu. Menus can be nested to any level. An **MMCMenu** object that has children cannot be selected by the user (that is, it defines a submenu).

The Click event is fired when the user selects the item represented by the **MMCMenu** object. It is fired on both the object and its containing **MMCMenu**. If the snap-in handles the event on the containing menu then the *Index* parameter indicates which element in its **Children** collection was clicked.

For more information on using menus in a snap-in see "Menus" in Chapter 34.

ContextMenu

ContextMenu represents the console's context menu and is used to add **MMCMenu** objects. It is passed as a parameter to the menu insertion events such as Views_AddTaskMenuItems. It has a single method **AddMenu** that receives the name of the menu being added. The designer runtime adds all of the items in **MMCMenu.Children** to the insertion point in MMC's context menu. This object cannot be used outside of these events.

MMCPropertySheet

MMCPropertySheet represents a Win32 property sheet displayed by the console. An **MMCPropertySheet** object is passed as a parameter to the SnapIn_CreateConfigurationWizard and Views_CreatePropertyPages events to allow the snap-in to add its pages to the wizard or property sheet.

Property pages that implement **IMMCPropertyPage** also receive an **MMCPropertySheet** object in the **IMMCPropertyPage_Initialize** method so that a reference to it can be stored in a module-level variable. This allows the property page to modify the state of the property sheet while it is running.

AddPage adds a property page to the sheet if it is a property sheet. It is usually called from the Views_CreatePropertyPages event but it can also be called from a property page to dynamically add a page to a running property sheet,

AddWizardPage adds a page for wizards. It can only be called before the property sheet is running. The object passed in the *ConfigurationObject* parameter will be available to the property page in its PropertyPage_SelectionChanged event in **SelectedControls(0)**.

For both **AddPage** and **AddWizardPage**, the page is identified by its name passed as a literal string.

GetPagePosition returns the one-based position of the property page within the property sheet.

InsertPage can be called from a property page to insert a new page at a specified position.

RecalcPageSize should be called from a property page after adding or inserting a page that is not the same size as the existing pages.

AddPageProvider can be called from a property page to pass the CLSID of a C++ COM object that will add pages to the property sheet. It creates the object and returns a reference to it along with the HWND of the property sheet. The caller can then pass the sheet's HWND to the object and it can use the Win32 PSM_ADDPAGE or PSM_INSERTPAGE message to add its pages. This mechanism allows using existing C++ property pages.

ActivatePage can be called from a property page to select a new page. This is the programmatic equivalent of the user clicking the page's tab.

RemovePage can be called from a property page to remove a page from a running property sheet.

SetTitle can be called from a property page to change the title of a running property sheet.

PressButton can be called from a property page to programmatically simulate the user pressing one of the property sheet's buttons.

ChangeCancelToClose can be called from a property page to change the **Cancel** button to a **Close** button. This can be used when the user has made changes that cannot be reversed.

SetWizardButtons can be called from a property page in a wizard to change the state of the wizard's **Back**, **Next**, and **Finish** buttons.

SetFinishButtonText can be called from a property page in a wizard to change the text of the **Finish** button and enable it. Also hides the **Back** and **Next** buttons.

RebootSystem and **RestartWindows** can be called from a property page to tell MMC to reboot the system or restart Windows after the property sheet is closed if the user clicked **OK**.

For more information see "Property Pages" in Chapter 34.

MMCPropertySheetProvider

MMCPropertySheetProvider is available as a property of the current **View**. It allows the snap-in to programmatically initiate the display of a property sheet or wizard.

CreatePropertySheet creates a new property sheet. The *Type* parameter determines whether the property sheet will contain property pages or a wizard. Wizard97-style wizards require using **Picture** objects on the property pages to hold the header and watermark bitmaps. For more information see "Creating Wizard97-Style Wizards" in Chapter 35. The *Objects* parameter can contain one or more objects that will be passed in the *Selection* parameter to the subsequent Views_QueryPagesFor and Views_CreatePropertyPages events. For property sheets, this object (or objects) will also available to the property page in its PropertyPage_SelectionChanged event in **SelectedControls**. For wizards, the object in **SelectedControls(0)** is the *ConfigurationObject* parameter to **MMCPropertySheet.AddWizardPage**.

AddPrimaryPages asks MMC to allow the snap-in to add its pages to the sheet. This causes the Views_QueryPagesFor and Views_CreatePropertyPages events to be fired.

AddExtensionPages asks MMC to allow extension snap-ins to add their pages to the sheet. Extension snap-ins implemented in Visual Basic will receive the ExtensionSnapIn_CreatePropertyPages event.

Show displays the property sheet or runs the wizard. The *Page* parameter specifies the page that should be shown first. It is the one-based ordinal position of the sequence in which pages were added in Views_CreatePropertyPages.

FindPropertySheet asks MMC to determine whether the property sheet for the specified object(s) is currently being displayed. If it is found then the sheet is made active and the method returns **True**.

Clear tells MMC to release all resources associated with the property sheet. This method should be called if a property sheet is created but not shown.

For more information see "Initiating Property Sheet and Wizard Displays Programmatically" in Chapter 34.

MMCConsoleVerbs

MMCConsoleVerbs is a fixed-size collection that represents the verbs exposed by the console: copy, cut, paste, rename, delete, open, properties, print, and refresh. It allows the snap-in to enable/disable verbs during the selection events Views_Select and ResultViews_DeselectAll (see "Views" in this chapter) and it can only be used during these events. The collection is indexed using the **SnapInConsoleVerbConstants** enumeration rather than by integers. This enumeration has values such as **siCopy, siCut**, and so on. Snap-ins cannot add or remove elements from this collection.

Verb execution occurs when the user clicks the corresponding context menu item, toolbar button, or presses the corresponding shortcut key. For example, when the user clicks the print button, the snap-in receives the Views_Print event. The following is a table of **SnapInConsoleVerbConstants** and their corresponding events:

The return value settings are:

Verb	Event
siCopy	None. Handled by MMC.
SICut	Views_Cut.
siDelete	Views_Delete.
siNone	None.
siOpen	ScopeItems_Expand (only for a scope item in the result pane).
siPaste	Views_Paste.
siPrint	Views_Print.
siProperties	Views_QueryPagesFor and Views_CreatePropertyPages.
siRefresh	Views_Refresh.
siRename	ScopeItems_Rename for a scope item or ResultViews_ItemRename for a list item.

The **DefaultVerb** property returns the verb that MMC executes when the user presses ENTER or double-clicks the selected items in the result pane. The default verb is also displayed in bold on context menus.

Visual Basic Snap-ins

The snap-in can set the default verb by setting **Default=True** on the corresponding **MMCConsoleVerb** object. For example, to make print the default verb the code is:

```
ConsoleVerbs(siPrint).Default=True
```

If open is the default verb and the selection is a single scope item in the result pane, then when the user double-clicks or presses ENTER MMC expands that scope item and selects it in the scope pane. If open is the default verb and the selection is a list item then MMC does nothing for a double-click or ENTER.

If the selection contains scope and/or list items and the default verb is properties then MMC initiates a property sheet display for a double-click or ENTER. In that case the snap-in will receive the Views_QueryPageFor and Views_CreatePropertyPages events.

For all other default verbs MMC does nothing on double-click or ENTER. To instruct MMC to always do nothing in response to double-click and ENTER set the default verb to none:

```
ConsoleVerbs(siNone).Default=True
```

For information on enabling and disabling verbs, See "MMCConsoleVerb" in this chapter.

MMCConsoleVerb

MMCConsoleVerb encapsulates the properties of a single console verb. Its properties determine whether MMC adds the corresponding toolbar and context menu items to its UI.

Enabled determines whether the verb is enabled for the selected items.

Hidden determines whether the verb's UI elements will be visible.

Checked determines whether a check mark will appear next to the corresponding context menu item and the toolbar button will appear pressed in with the checked style.

Indeterminate determines whether the corresponding toolbar button and context menu item will appear dimmed.

ButtonPressed determines whether the button is currently pressed.

MMCToolbar

MMCToolbar is similar to the Visual Basic Common Controls **Toolbar**. It is used to encapsulate the properties of toolbars and menu buttons added by the snap-in to MMC's control bar. Events are fired on the **MMCToolbar** object. A toolbar can be added to or removed from MMC's control bar in the Views_SetControlbar event for primary snap-ins and in ExtensionSnapIn_SetControlbar for toolbar extensions.

MMC does not allow mixing toolbar buttons and menu buttons within the same toolbar. This means that within a single **MMCToolbar** object cither all buttons have the drop-down style (for menu buttons) or they all have any of the other button styles (default, separator, checked, or group).

The **Name** property is used to identify the toolbar object in Visual Basic code. A toolbar created at design time becomes a module-level object in the snap-in at run time. It can be referenced by its design-time name, for example, **Toolbar1.Tag = 1**.

The **Buttons** property contains a reference to an **MMCButtons** collection that defines the buttons appearing on the toolbar.

The **ImageList** property references an image list that contains the bitmaps used for the toolbar buttons. All bitmaps in the image list must be 16x16 pixels.

The ButtonClick event is fired when the user clicks a toolbar button.

ButtonDropDown is fired when the user clicks a menu button before the designer runtime displays the drop-down menu. This allows the snap-in to change the state of and add or remove items on the drop-down menu.

ButtonMenuClick is fired when the user selects an item on a button's drop-down menu.

MMCButtons

MMCButtons contains a collection of **MMCButton** objects that represent the buttons on a toolbar. Buttons can be added or removed at run time before or after the toolbar is added to MMC's control bar.

MMCButton

MMCButton represents a single button on a toolbar. Except for **Style**, button properties can be changed at any time.

Style determines the type of button. If a button has the drop-down style then it represents a menu button and the snap-in must populate its **ButtonMenus** collection. MMC does not allow mixing buttons and menu buttons on the same toolbar. If one button has the drop-down style then all other buttons must also have that style.

Caption is used only for menu buttons. It contains the text that is displayed within the button on MMC's control bar.

ToolTipText contains the text for the tooltip displayed when the user holds the mouse over the button.

Image contains the index or key of the image for the button in the toolbar's image list. It is not used for menu buttons.

Enabled determines whether the button will accept user input.

Value determines whether the button is currently pressed.

Visible determines whether the button is visible.

MixedState determines whether the button appears in indeterminate state (dimmed).

ButtonMenus contains a reference to an **MMCButtonMenu** collection that defines the items displayed when a button menu drops down.

MMCButtonMenus

MMCButtonMenus is a collection of **MMCButtonMenu** objects that defines the items displayed when a button menu drops down. It is referenced in **MMCButton.ButtonMenus**. Button menus can be added or removed at any time except while the drop-down menu is displayed. Snap-ins typically use the MMCToolbar_ButtonDropDown event to adjust the contents of the collection prior to the display of the drop-down menu.

MMCButtonMenu

MMCButtonMenu represents an item displayed when a button menu drops down.

Text contains the text for the menu item.

Visible determines whether the menu is visible at run time.

Enabled determines whether the user can select the menu at run time.

Grayed determines whether the menu is dimmed and disabled at run time.

Checked determines whether the menu has a check mark displayed next to its caption.

MenuBreak indicates whether the menu item begins a new column.

MenuBarBreak indicates whether the menu item begins a new column with a separating vertical line.

Separator determines whether the item is a horizontal separator line.

Parent references the **MMCButton** object that owns the **MMCButtonMenus** collection that contains the menu item.

MMCControlbar

MMCControlbar represents the console's control bar and is used to add and remove the snap-in's toolbars and menu buttons. This object is only available within the Views_SetControlbar, Views_UpdateControlbar, ExtensionSnapIn_SetControlbar, and ExtensionSnapIn_UpdateControlbar events.

The **Attach** method adds a control to MMC's control bar.

The **Detach** method removes a control from MMC's control bar.

In MMC 1.1 and MMC 1.2 **MMCToolbar** is the only type of control that can be added to the control bar.

Taskpad

Taskpad encapsulates the properties of a snap-in taskpad. It is referenced from **MMCListView.Taskpad**.

Name identifies the taskpad in Visual Basic code. If a taskpad is defined at design time in the designer window then **Name** will be the same as the taskpad's name in the designer. It is also used as the group name. Primary Visual Basic snap-ins do not use the group name but extension snap-ins (both Visual Basic and C++) need to know the group name in order to extend the taskpad.

Type is an enumeration that indicates whether the snap-in is a taskpad, a list view taskpad, or a custom taskpad.

Title is a string displayed at the top of the taskpad.

DescriptiveText is a string displayed at the top of the taskpad beneath the title. This text can be a phrase that serves as a subtitle or instructions.

For list view taskpads **ListpadStyle** determines whether the listpad control on the taskpad is vertical or horizontal. The default is vertical. **ListpadTitle** contains the string displayed directly above the list view control. **ListpadHasButton** indicates whether a button is displayed to the right of the list pad title. If **ListpadHasButton=True** then **ListpadButtonText** contains the text displayed on the button. **ListView** contains the name of a list view defined at design time that is used to access the listpad control on the list view taskpad. At run time the snap-in uses **ResultView.ListView** just as it would for a list view in the result pane. If **Taskpad.ListView** is not set then the snap-in must initialize the properties of **ResultView.ListView** in ResultViews_Initialize.

For custom taskpads **URL** contains the res:// URL of the taskpad template.

For default taskpads and list view taskpads **BackgroundType** is an enumeration that indicates what type of background image the snap-in wants to display on the taskpad. The following table describes the different image types and the extra information required for each type.

Value	Meaning
siBitmap	**MouseOverImage** contains the res:// URL of a bitmap resource.
SiVanillaGIF	**MouseOverImage** contains the res:// URL of a custom resource containing a transparent GIF image where index 0 is transparent.
SiChocolatcGIF	**MouseOverImage** contains the res:// URL of a custom resource containing a transparent GIF image where index 1 is transparent.
SiSymbol	The image consists of a string of characters in a symbol font. **SymbolString** contains the string. **EOTFile** contains the res:// URL of the font file. **FontFamily** contains the font family name used to display the string.
SiNoImage	No image is used. No extra information is needed.

For more information on using images see "Using Resources in Taskpads" in Chapter 34.

Tasks contains a reference to the **Tasks** collection that defines the task buttons on a taskpad or list view taskpad.

Tasks

Tasks is collection of **Task** objects that define the task buttons on a taskpad or list view taskpad. For a taskpad defined at design time the collection is populated by the designer runtime prior to the ResultViews_Initialize event. Individual task properties can be changed before display in the ResultViews_Initialize event. For taskpads defined at design time that event should be used to populate the collection.

Task

The **Task** object defines a task button on a default taskpad or list view taskpad.

The **Text** property contains the text displayed underneath the task's image.

HelpString contains the text displayed in a tooltip when the user moves the mouse over the task's image or text.

Visible indicates whether the task should be displayed in the taskpad. It can be set in ResultView_Initialize. Typical usage of this property is to hide one or more tasks in a taskpad defined at design time.

ActionType is an enumeration that determines the type of action taken when the user clicks the task. The following table shows the different action types, additional information required, and the resulting action.

Value	Action	Additional information
siNotify	Snap-in receives ResultViews_TaskClick.	None.
siURL	MMC navigates to URL in the result pane.	**URL** property contains URL that MMC should navigate to.
siScript	Executes script code.	**Script** property specifies a string containing the script code to execute.

When using the **siScript** action the **Script** property can optionally begin with one of the following language identifiers: "VBSCRIPT:", "JSCRIPT:", or "JAVASCRIPT:". If the language is not specified then MMC assumes it is "JAVASCRIPT:". An example script is:

```
"JSCRIPT:alert('Message displayed from a script action')"
```

For VBSCRIPT MMC calls **window.execScript** to execute the script. For JSCRIPT and JAVASCRIPT MMC calls **eval** to execute the script. These calls are made within the DHTML code in MMC's default taskpad and list view taskpad HTML pages.

ImageType is an enumeration that indicates what type of image MMC displays for the task. Every task must have an image. The following table describes the different image types and the extra information required for each type.

Value	Meaning
siBitmap	**MouseOverImage** contains the res:// URL of a bitmap resource. This bitmap is displayed when the user moves the mouse over the task area. **MouseOffImage** contains the res:// URL of a bitmap resource displayed when the mouse is not over the task area. At least one of these properties must be set.
siVanillaGIF	**MouseOverImage** contains the res:// URL of a custom resource containing a transparent GIF image where index 0 is transparent. This image is displayed when the user moves the mouse over the task area. **MouseOffImage** contains the res:// URL of the same type of GIF displayed when the mouse is not over the task area. At least one of these properties must be set.
siChocolateGIF	**MouseOverImage** contains the res:// URL of a custom resource containing a transparent GIF image where index 1 is transparent. This image is displayed when the user moves the mouse over the task area. **MouseOffImage** contains the res:// URL of the same type of GIF displayed when the mouse is not over the task area. At least one of these properties must be set.
siSymbol	The image consists of a string of characters in a symbol font. **SymbolString** contains the string. **EOTFile** contains the res:// URL of the font file. **FontFamily** contains the font family name used to display the string.

For more information on using images see "Using Resources in Taskpads" in Chapter 34.

MMCMessageView

MMCMessageView encapsulates the properties of a message view in the result pane. It is referenced in **MMCListView.MessageView**.

TitleText contains the text displayed in the message view's title.

BodyText contains the text displayed in the body of the message view.

IconType is an enumeration that determines the icon displayed in the message view. These are similar to the standard icons used in a message box (error, information, question, warning, and none).

Extensions

Extensions is a collection of **Extension** objects that encapsulate the properties of all extensions registered for a particular node type. Snap-ins do not directly create **Extensions** collections. They are referenced in the following object properties:

Reference	Contents
SnapIn.RequiredExtensions	The set of all extensions registered for all of the snap-in's node types.
ScopeItem.DynamicExtensions	The set of dynamic extensions registered for the scope item's node type.
MMCListItem.DynamicExtensions	The set of dynamic extensions registered for the list item's node type.

Extensions.EnableAll enables all of the extensions in the collection.

Extensions.EnableAllStatic enables all of the static extensions in the collection.

For more information see "Extension" in this chapter.

Extension

Extension holds the registration database information for a snap-in registered to extend one of a snap-in's node types.

CLSID contains the extension's CLSID as a string. This is also used as the key for the **Extension** in the collection.

Name is the extension's name string in the registry. Snap-ins don't always register a name so this string can be empty.

ExtendsContextMenu, **ExtendsNameSpace**, **ExtendsPropertySheet**, **ExtendsTaskpad**, and **ExtendsToolbar** indicate which features the snap-in extends.

Type is an enumeration that indicates whether the extension is static or dynamic. A static extension is always loaded when the user invokes the extended feature for the node type. For example, a static context menu extension for one of a snap-in's scope items is always loaded when the user displays a context menu. A dynamic extension must be enabled before it can be loaded.

The **Enabled** property determines whether an extension will be loaded. If the **Extension** object is part of **SnapIn.RequiredExtensions** it can be enabled in SnapIn_Initialize to indicate to MMC that the extension should be loaded when the snap-in is loaded. If the **Extension** object is part of **ScopeItem.DynamicExtensions** or **MMCListItem.DynamicExtensions** then it can be enabled when the scope item or list item is created or when the particular feature event is fired (for example, a dynamic context menu extension could be enabled in Views_AddTaskMenuItems). When an extension collection is accessed for the first time, the designer runtime must read the registration database. If performance is critical then the snap-in should defer enabling dynamic extensions until the feature event is fired.

NameSpaceEnabled is used only for dynamic namespace extensions. If **NameSpaceEnabled** is set to **True** before the node it extends is expanded, then when the node later expands, the extension will be loaded and it will have the opportunity to add child nodes to the expanding node. If the extension is a Visual Basic snap-in then it will receive the ExtensionSnapIn_Expand event. If **NameSpaceEnabled** is set to **True** after the node it extends is expanded, then it will be loaded at that time.

For more information see "Developing Extension and Dual-Mode Snap-ins" in Chapter 34.

ColumnSettings

ColumnSettings is a collection of **ColumnSetting** objects that contain MMC's column persistence properties. The collection is referenced in **View.ColumnSettings**. If the collection is empty then MMC does not have any column persistence data. The snap-in can populate the collection and call **ColumnSettings.Persist** to create new column settings.

MMC's column persistence data is stored according to column set ID. **ColumnSettings.ColumnSetID** contains the ID. For more information on column set IDs and column persistence see "Using Column Persistence" in Chapter 35.

ColumnSettings requires MMC 1.2 or later.

ColumnSetting

The **ColumnSetting** object contains properties that define the customization of a single column in MMC's column persistence data.

Width contains the column's width.

Hidden determines whether the column is visible.

Position is the one-based location of the column in the list view. A user can change a column's position by using the **Customize** dialog box from the MMC **View** menu.

For more information on column persistence see "Using Column Persistence" in Chapter 35. **ColumnSetting** requires MMC 1.2 or later.

SortKeys

SortKeys is a collection of **SortKey** objects that contain MMC's column persistence sorting properties. The collection is referenced in **View.SortSettings**. If the collection is empty then MMC does not have any column persistence data. The snap-in can populate the collection and call **SortKeys.Persist** to create new column settings. As of MMC 1.2 there can only be one sort key.

MMC's column persistence data is stored according to column set ID. **SortKeys.ColumnSetID** contains the ID. For more information on column set IDs and column persistence see "Using Column Persistence" in Chapter 35.

SortKeys requires MMC 1.2 or later.

SortKey

The **SortKey** object contains properties that define the sort criteria of a single column in MMC's column persistence data.

Column contains the column number of the key.

SortOrder determines whether sorting on the column is ascending or descending.

SortIcon determines whether the column header displays an arrow icon indicating the sort direction.

For more information on column persistence see "Using Column Persistence" in Chapter 35. **SortKey** requires MMC 1.2 or later.

MMCStringTable

The **MMCStringTable** object provides a means of storing string data with the snap-in. MMC creates a string table in the console file (.msc) as needed for each snap-in.

The **MMCStringTable** object is a collection of strings in which every string has an ID that is a **Long**. The collection is indexed by the ID. The **Add** method adds a string and returns the ID. **Find** returns the ID of a string that was previously added to the collection.

Note that **MMCStringTable** is designed to work with specialized localization tools. Snap-ins without access to these localization tools will not benefit from using this object.

Visual Basic Snap-ins

IWizardPage

IWizardPage is an interface defined by the snap-in designer that must be implemented by property pages used in a wizard. Visual Basic uses COM property pages that were not originally designed to be used in the Win32 property sheets used by MMC. This interface allows the designer runtime to forward events, such as page activation and button clicks, to the property page. Using out parameters from **IWizardPage** methods, the property page can control the user's navigation among the pages.

Property pages use the **Implements** keyword at the top of the module as follows:

```
Implements IWizardPage
```

This informs Visual Basic that the property page module will implement all of the methods in this interface. In the code window, the left combo box will show **IWizardPage** and the right combo box can be used to navigate to its methods.

The **Activate** method is called when a page is about to be displayed. It asks the property page whether to enable the **Back** button and whether to display a **Next** or **Finish** button. If the snap-in chooses a **Finish** button then it can also choose the text to display in that button.

The **Back** and **Next** methods are called when the user clicks **Back** and **Next**. They both have a single *NextPage* **As Long** parameter that allows the property page to determine what will happen next. The following table explains the possible return values.

Returned value of NextPage	Action
0 (default)	Go to the next or previous page as the user intended.
−1	Stay on the current page.
>0	Go to that page number. Page numbers start at 1 and are implied by the order in which they were added to the wizard property sheet using **MMCPropertySheet.AddWizardPage**.

The **Finish** method is called when the user clicks **Finish**. It has an *Allow* **As Boolean** parameter that the property page can set to indicate whether the property sheet should be closed.

Most wizard pages will also need to implement **IMMCPropertyPage**. That interface has methods that provide both property sheet and wizard pages with information regarding the user's interaction with the page. For more information see "IMMCPropertyPage" in this chapter.

IMMCPropertyPage

Property pages can optionally implement an interface defined by the designer runtime called **IMMCPropertyPage**. This interface gives the property page access to extra functionality in MMC that is not part of a standard Visual Basic property page. Property pages use the **Implements** keyword at the top of the module as follows:

```
Implements IMMCPropertyPage
```

This informs Visual Basic that the property page module will implement all of the methods in this interface. In the code window, the left combo box will show **IMMCPropertyPage** and the right combo box can be used to navigate to its methods.

IMMCPropertyPage_Initialize is called when the page is created following the PropertyPage_SelectionChanged event. It receives a reference to the **MMCPropertySheet** object and the optional *InitData* parameter passed to **MMCPropertySheet.AddPage**. This allows the snap-in to communicate any extra data to the property page other than what is contained in the selected objects. While this parameter is available to all snap-ins, primary snap-ins should store any extra data in **ScopeItem.Tag** or **MMCListItem.Tag**. The *InitData* parameter is only needed for property page extensions calling **MMCPropertySheet.AddPage** in the ExtensionSnapIn_CreatePropertyPages event because they do not have access to any **Tag** properties.

The property page can store the **MMCPropertySheet** object passed to **IMMCPropertyPage_Initialize** in a module-level variable and use it to dynamically add and remove pages, activate pages, change button states, and request a reboot after the sheet is closed. For more information see "MMCPropertySheet" in this chapter.

Before the page is displayed, **IMMCPropertyPage_GetDialogUnitSize** is called to allow the page to determine its size using dialog units. For more information see "Creating Display-Independent Property Pages" in Chapter 35.

When the user clicks **Help** on the property sheet the runtime will call **IMMCPropertyPage_Help**. The property page can call the **MMCPropertyHelp** function (exported from mssnapr.dll) to ask MMC to display its integrated Help. See "MMCPropertyHelp" in this chapter for more information.

When the user attempts to cancel the property sheet by pressing ESC, clicking **Cancel**, or clicking the "**X**" button in the upper-right corner, then **IMMCPropertyPage_QueryCancel** is called. The page uses this method to decide whether to allow the cancellation request. If it is allowed then **IMMCPropertyPage_Cancel** is called for ESC or **Cancel** and **IMMCPropertyPage_Close** is called for "**X**".

MMCPropertyHelp

MMCPropertyHelp is an exported API function from the designer runtime (Mssnapr.dll) that allows a property page to invoke MMC's integrated HTML Help. A property page can call this function at any time but it is typically used when the user clicks the property sheet's **Help** button. Property pages can detect the **Help** button click by implementing the **IMMCPropertyPage** interface. **IMMCPropertyPage_Help** is called when the user clicks **Help**. To call **MMCPropertyHelp** the property page needs to declare the function as follows:

```
Private Declare Function MMCPropertyHelp Lib "mssnapr.dll"
↪ (ByVal HelpTopic As String) As Long
```

The *HelpTopic* parameter uses the same format as **SnapIn.Help**. The following is an example of calling **MMCPropertyHelp** to display this Help topic in this .chm file:

```
Private Sub IMMCPropertyPage_Help()
  MMCPropertyHelp
  ↪ "VBSnapInsGuide.chm::VBSnapInsGuide/VBSnapInsGuide_15.htm")
End Sub
```

For more information on the Help topic format see "Adding Help to a Snap-in" in Chapter 34.

Diagrams

The following diagrams illustrate some of the more commonly used object model elements as they relate to the MMC UI.

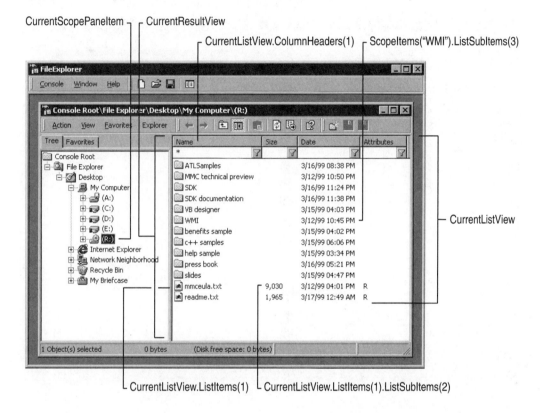

CurrentScopePaneItem ⌐ ⌐ CurrentResultView

⌐ CurrentListView.ColumnHeaders(1) ⌐ ScopeItems("WMI").ListSubItems(3)

CurrentListView

⌐ CurrentListView.ListItems(1) ⌐ CurrentListView.ListItems(1).ListSubItems(2)

ScopeItems("R:")

Views(1) (also CurrentView)

Views(1).ScopePaneItems("R:")
(also CurrentScopePaneItem)

ScopeItems("R:")

Views(2)   Views(2).ScopePaneItems("R:")

CurrentResultView.SetDescBarText

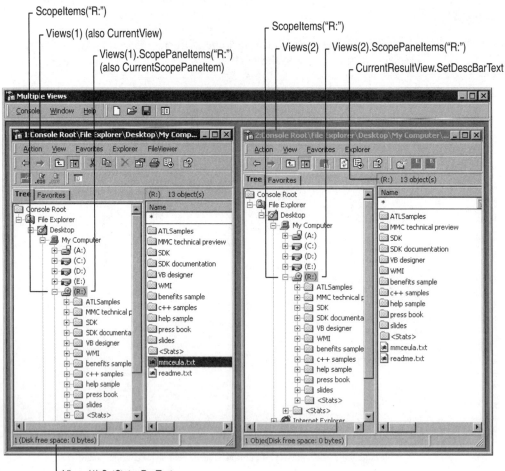

Views(1).SetStatusBarText

CHAPTER 37

Order of Events for Typical Scenarios

Loading a Snap-in

>SnapIn_Initialize
>
>SnapIn_Load

Expanding a Node

>ScopeItems_Expand (only occurs when node is first expanded in the namespace)
>
>ScopeItems_Initialize for every child added

Selecting a Scope Item That Will Display a List View

>ScopePaneItems_Initialize
>
>ScopePaneItems_GetResultViewInfo
>
>ResultViews_Initialize
>
>ResultViews_Activate
>
>Views_UpdateControlbar (scope item selected)
>
>Views_Select (scope item selected)
>
>Views_QueryPaste (target is scope item)

Deselecting That Same Scope Item

>Views_UpdateControlbar (scope item deselected)
>
>Views_Select (scope item deselected)

Selecting a List Item in the Result Pane

Views_UpdateControlbar (list item selected)

Views_Select (list item selected)

Deselecting That Same List Item in the Result Pane

Views_UpdateControlbar (list item deselected)

Views_Select (list item deselected)

Selecting a Scope Item in the Result Pane

Views_UpdateControlbar (scope item selected)

Views_Select (scope item selected)

Views_QueryPaste (target is scope item)

Deselecting That Same Scope Item in the Result Pane

Views_UpdateControlbar (scope item deselected)

Views_Select (scope item deselected)

Unloading a Snap-in

This scenario assumes that a scope item is selected in the scope pane and it is displaying a list view in the result pane.

Views_UpdateControlbar (scope item deselected)

Views_Select (scope item deselected)

Views_Deactivate

ResultViews_Deactivate

ResultViews_Terminate

Views_Terminate

ScopeItems_Terminate (once for each scope item)

SnapIn_Unload

SnapIn_Terminate

CHAPTER 38

Tips and Tricks

There are certain known issues that can affect usage of the designer. This section lists these issues and recommends workarounds where possible.

Designer Registration

The designer handles all registration and deregistration. When running under the Visual Basic IDE, after you press F5 or click the run button Visual Basic asks the designer to register itself. When you later press the stop button or click **End** on the **Run** menu the designer is asked to deregister itself. During the deregister operation all entries under the key **HKEY_LOCAL_MACHINE\Software\Microsoft\MMC** are removed. If you do not build your snap-in DLL before leaving the IDE then your snap-in will not be registered.

Another side effect of this deregistration in the IDE is that any extensions that registered themselves as extending your snap-in will have their extension entries removed (but not their own entries such as their **HKEY_LOCAL_MACHINE\Software\Microsoft\MMC\SnapIns** key). A workaround for this is to use a project group for your snap-in and all of its extension snap-ins. When you run in the IDE all projects in the group are compiled and registered. The FileExplorer sample and its extension use a project group for this purpose. To create a project group, open the main snap-in project. For each project to be added, click **File**, click **Add Project**, and specify the project's .vbp file. When all the projects have been added, click **File**, and then click **Save Project Group** to save the .vbg file that contains the project group information. To build all of the snap-ins in a project group, click **File**, and then click **Make Project Group**. To open a project group, select its .vbg file in the **Open Project** dialog box.

Taskpad Images Not Available Under Debugger

When debugging a snap-in in the Visual Basic IDE, taskpad images will not appear in MMC. This is due to the fact that the res:// URLs required by MMC cannot be created by the runtime when running under the debugger because the snap-in DLL is not loaded and may not even be built. If it is essential to see a taskpad image when debugging then you can use the following steps:

1. Temporarily change the taskpad properties to a fully qualified res:// URL using the path of your snap-in DLL on the development computer. For example: a bitmap normally specified as #2/MyBitmap should be changed to res://c:\MyProject\MySnapIn.dll/#2/MyBitmap.

2. Build the snap-in DLL.

3. Debug the snap-in in the IDE as desired. The snap-in code is executed within the IDE but the taskpad image will be taken from the built DLL.

4. When debugging is complete, change back the taskpad property and rebuild the DLL.

User Controls Not Created Under Debugger

When debugging a snap-in containing a user control that is used as an OCX view, MMC will not be able to display the OCX view. This problem can be seen when running the FileExplorer sample under the debugger. Select the static node and on the **View** menu click **Welcome to File Explorer**. Click the **About** task and you will see that the MMC splash screen is not displayed in the result pane. There is currently no workaround for this problem.

Moving the Visual Basic 6.0 Installation

If you remove your Visual Basic 6.0 installation and reinstall it at a different location on your hard disk then you must reinstall the snap-in designer.

"Retained in Memory" Project Option Cannot be Used

Visual Basic 6.0 has an option available on the **Project/Properties/General** page
called "Retained in Memory" that is used for Internet Information Services (IIS)
applications running on an IIS server. This option instructs the Visual Basic
runtime to keep itself and its project information loaded in memory even after the
IIS application has terminated. This option cannot be used with snap-ins in order
to keep the Visual Basic runtime loaded within Mmc.exe.

List View Does Not Repaint when Property Page Open Under Debugger

When running a snap-in under the debugger, if a property page is displayed for a
list item, the list view may not correctly paint the list items. To see the list items
just move the property sheet window.

Runtime Errors when Debugging Property Pages

Under certain circumstances on Windows NT 4.0, attempting to display property
pages while under the Visual Basic debugger will display the runtime error
&H800706F8, "The supplied user buffer is not valid for the requested operation."
If this occurs then Service Pack 6 is required on the Windows NT 4.0 system.

Tabbing in Property Pages Repeats Property Sheet Buttons

Under certain circumstances on Windows NT 4.0, attempting to display property
pages while under the Visual Basic debugger will display the runtime error
&H800706F8, "The supplied user buffer is not valid for the requested operation."
If this occurs then Service Pack 6 is required on the Windows NT 4.0 system.

Visual Basic Snap-ins

CHAPTER 39

Snap-in Designer Samples

The MMC Visual Basic sample snap-ins are installed as part of the Microsoft Platform SDK. Currently this location has a path similar to the following. Here, it is assumed that D: is the Platform SDK installation drive:

```
D:\Platform SDK\Samples\SysMgmt\MMC\
```

Software Requirements

- Microsoft Windows NT Workstation or Server version 4.0 with Service Pack 3 or later, or Microsoft Windows 2000 beta 3 or later, or Microsoft Windows 95 or Windows 98.
- Microsoft Visual Basic version 6.0 (no specific service pack required)
- MMC Snap-in Designer for Visual Basic
- Microsoft Management Console version 1.1 or later

Compiling the Samples

▶ **To compile the sample snap-ins**

1. Start Visual Basic 6.0.
2. On the **File** menu, click **Open Project**.
3. In the **Open Project** dialog box, click **MMCDesignerSamples.vbg**. This is a project group file that contains all of the sample projects.
4. Click **Open**.
5. On the **File** menu, click **Make Project Group**.
6. In the dialog box, click **Build** to start compiling.

Running the Samples

▶ **To run the sample snap-ins**

1. Start MMC.

2. On the **Console** menu, click **Add/Remove Snap-in**.

4. Click the **Standalone** tab, then click **Add**.

5. In the **Add a Standalone Snap-in** dialog box, click **File Explorer** in the **Available Standalone Snap-ins** list.

6. Click **Add**.

7. Answer the configuration wizard questions.

8. Click **Close**.

9. Click **OK**.

This procedure loads the FileExplorer sample into the console. The other samples are all extensions of FileExplorer and they will be loaded by MMC as needed.

Sample Functionality

The FileExplorer snap-in mimics the functionality of Windows Explorer in Microsoft Windows NT, Windows 2000, and Windows 95/98. It uses almost all the features of MMC in order to demonstrate their implementation in a Visual Basic snap-in. A configuration wizard asks whether to display network drives and whether to allow rename and delete for folders and files. If you save your console, FileExplorer will remember your configuration settings when it is reloaded.

FileExplorer is a dual-mode snap-in. It can be added to the console as a stand-alone snap-in, or in Windows 2000, it will appear as a namespace extension of Computer Management\System Tools. Its functionality is identical in both cases.

The static node has both a taskpad and a list view. If you are running MMC 1.2, or if you are running MMC 1.1 and your console has the option "Show taskpad views by default" selected, then the default result view for the static node is the taskpad. If you are running MMC 1.1 and that option is not selected, then the default result view is a list view showing the Desktop node.

Expanding the Desktop node reveals a My Computer node, and finally a list of the drives currently available on your computer. This includes all removable media, local hard disk drives, CD-ROMs, and network drives if you specified that in the configuration wizard.

In addition to the My Computer node, the desktop also contains the shell folders for Internet Explorer, Network Neighborhood, Recycle Bin, and My Briefcase. The Internet Explorer node uses a URL result view as a simple browser. To set the URL, display properties for the node. The **New** submenu on the node's context menu has a **URL** item that also displays the property sheet. Clicking the "MMC Home Page" task on the static node taskpad selects the Internet Explorer node and sets the URL to the MMC home page on www.microsoft.com. The other shell folder nodes are only for demonstration purposes and they do not display anything in the result pane.

The final node under My Computer is About FileExplorer. This node displays an OCX view in the result pane with some informational text and a button that invokes the same configuration wizard displayed when FileExplorer is added to a console. This demonstrates using the **MMCPropertySheetProvider** object from within an ActiveX control. Clicking the "About" task on the static node taskpad selects this node.

As in Windows Explorer, as you select specific drives or folders in the scope pane, the result pane is populated with a list of subfolders and files. When the view mode is set to Detail or Filtered, statistics for each file are displayed as well. The list view supports multiple selection. It also supports sorting on name, date, size, and attributes by clicking the column headers.

In Filtered view mode (available only on MMC 1.2), the name column supports some primitive filtering by name or by extension (*.*<ext>* or *<name>*.*). Click the filter button (in the lower-right corner of the column header) to display a pop-up menu that allows choosing which type of filtering should be used.

Rename and delete are supported for files and folders depending on the options specified in the configuration wizard.

Drag/drop and cut/copy/paste are also supported based on the configuration options. Targets can be folders or drives. The source can be any combination of folders and files.

Print is supported for files and, unlike Windows Explorer, it will handle multiple selection. Printing is done by invoking the system command processor's **print** command (for example, typing **print** *<file name>* at the command prompt).

Properties are supported for folders and files and are read-only (that is, you can't change a file attribute in the property page). Multiple selection is supported for property pages.

In addition to the console verbs described in the preceding paragraphs, FileExplorer has a number of custom actions that can be invoked from the context menu, a menu button, or a toolbar. These actions are as follows:

- **Run** can be used to launch applications. This can be done either by double-clicking a file name in the result pane or by highlighting the file and clicking the run button on the toolbar, the context menu item, or the menu button item. If the selected file is an application, it is launched immediately. If it is another type of file and the extension has an application associated with it, that application is launched with the file. **Run** also supports multiple selection.

- **RunAs** is similar to **Run** except that it brings up a dialog box with an edit control. Inside the edit control is the fully qualified path name of the selected file. The user can modify this command line by, for example, preceding the file path with "Notepad" (Notepad c:\Temp\Abc.xyz). In this way, a file can be launched using any application.

- **New Folder** creates a new folder underneath the currently selected folder or drive.

- On the **Explorer** menu button, there is a **Configuration** item that runs the same configuration wizard that is displayed when FileExplorer is added to the console.

FileExplorer also has a number of extension snap-ins that add functionality and demonstrate all the different extension features of MMC. These extensions are as follows:

- ComDetect is a very simple context menu extension that adds an item to the **All Tasks** submenu of MMC's context menu when a single DLL file is selected. It displays a message box saying whether the DLL is also a COM server. It determines this by using the Win32 API functions **LoadLibrary** and **GetProcAddress** to determine if the DLL exports the required **DllRegisterServer** function for in-process COM servers. Some DLLs might not load because some of the required additional DLLs may not be present.

  ComDetect is a dynamic extension and FileExplorer loads it only when a DLL file is selected.

- DriveStats is a dynamic namespace extension that adds a scope item underneath every drive. The scope item appears with the name <Stats> and has a list view showing the drive's properties.

  DriveStats also adds a <Stats> node under the My Computer node that displays a listpad showing the properties of the C drive. Clicking the listpad button displays a dialog box that allows selecting a different drive.

- FileViewer is a complex extension that extends FileExplorer's toolbar, menu buttons, property pages, taskpad, and context menus. FileExplorer loads it as a required extension.

FileViewer adds a toolbar button, a menu button, and an **All Tasks** context menu item that allow viewing the context of a file. FileViewer displays the file within a multiline edit control, so it is best suited for text files. It also adds a property page to the file's property sheet that displays the contents of the file. It supports multiple selection for property pages.

In an action unrelated to its name, FileViewer adds a property page to folder properties that displays some statistics about the folder. It is best to invoke this action on small folders that in turn reside within small folders because the statistics can take a while to gather.

FileViewer also adds an "About FileViewer" task to FileExplorer's static node taskpad.

The following diagram illustrates the various user interface objects added by FileExplorer and its extensions:

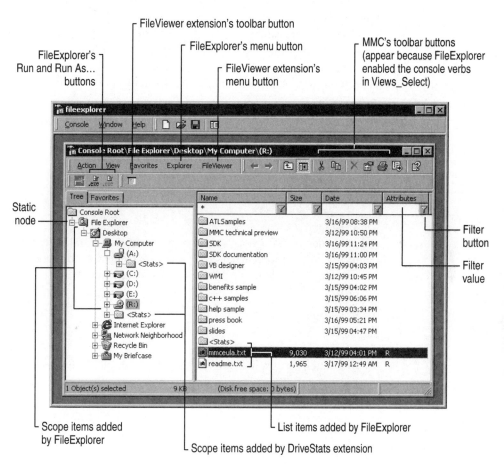

FileExplorer—Design-Time Objects

This section provides descriptions of the objects defined by FileExplorer in the snap-in designer.

Auto-Create Nodes

Auto-create nodes are defined using the snap-in designer in the Visual Basic IDE (integrated development environment). The nodes are customized using property pages. The snap-in designer takes this information and automatically creates each of these nodes at run time. Each auto-create node is represented by an entry in the tree view in MMC's scope pane. Each auto-create node is also accessible during run time by a corresponding **ScopeItem** object.

Name

Static Node

Description

This is the snap-in's static node and is the only one that is required for a primary snap-in. It is listed in the designer window with the name Static Node, but it will appear in MMC as File Explorer, as the direct child of the Console Root or of Computer Management\System Tools in Windows 2000.

Result Views

lvExplorerTop, ovAbout, uvMMCHome, StaticNodeTaskpad

Image Lists

imgSmallFolders, imgSmallOpenFolders, imgLargeFolders

Name

Desktop

Description

This node is defined as a child of the static node, and will appear directly under File Explorer when that node is expanded. Nodes are expanded either by clicking the node in the scope pane or by clicking the plus (+) sign to the left of it.

Result Views

lvExplorerFiles

Image Lists

imgSmallFolders, imgSmallOpenFolders, imgLargeFolders

Name

MyComputer

Description

This is a child of the Desktop node and will appear when the Desktop is expanded.

Result Views

lvExplorerMain

Image Lists

imgSmallFolders, imgSmallOpenFolders, imgLargeFolders

Name

Internet Explorer, NetworkNeighborhood, RecycleBin, MyBriefcase

Description

These are special shell folders that are also children of the Desktop node. They are added for the purpose of example but only Internet Explorer displays a result view.

Result Views

Programmatically defined URL view. Display properties for the node to select the URL. Context menu also has **URL** item on **New** submenu that displays the property sheet.

Image Lists

None

Name

About

Description

This is a child of the Desktop node and will appear when the Desktop is expanded. It displays an OCX view with informational text and a button that invokes the same configuration wizard displayed when FileExplorer is added to a console.

Result Views

ovAbout

Image Lists

None.

Other Nodes

Other predefined nodes are essentially templates for **ScopeItem** objects. They are not automatically created by the runtime, but can be used by the snap-in to dynamically create new nodes using all of the template's properties during the snap-in's execution. They are defined and configured just like auto-create nodes.

Name
Directory

Description
Used to create nodes for disk drives and folders.

Result Views
lvExplorerFiles

Image Lists
imgSmallFolders, imgSmallOpenFolders, imgLargeFolders

Name
ExtensionRoot

Description
The same as the static node but used as the root when File Explorer is created as an extension of Computer Management\System Tools in Windows 2000.

Result Views
lvExplorerTop, ovAbout, uvMMCHome, StaticNodeTaskpad, FAQListpad

Image Lists
imgSmallFolders, imgSmallOpenFolders, imgLargeFolders

List Views

FileExplorer defines the following list views:

Name
lvExplorerTop

Description
This list view is associated with the static node. It only displays the Desktop folder.

Default View Mode
Report

Image Lists
imgSmallFolders, imgLargeFolders

Column Headers
Name

Name
lvExplorerMain

Description
This list view is associated with the MyComputer auto-create node. It is defined to present drive-centric statistics.

Default View Mode
Report

Image Lists
imgSmallFolders, imgLargeFolders

Column Headers
Name, Type, Total Size, Free Space

Name
lvExplorerFiles

Description
This list view is associated with the Directory predefined node. It is used for displaying drives, folders, and files. It is also associated with those auto-create nodes that represent special folders that contain files, such as the Desktop and RecycleBin nodes.

Default View Mode
Report

ImageLists
imgSmallFolders, imgLargeFolders

Column Headers
Name, Size, Date Modified, Attributes

OCX Views

FileExplorer defines the following OCX view:

Name
ovAbout

Description
The result view for the About node under Desktop. Implemented by the user control **AboutCtl** that is part of the FileExplorer project. Contains a button that displays the same configuration wizard used when FileExplorer is added to the console.

ProgID
FileExplorerSample.AboutCtl

Taskpads

FileExplorer defines the following taskpad:

Name
    StaticNodeTaskpad

Description
    Displayed for the static node when the console's "Show taskpad views by default" option is selected.

Type
    Default taskpad

Tasks
    How to Use the File Explorer (URL: HTML page contained in custom resource)

    Start File Explorer (Notify: changes result view to lvExplorerTop)

    MMC Home Page (Notify: selects Internet Explorer and displays URL for MMC home page on www.microsoft.com)

    About (Notify: selects About node under Desktop)

Toolbars and Menu Buttons

Toolbars are not directly associated with any particular node or result view at design time. Toolbars are defined and configured in the designer window and are attached to the control bar for a particular view at run time. The control bar is the controlling entity for all the toolbars and menu buttons of a snap-in. Toolbars can be attached to and detached from the control bar at various times during the life of a snap-in. Because each toolbar is defined at design time, individual buttons on any toolbar can be accessed by code. It is therefore a simple matter to enable, disable, make visible, or hide any button(s) in response to any event as appropriate.

Menu buttons are defined by creating a toolbar in which all buttons have the **DropDown** style. Toolbar button styles must be consistent because MMC does not allow mixing toolbar buttons and menu buttons. This means that if one button in a toolbar has the **DropDown** style then they all must have that style.

FileExplorer defines the following toolbar and menu button:

Name
   tbrFileMgr

Description
   Defines FileExplorer's only toolbar.

ImageList
   imgButtons

Buttons
   Add (Adds a new folder)

   Run (Runs the selected file)

   RunAs (Prompts for a command line to run the selected file)

Name
   tbrMenuButton

Description
   Defines FileExplorer's only MenuButton

Buttons
   Explorer (ButtonMenus: **Add**, **Run**, **RunAs**, **Configuration**)

Menus

Menus, like toolbars, are not directly associated with any particular node or result view at design time. Menus are defined and configured in the designer window, and are attached to the console's context menus at run time. For every insertion point where the snap-in needs to insert menu items, a menu must be defined. That menu functions like a pop-up menu on a Visual Basic form, that is, it is not displayed but its contained items are.

FileExplorer defines the following menus:

Name
   mnuContext

Description
   Added to the top of the console's context menu for single and multiple file selections.

Items
   mnuRun (Runs the selected file)

   mnuRunAs (Prompts for a command line to run the selected file)

Visual Basic Snap-ins

Name

mnuNew

Description

Added to the **New** submenu of the console's context menu for folders and drives.

Items

mnuNewFolder (Creates a new folder under the selected drive or folder)

Name

mnuNewURL

Description

Added to the **New** submenu of the console's context menu for the Internet Explorer node.

Items

mnuURL (Displays property sheet for node that allows specifying URL)

Name

mnuFilterOp

Description

Displayed in response to a filter button click when the lvExplorerFiles list view is in filtered mode (MMC 1.2 only).

Items

mnuFilterByName (Filter displayed files using <filter value>.*)

mnuFilterByExt (Filter displayed files using *.<filter value>)

Image Lists

Image lists are collections of bitmaps. They logically group related bitmaps, and make accessing them easier. The first three image lists enumerated here actually work as a group. The imgSmallFolders and imgLargeFolders lists are both used by the list views, depending on the view mode. Each list item added to a list view must specify an image list index for its bitmap. The list view will determine which image list to use (one for Small, List, Detail, and Filtered view modes, and the other for Large view mode). Similarly, the scope pane will use both imgSmallFolders and imgSmallOpenFolders, depending on whether the scope item is selected. For this reason, the bitmaps in all three image lists must be coordinated. (For example, the LocalDrive image is at index 4 in all three image lists.)

FileExplorer defines the following image lists:

Name	Description	Images
imgSmallFolders	Provides the bitmaps for use in the scope pane nodes and in the list views (in the Small, List, and Detail view modes). All the bitmaps in this image list are 16x16 pixels, and are saved in 24-bit color.	Desktop MyComputer FloppyDrive LocalDrive CDRom RemoteDrive RemoteOfflineDrive Folder File Application AppExtension Unknown
imgSmallOpenFolders	Provides the bitmaps for use in the scope pane nodes, when a node is selected. All the bitmaps in this image list are 16x16 pixels, and are saved in 24-bit color.	Desktop MyComputer FloppyDrive LocalDrive CDRom RemoteDrive RemoteOfflineDrive Folder File Application AppExtension Unknown
imgLargeFolders	Provides the bitmaps for use in the toolbar. All the bitmaps in this image list are 32x32 pixels, and are saved in 24-bit color.	Desktop MyComputer FloppyDrive LocalDrive CDRom RemoteDrive RemoteOfflineDrive Folder File Application AppExtension Unknown
imgButtons	Provides the bitmaps for use in the toolbar. All the bitmaps in this image list are 16x16 pixels, and are saved in 24-bit color.	Add Find Properties Run RunAs

Property Pages

Property pages are used for displaying the properties of scope items and list items as well as for the configuration wizard. Property pages are not explicitly associated with a node or list view at design time. At run time, the snap-in is asked for its property pages and uses an **MMCPropertySheet** object to add its property pages to MMC's property sheet.

To ensure that property pages are properly registered they must be associated with **SnapInControl**, the user control that is part of every snap-in project.

FileExplorer defines the following property pages:

Name	Description
ppgGeneral	Displays properties for files and folders.
ppgWelcome	First page of the configuration wizard.
ppgNetDrives	Second page of the configuration wizard. Asks whether FileExplorer should display network drives.
ppgFolderAccess	Third page of the configuration wizard. Asks whether FileExplorer should allow renaming and deleting folders.
ppgFileAccess	Fourth page of the configuration wizard. Asks whether FileExplorer should allow renaming and deleting files.
ppgFinish	Final page of the configuration wizard.
ppgBrowser	Displayed for the Internet Explorer node. Allows the user to type a URL for display in the result pane.

User Controls

In addition to **SnapInControl**, an additional user control is used for the OCX view displayed in response to the "About" task in the static node taskpad.

FileExplorer defines the following user controls:

Name	Description
SnapInControl	This control is part of every snap-in project and is used to associate the snap-in's property pages.
AboutCtl	Used for the OCX view displayed for the About node. Displays some informational text and a button that displays the same configuration wizard used when FileExplorer is added to a console.

Forms

FileExplorer uses a form to display the **Run As** dialog box:

Name	Description
frmRunAs	Displays the dialog box for the **Run As** toolbar button and menu item.

Classes

FileExplorer uses a class to hold the configuration information collected by the configuration wizard.

Name	Description
ConfigData	Holds the configuration information collected by the configuration wizard. The properties of this class are serialized in the .msc file so that settings are preserved along with a saved console.

Resources

FileExplorer uses a resource to hold the HTML page that displays the user guide when the user clicks the "How to Use FileExplorer" task on the static node taskpad.

Custom Resources	USERGUIDE (Contains the HTML page for the user guide)

FileExplorer—Event Handling

The following topics describe the events handled by FileExplorer with a brief explanation as to why each one is implemented. For more information on how a particular event is implemented refer to the sample code, which contains detailed documentation for each handler.

SnapIn

FileExplorer handles the following events on the **SnapIn** object:

Event	Description
Initialize	Tells MMC that all static extensions are required. A required extension is preloaded when the snap-in is loaded. The only static extension is FileViewer but it is used so often that performance will be improved by preloading it.
QueryConfigurationWizard	Tells the snap-in manager that FileExplorer has a configuration wizard.
CreateConfigurationWizard	Adds the configuration wizard property pages to the snap-in manager's wizard property sheet.
ConfigurationComplete	Refreshes the scope pane after the configuration wizard is run from the menu button or from the **About** control.
WriteProperties	Saves the **ConfigData** class properties in the .msc file.
ReadProperties	Loads the **ConfigData** class properties from the .msc file.

ExtensionSnapIn

FileExplorer handles the following events on the **ExtensionSnapIn** object:

Event	Description
Expand	Used when FileExplorer is loaded as a namespace extension of Computer Management\System Tools on Windows 2000. Adds the ExtensionRoot node as a child of the expanding SystemTools node.

ScopeItems

FileExplorer handles the following events on the **ScopeItems** object:

Event	Description
Expand	If MyComputer is expanding, adds predefined nodes for all of the drives on the machine.
	If a drive or a folder is expanding, adds predefined nodes for all of its contained folders.
	If ExtensionRoot is expanding, adds the Desktop node. Note that the Desktop node is an auto-create child of the static node and does not need to be added when FileExplorer is created stand-alone. When created as an extension, Desktop must be added manually because it is not an auto-create child of ExtensionRoot. The auto-create children of Desktop will be created automatically in both cases.
Initialize	Defines column headers and sets list subitems for when the scope item is displayed in the result pane in detail mode. Column headers could be defined in the UI but it is done here as an example of adding them programmatically.
Rename	Renames the folder in the file system. Changes the **ScopeItem** object's display name and its column 1 text used for Detail mode.
Help	Displays this topic in this Help file. This Help file is merged with MMC's Help file because it is set as the value of the snap-in's **HelpFile** property at design time in the property browser.
PropertyChanged	Called when the property page for the Internet Explorer node (ppgBrowser) calls **ScopeItem.PropertyChanged** to inform the snap-in that the user has selected a new URL to display in the result pane. Reselects the Internet Explorer node and displays the specified URL.

Views

FileExplorer handles the following events on the **Views** object:

Event	Description
SetControlbar	Attaches the FileExplorer's toolbar and menu button to the console's control bar.
UpdateControlbar	Enables/disables toolbar buttons and menu buttons based on the current selection.
Select	Determines which console verbs to enable/disable based on the current selection. Updates the status bar with the number of selected objects and free disk space.
AddNewMenuItems	Adds FileExplorer's menu (mnuNew) that contains the items to appear on the **New** submenu of MMC's context menu. FileExplorer adds a **Folder** item to the **New** submenu when the selection is a drive or a folder.
AddTopMenuItems	Adds FileExplorer's menu (mnuContext) that contains the items to appear on the top of MMC's context menu. For single and multiple list items FileExplorer adds **Run** and **Run As** items.
QueryPaste	Tells MMC whether FileExplorer can accept a paste operation on the specified target **ScopeItem** object.
Paste	Copies or moves the specified folders and/or files to the folder represented by the target **ScopeItem** object.
Cut	Removes the moved **ScopeItem** objects. If there are moved list items and they are currently displayed in the result pane then removes them as well.
Delete	Deletes the folders and/or files from the file system and removes the corresponding **ScopeItem** objects and list items.
Refresh	Removes all the child **ScopeItem** objects (representing subfolders) of the target **ScopeItem** and then re-enumerates them in the file system and adds them back. This allows picking up any file system changes that might have occurred outside of FileExplorer (for example in Windows Explorer) because FileExplorer does not automatically detect external changes.
	If the target **ScopeItem** is also currently selected in the scope pane, refreshes the contents of the result pane.
Print	Calls the system command processor using
	`Shell Environ("ComSpec") & " /c PRINT "`
	for every file in the selection.
QueryPagesFor	If the selection contains folders and/or list items then returns **True**. If the selection is the static node then returns **True** because the user is running the configuration wizard from

	the **Explorer** menu button or from the button on the **About** control.
CreatePropertyPages	If the selection contains folders and/or list items then adds the property pages and uses the *InitData* parameter of **MMCPropertySheet.AddPage** to pass the index into **SelectedControls** of the object that the page should display properties for. If the selection is the static node then calls SnapIn_CreateConfigurationWizard because that event handler needs to do the same thing (call **MMCPropertySheet.AddWizardPage** for each of the configuration wizard pages).
GetMultiSelectData	Fired when the user selects multiple items in a list view. Allows the snap-in to export data for the multiple selection. Adds data formats for all the file names, file paths, and folder paths.

ScopePaneItems

FileExplorer handles the following events on the **ScopePaneItems** object:

Event	Description
GetResultViewInfo	Used when the user selects the Internet Explorer node. Sets **ViewType** to URL and uses "about:blank" for the URL.

ResultViews

FileExplorer handles the following events on the **ResultViews** object:

Event	Description
Initialize	Populates the list view with list items.
InitializeControl	Sets the following properties on **AboutCtl** so it can run the configuration wizard: text to display, **CurrentView.PropertySheetProvider**, and static node scope item.
Activate	Displays the count of objects in the description bar.
CompareItems	Called during a sort when the user clicks a column header. Does comparisons for size and date. For other columns does not return a result to indicate to the runtime that it should do a default string comparison (for example, for the Name column).
ListItemDblClick	For a file's list view calls the Win32 API **ShellExecute** for the file.

Event	Description
ItemRename	Does the rename operation in the file system and updates the file's display in the list view. Calls **MMCListItem.UpdateAllViews** to tell any other existing views that might be displaying the file to update their display too.
ItemViewChange	Fired in each view in response to the **MMCListItem.UpdateAllViews** in ItemRename event. Updates the list item's display.
TaskClick	Start FileExplorer (Change result pane for static node to lvExplorerTop)

MMC Home Page (Select Internet Explorer node with URL view displaying MMC home page on www.microsoft.com)

About (Select About node) |
TaskNotify	Called from the user guide HTML page using **MMCCtrl.TaskNotify**. Changes result pane for static node to StaticNodeTaskpad.
Print	Invokes the system command processor's **print** command to print the selected files.
Help	Displays this topic in this Help file. This Help file is merged with MMC's Help file because it is set as the value of the snap-in's **HelpFile** property at design time in the property browser.
FilterButtonClick	Displays a pop-up menu to allow the user to choose between filtering by name or by extension. (MMC 1.2 only.)
FilterChange	Refreshes the contents of the result pane. (MMC 1.2 only.)

Menus

FileExplorer handles the following menu events:

Event	Description
mnuNewFolder_Click	Creates a new folder under the selected drive or scope item.
mnuRun_Click	Calls the Win32 API **ShellExecute** for the file(s).
mnuRunAs_Click	Displays frmRunAs to prompt the user for a command line to run for the selected file(s).
mnuURL_Click	Displays the property sheet for the Internet Explorer node.

Toolbars

FileExplorer handles the following toolbar events:

Event	Description
tbrFileMgr_ButtonClick	Process new folder, run, and run as buttons as for context menu items.
tbrMenuButton_ButtonDropDown	Enables/disables menu items based on current selection.
tbrMenuButton_ButtonMenuClick	Process new folder, run, run as, and configuration items as for context menu items.

FileExplorer—Data Sources

In the FileExplorer sample, the source of the data being displayed is the **FileSystemObject** object from the Microsoft Scripting Runtime (Scrrun.dll). This is a separate COM object referenced by the snap-in. The direct user interface of the snap-in is coded in Visual Basic, but the data source does not have to be. In fact, every snap-in will acquire its data from a different source that is appropriate to that snap-in. These sources can be anything with which Visual Basic can communicate—Windows Management Instrumentation (WMI), ActiveX Data Objects (ADO) database connections, third-party COM objects, custom-built COM objects, legacy DLLs, host applications, socket connections, and so on.

FileExplorer—Component Files

The FileExplorer sample consists of the following files.

File name	Description
AboutCtl.ctl	Source for user control used in OCX view displayed for About node
AboutCtl.ctx	Serialized binary objects associated with **AboutCtl** (icons, bitmaps, and so on)
ConfigData.cls	**ConfigData** class source
FileExplorer.dca	Binary serialization of snap-in designer
FileExplorer.dll	The built FileExplorer snap-in DLL
FileExplorer.dsr	The snap-in designer source
FileExplorer.dsx	Serialized binary objects associated with the designer (icons, bitmaps, and so on)
FileExplorer.exp	Exported functions file created by linker during build process
FileExplorer.lib	Exported functions library created by linker during build process

File name	Description
FileExplorer.pdb	Symbolic debug information created by linker during build process
FileExplorerSample.res	Resource file containing taskpad bitmaps and user guide HTML page
FileExplorerSample.vbp	Visual Basic project file—contains project properties
FileExplorerSample.vbw	Visual Basic workspace file—contains workspace settings
frmRunAs.frm	Run As prompt form source
ppgBrowser	Source for Internet Explorer node property page
ppgFileAccess.pag	Source for file access property page used in configuration wizard
ppgFinish.pag	Source for final property page used in configuration wizard
ppgFolderAccess.pag	Source for folder access property page used in configuration wizard
ppgGeneral.pag	Source for property page used for folders and files
ppgNetDrives.pag	Source for network drives property page used in configuration wizard
ppgWelcome.pag	Source for first property page used in configuration wizard
SnapInControl.ctl	User control used to associate property pages so that they are correctly registered
SnapInControl.ctx	Serialized binary objects associated with **SnapInControl** (icons, bitmaps, and so on)
StartExplorer.bmp	Bitmap used for "Start File Explorer" task in StaticNodeTaskpad
mmc12.chm	This Help file
WizardSymbol.bmp	Bitmap used for configuration button on **AboutCtl**.

FileViewerExtension—Design-Time Objects

This section provides descriptions of the objects defined by FileViewerExtension in the snap-in designer.

Extensions

The Extensions node defines the node types that the snap-in extends and the type of extensions implemented for each node type. The designer uses this information to register the extensions under the extended snap-in's keys in **HKEY_LOCAL_MACHINE\SOFTWARE\Microsoft\MMC\NodeTypes**.

Name	Description	Extensions
Directory	FileExplorer's directory and drive **ScopeItem** objects	Property pages
FileExplorer	FileExplorer's static node	Taskpad
lvExplorerFiles	FileExplorer's files list view	Task menu Property pages Toolbar

Toolbars and Menu Buttons

Name	Description	Image list	Buttons
tbrViewer	Defines FileViewerExtension's only toolbar.	imgButtons	View File (Displays the file contents)
tbrMenuButton	Defines FileViewerExtension's only menu button.		FileViewer (ButtonMenus: View File)

Menus

Name	Description	Items
ViewerMenu	Added to the **All Tasks** submenu of the console's context menu for single file selections	ViewFile (Displays the contents of the selected file)

ImageLists

Name	Description	Items
imgToolbar	Provides the bitmap used in the toolbar	View File

Property Pages

Name	Description
ppgViewFile	Displays the contents of the file on a property page
ppgDirStats	Displays statistics about the selected folder

User Controls

Name	Description
SnapInControl	This control is part of every snap-in project and is used to associate the snap-in's property pages.
ctlFileViewer	Displays the contents of a file in a multiline edit control. Used by both ppgViewFile and frmFileViewer.

Forms

Name	Description
frmFileViewer	Displays the contents of a file

Resources

Bitmaps	VIEWER: used for task added to FileExplorer's StaticNodeTaskpad

FileViewerExtension—Event Handling

The following topics describe the events handled by FileViewerExtension with a brief explanation as to why each one is implemented. For more information on how a particular event is implemented refer to the sample code, which contains detailed documentation for each handler.

ExtensionSnapIn

FileViewerExtension handles the following events on the **ExtensionSnapIn** object:

Event	Description
AddTaskMenuItems	Adds the **View File** item to the **All Tasks** submenu of MMC's context menu
CreatePropertyPages	Adds ppgViewFile or ppgDirStats to MMC property sheet depending on selected item
SetControlbar	Adds tbrViewer and tbrMenuButton to the control bar
UpdateControlbar	Enables/disables toolbar button and menu button based on selection
AddTasks	Adds "About FileViewer" task to FileExplorer's StaticNodeTaskpad
TaskClick	Displays a message box with about information

Menus

FileViewerExtension handles the following menu event:

Event	Description
ViewFile_Click	Creates frmFileViewer to display file contents

Toolbars

FileViewerExtension handles the following toolbar events:

Event	Description
tbrViewer_ButtonClick	Processes **View File** button as for context menu
tbrMenuButton_ButtonDropDown	Enables/disables **View File** item based on current selection.
tbrMenuButton_ButtonMenuClick	Processes **View File** item as for context menu

FileViewerExtension—Data Sources

FileViewerExtension receives all of its information (file paths, folder paths, and so on) from data exported by FileExplorer.

FileViewerExtension—Component Files

The FileViewerExtension sample consists of the following files:

File name	Description
FileViewer.ctl	Source for user control used to display contents of files
FileViewer.ctx	Serialized binary objects associated with FileViewerCtl (icons, bitmaps, and so on)
FileViewerExtension.dca	Binary serialization of snap-in designer
FileViewerExtension.dsr	The snap-in designer source
FileViewerExtension.dsx	Serialized binary objects associated with the designer (icons, bitmaps, and so on)
FileViewerExtension.res	Resource file containing taskpad bitmap
FileViewerExtensionProj.dll	The built FileViewerExtension snap-in DLL
FileViewerExtensionProj.exp	Exported functions file created by linker during build process
FileViewerExtensionProj.lib	Exported functions library created by linker during build process
FileViewerExtensionProj.pdb	Symbolic debug information created by linker during build process
FileViewerExtensionProj.vbp	Visual Basic project file—contains project properties
FileViewerExtensionProj.vbw	Visual Basic workspace file—contains workspace settings
frmFileViewer.frm	Source for form that displays file contents
ppgDirStats.pag	Source for directory statistics property page
SnapInControl.ctl	User control used to associate property pages so that they are correctly registered
SnapInControl.ctx	Serialized binary objects associated with **SnapInControl** (icons, bitmaps, and so on)
Viewer.bmp	Bitmap used for toolbar button.

DriveStats—Design-Time Objects

This section provides descriptions of the objects defined by DriveStats in the snap-in designer.

Other Nodes

Name

DriveStats

Description

Added as a child of every drive node in FileExplorer.

Result Views

lvDriveStats

ImageLists

None. Uses default images supplied by MMC.

Name

MyComputerStats

Description

Added as a child of the My Computer node in FileExplorer.

Result Views

StatsListpad (uses lvDriveStats)

ImageLists

None. Uses default images supplied by MMC.

Extensions

The Extensions node defines the node types that the snap-in extends and the type of extensions implemented for each node type. The designer uses this information to register the extensions under the extended snap-in's keys in **HKEY_LOCAL_MACHINE\SOFTWARE\Microsoft\MMC\NodeTypes**.

Name	Description	Extensions
Directory	FileExplorer's directory and drive **ScopeItems**	Namespace
MyComputer	FileExplorer's My Computer node	Namespace

List Views

DriveStats defines the following list view:

Name
> LvDriveStats

Description
> This list view is associated with the DriveStats node. It displays various drive statistics. It is also associates with the StatsListpad result view used by the MyComputerStats node.

Default View Mode
> Report

ImageLists
> None. Uses default images supplied by MMC.

Column Headers
> Stat, Value

Forms

DriveStats defines the following form:

Name	Description
frmChooseDrive	Displayed in response to the listpad button click. Allows the user to choose a different drive to display in StatsListpad.

DriveStats—Event Handling

The following topics describe the events handled by DriveStats with a brief explanation as to why each one is implemented. For more information on how a particular event is implemented refer to the sample code, which contains detailed documentation for each handler.

ExtensionSnapIn

DriveStats handles the following event on the **ExtensionSnapIn** object:

Event	Description
Expand	If the expanding node is a FileExplorer drive, adds the DriveStats node underneath it. If the expanding node is FileExplorer's My Computer node then adds the MyComputerStats node underneath it.

ScopePaneItems

DriveStats handles the following event on the **ScopePaneItems** object:

Event	Description
GetResultView	If the lvDriveStats result view has been created once, then the DriveStats snap-in has requested to cache it in ResultViews_Deactivate and reuses it.

ResultViews

DriveStats handles the following events on the **ResultViews** object:

Event	Description
Initialize	Populates the list view with drive statistics
Deactivate	Tells the designer runtime that the result view should be cached
ResultViews_ListpadButtonClick	Displays frmChooseDrive to allow the user to choose a different drive to display in StatsListpad.

DriveStats—Data Sources

DriveStats receives all of its information (file paths, folder paths, and so on) from data exported by FileExplorer.

DriveStats—Component Files

The DriveStats sample consists of the following files:

File name	Description
DriveStats.dca	Binary serialization of snap-in designer
DriveStats.dsr	The snap-in designer source
DriveStats.dsx	Serialized binary objects associated with the designer (icons, bitmaps, and so on)
DriveStatsProj.dll	The built DriveStats snap-in DLL
DriveStatsProj.exp	Exported functions file created by linker during build process
DriveStatsProj.lib	Exported functions library created by linker during build process
DriveStatsProj.pdb	Symbolic debug information created by linker during build process
DriveStatsProj.vbp	Visual Basic project file—contains project properties
DriveStatsProj.vbw	Visual Basic workspace file—contains workspace settings
frmchoosedrive.frm	Form that allows user to choose drive in StatsListpad.
SnapInControl.ctl	User control used to associate property pages so that they are correctly registered

ComDetect—Design-Time Objects

The following section describes the design-time objects defined by ComDetect.

Extensions

ComDetect extends the following node:

Name	Description	Extensions
lvExplorerFiles	FileExplorer's files list view	Task context menu

Menus

ComDetect defines the following menu:

Name	Description	Items
mnuDetect	Added to the **All Tasks** menu for all files with the extension .dll	IsComServer (Displays message box indicating whether the selected file is also an in-process COM server)

ComDetect—Event Handling

The following section defines the events handled by ComDetect at run time.

ExtensionSnapIn

ComDetect handles the following event on the **ExtensionSnapIn** object:

Event	Description
AddTaskMenuItems	Adds the **Is this file a COM server?** item to the **All Tasks** submenu of MMC's context menu

Menus

ComDetect handles the following menu event:

Event	Description
IsCOMServer_Click	Uses Win32 API to check whether DLL exports the function **DllRegisterServer** and displays message box indicating whether the selected file is also an in-process COM server

ComDetect—Data Sources

ComDetect receives all of its information (file paths, folder paths, and so on) from data exported by FileExplorer.

ComDetect—Component Files

The ComDetect sample consists of the following files:

File name	Description
ComDetect.dca	Binary serialization of snap-in designer
ComDetect.dsr	The snap-in designer source
ComDetect.dsx	Serialized binary objects associated with the designer (icons, bitmaps, and so on)
ComDetectProj.dll	The built ComDetect snap-in DLL
ComDetectProj.exp	Exported functions file created by linker during build process
ComDetectProj.lib	Exported functions library created by linker during build process
ComDetectProj.pdb	Symbolic debug information created by linker during build process
ComDetectProj.vbp	Visual Basic project file—contains project properties
ComDetectProj.vbw	Visual Basic workspace file—contains workspace settings
SnapInControl.ctl	User control used to associate property pages so that they are correctly registered

Error Handling

Run-time errors in Visual Basic can come from many sources, and can potentially result from any statement or object access. For the purpose of these sample snap-ins, the error-handling mechanism is rather rudimentary. There is a small error handler set up for each method and event that will simply report the error that occurred and allow processing to continue. Obviously, in a real-life application error handling would need to be much more robust and fine-tuned. Not all errors are fatal. Some errors could trigger compensating logic that would allow the operation to be re-executed successfully. Some errors should merely be reported to the user. Some errors are catastrophic and will prevent the snap-in from continuing. The manner in which any snap-in handles errors should be carefully analyzed and designed into the snap-in.

A P P E N D I X   A

Snap-in Design Planning

Each part of this book addresses a specific aspect of creating snap-ins. What is not addressed is the process that must take place before snap-in creation begins—that of defining the management task and how the snap-in accomplishes this task. This appendix covers this process.

Snap-in design planning should not be undervalued. It is an ongoing process that begins before anything else on the project and runs throughout the development cycle. The process described in this appendix is used by Microsoft Corporation for snap-in design. It consists of six phases:

- Planning
- Research
- Definition
- Concept
- Detail
- Finalization

At Microsoft, the teams implementing these processes include people with a variety of skill sets: graphic designers, user interface designers, usability engineers, program managers, developers, technical writers, and marketers. The process outlined in the following pages, however, does not require a large team. The amount of time focused on each step varies depending on whether you are creating a snap-in for a new product or an older product. Take from this process whatever is practical for your situation.

Planning

The planning phase begins with the users. Visit customer sites to see how users are currently performing the management task for which you want to create a snap-in. If you are revising an existing product, contact product support and find out which problems users report. Establish a working relationship with targeted customers to gauge their satisfaction with the product and find out which specific areas they would like to see improved.

In this phase, try to:

- Evaluate the competition.
- Look at problems with the current version.
- Generate a vision of the new product or revisit the vision that you can verify with users.
- Identify basic product requirements based on user data.
- Gather data to determine if the snap-in will reside on just one computer or be distributed.
- Make an initial determination about whether the snap-in should be a stand-alone snap-in or an extension snap-in.
- Generate or revisit the product goals.
- Create a rough draft of the schedule.

Almost every step of the process is likely to be revisited with each draft and to be fine-tuned as you learn more about the users and how to meet their needs. Additionally, creating a preliminary schedule enables you to make an initial assessment of the resources needed to create the snap-in, and to compare your time-to-market with your staffing resources.

Research

In the research phase, try to learn as much as you can about your users' needs in order to determine how they will use the snap-in. Some methods for determining this information include: conducting customer site visits, focus groups, and user surveys. When conducting the user surveys, keep in mind how the tasks are being completed and the knowledge and experience the users have with the snap-ins or tools they are using to complete the tasks. You then create scenarios from your research results. Scenarios are short narratives that describe how a user implements the snap-in in a real-life setting. These scenarios will be used later to create and test the snap-in design.

Everett McKay, in *Developing User Interfaces for Microsoft Windows*, addresses the importance of this research:

> The goal behind this research is to really understand your program's users and their needs and goals. What you want to do is to create a framework that you can use to make good design decisions. You definitely want to avoid speculating on what tasks users might want to do or how they want to do them —work from the direct knowledge of your users that research gives you.

Use the site visits to learn what activity the snap-in should support and to gather a better profile of the typical user. Conduct surveys or use questionnaires to understand how the snap-in namespace should be organized to accommodate its use in a typical environment. Concerns here might include:

- Which tasks are the most common?
- What is the frequency of the task being performed?
- What parts of the task are rarely done?
- How should the parts of the task be subdivided?
- What categories do the tasks fall into: configuration, maintenance, or troubleshooting?

You should try to develop scenarios that encompass all possible ways that the product will be used. The more complete you make the scenarios, the more likely you are to create a snap-in that matches how users actually work. If you are working on a follow-up release of a shipped product, compile the feedback that you have from product support and others and prioritize the list. Take the problem areas from the user interface (UI) and take screen shots of all the steps a user would take to complete the task. Place the screen shots into a large flowchart in order to analyze the big picture and to better visualize the details of problems with flow, complexity, conceptual problems, writing, and so on to get at the cause of the problem. This can be done in conjunction with usability tests using scenario-based tasks to observe where users have trouble in the interface. The information gathered here is critical for the next phase, in which you actually start to create the snap-in.

Definition

In the definition phase, you develop goals for the snap-in design by using the data gathered in the planning and research phases. Your goals should state exactly what you expect the product to do. For creating an MMC snap-in, some general goals are:

- Learnability
- Efficiency
- Consistency
- Discoverability
- Error prevention

Learnability is a measure of how quickly and easily new users can master the snap-in. This goal must take into account the complexity of the task performed by the snap-in and the experience level of the users.

Efficiency is the degree of productivity gained by a user after he or she learns to complete the task.

Consistency is determined by how uniformly your snap-in adheres to the MMC guidelines and *The Windows Interface Guidelines for Software Design*. It also addresses internal uniformity. Does the snap-in consistently use the same UI for adding objects to the namespace?

Discoverability means how easily users can find the objects they need to complete their task.

Error prevention addresses how committed you are to designing a snap-in that precludes user mistakes, especially catastrophic ones. It also addresses the clarity and usefulness of generated error messages.

When creating your design goals, compare your most important goals against your less important goals and the constraints based on time and other factors.

During the definition phase, you should also create metrics that the design team can use to determine how closely the snap-in meets the design goals. Metrics are measurable goals that the design must meet to determine success. These metrics fall into two categories—performance metrics and preference metrics.

Examples of performance metrics are:

- Time required to complete the task
- Number and percent of tasks completed correctly without help
- Time spent in errors and in recovering from errors

- Number of commands used to complete the task
- Frequency of use of online Help or documentation
- Number of repetitions of failed commands
- Number of available commands not invoked
- Number of times the user expresses frustration or satisfaction
- Time spent calling product support services

Examples of preference metrics are:

- How useful the snap-in is
- How often the product matches expectations
- Appropriateness of the snap-in's functions to the user's tasks
- Overall ease of use or ease of learning
- Ease of setup and installation
- Rationale for preference of one prototype over another
- Rationale for preference of the product over a competitor's product

Concept

In the concept phase, take the first concrete steps to design the snap-in user interface. In this phase, conceptual models, scenario-based designs, and prototypes can be used to initiate the snap-in design.

Creating a conceptual model is very helpful at the beginning of this phase. A conceptual model is a logical representation of data, information, and behavior that meets a user's expectations. For a snap-in, the conceptual model is the foundation upon which the snap-in is built, both architecturally within the code and in the presentation of the UI to the user. Conceptual models come from a user's mental model, perception, or understanding of a task or activity. Once a conceptual model is developed, the team can work to simplify the model by reducing concepts and the number of objects. The conceptual model also helps to design the namespace.

Throughout the design process, you should be leveraging the scenarios that, as described earlier, will help you to understand the task of designing the snap-in. These scenarios can be used to create quick low-tech storyboards to map out the UI for a specific task screen-by-screen. Because these are static, they do not illustrate interactions well, but they do provide an excellent sense of the snap-in as a whole.

The scenarios you develop are an integral part of the process. Each scenario should reflect a real-life situation in which your snap-in is used to complete one or more management tasks. The substance of a scenario should be drawn from interactions with users. It is often helpful to sketch a drawing that captures the relationships involved in the scenario in order to make sure it is clearly understood.

Scenarios can be used to create test situations and to further plan the namespace. Make sure that the tasks required by the scenario can be accomplished easily using the namespace.

For example, consider the following scenario that was developed by the Exchange team as part of the development of Exchange 2000 Server. Use a sketch such as the one shown in Figure A.1 to illustrate the steps of the scenario.

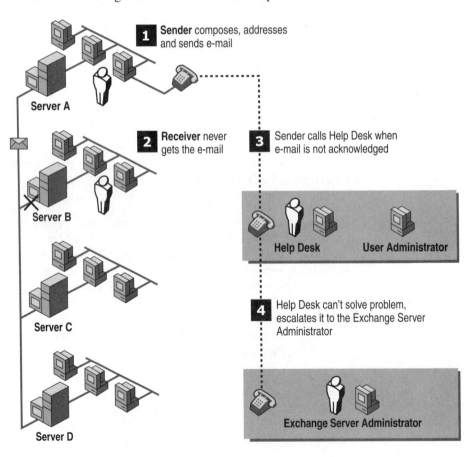

Figure A.1   Microsoft Exchange 2000 Server scenario

The figure illustrates a scenario involving a Microsoft Exchange 2000 Server mail service. The basis for the scenario is Juggernaut Insurance, which has about 2000 employees networked using four servers running Windows 2000 Server—servers A, B, C, and D. Juggernaut has several tier-one administrators, including those in directory service management and those who handle the help desk. There is a single tier-two administrator who handles advanced duties and troubleshooting.

A user, whose network home is on server A, addresses and sends e-mail to a user whose network home is on server D. The message does not go through. The sending user contacts the help desk and makes the tier-one administrator aware of the problem.

Because the problem is with server D, which appears to the tier-one administrator to be offline, the tier-one administrator escalates the problem to the tier-two administrator. The tier-two administrator resolves the issue and reboots server D, allowing the e-mail to be delivered.

Note that this scenario sets up a realistic situation in which the administrators use several Exchange tools to complete the task. As prototypes become more complete, you can test the ability of the snap-in to handle the scenarios you have developed. The more realistic the scenario, the better chance you have of completing a snap-in that operates as you expect and fulfills the needs of your users.

After studying the overview provided by the concept models and rough storyboards, you can begin to fine-tune your prototype. You don't need to make it fully functional yet, since it will merely be used to evaluate your first namespace organization design. You can add more substance to the prototype later as you gather information and refine the design process in the detail phase.

The scenario-based designs should identify the features (UI elements) the snap-in must contain to accomplish a particular management task. A careful study of the scenarios and user data helps you make these critical decisions.

In this phase, the prototype is of the namespace and can be created using the Snap-in Designer for Visual Basic. Ask users to walk through this prototype to compare the nodes with their intended task. Users should be able to quickly match the namespace parts with the task parts. Encourage users to think aloud as they work with the namespace prototype. A user's thoughts can help you not only to identify problem areas, but also to understand why they are problems.

Detail

In the detail phase, you create the UI for the snap-in. During this phase, you progress from prototypes to the actual resource files. There are several iterations of the design, each tested by users to ensure that the design goals are met. The namespace, menus, toolbars, and other UI elements are refined.

Continue to look at your goals to answer questions about the UI:

- Is the design as simple as possible?
- Can the user easily find nodes in the namespace to accomplish a given task?
- Is the UI consistent? Do similar tasks have the same UI?
- How does the system anticipate and prevent errors?

In this phase, look at the full range of the users' tasks. Think about how the context menus help or hinder usability for a given task. Look at the organization and hierarchy of information from the result pane down to the property pages. Here you can also start testing more detailed instructions with users in order to determine whether wizards or property pages should be used.

The detail phase should involve writers in the design process to make sure that the UI text is clear and to make Help as rich as possible. Make sure that you test the Help system when you test the UI with users. Also make sure that all the UI is designed according to accessibility and localization guidelines.

As you move further in this stage, you may find it useful to videotape users as they try to complete a task with the snap-in. The whole design team can then together evaluate the taped session and try to resolve issues that were uncovered.

Finalization

Finalization is the one phase of the design cycle that should not be iterative. At this point, the design is fairly solid, and the only changes to the UI that are required are visual layout and icons.

In this phase, testing of the snap-in moves from design testing to product testing. For an excellent short description of product testing procedures, see *Developing User Interfaces for Microsoft Windows* by Everett McKay.

During this phase, you should make sure that all the UI elements are presented as simply as possible, and that all screen layouts follow the guidelines presented in this book. Testing at this point should also ensure that the product meets the design goals that the design team set at the beginning of the design process.

Make sure that you finalize and lock down the UI elements so that there is plenty of time to document the UI completely.

APPENDIX B

Taskpad Wizard Icons

When you create taskpads, use meaningful icons to symbolize the various tasks. The appropriate icon helps users easily identify the purpose of a given task. To avoid confusion, you should also vary the icons you use. For example, if you create a taskpad that has several "add" tasks, and you use the Add icon for each task, users will find it difficult to distinguish among them. In such a case, you should use the icons that symbolize the objects that you are adding.

The following table lists the recommended meanings for MMC taskpad icons. Note that these are only recommendations; there may be cases where you use icons to symbolize tasks that are not included in this table.

	Symbol	Icon symbolizes	Alternate meaning	Notes
1		Add	Button	Use the Add icon for tasks that add existing objects to the UI. Use the New icon for tasks that create objects that did not previously exist.
2		Alert	Monitor, warning	This icon can also be used for notification tasks.
3		Cancel, remove	Button	Use the Remove icon for tasks that remove an object from the UI. Use the Delete icon for tasks that remove an object permanently from the computer.
4		Delete, close	Button, disable, uninstall, disconnect	Use the Remove icon for tasks that remove an object from the UI. Use the Delete icon for tasks that remove an object permanently from the computer.
5		Download	Arrow, move	This icon can also be used to symbolize disable.
6		Expand, uncompress	Tool, clamp, vise	
7		Export	Arrow, eject, push subscription	This is the preferred icon for *export*.
8		Export	Arrow, export using dts	
9		Import	Arrow, inject, pull subscription	
10		Link, shortcut	Button	
11		Move	Arrow, move	This icon can also be used to symbolize *open*.
12		New	Button, sparkle	Use the Add icon for tasks that add existing objects to the UI. Use the New icon for tasks that create objects that did not previously exist.

	Symbol	Icon symbolizes	Alternate meaning	Notes
13		Pause	Button, resume	
14		Play	Button, start	
15		Receive, send	Arrow, refresh	
16		Restart	Button	
17		Stop	Button	
18		Upload	Arrow, up	This icon can also be used to symbolize *enable*.
19		Information, alert	Message	
20		Cluster	Failover, server	
21		Computer	Client, cpu, disconnected, monitor	
22		Disk mirror	Hard drive	
23		Laptop	Computer, monitor, keyboard	
24		Mainframe		
25		Midi	Keys, music, piano	

	Symbol	Icon symbolizes	Alternate meaning	Notes
26		Server	Computer	
27		Site	Building	
28		Database	Cylinder, database	
29		Fax	Document, file, phone	
30		Fax jobs	Document, file phone, job, jobs	
31		Floppy Disks	Save, save as, disk, storage	
32		Hard drive	External, drive	
33		Hardware	Pci card, upgrade	
34		Modem	Phone	
35		Modem pool	Modem	
36		Mouse	Click	
37		Printer	Document, file, print	
38		Printer jobs	Printer, job, jobs	

	Symbol	Icon symbolizes	Alternate meaning	Notes
39		Remove media	Disc, disk, zip disk	
40		Software	Disc, disk, floppy disk, memory, storage	
41		Accessibility	Equal, monitor	
42		Application window	New window from here, create a view, monitor	
43		Table	Calendar	
44		View performance	Performance graph, graph control, monitor	
45		View, show	Network connection	
46		Code	Create a stored procedure, document, file	
47		Create a job	Server, job, jobs	
48		Desktop	Pencil, write	
49		Documents, files	Document, file	
50		Edit Document	Document, file, list, pencil, rename	
51		E-mail	Address, letter, mail, note	

	Symbol	Icon symbolizes	Alternate meaning	Notes
52		Files and folders	Document, file, container, folder	
53		Folders	Container, folder, open	
54		Help, troubleshoot	Document, file	
55		Inbox	Files, container	
56		Create a plan	Checklist, inventory, pencil, tasks	This icon can also be used to symbolize *properties*.
57		Properties, settings	Monitor	This icon can also be used to symbolize a list view.
58		Register	Address, checklist, letter, mail, pencil, task	
59		Reports	Log, notebook, view reports	
60		Check server	Performance, monitor, search, use profiler	
61		Find, search	Explore, magnifying glass, find...	
62		Search database	Search, find, query analyzer, server	
63		Search database	Find, magnifying glass, query analyzer, server	
64		Bell	Ring, service	

	Symbol	Icon symbolizes	Alternate meaning	Notes
65		Camera	Capture, shot, peripheral	
66		Erase, format	Drive, eraser	
67		Expenses	Money	
68		Home	House	
69		Internet	Internet, web, globe, world	
70		News	Article, newspaper	
71		Shaking hands	Agreement, hands, peace	
72		Under construction	Barrier, beta, construction, stop, warning	
73		Network access	Network, share, router, hub, connection	
74		Books online	Help, online help, shared publication	
75		Network connection	Cable, network	
76		Publish	Network, share	
77		Shared folders	Container, folder	

	Symbol	Icon symbolizes	Alternate meaning	Notes
78		Book	Publication	
79		Book	DSS tutorial, publication	
80		Configure replication	Arrow, book, publication	
81		Check package	Address, find, label, magnifying glass, search	
82		Access, permissions	Keys, security	
83		Certificate	License	
84		Password	Access, key, set password	
85		Security	Lock	
86		Setup	CD, CD-ROM, storage	This is the preferred icon for *Setup*.
87		Setup	Hammer, CD	
88		Finished	Complete, finish, flag, winner	
89		Off	Switch off	
90		On	Switch on	
91		Backup	Tape, memory, storage	

	Symbol	Icon symbolizes	Alternate meaning	Notes
92		Briefcase	Container, storage, offline	
93		Inventory	Memory, storage	
94		Tape drive	Tape, memory, storage	
95		Restore from backup	Tape, memory, storage	
96		Create backup	Tape, memory, storage	
97		Clock	Schedule, time	
98		Schedule	Date, pencil, calendar	
99		Adjust, tune	Tool, tune an index, wrench	
100		Component	Puzzle	
101		Compress	Clamp, vise	
102		Cube	DSS online	
103		Cubes	Olap concepts	
104		Gear	Cog, import/export using dts, service, settings	

	Symbol	Icon symbolizes	Alternate meaning	Notes
105		MMC symbol		
106		Services	Gears, automate administrative tasks, cog	
107		Wizard	Stairs, Steps	For wizards that add or create objects, use the Add or New icon. For other wizards, try to use an icon that more accurately represents the action of the wizard.
108		Change membership in group	Users, arrow	
109		Connected user	User, network, share	Avoid using this icon.
110		Connected users	User, network, share	Avoid using this icon.
111		E-mail distribution list	E-mail group	
112		Group	Users, people	
113		Grouped	Users, group	
114		User	Person	

Glossary

A

ActiveX Microsoft's brand name for the technologies that enable interoperability using the Component Object Model (COM). ActiveX technology includes, but is not limited to, OLE.

ActiveX control A user interface element created using ActiveX technology.

ActiveX designer An in-process ActiveX object that extends the functionality of the Visual Basic IDE. Visual Basic 6.0 ships with numerous ActiveX designers such as the Data Environment Designer, the DHTML Page Designer, webclasses, and so on. The Snap-in Designer for Visual Basic is an ActiveX designer.

application modal Refers to a type of user interface element (for example, dialog box, message box, property sheet) for which the user must respond to the user interface element before continuing work in the current application.

author mode Access mode to a custom console that grants the user of the console full access to all MMC functionality, including the ability to add or remove snap-ins, to create new windows, to create taskpad views and tasks, to add items to the Favorites list, and to view all portions of the console tree.

auto-create node A node in a Visual Basic snap-in that is defined at design time and that is automatically created in the console by the designer runtime when the parent of the node is expanded.

B

button menu A term used in a Visual Basic snap-in to represent an object that defines the properties of an item on a pop-up menu that is displayed when the user clicks a menu button.

C

chocolate GIF Enumerator value in the **MMC_TASK_DISPLAY_TYPE** enumeration, which defines the types of images that can be displayed for a task or the background on a taskpad. This value indicates that the image displayed for the task or background is a transparent GIF image where index 1 is transparent.

clipboard format A memory object on the clipboard with a specified data format. Each format is identified by an unsigned integer value. In MMC, clipboard formats are used for data transfer between MMC and snap-ins and between multiple snap-ins. Snap-ins register the clipboard formats that they support by using the **RegisterClipboardFormat** Win32 API function.

CLSID (class identifier) A COM term. A globally unique identifier (GUID) associated with a snap-in's primary object. Each snap-in (stand-alone and extension) should register its CLSID in the system registry so that MMC can locate the snap-in and load it in the console when it is required.

cocreatable class object (or class object)
A COM term. In MMC, a snap-in registers the CLSID(s) of its class object(s). MMC cocreates an instance of a stand-alone snap-in's class object in order to request interfaces from the snap-in such as **IComponentData**, **ISnapinAbout**, and **ISnapinHelp**. In the case of extension snap-ins, MMC cocreates an instance of an extension's class object to request interfaces such as **IExtendContextMenu**, **IExtendControlBar**, and **ISnapinHelp**.

code window   Window in the Snap-in Designer for Visual Basic in which snap-in developers write code for handling events sent to the snap-in during run time.

column configuration data   Used in conjunction with column persistence. Refers to the persisted column customization and sorting parameters that MMC stores in memory when the user customizes a list view column. Snap-ins can view and modify column configuration data using the methods of the **IColumnData** interface.

Visual Basic snap-ins can view and modify column configuration data using **View.ColumnSettings** and **MMCListView.ColumnHeaders**.

MMC persists column configuration data per column set per view per snap-in instance.

column filtering   MMC 1.2 feature, in which a list view can be displayed in filtered mode. The list view displays an edit control and a small button underneath each column header. The typical user action is to type a filtering criteria into the edit control and press ENTER. The snap-in then receives a notification to allow the snap-in to apply the new filtering criteria or to ignore the input.

If the user clicks the filter button, the snap-in receives a different notification. The snap-in should display a pop-up menu to allow the user to choose a filter operator.

column header   A term used in a Visual Basic snap-in to represent an object that defines the properties of a column displayed in a list view in detail or filtered mode.

column persistence   MMC 1.2 feature, in which MMC persists column customization and sorting parameters as the user moves between scope items in the scope pane. The feature allows a user to customize a list view, select another scope item in the scope pane, and then return to the original scope item with the customizations preserved.

MMC also allows snap-ins to view and modify persisted column customization and sorting parameters (also called column configuration data) by using the **IColumnData** interface.

Visual Basic snap-ins can view and modify column persistence data using **View.ColumnSettings** and **View.SortSettings**.

column set   Used in conjunction with column persistence. A set of columns inserted in the result pane by a snap-in when the user selects a scope item in the snap-in. When the user selects a different scope item in that snap-in, the same or a different column set may be shown by the snap-in.

MMC requires that every scope item specify a column set ID for the column set it inserts. MMC uses the ID of a column set to identify its persisted column configuration data within each view. If the snap-in does not explicitly supply one using the CCF_COLUMN_SET_ID clipboard format, then MMC uses the scope item's node type GUID.

Visual Basic snap-ins can view and modify the column set ID using **ScopePaneItem.ColumnSetID**.

column set ID   Used in conjunction with column persistence. Uniquely identifies a column set and its column configuration data. MMC persists column configuration data per column set per view per snap-in instance.

Completion page The last page of a Wizard97-style wizard. The Completion page typically has a bitmap image, called a watermark, to convey a specific message to the user. This is the same watermark image that is used in the Wizard97-style wizard's Welcome page.

Component Object Model (COM) An architecture for defining interfaces and interaction among objects implemented by widely varying software applications. A COM object instantiates one or more interfaces, each of which exposes zero or more properties and zero or more methods. All COM interfaces are derived from the base class **IUnknown**. MMC is built on the COM foundation.

composite data object Used in conjunction with multiple selection. During some multiple selection operations (for example, paste operations) MMC creates a data object consisting of an array of multiselection data objects provided by all the snap-ins involved in a multiple selection. This composite data object is forwarded to snap-ins, which can then use the CCF_MULTI_SELECT_SNAPINS clipboard format for extracting the array of multiselection data objects. The data format used with the clipboard format is the **SMMCDataObjects** structure.

Configuration Wizard A wizard that a snap-in can optionally display when the user adds the snap-in to a console by using the **Add/Remove Snap-in** dialog box. The snap-in can use the wizard to gather settings from the user during the insertion process that can be used for initializing the snap-in's state.

console Refers to an instance of the MMC application, as well as to the main MMC window. The term "MMC" is often used interchangeably with "console" in the MMC SDK documentation. A console does not perform any management function, but it hosts tools, called snap-ins, that provide the required management behavior. A console can have one or more MDI child windows, or views, in which snap-ins are hosted.

console file A file with an .msc (management saved console) extension that preserves the list of loaded snap-ins for a console, the arrangement and contents of open MDI child windows (views) in the main MMC window, the default mode, and information about permissions. All the configuration settings for the tools and controls are saved with the console and restored when the console file is opened. You can open a console file on different computers or even different networks and restore the saved settings for all the tools.

console taskpad MMC 1.2 feature. A taskpad that can be used to run tasks such as starting wizards, opening property pages, performing menu commands, running command lines, and opening Web pages. Console taskpads are implemented by MMC; this differs from standard taskpads, which are implemented by snap-ins.

console tree A hierarchical structure in the scope pane of a view. The console tree displays the static nodes and enumerated nodes associated with stand-alone and extension snap-ins.

container A scope item that has child scope items.

context menu extension An extension snap-in that extends the functionality of a primary snap-in by adding menu items to the scope and result items of a particular node type that are inserted by the primary snap-in.

control A child window that an application uses in conjunction with another window to perform simple input and output (I/O) tasks. Examples of controls in the main MMC window are the toolbar control and the menu button control.

control bar A control implemented by MMC to display and manage its own toolbars and menu buttons, as well as those added by snap-ins.

cookie Pointer-sized identifier within an instance of a snap-in that is associated with a particular scope or result item. When inserting an item in the scope or result pane, a snap-in passes to MMC the value that will be used as the item's cookie value. The value is solely determined by the snap-in.

MMC often requests a data object from the snap-in due to a user action. This data object is returned to the same snap-in or forwarded to an extension snap-in along with an appropriate notification message. When requesting the data object, MMC also passes the cookie value of the item on which the action is performed. The snap-in should store this cookie value in the returned data object, because this is the only way for a snap-in to determine the proper context when receiving the notification message.

custom OCX view See OCX view.

custom taskpad Taskpad view style in which the snap-in displays a custom DHTML page that contains tasks as well as other elements.

custom Web view See HTML view.

D

data object A COM term. Used for data transfer between MMC and snap-ins and between multiple snap-ins. A data object is an instance of a class that implements the **IDataObject** interface. MMC requests data objects from snap-ins that insert scope or result items by calling the **IComponentData::QueryDataObject** or **IComponent::QueryDataObject** method.

default list view taskpad See standard list view taskpad.

default taskpad See standard taskpad.

default verb The verb that specifies the default action for a scope item or result item when the user double-clicks or presses ENTER on that item. Default verbs appear in bold type.

designer window Window in the Snap-in Designer for Visual Basic in which snap-in developers can define most of the snap-in's user interface and run-time behavior.

details pane Term used in the MMC end-user documentation to refer to the result pane.

details view Term used in the MMC end-user documentation to refer to the result pane.

dialog unit Unit of measurement in Visual C++ used in dialog box templates to determine the size of dialog boxes and their contents. Also referred to as "dialog box units."

dual-mode snap-in A snap-in that operates both as a stand-alone snap-in and as an extension snap-in. An example of a dual-mode snap-in is the Event Viewer snap-in.

dynamic extension An extension snap-in that is added to a scope or result item programmatically at run time. A primary snap-in can dynamically add any type of extension to any of its own items.

dynamic-link library (DLL) A module containing functions and data that can be loaded at run time by a calling module (an executable file or another DLL). When a DLL is loaded, it is mapped into the address space of the calling process (module). The calling module can call the exported functions of the DLL to make use of the functionality provided by the DLL.

Snap-ins are implemented as in-process server DLLs that run in the process space of an instance of MMC.

E

enumerated node Subtree of nodes under a static node in the console tree. When the user selects or expands the static node in the scope pane, the snap-in associated with the static node is notified and can insert enumerated nodes as children of that static node. An enumerated node can have enumerated child nodes of its own. When the user expands an enumerated node for the first time, the snap-in that inserted the enumerated node is notified and can insert the child nodes.

exported data Snap-in data that is made available to other snap-ins. To export data, a snap-in must register its extendable node types and document their data formats so that other (extension) snap-ins will be able to interpret the snap-in's exported data. Documentation should include both the interface methods and the format of the data, including any clipboard formats that snap-ins must support to retrieve the data.

extension snap-in A snap-in that adds functionality to a stand-alone snap-in (or primary snap-in). Extension snap-ins can add their own scope items as children of a primary snap-in's scope item. They can also add context menu items, toolbar buttons, property pages, and taskpad tasks to extend the functionality of a primary snap-in.

An extension snap-in provides functionality on a per-node-type basis. The primary snap-in is responsible for registering its extendable node types, and the extension snap-in is responsible for registering itself as an extension (for example, namespace or toolbar) for an extendable node type. When the user selects a scope or result item in an MMC console, MMC checks to see if the node type of the selected item is an extendable node type. If it is, MMC allows all extension snap-ins that extend that particular node type to add their functionality. For example, one extension snap-in might add its own context menu items to the context menu of the selected scope or result item, while another extension snap-in might add its own property page to the property sheet for the selected item.

See also dynamic extension and required extension.

F

filtered view Standard list view for which column filtering is enabled.

G

GUID (globally unique identifier) A COM term. A 16-byte (128-bit) value that uniquely identifies some entity, such as a snap-in's CLSID or the node type of a scope or result item. A GUID is also referred to as a universally unique identifier (UUID).

H

handle Created by MMC to uniquely identify an inserted scope or result item. Scope item handles are of type HSCOPEITEM, while result item handles are of type HRESULTITEM.

A snap-in needs an item's handle in order to manipulate it using the methods of the **IConsoleNameSpace2**, **IConsole2**, and **IResultData** interfaces.

For all scope items other than the static node, MMC returns an item's HSCOPEITEM after the snap-in successfully inserts the item in the scope pane. In the case of the static node, MMC itself inserts it into the snap-in's namespace. MMC then passes the static node's HSCOPEITEM to the snap-in as the *param* parameter in the MMCN_EXPAND notification.

For all result items, MMC returns an item's HRESULTITEM after the snap-in successfully inserts the item in the result pane.

HRESULTITEM Handle to a result item.

HSCOPEITEM Handle to a scope item.

HTML Help collection file A merged HTML Help file (with the .col extension) that combines the information from the index and full-text search of multiple compiled Help (.chm) files and displays all the merged Help files in a single table of contents. For each console file, MMC maintains a collection file that merges the Help files of all snap-ins loaded in the console, as well as the Help files of enabled extension snap-ins and dynamic snap-ins.

HTML view A result pane view on the selected scope item in which the snap-in can display a custom Web page.

I

image list A collection of bitmaps that a snap-in can use as icons for items in the console tree in the scope pane, or in a list view in the result pane.

In a Visual Basic snap-in, an object that contains a collection of **Image** objects, where each object represents an image in the console tree or in a list view.

imported data Data from a C++ snap-in that is imported to a Visual Basic snap-in.

in-process server A server implemented as a DLL that runs in the process space of the client.

L

list item An object that defines the properties of a result item in a list view in a Visual Basic snap-in.

list pad See standard list view taskpad.

list sub-item An object that defines the column text for a list item in a Visual Basic snap-in when the list view is displayed in detail or filtered mode.

list view See standard list view.

lParam Member of a **SCOPEDATAITEM** structure or **RESULTDATAITEM** structure. Snap-ins must fill these structures when inserting scope or result items into their namespace. MMC uses the value of the **lParam** member as the cookie value of the scope or result item that a snap-in inserts.

M

main MMC window The MDI parent window that appears when the MMC application is started.

manually created node A node in a Visual Basic snap-in that is defined at design time and is explicitly created in the console by Visual Basic code in the snap-in.

menu bar Area of the main MMC window immediately beneath the title bar that contains pop-up menus such as **Console**, **Window**, and **Help**. The menu bar also contains menu buttons inserted by snap-ins.

menu button A pop-up menu on the main MMC window that is added either by MMC or by a stand-alone or extension snap-in.

menu button control MMC control for managing the pop-up menus in the main MMC window.

Message View An ActiveX control supplied by MMC that displays an icon, a title, and some message text. This can be useful when a snap-in needs to display an error message or other simple textual information in response to the selection of a scope item in the scope pane.

Microsoft Installer The Microsoft Windows Installer allows application developers to efficiently install and configure their products and applications. Snap-in developers can use the Windows Installer to load a snap-in installation into the Microsoft Directory Service and to have it downloaded automatically when the user tries to open a console file that references that snap-in.

modal Refers to a dialog box to which the user must respond before continuing work. A modal dialog box can be either application-modal or system-modal.

modeless Refers to a dialog box to which the user does not need to respond before continuing work. In MMC, property sheets displayed by snap-ins are modeless.

MSI package Required for a snap-in to be automatically downloaded and installed using the Microsoft Windows Installer. An installation package contains all the information that the Windows Installer requires to install or uninstall an application or product and to run the setup user interface (if there is one). Each installation package includes an .msi file, which contains an installation database, a summary information stream, and data streams for various parts of the installation. The .msi file can also contain one or more transforms, internal source files, and external source files or cabinet files required by the installation.

multiple-document interface (MDI)

A specification that defines a user interface for applications that enable the user to work with more than one document at the same time. Each document in an MDI application is displayed in a separate child window within the client area of the application's main window.

An MDI application has three kinds of windows: a frame window, an MDI client window, and a number of child windows. The frame window is the main window of the application. An MDI application does not display output in the client area of the frame window. Instead, it displays it in the MDI client window. The client window is a child of the frame window; it serves as the background for child windows. The client window is the parent window of all MDI child windows in the application.

In the MMC SDK documentation, the MMC application's frame window and MDI client window are referred to collectively as "main MMC window." MDI client windows are referred to as "views."

multiple selection (or multiselection)

Two or more (scope or result) items in the result pane selected at the same time. MMC supports a number of operations on a multiple selection, such as cut, copy, paste, and delete. Multiple selection is only allowed in the result pane.

multiselection data object

A data object that a snap-in creates when it receives the MMC_MULTI_SELECT_COOKIE special cookie value in a call to its **IComponent::QueryDataObject** method. MMC requests a multiselection data object during a multiple selection. This data object should supply the list of node types for all of the currently selected result items owned by the snap-in in the multiple selection. MMC requests this information from the data object by calling its **GetData** method with the CCF_OBJECT_TYPES_IN_MULTI_SELECT clipboard format.

MMC forwards the multiselection data object back to the snap-in during notifications that pertain to the multiple selection. For the snap-in to handle the notifications, the multiselection data object should also define some data structure that identifies the items currently selected in the result pane.

N

namespace   Collective term used to describe both the scope pane and the result pane of a console in which one or more snap-ins are loaded. A snap-in can add scope items and result items to its namespace—that is, it can add scope items in the scope pane and result items in the result pane of the console in which it is loaded. A namespace extension snap-in can add scope items to the namespace of a primary snap-in—that is, it can add scope items as children of scope items inserted by the primary snap-in.

namespace extension   An extension snap-in that extends the functionality of a primary snap-in by adding its own scope items as child items of a particular node type that are inserted by the primary snap-in.

node   An object in the console tree. There are two main types of nodes: static nodes and enumerated nodes. These nodes are also referred to collectively as scope items.

Static and enumerated nodes are implemented by snap-ins and offer the following viewing mechanisms: list view, HTML view, OCX view, and taskpad view.

A third type of node, called a built-in node, is implemented by MMC and does not interact with snap-ins. An example of a built-in node is the Console Root.

Node Manager   Used interchangeably with the term "MMC" in the MMC SDK documentation. The Node Manager implements a number of MMC COM interfaces and exposes them to snap-ins for their use.

node type   A scope or result item's most important property, represented by a node type GUID. An item's node type describes its overall type; for example, whether it is a user, a machine, a domain entry in a Domain Name System (DNS) database, or something else. A node type is defined by the individual snap-in rather than by MMC.

MMC uses an item's node type to determine whether it can be extended by any extension snap-ins.

node type GUID The GUID associated with a particular node type. GUIDs in this context have no COM significance, although they can be generated using Guidgen.exe just as with any other GUIDs.

Snap-ins must register the node type GUIDs of their extendable node types for extensions to extend the node types.

notification (or notification message)

A method of communication used by MMC to inform a snap-in that it needs to perform an action, usually in response to a user action such as selecting a scope item or a context menu item. MMC can send notification messages to the snap-in's **IComponentData::Notify**, **IComponent::Notify**, or **IExtendControlbar::ControlbarNotify** methods, depending on the notification.

O

OCX Used interchangeably with the term "ActiveX control" in the MMC SDK documentation.

OCX view A result pane view on the selected scope item in which the snap-in can launch an OCX control.

OLE Microsoft's object-based technology for sharing information and services across process and machine boundaries (object linking and embedding).

orphaned property page A term used in a Visual Basic snap-in to represent a property page displayed for one or more list items where the list view that owned the list items has been destroyed because the user selected a new node in the scope pane.

P

Policy Windows 2000 feature that allows administrators to determine access to tools and functionality on a group basis, for either computers or users. MMC administrators can use this feature to prevent individual users and groups of users from accessing specified snap-in functionality.

primary object A snap-in's cocreatable class object. For snap-ins that expose the **IComponentData** interface and the **ISnapinAbout** interface via two different cocreatable class objects, the primary object is the snap-in class object that exposes the **IComponentData** interface.

primary snap-in A snap-in (either a stand-alone snap-in or a namespace extension) that inserts scope or result items of node types that can be extended by one or more extension snap-ins. The primary snap-in is responsible for registering the node type GUIDs of its extendable node types.

property page A child window of a property sheet that contains control windows for setting a group of related properties. For example, a page can contain the controls for setting the font properties of an item, including the type style, point size, color, and so on. Each page has a tab that the user can click to bring the page to the foreground of the property sheet.

property page extension An extension snap-in that extends the funtionality of a primary snap-in by adding its own property pages to the property sheet of scope or result items of a particular node type that are inserted by the primary snap-in.

property sheet Window that allows the user to view and edit the properties of an item. A property sheet contains one or more overlapping child windows called property pages.

R

registry System-defined database in which applications and system components store and retrieve configuration data. MMC uses the registry to retrieve the location of snap-in DLLs and to determine whether a node type is extendable, and if so, which extension snap-ins extend that node type's functionality.

required extension An extension snap-in that is automatically added to a primary snap-in when the primary snap-in is loaded in an MMC console.

result item An item inserted by a snap-in in a list view.

result pane The right pane in a view. The result pane has one of four possible view types: standard list view; taskpad view; custom OCX view; custom Web view.

result view A term used in Visual Basic snap-ins to represent the contents of the result pane.

S

saved console file See console file.

scope item A static node or enumerated node in the scope pane of a snap-in.

scope node A term used in a Visual Basic snap-in to represent any node in the scope pane, regardless of its ownership.

scope pane The left pane in a view that contains the console tree. The user can choose to hide the scope pane in a view. The term "scope pane" is used interchangeably with "console tree" in the MMC SDK documentation.

scope pane item A term used in a Visual Basic snap-in to represent an instance of a scope item in the scope pane of a specific view.

snap-in An OLE InProc server that performs a server management task as part of an MMC console. MMC serves as a host for snap-in-defined user interfaces, but does not limit what the snap-ins can do or how they communicate with the managed services.

Snap-in Designer for Visual Basic
An ActiveX designer that allows a snap-in to be written entirely in Visual Basic. The Snap-in Designer is included in the Microsoft Platform SDK.

Snap-in Manager Term previously used in the MMC SDK documentation to refer to the **Add/Remove Snap-in** dialog box.

snap-in menu A menu button that a stand-alone or extension snap-in adds to the menu bar.

snap-in taskpad A taskpad implemented by a snap-in, as opposed to a console taskpad.

snap-in toolbar Section of the toolbar that contains the toolbar buttons added by stand-alone and extension snap-ins.

special cookie Nonstandard cookie that MMC sends to the snap-in's **IComponent::QueryDataObject** method in some situations. Special cookies are *not* associated with scope and result items, and their values are determined by MMC.

special data object Nonstandard data object that MMC sends to the snap-in's **IComponent::Notify** or **IExtendControlbar::ControlbarNotify** in some situations.

stand-alone snap-in A snap-in that, once loaded in a console, can perform its designated management task as the only snap-in loaded in the console.

standard list view Default result pane view type that displays a collection of items, each consisting of an icon and a label, and provides several ways to display and arrange the items.

standard list view taskpad Taskpad view style displays the taskpad title, a list control that displays items that can be selected, and tasks that can perform actions on the selected items.

standard taskpad Default taskpad view style that displays the taskpad title and tasks.

standard verb See verb.

static node A node in the MMC namespace that is present as long as the snap-in providing it is loaded. Only stand-alone snap-ins can have static nodes. Stand-alone snap-ins use their static nodes to store their setup configuration and relative placement in the console.

When a stand-alone snap-in is loaded in an MMC console, MMC inserts the snap-in's static node in the scope pane. All other nodes inserted in the scope pane (enumerated nodes) are inserted by the snap-in and by any number of namespace extension snap-ins.

system modal Refers to a type of user interface element (for example, dialog box, message box, property sheet) for which all applications are suspended until the user responds to the message box. System-modal message boxes are used to notify the user of serious, potentially damaging errors that require immediate attention, and should be used sparingly.

T

task An action on a taskpad, which consists of an image, a label, a description, and a mechanism for telling the snap-in to perform that action.

taskpad A result pane view on the selected scope item that is represented as a dynamic HTML (DHTML) page. The taskpad DHTML page lists actions, called tasks, that can be performed on the selected node.

taskpad extension An extension snap-in that extends the functionality of a primary snap-in by adding tasks to the taskpad view of scope items of a particular node type that are inserted by the primary snap-in.

taskpad view A result pane view that displays a taskpad.

toolbar Area of the main MMC window next to the menu bar that contains toolbar buttons.

toolbar button A button on the toolbar that consists of an icon, an associated action, and a mechanism for informing the owner of the button (MMC or a snap-in) to perform the action.

toolbar control MMC control for managing the toolbar in the main MMC window.

toolbar extension An extension snap-in that extends the functionality of a primary snap-in by adding its own toolbar buttons or menu buttons for scope or result items of a particular node type that are inserted by the primary snap-in.

trappable error A run-time error that occurs in a Visual Basic snap-in that can be detected and handled by the snap-in using the **On Error** statement.

U

Unified Modeling Language (UML)
Industry-standard modeling language for specifying and documenting both data and processes in software systems. The MMC SDK documentation uses UML to describe the sequence of interactions and collaborations between MMC and the objects of a snap-in.

URL view See HTML view.

user mode Access mode to a custom console that grants the user of the console full to limited access to MMC functionality. Three levels of user mode are possible: User mode–full access; User mode–limited access, multiple window; and User mode–limited access, single window.

V

vanilla GIF Enumerator value in the **MMC_TASK_DISPLAY_TYPE** enumeration, which defines the types of image that can be displayed for a task or the background on a taskpad. This value indicates that the image displayed for the task or background is a transparent GIF image where index 0 is transparent.

verb A command appearing in the context menu of a scope or result item. The MMC SDK specifies a number of standard verbs, such as cut, copy, and rename, that snap-ins can use as command identifiers in an item's context menu. When the user selects a standard verb in a context menu, MMC sends the snap-in that inserted the command a notification message to allow it to respond to the user action.

view An MDI child window within an MMC console that hosts snap-ins. When MMC is started from a command prompt or the **Run** dialog box, a single, empty view is displayed.

When the user adds a snap-in to the console, a view to the snap-in instance is provided in each open MDI child window. If the user later removes the snap-in, each open MDI child window loses its view of the snap-in instance.

Each view has a scope pane and a result pane.

virtual list view Also known as owner data. A virtual list view appears to the user as any other standard list view, but the underlying code to populate them is optimized for large data sets.

W

watermark Bitmap image used in a Wizard97-style wizard to convey a specific message to the user.

Welcome page The first page of a Wizard97-style wizard. The Welcome page typically has a bitmap image, called a watermark, to convey a specific message to the user.

Windows Management Instrumentation (WMI)
Microsoft's implementation of Web-Based Enterprise Management (WBEM), which is an industry initiative to develop a standard technology for accessing management information in an enterprise environment. WMI uses the industry-standard Common Information Model (CIM) to represent systems, applications, networks, devices, and other managed objects in an enterprise environment. MMC snap-ins can be used to display any information that is stored in WMI.

wizard A type of property sheet. Wizards are designed to present pages one at a time in a sequence that is controlled by the application. Instead of selecting from a group of pages by clicking a tab, users move forward and backward through the sequence, one page at a time, by clicking **Next** or **Back** buttons located at the bottom of the wizard. MMC allows a snap-in to add either standard wizard pages or Wizard97 pages.

Wizard97 page Wizard pages for use with a Wizard97-style wizard. Note that snap-ins are strongly encouraged to use the Wizard97 style for all wizards they create in order to have a consistent style throughout MMC.

Wizard97-style wizard A wizard style that greatly improves the usability of wizards by allowing the use of introductory (Welcome) and finish (Completion) pages, interior page titles, and a consistent presentation of information.

Index

P

R

T

U

Microsoft® Resource Kits— powerhouse resources to minimize costs while maximizing performance

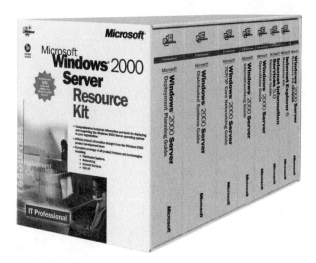

Deploy and support your enterprise business systems using the expertise and tools of those who know the technology best—the Microsoft product groups. Each RESOURCE KIT packs precise technical reference, installation and rollout tactics, planning guides, upgrade strategies, and essential utilities on CD-ROM. They're everything you need to help maximize system performance as you reduce ownership and support costs!

Microsoft® Windows® 2000 Server Resource Kit
ISBN   1-57231-805-8
U.S.A. $299.99
U.K.   £189.99 [V.A.T. included]
Canada $460.99

Microsoft Windows 2000 Professional Resource Kit
ISBN   1-57231-808-2
U.S.A. $69.99
U.K.   £45.99 [V.A.T. included]
Canada $107.99

Microsoft BackOffice® 4.5 Resource Kit
ISBN   0-7356-0583-1
U.S.A. $249.99
U.K.   £161.99 [V.A.T. included]
Canada $374.99

Microsoft Internet Explorer 5 Resource Kit
ISBN   0-7356-0587-4
U.S.A. $59.99
U.K.   £38.99 [V.A.T. included]
Canada $89.99

Microsoft Office 2000 Resource Kit
ISBN   0-7356-0555-6
U.S.A. $59.99
U.K.   £38.99 [V.A.T. included]
Canada $89.99

Microsoft Windows NT® Server 4.0 Resource Kit
ISBN   1-57231-344-7
U.S.A. $149.95
U.K.   £96.99 [V.A.T. included]
Canada $199.95

Microsoft Windows NT Workstation 4.0 Resource Kit
ISBN   1-57231-343-9
U.S.A. $69.95
U.K.   £45.99 [V.A.T. included]
Canada $94.95

mspress.microsoft.com

Here they are
in one place
practical,detailed
explanations of the
Microsoft networking APIs!

Microsoft has developed many exciting networking technologies, but until now, no single source has described how to use them with older, and even some newer, application programming interfaces (APIs). NETWORK PROGRAMMING FOR MICROSOFT WINDOWS is the only book that provides definitive, hands-on coverage of how to use legacy networking APIs, such as NetBIOS, on 32-bit platforms, plus recent networking APIs such as Winsock 2 and Remote Access Service (RAS).

U.S.A.	**$49.99**
U.K.	£46.99 [V.A.T. included]
Canada	$74.99

ISBN 0-7356-0560-2

mspress.microsoft.com

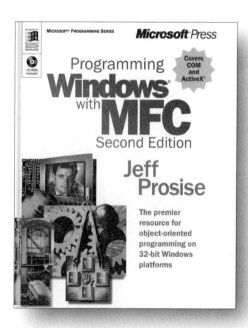

MICROSOFT LICENSE AGREEMENT

Book Companion CD

IMPORTANT—READ CAREFULLY: This Microsoft End-User License Agreement ("EULA") is a legal agreement between you (either an individual or an entity) and Microsoft Corporation for the Microsoft product identified above, which includes computer software and may include associated media, printed materials, and "online" or electronic documentation ("SOFTWARE PRODUCT"). Any component included within the SOFTWARE PRODUCT that is accompanied by a separate End-User License Agreement shall be governed by such agreement and not the terms set forth below. By installing, copying, or otherwise using the SOFTWARE PRODUCT, you agree to be bound by the terms of this EULA. If you do not agree to the terms of this EULA, you are not authorized to install, copy, or otherwise use the SOFTWARE PRODUCT; you may, however, return the SOFTWARE PRODUCT, along with all printed materials and other items that form a part of the Microsoft product that includes the SOFTWARE PRODUCT, to the place you obtained them for a full refund.

SOFTWARE PRODUCT LICENSE

The SOFTWARE PRODUCT is protected by United States copyright laws and international copyright treaties, as well as other intellectual property laws and treaties. The SOFTWARE PRODUCT is licensed, not sold.

1. **GRANT OF LICENSE.** This EULA grants you the following rights:

   a. **Software Product.** You may install and use one copy of the SOFTWARE PRODUCT on a single computer. The primary user of the computer on which the SOFTWARE PRODUCT is installed may make a second copy for his or her exclusive use on a portable computer.

   b. **Storage/Network Use.** You may also store or install a copy of the SOFTWARE PRODUCT on a storage device, such as a network server, used only to install or run the SOFTWARE PRODUCT on your other computers over an internal network; however, you must acquire and dedicate a license for each separate computer on which the SOFTWARE PRODUCT is installed or run from the storage device. A license for the SOFTWARE PRODUCT may not be shared or used concurrently on different computers.

   c. **License Pak.** If you have acquired this EULA in a Microsoft License Pak, you may make the number of additional copies of the computer software portion of the SOFTWARE PRODUCT authorized on the printed copy of this EULA, and you may use each copy in the manner specified above. You are also entitled to make a corresponding number of secondary copies for portable computer use as specified above.

   d. **Sample Code.** Solely with respect to portions, if any, of the SOFTWARE PRODUCT that are identified within the SOFTWARE PRODUCT as sample code (the "SAMPLE CODE"):

      i. **Use and Modification.** Microsoft grants you the right to use and modify the source code version of the SAMPLE CODE, *provided* you comply with subsection (d)(iii) below. You may not distribute the SAMPLE CODE, or any modified version of the SAMPLE CODE, in source code form.

      ii. **Redistributable Files.** Provided you comply with subsection (d)(iii) below, Microsoft grants you a nonexclusive, royalty-free right to reproduce and distribute the object code version of the SAMPLE CODE and of any modified SAMPLE CODE, other than SAMPLE CODE, or any modified version thereof, designated as not redistributable in the Readme file that forms a part of the SOFTWARE PRODUCT (the "Non-Redistributable Sample Code"). All SAMPLE CODE other than the Non-Redistributable Sample Code is collectively referred to as the "REDISTRIBUTABLES."

      iii. **Redistribution Requirements.** If you redistribute the REDISTRIBUTABLES, you agree to: (i) distribute the REDISTRIBUTABLES in object code form only in conjunction with and as a part of your software application product; (ii) not use Microsoft's name, logo, or trademarks to market your software application product; (iii) include a valid copyright notice on your software application product; (iv) indemnify, hold harmless, and defend Microsoft from and against any claims or lawsuits, including attorney's fees, that arise or result from the use or distribution of your software application product; and (v) not permit further distribution of the REDISTRIBUTABLES by your end user. Contact Microsoft for the applicable royalties due and other licensing terms for all other uses and/or distribution of the REDISTRIBUTABLES.

2. **DESCRIPTION OF OTHER RIGHTS AND LIMITATIONS.**

   - **Limitations on Reverse Engineering, Decompilation, and Disassembly.** You may not reverse engineer, decompile, or disassemble the SOFTWARE PRODUCT, except and only to the extent that such activity is expressly permitted by applicable law notwithstanding this limitation.

   - **Separation of Components.** The SOFTWARE PRODUCT is licensed as a single product. Its component parts may not be separated for use on more than one computer.

   - **Rental.** You may not rent, lease, or lend the SOFTWARE PRODUCT.

- **Support Services.** Microsoft may, but is not obligated to, provide you with support services related to the SOFTWARE PRODUCT ("Support Services"). Use of Support Services is governed by the Microsoft policies and programs described in the user manual, in "online" documentation, and/or in other Microsoft-provided materials. Any supplemental software code provided to you as part of the Support Services shall be considered part of the SOFTWARE PRODUCT and subject to the terms and conditions of this EULA. With respect to technical information you provide to Microsoft as part of the Support Services, Microsoft may use such information for its business purposes, including for product support and development. Microsoft will not utilize such technical information in a form that personally identifies you.

- **Software Transfer.** You may permanently transfer all of your rights under this EULA, provided you retain no copies, you transfer all of the SOFTWARE PRODUCT (including all component parts, the media and printed materials, any upgrades, this EULA, and, if applicable, the Certificate of Authenticity), **and** the recipient agrees to the terms of this EULA.

- **Termination.** Without prejudice to any other rights, Microsoft may terminate this EULA if you fail to comply with the terms and conditions of this EULA. In such event, you must destroy all copies of the SOFTWARE PRODUCT and all of its component parts.

3. **COPYRIGHT.** All title and copyrights in and to the SOFTWARE PRODUCT (including but not limited to any images, photographs, animations, video, audio, music, text, SAMPLE CODE, REDISTRIBUTABLES, and "applets" incorporated into the SOFTWARE PRODUCT) and any copies of the SOFTWARE PRODUCT are owned by Microsoft or its suppliers. The SOFTWARE PRODUCT is protected by copyright laws and international treaty provisions. Therefore, you must treat the SOFTWARE PRODUCT like any other copyrighted material **except** that you may install the SOFTWARE PRODUCT on a single computer provided you keep the original solely for backup or archival purposes. You may not copy the printed materials accompanying the SOFTWARE PRODUCT.

4. **U.S. GOVERNMENT RESTRICTED RIGHTS.** The SOFTWARE PRODUCT and documentation are provided with RESTRICTED RIGHTS. Use, duplication, or disclosure by the Government is subject to restrictions as set forth in subparagraph (c)(1)(ii) of the Rights in Technical Data and Computer Software clause at DFARS 252.227-7013 or subparagraphs (c)(1) and (2) of the Commercial Computer Software—Restricted Rights at 48 CFR 52.227-19, as applicable. Manufacturer is Microsoft Corporation/One Microsoft Way/Redmond, WA 98052-6399.

5. **EXPORT RESTRICTIONS.** You agree that you will not export or re-export the SOFTWARE PRODUCT, any part thereof, or any process or service that is the direct product of the SOFTWARE PRODUCT (the foregoing collectively referred to as the "Restricted Components"), to any country, person, entity, or end user subject to U.S. export restrictions. You specifically agree not to export or re-export any of the Restricted Components (i) to any country to which the U.S. has embargoed or restricted the export of goods or services, which currently include, but are not necessarily limited to, Cuba, Iran, Iraq, Libya, North Korea, Sudan, and Syria, or to any national of any such country, wherever located, who intends to transmit or transport the Restricted Components back to such country; (ii) to any end user who you know or have reason to know will utilize the Restricted Components in the design, development, or production of nuclear, chemical, or biological weapons; or (iii) to any end user who has been prohibited from participating in U.S. export transactions by any federal agency of the U.S. government. You warrant and represent that neither the BXA nor any other U.S. federal agency has suspended, revoked, or denied your export privileges.

DISCLAIMER OF WARRANTY

NO WARRANTIES OR CONDITIONS. MICROSOFT EXPRESSLY DISCLAIMS ANY WARRANTY OR CONDITION FOR THE SOFTWARE PRODUCT. THE SOFTWARE PRODUCT AND ANY RELATED DOCUMENTATION ARE PROVIDED "AS IS" WITHOUT WARRANTY OR CONDITION OF ANY KIND, EITHER EXPRESS OR IMPLIED, INCLUDING, WITHOUT LIMITATION, THE IMPLIED WARRANTIES OF MERCHANTABILITY, FITNESS FOR A PARTICULAR PURPOSE, OR NONINFRINGEMENT. THE ENTIRE RISK ARISING OUT OF USE OR PERFORMANCE OF THE SOFTWARE PRODUCT REMAINS WITH YOU.

LIMITATION OF LIABILITY. TO THE MAXIMUM EXTENT PERMITTED BY APPLICABLE LAW, IN NO EVENT SHALL MICROSOFT OR ITS SUPPLIERS BE LIABLE FOR ANY SPECIAL, INCIDENTAL, INDIRECT, OR CONSEQUENTIAL DAMAGES WHATSOEVER (INCLUDING, WITHOUT LIMITATION, DAMAGES FOR LOSS OF BUSINESS PROFITS, BUSINESS INTERRUPTION, LOSS OF BUSINESS INFORMATION, OR ANY OTHER PECUNIARY LOSS) ARISING OUT OF THE USE OF OR INABILITY TO USE THE SOFTWARE PRODUCT OR THE PROVISION OF OR FAILURE TO PROVIDE SUPPORT SERVICES, EVEN IF MICROSOFT HAS BEEN ADVISED OF THE POSSIBILITY OF SUCH DAMAGES. IN ANY CASE, MICROSOFT'S ENTIRE LIABILITY UNDER ANY PROVISION OF THIS EULA SHALL BE LIMITED TO THE GREATER OF THE AMOUNT ACTUALLY PAID BY YOU FOR THE SOFTWARE PRODUCT OR US$5.00; PROVIDED, HOWEVER, IF YOU HAVE ENTERED INTO A MICROSOFT SUPPORT SERVICES AGREEMENT, MICROSOFT'S ENTIRE LIABILITY REGARDING SUPPORT SERVICES SHALL BE GOVERNED BY THE TERMS OF THAT AGREEMENT. BECAUSE SOME STATES AND JURISDICTIONS DO NOT ALLOW THE EXCLUSION OR LIMITATION OF LIABILITY, THE ABOVE LIMITATION MAY NOT APPLY TO YOU.

MISCELLANEOUS

This EULA is governed by the laws of the State of Washington USA, except and only to the extent that applicable law mandates governing law of a different jurisdiction.

Should you have any questions concerning this EULA, or if you desire to contact Microsoft for any reason, please contact the Microsoft subsidiary serving your country, or write: Microsoft Sales Information Center/One Microsoft Way/Redmond, WA 98052-6399.

PN 097-0002296

OWNER REGISTRATION CARD   *Register Today!*   0-7356-1038-X

Return the bottom portion of this card to register today.

Microsoft® Management Console Design and Development Kit

FIRST NAME   MIDDLE INITIAL   LAST NAME

INSTITUTION OR COMPANY NAME

ADDRESS

CITY   STATE   ZIP

(   )

E-MAIL ADDRESS   PHONE NUMBER

U.S. and Canada addresses only. Fill in information above and mail postage-free.
Please mail only the bottom half of this page.

For information about Microsoft Press®

products, visit our Web site at

mspress.microsoft.com

Microsoft®